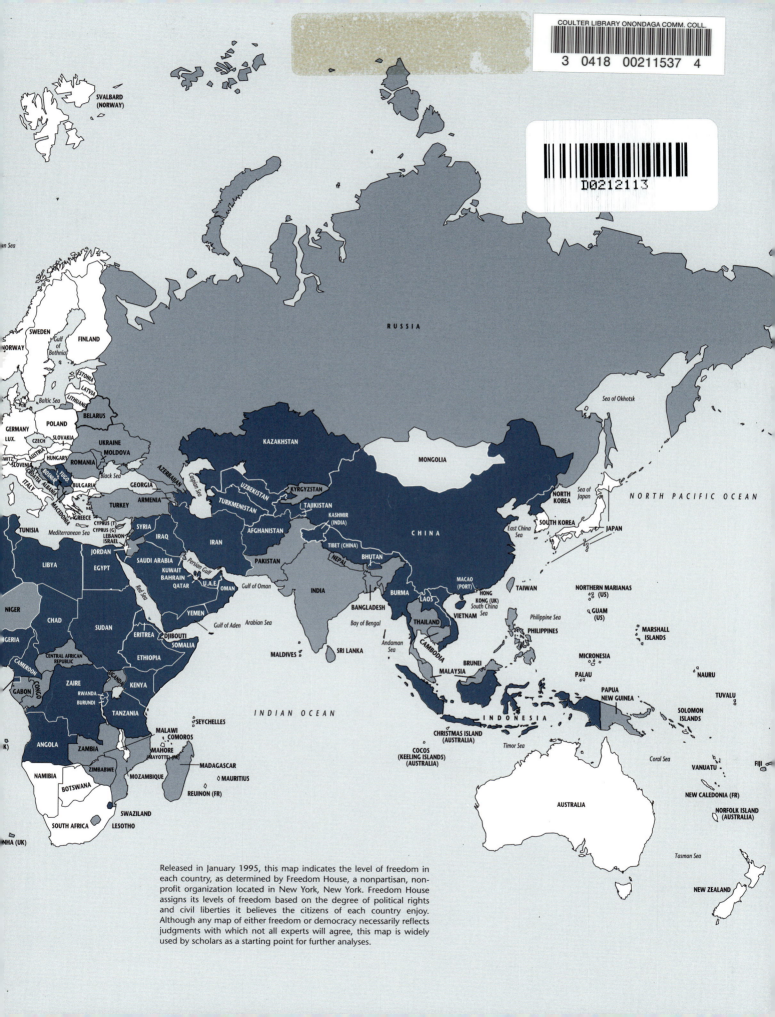

Released in January 1995, this map indicates the level of freedom in each country, as determined by Freedom House, a nonpartisan, nonprofit organization located in New York, New York. Freedom House assigns its levels of freedom based on the degree of political rights and civil liberties it believes the citizens of each country enjoy. Although any map of either freedom or democracy necessarily reflects judgments with which not all experts will agree, this map is widely used by scholars as a starting point for further analyses.

THE ENCYCLOPEDIA OF DEMOCRACY

THE ENCYCLOPEDIA OF DEMOCRACY

SEYMOUR MARTIN LIPSET

Editor in Chief

VOLUME III

 CONGRESSIONAL QUARTERLY INC.
Washington, D.C.

Published in the United Kingdom by Routledge

11 New Fetter Lane, London EC4P 4EE

Book design and production by Kachergis Book Design,

Pittsboro, North Carolina

Printed and bound in the United States of America

The paper used in this publication meets the minimum requirements of the American National Standard for Information Sciences—Permanence of Paper for Printed Library Materials, ANSI z39.48-1984.

LIBRARY OF CONGRESS CATALOGING-IN-PUBLICATION DATA

The encyclopedia of democracy / Seymour Martin Lipset, editor in chief.
    p. cm.
  Includes bibliographical references (p.) and index.
  ISBN 0-87187-675-2 (set : alk. paper)
  ISBN 0-87187-886-0 (v.1 : alk. paper)
  ISBN 0-87187-887-9 (v.2 : alk. paper)
  ISBN 0-87187-888-7 (v.3 : alk. paper)
  ISBN 0-87187-889-5 (v.4 : alk. paper)

  1. Democracy—Encyclopedias.   I. Lipset, Seymour Martin.
JC423.E53   1995
321.8'03—dc20   95-34217
                                  CIP

ABOUT THE EDITORS

GAIL W. LAPIDUS is senior fellow at the Institute for International Studies, Stanford University, and professor emeritus of political science at the University of California, Berkeley. She received her Ph.D. from Harvard University. She is the author of *State and Society in the USSR* and *Women in Soviet Society: Equality, Development and Social Change.*

AREND LIJPHART is professor of political science at the University of California, San Diego, and president of the American Political Science Association. He received his Ph.D. from Yale University. Among his many publications is *Electoral Laws and Party Systems in Western Democracies, 1945–1990.*

JUAN J. LINZ is Sterling Professor of Political and Social Science at Yale University. He received his Ph.D. from Columbia University. He is the author or coeditor of several books, including *The Breakdown of Democratic Regimes: Crisis, Breakdown, and Reequilibrium.*

THOMAS L. PANGLE is professor of political science at the University of Toronto and a fellow at St. Michael's College. He received his Ph.D. from the University of Chicago. He is the author of several books, including *The Ennobling of Democracy as the Challenge of the Postmodern Age* and *The Spirit of Modern Republicanism: The Moral Vision of the American Founders and the Philosophy of Locke.*

LUCIAN W. PYE is Ford Professor of Political Science at the Massachusetts Institute of Technology. He received his Ph.D. from Yale University. He is a past president of the American Political Science Association. His many publications include *The Mandarin and the Cadre: The Political Culture of Confucian Leninism* and *Asian Power and Politics.*

GEORGE H. QUESTER is professor and chairman of the Department of Government and Politics at the University of Maryland. He received his Ph.D. from Harvard University. He is the author of *Deterrence before Hiroshima* as well as many other books, articles, and monographs.

PHILIPPE C. SCHMITTER is professor in the Department of Political Science at Stanford University. He received his Ph.D. from the University of California, Berkeley. He is coeditor of *Transitions from Authoritarian Rule: Prospects for Democracy* and *Private Interest Government and Public Policy.*

CONTENTS

THE ENCYCLOPEDIA OF DEMOCRACY

L

Labor

See *Class relations, Industrial; Industrial democracy*

Laissez-faire economic theory

An economic theory that is based on a peremptory rejection of government interference with economic affairs and a faith in unrestricted private decision making as an instrument for promoting the public welfare. The origin of the term *laissez faire* is generally credited to an eighteenth-century French trademark inspector, Vincent de Gournay. Exasperated with government trade regulations, he reportedly exclaimed, *"Laissez faire! Laissez passer!"* ("Let [them] do [as they please]! Let [them] pass!"), calling for noninterference in enterprise and trade.

The Eighteenth and Nineteenth Centuries

Following the lead of François Quesnay and Anne-Robert-Jacques Turgot (who were members of the eighteenth-century French school of economics known as the physiocrats), the classical economists of the British liberal school made laissez-faire the centerpiece of their attack on state mercantilist economic policy. In his landmark treatise, *The Wealth of Nations* (1776), for example, the Scottish economist Adam Smith expounded what he called the natural economic system wherein self-interest, the private pursuit of profits, and individual freedom to trade would be guided—as if by an "invisible hand"—to promote the social welfare. The system would compel individuals to utilize their resources in accordance with consumers' wants and to strive to do so in ever more efficient and technologically superior ways. These socially beneficial

The Scottish economist Adam Smith laid out the fundamental principles of laissez-faire economic theory in his seminal work *The Wealth of Nations* (1776).

outcomes would be the result, Smith argued, not of altruistic motives but of the narrow-minded pursuit of individual self-interest. As he put it, it is not from the benevolence of the butcher, the brewer, or the baker that we obtain our dinner but from their efforts to provide what others desire and what, therefore, is profitable for them to produce.

Although Smith identified some major deficiencies in private enterprise as a system of economic organization, and although he explicitly assigned certain responsibilities to government, his advocacy of private enterprise has served for more than two centuries as an ideological justification for opposing government economic policies as "dangerous" and "unnatural."

Social Darwinism, or economic Darwinism, as articulated in mid-nineteenth century England by Herbert Spencer (*The Man versus the State*, 1884) and in late nineteenth century America by William Graham Sumner (whose views were posthumously collected in *The Challenge of Facts and Other Essays*, 1914) reinforced and buttressed the doctrine of laissez-faire. (Actually, Spencer's work preceded, and to some degree shaped, Darwin's conjectures about the evolution of animal species.) According to this view, the press of the economic environment, coupled with unrestrained competition among individuals for income, forces the development of socially beneficial talents and aptitudes. Life rewards those who succeed in proving themselves to be most fit in these regards, while punishing those who are less fit.

Spencer and Sumner, for example, argued that government programs to protect the poor—to provide food, shelter, and education for them—only worsened their lot by depriving them of the energy and incentive to improve their economic condition. Similarly, Spencer contended that government should not in any way regulate the sale of lethal quack medicines, on the grounds that the fatal decisions made by some would encourage more intelligent decision making by everyone else and that the misfortune of one would serve as a powerful lesson for thousands of others. In general, according to this school, any government cure is far worse than the disease itself: government interference in economic matters violates natural social laws, weakens the strong, dulls initiative, and saps a society's economic vitality.

Twentieth-Century Thought

A later version of laissez-faire thinking emerged during the 1930s and became known as the Austrian school of economics, named in honor of its progenitors, Friedrich von Hayek and Ludwig von Mises. Economic systems, they argued, are fraught with uncertainty and subject to continual change in unpredictable and unanticipated ways. Only private individuals possess both the incentives and the abilities to obtain, interpret, and act expeditiously upon information concerning the nature and significance of these unforeseeable changes. Although the state could in theory duplicate the performance of the private marketplace in a static world, the information and decision-making requirements in the dynamic environment of the real world preclude government from acting in a fashion capable of promoting the public welfare.

More recently, the laissez-faire doctrine has been supported by the public choice school of economic analysis. This view, which emerged during the 1960s, applies economic theory to question the very foundations of democracy. It concludes that, in practice, the democratic political process suffers from inherent flaws. As a result virtually all government economic policies—no matter how well intentioned—are likely to fail. The political process is defective, it claims, because voters in a democracy are "rationally ignorant": they recognize that their individual vote cannot alter the outcome of elections and that the personal cost to them of informing themselves about issues and candidates far outweighs any benefits they might personally derive from casting an informed vote. Moreover, the political process is believed to yield questionable results because it typically is manipulated by special-interest groups in order to produce benefits for themselves at society's expense. Finally, government officials are considered prone to pursuing their personal self-interest. Self-interest induces them to exacerbate the problems they are ostensibly responsible for resolving, in order to secure their personal employment and enhance their income. Therefore, according to the public choice theorists, although private enterprise may generate social problems, government cures are, once again, worse than the disease.

Finally, the Chicago school of economics, which reached its apogee of influence during the 1980s, represents a latter-day reincarnation of nineteenth-century social Darwinism and a repository for all these various strains of laissez-faire thinking. Like Spencer and Sumner a century earlier, the Chicago school's most forceful advocate, Milton Friedman, has long condemned government welfare programs for the poor, reasoning that welfare programs weaken incentives to work and save and that they produce a permanent underclass bereft of motivation and self-reliance. Like Spencer, he has opposed consumer protection legislation, arguing that the private marketplace will protect consumers better than government agencies can do. If a consumer is sold rotten meat by one grocer, Friedman says, the consumer can switch to another store. The market will force the first shop to improve the quality of its meat or go out of business.

Criticisms of Laissez-Faire

The laissez-faire doctrine has not escaped virulent criticism. Some have attacked it as nothing more than a naïve rationalization—a simplistic faith that "whatever is, is right," an excuse for egregious inequalities, a shield for domination by unregulated and uncontrolled private power blocs. Adam Smith's invisible hand may be a powerful force for compelling socially desirable decision making, they say, but only so long as markets are protected from subversion by private cartels and monopolies. But laissez-faire slogans developed by Smith to destroy monopoly may, ironically, become monop-oly's bulwark when used to oppose government actions that would preserve, restore, or promote the competition Smith advocated.

Others argue that the doctrine is self-contradictory. On the one hand, it demands that government refrain from interfering with "private" economic affairs. On the other hand, it ignores the fact that the capacity of individuals to engage in such activities hinges on the "interference" of the state in myriad ways—specification of legal title to property, provision of courts to enforce and adjudicate commercial contracts, statutory provision of the advantages of the corporate form of organization, and so forth.

Moreover, as John Kenneth Galbraith and others contend, a more active economic role for government may have enabled the market system to endure, by softening the harshest edges of unregulated capitalism. Darwinian survival of the fittest, they say, is fundamentally inappropriate when applied to human affairs, because all human advances—from scientific agriculture to high-technology medical care—stem at bottom from deliberate efforts to interfere with the "natural" environment.

Most generally, as the economist John Bates Clark pointed out in *The Control of Trusts* (1912), championing survival of the fittest begs the critical question, fittest to do what? Survival in the prize-fighting ring, he observed, means fitness for pugilism but not necessarily for bricklaying. Only with the right kind of rules can the right kind of fitness emerge. Determining these rules, and harnessing self-interest to best serve the common good, is the central economic challenge in a free society.

See also *Regulation*.

Walter Adams and James W. Brock

BIBLIOGRAPHY

Adams, Walter E., and James W. Brock. *Antitrust Economics on Trial: A Dialogue on the New Laissez-Faire.* Princeton: Princeton University Press, 1991.

Friedman, Milton, and Rose Friedman. *Free to Choose.* New York: Avon Books, 1980.

Galbraith, John Kenneth. *The New Industrial State.* Boston: Houghton Mifflin, 1967; Harmondsworth: Penguin Books, 1991.

Hayek, Friedrich von. *The Counter-Revolution of Science: Studies in the Abuse of Reason.* Glencoe, Ill.: Free Press, 1952.

Hofstadter, Richard. *Social Darwinism in American Thought.* Boston: Beacon Press, 1955.

Lippmann, Walter. *The Good Society.* Boston: Little, Brown, 1937.

Smith, Adam. *An Inquiry into the Nature and Causes of the Wealth of Nations.* 2 vols. Oxford and New York: Oxford University Press, 1979.

Laos

See *Asia, Southeast*

Laski, Harold

English political scientist, teacher, and socialist intellectual. Laski (1893–1950), who was from a middle-class Jewish background in Manchester, earned a degree at Oxford University in 1914. After teaching at McGill University in

Montreal for two years, he moved to Harvard Law School, where he established himself as a major political theorist. In 1919 he offended the Boston elite by supporting the police strike, and the next year he returned to England to take up a lectureship in politics at the London School of Economics. Promoted to a full professorship at the age of thirty-two, he was an inspiring teacher who influenced generations of students from all over the world. Laski's prolific works, including *A Grammar of Politics* (1925), *Democracy in Crisis* (1933), and *The State in Theory and Practice* (1935), were major texts in socialist thought.

Convinced that academic life must not be confined to the "ivory tower," Laski was also a political activist. He was a prominent member of the Labour Party's executive committee and a friend of leading members of Franklin D. Roosevelt's New Deal administration. His influence was felt in the United States, India, and continental Europe as well as in Britain. Such fame, however, also brought about Laski's downfall. During Britain's 1945 general election campaign, he achieved notoriety when he tried to ensure that Clement Attlee, the Labour Party leader, would follow the party's foreign policy rather than continuing with that of the wartime coalition. He became the focus for right-wing propaganda attacks and was even accused of advocating violent revolution. Although this allegation was false, Laski lost a libel action in 1946, and his reputation declined. He was discredited in the West during the cold war era, and since his death he has received less recognition than he deserves.

Laski's earliest major writings, *Studies in the Problem of Sovereignty* (1917) and *Authority in the Modern State* (1919), contributed to the theory of pluralism, which stressed the importance of groups in society and questioned the need for a strong central state. Arguing that a healthy body politic was dependent upon active participation by its citizens, Laski maintained that citizens felt their primary allegiance was to associations such as churches and trade unions. In his view these were the lifeblood of the community and should be encouraged through a decentralization of power in a system of both functional and territorial federalism. The other side of the coin was his denial of state sovereignty, both as an ideal and as a reality. People had a "plurality" of loyalties and freedom depended upon their activity in associations: the state should win their support but could not demand it through invoking bogus doctrines to justify obedience.

These early writings reflected Laski's enduring assumptions about the nature of a vibrant democracy. He also adhered to other values, however, which were not easily reconcilable with pluralism. In particular, he held that capitalism was corrupted by class inequality and that fundamental change was necessary to enable working-class people to share in both the material and the spiritual benefits that society could offer. While continuing to describe his work as "pluralist," he thus ascribed an increasingly important role to the state in bringing about the socioeconomic reforms that would make liberty a reality for the masses. *A Grammar of Politics,* probably his most influential book, argued that liberty was impossible without substantial equality and elaborated the practical measures necessary to convert political democracy into full democracy. This was a major text that offered a rationale for a program of peaceful, constitutional change.

From the latter half of the 1920s, however, Laski's position gradually became less optimistic as the evidence suggested that those who benefited from the existing distribution of property would never agree to the changes that he deemed necessary. Because he also believed that it was both morally right and historically inevitable that the working classes would seek "economic democracy," he feared that their demands would result in violent confrontation or the establishment of a right-wing dictatorship by the ruling classes. The collapse of the second Labour government in 1931, the worldwide economic depression, and the proliferation of dictatorships in Europe reinforced his pessimism. In *Democracy in Crisis* he argued, with great passion, in favor of liberal democracy but warned that the system could not be saved unless progressive movements attained far greater determination and understanding and conservative forces recognized that reform was the only alternative to violence or repression. In this period Laski was torn between an intellectual attraction to Marxism, which implied that capitalists would turn against democracy if it threatened their interests, and liberalism, which suggested that such values as freedom and reason would eventually triumph.

Hitler's accession to power in Germany in January 1933 appeared to reinforce the Marxist influence on Laski and his fear that capitalist democracy would be replaced by fascism. As an alternative, Laski thought that Stalinism might promise a new civilization. Because of his deep-seated belief in liberal values, however, he recoiled from wholehearted endorsement of the Soviet regime and frequently criticized its excesses. Instead he saw Roosevelt as the beacon of hope for democracy throughout the world, and he sought to persuade Americans that all obstacles to the New Deal must be surmounted. In particular, *The American Presidency* (1940) was a justification for strengthening presidential power as the sole way of effecting vital reforms through democratic means.

Despite his hatred of violence, Laski saw the war against Hitler as an opportunity for reinvigorating democracy. In such works as *Reflections on the Revolution of Our Time* (1943), he called for a "revolution by consent," which would bring about extensive welfare reforms and public control of the economy, thereby securing mass support and thwarting any recurrent tendencies to fascism. His optimism again evaporated, however, as he came to believe that Britain and the United States were fighting to restore the old elites rather than to encourage the social forces that he saw as the basis for enduring democratic systems.

In the postwar period Laski became increasingly disillusioned, particularly with the United States. His last major work, *The American Democracy* (1948), was a sustained indictment of the system. In this monumental work he argued that the spirit and institutions of democracy were corrupted by the dominance of business over every facet of life. He was equally damning of both the theory and the practice of communism, however, and continued to stress the importance of democratic values. Indeed, some of Laski's last writings reaffirmed his early pluralist themes of decentralization and the diffusion of power. He was clearly seeking a more participatory society than that suggested by the model of democratic elitism that tended to dominate Western thinking.

Laski never brought together his work into an overall theory of democracy. Convinced that the problems of his time were too urgent for leisurely, academic analysis, he wrote too much, overestimated his influence, and sometimes failed to distinguish sufficiently between theory and polemic. But his search for a synthesis between liberty and equality defined an approach to democracy that was highly influential in his time. Now that the cold war is over, its importance may again be appreciated.

Michael Newman

BIBLIOGRAPHY

Kramnick, Isaac, and Barry Sheerman. *Harold Laski: A Life on the Left.* New York: Viking; London: Hamilton, 1993.

Newman, Michael. *Harold Laski: A Political Biography.* London: Macmillan, 1993.

Zylstra, Bernard. *From Pluralism to Collectivism: The Development of Harold Laski's Political Thought.* Assen, The Netherlands: Van Gorcum, 1968.

Lasswell, Harold D.

Pioneer in the theory and practice of policy sciences. The son of a teacher and a Presbyterian minister, Lasswell (1902–1978) grew up in small towns in Illinois. He earned a doctorate in political science at the University of Chicago and served as a member of the faculty until 1938. After a decade in Washington, D.C., affiliated with various research organizations, Lasswell moved to the Yale Law School, his base from 1947 until retirement in 1973. Extensive travel throughout his career brought him into contact with many of the major intellectual and political figures of his time.

Lasswell defined democracy as the sharing of power (by which he meant participation in the most important decisions) and affirmed it as part of a broad commitment to human dignity for all. His concern, however, was not to redefine democracy or to rejustify it: the moral heritage was already adequate. His concern was to help to realize democratic aspirations. Progress, he believed, depended on a policy science dedicated to the understanding and possible control of factors affecting democracy. In the first half of the twentieth century it was clear that democracy could fail; with scientific knowledge it might succeed.

Lasswell's contributions to the policy science of democracy were grounded in research published in *Psychopathology and Politics* (1930). In the psychoanalytic understanding of personality, an individual's adaptation to changing reality (the ego function) is complicated by emotional impulses and inhibitions arising from primitive structures (the id and superego), which influence adult behavior in more or less disguised forms. For example, as the ego develops, the child discovers that the wisdom and might of the authoritative parent has been exaggerated. But the adult displaces the continuing unconscious need for an ideal parent onto a leader, the state, or another symbol of authority. Displacements are part of the personality's struggle to maintain internal equilibrium in a changing environment.

The ego, or reasoning function, is particularly handicapped when military defeat, unemployment, violence, or other widespread disturbances upset the internal equilibrium for many people at the same time, thereby raising the level of social tension, releasing emotional affects from previous objects of displacement (such as authority symbols), and creating a susceptibility to alternatives. In response, political elites struggle to organize public opinion and mobilize public support by circulating symbols that purport to diagnose the causes of the crisis and to prescribe solutions. The symbols that compete most successfully become focal points for the displacement of private affects; they meet the diverse emotional needs of an aroused public, not necessarily the tests of reason. Hence public opinion organized by these symbols may bear little relation to policies that might in fact permanently reduce the level of tension. The symbols of Nazism, which led Germany to devastation by the end of World War II, are a case in point.

Many scholars denied these psychoanalytical insights into political behavior, while others used them to question faith in public opinion and the viability of democracy. Lasswell, in contrast, accepted these insights as verified by systematic observations of individual personalities and political crises. He considered ways to strengthen the ego function of the public and public officials alike. Strengthening the ego function depended on improving the stream of facts and interpretations on which moral and rational judgments are based. And such improvements in turn depended on scientists and other experts whose proper role was to give guidance, not to make decisions.

Lasswell dissociated himself from those who are contemptuous of the public and express their contempt by addressing themselves exclusively to the powerful or conceal their contempt by addressing the public as ignorant masses easily seduced with words.

In Lasswell's view, the success in establishing and maintaining democracy depends upon many factors working together. The structural framework includes standards of character and education that encourage individual restraint and responsibility in the uses of power; political structures, such as the checks and balances prescribed by the U.S. Constitution, that constrain abuses of power and leave decisions open to challenge; and patterns of social control that permit impartial access to wealth, skill, and other values on which power depends. By denying impartial access (or equal opportunity), an elite might consolidate itself as a closed caste beyond control of the masses.

Democratic structures are supported by policies that moderate the level of tension and facilitate smooth adjustments to changing conditions. Erratic rates of change and other maladjustments heighten uncertainty, generate frustration, and exacerbate destructive impulses that threaten democracy. To support continuing refinements in the science of democracy, Lasswell emphasized the need for improvements in data and methods of observation. He advocated the use of the prolonged interview (which he considered Freud's most distinctive innovation) and the need for content analysis of media that include political symbols.

To guide policy research, Lasswell created tentative models of the past and future of world politics. In *World Politics and Personal Insecurity* (1935), he recognized the shift from the class struggle of Marxist theory to a skill revolution, dominated by rivalries and alliances among specialists skilled in manipulating violence, symbols, and goods and services. In a 1937 variant of the skill revolution, he noted the rise of specialists in violence—the military and police—whose supremacy might be consolidated into the closed castes of a garrison–police state through prolonged security crises. In a 1965 variant, he noted the quiet rise of symbol specialists—the modernizing intellectuals—whose power is based on their skill in relating knowledge to complex problems of decision in the modern era. Although the rise of modernizing intellectuals has less obvious and ominous implications for democracy than does the garrison-state, the implications are not altogether benign.

Lasswell wrote for the general public as well as for experts. *Democracy Through Public Opinion* (1941) responded to people's shaken faith in public opinion and democracy. *World Politics Faces Economics* (1945) anticipated postwar economic problems and elements of the Marshall Plan, which assisted in rebuilding Europe. And *National Security and Individual Freedom* (1950) considered how to protect civil liberties jeopardized by the security crises of the cold war.

Lasswell also helped to design and field-test prototypes of democracy for adaptation to particular situations. In the 1950s at Vicos, a Peruvian hacienda, he worked with anthropologists from Cornell University to devolve power to the peasants and initiate a democratic and self-sustaining process of development. In the 1960s at the Yale Psychiatric Institute he worked with the staff to share power with resident mental patients as part of the patients' therapy. With Myres S. McDougal at the Yale Law School, Lasswell led a program in law, science, and policy that, over several decades, influenced decisions worldwide through research and practice by lawyers trained as agents of democratic progress.

Finally, Lasswell worked extensively with public officials, on a confidential basis that has obscured connections between his advice and specific decisions. Clearly, however, he reinforced and enlightened those predispositions of the public and public officials that were consistent with the needs of democracy and human dignity in his time. Thus he exemplified the ideal of the policy scientist.

See also *Intellectuals; Psychoanalysis; Science.*

Ronald D. Brunner

BIBLIOGRAPHY

Dobyns, Henry F., Paul L. Doughty, and Harold D. Lasswell. *Peasants, Power and Applied Social Change: Vicos as a Model.* Beverly Hills, Calif.: Sage Publications, 1971.

Lasswell, Harold D. "Democratic Character." In *The Political Writings of Harold D. Lasswell.* Glencoe, Ill.: Free Press, 1950.

———. *A Pre-View of the Policy Sciences.* New York: Elsevier, 1971.

———. "The World Revolution of Our Time: A Framework for Policy Research." In *World Revolutionary Elites,* edited by Harold D. Lasswell and Daniel Lerner. Cambridge: MIT Press, 1965; London: Greenwood, 1980.

———, and Myres S. McDougal. *Jurisprudence for a Free Society: Studies in Law, Science and Policy.* 2 vols. New Haven, Conn.: Yale University Press; Dordrecht, The Netherlands: Nijhoff, 1992.

Latvia

See *Baltic states*

Leadership

The guidance of a group, party, or political entity, typically undertaken by an individual. Although styles of leadership vary in scope and manner, it is expected that leaders will avoid merely representing (as would a clerk) the tallied demands of followers, on the one hand, or engaging in violence or duplicity against them, on the other. The term can refer either to leading a part of a polity in need of defense against the whole or to acting and thinking on behalf of a whole people or nation whose parts (or parties or interest groups) would, in its absence, be deadlocked or too shortsighted for prudent action.

Leadership is counted on not only to advance interests but also to overcome the warring of clashing interests and even to undertake the education and elevation of those interests to broader and deeper views. At the same time, leadership is expected to cut through the deliberation—and, if Niccolò Machiavelli (1469–1527) is to be believed, the morality—of political partisans, supplying the morally suspect, though politically necessary, qualities of decisiveness, secrecy, and dispatch. The leader must combine something of the diverse qualities of the partisan political infighter, the farseeing nation-building founder or legislator, and the inspiring and daring general.

Democracy's Ambivalence Toward Leadership

The relationship of democracy to leadership is complex and controversial. Historically democracies have taken pride in being schools for statesmen but have also suspected and even ostracized them. Theoretically, democracy has been understood both to require particularly virtuous and astute leadership and to require the rejection of all leadership as such. In the contemporary United States there is, at the popular or journalistic level, a continuous (and, it seems, an increasingly desperate) admission of a "need for leadership." This call receives two quite disparate responses from political scientists. Those engaged in leadership studies generally are sympathetic to the demand and try to encourage the phenomenon through a proper understanding of it. Increasing numbers of democratic theorists, on the other hand, ignore or condemn this demand, maintaining that democracy requires first and foremost a vigorous and self-directing citizenry, confident enough in its ability to exercise political judgment that it can dispense with leaders. Although this latter group claims to be invoking Jeffersonian democracy, it should be noted that Jefferson expected citizens to become competent only in selecting what he called the "natural aristoi" to lead them.

In some sense, leadership constitutes democracy's (or, at any rate, liberal democracy's) greatest embarrassment. Democracy, of course, means "rule by the people." And liberal democracy is premised on the view that all are born free by nature and so no one has a right by nature to rule another. Accordingly, in a liberal democracy, there are no leaders by divine right or tradition or family background: citizens must choose or consent to their leaders. If we believed that anyone could do the job, we would adopt what Aristotle refers to as the purely democratic mode of selecting leaders—namely, lot. In electing our leaders, we implicitly concede that some are better than others for this important job. (Thus Aristotle refers to election as an aristocratic mode of selection.) And this admission, in turn, is tantamount to conceding that democracy requires some supplemental principle by which to govern itself. A democracy's attitude toward leadership, then, reveals whether it seeks a form of radical or direct democracy, which would consist wholly of citizens directing themselves, or a moderate democracy (as conceived by the Framers of the U.S. Constitution and most older democratic theorists), which would accept the need for a mixture of some nondemocratic elements in a regime.

Democracy's attitude toward leaders thus is related to its attitude toward greatness or superiority generally. The most abiding criticism made of democracy is that it is leveling—that is, it comes to be irritated by any distinction, however legitimate. This irritation, strangely enough, is today more frequently voiced by "elite" spokesmen for democracy (for example, democratic theorists) than by citizens of democracies. Thus we see the spectacle of (some) democratic theorists condemning the admiration for the great man as an undemocratic tendency. This criticism of ruling appears to have had an effect, though not perhaps the one expected. Citizens of democratic states still long for strong leadership, but the potential leaders who might answer that call seem increasingly hesitant to lead. Some students of leadership have suggested that reluctance to exert power is more a problem today than is the reluc-

tance to follow. Leaders still exert power, but they do so in spite of, not with the guidance and blessing of, the predominant political sentiment. Condemned to lead with a bad conscience, they lead less well than they might.

Despite these objections, some argue that democracies are particularly in need of leadership. Put simply, democratic equality is strong on gaining wide-ranging and diverse input but weak on taking decisions or on ranking alternatives. Moreover, liberal democracies invite citizens to take their private lives seriously, leaving the tiller of the ship of state unattended. Leaders then must decide while others are satisfied with deliberating; they must concern themselves with politics or the public good while others concern themselves with private life; and they must break to some degree with the prevailing democratic ethos even as they seek to serve it.

Democratic Theory and Leadership

In some sense our understanding of leadership derives from the social contract theories of Thomas Hobbes (1588–1679) and John Locke (1632–1704), which—in spite of the continued and increasing theoretical criticism to which they are exposed—lie at the root of our political system. Such theories aim at avoiding the bad, not at achieving the good. Yet, according to the same theories, an executive—perhaps even an energetic executive—is necessary to ensure the execution of laws (the chief means by which the bad is avoided). The appropriate status of that executive thus becomes a major problem in liberal democratic theory. Some, chiefly Hobbes, have asserted the need for an absolute sovereign who would constrain citizens through fear so as to secure them. Others, specifically Locke, have accepted Hobbes's premises but condemned Hobbes's politics.

Locke, however, did not deny the inescapable need for an executive, and one, moreover, armed with the prerogative of acting in the absence of the law, and sometimes even against it. Leadership could never simply be reduced to the rule of law. For the law sometimes cannot be sovereign, as in the managing of foreign affairs, and sometimes is dormant, silent, self-contradictory, or simply too weak to accomplish much good. Hence leaders or executives are needed to supply the wisdom or prudence—or merely the brute strength—sometimes lacking in law. Contemporary liberals often have been unwilling to concede the necessary inadequacy of law. Emphasizing one strand of liberal thought, such liberal democrats, for all their talk of the need for leadership, ultimately seem more concerned with limiting the potential of bad or dangerous leaders than with guaranteeing the potential of good or helpful ones. Often only a serious crisis—a depression or a war—will reconcile some democrats to leadership.

Modern political theory has consisted, in large measure, of the liberation of political leadership from the cumbersome restraints of ancient and Christian morality, followed by a series of subsequent efforts to "tame" or domesticate such ferocious princes. Machiavelli, the first political philosopher to side with the people, nevertheless argued that a people can attain nothing without leaders. But, as modern democracy took root and flourished, it became increasingly ambivalent about leadership as such. (The ambivalence sometimes seemed to grow in proportion to the flourishing.) Machiavelli's followers focused on limiting government rather than on strengthening it. They invented the separation and balancing of powers, which turned leadership against itself, and promoted a politics of commerce, which, according to Montesquieu (1689–1755), would render authoritative leadership increasingly clumsy and unnecessary. Yet Montesquieu also defended the need for an executive and eloquently described the compatibility of democracy and leadership, warning against the potential egalitarian hostility toward all leaders.

The case of the United States reveals the democratic ambivalence about leadership at its origin. On the one hand, Alexander Hamilton called for an "energetic" executive and pointed to the Roman use of the dictator as evidence of the compatibility of republicanism (and, by extension, of democracy) and leadership. On the other hand, James Madison spoke disparagingly of leaders apt to quarrel amongst themselves for private purposes and proudly defended the American regime for not relying on the presence of "enlightened statesmen" (*Federalist* Nos. 10 and 70). The remarkable innovations of modern political science—separation of powers, checks and balances, extended sphere, representation, and so forth—seemed to hold out the hope that rightly constructed institutions could do away with the need for any further reliance on leadership, a hardly dependable commodity in any event.

As these suspicions of leaders hardened into opposition, a certain counterrevolution occurred. Inclined to the view that democratic envy or herd mentality (or simply an excessive reliance on institutions and laws) rather than sound political or moral judgment lay at the root of this opposition to leadership, supporters and practitioners of the idea of leadership began to enter the debate. In the nineteenth century, Alexis de Tocqueville warned that, just as aristocracies tended to overestimate the capacity of one man to change the course of history, so democracies tend to underestimate it. And this latter error is more damaging than the former because it reinforces an already debilitating materialism and determinism that is fatal to self-government. At the practical level, Abraham Lincoln's rise to prominence with his criticism of Stephen Douglas's thesis of popular sovereignty in the 1850s implies that a leader will always be needed, at least in the hard cases, to remind people of their principles lest they succumb to a base, narrow self-interest or a lazy compliance with circumstance.

Responsibilities of Leadership

The fundamental responsibility of leadership might best be understood as the need to navigate between the two major tensions present in modern, liberal democratic politics: between the good (or utility or security) and justice (or rights) and between wisdom and consent. If one element of either of these pairs comes to dominate the other, liberal politics, and hence individual happiness, will be at risk. Seeking the good (healthy souls or efficiency, for example) without respecting rights is illiberal (and, according to liberalism's founders, conducive to civil war), while defending rights without a concern for the consequences will likely prove damaging to such things as community, family, church, and moral fiber. Similarly, granting wisdom unrestricted sway smacks of an elitist contempt for people's preferences and sensibilities, while an unlimited deference to consent likely will lead either to confusion (as when various incompatible policies are simultaneously consented to) or to majority tyranny. Leadership then must balance competing ends (the good and justice) as well as competing means (reason and consent). A genuine or effective leader must be both flexible (without being vacillating or merely reactive) and principled (without being obstinate or absolutist).

Although the securing of rights is said by the American Declaration of Independence to be the purpose of government, rights cannot be secured except by an existing and relatively stable government, able as well as inclined to secure them. Hence there arise occasions, so troubling to principled defenders of liberal democracy, on which civil rights must apparently give way to such concerns as the common good, civic order, and national security. President Lincoln, in defending as constitutional his suspension of the constitutionally mandated writ of habeas corpus during the Civil War, has supplied the necessary justification for such actions in asking whether we must sacrifice the workings or existence of the government as a whole to the sanctity of each and every law. Vigilant defenders of liberty nevertheless are right to warn against the danger of the slippery slope.

The other difficulty that leadership must confront is the tension between what wisdom or sound administration or expertise demands and what the people have actually or presumptively consented to. The German philosopher Johann Fichte (1762–1814), embracing one horn of the dilemma, argued that whoever possesses reason has the right to compel everyone else to follow his views. This sort of leadership presents obvious difficulties for societies premised on the notion of consent, as societies do not always consent to what is rational. On the other hand, people can be presumed to have consented to that government and those policies which can reasonably be expected to secure their rights. Again Lincoln points to the most tenable solution to this problem when he suggests that public sentiment is decisive: whoever molds public sentiment makes it either possible or impossible to have a law-abiding polity. Simply stated, the chief responsibility of liberal democratic leadership is to educate public sentiment, through the use of rhetoric, so as to enable the people to consent to what is reasonable.

Leadership styles can be broadly related to two preferred manners of setting goals—either allowing goals to percolate up from a slowly building national consensus (the leader as agent) or having them devolve from the top down, that is, from an active executive branch (the leader as independent actor). But this dichotomy is in some ways misleading, as Lincoln's observation implies. For leadership is constrained by public opinion even as it seeks to educate or change it. Liberal democratic leadership neither dictates nor simply submits to public opinion. This "dialectic" does not exist in a political vacuum, however, but rather—in the case of the United States—within the context and boundaries of the Constitution, which sets the goals of American politics. A leader thus defends the constitutional interests of the people against the whims, fancies, and even settled but improper tendencies of the people.

Leadership and Statesmanship

Finally let us consider leadership as a variant of—or replacement for—statesmanship. Behind these terms lie two fundamentally different understandings of what the relationship between ruler and ruled should be. There are, in turn, two views of leadership itself. In one, leaders, by virtue of inspiration or charisma, supply their followers with a vision that functions as a map to new and uncharted regions. Such leaders, according to the German sociologist Max Weber (1864–1920), the discoverer of charisma, owe their authority neither to tradition (in the sense of being elders steeped in the tried and true ways of the community) nor to rationalism (in the sense of bureaucratic legalism and its putative standards of merit) but, rather, to their divine inspiration and mission. Such leadership is vindicated by nothing so formal as consent or election or representativeness but solely by the attainment of its initially mysterious end: no miracle accomplished, no more charismatic authority. As to the followers, they cannot know what they are in for until they get it.

In the second view, the leader discerns, through a peculiar talent for deft and sensitive listening, from the followers' discordant debating, or even from their pregnant silences, the vision implicit in what they are or desire. Woodrow Wilson, impatient with formalistic constraints (here, those of the Constitution), made the soundest argument for this type of leader. According to Wilson an almost biological imperative for societies to develop and progress exists, but it has been thwarted by unsound political structures (chiefly a division of powers that divides leadership against itself) and by the absence of leaders genuinely ready to listen sympathetically (and perhaps a bit creatively) to the spirit of their times. Wilson sensed and denounced the dangers of demagoguery inherent in the charismatic alternative, though his condemnation seems to have arisen despite, rather than because of, his theories. Here we have leadership of opinion, an effort to give voice to the people as against the people's representatives, with their secretive and conservative interests. In either case, the relevant metaphor for leadership is that of the journey, designed to broaden us by opening us up to new possibilities and showing us new horizons.

Statesmanship, on the other hand, implies neither the creativity of the former view nor the docility of the latter. (Wilson, it must be noted, spoke of the ultimate need for leaders to submit to what the public wants, if they are unable to convince it otherwise.) It involves turning one's gaze from the implicit and unformed yearnings of the citizens to the state or, better, to the political regime in which the statesman and the citizens find themselves. The statesman confronts the twin challenges of maintaining both the regime's existence and its character. In the view of a democratic people, the latter enhances the former: a democracy is made more secure by being made more democratic. Where a leader would tend, perhaps after some foot dragging, to comply with such a popular demand, a statesman would look to the regime, taking as his responsibility the occasional need to limit, rather than extend, the principle of the regime. Accordingly, the statesman's primary goal is not to propose something altogether new but to defend or improve the political regime by deepening its attachment to the political and moral principles already undergirding it. The relevant metaphor here then is the gymnastic trainer, who challenges us to be more fully what we already are.

It should be apparent by now that, to those bemoaning the "need for leadership," the statesman will often appear to be unimaginative, sluggish, lacking in daring, and unaccountably ready to side with the security-minded and even conservative citizens against their justice-loving and progressive fellows. The great African American abolitionist Frederick Douglass conceded that such was his initial view of Lincoln, the "white man's president." But when he came to recognize the harsh demands of the events under which Lincoln was laboring, he began to appreciate Lincoln as a veritable radical from the point of view of his people, a genuine statesman who sought and achieved a considerable measure of liberty and progress.

See also *Aristotle; Elite theory; Elites, Political; Hamilton, Alexander; Hobbes, Thomas; Jefferson, Thomas; Lincoln, Abraham; Locke, John; Machiavelli, Niccolò; Madison, James; Montesquieu; Rhetoric; Tocqueville, Alexis de; Weber, Max; Wilson, Woodrow.*

Richard S. Ruderman

BIBLIOGRAPHY

Burke, Edmund. "Speech to the Electors of Bristol." In *Burke's Politics,* edited by Ross J. S. Hoffman and Paul Levack. New York: Knopf, 1949.

Burns, James MacGregor. *Leadership.* New York: Harper and Row, 1978.

Charnwood, Lord. *Abraham Lincoln.* London: Constable, 1919.

Jones, Bryan D., ed. *Leadership and Politics.* Lawrence: University Press of Kansas, 1989.

Mansfield, Harvey C., Jr. *Taming the Prince.* New York: Free Press, 1989.

Tulis, Jeffrey. *The Rhetorical Presidency.* Princeton: Princeton University Press, 1987.

Weber, Max. "Politics as a Vocation" and "The Sociology of Charismatic Authority." In *From Max Weber.* Translated by Hans H. Gerth and C. Wright Mills. New York: Oxford University Press, 1946.

League of Nations

The League of Nations was the first serious move in history toward world government—or at least toward an international organization designed to prevent wars. Established after World War I (1914–1918) as part of the Treaty of Versailles, the League handled a number of minor issues fairly well from 1919 into the 1930s. But it failed in its most important task, that of keeping the peace. The League of Nations played no role during World War II and was superseded by the United Nations after 1945.

The League was based largely upon the designs of Woodrow Wilson, who was president of the United States when that nation entered World War I in 1917. In 1919 the U.S. Senate rejected the League by failing to cast the two-thirds vote required to ratify the Treaty of Versailles. The League went ahead without American participation, but it drew in most of the independent nations of the world.

Self-Determination and Collective Security

Wilson and other supporters of the League of Nations had spoken of entering the war to "make the world safe for democracy," but they could just as well have spoken of making the world safe *by* democracy. Advocates of the League believed that many of the problems and wars inherited from nineteenth-century European diplomacy had emerged because self-determination was not the guiding principle in establishing political boundaries. Ethnic groups and even entire countries were governed against their preferences. The solution—either by the terms of the peace treaties ending World War I or by plebiscites to be administered thereafter by the League of Nations—would be to allow people to choose which country they were to be part of, what language they were to speak, and what flag they were to salute.

Given the revulsion against the slaughter and destructiveness of World War I, the League was intended to promote peace at least as much as it was designed to foster democracy. Yet the assumption was that the two went together. For example, the architects of the League believed that Germany, which was blamed for initiating the war, could be trusted only when it became democratic and that the ethnic disputes of Central and Eastern Europe might be manageable if each geographic area were governed according to the wishes of the people who lived in it.

The priority of peace called for the League to come

down against the initiator of any war. Whereas the old balance-of-power system would have called for intervention against the likely winner of any war, to prevent a hegemonic, or dominant, power threat from emerging, the new collective security logic of the League of Nations called for intervention against the nation that had started the war. The objective was to establish the principle that all wars must be avoided.

In the old balance-of-power system of diplomacy the ideal number of participating nations was often thought to be five. Rulers (typically hereditary monarchs) of the separate states were constantly on guard against anyone attempting to establish an empire over the entire system. Whenever any two states waged war, the other states typically would wait to see who was winning and then would intervene to keep the weaker side from being defeated and absorbed. The goal was to keep any conglomeration of power from emerging that could then defeat and absorb all the separate states.

Under the League of Nations, however, the ideal number of participants was much larger—perhaps between fifty and a hundred or more. In case of war the League might require large numbers of unbiased and unprejudiced fact finders to take on a "jury duty" role and determine which nation had initiated hostilities. In deciding to impose economic sanctions or collective political intervention, a fair determination of which country had struck the first blow would be crucial. Moreover, if the principle of self-determination were successful, the total number of sovereign countries would increase. A growth in numbers would not have worked under the old balance-of-power system, but it fit well with the structure of a collective security arrangement.

With the toppling of Czar Nicholas II in Russia, in 1917, the Allies (the victorious nations in World War I), which were joined with the United States in drafting the Charter of the League of Nations, were all political democracies. Although it was soon clear at Versailles that France, Great Britain, and Italy had retained some of their traditional power and territorial interests, their domestic political style was based on free elections and thus was not inconsistent with a commitment to democracy as part of a new international order.

France's traditional enmity with Germany, however, suggested that the French would not be happy to see the Austrians, as a result of self-determination, joined with Germany or to see the German minorities in Czechoslovakia and Poland merged with Germany. France in partic-

ular was more concerned about future relationships with its neighbor than about the League of Nations as a vehicle for the democratic self-determination of all of Europe. These priorities persisted even when democracy was tried in Germany. The German Weimar Republic, which lasted only from 1919 until 1933, was beset with economic problems and bitterness about Germany's defeat in World War I and thus lacked deep popular support.

Wilson and his supporters were dismayed by the persistence of such attitudes at Versailles. They were disappointed at the secret agreements that the Allies had negotiated among themselves before the United States entered the war. These agreements often ran flagrantly counter to the ethnic preferences of the territories being swapped. Wilson reluctantly went along with some of these arrangements, expecting that the League of Nations would provide the mechanism for rectifying territorial discrepancies and bringing self-government to any border territories that had been so cavalierly handled.

Structure of the League

The internal voting arrangements established for the League of Nations mirrored its proponents' general commitment to democracy. As noted, a larger rather than smaller number of members was implicit in the new system. Over its history, the League had sixty members altogether, as members joined and withdrew. Germany was not permitted to join the League until 1926, when its democratic nature under the Weimar Republic and a new constitution seemed reasonably established. Adolf Hitler's Nazi regime withdrew Germany from the League in 1933. The Soviet Union was allowed to join in 1934 but was expelled after it invaded Finland in 1939. The United States was the only major independent state never to be a member.

Based in Geneva, Switzerland, the League worked through its two most important components: the Assembly, in which all members voted, and a smaller Council. As a concession to the larger states, permanent membership in the Council was accorded to the major powers. The remaining Council seats rotated among the other members. Important decisions of either the Assembly or the Council required unanimous votes, but parties to a dispute were not allowed to vote on that dispute. Unlike the later United Nations, the League did not endow the major powers with any special veto.

The Council had no exclusive responsibilities. It was formed on the assumption that in a time of slow communication and transportation it would be difficult to convene meetings of the entire Assembly on short notice; the smaller Council, however, could be drawn together more rapidly.

Because the premise of the League of Nations was that force, as in domestic society, should never be used to settle international disputes, there obviously had to be some sort of court, as in domestic government, to hear grievances. A Permanent Court of International Justice was established as part of the League to hear and adjudicate disputes. This judicial body, renamed the International Court of Justice, was later retained as part of the United Nations. Also under the League's overarching umbrella were several specialized international agencies, such as the World Health Organization, World Meteorological Association, and International Labor Organization. Some of these had existed before 1919, and most survived to be incorporated into the United Nations.

Reasons for Failure

It is commonly remembered that the League's failure to maintain peace occurred because the United States did not become a member. Considerations of democracy played an important role here, in several ways. The U.S. Constitution requires that something as momentous as a commitment to an international organization be ratified by more than a simple majority of the Senate. It is easy today to forget that a majority of Americans in 1920 were probably in favor of joining the League of Nations and that a majority of senators were ready to endorse it, albeit not the required two-thirds.

One powerful argument against the League was the threat to American democracy and self-determination that an international organization could pose. Great Britain was a democracy, most Americans would have agreed, but the League provided for each of Britain's overseas dominions to be a member, including even India, which was in no sense self-governing. Furthermore, the British and French demands and secret treaties revealed at Versailles disillusioned many Americans who had seen the war as a struggle between good and evil, between self-determination and power-hungry imperialism.

The United States also had mixed feelings about according each country, regardless of size, an equal membership in the League of Nations. Americans would insist on their own sovereignty as protection for their own political democracy and freedom. But such a recognition of separate sovereignty and equal votes in a world organiza-

tion, given that most countries were much smaller than the United States, would be inconsistent with the democratic ideal of equal voting power for equal-size population groups. Thus, for some Americans, the only solution was to oppose membership in the League.

Not all the disappointments with the League of Nations can be blamed on the failure of the United States to participate, however. League-sponsored attempts to promote self-determination across Central and Eastern Europe during the years between the two world wars were disappointing. Every country but Czechoslovakia succumbed to a dictatorship of one kind or another. Furthermore, these countries did not demonstrate fair-mindedness or concern about self-determination where ethnic minorities were concerned. Just as many Americans had become disillusioned with the inability of the Latin American republics (all of which joined the League of Nations) to maintain democratic practices domestically, the record of Europe after 1919 upset the link between democracy and collective security, reducing rather than increasing U.S. support for the League.

As an instrument of peace, the League was thwarted when it confronted so blatantly nondemocratic a regime as Benito Mussolini's Italy or Adolf Hitler's Germany. Wilson and other architects of the League of Nations assumed that the entire world would desire peace after the carnage of World War I, and that democratic governments in particular would want peace. Mussolini and Hitler would turn this assumption around, announcing that Italy and Germany were not so addicted to peace because they had transcended and abolished democracy. Their message to the League was the fundamental challenge of the bully: If you want to maintain peace, stand aside as we annex territories. The League's aversion to war, stemming in important part from its democratic origins, made the threat of going to war to repulse aggressions appear a bluff. Germany, Italy, and imperial Japan saw their own advantage in such contests of resolve against the League of Nations and were able to act precisely because they were not democratic.

Analysts differ in explaining why the League of Nations failed. The most common explanation is that the absence of the United States left the League unequal to the demands of confronting Germany and Japan. Some, however, conclude that the basic premise of collective security, that war could be ruled out as a means of resolving disputes, was unrealistic. Related to this view is the belief that Wilson and other advocates of the League were premature in expecting democracy to spread and in expecting democracies to be peaceful.

International organizations depend to a great extent on what happens in domestic politics. In the contemporary world, if democracy takes hold across the former Soviet Union and Eastern Europe and in Latin America, and if economic reforms in China lead the Chinese toward political democracy, the international order can be based on democracy, as Woodrow Wilson and other proponents of the League of Nations had envisaged. If political democracy fails in many of these countries, however, the international order will revert to a form more familiar to the believer in power politics.

See also *International organizations; United Nations; Wilson, Woodrow; World War I.*

George H. Quester

BIBLIOGRAPHY

Claude, Inis L. *Swords into Plowshares.* New York: Random House, 1971.

Fleming, Denna Frank. *The United States and the League of Nations.* New York: Russell and Russell, 1968.

Joyce, James Avery. *Broken Star: The Story of the League of Nations.* Swansea: C. Davies, 1978.

Marks, Sally. *The Illusion of Peace: International Relations in Europe, 1918–1933.* New York: St. Martin's; London: Macmillan, 1976.

Northedge, F. S. *The League of Nations: Its Life and Times, 1920–1946.* New York: Holmes and Meier, 1986; London: Leicester University Press, 1988.

Stone, Ralph A., ed. *Wilson and the League of Nations: Why America's Rejection?* New York: Holt, Rinehart, and Winston, 1967.

Walters, Francis Paul. *A History of the League of Nations.* New York and Oxford: Oxford University Press, 1952.

Lebanon

A constitutional republic located on the eastern end of the Mediterranean Sea, bordered on the east by Syria and on the south by Israel. For more than three decades—from independence in 1943 until the collapse of civil order in 1975–1976—Lebanon had the only continuous democratic political system in the Arab world. To be sure, Lebanese democracy was limited and flawed in many ways, but it could boast regular, free, and competitive elections and an impressive degree of open political debate and activity. The ruinous civil war that claimed at least 120,000 lives between 1975 and 1990 ended with the resto-

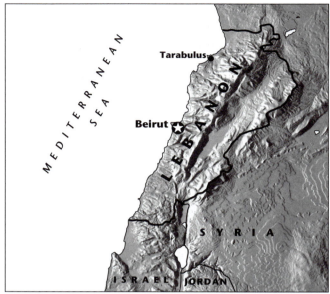

ration of the old parliamentary system, considerably modified, and with the country's politics dominated by its bigger neighbor, Syria.

Although modern Lebanon, in terms of territory and political structure, is a recent creation—dating only to the establishment of the French mandate in 1920—historic Lebanon, according to the mythology of some Lebanese nationalists, is rooted in ancient Phoenicia and early Christianity. Traditional "Mount Lebanon" encompassed the area from the Mediterranean just north of Beirut and south of Tripoli to the Lebanon mountain range. Owing in part to its rugged terrain (useful for defensive purposes), Lebanon became the refuge and home of numerous Christian and Muslim sects: Maronites, Greek Orthodox, Greek Catholics, Roman Catholics, Sunnis, Shi'ites, Druze Muslims, and many other smaller communities. It also developed a complex quasi-feudal social structure during the Ottoman Empire.

Because of its many sects and complex society, Lebanon was not a place that could be governed, even by a powerful empire, without mechanisms for balancing the various communities and interests found there. It was perhaps this diversity rather than any common orientation that set Lebanon apart from neighbors and gave it a kind of "negative identity."

In 1920, after World War I, France created two new states in former Ottoman territory: Lebanon and Syria. "Greater Lebanon" comprised the traditional Mount

Lebanon as well as the territories now known as North Lebanon, the Biqa, South Lebanon, and Beirut—territories that, significantly, were composed overwhelmingly of Sunni or Shiʿite Muslims. France's political control over Lebanon came to an end in 1943, allowing a coalition of Lebanese nationalists (Christians and Muslims) to achieve a relatively bloodless independence. An act of creative statesmanship by two liberal politicians (Bishara al-Khuri, a Maronite Christian, and Riyad al-Sulh, a Sunni Muslim) produced in 1943 the National Pact, often dubbed Lebanon's "real" constitution.

The National Pact

The National Pact solved the problem that had paralyzed politics under the French mandate: it brought the Muslims back into the system. It did so by allocating major offices according to a more equitable formula than had previously been used and by stipulating a foreign policy that would avoid entangling alliances with either the Christian West or the Arab-Muslim East. The National Pact ensured that the president would always be a Maronite Christian, the prime minister a Sunni Muslim, and the president of the Chamber of Deputies a Shiʿite Muslim. It also provided that legislative and executive positions would be allocated on a 6 to 5 basis between Christians and Muslims, with an equitable distribution among the various Christian and Muslim sects as well.

Thus the National Pact, a constitution in 1926, and subsequent electoral laws brought about a fairly faithful replication of the consociational democracy model, in which elites representing mutually hostile ethnic groups share power according to fixed rules. Sects were represented proportionally within the government, and the system encouraged the integration of all sects at the elite level. It also furthered elitism within the sects. Landowners, business leaders, and lawyers were able to manipulate the electoral system so as to enhance their prestige and power in the emerging Lebanese state.

For three decades Lebanon's consociational arrangements ameliorated the problem of sectarian insecurity and rivalry. But Lebanon's politicians were never able (nor indeed was it in their interest) to eliminate political sectarianism altogether. By the mid-1950s the demographic rationale for Christian (especially Maronite) predominance was widely thought to have evaporated. The only formal population census had been taken under the French in 1932. But higher Muslim birthrates and higher Christian emigration after that time led many to think that non-Christians were now a majority. Compounding the problem was the rise of Arab nationalism in the 1950s. Lebanese Muslims felt that the Christian president was siding with the "imperialist West," while Lebanese Christians feared a Muslim-led, pan-Arab takeover that might extinguish the country's Christian character, if not its very existence. Socioeconomic tensions also were growing, driven by uneven development and rapid urbanization. The carefully calibrated sectarian system made it difficult for government to respond to these challenges.

In theory, the president should have been able to provide dynamic and creative leadership because his powers exceeded those of any other politician or institution, including the prime minister and the Chamber of Deputies. In practice, however, independent Lebanon's first two presidents, Bishara al-Khuri (1943–1952) and Camille Chamoun (1952–1958), concentrated their energies on consolidating their winning coalition in Parliament and in the country, and both sought to renew their terms despite a constitutional prohibition. In both cases disgruntled notables—traditional leaders of sects or regions—banded together to challenge the president and drew on the increasingly radicalized young people from the middle and lower classes to rally around their "reformist" opposition. President al-Khuri was replaced after a constitutional crisis in 1952, and President Chamoun precipitated a brief civil war in 1958. An American diplomat, Robert Murphy, helped to negotiate Chamoun's resignation and his replacement by the commander of the Lebanese army, Gen. Fuʾad Shihab.

The 1958 crisis revealed the fragility of Lebanon's consociational democracy. A formula designed to neutralize sectarian divisions was unable to adapt to changing demographic and social conditions, nor could it bridge the growing divide between Lebanese Christians and Muslims over Lebanon's position in the "Arab cold war" between Western and Arab nationalist orientations. The "military solution" to the 1958 crisis, in the person of General Shihab, resembled more the Turkish model of temporary corrective intervention than the Arab model of intervention by military figures in nationalist garb who often seek to make the presidency a lifetime position. Shihab's reform program, however, began to run out of steam by the end of his term in 1964, and his handpicked successor, Charles Hilu (1964–1970), lacked the authority and leadership to regain the momentum.

The traditional politicians, mostly Christian, who had been shoved aside by "Shihabism" gradually recovered and were able to exploit the inefficiency, corruption, and occasional repressiveness of the Shihabists. The regional turmoil churned up by the defeat of neighboring Arab regimes at the hands of Israel in the 1967 Six-Day War stimulated the growth of the Palestinian resistance movement in Lebanon and elsewhere. Many Lebanese Christians feared that the growth of this movement threatened Lebanon's delicate sectarian balance. For their part, many Lebanese Muslims (and some Christians) lent enthusiastic support to the Palestinian guerrillas who had emerged in the wake of Arab government defeats in 1967. While the leading Palestinian group, al-Fatah, emphatically denied any interest in becoming involved in Lebanese affairs, Palestinian leaders felt it prudent to cement relationships with friendly Lebanese Muslims in order to offset growing Lebanese Christian hostility. Lebanese Muslim politicians feared that right-wing Christians might control the Lebanese army, and they also observed that Christian politicians were building their own militias. Because they lacked comparably powerful militias, they turned to the well-organized and well-equipped Palestinians.

Driven by worst-case, self-fulfilling prophecies, all these players found themselves marching toward civil war. Between 1970 and 1975 the coherence, authority, and relevance of the Lebanese state dwindled. Not only was the multisectarian consociational Lebanese elite disintegrating, but the masses too were increasingly riven by sectarian fear and hatred. The parliamentary election of 1972, though broadly representative of the sects and major traditional leaders, was unable to bridge the growing cleavages.

There would not be another such election for twenty years. In 1975 Lebanon was plunged into a fifteen-year civil war that wrecked the country's economy and society. Armed militias displaced the authority of the state; democratic processes were paralyzed. Complicating matters was the involvement of external actors, notably Israel, Syria, Iran, and the Palestinians.

Ta'if Accords

The civil war was formally brought to an end with the signing of the National Accord Document for Lebanon, issued in Ta'if, Saudi Arabia, on October 24, 1989. The Ta'if accords, composed with the active participation of Syria, Saudi Arabia, and the United States and signed by nearly all of the surviving members of the 1972 Chamber of Deputies, were the blueprint for the restoration of the Lebanese state.

The accords may have modified the rules of the game of the First Republic, but they did not alter the basic character of the rules. Postwar Lebanon—in form—is still more or less a consociational democracy. Sectarian proportionality remains in place, but the proportion of Muslim to Christian legislators and officials has been increased to 50-50. For the foreseeable future the president of the republic remains a Maronite Christian, but the powers of the office have been substantially reduced. The prime minister remains a Sunni Muslim, but the powers of the Council of Ministers, chaired by the prime minister, have been increased. The office of president of the Chamber of Deputies still goes to a Shi'ite, but the term has been increased from one year to four and the influence of the office has also increased. The power of the Chamber itself was increased by the elimination of the old provision allowing the executive to pass "urgent" legislation without parliamentary involvement. At the same time, the Ta'if accords explicitly called for a gradual phasing out of political sectarianism.

Other provisions of the Ta'if accords relating to Lebanon's external relations were more controversial. For example, in proclaiming that Lebanon was Arab in identity, the accords went farther than the 1943 National Pact and thus alarmed some Christians. Even more alarming was the provision authorizing a special relationship between Lebanon and Syria, which would give Syria a privileged position in certain matters, including national security. Moreover, a pledge by Syria to redeploy its forces in Lebanon east of the Lebanon mountain range within two years of the formal ratification of the Ta'if accords (in 1990), the holding of a new presidential election, and the formation of a new cabinet also were conditional on the approval of political reforms (by which was meant the beginning of the process of desectarianization). Two years later, in 1992, with a new president and cabinet in place, the Syrians refused to redeploy on the grounds that not all of the political reforms had been achieved. Furthermore, as long as Israel controlled its self-styled "security zone" in southern Lebanon, Syria could justify keeping its own military presence in the country.

Many Maronite Christians either opposed the Ta'if accords outright or accepted them with great reluctance. They also opposed holding new parliamentary elections in August and September 1992, but Syria refused all requests to delay them, even for technical reasons such as the difficulty of updating the electoral rolls after the vast demographic upheavals of the previous seventeen years.

The elections were held, notwithstanding the shadow of Syria and a boycott in much of the Maronite heartland of Mount Lebanon. The new Parliament was welcomed in most other parts of the country as an important, if flawed, step on the road back to stable representative government.

There were several striking trends in the political makeup of the new Chamber of Deputies. Some 47 percent of the new deputies were affiliated with a political party or movement (as opposed to a traditional grouping or independent status), compared with 31 percent in the 1972 Parliament. Some of the parties showed continuity—for example, the Baʿath, Druze leader Kamal Junblat's Progressive Socialist Party, and the Armenian Revolutionary Federation (Dashnak). More striking was the disappearance of many traditional Maronite actors. Absent too were the prominent anti-Syrian militia chiefs of the civil war. Many Maronites of Mount Lebanon looked upon these results as depressing evidence of the end of Maronite hegemony. But not only were traditional Christian players missing, there also were new Islamic actors on the parliamentary scene. The Shiʿite parties Amal and Hizballah now constituted the largest blocs in Parliament—twelve seats for Hizballah and twenty for Amal. There also was small but significant representation from two Sunni Muslim Islamist parties.

Even Lebanese observers who detested Syria's involvement in Lebanese politics admitted that Damascus had on the whole acted skillfully to implant its influence in postwar Lebanon while allowing quite a broad spectrum of traditional and new political forces a place on the stage. But if Lebanon was to emerge definitively from its past agony, the traditional Christians of Mount Lebanon would have to be brought back into the formal system in one way or another. The presidential election scheduled for 1995 and the parliamentary elections in 1996 would provide important tests of the inclusiveness of the postwar order.

The Lessons Learned

Modern Lebanon has exhibited a limited form of liberal democracy because of its exceptional cultural and social diversity. As perhaps the most heterogeneous region in the Ottoman Empire it was too hard to rule directly. There was a functional imperative for institutionalized procedures for consultation and representation. As a quintessentially plural society, Lebanon developed pluralist political structures long before it emerged as a modern state. The liberal bourgeois founders of independent Lebanon

sought with considerable success to integrate traditional pluralism with a European parliamentary model.

In the early 1950s, when liberal experiments in neighboring Arab countries such as Syria, Egypt, and Iraq were giving way to anti-Western nationalist authoritarianism, Lebanon's Christian-dominated elite managed to deflect similar tendencies, but only with great difficulty. The 1958 crisis, in retrospect, should have sounded the alarm that the system was insensitive to internal socioeconomic pressures that were undermining the sectarian formula, and that regional ideological challenges were growing. The failure of the Shihabist reforms and the resurrection of the parochial Maronite leaders paved the way for the total collapse of the system in 1975.

What are the lessons of the civil war? The first reaction might be that Lebanon has given democracy a bad name. If democracy failed in Lebanon—the only Arab country where it had worked—why should anyone recommend its application elsewhere in the region? Indeed, why should anyone recommend a return to democracy for postwar Lebanon itself? This issue has been hotly debated in Lebanon, with some arguing that the civil war was almost totally the result of outside pressures and others insisting that the domestic sociopolitical order was the principal weakness. Without minimizing the complexity and multiple causes of the war, one might propose that Lebanon's problem was not too much democracy but rather too little. More precisely, the built-in sectarianism that defined Lebanon's elitist, consociational democracy carried the seeds of future disaster. The consociational medicine that relieved immediate sectarian tension lost its potency as Lebanon's society and demography changed. Furthermore, the side effects—parochialism and a certain immobilism and insensitivity in policy making—tended to impede effective responses to many other issues that were threatening social order and political stability. To blame Lebanon's troubles simply on "democracy," then, would risk throwing out the democratic baby with the consociational bathwater.

See also *Middle East*.

Michael C. Hudson

BIBLIOGRAPHY

American Task Force for Lebanon. "Working Paper: Conference on Lebanon." Washington, D.C.: American Task Force for Lebanon, 1991.

Baaklini, Abdo I. *Legislative and Political Development: Lebanon, 1842–1972.* Durham, N.C.: Duke University Press, 1976.

Hudson, Michael C. *The Precarious Republic: Political Modernization in Lebanon*. New York: Random House, 1968; Boulder, Colo.: Westview Press, 1985.

Khalaf, Samir. *Lebanon's Predicament*. New York: Columbia University Press, 1987.

Salibi, Kamal. *The Modern History of Lebanon*. London: Weidenfeld and Nicolson, 1965.

Legislatures and parliaments

Assemblies of elected representatives from geographically defined constituencies, with lawmaking and other functions in the governmental process. Legislatures, called parliaments in most countries, exist in nearly all contemporary political systems, although they are particularly associated with democracies.

The size of legislatures is related imperfectly to the size of the populations of their countries. Most are composed of 100–300 members. Countries with small populations may have parliaments as small as the 15-member Diet of Liechtenstein. Large countries may have congresses of more than 1,000 members, as Russia did between 1990 and 1993. The U.S. Senate, with 100 members, is at the low end of the range of major legislatures. The U.S. House of Representatives has 435 members, and some of the oldest parliaments of European countries have more than 600 members.

Members of legislatures base their authority on the claim that they represent the citizens. Since each member is equally a representative, each is equal to every other in formal authority and status. To transform the strong and often contentious views of such a large number of individuals into collective decisions requires distinctive procedures. These have developed through centuries of experience and have been passed from older to newer parliaments.

At minimum, all legislatures are public forums for the discussion of major issues, an important function in democracies. In some cases, notably in the United States, legislatures are important lawmaking and budget-making bodies. In most countries, however, their role in lawmaking and in the formulation and enactment of the budget is subordinate to that of the executive branch. The executive drafts most bills, proposes the budget, and manages the passage of items through the legislature. In parliamentary systems of government the legislature participates in se-lecting the chief executives of government. They are generally chosen from among leaders of the dominant party or parties in the legislature. In most systems, legislatures supervise the executive branch in various ways, exercising what is known as oversight. As the capacity of legislatures to make laws and budgets has become more limited everywhere, this oversight has gained in political importance.

Legislatures exercise different functions from time to time and from place to place, but they have a characteristic structure that determines how they work and that distinguishes them from the executive branch of government. Members of a legislature do not stand in a relationship of authority and subordination to each other but are formally equal. They base their authority on their claim to represent others, rather than on a claim of their own subject expertise. Legislatures conduct their business at least partly in the public view. The decisions of legislatures are made collectively rather than by the command of superiors.

The capacity of several hundred men and women to reach collective decisions depends on the complicated patterns of influence that develop among these nominally equal individuals when they become members of the legislature. These patterns are a product of (1) the legislature's institutional history; (2) the relationship of representation between members and the outside world; (3) the legislature's distinctive organization; and (4) its distinctive procedure.

Predemocratic History

Parliaments predate the advent of democracy. They arose in medieval Europe as early as the twelfth century. Many of the procedures of modern legislatures have evolved from their long historical experience. These procedures have been preserved by successive generations of parliamentarians in the form of parliamentary precedents. The parliamentarians of the British House of Commons were particularly adept at recording and maintaining these precedents. The concept of representation, on which the authority and the composition of legislatures rests, also has medieval origins. Thus the legislature is a product of medieval European civilization, transformed in the age of democracy to suit the needs of a great variety of contemporary political systems, including some systems in which the legislature serves largely to legitimate nondemocratic authority.

In the five centuries preceding the American Revolution, the normal form of government in Europe was

The legislative assemblies of many nations trace their procedures and practices to the House of Commons, the lower house of the British Parliament.

monarchy. Monarchs reigned over societies in which the Catholic Church, the landowning nobility, and trading organizations in the towns claimed rights and privileges from the crown. These varied groups—called orders, corporations, colleges, or, more generally, estates—composed a society of status groups. The state that was built on the distribution of power among these groups was appropriately called a *Ständestaat,* a state of estates. The privileges that these estates claimed were based on custom, contract, or civil and church law.

To come to terms with these centers of power, monarchs found it prudent to assemble leading members of these groups from time to time to consult them concerning important questions of war and peace, of taxation, and of the administration of justice. In some countries monarchs met separately with the nobility; this pattern led to bicameralism, or parliaments composed of two houses. These assemblies, which usually met irregularly, existed in most of the countries of Europe west of Russia. They were variously called *Cortes* (Spanish), *Etats-*

Généraux (France), *Landtag* (German), *Parlemento* (Italian), or *Riksdag* (Swedish). Such names denoted the place or day of meeting or the group's composition or activity. The name *legislature* came much later, during the seventeenth-century revolution in England, when the House of Commons claimed to be the lawmaking body, a claim that the institution did not finally achieve in Great Britain. The claim, however, was heard and remembered by the British settlers in North America, who used it successfully to gain autonomy from the king by insisting on the lawmaking powers of their own assemblies. Thus the institution has been called the legislature in the United States, while almost everywhere else its name does not connote a lawmaking function.

To the extent that these assemblies, by whatever name, developed a sense of their collective power, that power was justified by the idea that they were a representation of society: when they met it was the meeting of the country in the presence of the monarch. These early assemblies exercised influence on government at the provincial and national levels throughout Europe for five centuries before the advent of democracy. They were therefore familiar political institutions at the dawn of democracy in the late eighteenth and early nineteenth centuries. Furthermore, because their influence was based on their capacity to speak for and make commitments for the most powerful groups in society, these assemblies could be adapted to the requirements of democracy when participation in politics expanded to new groups of the population.

Indeed, democratic movements in Europe regarded a parliament as an instrument for imposing the will of the people on the monarch. Parliaments therefore arose out of the needs of a predemocratic but pluralistic society and out of efforts to restrain executive power. Although they were not the invention of democracies, they proved to be the most suitable instruments of democracy among the traditional institutions of European government.

Some medieval European parliaments, like the Estates General of France, fell victim to the democratic revolutions of the late eighteenth and early nineteenth centuries because they were too strongly associated with the privileges of the medieval estates, communities, or corporations. Their composition could not withstand the democratic claim that the nation was composed of individuals deserving representation as equals. Others, like the British Parliament and the provincial German Landtage, were reformed and became instruments of democracy. Whether the democratic parliaments were new creations or modifications of traditional parliaments, their composition continued to rest on the principle of representation, and their organization and procedures were based on those of the medieval assemblies. Without the centuries-old traditions accumulated by the medieval European parliaments, the modern institution is unimaginable.

Representation

A legislature whose members claim to be representative of a democratic society must have its members elected by the people at regular intervals. Some democracies may tolerate appointed second chambers as vestiges of a class-based society, like the House of Lords in the United Kingdom. All democracies, however, insist that the dominant parliamentary chamber be elected by a broad franchise. The idea of "virtual" representation—that constituents who have not voted are nevertheless represented in Parliament—may have been credible to defenders of the unreformed House of Commons in Great Britain in the nineteenth century. The concept is inconsistent with demo-

cratic thought, however, except as it may pertain to children and others who are incapable of exercising the franchise. Consequently, the democratization of legislatures has consisted of defining and expanding the electorate, organizing the massive electorates characteristic of modern states, and broadening eligibility for membership in Parliament.

One-third of the world's parliaments consist of two houses. The members of half of these second chambers are directly elected, while those of the other half are either elected indirectly or appointed. In the twenty-five years after World War II, three countries replaced a bicameral legislature with a one-house, or unicameral, legislature: Denmark, New Zealand, and Sweden. When parliaments were democratized in Central and Eastern Europe following the withdrawal of the Soviet Union from support for communist regimes, Poland added a second chamber to its parliament. Still other countries contemplate the establishment of a second house. There is no clear trend away from bicameralism, despite its predemocratic roots. Indeed, a house to represent constituencies not based on equal populations continues to be attractive, particularly in federal states where one house, like the U.S. Senate or the German Bundesrat, is used to represent the component states.

Nevertheless, the effort to democratize parliaments principally has consisted of extending the right to choose members. Thus a franchise limited to property holders was expanded to "universal" manhood suffrage and then to suffrage without regard to gender, race, or ethnicity and finally to eighteen-year-olds. This development began in the United States early in the nineteenth century, in Great Britain with the first reform of parliamentary representation in 1832, and on the continent of Europe after the revolutions of 1848. It was completed in most countries in the second half of the twentieth century and had profound consequences for the composition and internal organization of parliaments.

The democratic franchise created mass electorates that needed to be organized in order to be able to act at all. To that end modern legislatures retained the medieval notions that the country consists of geographic communities and that the representative assembly should be a house representing these communities, or *commons*, as the British called them. Thus the British elected chamber is the House of Commons. By comparison, the notion that the country consisted of estates or orders was generally abandoned. Also abandoned were attempts to give a modern, functional form to the medieval corporations by establishing a chamber representing professions, occupations, and interest groups. The electoral process by which members of legislatures are chosen is therefore organized territorially, with geographically defined constituencies electing single or multiple representatives.

The mass electorate is also organized by political parties, successors to the factions that existed within predemocratic parliaments. Unlike factions, parties work outside parliaments as well as within them, linking groups of like-minded members with their voters. Parties nominate candidates for parliament, mobilize the voters, formulate electoral programs, and attempt to hold the elected members accountable to their voters. Democratic legislatures are distinguished from legislatures in dictatorships by the fact that their members are selected in competition between candidates of two or more political parties. The organization of democratic electorates has therefore taken two forms: territorial and partisan. There is considerable variation from one country to another in how territorial constituencies are drawn and how party competition is regulated.

In the United States, as in most federal states, constituencies are divided first among the component states by a formula that reflects their relative populations. The state legislatures then draw congressional constituency boundaries, under supervision by the courts to make certain that two basic criteria of fairness are followed. First, constituencies must have strictly equal populations. Second, racial and ethnic minorities must have a chance to win their proportional share of seats. The votes of minorities may not be "diluted" by the way constituency borders are drawn. In Great Britain, Germany, and many other democratic countries, boundaries are drawn by nonpartisan, quasi-judicial commissions, and expectations of fairness are different. In most countries the principle of population equality is not as strictly enforced as in the United States, and regard for the representation of minorities varies greatly. The populations of British parliamentary constituencies can deviate by more than 20 percent from the national average. Especially in countries having multiparty systems, the expectation that the partisan preferences of the electorate should be fairly represented in parliament is more highly developed than in the United States.

In about half of all democratic countries, each parliamentary constituency is represented by several members. This makes it possible to have proportional representation, or the election of candidates of the various political parties in proportion to their relative number of votes. The precision of this proportionality depends on the number of representatives elected for each constituency. Partisan proportionality avoids the dominance of a single party over time, like Democratic Party dominance in the U.S. House of Representatives. It results, however, in an increase in the number of political parties that win seats in parliament.

The preference for proportional representation developed in Europe after World War I, expressing a democratic sense of fairness toward the whole spectrum of political parties. As a result, political parties proliferated, causing an early form of gridlock in parliaments. After World War II many countries limited proportional representation by requiring parties to obtain at least 5 percent of the vote in the entire country before they could claim their proportional share of seats in parliament. This "threshold" provision was also adopted by most of the newly democratic legislatures that were established in Central and Eastern Europe after 1989. The structure of representation therefore has direct consequences for the party composition of legislatures and for the process of decision making in the legislatures, in which parties play an important role.

In addition to the expansion of the electorate, democracy required the expansion of eligibility for membership in parliament. Most countries impose criteria for election of members that are more exacting than the criteria for voting. They do this not from an antidemocratic impulse but to increase the probability that members of legislatures will be qualified to carry out their responsibilities. Most countries require members to be at least twenty-one years of age, even if voters need only be eighteen. In the United States members of the House of Representatives must be at least twenty-five, and members of the Senate must be thirty years old. Most countries also require members to have been citizens and residents of their country for a specified number of years, and many bar candidates who have serious criminal records or other legal incapacities. To avoid conflicts of interest, many countries establish the ineligibility for parliament of holders of certain public offices or even members of certain occupations.

Broadening the right of the population to participate in the selection of members of parliament and broadening eligibility for membership do not ensure that the composition of the legislature will appear to be representative of the population. A few hundred representatives cannot fully mirror a large population, but democratic publics do expect representative institutions to resemble them in salient respects. All countries expect that the membership of the legislature should reflect the geographic diversity of the population, and most expect that the party composition of the legislature should bear a reasonably close relationship to the distribution of the vote by party in the electorate.

On the continent of Europe there have long been expectations that parliaments should be composed of members from a wide range of professions and occupations. Many countries are sensitive to balance within parliament among members belonging to the principal religious, ethnic, or tribal groups. The nomination of candidates by the political parties is the mechanism by which the composition of the legislature is made to correspond to public expectations, but that mechanism is imperfect. The sensitivity of the parties may lag behind voter expectations, and election outcomes may in any case be governed by the accidents of the distribution of votes across constituencies. The very slow increase in the number of women in legislatures exemplifies many of the imperfections in the mechanism by which changing cultural expectations are translated into changes in the composition of legislatures. Over time, however, legislatures do tend to mirror the expectations of the electorates regarding what constitutes "representativeness." Failing this, their authority is impaired.

The "electoral connection" between members of the legislature and the population is a critical aspect of democratic representation. It provides the incentive for members to be responsive to their voters. The influence of the electoral connection on responsiveness is in part determined by the frequency of elections. Only the U.S. House of Representatives has a term of office as short as two years. In other countries the normal term is four or five years, but in parliamentary systems the term may end abruptly if parliament has voted its lack of confidence in the executive branch and the prime minister responds by dissolving parliament and calling new elections.

The advantage enjoyed by incumbents in seeking reelection—notably greater in U.S. elections than in the more party-oriented legislative elections of most other countries—raises the question of the desirability of limiting the number of terms that a legislator may serve. The purpose would be to maintain the competitiveness of elections. Only nondemocratic parliaments limit members to single terms, because inexperience in members contributes to a legislature's weakness. In the United States, several states have imposed term limits on their own legislators and have attempted to impose them on their representatives in Congress as well. In other democratic countries, where the advantages of incumbency have not been so conspicuous, no term limits exist.

An idealized image of responsiveness would measure its achievement by the extent of congruence between the views of constituents and those of their representatives. Such an idealized image would overlook two very important political realities. First, there is usually no unanimity of views within single constituencies and certainly no unanimity across the constituencies of a nation. Second, political issues are of peripheral concern to most citizens, who therefore have no views at all, or no stable views, on most issues.

As a result of these realities, representatives cannot be delegates of their constituents or merely mirror their views. By their engagement in parliamentary politics, organization, and procedure, they develop information and views about politics that their constituents lack. They are bound to have views that differ from those of their constituents. Thus representatives often act as trustees of the interests of their voters. This in itself does not violate their obligations as representatives. Rather, their role as representatives includes that of formulating the political agenda, proposing alternative solutions, seeking public support for these solutions, and responding to public wishes when these are clearly expressed. Edmund Burke, a member of the British Parliament at the time of the American Revolution, gave classic expression to the view that a member is not a mere delegate of a constituency in the medieval sense but a trustee of constituents, owing them his "unbiased opinion, his mature judgment, his enlightened conscience."

Experienced legislators recognize that their constituents are not attentive to most issues. They rely on their similarity to their constituents to avoid conflict between their own judgment and what their voters would accept. They act as agents of their constituents, however, when constituents press their individual needs or requests. Indeed, constituency service in this sense is a universal function of members of legislatures and parliaments. Members characteristically hold office hours in their constituencies, intervene with government agencies on behalf of their constituents, answer mail, and issue newsletters. With their large personal staffs, members of the U.S. Congress develop and attend to a much larger volume of constituency "casework" than do members of other legislatures. The activity itself is universal among members of legislatures and parliaments in all countries.

The "electoral connection" is an important bond between the individual member and his or her voters, but the sum of these bonds of the individual members to their individual constituencies does not necessarily serve the interest of the entire population. Achieving that ideal requires methods for identifying the interests of the population of each constituency. These interests, and the incentives that each member has to advocate the plurality of these constituency interests, then have to be transformed into collective decisions that will serve the common interest. Parliamentary organization and procedure are the means for achieving that transformation. These turn an assembly of equals into a structure in which a division of labor and an implicit hierarchy of influence make it possible for the members to be true representatives of the people.

Organization

The complexity of modern society makes it particularly difficult to identify the general interest of the represented. Many aspects of the organization of legislatures help members identify interests, however, and then induce them to reconcile the sum of these interests with the general interest. The method of selecting the members of a legislature leads them to identify and advocate the multiple geographic interests in a society. The dependence of the members on regular reelection causes them to be particularly attentive to interest groups in their constituencies that provide them with valuable information on issues, organizational skills, and possibly campaign contributions. Although members of these groups may be included in the membership of the legislature, this occurrence is less common in the United States than in Europe. To the extent that interest group members do not sit directly in the legislature, their external organizations contact legislators, an activity called *lobbying*.

In addition to the external pressure of interest groups, legislatures have a special propensity to respond to the plurality of interests because they organize themselves into committees specializing in particular subject areas. The U.S. Senate has 16 specialized standing committees as well as 86 subcommittees, and the U.S. House of Representatives has 22 standing committees with 115 subcommittees. Committee specialization in the U.S. Congress exceeds that in other national legislatures. The number of committees ranges from just 6 in each house of the French parliament to 29 in the directly elected house of the Dutch parliament. The usual number is 10 to 20 committees, and subcommittees are seldom used.

In the British Parliament most committees are organized on an ad hoc basis, appointed anew for each bill. This limited specialization among members reflects the limited lawmaking function of the House of Commons and places members at a great disadvantage in relationship to party leaders in the executive branch and their civil servants in the bureaucracy. To offset this liability, and to improve the ability of members of Parliament to supervise the executive branch, a system of what are now 14 specialized select committees was established in 1979. The British approach to committee organization reveals the subordination of the British Parliament to party leaders and the bureaucracy. Elsewhere legislatures have long relied on specialized committees to develop their own specialized knowledge.

To the extent that legislatures adopt a specialized committee system, they emulate the executive branch. This is true especially because the subject jurisdiction of legislative committees tends to reflect the specialization among cabinet departments. This is in part the result of the committees' role in exercising oversight over executive departments, a role as important as lawmaking and appropriations even in the United States.

Legislators naturally prefer assignment to committees whose subject areas are familiar to them and whose subjects serve their constituents. This means that committee members start out with specialized knowledge and interest in the area of their committees, and they gradually develop further expertise. Their specialization is aided by professional committee staffs, which are very extensive in the United States and have now been established in most democratic legislatures. The U.S. Congress employs more than 3,000 committee staff members. No other national legislature has a staff even one-tenth as large. Still, many U.S. state legislatures have developed good-sized staffs, as have the parliaments of Western Europe and Japan. Through the specialization of their members and staffs, these committees produce a range of expertise on the major issues of politics. In most legislative bodies, that expertise does not approach what is available to the executive branch; however, it comes closer in the U.S. Congress than anywhere else.

Geographically defined constituencies and committee specialization clearly help legislators to identify the special interests of their constituents and to serve them. This emphasis on particular interests, however, presents obstacles to the formation of legislative majorities. One way members overcome these obstacles is by trading votes with each other. Relying on differences in the intensity of their various preferences, legislators exchange support on matters of indifference to them for support on matters they regard as extremely important to their constituents. This is the basis of "pork barrel" legislation, in which appropriations measures provide individual benefits for every member's constituency at a cost greater than what would be economically efficient for the entire nation. This pattern is called *distributive politics,* in which everyone appears to win but the collectivity is ill served.

Two major countervailing pressures limit the effect of distributive politics. One limit is imposed by political parties, which combine the interests of individual legislators into general policies attractive to their electorates nationally. Parties are organized within legislatures into what are called *caucuses* in the United States and *parliamentary parties* in Great Britain. These groupings of legislators belonging to the same party organize to choose their floor leaders and whips, as well as the presiding officer of each chamber, called the *speaker* in the English-speaking world or *president* elsewhere. They may allocate committee chairmanships to the extent that these are not automatically assigned by a seniority system, as in the United States, or by a system of proportional representation among the parties. These groupings also endeavor to negotiate committee assignments among their members. They attempt to formulate party policy on issues before the legislature, often employing their own specialized party committees for the purpose. They try to persuade members to maintain a common position on important issues. If more than five or six parties are represented in parliament, their contribution to the aggregation of interests and to the organization of work is obviously limited.

As a result of party organization within the legislature, and of the capacity of parties to influence the nomination of candidates and election campaigns, the voting behavior of members of legislatures exhibits considerable party cohesion. This is the case particularly in European parliaments that have long-established party systems in which the electorate is strongly influenced by party labels in choosing representatives. Even in the United States, where members of Congress contest their seats far more as individuals than as party members, half the votes on the floor of the two houses are party votes in the sense that a majority of Democrats vote together against a majority of Republicans. Furthermore, members have shown a growing tendency to vote with the majority of members of their party. By the early 1990s the proportion doing so reached 80 percent among House Democrats and was even higher on crucial issues, such as the budget.

Party discipline exceeds 90 percent in most democratic parliaments outside the United States, except on matters of individual conscience. In the 1980s and 1990s Democrats and Republicans in the U.S. Congress also attained this level of cohesion on important issues. In parliamentary systems, when the prime minister and the cabinet consist of leaders of the party or parties holding a majority in the assembly, party discipline adds to the authority of the executive. In the U.S. presidential system, where the presidency and Congress are often in the hands of different parties, party discipline may make for divided government. In that case the presidential veto becomes an important source of executive influence over the legislature, limited only by the capacity of the Congress to override the veto by a two-thirds vote.

A second countervailing influence on the propensity of members to engage in distributive politics is their uncertainty about the consequences of particular policies. In a complex modern society the outcomes of legislative actions are often so unclear that legislators cannot make reliable calculations about the political consequences of their votes. Outside the areas of their own expertise, legislators are often uncertain about the policy implications of a particular vote, about probable voter reaction, and about possible policy alternatives. Such uncertainty leads members to defer to the experts among them. They thus have a tendency to trade specialized information as well as votes based on their specialized interests.

The effect of information trading on the collective decisions of the legislature is different from the effect of vote trading. Expert information is likely to reflect a large variety of considerations, technical expertise supplied by committee staffs and executive departments, nationwide party interests, and calculations about the eventual outcomes of a particular policy decision. To the extent that members defer to it, their decisions are likely to serve the general interest rather than narrow interests. The committee, party, and interest group structure of legislatures thus enables members to identify both the multiple interests of the represented and the general interest—at least to the extent that deliberation among the best informed leaders of government and politics can determine it.

Procedure

The patterns of influence that committees and parties have on the decisions of the entire legislature are determined by its procedure. Procedure governs three very important aspects of parliamentary activity: the lawmaking and budgetary process, the resolution of differences between the two houses in bicameral systems, and the conduct of public debate. Procedure is set out partly in written regulations, partly in interpretations and precedents based on the written rules, and partly in informal norms of conduct. Although legislatures generally have the authority to make their rules of procedure, in practice most newly elected legislatures readopt the procedures of their predecessors. Newly established legislatures generally borrow the procedures of long-established parliaments in other countries. Although rules of procedure vary from one legislature to another, many contemporary versions of parliamentary rules can be traced back to the procedures of the British Parliament in the predemocratic era.

The uninterrupted 500-year history of British parliamentary procedure was carefully recorded in its journals and in compilations of precedents. This history was transmitted to the colonial legislatures of North America and later to the legislatures of the British Commonwealth. The diffusion of British parliamentary experience sometimes took the form of direct imitation, as in the manual based on the procedure of the British House of Commons that Thomas Jefferson prepared when he presided over the U.S. Senate. Sometimes it occurred through the writings of political theorists, such as Jeremy Bentham, whose *Essay on Political Tactics* (1816) influenced Belgian, French, and later German legislative practice. When parliaments were established in newly independent states in Asia and Africa after World War II, the British Parliament provided technical assistance to parliamentarians in those countries. The U.S. Congress provided similar assistance to the newly democratic parliaments of Central and Eastern Europe after 1989.

Legislatures take a traditional approach to their own procedures because they recognize the difficulty of designing ways to reconcile the wills of the members of a large assembly. In most legislatures members develop great respect for the historical experience of the institution and the parliamentarians who interpret that experience. Legislative procedure tends to evolve over time, deriving its authority more from tradition, precedent, and custom than from explicitly enacted rules.

Even such a deceptively simple proposition as "deci-sions must be taken by a majority" is by itself quite inadequate for reaching conclusions in legislatures. Unlike voters in general elections, legislators vote on a constant stream of related issues. As they do so, they interact with each other, taking a variety of interests into account and negotiating compromises. As soon as there are more than two alternatives on which legislators must vote, each successive pairing of alternatives may have a different result, leading to an endless cycle of majority votes with different outcomes. The varied preferences of a group of legislators choosing among many alternative solutions to an issue will not naturally lead to a single majority decision. Subsidiary rules must determine the sequence in which alternatives are considered and the point at which a vote becomes final.

Outsiders often mistakenly disparage legislatures that wrangle over "mere procedural questions." Rules have an effect on decisions, so they are potentially extremely controversial. They allocate authority among committees, between committees and the whole house, between majorities and minorities, between decisions made at different points in time, and, in parliamentary systems, between the leaders of parliament in the cabinet and their "back bench" followers. The rules determine the sequence of actions—for example, the order of consideration of bills and amendments. They can themselves arouse intense conflict even as they seek to structure conflict over substantive issues.

The lawmaking process begins with the introduction of bills. Bills are introduced in one of several ways: by individual members, as in the U.S. Congress; by the cabinet, in parliamentary systems of government where the cabinet consists of leaders of parliament; by the component states in a federal system, as in Germany; by voters in the form of an initiative, as in Switzerland and many of the states of the United States; or by committees, as in half the world's legislatures. Bills are nearly everywhere referred to committees, which may revise them substantially before reporting them back to the full chamber. In the United States a committee often fails to report a bill back at all. This is because each member of the U.S. Congress may propose unlimited numbers of bills, a procedure that results in 10,000 bills in each biennial Congress, far more than in any other legislature.

Procedure determines the sequence by which bills are reported back and the restrictions, if any, on their further amendment on the floor. In the U.S. House of Representatives, the Rules Committee proposes a special rule for each important bill, to govern the particular circumstances under which it will be considered by the whole chamber. Special restrictive rules thus determine the influence of the committee version on the final outcome. In the U.S. Senate the sequence of business must be negotiated among the party leaders to achieve the "unanimous consent" of all 100 members, for senators are unwilling to delegate this important matter to a committee on rules.

A special process generally governs the appropriation of public funds, in recognition of the technical expertise required to formulate a national budget and of the temptation of legislators to appropriate funds in excess of what they are willing to vote in taxes. Despite the conviction rooted in U.S. history that the appropriation of funds should be the province of the legislature—and the special province of the House of Representatives—the executive branch has the obligation to present an annual budget even in the United States. In Great Britain the House of Commons abdicated its right to introduce money bills nearly three centuries ago.

Most countries place limits on the right of legislatures to raise the level of appropriations recommended by the executive branch. The U.S. Congress long insisted on full power to raise and cut expenditures. It, however, passed a series of laws, beginning with the Congressional Budget Act of 1974, by which it developed special procedures that compel it to set budgetary priorities and provide the staff to match the expertise available to the executive.

The collective decision of a legislature takes the form of a vote of its members. Procedure determines whether the decision is by a simple majority of voting members, by an absolute majority of all members whether voting or not, or by a qualified majority of three-fifths, two-thirds, or three-quarters of the members. Procedure also determines how the vote is taken: orally by calling for "ayes" and "nays"; visually by show of hands or by asking members to stand; by a secret ballot (provided for the election of leaders or prime ministers in some parliaments); or by a call of the roll of members. The traditional "roll call vote," by which members' decisions are readily reported to their constituents, has been replaced in the U.S. Congress and many other legislatures by electronic voting, which allows members to cast instantly recorded votes from their seats by pushing buttons. The method of voting affects the public visibility of the members' votes and the opportunities for last-minute bargaining during the conduct of a vote. In the British Parliament the substitute for roll calls or electronic voting is an efficient procedure called a *divi-*

sion. In a division, members leave their seats and reenter the House through opposite doors, one for the "ayes" and one for the "nays," while tellers record their vote.

At least as important as the form of the vote is the sequence by which amendments are considered, for this directly affects the final outcome. The importance of this sequence has always been understood by experienced legislators, who often become skilled in exploiting particular sequences to their own advantage. Informed observers can distinguish between "tactical" and "sincere" voting. Legislators vote tactically, for example, if they support an amendment that they dislike because they calculate that this amendment would increase the prospects for passage of a bill that they favor. Sophisticated research employing mathematical models has demonstrated the calculations involved in such a voting sequence.

The existence of two chambers in a legislature, as in France, Germany, Great Britain, and the United States, adds to the complexity of the legislative process. Special procedures govern the ways in which the separate decisions of the two houses can be reconciled. In the United States a joint conference committee attempts to formulate a compromise that can be adopted in identical form by each house. The joint committee may consist of more than 100 members of the two houses and is sometimes divided into subcommittees. Its role late in the legislative process gives subject specialists who dominate conference committees important influence on the final text of legislation. In other countries, such as Australia, Canada, and France, bills shuttle back and forth between the chambers until an identical text is adopted by both. Some parliaments use a combination of these procedures. Some, such as France, Germany, and the United Kingdom, grant the directly elected house the last word, giving it power in relation to the number of shuttle trips permitted.

Public debate in parliament is important for its effect on particular decisions within the chamber, as in the case of debate over a piece of legislation. It also has an effect on the policies of the executive branch and on the public. Procedures governing debate determine the opportunities for public deliberation and the allocation of time among speakers. Debate on legislation generally takes place in three stages, called *readings.* Debating time is limited, both by general rules and by rules specific to a particular item of business. An exception is the U.S. Senate, which allows members to speak without time limit unless "closure" of debate is adopted by a three-fifths vote. The Senate's unlimited debate is an extreme example of a procedure to protect minorities against majority rule. In most legislative bodies debating time is allocated to individual members by the leaders of their parties, after the parties agree on an allocation of time among themselves. The presiding officer may have influence in recognizing individual members, but above all he or she has the duty to maintain orderly debate and to stop inflammatory remarks. The British House of Commons has a fully developed set of precedents regarding what constitutes unparliamentary language; most other parliaments follow its example in ways consistent with their own national cultures.

Debate for the purpose of influencing the executive branch or the public takes a variety of special forms, most of them originally developed in Great Britain. A regular hour for questioning the prime minister and members of the cabinet has become a favorite vehicle for the parliamentary interrogation of executives, in part because it offers an opportunity to air ministerial actions publicly. It is equivalent in some respects to presidential press conferences in the United States or to committee hearings. These procedures all tend to attract television coverage, which enhances their intended effect on the public. Most parliaments also afford their members an opportunity to debate government policies generally, without attaching the debate to a particular item of business. The purpose may be to persuade the electorate rather than other members of the legislature or the executive.

Together, parliamentary organization and procedure produce the informal hierarchies and asymmetries by which assemblies of equal members are turned into working bodies capable of decision making. The subtle, implicit codes of courtesy and good conduct among members—often called *informal norms*—contribute to members' ability to work together. In most effective parliaments there is reciprocity in interpersonal relations. This consists of showing courtesy even when sharp substantive differences exist, of keeping promises even during intense tactical maneuvering, and of cooperating even in the face of competition. Members learn that they must work with each other and respect each other's burden of work. They learn that even the fiercest political differences are best acted out when they are depersonalized. These informal norms contribute to the transformation of a collection of individuals into a corporate body.

Legislatures in Democracies

Parliament seemed so ideally suited to be the central institution of democracy that liberal democrats regarded

government based on it as a perfect form of government. It permitted the people to exercise controlling power through their representatives. Exaggerated expectations led to exaggerated disillusionment when proponents were faced with the uneven quality of members, their partisanship, and the inattention of the public. Much of the criticism reflected predemocratic conceptions of a representative assembly composed of "elites," coupled with unrealistic expectations of public interest in government.

Unrealistic expectations of parliaments were expressed again with regard to the newly independent states of Africa and Asia after World War II and the newly democratic states of East Central Europe after 1989. Experience in both the old and the new democracies indicates that parliaments do not necessarily produce politically enlightened publics or responsive governments. They do, however, perform indispensable functions in modern political systems. They attract public attention to politics. They recruit and train political leaders. They provide governments with crucial information about what the public wants and what it will accept, and this affects the formulation of public policies and budgets. Finally, a parliament helps define a nation.

The last of these functions proved especially important in the second half of the twentieth century in the newly independent nation-states of Africa and Asia, and in Central and Eastern Europe after the dissolution of the Soviet Union. In many of these places populations seriously divided by tribal and ethnic loyalties had no commitment to being governed together as members of a single political community. At best they had been tied together by a common hostility to their former colonial or Soviet masters. When they gained independence they faced the challenge of agreeing on institutions of government and on solutions to their most urgent social and economic problems, even though they lacked a sense of their common political identity. In these circumstances legislatures played a nation-building function, defining the constituencies of the nation, linking these constituencies to the central government, training a political leadership as well as an opposition, and providing a symbol of the new state. Parliaments had earlier performed this function in the nation-building stages of European history.

Although legislatures and parliaments supposedly represent the public and are second only to presidents and prime ministers in their public importance, they are surprisingly unpopular. Public opinion in all countries generally takes a dim view of their work. Two characteristics of the institution help to explain this paradox. First, the internal organization of legislatures is complicated and relatively inscrutable, and the private sector has nothing that resembles it closely. Second, members of legislatures emphasize how they serve their own constituencies, whether geographic units, political parties, or interests. Yet to be effective these same members must reach compromises, which they find difficult to explain, let alone defend, to their own constituents. Legislators therefore are tempted to blame their colleagues publicly for what they have arranged with them quietly, and this fuels public criticism of the institution. They practice one style of politics at home and another style in the legislature, and their failure to reconcile the two leads to public distrust. Individually, members of legislatures are able to champion the causes of their constituents and thereby to personalize government. Collectively, however, legislatures and parliaments appear destined to be the target of much of the criticism that government policies in a democracy attract.

The evaluation of parliaments by the general public depends largely on public satisfaction with government policy, and it fluctuates accordingly. In new states facing exceptionally severe and urgent problems, legislatures have few opportunities to act in ways that produce public satisfaction. Yet attentive citizens and political leaders have a strong commitment to the institution. The number of cases in which legislatures have been abolished by political elites is much smaller than the number of cases in which legislatures have been created or re-created. In most countries political leaders are the products of legislatures. Political careers begin with service in local or provincial legislatures, and positions of leadership in the executive branch are achieved in parliamentary systems primarily by leaders of parliament.

Regardless of the ups and downs of public attitudes toward the legislature, political leaders in democratic states are committed to it. Their challenge is to employ the institution in such a way as to maintain political stability. Working in their favor is the absence of attractive alternatives. In the last decades of the twentieth century nonparliamentary political elites abdicated in many states—in southern European and Latin American states, where the elites had seized power from democratic predecessors and in the former communist states that had depended on the support of the Soviet Union.

The principal challenges to parliaments continue to be identifying the interest of the represented and responding to that interest in the formulation and adoption of public policies and budgets. The organization and procedure of legislatures are designed to provide members with the capacity to gather information on political issues from the greatest variety of sources, to combine that information, to exchange interpretations of it, eventually to reach conclusions based on it, and then to seek the endorsement of their constituents. Viewed from this perspective, legislatures and parliaments make distinctive informational contributions to the governmental process. When bureaucratic executive institutions dominate political systems—as they did during communist rule in Central and Eastern Europe between 1945 and 1990, and at various times in newly independent, developing countries—governments are deprived of both the information and the public support that effective parliaments can provide. The distinctive role of legislatures in modern democracies is to help identify the public policies that a nation's ablest experts are able to devise and to reconcile them with the expectations of the nation's citizens.

See also *Federalism; Interest groups; Parliamentarism and presidentialism; Parties, Political; Proportional representation; Representation.*

Gerhard Loewenberg

BIBLIOGRAPHY

Converse, Philip E., and Roy Pierce. *Political Representation in France.* Cambridge: Harvard University Press, 1986.
Dodd, Lawrence C., and Bruce I. Oppenheimer, eds. *Congress Reconsidered.* 5th ed. Washington, D.C.: CQ Press, 1993.
Fenno, Richard F., Jr. *Home Style: House Members in Their Districts.* Boston: Little, Brown, 1978.
Inter-Parliamentary Union. *Parliaments of the World.* 2d ed. New York: Facts on File, 1986.
Jennings, W. Ivor. *Parliament.* 2d ed. Cambridge: Cambridge University Press, 1957.
Keefe, William J., and Morris S. Ogul. *The American Legislative Process: Congress and the States.* 8th ed. Englewood Cliffs, N.J.: Prentice Hall, 1993.
Kim, Chong Lim, Joel D. Barkan, Ilter Turan, and Malcolm E. Jewell. *The Legislative Connection: The Politics of Representation in Kenya, Korea, and Turkey.* Durham, N.C.: Duke University Press, 1984.
Krehbiel, Keith. *Information and Legislative Organization.* Ann Arbor: University of Michigan Press, 1992.
Loewenberg, Gerhard, and Samuel C. Patterson. *Comparing Legislatures.* Boston: Little, Brown, 1979. Reprint, Lanham, Md.: University Press of America, 1988.
Loewenberg, Gerhard, and Malcolm E. Jewell, eds. *Handbook of Legislative Research.* Cambridge: Harvard University Press, 1985.
Matthews, Donald R. *U.S. Senators and Their World.* Chapel Hill: University of North Carolina Press, 1960.

Mayhew, David R. *Congress: The Electoral Connection.* New Haven: Yale University Press, 1974.

Norton, Philip, ed. *Legislatures.* New York: Oxford University Press, 1990.

Pitkin, Hanna Fenichel. *The Concept of Representation.* Berkeley: University of California Press, 1967.

Taagepera, Rein, and Matthew S. Shugart. *Seats and Votes.* New Haven: Yale University Press, 1989.

Legitimacy

An accepted entitlement or sanction to rule. All governments depend on some combination of coercion and consent for survival. Democracies, however, differ from autocracies in the degree to which their stability rests on the consent of the majority of those governed. Too great a reliance on coercion to keep order would stifle the political competition and liberty that constitute much of the essence of democracy.

Almost as a given, theories of democracy stress that democratic stability requires legitimacy. Elites and the masses must share the belief that the system—that is, the set of constitutional arrangements, not the particular administration—is the best form of government (or the least evil). Hence elected officeholders are morally entitled to demand loyalty and obedience—to tax and draft and regulate, to make laws and enforce them—even from those who voted against them or are strongly opposed to their policies.

Legitimacy of any kind is derived from shared beliefs; such consensus develops slowly. That is not to say that everyone in a society must share basic beliefs about governance. In any population some people do not care at all, or do not feel deeply, about the polity. In any given society many who believe that democracy is a desirable form of government are not ready to fight for it or to make any effort to defend it from danger. In every democracy some who consider freedom desirable in principle do not believe that political freedoms are appropriate in the particular circumstances of their country. Some people (and at some historical moments, perhaps many) who value democracy may consider certain other objectives more important or believe that different ways of organizing political life are more efficient for attaining their goals.

The attitudes of a society's members toward democracy as a political system should not be confused with their evaluation of the performance of specific institutions or with their judgments about particular officeholders. Certainly a negative opinion over a long period of time about democratic outcomes, about chronic failures or corruption among democratically selected leaders, as in Italy in the 1980s and 1990s, will erode legitimacy. But opinions about the legitimacy of democracy and the effectiveness of democracy have to be distinguished and analyzed separately.

Democratic legitimacy derives, when it is most stable and secure, from a commitment to democracy as an end in itself, as the best form of government, even in very difficult circumstances. Although no regime is entirely immune to breakdown, highly legitimate democratic systems can survive serious crises and challenges. Generally, the deeper the legitimacy of a regime, the more likely it will be able to endure intense stress.

Democratic stability is supported by the interplay of legitimacy and effectiveness. Regimes that are both legitimate and effective generally enjoy high levels of voluntary compliance. Systems with neither legitimacy nor effectiveness by definition will have to deal with insubordinate citizens and may even break down, unless they are dictatorships that can maintain themselves by force and guile. Thus democratic regimes with strong legitimacy have tended to survive failures of effectiveness, as did the Netherlands, the United Kingdom, and the United States during the Great Depression of the 1930s. Those in which support for democracy is based only on effectiveness are likely to break down, as did the German Weimar Republic in 1933, where the government's legitimacy was never accepted by the many who favored the monarchy, or the post–World War I regimes of Eastern Europe, which lacked any historic claim to govern.

The Role of Elites

Despite the presumably strong linkage between democracy and popular participation and support, the legitimacy of popularly based systems depends first on backing from political elites—mainstream political leaders, military officers, civil servants, business and labor officials, and religious and other opinion leaders. Considerable research indicates that the impetus for the transition to democracy (and to a considerable extent for democratic consolidation as well) comes from the political choices, actions, and skills of contending political elites in both government and opposition.

If important minorities (not to mention majorities)

among the elites question the value of democracy (either for their society or in principle), or even if they are indifferent about the desirable type of regime, democracy is in danger. This situation occurred in the early 1920s in Italy, and more recently in much of Eastern Europe and in the successor states to the Soviet Union. Such elites tend to have the resources, the mobilizing capacity, and the strategic position to produce a crisis in the regime if they are not committed to the system. Masses, even where they are organized, typically have a much less forceful and rapid impact, in part because their major resource—numbers—makes it difficult for them to act decisively on their own.

If elites do not harbor democratic sentiments, even if democracy in principle has wide popular support, the chances of preserving a free system are slim. On the other hand, elites may establish a majoritarian regime even in the absence of significant democratic loyalties on the part of the citizenry, as in Portugal after António Salazar died in 1970 and in Spain after Francisco Franco died in 1975. The construction of democracy, like its overthrow, is largely engineered by elites.

Nevertheless, popular attitudes can influence elite choices. The more widespread the democratic commitment and the more deeply it is rooted throughout society, the more likely it is that systems will be able to handle crises. The progressive erosion of democratic legitimacy, or the crystallization of doubts as to its effectiveness, emerges with stunning regularity as a critical factor in many cases of regime breakdown. Weak and eroded democratic legitimacy has permitted weak civilian rulers or military elites in many countries to constrict or shut down democracy, as in France on at least ten occasions since 1789, in Russia in the October 1917 Bolshevik revolution (which overthrew an eight-month-old democracy), in Argentina from the 1930s on, or in Haiti repeatedly. By contrast, intrinsic legitimacy is associated with the persistence of democratic regimes even through very stressful times, as in Costa Rica in the late 1940s and in the United States during the Watergate crisis in the 1970s. How legitimacy is produced and lost, and how it contributes to democratic stability, are among the most important issues in understanding the persistence, failure, and renewal of democracy.

Global Trends

How do elites (and the larger society) become convinced that democracy is the best form of government? Since the 1980s a diffuse climate of opinion has played a central role in creating these democratic convictions. This pro-democracy climate has become increasingly global and has been supported by international institutions such as the European Community (now the European Union), the World Bank, and the International Monetary Fund.

Legitimacy is inherently relative. To judge that a political system is not merely satisfactory or efficacious but the best type of government for a country involves a weighing (explicitly or implicitly) of alternatives. And people judge not only the comparative experience of other countries but also their own historical record. The legitimacy (still weak) of the new democratic regimes that emerged in South America in the 1980s derived from a renewed appraisal of democracy in the light of the preceding authoritarian regimes. Repressive systems, like those in Argentina, Spain, or the former totalitarian states, may "inoculate" their citizens to reject antidemocratic appeals.

To say that legitimacy is relative, then, implies that people may come to view democracy as preferable by default—because there is no other appealing or plausible model, because it is the "least bad" alternative. This is often the judgment (especially among elites) by which democracy gains a purchase in unstable and conflict-ridden political circumstances. Although its relative merit can serve perfectly well to initiate democracy, being the least bad form of government is not a promising foundation for intrinsic legitimacy. Ultimately, democracy will be most stable when it is viewed as a positively good form of government.

Historical Traditions and Charisma

As the German sociologist Max Weber (1864–1920) recognized in his classic writings on the subject, historical traditions can provide a natural source of legitimacy. This source may be particularly important for societies in the early stages of political liberalization and democratization. If previously entrenched social forces feel threatened by democratic change, they may work to undermine democracy by playing on the conflict between tradition and modernity.

Some legitimate traditional institutions, such as monarchy, have facilitated democratic change. It remains one of the enduring ironies of comparative politics that most of the world's longest-standing democracies are monarchies. In these (predominantly northern European) countries, democracy emerged through a gradual process in which monarchs first shared their right to rule and later surrendered it to democratically accountable governments, while remaining in place as the head of state and source of authority, distinct from the temporary elected agents of authority.

The most successful nonmonarchic polity, the United States, attributes legitimacy to what has become a hallowed authority, the U.S. Constitution. But it took well over a century for the nation to acquire legitimacy. During its first seventy-five years of existence, it faced at least five threats of secession, from the New England states during the War of 1812 to the South in 1860–1861, and national authority was clearly not legitimate south of the Mason-Dixon line for many decades after the Civil War. The post–Civil War United States acquired legitimacy as it became the most productive economy with the highest standard of living in the world. Postrevolutionary France, in contrast, was unable to form a legitimate democratic polity until very recently. It had seven regimes between 1789 and 1871, and then gave birth to three republics under distinct constitutions from 1871 to 1958.

Given the inherent lack of legitimacy in new systems, rulers who wish to reduce the need for force to maintain control often resort to a cult of personality. As Weber emphasized, legitimation through charisma—the imputation of extraordinary qualities to the leader—appears frequently where traditional authority is weak. Marxist theory deprecates the role of leaders in making history. Yet most communist countries have violated this tenet and have imputed charismatic qualities to their heads: V. I. Lenin and Joseph Stalin in the former Soviet Union, Mao Zedong and Deng Xiaoping in China, Ho Chi Minh in Vietnam, Josip Tito in Yugoslavia, Enver Hoxha in Albania, Nicolae Ceausescu in Romania, and others. Similar developments have occurred in many Asian and African new states.

Charismatic leadership, moreover, because it is so dependent on the actions of one person, is extremely unstable. The source of authority is not distinct from the actions and agencies of authority, so particular dissatisfaction can easily become generalized disaffection. Therefore, the charismatic leader must either make open criticism impermissible or must transcend partisan conflict by playing the role of a constitutional monarch. Even where opposition to specific policies on an individual basis—or informal factional basis—may be tolerated, no opposition party with its own leader can be formed. Hence charisma has rarely laid the ground for legitimate democracy.

The Role of Success

Entrenched legitimacy often evolves from prolonged success, that is, from efficacious results. Comparative work on democratic transitions has shown that, initially, elites often choose or settle on democracy because it is the best, or the safest, institutional means for managing their current divisions and achieving their other goals—not from any intrinsic value commitment to it as the best possible system in all conditions. As they practice democracy over a long period of time, however, its values and habits can become embedded in a political elite and (eventually) in a broad societal consensus. Historically, the longer and more successfully a regime has provided what its citizens (especially the elites) want, the greater and more deeply rooted its legitimacy becomes. A long record of achievement tends to build a large reservoir of legitimacy, enabling the system better to endure crises and challenges.

New democratic regimes are particularly dependent on current achievements for legitimacy. They lack a tradition of democratic loyalty and a record of past accomplishments to which they may point as proof of the regime's efficacy in the face of presumably temporary failures. The link between immediate performance and regime legitimacy is also intensified when there is inadequate separation between the source of democratic authority (the constitution or constitutional monarch) and the elected agent, the temporary incumbent of that authority.

Political leaders, movements, and parties that have brought about the transition to democracy often become identified with the new regime itself. Their failures, instead of being attributed to individual or partisan flaws, may be attributed to democracy as a system. This was true for most of the postcolonial new states of Africa, and has been one of the most acute challenges facing the new democratic regimes of Eastern Europe as the euphoria of overthrowing communism quickly gives way to the pain and dislocation of the economic transition from state socialism to a market system.

The capacity to find solutions to the pressing problems of society is necessary for the stability of all polities, authoritarian as well as democratic. Apart from their need for legitimacy to survive, democratic regimes also depend more on effective performance than do nondemocracies. This is so because failures in performance of democratic regimes are transparent to a unique degree. Being open societies, democracies provide much more complete and accurate information on how they are doing, and they allow specialists, the mass media, and the general public to criticize, publicize, and protest their failures.

The simple passage of time is an element in legitimating democracy. To the extent that a system works well enough to endure across generations, successive age cohorts become socialized into a fully functioning democratic polity so that elites and citizens seem to become "habituated" (to use Walt Rostow's term) to democracy. Reviewing fifty-two cases of internal breakdown of democracy between 1900 and 1985, Robert Dahl found that only in one case, Uruguay, did democratic breakdown occur in a country that had experienced at least twenty years of continuous democracy.

When democracy is institutionalized in nontraditional systems, its legitimation generally follows a pattern that Weber described as rational-legal. That is, prolonged effectiveness has led to the widespread and deep acceptance of the basic system of rules that determine minority rights and the ways in which the opposition may compete to win office. But that basic law, if accepted as the source of legitimacy, takes on an exceptional character, as with the U.S. Constitution.

Political Performance

It is often said that modern governments live and die on their economic records. This is often true, not only in industrialized countries but also in developing ones. However, withdrawal of support for a particular government (a temporary agent of authority) by no means implies loss of faith in the democratic regime. Moreover, even as a legitimating factor, performance does not encompass economic matters alone. No doubt growth in individual income and material improvement in the conditions of daily life are among the most universal personal aspirations and expectations of government. But there are others as well.

Regime performance encompasses a number of political dimensions. Everywhere, to a greater or lesser degree, people want government to maintain order, to resolve conflicts peacefully, to provide a climate of peace and security in which people can go about their daily lives unfettered and without fear of harm to themselves or their families. Citizens expect their government to be able to formulate policies to respond to the basic problems facing their society; in other words, they expect a certain minimum level of political efficacy in the conduct of governmental affairs. Especially in democracies, citizens desire fair and equal treatment by government authorities, and they trust that those officials will use public resources for the defined purposes of government and not for their own advantage and enrichment.

Finally, there is a special expectation of democratic regimes: citizens of free societies believe that, if nothing else, their polities should excel at being democratic, at safeguarding civil and political liberties, honoring the provisions of the constitution or basic laws, ensuring a rule of law and free and fair elections, and being responsive and accountable to the citizenry. To the extent that elected, putatively democratic governments behave in an authoritarian fashion, their citizens are likely to see little point in putting up with them unless they can point to other great accomplishments.

There is substantial evidence of the danger posed by economic crisis and decline to new, fragile, and embattled democracies. This point raises a pertinent question: Why, in spite of low legitimacy, have so many of the newly restored democracies of Latin America and the formerly communist countries of Eastern Europe survived since being formed in the 1980s? How could they have lasted in economic circumstances far worse than those that accompanied most of the breakdowns of the 1960s and 1970s? These countries have seen high inflation rates; decreasing standards of living; drastic increases since 1985 of the numbers of people living below the poverty line; deteriorating health, education, and other public services; widespread unemployment and underemployment; and severe reductions in real wages. These economic circumstances have had profound social and political effects, producing a drastic loss of confidence in major institutions. But why have these developments not undermined the fragile legitimacy of the new democracies?

There are several reasons why some of the new democracies have survived. First, most of their economic crises predate the new regimes, and their citizens still hold the preceding dictatorships responsible for many of the problems. (With time, however, the new governments' freedom from responsibility will progressively erode.) Second, many influential people understand that the circumstances, including heavy foreign debt and weak commodity prices, lie outside the immediate control of their own governments and that there may simply be no alternative to painful economic restructuring. The military, in particular, may not try to take over governments because the problems would come along with power. Third, because of the unprecedented repressiveness of the preceding regimes, and because the alternatives may not be viable or attractive, the new democracies of the 1980s and 1990s have had considerably greater initial acceptance—legitimacy by default—than have earlier constitutional regimes. This fragile legitimacy enables them to stagger on, painfully, for a while.

Beyond Economics

Three points bear emphasis beyond the linkage between economic achievement and democratic legitimacy. First, people value other dimensions of regime performance, particularly freedom, order, and personal security. Clearly freedom, participation, and lawfulness were of high salience in post-Franco Spain after several decades of authoritarian rule, as they are in Latin America. Most new democracies have done much better in satisfying these popular expectations than the economic ones.

Second, the impact of economic downturns (or other performance declines) on legitimacy will be moderated by considerations of whether any other type of regime could govern more effectively. It has been argued that the key to avoiding democratic breakdown is the ability of leaders to form new coalitions or reaffirm old ones in order to give direction to the national economy. The degree to which political leaders are adept at managing adversity determines whether economic crisis will be blamed on the regime.

Although good performance can serve as a foundation of legitimacy, some level of legitimacy is a precondition for efficient governance. As noted, regimes that cannot command the voluntary compliance of citizens must rely on extensive force to ensure order and govern effectively. Democracies cannot govern primarily on the basis of force and remain democracies.

Because regimes begin with little legitimacy, it is difficult for new democracies to make the necessary tough policy decisions. Key economic and military actors may challenge the government's authority with impunity, leaving it little effective power to meet popular expectations. It is easy to understand why in such systems, those who come into power can squeeze personal profit from the system, setting in motion a dynamic of intense corruption and violence that leads to the breakdown of democracy. Not surprisingly, most efforts to institutionalize democracy in postrevolutionary and postcoup systems or in newly independent states have failed. The success of the American Revolution is truly exceptional.

For the long-run success of democracy, there is no alternative to economic stability and progress. Unless today's new regimes implement the kinds of market-oriented changes that stimulate economic growth, they will be doomed at best to limp along indefinitely with fragile legitimacy. To succeed, new systems often require a political pact and coalition among several parties. They may also need broad social and economic agreement among business, labor, and political groups to share the sacrifices needed for growth and stability. To make such changes has often been impossible.

See also *Elites, Political; Monarchy, Constitutional; Political culture; Weber, Max.*

Larry Diamond and Seymour Martin Lipset

BIBLIOGRAPHY

Bendix, Reinhard. *Max Weber: An Intellectual Portrait.* Garden City, N.Y.: Doubleday, 1962.

Dahl, Robert A. *Polyarchy: Participation and Opposition.* New Haven and London: Yale University Press, 1971.

Dogan, Mattei. "The Pendulum between Theory and Substance: Testing the Concepts of Legitimacy and Trust." In *Comparing Nations: Concepts, Strategies, Substance,* edited by Mattei Dogan and Ali Kazancigil. Oxford: Blackwell, 1994.

Linz, Juan. *Breakdown of Democratic Regimes: Crisis, Breakdown, and Reequilibration.* Baltimore and Northampton: Johns Hopkins University Press, 1978.

———. "Legitimacy of Democracy and the Socioeconomic System." In *Comparing Pluralist Democracies: Strains in Legitimacy,* edited by Mattei Dogan. Boulder, Colo.: Westview Press, 1988.

Lipset, Seymour Martin. *Political Man: The Social Bases of Politics.* Expanded and updated ed. Baltimore: Johns Hopkins University Press, 1981; Aldershot: Gower, 1983.

Powell, B. Bingham. *Contemporary Democracies.* Cambridge, Mass., and London: Harvard University Press, 1992.

Sternberger, Dolf. "Legitimacy." In *International Encyclopedia of the Social Sciences,* edited by David L. Sills. New York: Macmillan and Free Press, 1968.

Weber, Max. *From Max Weber: Essays in Sociology.* Translated by Hans H. Gerth and and C. Wright Mills. New York: Oxford University Press, 1946.

Leninism

The aims, policies, and organization of the Bolshevik faction of the Russian Marxist party as formulated by the Russian revolutionary Vladimir Ilich Lenin (1870–1924). Bolshevism represented one attempt to apply Marxist ideas and programs in czarist Russia; the Bolsheviks brushed aside the notion that Marxism might not be applicable in Russia.

In the nineteenth century Friedrich Engels and Karl Marx had argued, in effect, that genuine political democracy presupposes economic equality. Marxism accepted that the material preconditions for such a community—that is, an economy of abundance—had been created by capitalism, but only in Western Europe. Czarist Russia differed from Western Europe in several important ways: economic development, social structure, level of education, and other indicators of modernity. Although constitutional government and citizens' participation in public life were the rule in Western Europe, in Russia the czars and their bureaucrats still ruled without any constitutional checks on their powers. Disregarding these differences, some Russian radicals turned to Marxism and founded the Russian Social-Democratic Workers Party in 1898.

Bolshevism originated in 1903 in a dispute over the organization and membership criteria of the Russian Social-Democratic Workers Party. The faction developed its broader views and programs and, ultimately, its identity as a separate party in the years between 1905 and 1911. At that time it had a dual identity and two leaders. On the one hand, the Bolshevik Party was an underground workers' movement within Russia led by A. A. Bogdanov. On the other hand, it was a small circle of Bolsheviks living in Central European exile and led by Lenin.

The ideas of these two leaders increasingly diverged, and they fought over the right to define Bolshevism, lead the party, train its cadre, and dispose of its funds. Bogdanov (whose real name was Malinovsky) was the son of a school teacher, trained as a physician, scientist, and philosopher. His compassion for the poor turned him toward revolutionary activity. Lenin (whose real name was Ulyanov) was the son of a high-ranking czarist official of noble rank. Lenin was a lawyer. He had turned toward radicalism when his older brother was hanged for having conspired to assassinate the czar.

Believing that the workers would not rebel against their exploitation, Lenin wanted a highly disciplined party of professional revolutionaries drawn from the educated classes, who would act as the general staff of the revolution. In contrast, Bogdanov placed his faith in the working class and in a workers' intelligentsia. Lenin's aim was to overthrow the power of money in a political revolution, while Bogdanov argued that such an event would have to be complemented by a cultural revolution—that is, by changing people's attitudes and styles of behavior. Bogdanov believed that the Bolsheviks would have to create a distinct workers' culture as well as to mobilize the masses politically.

Leninism took as its model the radical leaders of the French revolutions of 1789 and 1848, who believed that the

seizure of power by an enlightened vanguard would effect revolutionary change. Lenin insisted on the thoroughly bureaucratic organization of such a revolutionary party. Bogdanovism took its cue from radical theorists who believed that revolutions needed to begin from the grass roots, not in the actions of any leadership. In this case, Bogdanov believed, the revolution had to spring from the spontaneous action of militant labor unions. Thus the preferred revolutionary strategy of Bogdanovism was the general strike.

Bogdanov wanted to incorporate some aspects of religion into the Bolshevik movement. He sought to mobilize Russia's so-called Old Believers. The Old Believers were a fundamentalist sect that had split from the Russian Orthodox Church in the seventeenth century and ever since had been persecuted by the authorities. Lenin, however, defended a dogmatic atheism.

Lenin insisted on adherence to the dialectical materialism preached by the theorists of "orthodox" Marxism, such as Karl Kautsky and Georgy Plekhanov. Bogdanov wished to integrate into Marxist philosophy the new theories of modern physics, especially those of Ernst Mach. His vision of the future was colored by the seemingly unlimited possibilities of advanced technology.

By 1909 Lenin had managed to discredit Bogdanov and his associates and to gain control of the Bolshevik faction, including its treasury. From then on Leninism and Bolshevism were one.

Leninist Revolutionary Strategy

Leninist strategy foresaw two revolutions for Russia: a "bourgeois" revolution that would remove Russia's precapitalist vestiges, and a "proletarian" revolution that would bring about the dictatorship of the Bolshevik Party, which claimed to represent the proletariat. The first revolution would introduce "capitalism American style." This meant some sort of Jeffersonian democracy, also called the revolutionary-democratic dictatorship of workers and peasants.

To bring about the first revolution, Lenin sought to mobilize not only Russia's industrial workers but also the peasants and the national minorities. The peasants, who made up most of the population, resented the oppressive financial burdens they had to carry and the privileges of the nobility with their vast land holdings. The non-Russians, numbering in the millions, felt persecuted and threatened by the dominant Russian nation. In 1917 Leninist propaganda added to these potential allies the war-weary troops who had been poorly led during World War I and had suffered tremendous hardships. Grassroots democracy in the new regime was to be exercised by councils formed in villages, factories, and troop units; the Russian word for these action councils is *soviet*.

Lenin expected that a Russian revolution would spark a worldwide chain reaction of proletarian revolutions, which would ensure the success of the Russian one. He believed that the outcome of these revolutions would be a genuine democratic community in which the burdens and benefits of citizenship would be shared equally. People would learn to be cooperative and productive without the incentive of profit. Coercive institutions and political elites would gradually become superfluous. The remaining administrative tasks could then be rotated among all citizens.

Lenin believed that his views and activities were well in tune with democratic ideas. But his conception of democracy was substantive rather than procedural. Procedural democracy is a method of mitigating conflict through institutions that afford all citizens structured and limited participation in the discussion of issues and the choice of representatives. Its goal is to arrive at compromise solutions that all can accept. Substantive democracy means rule by, and policies benefiting, the masses of the poor. This is the definition of democracy that was generally accepted before the nineteenth century. From this viewpoint, mitigating conflict through compromise would be undemocratic. Thus substantive democracy is identical with the dictatorship of the proletariat or with government by soviets.

The substantive theory of democracy also contains the notion that the worth of any society is judged by its treatment of those at the bottom. Lenin included workers, peasants, and national minorities among the exploited. More globally, his writings point toward a theory of capitalism in which entire nations can be placed under class categories. For example, in his book on imperialism Lenin suggested that the affluent nations of Europe and North America were playing the role of a ruling class, while their colonies, as well as the underdeveloped nations of Asia, Africa, and Latin America, had become the global proletariat. The overthrow of imperialism thus became part of his program for a worldwide proletarian revolution.

World War I was disastrous for Russia. Heavy military losses and painful defeats, economic dislocation and grave civil disorders (including bread riots), continued corruption, and inefficiency in high places put the Russian peo-

Vladimir Ilich Lenin seized power after the Russian Revolution in 1917 and, as first head of the new Union of Soviet Socialist Republics, led his country to become the first communist state.

ple in a rebellious mood. In early 1917 the first riots occurred in the capital city. The system promptly collapsed; the czar abdicated, and nobody wanted to occupy the empty throne. The Leninists hailed the fall of czarism as the expected bourgeois revolution. At Lenin's urging, the Bolshevik Party almost immediately began planning to lead the next phase—the proletarian revolution. Eight months after the czar's abdication it seized power. What explains this success?

After more than three years of war, Russia was exhausted, its people starving, its economy ruined. The end of czarism aroused expectations for the solution of many burning problems. Russians wanted a democratic constitution, equitable land reform, an end to hunger, and lasting peace. A growing number of voters wanted these goals achieved at once, but political leaders argued that such weighty issues needed to be discussed at length. The Bolsheviks stoked the fires of discontent, and only Lenin's party chimed in with answers to the utopian demands of the masses. As a result the Leninists had significant popular support when they seized power.

The Leninist Theory of Governance

The expected worldwide chain reaction of proletarian revolutions did not occur. Moreover, the membership and clientele of the Bolshevik Party were unprepared for the tasks of governing a country ruined by previous misgovernment, by war and civil war. From the beginning, rule by the party was crisis management. In the last few years of his life, Lenin established some guidelines for ruling, which one might call the Leninist principles of governance.

First, Leninists wish to govern a strong unified state not weakened by any checks and balances. The citizens' organizations, the soviets, combine legislative and executive functions. But the soviets are to be controlled by the single party that claims to represent the working class; all other parties are to be outlawed.

Second, in all its functions the ruling party is to adhere to the rules of "democratic centralism." This formula is designed to combine democratic and bureaucratic principles. Lenin held that under democratic centralism, pending issues could be debated freely by the party membership. Once a decision was made, members had to accept it without further questioning. In practice, however, Leninist political culture—especially when linked with a ban on the formation of factions—discouraged and eventually outlawed all free discussion.

Third, a Leninist definition of citizenship stresses duties instead of rights and the interests of the collective rather than those of individuals. It boldly favors people from the lower classes while discriminating against those who previously had enjoyed wealth, education, or social status. Some of this discrimination takes the form of "revolutionary justice," allowing security forces to punish alleged class enemies, whether or not they have committed any crimes.

Fourth, the principal task of the Leninist state, once it is secure from enemies inside and outside its borders, is to promote modernization. This means introducing technology and the skills associated with it—what Lenin called "learning from capitalism." Equally important, modernization implies the difficult task of resocializing the Russian peasantry and other "backward" elements of society by making them unlearn their traditional habits and outlooks. Lenin defined this as a cultural revolution.

Finally, in world affairs, Leninism is committed to two tasks: promoting the spread of the anticapitalist and anti-imperialist revolution throughout the world and securing the continued existence of the Soviet state by cementing fruitful relations with "capitalist" states. In fact, these two tasks were incompatible. By pursuing both tasks at the same time, the Russian Leninist state ultimately failed in both.

After Lenin's death the Bolshevik Party was deeply divided over the policies to be derived from these principles of Leninism. The aspiring leaders all sought to justify their views by reference to Lenin; the term *Leninism* was coined at this time. The disputes over Lenin's intellectual heritage suggest that the totalitarian excesses of his successor, Joseph Stalin, were one possible result of the spirit of Leninism, but not necessarily the only one.

The conflict within the party concerned the best method of modernizing the Soviet Union, since modernization was seen as the precondition for socialism. Advocates of gradual, relatively painless methods clashed with those who recommended drastic methods. In the end, the radical group won, and under their leader, Joseph Stalin (whose real name was Dzhugashvili), managed a crash program of industrialization that modernized the Soviet Union and helped it win over a very strong enemy in World War II. The success, however, came at the cost of transforming the country into a totalitarian dictatorship. Under Stalin, Leninism turned into a reactionary ideology justifying every hardship and sacrifice that the party was imposing on the people.

See also *Communism; Marxism; Russia, Pre-Soviet; Union of Soviet Socialist Republics; World War I.*

Alfred G. Meyer

BIBLIOGRAPHY

Daniels, Robert V. *The Conscience of the Revolution: Communist Opposition in Soviet Russia.* Cambridge: Harvard University Press, 1960.

Haimson, Leopold H. *The Russian Marxists and the Origins of Bolshevism.* Cambridge: Harvard University Press, 1955.

Meyer, Alfred G. *Leninism.* Boulder, Colo.: Westview Press, 1986.

Sochor, Zenovia A. *Revolution and Culture: The Bogdanov-Lenin Controversy.* Ithaca, N.Y.: Cornell University Press, 1988.

Williams, Robert C. *The Other Bolsheviks: Lenin and His Critics, 1904–1914.* Bloomington: Indiana University Press, 1986.

Lesotho

See *Africa, Subsaharan*

Levellers

Supporters of a movement in seventeenth-century England that advocated government based on popular sovereignty. The movement emerged from the Civil War (1642–1651), when Parliament took to the field against the king, Charles I. Although it had no qualms about preserving a political system in which wealth and inheritance were the bases of power and authority, Parliament demanded a greater say in royal councils. Many members also hoped to erect a national, compulsory Presbyterian church in place of the Royalist proto-Anglican one.

Against this background the Leveller movement took shape around principles of religious toleration, separation of church and state, equal application of the law, and freedom in the pursuit of trade and vocation. At the height of their activities, the Levellers called for an extension of the franchise that foreshadowed universal male suffrage. The designation "Levellers" was given in derision by their enemies, who perceived that such principles of equality posed a threat to a social order based on tradition and hierarchy.

The movement coalesced in 1645 around the figure of John Lilburne. Lilburne, who had been arrested in 1638 for smuggling Puritan pamphlets into the country, was imprisoned until 1640. With the outbreak of war, he joined the parliamentary army but resigned his commission when Parliament demanded an oath of loyalty from its adherents. Imprisoned for refusing to answer at an official tribunal, Lilburne complained that Parliament was acting tyrannically and claimed that, as a free-born Englishman, he should be accorded the rights guaranteed by existing legislation. His plight provoked sympathetic responses from others already active in the cause of toleration.

Within two years, the Levellers had become a discernible political party with fund-raising capabilities and a political program. In 1647, after the defeat of the Royalists, they sought to accomplish this program by proposing their first Agreement of the People. The agreement asserted that the authority of a governing power comes from the people whom it represents. It spelled out the areas of public responsibility: making laws that were to be applied to all citizens without distinction, dealing with foreign states, and appointing and calling to account officials at every level.

More important, the agreement affirmed the limited jurisdiction of the state. Levellers insisted that government had no authority over the individual conscience, which was sovereign and answerable only to God. Consequently, the state could not compel belief. The state should not coerce individuals into forswearing themselves at courts of law; much less should it command a single form of worship. Liberty of conscience was the fundamental tenet upon which all other Leveller principles were constructed; an aspect of popular sovereignty, it was also the single most important item attracting a broad basis of support from opponents of a state-imposed religious orthodoxy.

Much more contentious than religious freedom was the idea of consent. Leaders of the movement agreed that consent came from the electoral process and argued that all those who lived under a particular government had the right to give or withhold consent to it. The Leveller program suggested the enfranchisement of the poor and the propertyless. Critics suspected that such people threatened political stability. As property was the prevailing basis for electoral privilege, the idea of universal consent was generally believed to be a route to anarchy. Levellers were willing to compromise on the issue of the electorate but not on the principle of consent.

Support for the movement fell away when Parliament, after executing the king and instituting its own conservative settlement in 1649, tacitly offered a measure of toleration. At the same time, after denouncing Parliament's settlement, Lilburne and others were arrested, and more militant Levellers in the army were executed for insubordination and mutiny. Henceforth, with its leaders imprisoned and its supporters scattered or cowed, the movement lost momentum. Lilburne remained a popular figure until his death in 1657, but he never again galvanized support as he had in the 1640s.

Yet the impact of the Levellers was profound. More lobbyists than politicians, they did not seek to seize power. Still, the English Civil War was transformed into a revolution as public debate followed the issues set forth by the Levellers. And the revolutionary ideology of the rights of conscience protected by a written constitution was fulfilled by Oliver Cromwell, who became Lord Protector of England in the 1650s. Leveller thinking might well have provoked some of the arguments of Thomas Hobbes, and it informed the political philosophy of John Locke. Today it occupies a hallowed place in the British democratic tradition as represented by the Labour Party.

See also *Hobbes, Thomas; Locke, John; Popular sovereignty; United Kingdom.*

Adriana McCrea

BIBLIOGRAPHY

Aylmer, Gerald E., ed. *The Levellers in the English Revolution.* Ithaca, N.Y.: Cornell University Press, 1975.

Davis, J. C. "The Levellers and Democracy." In *The Intellectual Revolution of the Seventeenth Century,* edited by Charles Webster. London: Routledge and Kegan Paul, 1974.

Thompson, Christopher. "Maximilian Petty and the Putney Debate on the Franchise." *Past and Present* 88 (August 1980): 63–69.

Wolfe, Don, ed. *Leveller Manifestoes of the Puritan Revolution.* New York: Nelson, 1944.

Wootton, David, ed. *Divine Right and Democracy: An Anthology of Political Writing of Stuart England.* Harmondsworth: Penguin Books, 1986; New York: Viking Penguin, 1987.

Liberalism

A theory of limited government aimed at securing personal liberty. Toward this end, the chief concern of liberalism is opposing political absolutism and arbitrariness. To guard against political absolutism, liberal government is limited in its purposes and the scope of its legitimate powers. To guard against arbitrariness, it treats individuals according to known, settled laws, impartially applied. Its defining institutions are constitutionalism and the separation of powers, including an independent judiciary; the rule of law; a system of political representation; and enforceable civil rights to secure the liberties of individuals and minority groups. Although it sometimes is confused with a particular social structure (bourgeois society), economic organization (free market economy), epistemological stance (skepticism), or philosophy of the person (moral autonomy), liberalism is first of all a theory of government with personal liberty as its goal.

Specific rights guarantee liberty and protect against official abuse. These fundamental rights should be secured to all adult citizens without regard to race, class, sex, or social or cultural affiliation: freedom of religion, freedom of speech and association, freedom to own property, and freedom to travel. Particularly important are the rights associated with due process of law. Among these rights are habeas corpus, which protects individuals against arbitrary imprisonment or detention; freedom from unwarranted search and seizure; and protections for the accused in criminal matters, such as trial by jury. In addition to these civil rights, essential political rights include the right to vote and to run for public office. This list is not exhaustive.

Limited Government and Guarantees of Liberty

Various mechanisms have been devised to limit government. Institutional design, through which power is divided between elements of government, is one mechanism. The French philosopher Montesquieu (1689–1755) and the American statesman James Madison (1751–1836), who was influenced by Montesquieu's thought, are the principal theorists of constitutionalism and the separation of powers. The elements of government—the chambers of the legislature in bicameral systems, the executive, the judiciary, and federalist arrangements—are designed to divide authority and check one another. Montesquieu reflected on the British tradition of unwritten constitution in his *Spirit of the Laws* (1748). In this account, the branches of government correspond not only to separate governmental functions but also to separate social estates—the king, the aristocracy, and the common people. The constitutional ideal was a balance among them. In the 1780s, in *The Federalist Papers,* Madison developed the modern idea that popular conventions draw up written constitutions and that all branches and levels of government, including the executive office and senate, represent the people generally. Both Montesquieu and Madison thought that liberty should not have to depend on enlightened statesmanship or strenuous civic virtue. Institutions could limit government if they were designed to balance opposite and rival interests and to make ambition counteract ambition.

Another safeguard for civil liberties and limited government is a pluralist civil society with a wide range of religious, economic, cultural, and ideological groups. The political justification for individuals to be free to amass private property and form economic associations is that this freedom disperses power and provides material and social resources for resisting official injustice. The political justification for freedom of association for voluntary groups organized around a virtually unlimited array of noneconomic interests and opinions is the same: associations are sources of resistance against absolutism and arbitrariness. If pluralist groups are brought into the framework of government through a system of representation, Madison argued, they check one another and prevent the formation of a permanent, potentially tyrannical majority. Liberalism and pluralism are mutually reinforcing. Pluralism helps guard against tyranny, and civil liberty encourages the formation of secondary associations and a diverse civil society.

A third security for civil liberties is an attitude of mistrust toward government. John Locke (1632–1704) warned in *The Second Treatise of Government* (1689) that governors are potential lions who will use power cruelly and arbitrarily to advance their sinister interests. Institutional mechanisms and social pluralism only protect against abuse of power if citizens are vigilant; if they care about the liberty of others, not just their own; and if the disposition to resist oppression is sufficiently widespread. Popular vigilance and mistrust are made effective by publicity and a free press, which writers as different as the German philosopher Immanuel Kant (1724–1804) and the British utilitarian Jeremy Bentham (1748–1832) saw as the key to liberty. Government must be open to public inspection, policy must be publicly justified, and public criticism must be permitted.

Limited government does not mean weak government incapable of collective action, however. Political authority must be strong enough to eliminate inherited privileges, entrenched hierarchies, and private coercion. Government must be able to enforce equal civil liberties against opposition from many quarters: a feudal nobility, traditions of caste and exclusion, large concentrations of landed wealth, powerful business corporations, and dominant cultural or racial groups who would deny rights to minorities.

Finally, limited government does not mean inactive government. It is neither logically nor historically tied to libertarianism, which advocates a minimal state restricted to maintaining order and defense against external aggression. Nor is liberalism tied to a laissez-faire doctrine in economic affairs. Liberal government is compatible with economic orders that regulate production, exchange, and the conditions of labor in different ways and to different extents. Various kinds and degrees of free enterprise and public ownership are found in liberal governments. Some are expansive welfare states, while others are mixed systems that combine capitalist economic freedoms and inequalities with welfare state egalitarian policies.

Changing Concerns

Liberalism approaches questions of social justice and active government out of concern for liberty. If all citizens are to exercise their rights in practice, redistribution of social resources and opportunities may be necessary. State-provided legal representation, for example, is necessary to make due process of law as effective for the poor as for those who can afford private counsel. Policies of "affirmative action" in hiring may be necessary to ensure equal op-

portunity in employment for members of groups that historically have suffered systematic discrimination. Liberals disagree about the social conditions and degree of equality necessary for realizing full liberties for all citizens and debate these questions of social justice as ardently among themselves as with their ideological opponents. But the outlines of liberal social justice are clear. Although liberty does not necessarily have priority over other goods, such as social justice, particular liberties do have priority. Expansion of public purposes and growth of government cannot violate basic civil rights (such as the freedom to choose one's occupation) or eclipse certain guaranteed spheres of personal liberty (such as the decision whether and whom to marry).

The content of rights and the boundary between public and private is always shifting. Religious practice was the first activity designated private and protected from government interference and control, and churches were the first institution to benefit from the principle of autonomy for the internal life and the governance of private associations. As the free exercise of religion indicates, personal liberty is not restricted to the inner citadel of thought and belief but extends to conduct. The critical question for liberalism is, What areas of life are legitimate objects of political control and what are sacrosanct?

Today, feminists are among those recasting the divide between the public and the private. The practice of restricting women to the domestic sphere and denying them rights to hold property, to sue in court, to conduct business, to sit on juries, and to vote made them vulnerable to exploitation and domination, as the British philosopher John Stuart Mill (1806–1873) described in *On the Subjection of Women* (1869). Once considered private and beyond the reach of government, the justice of family arrangements and the rights of individual family members against one another have become appropriate subjects of legislative reform. At the same time, feminists understand reproductive decisions to be irretrievably private and beyond the reach of criminal law. Where the line between public and private is drawn is a matter of changing principles, technology, and experience.

Opposition to liberalism comes from Marxism and other varieties of socialism, authoritarianism, fascism, totalitarianism, racism, social Darwinism, antiliberal nationalism, imperialism, and militarism. It also comes from some forms of democracy. Throughout the course of its three-hundred-year history, liberalism has been the exception, even in Western Europe and North America. The

United States was a liberal state in name only until civil and political rights were extended to African Americans and to women. French and German liberalism has had a precarious existence in the twentieth century. The effectiveness of the Soviet empire in Central and Eastern Europe, and powerful challenges to liberalism's emergence in newly independent states, both former colonial and former Soviet countries, should dispel any notion of steady liberalization. Even in stable, liberal democracies, individuals continue to be excluded from rights and opportunities on the basis of gender, race, or cultural affiliation. And opposition to liberalism from ideological tendencies such as racism and sexism remains strong.

Tension Between Liberalism and Democracy

There is a difference between the democratic question "Who governs?" and the liberal question "What are the limits of government?" Direct self-government and a duty to participate in public affairs are not defining characteristics of liberalism. In fact, liberalism is in tension with many forms of democracy, as became evident when the liberal French Revolution of 1789 was transformed into the Terror of the democratic revolution of 1793. The French thinker Benjamin Constant de Rebecque (1767–1830) observed that it makes no difference whether individual liberty is crushed by despotism or by popular sovereignty. Unconstrained majoritarianism is only one form of democratic tyranny. Neither democracy modeled after the "general will" of the philosopher Jean-Jacques Rousseau (1712–1778) nor deliberative ideals aimed at consensus and a single idea of the common good are committed to or protect minority rights. They put self-government in the service of some higher ideal—public order, economic progress, equality, or a particular vision of the good life, which takes priority over basic liberties. Both Mill in *On Liberty* (1859) and Alexis de Tocqueville in *Democracy in America* (1835–1840) warned about the tyranny of the majority, which does not recognize limits on the power that can legitimately be exercised over individuals. Mill and Tocqueville also warned that even apart from laws, democratic society tends to exercise a tyranny of opinion that demands conformity and inhibits individuality and independence. Thus a disposition to tolerate diversity is at the heart of liberalism.

Despite the potential for conflict, liberalism today accepts a marriage of convenience with democracy and sees some form of representative government as essential. Temporary, elected representatives are necessary to coun-terbalance executive power, to ensure that social interests are not ignored or trespassed, and to hold officials accountable. The American revolutionary demand for "no taxation without representation" has not stopped at fiscal matters. The idea that everyone has interests and opinions to advance and defend through political representation has led to the extension of political rights to previously excluded groups. The expectation is that new political groups and social movements will bring ever changing notions of interests, needs, and values into public arenas. Unlike many forms of democracy, liberal democracy does not imagine that well-devised systems of representation and deliberative procedures can harmonize interests or produce moral consensus. Rather, the hope is that within an agreed-upon procedural framework conflicts can normally be negotiated, many interests can be accommodated, and a modicum of agreement can be reached on the basic requirements of social justice.

Majoritarianism and the utopian hope for consensus on a common good are not the only sources of tension between democracy and liberalism. Liberalism and democracy are in conflict wherever a particular cultural, religious, or racial identity is made key to the enjoyment of rights of citizenship and of effective political participation. Constitutionalism and rights are purely formal and fail to secure the liberties of individuals and minorities where the purpose of democratic self-government is the preservation and promotion of the culture, values, and historical goals of a particular national group. Democracy is not liberal if the dominant ethnic, religious, or racial group's interest defines the rights and liberties of others in a multinational society. Indeed, where the justification for democracy is self-government by and for a nationally defined people, nothing is more common than minorities suffering exclusion, legal discrimination, and in the worst cases exile, torture, or massacre.

Liberal democratic citizenship is a legal category, not a social or cultural one. It encompasses all native-born adults or long-time residents who want naturalization. In the United States, for example, the guarantee of equal protection of the law is supposed to ensure that offices and occupations are open to individuals without regard to race, religion, sex, or national origin. The liberal promise is that rights and benefits are secure, whether individuals are members of one group or of none. People of mixed ethnic or cultural backgrounds and individuals who resist being identified with a particular group are not at a disadvantage in the public distribution of social goods, and political participation is not tied to social identification.

At the same time, liberal democracy may encourage political recognition and representation for powerless minority groups when the object is to remedy systematic discrimination and to eliminate caste. Liberalism invites the formation of voluntary associations dedicated to preserving the cultural identity of groups. It may allow a degree of cultural autonomy in order to sustain fragile communities. The Amish in the United States, for example, are exempted from the general obligation to send their children to school until the age of sixteen. Aboriginal tribes in many places are afforded autonomy. The difficulty for liberalism is to strike a balance between freedom for groups and voluntary associations, on the one side, and excessive autonomy for subcommunities uncommitted to a political society of equal rights and liberties, on the other.

Evolution of the Liberal Tradition

Liberalism has taken a different course in Britain, France, Italy, Germany, and the United States. It arose in different political conditions, and different social groups (barons, merchants, and landowners) were its initial advocates and enemies. In some places its first task was to limit absolute authority; in others it was to strengthen government against powerful private groups in order to ensure equality before the law. The history of liberalism's shift in the direction of democracy differs from country to country, as does the extent to which democracy, when it arose, was liberal. Doctrinally, too, liberalism has national variations, depending on whether its principal theorists were jurists and historians (as in France) or philosophers (as in England). Despite political vicissitudes and national variations in the theoretical underpinnings of limited government, we can still speak of a liberal tradition and survey briefly some of its historical highlights.

The rise of liberalism occurred in post–Reformation Europe in the seventeenth century. Religious persecution and wars of faith provided the impetus to one of the first limits on government. Public officials were prohibited from enforcing religious practices on nonbelievers and from dictating matters of faith. Locke's *Letter on Toleration* (1690), although it did not make the argument for separation of church and state familiar from the U.S. Constitution, argued for toleration of dissenters from official orthodoxy. A policy of religious liberty is not liberal if it is a pragmatic tool of government for maintaining public order, however, or if it is the work of one dissenting sect winning the privilege of religious liberty for itself while permitting the repression of rival faiths.

Principled toleration, Locke argued, rests on the inviolability of conscience in matters of faith. It follows that people are justified in religious dissent from the state church and in political dissent from government if government trespasses on this liberty. The original connection between conscience and liberal freedoms lies here. Principled toleration is part of the broader idea that the legitimate purposes of public authority are limited and stop short of favoring or enforcing a particular religious faith or philosophy of the good life. Religious nonconformism is part of the broader idea that peace and liberty are compatible with social and moral diversity.

In its origin, liberalism was a revolutionary doctrine that provided a theory of legitimate resistance to absolute and arbitrary rule. John Locke's *Second Treatise of Government* is the classic statement, echoed in the American Declaration of Independence of 1776. When governors exercise force without right, they put themselves in a state of war with the people. Invoking a violation of the social contract or of universal natural rights, or simply the experience of a long train of abuses, people have a right to resist tyranny. Like liberal government, liberal revolution is limited. Its object is to remove arbitrary and corrupt rulers and restore a government that will secure liberties; it is political, not social, revolution. The revolutionary import of liberalism remains powerful today.

A recurrent strain of utopianism in liberal thought dates from the Enlightenment of the late eighteenth century. The French philosopher the Marquis de Condorcet (1743–1794) wrote that liberalism weakened the hold of political authority and with it other authorities such as the church and tradition. By liberating human reason from superstition and dogma, it made infinite perfectibility possible. In the same spirit, the American revolutionary Thomas Paine (1737–1809) believed that liberal democracy provided freedom for continual experiments in happiness. Paine looked forward to a progressive revolution in every generation.

From its inception, a defining element of liberalism was the right of private property. This idea does not reflect the view that possessive individualism characterizes liberals or that acquisitiveness and competitiveness are moral virtues. Instead, private property was thought to serve political purposes. It was a source of independence and of resistance to political authority. Thinkers of the Scottish Enlightenment, among them David Hume (1711–

1776) and Adam Smith (1723–1790), saw private property as a support for liberal practices and institutions. The habits of rule following, contracting, and regularity associated with manufacture and trade were conducive to legalism and civil peace. Measured calculations of economic interests were thought to counterbalance more disturbing passions, such as the aristocratic pursuit of honor or military glory. Montesquieu argued that trade promotes tolerance by requiring people to deal with one another fairly and impersonally, regardless of religious or other differences. Kant went a step further: he predicted that, because war is intolerably disruptive of commerce and the legal order on which it rests, a peaceful cosmopolitan order would arise among liberal states.

The classic economic doctrine of laissez-faire, familiar from Adam Smith's seminal work *The Wealth of Nations* (1776), was directed against feudal or customary obstacles to the free flow of labor and capital and toward freedom of contract. Among those obstacles were local tariffs, royal monopolies and privileges, the guild structure of occupations, the restriction of certain occupations to particular castes, and legal restraints on inheritance and the sale of land. Laissez-faire was a program of legal reform aimed at overcoming these impediments to economic liberty. Its proponents did not anticipate the regulation of property or labor conditions by democratic governments or taxation for the purposes of social welfare. In the twentieth century, in reaction to modern government regulation of the economy, neoclassic liberals such as the Austrian economist Friedrich von Hayek (1899–1992) called regulation the road to serfdom, and "libertarian" liberals made a nearly absolute right of private ownership and control the premier liberty.

For the most part, however, since the late nineteenth century, liberal thinkers and governments have recognized powerful nongovernmental obstacles to freedom. Civil and political liberties can be effectively diminished if people are forced by economic necessity to accept any conditions others impose in return for having basic needs met. Endorsing ideas shared by socialists, liberals argued that true freedom of contract requires measures to counterbalance the inequality of contracting parties, such as legislative protection for wages and working conditions and the legalization of trade unionism. Increasingly the question for liberalism has been, In what conditions do liberties have equal worth to citizens, and what is the responsibility of government for creating those conditions?

Justifications

There are three main philosophic and political justifications for liberalism: self-protection, natural rights, and moral autonomy. Each has a long history, and each draws attention to a particular facet of liberalism's preoccupation with personal liberty.

The first justification is the right of self-protection. The experience of unlimited power, torture, and war by governments against their own citizens has been sufficiently common to demonstrate the benefits of liberal institutions as a defense of the relatively powerless against public officials. Fear is a universal reaction to absolutism and arbitrariness. One justification of liberalism is based on the recognition that fear is paralyzing, it makes every endeavor impossible, and it is incompatible with human dignity. The universal disposition to avoid fear is the moral force behind limiting government, enforcing rights, and guarding against extralegal, arbitrary, unnecessary uses of public power. This justification focuses on what is to be avoided by enforcing rights and limiting government. It highlights self-protection and "negative liberty"—that is, freedom from government regulation and control.

A second justification of liberalism is the doctrine of natural rights, which says that people are governed by natural laws and endowed with natural rights discoverable by reason. Rights may be divinely given or reflect the secular moral order of the universe and human nature—for example, rights of self-preservation and self-defense and imperatives against needless cruelty. In either case, natural laws and rights point to a basis for the moral equality of individuals outside custom and convention. They establish universal standards for judging political arrangements. Natural rights direct us to preserve our lives, liberty, and property and to punish transgressors. They recommend consent to political authority in order to enforce rights effectively and impartially. Natural laws instruct us in our obligations, such as keeping promises, but they also set limits to the obligations we can assume. Consent is not unconditional but is regulated by natural law, and natural rights are inalienable. Natural law prohibits consent to slavery or to absolute authority, for example. In short, natural laws describe a moral order that government should guarantee to all, and natural rights prescribe legitimate grounds of resistance when governments violate this order. This justification highlights liberalism's revolutionary potential and the moral basis of equal liberties.

A third justification of liberalism rests on a particular philosophic notion of the individual as morally autonomous. Moral autonomy comes into play when individuals are independent of authority, determining for themselves which obligations are binding and making their own choices about happiness and the good life. Because liberalism limits authority and guarantees a sphere of personal liberty, it is the most favorable political condition for pursuing and even conceiving various ends. As Mill argued in *On Liberty*, moral autonomy is exercised where there is pluralism and liberty to choose among values and ways of life. Liberalism, however, is more than just a background condition for the exercise of moral capacities. Its institutions have an educational character and impose a positive obligation to respect the moral dignity and rights of others. In romantic justifications of liberalism, the notion of men and women as essentially morally autonomous is replaced by a focus on individual self-expression. The conditions for developing each individual's unique personality form the basis of Wilhelm von Humboldt's romantic defense of liberalism.

No justification of liberalism translates directly into a specific account of the limits of government or the boundary between public and private life. Each can be used to support diverse notions of social justice and prescriptions for government activism or restraint. But together they provide an overlapping consensus for constitutionalism, the rule of law, universal civil and political rights, and tolerance of diversity, as securities for liberty.

See also *Conservatism; Constitutionalism; Enlightenment, Scottish; Laissez-faire economic theory; Locke, John; Montesquieu; Pragmatism; Revolutions; Rousseau, Jean-Jacques; Separation of powers; Theory, Postwar Anglo-American; Theory, Twentieth-century European; Tocqueville, Alexis de.*

Nancy L. Rosenblum

BIBLIOGRAPHY

Berlin, Isaiah. "Two Concepts of Liberty." In *Four Essays on Liberty*. Oxford: Oxford University Press, 1969.
De Ruggiero, Guido. *The History of European Liberalism*. Translated by R. C. Collingwood. Oxford: Oxford University Press, 1927.
Hirschman, Albert O. *The Passions and the Interests*. Princeton: Princeton University Press, 1977.
Kymlicka, Will. *Contemporary Political Philosophy: An Introduction*. Oxford: Oxford University Press, 1991.
Locke, John. *A Letter Concerning Toleration* and *Two Treatises of Government*. Edited by Peter Laslett. Cambridge: Cambridge University Press, 1967.
Merquior, J. G. *Liberalism Old and New*. Boston: Twayne, 1991.
Shklar, Judith. "The Liberalism of Fear." In *Liberalism and the Moral Life*, edited by Nancy L. Rosenblum. Cambridge: Harvard University Press, 1989.

Liberia

See *Africa, Subsaharan*

Liberum veto

See *Veto, Liberum*

Lincoln, Abraham

Sixteenth president of the United States. Lincoln (1809–1865) was born to nearly illiterate parents on the Kentucky frontier at the dawn of the American Republic. He moved west with his family, first to Indiana, where his mother died when he was only nine, and then to Illinois, where he spent the remainder of his life except for two sojourns in Washington. At age thirty-three he married Mary Todd. They had four sons, only two of whom survived him. As president, Lincoln led his country during its great Civil War (1861–1865). Under his leadership the union of the states was saved, slavery was abolished, and the country turned decisively toward the future.

Lincoln's Gettysburg Address (November 19, 1863) and his Second Inaugural Address (March 4, 1865) are two of the finest political statements of the Western world. In the first he spoke of saving the "government of the people, by the people, for the people"; in the second he promised a policy "with malice towards none; with charity for all." Along Lincoln's road to greatness he transformed himself from a barefoot boy into a frock-coated lawyer and politician. But he never lost his common touch.

His public life divided into three parts. During the first, his Whig years, from 1832 to 1854, Lincoln's politics found meaning in staunch championship of economic development and the right to rise. At the heart of his persuasion was an intense and continually developing commitment to the ideal that all people should receive a full, good, and ever increasing reward for their labor so that they might have the opportunity to get ahead in life. The policies he advocated paved the way for what later came to be called the American Dream.

Lincoln wanted Illinois, and the nation, to build roads, canals, and railroads; dredge rivers and harbors; create inventions; and, in short, make great "internal improvements," as Americans said. These went hand in hand with the creation of credit and a sound currency through banks, however much people misunderstood and suspected them. In a related policy, tariff protection was to encourage native industries. Taxes, however hateful, would be needed and had to be made just. Forging ahead thus—changing the nation, letting and making it grow—also required education and a temperate society. Such a society could be achieved by abstaining not only from toxic substances like alcohol but also from extremist politics, which some feared might lead to dictators and degenerate into mob violence or war. Finally, there had to be political liberty.

The 1850s brought a revolution in American politics. Slavery, an institution Lincoln had always hated, occupied center stage, and so the second period of his public life commenced. He joined the Republican Party and ran for the U.S. Senate twice. He was defeated both times, but his second try in 1858, against Stephen A. Douglas, perhaps America's best-known politician, made Lincoln famous.

The Lincoln-Douglas debates, a series of seven one-on-one encounters, captured the imagination of Illinois, the nation, and posterity. Lincoln opposed the extension of slavery to the West, where it did not yet exist; Douglas favored popular sovereignty—letting local territories decide the issue for themselves. Lincoln tried to infuse the debates with his deep sense of morality and insisted that chaining down black people endangered the freedom of all people. He conjured up the false specter of a proslavery conspiracy among his Democratic opponents even as he denied seeking political or social equality for black people. Yet the issue he and the Republicans presented to the America of the 1850s was huge enough: Could the nation, he asked, continue to be half slave and half free forever?

Lincoln himself gave one answer when he accepted the Republican nomination for senator in 1858: "A house divided against itself cannot stand." But Lincoln and the nation were unprepared for the violence that came with the answer, although Douglas and others had warned of it. Lincoln was a pacific man, and as a mature adult he denounced war and military glory. Then at age fifty-two he became the leader of a nation at war with itself. The third and final stage of his public life was at hand.

Lincoln's election to the presidency in November 1860 precipitated the secession of the Southern states, which formed the Confederate States of America. War followed and with it the last stage of Lincoln's public life. The fuse was set off at Fort Sumter, in Charleston harbor in South Carolina. In mid-April 1861 Lincoln sent supplies to Fort Sumter's beleaguered garrison, and his Confederate counterpart, Jefferson Davis, ordered the fort attacked. It fell, and the war between the Union and the Confederacy was on. During the next four years the president had two chief tasks. One was to keep the armies in the field until the Union forces achieved victory; the other was to keep the people of the North behind the war effort, which was growing ever more costly. He succeeded at this and more: during his presidency the nation laid the foundations for modern America.

Lincoln appointed a strong cabinet, including in it his chief rivals for the Republican leadership, and set about creating an army. As enthusiasm for the war waned and one bloody year followed another, the Union had to resort to conscription for the first time in American history. The Confederacy also instituted a draft. Lincoln weakened civil liberties in other ways, suspending the writ of habeas corpus, for example. His principal goal was to aid the war effort and not to obtain political gain. What is remarkable is how little liberty suffered during a bloody civil war. Yet tensions from the draft, and the changes in society brought on by the war, led to civil disturbances. Some of the victorious troops from Gettysburg, in Pennsylvania, were called to put down a huge riot in New York City.

The Battle of Gettysburg on July 1–3, 1863, together with the surrender, at the same time, of Vicksburg on the Mississippi River, signaled the military turning point of the war. Until then the war had not gone well for the Union, especially not in the East. After Gettysburg, a military victory seemed unlikely for the Confederacy. Its chief hope was that war-weariness in the North would lead to the Union's defeat. Lincoln not only served as the commander in chief, exercising strong civilian control over the military, but at times served as his own general in chief. He was the architect of victory.

Lincoln also played a crucial role in laying the groundwork for a new America. The economic policies at the center of much of his public life were institutionalized during his administration. Banking was centralized, a uniform currency created, protection for industries established, organized labor given some encouragement, the foundation of public universities laid, a homestead act passed, and scientific agriculture promoted. Corruption and the abuses that climaxed a decade later in the Gilded Age also began at this time.

Lincoln ably faced up to the crucial problem of slavery, transforming the war from one for the Union into one for emancipation as well. With brilliant timing and a clear understanding of the limits of the possible, he moved an often reluctant North toward freedom for black people. The Emancipation Proclamation, issued on January 1, 1863, served as the symbolic turning point of the war. It was followed by a slow but steady movement toward turning the slaves into soldiers and citizens. Lincoln also played an important part in the passage of the Thirteenth Amendment to the Constitution, which ensured the ending of slavery.

The European reaction to emancipation ranged from the skeptical to the ecstatic, but the scoffers eventually melted away. During the war Lincoln could not entirely discount the possibility of British and French intervention on the side of the Confederacy, but the latter never produced the prerequisite of decisive victory on the battlefield.

As the war dragged on, Lincoln became one of the most unpopular presidents in the history of the United States. Soon after Confederate cavalry made a raid within two miles of the White House in the summer of 1864, Lincoln concluded that he could not win the presidential election scheduled for that fall. But he did so (having never contemplated the possibility of postponing the election) because the fortunes of war once again turned in favor of the North. At last, the end of the great American tragedy was in sight.

Lincoln favored a generous peace with his once and future countrymen, the whites of the South; but he also wished to protect the freedmen, and by the end of the war, he supported partial black suffrage. He did not live to see the tension between his hopes flare into open conflict. On April 14, 1865, a Confederate-sympathizing actor, John Wilkes Booth, assassinated the president in Ford's Theatre, Washington, D.C.

See also *Abolitionism; Slavery.*

Gabor S. Boritt

BIBLIOGRAPHY

Boritt, Gabor S. *Lincoln and the Economics of the American Dream.* Memphis: Memphis State University, 1978. Reprint. Urbana: University of Illinois Press, 1994.

Cuomo, Mario M., and Harold Holzer, eds. *Lincoln on Democracy.* Urbana: University of Illinois Press, 1990.

Mellon, James. *The Face of Lincoln.* New York: Viking, 1979.

Neely, Mark E., Jr. *The Fate of Liberty: Abraham Lincoln and Civil Liberties.* New York: Oxford University Press, 1991.

Oates, Stephen B. *With Malice toward None: The Life of Abraham Lincoln.* New York: Harper and Row, 1977.

Paludan, Phillip Shaw. *The Presidency of Abraham Lincoln.* Lawrence: University Press of Kansas, 1994.

Peterson, Merrill D. *Lincoln in American Memory.* New York: Oxford University Press, 1994.

Wills, Garry. *Lincoln at Gettysburg: The Words That Remade America.* New York: Simon and Schuster, 1992.

Lippmann, Walter

Pulitzer Prize–winning American political journalist and writer. Lippmann (1889–1974), who graduated from Harvard University in 1910, founded a socialist club as a student. Throughout his life he shared with others the hope that through democratic institutions the social environment could be shaped to fulfill the best human im-

Walter Lippmann

pulses. He believed that democracy contained the possibility of mastering public problems.

Lippmann began his book-writing career in 1913 with *A Preface to Politics.* He was then part of the Progressive movement, and Theodore Roosevelt—who ran as the Progressive candidate for U.S. president in 1912 after serving two terms as a Republican (1901–1909)—remained a lifelong influence on him. Although Lippman's early work was reformist and left wing, he shifted his political allegiances soon after Woodrow Wilson's presidency began in 1913.

The unexpected coming of World War I in 1914 forced Lippmann, like others at the time, to try to reconcile his conception of democracy with a nation's need to function in international affairs. His *Stakes of Diplomacy* (1915) was therefore pathbreaking. He helped to draft propaganda on behalf of the Allied cause, and later he played an important part in drawing up Wilson's Fourteen Points as objectives of the war. Lippman, however, viewed the Treaty of Versailles, which set the terms for peace, as a great betrayal of his liberal Wilsonian expectations, and he felt forced to

reconsider the ideals of self-government in the light of what he had seen of democracy in action. He began to examine his ideas about the problem of publicity and propaganda in *Liberty and the News* (1919).

Before World War I, Lippmann had been one of the first American writers to recognize the significance of Sigmund Freud's findings, and he became a persuasive publicist for the implications of psychoanalytic thinking for democratic theory. His most influential work, *Public Opinion* (1922), concerns the role of the irrational in democratic politics. The first chapter in the book contrasts the complexities of the outside world with the distortions inherent in the human need to create simpler mental images. This dichotomy between the immense and almost unknowable social environment in which we live and our ability to perceive it only indirectly has continued to haunt democratic thinkers. Leaders acquire fictitious personalities, and symbols can govern political behavior. In certain conditions, people respond as readily to fictions as they do to realities, and in many cases they help to fabricate the very fictions to which they respond.

Between each person and the outside world there arises what Lippmann called a pseudo-environment. He conceived of political behavior as a reaction not to the real world but to those pseudo-realities that everyone constructs about phenomena that are beyond direct knowledge. Lippmann discerned implications that went beyond the importance of propaganda, although his thinking was permanently influenced by his exposure to public relations devices during World War I. Along with other critics of utilitarian psychology, he held that social life cannot be explained in terms of calculations of pleasure and pain. He wanted to explore how people come to perceive their self-interest in one way rather than another.

Censorship posed a special threat for a functioning democracy, and Lippmann saw how news from a different culture can be arranged to suit practical and ideological purposes. He was troubled by the limited possibilities for the circulation of ideas and for genuine tolerance. Constraints on time and attention, combined with the effects of our various social circumstances and modern means of communication, mean that each of us is necessarily less open and responsive than we usually choose to think we are. Lippmann was noteworthy for establishing the role of stereotypes in the making of public opinion; we simplify perception in terms of our preferences as well as to defend our position in society.

In the light of these psychological insights, it is no

wonder that Lippmann questioned idyllic concepts of democracy. He thought it was hard for many people to accept the degree to which democracy, even if designed for harmony and tranquillity, has to rest on symbols of unity, the manufacture of consent, and the manipulation of the masses. He became skeptical about dogmas of popular sovereignty. He tried to rebuild an enduring image of how to reconcile public knowledge and participation in government, a problem that persists today.

In the end, Lippmann shared the commitments of traditional liberal culture. He sought to study the world in order to help legislators and bureaucrats govern it. His optimism about the possibilities of truth persisted, though he knew some of the inadequacies of the classic doctrine of civil liberties and understood how a stylized version of reality gets reported in the news.

After the 1929 economic crash, Lippmann became an early proponent of countercyclical economic planning, though he turned into a tough critic of Franklin Delano Roosevelt's New Deal. Always cosmopolitan, he did not hesitate to propose American involvement in Europe in the late 1930s, and yet after World War II he cautioned against American overinvolvement in the affairs of the world. In each of these different and often inconsistent phases, Lippmann did not try to be a moral prophet but expressed his likes and dislikes by means of a reasoned analysis of the issues at stake.

Perhaps the peak of Lippmann's conservatism, which can be said to have begun with *Public Opinion,* came during Dwight D. Eisenhower's presidency in the 1950s, when what he saw as incompetent businessmen in high public office brought out his most elitist proclivities. His writing, however, continued to belie his most reactionary principles; in seeking over the years to be a public educator, Lippmann never lost faith that clearheadedness on public matters can be communicated to the people effectively. He did not relinquish the democratic ideal that the people can be rallied to the defense of the public interest.

In *The Public Philosophy* (1955), a critique of democratic government, Lippmann argued that the rise of modern dictatorships can be traced to what he called the paralysis of government; popular government was, he held, increasingly unable to cope with its own affairs. By the end of his career as a publicist, during the height of the controversy over President Lyndon B. Johnson's conduct of the war in Southeast Asia, Lippmann notably crossed swords with the administration, appealing to the educated public's capacity to reason.

Lippmann was troubled by the inability of a modern electorate to secure the necessary information on which to act rationally. Although he doubted that democracy could survive in the complicated conditions of twentieth-century life, he devoted his journalistic talents to the democratic ideal of purifying the news for the public. Despite the temptations of being close to power, he stood his ground and remained a critic. He was willing to change his mind but not to abandon his independence.

See also *Psychoanalysis.*

Paul Roazen

BIBLIOGRAPHY

Auchincloss, Louis. *The House of the Prophet.* Boston: Houghton Mifflin, 1980.
Blum, John Morton, ed. *Public Philosopher: Selected Letters of Walter Lippmann.* New York: Ticknor and Fields, 1985.
Lippmann, Walter. *Public Opinion.* New York: Macmillan, 1922.
———. *The Public Philosophy.* Boston: Little, Brown, 1955.
Steel, Ronald. *Walter Lippmann and the American Century.* Boston: Little, Brown, 1980.

Lipset, Seymour Martin

American social scientist who has shaped, arguably more than any other contemporary social scientist, the study of the conditions, values, and institutions of democracy in the United States and throughout the world. Lipset (1922–) is the author of several seminal works. *Political Man,* an immensely influential book, analyzes the bases of democracy across the world. *Agrarian Socialism* investigates the conditions of radicalism in the United States and Canada. *The First New Nation* looks at democracy and its development in the United States from a comparative perspective. *Consensus and Conflict* is a wide-ranging study of how democracies are shaped by social cleavages. And *Continental Divide* compares culture, society, politics, and economy in the United States and Canada.

After finishing undergraduate work at City College of New York, Lipset completed work for a Ph.D. at Columbia University in 1948. He has taught at several universities, including the University of California, Berkeley; Columbia; Harvard; Stanford; George Mason; and the Hoover Institution. Lipset has been president of the World Association for Public Opinion Research, president of the International Society of Political Psychology, and vice president

Seymour Martin Lipset

of the International Political Science Association. With his election in 1991 to the presidency of the American Sociological Association, he became the only social scientist ever to serve as president of both this organization and the American Political Science Association. The author or coauthor of twenty-one books and numerous scholarly articles, he has edited or coedited another twenty-five books. No living political scientist or sociologist is more frequently cited by other scholars.

In elaborating the liberal, pluralist approach to the conditions of the democratic order that pervades his writing on the subject, Lipset has been deeply influenced by classical political thinkers, dating back to Aristotle. He frequently acknowledges this intellectual debt, as he did with the selections from Aristotle that introduce *Political Man.* These passages emphasize the crucial link between political order and the rule of law; the dangers of political ex-

tremism and unfettered populism; and the importance to democracy of limited inequality, a large middle class, and political moderation. These themes, which resonate throughout Lipset's writings, underpin his theoretical and philosophical approach.

Lipset's thinking has been strongly influenced by Robert Michels, Talcott Parsons, Karl Marx, and, perhaps most of all, Max Weber. With reference to the conditions of democracy, Lipset has an especially close intellectual affinity with Alexis de Tocqueville. Lipset observes in the introduction to *Political Man* that Tocqueville, struggling with many of the same momentous issues and conflicts as Karl Marx, came to very different conclusions. He notes that Tocqueville emphasized the coexistence of political cleavages and political consensus while rejecting the desirability or inevitability of conflict polarization and revolution. The analysis of factors that contain political conflict within a framework of consensus has been a consistent theme in Lipset's writings on democracy and society. Following Tocqueville, he has developed an intellectual and normative interest in gradual change, political accommodation, and the sources of political legitimacy; in limiting the power of the state; and in independent, voluntary associations as one important means for controlling the state and developing the social infrastructure of a free society.

One of Lipset's enduring contributions to our understanding of democratic stability is the notion of cross-cutting cleavages—multiple bases of political conflict that cut across rather than reinforce each other. These cleavages reduce the intensity of political emotions and assure individuals who are in the minority on one issue that they may form the majority on other issues. His analysis of the dynamics of legitimacy and the effects of cleavage structure are among the most compelling in political sociology. These and related issues of democratic development are advanced in *The First New Nation,* which highlights the importance of political leadership and political values and examines the determinants and consequences of party systems.

Few scholars, if any, of the conditions of democracy have been more concerned than Lipset with the sources and consequences of political conflict and competition. A requirement of democracy, Lipset argues in *Political Man,* is to have institutions that both permit conflict and sustain consensus. Lipset is clearly in the tradition of Joseph Schumpeter in his belief that free competition among political parties is a defining feature of democracy.

One of the most important currents in Lipset's work

has concerned the conditions of the democratic order. Few contributions on this theme have proved more seminal and durable over time than his 1959 article in the *American Political Science Review,* "Some Social Requisites of Democracy: Economic Development and Political Legitimacy" (republished in *Political Man* as "Economic Development and Democracy").

Lipset has explored the bases of democracy in voluntary organizations as well as in the larger polity. In *Union Democracy,* written with Martin Trow and James Coleman, he challenged Robert Michels's thesis that political organizations are subject to an iron law of oligarchy, which renders them inherently undemocratic, by analyzing the conditions of durable two-party democracy in the International Typographical Union. The book is a model of the case study in the social sciences.

From the time of his Ph.D. dissertation and first published book, *Agrarian Socialism,* which compared the contrasting experiences of leftist radicalism in Saskatchewan and the American Northwest, to *Continental Divide,* which compares diverse aspects of the United States and Canada, Lipset has sought to explain the unique character of American politics. In this endeavor he has consistently elaborated the view that the United States is exceptional among the English-speaking settler societies. The most striking evidence of this uniqueness is the absence in the United States of a socialist or labor party, the relative weakness of class consciousness and labor organization, and the relative paucity of welfare provision, topics that Lipset has explored in many publications spanning the past four decades.

Virtually all Lipset's writings on the conditions and character of democracy in the United States and throughout the world are comparative. *The First New Nation, Continental Divide,* and *American Exceptionalism* are motivated by the conviction that an understanding of American politics and society involves a comparative perspective that is best pursued by comparing the United States with the countries to which it is most similar—that is, English-speaking developed countries, particularly Canada. Lipset's classic analyses of the economic conditions of democracy (in *Political Man)* and the development of party systems (written with Stein Rokkan and republished in *Consensus and Conflict)* are wide-ranging, cross-national comparisons. In staking out new areas of inquiry and guiding subsequent research, Lipset's writings demonstrate the scope and power of comparison in the study of society.

See also *Aristotle; Theory, Postwar Anglo-American; Schumpeter, Joseph; Tocqueville, Alexis de.*

Gary Marks

BIBLIOGRAPHY

Diamond, Larry, and Gary Marks. "Seymour Martin Lipset and the Study of Democracy." In *Reexamining Democracy,* edited by Gary Marks and Larry Diamond. Beverly Hills, Calif., and London: Sage Publications, 1992.

Lipset, Seymour Martin. *Agrarian Socialism: The Cooperative Commonwealth Federation in Saskatchewan.* Rev. ed. Berkeley: University of California Press, 1971; Chicester: Wiley, 1972.

———. *American Exceptionalism: The Double-Edged Sword.* N.Y.: Norton, 1995.

———. *Consensus and Conflict: Essays in Political Sociology.* New York: Transaction, 1985.

———. *Continental Divide: The Values and Institutions of the United States and Canada.* New York: Routledge, 1990.

———. *The First New Nation: The United States in Historical and Comparative Perspective.* New York: Basic Books, 1973; London: Norton, 1980.

———. *Political Man: The Social Bases of Politics.* Expanded and updated ed. Baltimore: Johns Hopkins University Press, 1981; Aldershot: Gower, 1983.

———, Martin Trow, and James Coleman. *Union Democracy: The Internal Politics of the International Typographical Union.* New York: Free Press, 1956.

Lithuania

See *Baltic states*

Local government

The institutions and procedures through which small districts—such as counties, townships, cities, and villages—are ruled. In a democracy, local government is conducted by representative bodies, assisted by paid administrators. Indeed, local government is where democracy developed, often sooner and more powerfully than in national governments. The direct participation of citizens in electing local leaders has long been identified as a classical source of democratic patterns.

Democracy is rooted in ancient Greek city-states, although Greek democracy was restricted to patricians and was therefore autocratic. Later, in the heyday of medieval Europe, free cities such as Hamburg and Venice, which accepted migrants from the surrounding feudal hierarchies, fostered international free trade, a spirit of individualism, and democracy. Their local parliaments were elected both by the voters in territorial units and by guilds organized for various crafts. Unlike in the ancient Greek city-states, patricians seeking political influence were often required to enter guilds where they could be outvoted. As rich and powerful conduits for the Renaissance of Western culture from the 1300s onward, the free cities rediscovered Greek concepts of democracy.

After the Renaissance, nation-states in Europe absorbed the free cities, and monarchies curtailed local democratic practices. City governments under royal patronage became self-perpetuating oligarchies, frequently controlled by powerful merchant guilds, while rural governments were closely controlled by the landed aristocracy or the church.

Fully democratic local government reemerged in Western Europe in the late nineteenth century only after democracy was achieved nationally. For example, in France it was not until 1880, ten years after the creation of the Third Republic, that a mayor was elected, not appointed, by a communal council. In England, counties became democratic in 1888, twenty-one years after the Second Electoral Reform Act gave the vote to most urban men. Was local democracy suppressed by centuries of hierarchical nation-states? Apparently not. The medieval Italian free cities continued to retain some elements of local democracy until late in the twentieth century, through voluntary and neighborhood associations that opposed the national hierarchical-bureaucratic traditions. In 1921 German sociologist Max Weber stressed the transitional role of medieval cities in encouraging democratic practices, but he also warned that in the future democracy might be suppressed by massive nation-states and corporations.

Legal Structures of Local Democracy

Many of the modern legal structures of local democracy were formed in the late nineteenth century. In Europe, for example, local democracy was typically modeled on the national representative government. Similarly, in most European states today local councilors are elected from geographically distinct wards every four to six years. The councilors then select the mayor or, in Britain, the acting political head. The mayor, with the support of a council majority, determines which councilors will head each executive committee. The mayor normally sets the policy direction of the council.

Since 1945 most European local elections have been contests among political parties, reflecting national multi-party systems. Many cities are governed by coalitions of the dominant party groups, which set policy directions. Thus the success rates of candidates for office or of those wishing to influence local policy normally depend on the local party machines.

Several European countries do things differently. Some elect councilors using proportional representation, encouraging coalition party government by breaking the link between the councilor and the area-based ward. Instead of voting for a person in their district, voters choose parties or party-affiliated, ranked lists of candidates. This method weakens the individual representative and ward/neighborhood and strengthens party leaders in the council, who often become key actors, negotiating coalitions and compromises with other council party leaders. In Italy *la quinta,* an inner group on larger councils, determines policies thrashed out by coalition party leaders. In some Scandinavian countries power is concentrated in a few senior commissioners, who became dominant, full-time, salaried councilors.

In the United States, although some local governments have used the European legislative model (known as the weak mayoral system), the majority, particularly cities, have settled on a presidential style of government (known as the strong mayoral system). In the latter, the mayor, who is popularly elected, serves as political and executive head with veto power, although council support must be secured to pass important legislation. In contrast to the situation in Europe, then, the personalities of American mayoral candidates loom larger, and American political parties are less important.

In the late nineteenth century, party machines in many American cities were pronounced corrupt by reform movements. In the restructuring of many local systems that followed, party-sponsored candidates were disqualified from participating in elections and nonpartisanship prevailed. The fewer councilors then elected represented the city "at large" rather than individual geographic wards, and professional city managers were hired to lead staffs that were protected by civil service codes and boards. Today, some 40 percent of U.S. cities have such reform institutions, which have the cumulative effect of weakening the mayor and strengthening the council and staff.

The reform movement often reflected resentment by civic and business interests of the high-spending policies of recent immigrants who had begun to control city governments in the late nineteenth century and who used their positions to distribute sinecure jobs—a form of issuing social welfare benefits. With the growth of federal and state welfare systems, however, the social security activities of city boss politics declined. Reform structures remain, but some studies suggest that they have not measured up to their democratic pretensions and are less sensitive to local popular opinion than the party-based strong or weak mayoral structures. Since the 1970s, though, many reform governments have grown more politicized and more responsive to ethnic minorities.

In Asia, Latin America, and Africa local democracy usually reflects national democracy. India, for example, has had a democratic tradition since its independence in 1947, but local democracies vary among communities. In rural areas village authorities are not popularly elected but are delegates from the village council. Several developing countries usually classed as democracies do hold open elections for their national assemblies but do not extend this principle to localities. Malaysia, for example, has open elections for its federal government, but its state government appoints local government councilors.

Professional Bureaucracy

To flourish in the late twentieth century, local democracies have had to incorporate the kind of professional expertise found in national bureaucracies: full-time experts to manage technical services such as water treatment, highway maintenance, and care for the mentally ill. But tension between such bureaucratic expertise and democracy is longstanding.

Throughout history, despotic political leaders have often built large bureaucracies to control their populations and to discourage democracy, especially local democracy. From the Roman Empire to Louis XIV, Napoleon Bonaparte, and Joseph Stalin, a strong central bureaucracy was imperative for military domination and economic management. Indeed, the French monarchs lured local patricians to the palace at Versailles and replaced them with administrative officials called *intendants* (later *préfets*). As national democracies emerged in the late nineteenth century, the massive state bureaucracies they inherited were, for the most part, redirected toward increasing equality and providing equal access to national government services. Otto von Bismarck, who launched the Prussian welfare state in the 1880s, was followed by more egalitarian national leaders in most of twentieth-century Western Europe.

Until midway through the twentieth century, "social democracy" was largely synonymous with a strong central

welfare state that assumed equal treatment of all citizens. Local democracy was sometimes viewed as antithetical to this notion, since local autonomy could potentially undercut the uniform national standards of social programs. In the 1970s and 1980s, however, even leftist parties shifted their positions to favor more autonomy for local government as decentralization once again came into vogue. Because the ever growing array of complex social services had begun to overload the central states, many services were delegated to local officials, whose proximity to service recipients was thought to make them use limited funds more responsively. The most extreme examples of this situation were the former communist countries. After 1989 Czechoslovakia and Hungary doubled their numbers of democratic local governments by restoring many small units abolished under communism. Major national programs were dismantled or decentralized. Many other forms of decentralization have been implemented since the 1960s, with the largest national welfare states in Western Europe often in the lead. The Scandinavian countries, for example, experimented with easing national regulations for certain "free cities," to permit them to pursue policies otherwise impossible. Observers suggest that such decentralization has made the Scandinavian national welfare states more locally responsive.

The questions of professional bureaucracy that have troubled democratic practitioners of the late twentieth century have prompted them to review earlier successes and failures. The Prussian model of the welfare state is still important, particularly in developing countries where professional expertise outshines amateur democracy. Another model is the civil service ideal of the Victorian English reformers, who developed a nonpartisan civil service corps to implement policies set by democratically elected leaders. Its success depended on separating "politics" from "government," leaving day-to-day decisions to bureaucrats. The British Empire spread these ideals around the world. For example, Canada, New Zealand, and Australia, settled heavily by British immigrants, have maintained these civil service ideals.

The United States, after extensive non-British immigration in the late nineteenth century, saw such non-British influences as corruption and patronage politics surface, for which Irish Catholic local officials, in particular, were blamed. This in turn spawned a reform movement to curtail such practices. In much of Africa and Asia the civil service reform ideals have seen varied success. Debates held from the 1970s to the 1990s about welfare states often started with national governments but concluded that local governments might do better. Searches for improving government at each level were thus intertwined.

Styles of Democracy

Local governments' conceptions of democracy shape the realities of decision making and popular participation in government. In much of Western Europe, in France in particular, local democracy is based on the collectivist ideas of philosophers Jean-Jacques Rousseau (1712–1778) and G. W. F. Hegel (1780–1831), which stress mutual social interactions and local consensus. These ideas reveal themselves in the mayor's role as the sometimes autocratic representative of an entire community who tolerates little deviance from the establishment. In fact, mayors of small French towns have been known to monitor their citizens to ensure that they vote on election day. Those who do not vote by midafternoon may receive a personal visit and encouragement to do so. Turnout often exceeds 90 percent.

The Swiss also drew on Rousseau for democratic inspiration, but almost no Swiss communes (the smallest administrative district of local government) have mayors; rather, a collective executive of several councilors seeks to remain close to the people. Indeed, to label one councilor "mayor" would elevate that official unduly.

A powerful monitoring tool, the referendum, is used to hold elected officials close to their constituents. Referendums on specific policies and annual budgets are held in many Swiss communes each year. Special interests are curtailed by the ever present threat of calling a referendum if any single group threatens to violate the majority position. Internationally, the Swiss commune is an exemplar of a consensual, active democratic practice.

In Britain, Canada, and the United States democracy has often been conceived as a safeguard for individual liberties. In the early years of the United States, liberal democratic values, as established by the Federalists, emphasized freedom from the kind of arbitrary government so favored by European national governments and monarchs in eighteenth-century Europe. These values underpinned the town meetings of New England, in which each adult citizen would participate and vote. Over the nineteenth century the growth of cities encouraged a representative system (where citizens elected council members to represent them). But special interests such as ethnic groups, parties, and business grew more vital and noticeable too.

Conflicts between such democratic ideals and actual practices have generated research as well as reform political movements. For example, studies of elite power in American cities in the 1950s stimulated other scholars to research less elite forms of power and leadership. Most prominent was Robert Dahl, whose 1961 study of New Haven, Connecticut, became a classic in the sphere of democratic politics. Dahl's theory of pluralism suggested that leadership consisted essentially of multiple, competing interest groups, which shifted in importance and composition from one "issue area" to the next. Citizens could mobilize new groups and displace old elites if they strayed far from citizens' preferences. Economic determinism was an insufficient explanation for political outcomes since a wide range of noneconomic resources (such as votes, media access, and group membership) could be "pyramided" to affect decisions. Most political systems could be characterized as "slack," since not all resources were mobilized at any one time. This slack permitted new groups to enter by mobilizing new resources. Still, most citizens were not highly interested or informed about specifics; leaders of organized groups were the critical carriers of democratic norms and practices, which they tended to impose on one another. The "decisional" method was developed by Dahl to identify leaders in distinct decisions, as opposed to the "reputational" method, which did not ask about actual decisions or differences across issues.

This research generated considerable controversy. Some researchers suggested that resources were more heavily stratified than Dahl suggested. Others invoked the concept of nondecisions, suggesting a mobilization of bias in the status quo that disadvantages minorities. Such debates have been intellectually fruitful in stimulating the development of key concepts to capture nuances of power and related phenomena. Findings have varied, but there has been a cumulative refinement in the understanding of specifics.

Some later community power researchers strongly disagreed with Dahl. For example, a 1976 study of pluralism in the British city of Birmingham concluded that most council leaders were responsive to a small coterie of wealthy and nationally organized interests. Further studies of British cities were even more pessimistic, suggesting that local elections just reflected national political trends, not local policies. But several studies of the postcommunist democracies in Eastern Europe have reported competition among elites, rapid turnover, and openness quite reminiscent of Dahl's New Haven study.

Who governs and who holds community power have been heated issues for decades. Widespread research has generated subtle concepts and measures of democracy, which in turn have been applied to localities as well as to national governments, political parties, and organizations. In fact, more than two hundred studies of local democracy have been conducted since 1945. Early findings were often ambiguous because of the diversity of researchers' conceptualizations and measures. In the late 1960s comparative research was launched in the United States using directly comparable surveys in large numbers of cities. Precise differences among cities were documented, thereby avoiding the criticism that researcher X used a method not comparable to that of researcher Y who was studying a different city. Similar comparative efforts were under way in other countries. The largest example was the Fiscal Austerity and Urban Innovation (FAUI) project involving thirty-six countries. The results show some national differences that match historic traditions but frequently document remarkably comparable cross-national patterns. (See Figure 1.)

One burning issue in the measurement of democracy has been determining which groups are most powerful. For example, do business groups and capitalists dominate parties, elected officials, and organized groups? There are differences across nations in the FAUI scores of group power, but, surprisingly, the differences often are smaller than national histories of local democracy suggest. For example, French political observer Alexis de Tocqueville wrote in the nineteenth century that Napoleon destroyed voluntary associations in France, whereas in the United States they were the engines of democracy. Yet by the 1980s French and U.S. local governments were remarkably similar in overall importance of voluntary associations, despite a few differences in specific group scores.

As for measuring citizen participation, how much is necessary for a political system to be democratic? In the 1950s and 1960s Robert Dahl and others developed the elitist theory of democracy, which suggested that it was naïve to expect populist democracy, in which all citizens were personally knowledgeable and participated actively in important decisions, to be widespread. Dahl held simply that a political system was democratic if it provided regular opportunities for its citizens to elect new leaders. Accordingly, most citizens were expected to judge their leaders only after policies were implemented (rather than guiding policy, as populists have suggested).

In the late 1960s pressures mounted around the world

FIGURE 1. Responsiveness of Mayors and Council Members to Their Constituents, Across Countries (*national averages of responses*)

Question: Sometimes elected officials believe that they should take policy positions that are unpopular with the majority of their constituents. About how often would you estimate that you took a position *against* the dominant opinion of your constituents?

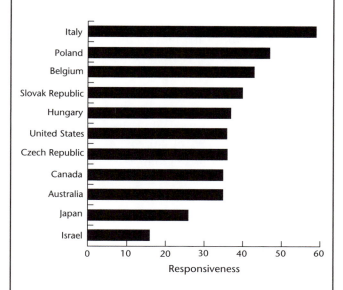

SOURCE: Prepared by Terry Nichols Clark from data gathered by the Fiscal Austerity and Urban Innovation Project.

NOTE: Surveys were conducted by national teams for the Fiscal Austerity and Urban Innovation Project. Most surveys were conducted from 1985 to 1988; for the Czech Republic, Hungary, and the Slovak Republic, surveys were conducted from 1990 to 1992.

RESPONSES: 0 = never or almost never; 25 = only rarely; 50 = about once a month; 75 = more than once a month; 100 = regularly.

to increase direct citizen participation. "Elitist" concepts of democracy were attacked in efforts to achieve "maximum feasible participation," the famous phrase written into national legislation during the U.S. War on Poverty in the 1960s. Specifics were fought out locally as some cities embraced highly populist modes of citizen participation, while others (such as Chicago) strongly resisted such efforts. At the same time student and worker movements based on such issues as environmental protection and minority rights emerged worldwide, pressing for more citizen participation in government. Decentralization and self-management were the watchwords used to attack elites from Chile to Yugoslavia. Major changes were implemented in many countries. In France and Italy the national governments delegated decisions to regional governments and neighborhood councils.

But countries found that if the unit (for example, a neighborhood) is very small, campaigns are less active; if voter turnout declines, local politics can fall under the control of special-interest groups, such as schoolteachers unions in New York City. Indeed, from the 1960s to the 1980s voter turnout for elections at all levels of government declined by as much as half in many Western countries, yet participation in nonelectoral activities (such as environmental groups) more than doubled. Thus alternatives to direct voter participation have been explored; among these are surveys of citizens on specific policies, referendums, and focused group meetings that discuss important policy issues. Many such mechanisms have emerged locally and spread to other cities, sometimes even to national governments. These mechanisms have increased in importance as political parties have weakened in many countries. In contrast to the situation found a few decades ago, especially in Europe, more policies are now based on the issue-specific preferences of citizens and organized groups than on the left and right ideologies of political parties.

Contribution to National Democracy

Local government influences national democracy in three ways: (1) it generates local authorities that are internally democratic; (2) it contributes competing perspectives to national democratic processes; and (3) it fosters local innovations that can spread nationally. Each is considered briefly here.

Democracy is quintessentially local. For that reason, many observers have argued, from the Greeks through Dahl, that large cities and, even more, national governments are less democratic. To preserve a democratic culture, they have asserted, one should break up the largest units into smaller units that can be responsive to their constituents. Many cities, from Paris to Warsaw, have done this. The explosion in the number of suburbs is in part an analogous phenomenon. But, while this decentralizing, "small is beautiful" outlook may heighten democratic practice, at the same time it generates problems of coordination on such issues as clean air, public transit, and social services, which cover wide areas.

Local governments enhance national democracy by encouraging distinct local interests to counter central control. For example, autonomous local governments help to guarantee that political decisions are not the sole product of the national government. Communities are not uniform aggregations of citizens; they vary in size and needs. A state imposing uniform standards for services on all localities loses local richness. The dispersion of power among different levels of government facilitates a national system of government with checks and balances among its separate branches.

While decentralization and enhanced local participation have spread across much of the world since the 1960s, an important exception is Britain and many former British Commonwealth countries, which either have not changed much or have become more centralized. In the 1980s a fierce political battle raged in Britain between Conservative prime minister Margaret Thatcher and certain local authorities controlled by the Labour Party and unions. The Labour authorities actively resisted central government policies (such as privatizing and encouraging competition between government providers and private vendors for such services as garbage collection). Consequently, in seeking to extend their programs, many Thatcher administrators curtailed local autonomy. In addition, Britain has remained notably unenthusiastic about the adoption by the European Union of the principle of "subsidiarity," which calls for delegating power to the lowest unit capable of making a decision on a particular issue. This principle was long debated among liberal political theorists and even denied by British economist and philosopher John Stuart Mill (1806–1873), who maintained that the principal business of the central authority was to give instruction and the principal business of the local authority was to apply it. From Ireland to Australia similar centralist tendencies have prevailed.

Finally, local autonomy in a national system can foster an innovative spirit among the local units that will help them to adapt to changing conditions. Major examples are the postcommunist European countries, which emphatically embraced local democracy after 1989. Yet the magnitude of problems in these countries—economic transition, ethnic conflict, and crime, among others—leads even optimistic observers to be cautious about the capabilities of democratic systems to address severe social and economic problems. Nevertheless, compared with the centralist state alternative, local democracy is a major source of innovative ideas and specific practices from which all levels of government can learn in years of turbulence.

See also *Accountability of public officials; Associations; Dahl, Robert A.; Decentralization; Elite theory.*

James A. Chandler and Terry Nichols Clark

BIBLIOGRAPHY

Chandler, J. A. "The Liberal Justification for Local Government: Values and Administrative Expediency." *Political Studies* 37 (1989): 604–611.

Clark, Terry Nichols. "Local Democracy and Innovation in Eastern Europe." *Government and Policy* 11 (1993): 171–198.

———, Seymour Martin Lipset, and Mike Rempel. "The Declining Political Significance of Social Class." *International Sociology* 8 (September 1993): 293–316.

Dahl, Robert A. *Who Governs?* New Haven: Yale University Press, 1961.

Elazar, Daniel. *Exploring Federalism.* Tuscaloosa: University of Alabama Press, 1987.

Fiscal Austerity and Urban Innovation Project. *The International Mayor.* Chicago: University of Chicago, Fiscal Austerity and Urban Innovation Project, 1991.

Jeanrenaud, Claude, and Terry Nichols Clark. "Why Are Most Swiss Leaders Invisible? The Swiss Communal Ethic." In *New Leaders, Parties, and Groups,* edited by Harald Baldersheim et al. Paris and Bordeaux: CERVEL, 1989.

Putnam, Robert D. *Making Democracy Work.* Princeton: Princeton University Press, 1993.

Tocqueville, Alexis de. *Democracy in America.* Edited by J. P. Mayer. Translated by George Lawrence. Garden City, N.Y.: Anchor, 1969.

Weber, Max. *The City.* Glencoe, Ill.: Free Press, 1958.

Locke, John

English philosopher whose writings helped lay the foundations of modern liberal democracy. Locke (1632–1704) studied, taught, and practiced medicine at Oxford University from 1652 until 1667. He then became secretary to the Whig leader Anthony Ashley Cooper (later Lord Shaftesbury), who had him appointed secretary to the Board of Trade and sent him on a diplomatic mission. He was expelled from Oxford for his anti-Royalist politics and fled to Holland in 1683, returning to England in 1689.

Whether Locke advocated a democratic form of government remains controversial, though he did develop many of the principles of liberalism that were influential in the history of democratic theory. These fundamental principles included the natural liberty and equality of human beings; individuals' rights to life, liberty, and proper-

John Locke

ty; government by consent; limited government; religious toleration; the rule of law; the separation of powers; the supremacy of society over government; and the right of revolution.

Locke's most important work of political theory was the *Two Treatises of Government,* published in 1689 to vindicate the Whig revolution of 1688, in which the English Parliament replaced James II with William and Mary and reasserted its own constitutional role (though most of the book was written earlier). In the *First Treatise* Locke refuted the theory of the divine right of kings as advanced by Sir Robert Filmer (1588–1653). This theory was widely invoked in Locke's time by the Tory advocates of royal power. Locke rejected Filmer's derivation of political principles from obscure scriptural passages, his assumption that a particular form of government and even particular rulers were divinely ordained, and his acceptance of the patriarchal family as the model for politics. Locke thus cleared the ground for his own *Second Treatise,* which derived political principles from human reason, relegated forms of government and rulers to human choice, and considered family and politics as separate spheres of human activity.

The State of Nature and the Idea of Consent

Locke's fundamental hypothesis in the *Second Treatise* is what he called the *state of nature*: the natural condition of all human beings as one of freedom and equality. By nature human beings are constrained only by their own reason (the dictates of which Locke called the *law of nature),* not by the will of any other human being. This hypothesis contrasts sharply with the theory of divine right, which asserts that God subordinates some human beings to others, as well as with Aristotle's claim that natural inequalities subordinate some human beings to others.

Locke argued that in a state of nature, prior to government, individuals could acquire property through their own labor without help from God or a human sovereign. Others would be obligated by the law of nature to respect private property. Individuals could give away, exchange, sell, or accumulate property. Locke's justification for such natural economic rights was that human labor produced almost all value, with nature providing only the raw materials, which he deemed almost worthless, and that accordingly private appropriation and accumulation did not lessen but increased the amount left for others. In *Several Papers Relating to Money, Interest, and Trade* (1696), Locke argued against government limitation of interest rates and currency depreciation, contending that civil laws cannot successfully thwart the laws of value or supply and demand resulting from the actions of individuals. These claims have led to Locke's being considered one of the originators of the spirit of capitalism. His theories laid the groundwork of modern political economy as developed by Adam Smith in *Wealth of Nations* (1776).

Men and women in a state of nature could form families through voluntary conjugal contracts. It was the duty of parents to preserve, nourish, and educate their children until the children reached the age of reason. Locke's account of these natural relations, which gives the economic and familial spheres a kind of priority to and independence of government, also helps to clarify the distinctive features of political power. Unlike economic and familial power, political power includes power over life and death. But political power does not belong to its owners as a kind of property to be used or sold for their benefit, nor does it consist in paternalistic education of irrational individuals by rational ones.

In the state of nature individuals enjoy and defend rights not only to their lives (as in Thomas Hobbes's account) but also to their liberty and property. Liberty is the basic fence protecting life; any threat to one's liberty, any attempt to place one individual under another's arbitrary power, may be resisted as an attack on one's life. No one can reasonably consent to slavery, a condition that may be worse than death, though slavery may be the penalty imposed on those who have violated the law of nature. In the state of nature it is each individual's right to execute the law of nature by all penalties including death. Because, in the state of nature, every least difference is apt to end in war, and war once begun tends to continue, the enjoyment of natural rights to life, liberty, and property is uncertain. Thus it is reasonable for individuals to leave the state of nature and establish civil society.

Because adult human beings are by nature free and equal without any natural subordination of one to another, all rightful political power exists only by consent. Locke's view contradicts any justification derived from conquest as well as the classical conviction that superiority in wisdom or virtue carries with it a right to rule. By consenting to membership in a society, individuals give up entirely the right possessed in a state of nature to punish others. But the liberty they enjoyed there is surrendered only as far as is necessary to preserve themselves and the other members of society.

The tacit consent indicated merely by being within the territory of a government and enjoying the protection of its laws obliges people to obey those laws; however, the consent that makes them permanent members of a civil society and that renders its government rightful must be the express consent of living individuals (not long-dead ancestors), such as that expressed in freely taken oaths of allegiance by adults. (Locke would regard as nonsensical pledges of allegiance by children not yet of the age of consent.) Governments that do not enjoy the consent of the governed are not entitled to obedience.

The Limited End and Power of Government

As Locke conceived of individuals as possessing rights to life, liberty, and property in a state of nature, so he regarded the end of government as the protection of the lives, liberties, and properties of all members of society as far as possible. (Locke sometimes called the end of government the preservation of "property," referring to these three rights collectively, because each is conceived of as property, something that individuals cannot rightfully be deprived of without their consent.) Governments may deprive individuals of life, liberty, or property only as required by that end, and they may protect individuals only from force or fraud by others, not from their own negligence or prodigality. This limited end of government, which is the heart of modern liberalism, contrasts sharply with classical and medieval conceptions of the end of government as the improvement or salvation of souls, the punishment of vice or sin, the propagation of the truth, or the glorification of God.

This limitation and contrast are especially important in Locke's *Letter concerning Toleration* (1689), in which he argued that the civil power is confined solely to the care and advancement of civil goods (such as life, liberty, health and freedom from pain and possession of property) and that it neither can nor ought to be extended to the salvation of souls. Locke concluded that government should tolerate all religious opinions and practices except those that interfere with the civil rights of others or the preservation of civil society or that reject the duty of such toleration. Although few denominations might have met that test in Locke's time, through *The Reasonableness of Christianity* (1695) he contributed immensely to the modern liberalization of religion, which allows it to meet those conditions for toleration.

In the *Second Treatise* Locke tried to limit not only the end of government but also its power. Government cannot possess absolute arbitrary power over the lives and property of the people. This limitation of power is a corollary of the limitation of end: a power given only for the end of preserving life, liberty, and property cannot be used to destroy, enslave, or impoverish its subjects. Locke also stated this limitation in the traditional terms of the priority of the public good and natural law over civil law. But, in the new understanding of liberal individualism, he took the public good and natural law to mean the preservation of society and the good of every particular member of society as far as by common rules it can be provided for. Government cannot rule by decree without officially published laws and authorized judges: rule of law distinguishes civil society from a state of nature in which the law of nature is unwritten and unrecognized by human beings swayed by passion and interest.

Government likewise cannot take any part of an individual's property without consent, which Locke equates with the consent of the majority or their representatives. Locke also treats this limitation as a direct consequence of the definition of the end of government as the preservation of property. It is this limitation that inspired the American revolutionary slogan "no taxation without representation." Finally, rulers cannot transfer power as if it were their own property to hands other than those designated by the people.

Forms of Government

One of the most democratic elements of Locke's political theory is that once individuals have consented to government, political power belongs to the people acting by majority decision, constituting what Locke calls a perfect democracy, unless or until they establish another form of government. Even in a form of government other than a direct democracy, political power therefore should ultimately be derived from democratic action. The people, or society acting through the majority, are prior and superior to the government or state. Locke, however, avoided saying that the people are sovereign: the limitations he set on the end and power of government were meant to limit even the people and to counter any doctrine of sovereignty understood as absolute arbitrary power.

Locke's principles of government by consent with limited end and power and ultimate popular supremacy laid the ground for liberal constitutionalism. The people by majority decision establish the form of government by a voluntary grant, which Locke calls the *original constitution*. Because this constitution is the original and supreme act of the society, antecedent to all other laws, and because it depends wholly on the people, no inferior power can alter it. Thus Locke establishes the basis of the position that a constitution is paramount over ordinary laws: it is prior to them, it is what authorizes the legislature to make them, and it is the act of the people themselves rather than the act of the legislature (a position argued in its classic form by Alexander Hamilton in 1788 in *Federalist* No. 78). Locke was a constitutionalist rather than a populist. Once the people have delegated their authority through the constitution to the authorities it constitutes, they do not resume that authority as long as that constitution and government last. Locke was not, however, a doctrinaire constitutionalist; he recognized that the uncertainty of human affairs may prevent the framers of a government from settling important questions and compel them to entrust such matters to the prudence of later governors. He also recognized that the people may be irrationally averse to amending even the acknowledged defects of the original constitution, so much more powerful is custom than reason.

Unlike Plato and Aristotle, Locke was concerned less with sketching a best form of government than with delineating the origin and extent of government and thereby distinguishing rightful governments that subjects are obligated to obey from illegitimate ones they are entitled to resist. Indeed, his claim that the majority may exercise legislative power themselves as a perfect democracy, put it into the hands of a few men and their heirs or successors as an oligarchy, give it to one man as a monarchy, or create a mixed form of government, as they think good, suggests almost an indifference to forms of government, the central subject matter of classical political philosophy. Allowing the majority to establish the form of government they think good might seem both more democratic and less democratic than insisting that they establish a democracy and regarding any other form of government as illegitimate.

But Locke allowed the majority less latitude in choosing a form of government than first appears. First of all, he ruled out absolute monarchy as inconsistent with civil society and therefore not a form of civil government. For civil society implies the possibility of appeal, in a dispute between any two persons, to common laws and recognized judges. By uniting all legislative and executive power in one man, absolute monarchy leaves him still in the state of nature in regard to those under his dominion. Second, Locke's stipulation that government may not take property without the consent of the majority or their representatives effectively requires every form of government to include one democratic branch for purposes of taxation (as the English mixed constitution was supposed to do with its king, lords, and commons). Indeed the breadth with which Locke sometimes used the term *property* and the wording of other passages in the *Second Treatise* suggest that the consent of a representative body may be required not only for taxation but for all legislation. Thus, although Locke did not insist on an unmixed government composed entirely of democratic elements, he did require that the government established by the majority in the original constitution must include at least one representative democratic component.

The Structure of Government

Whatever the form of government, Locke argued that the same persons should not control both the legislative and the executive powers. It is too great a temptation for human beings apt to grasp at power to enable the persons charged with making laws to exempt themselves from their execution. Legislators who are themselves subject to the laws are compelled to make laws that serve the public good. The legislative power is the supreme power because the power that can give laws to another must be superior to the power that merely executes those laws. Legislative supremacy appears to be a corollary of the rule of law: if individuals are to be free from absolute arbitrary power, they should be subject only to general laws and those commands necessary to enforce them.

In addition to the legislative and executive powers familiar from later versions of the theory of the separation of powers, Locke discussed what he called the *federative power*—the power over war and peace, leagues and alliances, and all transactions with persons and communities outside the commonwealth. This power is an extension of the power possessed by every individual in the state of nature. Locke acknowledged that the executive and the federative powers are almost always united in the same hands because both require control over the armed force of the society. He insisted, however, that they are really distinct. Although the executive power is subordinate to the legislative power, the federative power is much less capable of being directed by laws and so necessarily must be left to the prudence of those who wield it. General laws cannot direct in advance the actions of foreign powers as they can those of subjects; foreign policy must instead flexibly take account of other countries' varying actions, designs, and interests.

Foreign policy is not the only area in which Locke qualified legislative supremacy. Where the executive shares in the legislative power (as the English monarch formerly did and the American president does in a qualified way through the veto), Locke conceded that the executive may also be called supreme. More generally, Locke argued that because it is impossible to foresee all accidents and necessities, the good of the society requires that many decisions must be left to the discretion of the executive, both where the law is silent and sometimes even against the law. This doctrine of executive prerogative seems to contradict not only legislative supremacy but the rule of law itself. Locke, however, believed that the people may judge whether the exercise of such prerogative tends toward their good. If necessary, they can limit executive prerogative through laws passed by the legislature. Because prerogative exists only for the people's good, and indeed is nothing but what the people allow and acquiesce in, such limitations are not encroachments on a power belonging inherently to the executive.

Revolution and Education for Liberty

Although Locke considered the legislative power to be supreme within any form of government, it is a fiduciary power given by the people as a trust to be employed for their good and is forfeited when used contrary to that trust. The people retain the supreme power to remove or alter the legislative power. This supremacy of the people or society over the government or state is expressed in the election of representative legislative bodies and ultimately in the right of revolution. Transgression of its limits dissolves a government and the obligation of its subjects to obey it. Political power reverts to the society acting through its majority, which must act to remove the offending rulers and establish a new government before society dissolves under the pressure of tyranny.

Balancing this sense of vigilance and urgency in the exercise of the right of revolution is the people's obligation to be sure the violated right is worth the cost of vindicating it. They may well tolerate great mistakes, and even many wrong and harmful laws, and overlook the oppression of one or even a few unfortunate individuals. But if acts of oppression extend to the majority or to a few individuals in such a way that the precedent and consequences threaten all, if a long train of abuses and the general course of things manifest a design against liberty, resistance becomes a moral necessity. This justification of resistance was echoed by Thomas Jefferson in the American Declaration of Independence of 1776.

Although, according to the *Second Treatise,* the end of government is limited to the protection of rights rather than the cultivation of virtue, Locke in other works was concerned with the education of human beings in the virtues required for liberty, an endeavor with which later theories of the democratic personality should be compared. In *An Essay concerning Human Understanding* (1690) he argued against the doctrine of innate ideas, which he regarded as a justification for subservience to prejudice, superstition, and intellectual tyranny. He encouraged readers to question the opinions others would impose on them by authority and to refrain from imposing their own opinions on others by authority. Drawing on his own experience as a tutor, he showed in *Some Thoughts concerning Education* (1693) how children could be educated in the virtues necessary in a free society: respect for the rights of others, civility, liberality, humanity, self-denial, industry, thrift, courage, and truthfulness. These virtues were to be inculcated not through coercion but through appeals to our love of liberty, our pride in human rationality, and our sense of what is suitable to the dignity and excellence of a rational creature.

See also *Capitalism; Consent; Constitutionalism; Hobbes, Thomas; Montesquieu; Natural law; Republics, Commercial; Revolutions; Separation of powers; Spinoza, Benedict de.*

Nathan Tarcov

BIBLIOGRAPHY

Dunn, John. *The Political Thought of John Locke: An Historical Account of the Argument of the "Two Treatises of Government."* Cambridge and New York: Cambridge University Press, 1969.

Grant, Ruth W. *John Locke's Liberalism.* Chicago: University of Chicago Press, 1987.

Kendall, Willmoore. *John Locke and the Doctrine of Majority Rule.* Urbana: University of Illinois Press, 1965.

Pangle, Thomas L. *The Spirit of Modern Republicanism: The Moral Vision of the American Founders and the Philosophy of Locke.* Chicago: University of Chicago Press, 1988.

Tarcov, Nathan. *Locke's Education for Liberty.* Chicago: University of Chicago Press, 1984.

Vaughan, Karen Iversen. *John Locke: Economist and Social Scientist.* Chicago: University of Chicago Press, 1980.

Low Countries

Three independent states—Belgium, Luxembourg, and the Netherlands—all constitutional monarchies, situated in Western Europe. Known colloquially as the Low Countries, and officially as the Benelux countries, these states have much in common. In the recent past all three have been characterized as consociational or consensus democracies, combining political stability and democracy despite deep social divisions.

The Low Countries were part of a single state from 1543, when Charles V, the Hapsburg Holy Roman emperor, united most of their territories into seventeen provinces, until 1648, when the Peace of Westphalia gave independence to the northern provinces now known as the Netherlands. After the Napoleonic era, the three countries were reunited in 1815, when the Congress of Vienna joined the Netherlands and Belgium into a single kingdom under the House of Orange, which also provided the grand duke of Luxembourg. After a brief struggle Belgium became an independent kingdom in 1830. When the House of Orange had no male heir in 1890, the Grand Duchy of Luxembourg severed its ties with the Netherlands (although the national flags are still similar).

In addition to shared historical experiences, the three countries have economic similarities, although Belgium and Luxembourg relied more on coal and steel than did the Netherlands. All three countries have open economies, and the dependence on international trade constrains the national economic policies of the three governments. Since 1922 Luxembourg has joined in an economic and monetary union with Belgium. After the Second World War the three countries formed the Benelux Economic Union to further economic cooperation. This organization, however, was soon overtaken by the European Union (formerly called the Common Market and then the European Community), of which the Netherlands, Belgium, and Luxembourg are founding members. The capitals of Belgium and Luxembourg—Brussels and Luxembourg, respectively—also serve as governmental centers for the European Union. Compliance with, or anticipation of, European regulation across national boundaries, is an important dimension of policy making in the three polities.

Pillarization: Language, Class, and Religion

In terms of their political cultures, all three countries have at one time or another been classified as consociational democracies—that is, as deeply divided countries that maintained political stability through elite cooperation rather than elite competition or polarized mass parties. For the Netherlands and Belgium this situation is largely due to the Roman emperors and the popes of the Middle Ages and Renaissance. The ancient Roman highway from Cologne in Germany, through Belgium, to the French coast eventually became a rough dividing line between francophones, or French speakers, in the south, and Dutch speakers in the north. After the religious struggles of the Reformation, the rivers Rhine and Meuse, which flow through the Netherlands, came to form a religious border between Protestants in the north and Roman Catholics in the south. The official border between the Netherlands and Belgium coincides with neither the linguistic nor the religious border, thus creating two culturally segmented countries. In both countries this segmentation is known as "pillarization," the metaphor implying that the various pillars stand apart but together carry the "roof" of the individual Dutch and Belgian states.

In the Netherlands these pillars were defined by class and religious cleavages. There were two religious pillars (Catholics and Protestants)—or three if the two main Protestant denominations are distinguished—and two secular pillars (the secular working class, the Socialists, and the secular middle class, the Liberals). Each of these pillars consisted of a network of social and cultural organizations (schools, mass media, health care, unions, and so forth) and a political party. Thus, notwithstanding a large number of smaller parties on the right and on the left, Dutch politics was traditionally dominated by five parties—the Catholic People's Party, the Protestant Anti-Revolutionary Party and Christian Historical Union, the liberal People's Party for Freedom and Democracy, and the social democratic Labor Party—until the three religious parties merged into the Christian Democratic Appeal in 1977. Since the late 1960s pillarization has gradually declined. Subcultural loyalties weakened; organizations belonging to different pillars merged or had to face competition from new rivals that were not associated with any of the pillars. New political parties came and went, but at least one of them, Democrats 66 (a democratic reform party, founded in 1966), carved out a more permanent niche for itself.

In Belgium, until the 1950s, similar pillars and parties could be discerned (with the obvious exception of Protestant groups): Christian Democrats, Socialists, and Liberals. After the conflict over state financing of religious schools was resolved in 1958, and after economic power started to shift from Wallonia in the south to Dutch-speaking Flanders in the north, the formerly latent linguistic cleavage gradually became the dominant line of conflict in Belgium. Support for the three main linguistic parties (one for Flemish speakers, one for Walloon speakers, and one for francophones in Brussels) increased during the 1960s. Eventually, the three national parties fell victim to the linguistic pressures: in 1968 the Christian Democrats split into the Flemish Christian People's Party and the francophone Social Christian Party; in 1972 the Liberals split into the Flemish Party for Freedom and Progress and the francophone Liberal Reformation Party; and in 1978 the Socialist Party was divided into the Flemish Socialist Party (SP) and the francophone Socialist Party (PS). None of these six parties, however, has so far entered a government without its ideological neighbor from across the linguistic border, even though the Christian Democrats are stronger in Flanders, and the Socialists in Wallonia.

Pillarization has not weakened in Belgium to the extent that it has in the Netherlands, in part because the linguistic cleavage continues to mobilize people in Belgium more than the religious and class cleavages do in the Netherlands. In addition, the Belgian pillars and parties have developed into patronage networks that provide people with more than ideological incentives to remain loyal to the pillar.

The cleavage structure and party system of Luxembourg resemble those of the Netherlands rather than those of neighboring Belgium. Three languages are spoken in Luxembourg (Luxembourgeois, German, and French), but they have not given rise to distinct communities. Education is conducted largely in German, whereas French dominates official documents; newspapers use all three languages in the same edition.

Political Structures

All three states are constitutional monarchies. Bitter controversies over the alleged collaboration of the monarch with German occupying forces culminated in referendums in Luxembourg in 1919 and in Belgium in 1950. In Luxembourg a large majority supported the continuation of the monarchy, but in Belgium only 58 percent nationwide, and a minority of the francophones, voted for the return of the king. Since then, however, the monarchs in these two countries, as in the Netherlands, have been unifying symbols in their divided societies. The political roles of the Dutch queen, the Belgian king, and Luxembourg's grand duke are confined largely to overseeing the formation of a new government after elections. The ministers in each government are responsible to the parliament for the government's policies.

Although the electoral systems of all three countries are based on proportional representation, there are important differences. Unlike Belgium and Luxembourg, the Netherlands has no electoral districts. This results in an extremely low threshold for winning one of the 150 seats in the popularly elected Second Chamber, as 1/150 (or .66 percent) of the vote suffices. It also has the effect that geographical representation is absent in Dutch politics. In Luxembourg each voter has as many votes as there are seats to be won in his or her district. Compulsory voting is still found in Belgium and Luxembourg, but it was abolished in the Netherlands in 1970.

Since the Second World War, with a few exceptions in Belgium, no party has obtained an absolute majority in the elections, and the custom of elite cooperation does not allow for minority governments. Consequently, elections in all three countries are followed by negotiations to form a majority coalition. In the Netherlands in particular, these negotiations are often protracted, with a record length of 208 days in 1977 and with an average of one month per year spent in forming governments. On the other hand, Dutch government coalitions tend to be relatively stable (lasting almost 2.5 years), at least compared with Belgian governments (which last less than 1.5 years). In Belgium the constitution requires the cabinet to be made up of equal numbers of French-speaking and Dutch-speaking ministers (with the possible exception of the prime minister). In all three countries, the Christian Democrats are most likely to be in government, reflecting their centrist position on socioeconomic issues; in Belgium and the Netherlands, however, they occasionally have been in opposition.

Once sworn in, these governments are dependent on the confidence of a majority in the parliament. Luxembourg is the only country with a unicameral parliament, although its Council of State, an appointed advisory council, takes on some of the functions of a senate; bills must be passed by the parliament twice, unless the Council of State grants an exemption. In the Netherlands the First Chamber is elected by an electoral council composed of all members of all Provincial Councils. It has only a right of veto (it cannot initiate or amend legislation) and consists of part-time politicians. The directly elected Second Chamber is the real political arena. In Belgium one part of the Senate is elected directly and another is elected by the Provincial Councils; a third part is chosen by the elected senators. A reform of the Senate is planned along federal lines. Both the Senate and the House of Representatives share equally in the exercise of the powers of the parliament. Unlike the Dutch legislature, however, the Belgian parliament as such rarely plays a significant role in policy making. On several occasions it has adopted a special law temporarily relinquishing some of its powers to the government in power.

Both the Netherlands and Luxembourg are highly centralized states. The municipalities in Luxembourg, and the provinces and municipalities in the Netherlands, enjoy little autonomy. The situation is very different in Belgium, where the linguistic conflict could be alleviated only by gradually granting more powers to the Dutch-speaking and francophone communities. Finally, Belgium declared itself a federal state with the new constitution of 1989. Belgium was divided into nine provinces, three communities (French, Flemish, and German speaking), and, most important, three regions: Wallonia (covering the francophone and German-speaking parts), Flanders, and the (bilingual) Region of Brussels-Capital. Each region, with its own government and parliament, has extensive powers.

Policy making in all three countries is characterized by the direct and regular incorporation of powerful interest groups into the decision-making process. As a consequence, the three Benelux countries are known not only as examples of consociational democracy but also of neo-corporatism, in which competition for government favors by interest groups is replaced with joint efforts of interest group representatives and government officials to coordinate economic activity. The history of cultural segmentation, the continued minoritarian status of all parties, and the continuous consultation of interest groups have given politics in these democracies a distinctly consensual style.

See also *Europe, Western.*

Rudy B. Andeweg

BIBLIOGRAPHY

Andeweg, Rudy B., and Galen A. Irwin. *Dutch Government and Politics.* London: Macmillan; New York: St. Martin's, 1993.

Daalder, Hans, and Galen A. Irwin, eds. *Politics in the Netherlands: How Much Change?* London and Totawa, N.J.: Frank Cass, 1989.

Dewachter, Wilfried. "Changes in a Particratie: The Belgian Party System from 1944 to 1986." In *Party Systems in Denmark, Austria, Switzerland, the Netherlands, and Belgium,* edited by Hans Daalder. London: Pinter; New York: St. Martin's, 1987.

Fitzmaurice, John. *The Politics of Belgium: Crisis and Compromise in a Plural Society.* 2d ed. London: Hurst, 1988.

Lijphart, Arend. *Conflict and Coexistence in Belgium: The Dynamics of a Culturally Divided Society.* Berkeley: University of California Press, 1987.

———. *The Politics of Accommodation: Pluralism and Democracy in the Netherlands.* 2d ed. Berkeley: University of California Press, 1975.

Weil, Gordon. *The Benelux Nations: The Politics of Small Country Democracies.* New York: Holt, Rinehart, and Winston, 1970.

Luxembourg

See *Low Countries*

Luxemburg, Rosa

Polish-born German revolutionary leader who advocated a militantly libertarian Marxism opposed to both bureaucratic reformism and communist authoritarianism. Luxemburg (1871–1919) based her conception of democracy on a refusal to identify freedom with any set of institutions and a concern with furthering the self-administrative capacities of working people. Thus her influence has largely been confined to movements and thinkers critical of both the socialist and communist mainstream.

Born in Russian Poland, Luxemburg became involved in anti-czarist politics as a teenager. Forced into exile, she entered the University of Zurich, where in 1898 she completed a dissertation on the industrial development of Poland. The internationalism evident in this work became her trademark.

Luxemburg feared that nationalism would divide workers, foster militarism, generate class compromise, and threaten the values of socialist democracy. Her most important work, *The Accumulation of Capital* (1913), attempts to demonstrate how capitalism generates militarism, nationalism, and imperialism. Because of these views, she remained a pacifist during World War I, spending much of the war in prison.

Luxemburg gained notoriety with her contribution to the revisionism debate. The chief advocate of revisionism, Eduard Bernstein, sought to replace the revolutionary ideology of the labor movement with evolutionary reform. He aimed to substitute a politics of class compromise for visions of a future capitalist collapse. Luxemburg, in *Social Reform or Revolution* (1899), insisted that reform is limited, that a systemic breakdown is unavoidable, and that a policy of class compromise will only empower party bureaucrats.

Luxemburg's *Organizational Questions of Social Democracy* (1904), in the same vein, criticized V. I. Lenin's concept of the "vanguard party." During the following year she participated in the Russian revolution of 1905. The experience inspired perhaps her finest theoretical work. *Mass Strike, Party, and Trade Unions* (1906) emphasized the spontaneity of revolutionary uprisings and the ability of the working class to rule society in a democratic fashion. The pamphlet anticipates her most famous work, *The Russian Revolution,* written in 1918, while she was in jail. In this work Luxemburg criticized Lenin's dictatorship by claiming that political democracy with full civil rights must serve as the precondition for socialism.

When Luxemburg was released from prison in 1918, proletarian uprisings were sweeping Europe. She became president of the new German Communist Party and participated in the attempt to bring a new regime of soviets,

Rosa Luxemburg

or workers' councils, into being. In 1919 she was murdered by the right-wing militia employed by the first government of the Weimar Republic.

See also *Bernstein, Eduard; Marxism.*

Stephen Eric Bronner

M

Macedonia

See *Europe, East Central*

Machiavelli, Niccolò

Florentine bureaucrat, writer, and political theorist. Machiavelli (1469–1527), the son of a lawyer, served the Florentine Republic in several important administrative and diplomatic capacities, including leading missions to France, Germany, and other Italian city-states. He was exiled by the Medici, the ruling family of Florence, when they were restored to power in 1512 after being expelled in 1494. He spent his remaining years in retirement writing at his estate just outside Florence.

Machiavelli's most famous work, *The Prince,* is a handbook on how an aspiring dictator might gain and retain power. Among other things, Machiavelli supported the use of deceit and craftiness in the interest of political expediency. In the *Discourses on Livy,* he widened the discussion to other kinds of regimes, beginning with those described in the writings of the ancient political philosophers: monarchy, aristocracy, and democracy. He argued for a free, well-ordered republic.

In the *Discourses,* Machiavelli looked back to the Roman Republic as his ideal. Rome's greatness was based on the *virtù* (which means strength and ability as much as civic virtue) of its citizens. According to Machiavelli, the tribunes of the people (elected officials responsible for protecting the interests of the Roman people against those

of the nobility) were essential to the success of the republic. An equilibrium between the aristocratic Senate and the common people made the republic strong and stable. Machiavelli warned that the formidable power of the people must be taken into account.

The supreme political realist, Machiavelli separated questions of religion and morality from politics. His primary concern was the survival of the state. He considered a republican government superior to a state ruled by a prince—when the people have sufficient *virtù*—because a republic is more stable. A successful republic, however, must have a mechanism for turning to an autocratic ruler in times of emergency.

Although he was no democrat, Machiavelli believed that the people must have a share in power for a state to maintain political stability. Finally, he argued, it would be difficult for an autocrat to overthrow an effective republican government.

See also *Classical Greece and Rome; Critiques of democracy; Leadership; Republicanism; Virtue, Civic.*

Ann Davies

Macpherson, C. B.

C. B. Macpherson

Canadian political theorist who coined the term *possessive individualism* to describe the self-centered and consumerist aspects of liberal democracy. After studying with Harold Laski at the London School of Economics, Macpherson (1911–1987) returned to his native Toronto in 1935. There he took a position teaching political theory at the University of Toronto, where, with the exception of some visiting appointments, he remained throughout his academic career.

In 1962 Macpherson published his best-known book, *The Political Theory of Possessive Individualism.* In it he argued that the emerging capitalist market of seventeenth-century England produced a culture in which possession of commodities was life's main purpose and in which people's capacities were viewed by themselves and others as commodities to be bought and sold. Such an attitude was evident, Macpherson maintained, in the works of Thomas Hobbes and John Locke, and it even infected the egalitarian thinking of the Levellers. In the nineteenth and twentieth centuries the marriage of liberalism and democracy was torn, as in the thought of John Stuart Mill, between this possessive individualist culture and an alternative conception according to which democracy requires the development by every human being of capacities for such things as understanding, friendship, and creativity.

In later works Macpherson criticized twentieth-century theories of democracy, including Joseph Schumpeter's entrepreneurial model and Robert Dahl's version of plural-

ism. He claimed that these models redefined democracy to fit a competitive market economy and that they were biased against widespread democratic participation. In Macpherson's view such participation was central to an alternative model of democracy, which he called developmental democracy.

In *Democratic Theory: Essays in Retrieval* (1973), Macpherson argued that democratic progress could be made if some developmental values in the historical background of liberal democracy were revitalized. For example, while endorsing a liberal-democratic emphasis on the importance of individual freedom, Macpherson criticized liberal theorists such as Isaiah Berlin, for whom liberty is nothing but the absence of deliberate interference with people's ability to act on their preferences. Macpherson favored a positive conception according to which people are free to the extent that they are able to develop their capacities to the fullest.

Macpherson also believed that two concepts of individual property coexisted in seventeenth-century thought. Some defined property as a right to the exclusive use of something; others, as a right of access to means for self-development. Although the first of these concepts became dominant in modern times, Macpherson held that retrieval of nonexclusionary property rights, like retrieval of positive liberty, was essential for a robust democracy.

Macpherson—who, like Laski, favored some form of democratic socialism—employed economic class analysis and other components of Marxist theory. Also like Laski, however, he broke from traditional Marxism in placing his primary emphasis on democracy. In a series of radio lectures, published as *The Real World of Democracy* (1965), Macpherson argued that liberal democracies, socialist societies (as they existed then), and developing nations each contained unique potentials for and impediments to democracy. Democratic progress therefore requires attention to the economic circumstances and the political and cultural contexts in which it is sought.

See also *Berlin, Isaiah; Dahl, Robert A.; Laski, Harold; Schumpeter, Joseph.*

Frank Cunningham

James Madison

Madagascar

See *Africa, Subsaharan*

Madison, James

A founder of the American political system and fourth president of the United States. Born at Port Conway, Virginia, Madison (1751–1836) was taught by a private tutor until he entered the College of New Jersey (now Princeton University). In 1776 he was elected to the convention that declared Virginia's independence from Great Britain and that drafted both the first state constitution and the first state bill of rights. He was elected to the General Assembly under the new state constitution. He served in the Continental Congress as a delegate from Virginia from 1780 to 1783.

In 1784 he was again elected to the Virginia General Assembly, where, the following year, he drafted the *Memorial and Remonstrance,* which helped bring to passage Thomas Jefferson's historic Bill for Religious Liberty. In 1786 Madison was the delegate from Virginia to the Annapolis Convention, which called for a constitutional convention to revise the Articles of Confederation (the original framework for the federal union).

It was as a delegate from Virginia to the Constitutional Convention meeting in Philadelphia in 1787, and as a defender of the Constitution drafted there, that Madison established his reputation as a preeminent political theorist and practical politician. He brought to the convention the benefits not only of his years of study of political systems but also of his experience in a variety of public offices. To these must be added his desire for a firm, national political union and his acknowledged zeal for a republican form of government. Madison kept careful notes on what was said and done that spring and summer in Philadelphia; these notes have been the primary source for scholarship on the Constitution of the United States.

When the new constitution was sent to the states for ratification, the vote on the issue was expected to be close in several of the states, particularly in New York and Virginia. Alexander Hamilton asked Madison to join John Jay and himself in writing a series of articles for the New York newspapers to support ratification. Eighty-five articles, known as *The Federalist,* were written. Of these Madison wrote twenty-nine, including two of those most frequently cited, Nos. 10 and 51.

In framing a government, Madison wrote in *Federalist* No. 51, it was necessary to ensure not only that the government controlled the governed but that it controlled itself. A system of elected representatives would help keep the government responsive to the citizenry; but such a system would not prevent the majority from tyrannizing the minority. Society was composed of separate interests and different classes. Wherever the interests of the majority were united, the interests of the minority would be insecure. In the federal republic, society would be composed of such a numerous variety of interests that it would be difficult to unite them in a tyrannical majority. In the same way that a multiplicity of sects protects religious rights, a diversity of interests would protect minorities from the usurpations of a majority.

A further precaution, Madison noted, was in the structure of the government. The separation of powers into different branches of government, each possessed of the constitutional means to protect itself from the encroachment of others, would check any moves toward a concentration of power in any office. Moreover, the ambitions of officeholders in each department would serve as a check on any dangerous enlargement of powers advanced by another department.

Among the objections of those opposed to the new constitution was the claim that republican government could survive only in a small state. In *Federalist* No. 10, Madison turned the argument around. A large federal republic, he asserted, could better resist the turbulence of factionalism than a small republic, for the greater the area encompassed by the republic, the greater would be the number of diverse interests encompassed in it. So many interests would be present that it would be difficult to find a majority united in a purpose that might endanger a minority. He believed also that the quality of representatives would improve in a large state, where there would be more potential candidates to choose from.

When Madison was writing *The Federalist,* he did not believe that a bill of rights was needed in the Constitution.

He changed his mind, however, when he listened to the objections of the Antifederalists. As a delegate to the Virginia ratifying convention, he promised that if the Constitution was ratified he would prepare a bill of rights for Congress to propose as amendments. Elected to the House of Representatives in the first Congress, he prepared the amendments now known as the Bill of Rights.

Before Madison was forty years old he had helped to create the Virginia constitution (1776), the Virginia bill of rights (1776), the Virginia statute for religious liberty (1786), the Constitution of the United States (1787), and the first ten amendments to that Constitution (1789). He had been elected to the legislatures of both Virginia (1776–1777, 1784–1786) and the United States (1789–1797).

Madison retired from Congress in 1797 expecting to return to private life. But he was soon drawn back into politics. The Alien and Sedition Acts, passed by Congress in 1798, prompted him to draft the Virginia Resolution, companion to Jefferson's Kentucky Resolution, which called on the states to consider whether Congress had enacted unconstitutional legislation. Many states' rights politicians saw these resolutions as support for nullification of congressional acts by states that thought them to be unconstitutional.

From 1801 until his election as president in 1808 Madison served as Jefferson's secretary of state. As president (1809–1817) he was concerned mainly with international affairs, searching for a safe course for the nation amid the international turmoil caused by the Napoleonic Wars. His policy of embargo and nonintercourse failed to check the hostile acts toward the United States of either Great Britain or France, and in 1812 he declared war against Britain. Before a treaty of peace was signed in 1814, the British had entered Washington and burned the White House.

In 1829 Madison came out of retirement again to participate in Virginia's constitutional convention. He made his most enduring contribution to democracy, however, in the early years, when he was one of the Founders of the American political system. He was the last survivor of those who had attended the Philadelphia Convention.

See also *Antifederalists; Federalists; Majority rule, minority rights; States' rights in the United States; United States Constitution.* In Documents section, see *Constitution of the United States (1787).*

Alan P. Grimes

BIBLIOGRAPHY

Brant, Irving. *James Madison.* 6 vols. Indianapolis: Bobbs-Merrill, 1961.

Burns, Edward. *James Madison, Philosopher of the Constitution.* New Brunswick, N.J.: Rutgers University Press, 1938. Reprint, New York: Octagon Books, 1968.

Ketcham, Ralph L. *James Madison: A Biography.* New York: Macmillan, 1989.

McCoy, Drew R. *The Last of the Fathers: James Madison and the Republican Legacy.* Cambridge and New York: Cambridge University Press, 1989.

Miller, William Lee. *The Business of May Next: James Madison and the Founding.* Charlottesville: University Press of Virginia, 1992.

Morgan, Robert J. *James Madison on the Constitution and the Bill of Rights.* Westport, Conn., and London: Greenwood, 1988.

Rutland, Robert A. *James Madison, the Founding Father.* New York: Macmillan, 1987.

Magsaysay, Ramón

President of the Philippines from 1953 until his death in 1957 in an air crash while campaigning for reelection. As president of the Philippines, Magsaysay (1907–1957) helped his country achieve democracy after it gained independence from the United States in 1946. He stands out among Filipino leaders because of his commitment to democratic procedures, his reform policies designed to relieve the poverty of the common people, and his opposition to the powerful landowning class.

First known as a resistance leader during World War II, Magsaysay became a member of the Filipino Congress and then secretary of defense. As defense minister in the early 1950s, he successfully put down the communist-led rebellion of the Huk peasants. His strategy was to improve the level of development in Huk areas by providing land, shelter, and agricultural implements to Huk rebels who surrendered. His evenhanded, nonideological policies as head of the military catapulted him into the presidency.

In the 1953 election campaign, Magsaysay opposed Elpidio Quirino, the incumbent president who had appointed him secretary of defense. Magsaysay resigned from the Liberal Party to become the candidate for the rival Nacionalista Party. He won the election by the largest landslide since independence.

As president, Magsaysay continued his policy of community development, which included reforming the land tenure system, building roads, and providing farmers with credit. He established a presidential commission to bring new roads, bridges, canals, and irrigation facilities to rural areas. He opened the doors of the presidential residence to the common people. Because of his great popularity, his sudden death in 1957 was especially traumatic for the Filipino people.

For some Filipinos, Magsaysay's impeccable reputation was marred by evidence that the U.S. Central Intelligence Agency had supported his presidential campaign. Nevertheless the charismatic Magsaysay remains a symbol of the period when the Philippines was known as the "showcase of democracy" in Asia.

See also *Philippines.*

Clark D. Neher

Majority rule, minority rights

Majority rule and *minority rights* are terms that incorporate the essential tension in democracy between the need for collective decision making and respect for equality and individual choice. As an abstract idea, democracy requires that the governed decide matters of public importance. There is no higher authority than the citizenry. As a practical matter, political issues of importance are rarely resolved by unanimous decision. In virtually every instance, some people will win in the public deliberations and some will lose. The best justification for majority rule therefore is that it provides a legitimate and realistic way to make collective decisions while requiring the smallest number of citizens to accept the decisions of others as their own. Although it minimizes the number of citizens who must obey laws to which they did not consent, majority rule is nevertheless in tension with the democratic principle that individuals are most free when they are obligated by laws of their own making.

Majority Rule and Democracy

Majority rule is implicit in the concept of democracy, but it also logically follows from two other principles: equality and respect for the autonomy of individuals. Majority rule treats all individuals as equals. The decision of a numerical majority thus carries the most weight; in contrast, accepting the decision of the minority would mean a relative devaluation of the vote of each member of the majority. Because majority rule respects the individual choices made by the majority of the citizenry, it implies a utilitarian theory of justice. If people vote according to their own perceived best interest, majority rule will result in policies that are perceived to benefit the most people. Majority rule presumes that all individuals are capable of understanding their own interests and that no single group has a monopoly on truth or political wisdom. Majority rule therefore is not compatible with claims to possess and enforce the singular truth about human nature, the good life, or the just society.

Although majority rule is a pragmatic solution to the problem of who shall rule, it does not fully capture the essence of democracy. Constitutional democracies attempt to balance majority rule with the equally important principle of minority rights. Minority rights serve as a counterbalance to majority rule by preserving such liberal democratic principles as liberty, equality, and respect for individual choice.

If the principle of equality is to be upheld, for example, minorities cannot be excluded entirely from access to institutions of power. Such exclusions compromise the principle of equality, which is the ultimate justification for majority rule itself. If members of a minority cannot participate fully in democratic decision making, there is no rational reason for them to consider government legitimate. Similarly, when the state singles out a group for adverse treatment under its laws, that group has less to gain by upholding those laws. When such abuses target a single group, the state not only exceeds its legitimate power; it also violates the principle of equality.

Actions by the state that are overly broad and unjustified violate the liberal theory of limited government, which is itself based on a respect for individual choice and personal liberty. In constitutional democracies, the government may be prohibited from making decisions that are properly made by other social institutions, such as families or religious organizations, or that are matters of personal conscience. The state may be prohibited from taking certain actions if those actions deprive individuals or groups of something to which they have a protected right, such as property, or if an action is arbitrary and harms an individual or group without furthering the state's legitimate purposes.

Constitutionalism

The balance between rule by majorities and the rights of minorities is at the core of constitutionalism, which may be defined as the principle that governments should follow their own laws regarding the exercise of state authority. A nation's constitution (which is not limited to the idea of a written constitution) can refer both to the composition of its citizenry and to relationships among its political institutions. The idea that a constitution was the sum total of all relationships between the state and society, and among social classes, was particularly strong in ancient and medieval republics, in which the different social classes were given offices and institutions to represent their interests. Although such republican constitutions allowed for the representation of all interests, they were not democratic because they treated individuals of different classes unequally, providing them with different mechanisms by which to influence political decisions. Majoritarian institutions require first that all citizens are at least formally equal in their legal and political rights and in their ability to influence decisions on matters of public policy.

The antimajoritarian institutions of early republics originated in the wealthy minority's fear that the poor majority might expropriate their riches. The danger that the majority might be uncontrollable was particularly strong when there were great differences between rich and poor, slave and free. What Aristotle referred to as a "mixed" constitution was an established mechanism for balancing the interests of all recognized factions: all constituent classes were represented through their own institutions, and each class would check the ambitions and interests of the others. Many modern liberal democracies, especially constitutional monarchies such as Great Britain, evolved out of mixed constitutions through which the monarch shared power with both nobles and representatives of the Commons.

The liberal democracies of Australia, Canada, New Zealand, and the United States are distinctive because they have no history of feudal institutions. In these societies, class and status are more fluid and less easily identifiable with specific political and economic interests than in the European democracies. Majority rule in these states has been based on aggregations of individuals, without resort to the representation of different social estates based on a feudal past. These nations, however, have been troubled with the task of accommodating the rights of cultural and racial minorities. Indigenous peoples were not extended full rights until late in each nation's history. The United States has had the distinctive problem of extending full rights to African Americans, who were first enslaved and later discriminated against and systematically excluded from the nation's political and legal institutions.

Although liberal states have faced constitutional struggles in protecting racial and cultural minorities against discrimination by the majority, the protection of the propertied minority against the aspirations of the laboring majority evolved gradually, notwithstanding the expansion of the electoral franchise during the nineteenth and twentieth centuries. Rather than basing the protection of private property on the ability of the propertied to reject unfavorable legislation, liberal democracy has instead understood expropriation by the state to be unacceptable because it exceeded the legitimate power of the state. Guarantees of personal liberty and private property limited the state's ability to regulate private decisions and transactions between individuals.

The development of the welfare state in industrial democracies, beginning in the late nineteenth century, required some modification of this understanding. In the United States, where the judiciary had zealously protected property rights from governmental regulation, special constitutional protections for the wealthy left a legacy of suspicion of minority rights and a belief that unelected institutions such as the Supreme Court should not obstruct implementation of the will of the majority in economic matters. When the Supreme Court rejected special constitutional protections for wealth, however, it articulated a new role of protecting the fundamental personal rights of very different kinds of minorities—those without power or privilege.

Defining Majorities and Minorities

The rights of minorities are not reducible solely to individual rights. Minorities are not merely smaller aggregates of individuals than majorities. Both majorities and minorities may be groups composed of individuals with similar interests, attributes, or beliefs. Often, however, they are not. Majorities may be unstable, composed of shifting combinations of minorities who bargain and cooperate to further their own particular interests. James Madison believed that such a system of competing and countervailing "factions" would, along with proper constitutional constraints, prevent majority tyranny by making such majorities rare and fragmented. Members of the current majority may be induced to behave more conscientiously, knowing that they might in the future be in the minority themselves.

The seriousness of the threat that majority rule may result in tyranny or intolerance thus depends on whether there is a stable and well-organized majority. In many countries, political parties represent well-defined social, economic, or cultural interests on a variety of issues. Although popular support may shift between parties, even in strong party systems, political parties contribute to the identification of minority and majority political agendas. The danger of a strong party system is that the majority can more easily transform its own agenda into policies unacceptable to the minority. In countries that lack strong party systems, and where politics is characterized by the particular concerns of interest groups (as factions have become known), it is more difficult to form and preserve majorities to implement new governmental policy. Minorities in a fragmented political system may benefit from their ability to negotiate and trade votes on particular issues, building temporary majority coalitions to pass or block those policies about which they feel strongly. In a fragmented system, however, it may be especially difficult to build majorities that are sensitive to minority rights.

Minorities thus may play an important part in forming and preserving majorities. The protection of minority rights is not justified merely by the existence of a minority; to extend such protection would completely undermine the principle of majority rule by automatically conceding a veto power to those who lose in the political process. Minority rights, however, can be extended to groups who lose regularly because of social or political practices that violate the equality principle. In the United States, the Supreme Court, as a nonmajoritarian institution, has been particularly instrumental since the New Deal of the 1930s in protecting the rights of minorities against abuses by the majority. The Canadian Charter of Rights and Freedoms (1982) has also provided the Canadian judicial system with the authority to enforce the rights of cultural minorities in that country. Many civil law countries have separate constitutional courts that may hear challenges to discriminatory treatment.

A matter of constant dispute is whether the legislature or the judiciary should assume primary responsibility for protecting minority rights. Although some nations may protect cultural or racial minorities through special legislation, judicial protection of minorities may also be required to sustain democratic ideals of equality. Where such protections are not specifically provided for through the legislative process, the difficult task of defining which groups qualify as protected minorities may fall to the judiciary. The requirement that a protected minority be easily identifiable and bounded prevents confusion between those groups that have merely lost in the political process and those that have been unfairly denied the opportunity to participate in it. Because not all minorities can be protected equally (except in theory), there is often intense competition for protected status. Although conditions change, and some minorities do achieve vindication of their constitutional rights, few are willing to give up the advantages of identification as an oppressed minority.

In the United States groups that desire protected status must demonstrate that the state or private organizations have previously enforced policies that disproportionately burdened members of that group for no legitimate reason. Thus groups that desire enhanced protection of their voting rights must demonstrate that states employed seemingly legitimate tests or qualifications with the effect of depriving their members of the right to vote, and those seeking affirmative action requirements in employment or education must demonstrate that the organizations they have targeted have previously imposed requirements that benefited members of the majority group at their expense.

There is also considerable debate about whether, and when, rights attach to members of minority groups because of that membership and when rights are extended only to individuals who may, or may not, be minority group members. The basic theory of American constitutional law is that rights are individual even though deprivation of rights may be attributed to group membership; thus rights cannot be reserved for minority group members. Whites as well as blacks, for example, may invoke the protection of civil rights laws. In limited instances such as affirmative action in employment, school admissions, and electoral representation, however, special remedial rights and protections may be afforded to individuals solely because of their race, ethnicity, or gender.

Minority Representation

Because most political decisions in a democracy are made directly or indirectly through representative institutions, the rules governing how citizens will be represented have an important effect on the balance between majority and minority interests. The liberal tradition of representative democracy has grouped individuals by geographic area or political subunit and has been unsympathetic to claims to representation on the basis of cultural or racial affiliation. Democratic representation includes decisions about how social or political minorities may be made more or less efficacious. In particular, governments may act to protect a group's right to political participation when that right has been arbitrarily abridged. In the United States, for example, special protections have been devised for minorities who have been stable over time, whose members act or vote in concert, whose rights have been perpetually denied, and whose political efforts to achieve redress have been consistently frustrated by an identifiable majority that also acts or votes cohesively.

Different systems of representation may increase or decrease the prospects for majority rule or may even exclude minorities from political power. Single-member electoral districts, which are prevalent in the United States, perpetuate majority rule; candidates must focus on gaining at least a plurality of votes to win. Where minorities are residentially segregated and comprise a substantial portion of the population, at-large elections for multimember districts may dilute their voting strength and favor majority candidates. Proportional representation allows for greater minority representation by including legislative seats for groups that can muster a significant level of support, even if they are not a plurality. However, when a limited number of seats are distributed among many competing and qualifying groups within a proportional system, as in Israel, minorities may be overrepresented. The structural representation of small minorities may reduce the incentives for stable majority rule, although it may also promote the formation of semipermanent coalitions.

Conflict over representation centers on two issues: the apportionment of legislative seats and equal treatment in the political process. Conflict arises when the apportionment of legislative representatives does not reflect the principles of majority rule. Legislative districts may be based on geography, types of economic development, or political subunit, thus providing smaller populations with the same amount of representation as larger ones. Or legislative districts initially drawn on the basis of equal representation may not be revised periodically to reflect changes in population, resulting in severe malapportionment.

In the United States the Supreme Court has chosen to reaffirm the principle of majority rule based primarily on population ("one person, one vote"). The Court held in 1964 that the equal protection clause of the Fourteenth Amendment required that all voters have an equal voice in the election of state legislatures and other elected government bodies. A similar principle was applied to elections for the U.S. House of Representatives.

In the United States, where representation is based primarily on population, designing systems of representation that protect the interests of disadvantaged minorities is particularly problematic. Until the 1990s the Supreme Court interpreted the Voting Rights Act of 1965 to mean that states shown to have discriminated against African Americans in the past should devise electoral districts in such a way as to maximize the number of majority African American districts so long as the geographic boundaries of those districts were not drawn solely on the basis of the districts' racial characteristics. In the 1990s the Court began to challenge the validity of this view, ruling that race may be more important than many other criteria, but it is not exclusive of other interests in representation. The claims of other underenfranchised minorities have not been considered to the same extent, although in theory the principle of affirmative action should also apply to large concentrations of other minorities.

Another strategy, useful in systems that use multimember districts, is to provide voters with several votes that they can allocate as they choose among several candidates. Instead of casting one vote per vacant seat, minority voters can choose to use all their votes to support one or two candidates ("bullet voting"). Of course, majority voters would not use this strategy since their goal is to maximize the number of seats their preferred candidates would receive. Such a form of representation might better reflect actual public opinion, and it would account for intensity of interest in a way that single-member-district voting cannot. Because most electoral systems in the United States involve single-member districts, however,

balancing the interests of majority and minority groups in representation must be accomplished through manipulation of the districts' geographic boundaries. Apart from the Voting Rights Act requirements, the Supreme Court has approved a modest amount of "political" gerrymandering while maintaining, somewhat inconsistently, that racial gerrymandering is unconstitutional except as required under the act.

Voting rights law also responds to the second problem in political participation by minorities: unequal treatment. Exclusion from political participation is an especially damaging form of infringement of rights. Denying minorities a fair opportunity to change the policies that disadvantage them invites destabilizing protest strategies. Majority groups, although they are favored by majority rule, may nonetheless attempt to deny minorities access to political power. Their fear is that minorities will become a political force by allying themselves with factions of the majority or by cooperating with other minority groups to form a new majority or displace a powerful plurality. More commonly, however, the denial or obstruction of political participation is based on racial animosity, cultural disagreements, or other conflicts external to the structure of the political process.

Special majorities are needed for certain types of decisions, such as amending constitutions. Constitutional change requires extraordinary majority support to ensure legitimacy. Neither mere bargaining nor a slight preference on the part of the majority is adequate for fundamental structural change. Requirements for ratification of amendments by a substantial majority of regional or administrative subunits (such as ratification of an amendment to the U.S. Constitution by three-quarters of the states) help to keep regional coalitions from forcing an unpalatable decision on other regions. Similarly, in many U.S. states, changes in state constitutions require two legislative votes separated in time by an intervening election. Such requirements ensure that the majority that authorized the change is stable and cohesive and give the electorate a chance to express an opinion.

Minority Rights in Civil Society

Many minority rights are protections against unequal treatment or abuse by political majorities; others are both created and curtailed by the liberal concept of the limited state. The liberal distinction between the state and civil society requires that the state not interfere with the internal decisions of the institutions of civil society unless they adversely affect the larger society. At the same time, those institutions—economic, social, and cultural—may be actively hostile toward or intolerant of minority groups, so that the state must intervene to preserve the democratic principles of equality of access and, sometimes, equality of outcome.

Majority rule is not unrelated to rule by popular opinion. Nineteenth-century liberal theorists such as John Stuart Mill and Alexis de Tocqueville wrote of the dangers of tyranny arising through popular opinion in a democratic society. They argued that the need for vigilance against social pressure becomes greater as people become more equal and less likely to tolerate differences. Minority rights are often asserted in an atmosphere of hostility and social pressure. Therefore, to obtain their rights, minorities may need to call on governmental institutions to enforce constitutional norms. Government protection may thus provide symbols of minorities' right to assert their rights. Government action on behalf of minority rights is evidence that majorities accept this general principle.

The awareness of being a marginalized or excluded group pervades the assertion of rights by minority communities, particularly cultural minorities who feel pressured by what they view as the assimilationist institutions of the majority. Such minorities may demand special cultural or social exemptions in order to protect their identity or heritage. Cultural minorities may seek to protect and preserve their language, for example. French-speaking Canadians' claim of cultural autonomy in Quebec underlies much of their conflict with English-speaking Canadians over the language used in public education, in broadcasting, and even on the signs used by private stores. French Canadians claim that their identity as a distinct group is threatened by the dominance of the language and culture of English-speaking Canada. They therefore demand—and have largely received—the special right to promote their own heritage and to prohibit the majority culture from intruding into those social practices that they view as integral to the maintenance of their identity. In the United States, similarly, assertions about the need for bilingual education have been made by Hispanic groups; and some African Americans have called for tolerance of, if not education in, "black English." The former has been incorporated into the Voting Rights Act; the latter remains very much in dispute.

As in many of the countries where there are strong cultural differences, the Canadian compromise on language has focused on federalism. Establishing provinces and au-tonomous zones has allowed many countries, such as India and Russia, to incorporate majority rule on matters of economics or foreign policy while accommodating indigenous minorities' desire to control their own internal affairs. Such solutions are always controversial. The strict laws that have been passed in Quebec, for instance, have led many English-speaking residents to claim that *they* have been discriminated against as a minority. More dramatically, the disintegration of the Soviet Union and the dismemberment of Yugoslavia have instilled the fear among many ethnic groups that the creation of a smaller state might leave them as a minority under the domination of another, possibly hostile, ethnic group. The violent conflict among Serbs, Croats, and Muslims in the former Yugoslavia attests to the difficulty of holding together such a volatile mixture. The Commonwealth of Independent States faces a similarly difficult challenge in establishing working relationships among the states that once constituted the Soviet Union.

Finding the Balance

The ultimate justification for minority rights is that majorities are not always right, fair, or just. Indeed, majorities are not always majorities. Representative institutions do not always directly reflect public opinion. Perhaps necessarily, representation in two-party states compels citizens to condense their positions on many different issues into a single vote or to vote on one or another side of an issue about which they are ambivalent, have only a slight preference, or would prefer a third alternative. Thus a common condition in democracies is "minorities rule" in the name of the majority.

A powerful justification for majority rule, whatever its imperfections, lies in the need for governmental legitimacy and public respect for the government and the law. The greater the agreement with a law, the more likely it is to be obeyed. When a law is systematically ignored or flouted, its legitimacy is threatened. Requiring majority approval of a law or other governmental policy ensures that governments retain their legitimacy by promulgating only policies that people will comply with and that will need minimal coercive enforcement. Such a consent theory of majority rule may more accurately reflect reality than theories that merely assume that majority rule reflects the will of the people. Minorities may be able to secure the passage of legislation that favors them if there is minimal opposition by the majority, and majorities may be indifferent at times to the measures passed in their name. Majorities, however, must be wary of measures that will be strongly opposed by others.

Securing a balance between majority rule and minority rights is critically important, therefore, because it provides both majorities and minorities with a stake in the democratic process. Although the principle of majority rule means that the majority generally will be victorious in political disputes, the principle of minority rights means that those victories will have limits. Minorities may be defeated at times, even often, but they must always have a chance to participate and some confidence that their very existence and identity are secure.

A democratic state may accomplish these tasks through constitutional mechanisms that feature countermajoritarian institutions, such as courts, or forms of representation that serve both majority and minority interests. Nations may legislate special treatment for certain minority groups while reserving other rights for the majority. But for all of these different institutions and procedures, the goal remains to tolerate the choices of the few while expressing the will of the many.

See also *Affirmative action; Aristotle; Consent; Constitutionalism; Decision making; Federalism; Interest groups; Justifications for democracy; Madison, James; Multiethnic democracy; Popular sovereignty; Property rights, Protection of; Proportional representation; Relativism; Representation; Utilitarianism.* In Documents section, see *Canadian Charter of Rights and Freedoms (1982).*

Joel B. Grossman and Daniel M. Levin

BIBLIOGRAPHY

Chapman, John W., and Alan Wertheimer, eds. *Majorities and Minorities.* New York: New York University Press, 1990.
Commager, Henry Steele. *Majority Rule and Minority Rights.* New York: Oxford University Press, 1943.
Dahl, Robert A. *A Preface to Democratic Theory.* Chicago: University of Chicago Press, 1956.
Mayo, Henry B. *An Introduction to Democratic Theory.* New York: Oxford University Press, 1960.
Mill, John Stuart. *Utilitarianism, On Liberty, and Representative Government.* New York: Dutton, 1912.
Spitz, Elaine. *Majority Rule.* Chatham, N.J.: Chatham House, 1984.

Malawi

See *Africa, Subsaharan*

Malaysia

A federation, located in Southeast Asia, of Malaya, Sarawak, and Sabah, which has been independent from the British since 1957. In contrast to neighbors who fought wars of independence, Malaysians had the advantage of not having to struggle against the return of their colonialist ruler, Great Britain. Independence was granted peacefully and was received with some reluctance by the Malaysians, who feared their country's continued existence would be jeopardized without the support of Great Britain.

When Malaysia received its independence from British rule on August 31, 1957, the new country was called Malaya and consisted of the peninsular area south of Thailand to Singapore. The country's multiethnic nature was reflected in its politics. Ethnic Malays constituted nearly half the population, and the Chinese made up about one-third. Indians, aborigines, and Europeans were smaller minority groups. The Chinese and Indians had been brought to Malaya by the British in the nineteenth century to work on fruit plantations and in the tin mines.

Malaya was transformed into the Federation of Malaysia in 1963, when Sabah, Sarawak, and Singapore were incorporated. The creation of the federation was due in part to the communal (multiethnic) nature of Malaya. Sabah and Sarawak, on the island of Borneo, were populated by ethnic Malays and hence balanced the new Chinese from Singapore. The new federation lasted only two years in that form. In 1965 Prime Minister Tunku Abdul Rahman, the leader of Malayan independence, requested that Singapore leave the federation. With its overwhelmingly Chinese population, Singapore threatened the fragile balance achieved by the Malaysian government, which promised the ethnic Malays political dominance.

Postindependence Government

The Malaysians adopted the British model of governance, including regular competitive elections, a representative parliament, separation of powers, civilian supremacy, and civil liberties. This choice is especially noteworthy because Malaysian elites tend to hold a formalized view of democracy, which crumbles when it faces more deeply held values; stability and security, for example, take precedence over democratic values. In terms of the achievement of democracy, political stability, and economic de-

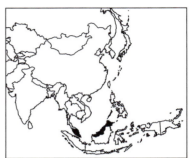

velopment, Malaysia is the most successful country of Southeast Asia.

The distinctive Malayan contribution to the constitutional arrangements was the creation of the position of paramount ruler *(yang di-pertuan agong),* selected from each Malay state in turn every five years. Nine states in the federation have hereditary rulers, known as sultans, and together these constitute the Council of Rulers. The paramount ruler is chosen from this body. This king, who has ceremonial and religious duties and powers of appointment, can delay (but not kill) certain legislative bills; the parliament can overrule the veto.

The most traumatic event of the postindependence period occurred in 1969, when ethnic riots erupted in the capital city, Kuala Lumpur. Dozens of people were killed in the racial violence. To bring order to the country, democratic institutions were temporarily disbanded, and total authority was granted to a National Operations Council. It was clear that a return to parliamentary rule would be disastrous unless significant changes were made in Malaysian politics. To preserve stability, several pieces of legislation were passed that limited the rights of Malaysians. These acts provided Malays with special rights and prohibited discussion of "sensitive issues," such as the prerogatives of the Malay rulers and the official status of the Malay language. Malay was required to be used in all the nation's schools; no debate was allowed regarding its official status, despite the views of many academics that English should also be allowed in the schools.

A modified parliamentary government returned to Malaysia in 1971. Political stability was restored, and a new united front, called the National Front, was established among the major political parties. The National Front consisted of the leading Malay, Chinese, and Indian political parties and continued to dominate every election in the following years.

In 1981 Mahathir bin Mohamad was elected the first "commoner" prime minister—that is, the first leader with no roots in the traditional aristocracy. Mahathir became a vigorous symbol of the modern Malaysian technocrat. He set forth a "Look East" economic policy, arguing that the Western nations were not appropriate models for Malaysia to follow. Mahathir's policy emphasized adoption of the work ethic and methods of Japan and South Korea; a market-oriented economy featuring the privatization of public utilities, communications, and transportation; and increased trade with Asian neighbors. Mahathir viewed the authoritarian societies of South Korea and Taiwan, in particular, as worthy of emulation. He argued that at Malaysia's stage of development, authoritarian leadership was more effective than Western-style democratic government. The success of these programs led economists to predict that Malaysia would be the next newly industrialized country, joining Singapore, Taiwan, South Korea, and Hong Kong as Asia's fifth "tiger."

Communalism, Religion, and Ethnic Identity

During Mahathir's administration, communalism continued to be the central issue in Malaysia. This was especially so because of the rise of Islamic fundamentalists who demanded an Islamic state. The excellent economic growth among most sectors during Mahathir's term, however, provided a cushion for the Malaysian government. Communal tensions remained beneath the surface because the people perceived that their needs were being met.

In the early 1990s Malaysia continued to be ruled by the National Front. Three parties made up the alliance: the United Malays National Organization, the Malaysian Chinese Association, and the Malaysian Indian Congress. These parties accepted the alliance formula in order to legitimize the interests of the three major ethnic groups, which they represented. The formula required that each group accept the basic societal division: Malays dominate the political sphere, and Chinese and Indians dominate the economy. Every Malaysian prime minister has reached that position because he led the United Malays National Organization.

In Malaysia, all Malays are Muslim by legal definition. Islam provides Malays with both legal and political privileges. The loss of these privileges would amount to renunciation of the Malay way of life. Islam, which does not separate secular from religious activities, is tightly organized from the village up to the state level. Muslim youth, many of whom are fundamentalist, call for rigid codes of conduct and the implementation of Islamic law. This increase in Islamic militancy is viewed as threatening by the non-Muslim population.

The religious element is central to the political party orientations of Malaysians. During the independence period some of the parties that were formed were defined almost exclusively in terms of their degree of Islamic orthodoxy. Through the early 1990s moderate Islamic parties were dominant in the ruling alliance. The principal opposition parties have been made up of Islamic fundamentalists, who used their religious doctrines for political objectives.

Chinese citizens also join political parties that reflect their ethnicity. Most Chinese have joined moderate parties, such as the Malaysian Chinese Association. Radical parties have also arisen, out of fear of Islamic militancy and as a reaction to economic policies that threaten the leading Chinese role in the economy.

Quasi-Democracy

Since independence, Malaysia has held eight national elections. Four orderly successions of power have taken place. Despite this record, Malaysia is regarded as a quasi- or semidemocracy because of limitations on civil liberties. The explanation given for the necessity of quasi-democracy is that the communal situation in Malaysia is unique.

In the context of communal issues, an election loss by the National Front would mean the perceived end of the primary rights of the Malays.

Malaysia's Official Secrets Act, Internal Securities Act, and Sedition Act have imposed a culture of silence on citizens. Newspapers, television, and radio are controlled by the government or the United Malays National Organization and are generally compliant with regard to all communalism issues. Newspapers that raised "sensitive issues" were shut down when Prime Minister Mahathir invoked the Internal Securities Act.

Mahathir moved toward authoritarian rule in 1987, when factionalism arose in the National Front. His administrative style was characterized more by confrontation than by consensus. His opponents responded in kind, thereby departing from the traditional ways of leading the nation. By 1993 Mahathir had succeeded in taming the bureaucracy, the political parties, the judiciary, the press, and the state rulers (sultans).

Malaysia's economic growth was among the highest in the world during Mahathir's terms in office. As a result, Malaysians appeared willing to let him rule in a more authoritarian manner than his predecessors. With a gross domestic product (GDP) of almost $3,000 per capita, Malaysia surpassed the European nations of Portugal and Hungary in the world rankings. The standard of living had clearly continued to improve since independence. Clean water, electricity, televisions, and education were universally available. In 1966 just 4 percent of Malay families owned a television; in 1990 more than 90 percent owned one. In this same period, dirt roads were paved, telephone lines were installed, and schools were built.

Under Mahathir, Malaysia emphasized a market-oriented economy. Formerly public enterprises were privatized. Malaysia became integrated into the world capitalist system, as the world's largest exporter of semiconductors and one of the largest exporters of air conditioners, textiles, and footwear.

The October 1990 parliamentary election continued the established pattern of authoritative decision making, with the National Front leading an alliance of parties. Malaysia continued to prosper, and there was a general perception that the government was meeting the needs of the people. It appeared that Malaysians would continue to achieve political stability in the context of a quasi-democracy.

See also *Abdul Rahman, Tunku; Asia, Southeast; Singapore.*

Clark D. Neher

BIBLIOGRAPHY

Jomo, Kwame Sundaram. *A Question of Class: Capital, the State, and Uneven Development in Malaya*. New York: Oxford University Press, 1986.

Mauzy, Diane K. *Barisan Nasional: Coalition Government in Malaysia*. Kuala Lumpur: Marican and Sons, 1983.

Ness, Gayle D. *Bureaucracy and Rural Development in Malaysia*. Berkeley: University of California Press, 1967.

Roff, William R. *The Origins of Malay Nationalism*. New Haven: Yale University Press, 1967.

Scott, James C. *Weapons of the Weak: Everyday Forms of Peasant Resistance*. New Haven and London: Yale University Press, 1983.

Tilman, Robert O. *Bureaucratic Transition in Malaysia*. Durham, N.C.: Duke University Press, 1964.

Von Vorys, Karl. *Democracy without Consensus: Communalism and Political Stability in Malaysia*. Princeton: Princeton University Press, 1975.

Mali

See *Africa, Subsaharan*

Mandela, Nelson

President of the African National Congress and, following South Africa's first nonracial elections in April 1994, the first president of a democratic South Africa. Mandela (1918–   ) led the liberation forces in negotiating a transition to a nonracial democracy in his country.

Born into an important family in the Xhosa tribe, Mandela was positioned to succeed his father as chief of the Tembus, a large clan in the Transkei homeland. He rejected this traditional leadership role and chose to become a modern political leader. Believing that all people, regardless of their birth, have a right to participate in national institutions and politics, he became an eloquent advocate of democratic values.

From youth, Mandela seemed destined for greatness. He acquired an education in a period when most of his black peers did not. Like many Africans schooled in the 1920s, he was educated by Christian missionaries from the West. He excelled and in 1940 enrolled for a law degree at the University of Fort Hare. In his second year of study, he was expelled for participating in a student strike. He later completed his legal studies as a part-time student at the University of South Africa. While at Fort Hare, however, Mandela met a generation of future political leaders in Southern Africa, including Robert Mugabe, later president of Zimbabwe, Yoweri Museveni, later president of Uganda, and Oliver Tambo, then president of the African National Congress (ANC). Mandela's formative years as a political activist were spent at Fort Hare, and his friendships and experiences there had a lasting effect on him.

Soon after his expulsion from the university, Mandela participated in founding the ANC Youth League, a militant organization that helped convince the ANC to adopt radical methods of struggle. The Youth League conceived the program of action adopted by the ANC in 1949. Strikes, stay-at-home protests, and demonstrations replaced more passive methods of political influence, such as deputations and petitions to the authorities.

The 1950s saw the largest, most intensive mobilization of anti-apartheid forces in South African history. So powerful was the anti-apartheid movement that the government in 1960 proscribed the ANC and the Pan-Africanist Congress (PAC). Mandela and more than a hundred other ANC leaders were arrested in 1956 and charged with treason. This charge was based solely on the ANC's Freedom Charter, a pro-democratic treatise that still guides ANC policy. Among the last to be discharged in 1961, when the trial finally ended without a conviction, Mandela went underground with other ANC and PAC colleagues.

Soon thereafter Mandela was sent abroad to elicit support from a number of African countries to continue the struggle, by force if necessary. He met with African nationalist leaders, many still engaged in anticolonial struggle, and trained in Algeria with the National Liberation Front during their armed fight against the French. After slipping back into South Africa, Mandela helped to form an ANC guerrilla army and became its first commander in chief.

When the ANC began sending some of its key members abroad, Mandela remained in South Africa to help lead the resistance to apartheid. In August 1962, however, he was arrested for leaving the country illegally. He was sentenced in November to five years in prison. In 1963, while serving this sentence, he was tried for sabotage; he and seven other ANC leaders were found guilty and sentenced to life imprisonment. It was during this trial that Mandela, anticipating a possible death sentence, made his

Nelson Mandela

tiations was laid. Because Mandela's participation was seen as critical to a peaceful settlement, he was released on February 11, 1990, by the new state president, Frederik W. de Klerk. Mandela's release, which followed the lifting of the ban on the ANC and other liberation organizations on February 2, signaled the start of negotiations for a new political system in which he would assume a leadership role. Soon thereafter political exiles returned and more political prisoners were released. In a four-day meeting in May 1992 to mark its evolution into a political party, the ANC elected Mandela its president, virtually assuring him of becoming the first head of a democratic nonracial South Africa.

May 1992 also saw the collapse of the first round of negotiations between the ANC and de Klerk's National Party, in the Convention for a Democratic South Africa. In the subsequent two years, Mandela led the ANC through a tortuous negotiating path to an interim constitution and the first free, nonracial elections in the country's history. The success of these negotiations was owing in no small measure to Mandela's extraordinary leadership abilities: his vision, integrity, tolerance, and self-confidence; his commitment to peaceful change in the face of rising political violence and intimidation from the extremists; and his capacity to forge an effective working relationship with his National Party counterparts, particularly President de Klerk, while holding disparate factions of the ANC together in a united party. Ultimately, the participation in the elections of both conservative Afrikaners and the militant Inkatha Freedom Party, led by Chief Mangosuthu Buthelezi, owed much to the tireless joint efforts of Mandela and de Klerk to reach a broad accommodation.

Mandela led the ANC to a decisive victory in the elections held April 26–28, 1994, when he won 63 percent of the vote and was elected by Parliament the first president of a democratic South Africa. In office, at the helm of an ANC-dominated government of national unity, Mandela continued to lead vigorously, setting a tone of moderation and racial reconciliation while launching an ambitious reconstruction and development program to revive the economy and promote social justice. While the challenges to democratic consolidation remained formidable, Mandela's presidential leadership, which commanded broad popular approval, established a foundation of democratic commitment and hope.

See also *De Klerk, Frederik Willem; South Africa.* In Documents section, see *African National Congress Freedom Charter (1955).*

Khehla Shubane

now famous "I am prepared to die" speech from the dock.

Mandela and his colleagues were among the first prisoners to be sent to Robben Island. They organized hunger strikes and other peaceful actions to protest the harsh conditions. Although banned, the ANC continued to function underground inside the prison, and Mandela turned to it for consultation on major issues. In March 1982 Mandela was transferred to Polsmore Prison in Cape Town, where he served most of his sentence. Later he was transferred to Victor Verster in Paarl, where he was detained in a house.

In a historic development, on July 9, 1989, South African president Pieter Botha met with Mandela, still a prisoner, in Cape Town. During these talks the basis for nego-

BIBLIOGRAPHY

Benson, Mary. *Nelson Mandela: The Man and the Movement.* New York: Norton, 1986.

Johns, Sheridan, and R. Hunt Davis, Jr., eds. *Mandela, Tambo, and the African National Congress: The Struggle against Apartheid, 1948–1990.* New York: Oxford University Press, 1991.

Mandela, Nelson. *Long Walk to Freedom: The Autobiography of Nelson Mandela.* Boston: Little, Brown, 1994.

———. *Nelson Mandela: The Struggle Is My Life.* Rev. ed. New York and London: Pathfinder Press, 1990.

Meli, Francis. *South Africa Belongs to Us: A History of the ANC.* Harare: Zimbabwe Publishing House; Bloomington: Indiana University Press; London: J. Currey, 1989.

Mannheim, Karl

Hungarian-born sociologist best known for his sociology of knowledge—the study of the organization, institutions, and development of learning and understanding. Mannheim (1893–1947) grew up in a Jewish family in Budapest. Influenced by German thinkers such as Immanuel Kant, G. W. F. Hegel, Karl Marx, and Max Weber, he explored democratic planning as a process of rational and conscious guidance and creation of values and institutional arrangements, with the purpose of predicting and influencing social development.

After the collapse of the social democratic and communist parties in Hungary in 1920, Mannheim fled to Heidelberg, Germany. He taught at the University of Heidelberg and at the University of Frankfurt am Main. Dismissed in 1933, when the Nazis came to power, he took refuge in England, where he taught at the London School of Economics and the University of London.

Mannheim studied the social and cultural context of what people know and think and the connections between the various spheres of their activities. He argued that the sociology of knowledge should be central to every attempt to bring politics and reason together. The knowledge of social psychology is of value to leaders as a technique for mass manipulation; in this limited sense, politics as a science clears the way for action. The sociology of knowledge may also explain why socially unattached intellectuals seek a synthesis between conflicting ideologies.

Mannheim's personal life as an exile and the specter of social dissolution influenced his major themes. These were his sociology of knowledge; his theory of societal planning; his emphasis on the importance of the role of mass education in fostering ideological unity within a country; and his plan for social justice and freedom at the roots of militant and fundamental democracy.

Mannheim believed that the sociology of knowledge influences political awareness in three ways: it can be an analytical tool and a guiding force for those who are active in politics; it is a way to understand the dual process of rationalization and assertion of the self in contemporary societies, allowing people to make choices that are free, rational, and conscious; and it provides a way to counter prevailing myths about public order and fair political conduct, by stressing how democratically educated leaders may use authority and law to maintain order and settle conflicts in complex societies.

Two of Mannheim's works, *Ideology and Utopia* (1929) and *Structures of Thinking* (1980), present his theoretical investigations into the conditions in which intelligence and thought emerge, the role of ideas in political and social movements, and the value of knowledge in controlling social reality. The essay *Conservatism: A Contribution to the Sociology of Knowledge* (1927) is a model of empirical research into how styles of thinking are rooted in experience. This work examines modes of scientific inquiry leading to political knowledge and shows the range and limits of an individual's comprehension of ultimate reality.

Mannheim saw the science of politics as a major contribution of liberal democratic thought. In his understanding of politics as the dynamic unfolding of conflicting forces, he welcomed the socially independent and intellectually open elites' dynamic balancing between cultural tradition and social change.

In Mannheim's view, democratization alters the number, function, and recruitment of political elites; it increases free competition, which forces individuals to adapt and to take the initiative; and it diminishes the social distance between classes. But the state and political parties also marginalize minority political views for the sake of stability. Democracies proclaim that all socially useful work is noble; that law serves to maintain order and settle conflicts, though peaceful methods are not always possible; that authority is vested in political leaders who claim to serve the will of the people; that love, freedom, and justice are primary social goals; that political parties compete for power within the state, legitimized by plebiscites or elections; and that the executive is given the chief initiative of government but is checked by other political institutions.

In his later works, Mannheim diagnosed a societal crisis brought on by a parody of the democratic principle of merit and pervasive egalitarianism, the disappearance of traditional and partisan forms of organization, and an excessive role for nonvoters and emotional younger generations. He proposed reforms to stop personal and social disintegration. In the 1940s he proposed government control over a planned economy and over mass education and a complete revision of democratic values (intended to halt the drift toward anomie and rootlessness), educational practices, and the role of intellectuals. But he did not fully address some important questions: how to avoid violence in political life and coercion in social control, how to develop the competence of parties, and how to determine who should devise the goals of, and techniques for, social change.

Counterculture intellectuals in the 1960s and 1970s greatly admired Mannheim's sociology of knowledge. His sociology of planning has been a crucial component of contemporary theories of societal guidance, linking systematic knowledge with organized action and imposing new obligations upon all responsible members of society.

See also *Education; Hegel, G. W. F.; Kant, Immanuel; Marx, Karl; Weber, Max.*

Brigitte Vassort-Rousset

BIBLIOGRAPHY

Mannheim, Karl. *Diagnosis of Our Time: Wartime Essays of a Sociologist.* London: Kegan Paul, 1943; New York: Oxford University Press, 1944.

———. *Freedom, Power, and Democratic Planning.* Edited by E. K. Bramsted and H. Gerth. New York: Oxford University Press, 1950; London: Routledge and Kegan Paul, 1951.

———. *Ideology and Utopia.* Translated by Louis Wirth and Edward Shils. London: Routledge and Kegan Paul; New York: Harcourt, Brace, and World, 1936.

———. *Man and Society in an Age of Reconstruction: Studies in Modern Social Structure.* Translated by Edward Shils. London: Routledge and Kegan Paul; New York: Harcourt, Brace, 1940; 2d rev. ed. London: Routledge, 1991.

———. *Systematic Sociology. An Introduction to the Study of Society.* Edited by J. S. Erös and W. A. C. Stewart. London: Routledge and Kegan Paul; New York: Oxford University Press, 1957.

Maritain, Jacques

French Roman Catholic philosopher best known for his interpretation of the thought of the medieval Italian theologian and philosopher Saint Thomas Aquinas and for his own philosophy based on Aristotelianism and Thomism. Maritain (1882–1973) was perhaps the most influential Catholic thinker in changing the church's position on democracy and the modern world. Through his wide-ranging work on religion, culture, and contemporary politics, he took part in the controversy over Thomist political philosophy in the early twentieth century—a controversy that concerned the church's involvement in secular matters. He believed that democracy should serve as the central issue in political philosophy and suggested that the democratic ideal itself was the lay name for the ideal of Christianity.

Influenced by Christian mystics as well as by Thomas Aquinas, Maritain initiated an important spiritual trend in French interwar Catholicism. From 1914 to 1939 he taught at the Catholic Institute in Paris. He and the Dominicans analyzed the moral and political debates of the time from a Christian perspective in an attempt to reconcile spirituality with emancipation, and political activity with culture. Such religious renewal spurred Christian think tanks, social commitment, and trade unionism. Yet Maritain longed for the creation of a movement inspired by Christian principles that would serve as the political expression of the intermediate, secular ends of Christian faith and of the struggle for freedom.

After France was defeated by the Germans during World War II, Maritain wrote brochures in defense of freedom from the United States, where he taught at Princeton and Columbia Universities. He returned to Princeton as emeritus professor in 1948 after serving as French ambassador to the Vatican. In 1958 the University of Notre Dame established the Jacques Maritain Center for the study of his philosophy. In 1970 he took religious vows in Toulouse, France, where he had lived since 1960.

According to Maritain the philosopher's role is to set principles for social relationships among people and to foster ethical reflection on challenges to equality, tolerance, and mutual respect; on individual dignity and rights; and on the search for peace. Applied philosophy, he believed, gives people a supernatural purpose and the sense that freedom and truth are the basic conditions for thinking and interpreting facts. It roots democratic principles in the interaction of the spiritual and the secular.

The Vatican's condemnation in 1926 of *L'Action Française*, the pro-monarchy movement of French political theorist Charles Maurras, signaled Maritain's rejection of anthropocentrism and the articulation of his moral philosophy on the intrinsic subordination of politics to ethics and ethics to religion (*Primauté du spirituel*, 1927) and on the obligation of justice toward the working class. Basing his observations on the global crisis created by World War I, Maritain held that political, social, and economic relationships should stem from theocentric or integral humanism that serves the public good and individual spiritual freedom. Brotherly love, civic friendship, and acceptance of strangers are worldly evidence of evangelical inspiration and are aimed at reaching for an end above the state. In times of crisis, growth, or renewal, he pointed out, the energy and moral responsibility of prophetic leaders are crucial: freely and variously organized and selected from all social strata through dedication and heroism, they inform people that democratic principles reach beyond the individual.

From the mid-1930s Maritain considered democracy to be a state of mind and a philosophy rather than a political regime; yet he believed that the people's freely elected rulers are endowed with the right to rule in certain conditions, though controlled periodically by representatives and assemblies. The authority of rulers rises up from the people, who possess God's transcendental authority. Universal suffrage, however fundamental, is not sufficient to establish justice and law. Democratic principles are personalist, community oriented, pluralist, and Christian, as well as respectful of such intermediate ends as individual liberty and the autonomy of the secular realm in relation to otherworldliness.

In political ethics, authority and the rationale for the public good are derived from the transcendental foundation of law. Democracy prospers within clearly distinct yet organic links and cooperation among religious institutions, the state, and the citizenry. A legally formulated and established constitution should protect personal and social rights as well as the tenets of the state and of social relationships.

Functions of the presumably republican state are limited to coordinating, checking, and guiding autonomous activities. Political parties should become political schools educating public opinion, and justice should restore equality before the law since equal dignity is granted to all human beings. Private property, justified by hard work, should be welcome when serving the public good. Finally, democratic considerations may be extended to any peace-oriented framework of international relations, to be constructed on pluralism and free will.

Brigitte Vassort-Rousset

BIBLIOGRAPHY

Evans, J. W. *Jacques Maritain: The Man and His Achievement.* New York: Sheed and Ward, 1963.
Maritain, Jacques. *Christianisme et démocratie.* New York: Editions de la Maison Française, 1943.
———. *Les droits de l'homme et la loi naturelle.* New York: Editions de la Maison Française, 1944.
———. *Humanisme intégral.* Paris: Aubier, 1936.
———. *Man and the State.* Chicago: University of Chicago Press, 1951.

Market theory

A theoretical approach that develops models of the effect of economic markets on politics and society. Since the early 1800s the tension between markets and political democracy has been a dominant theme in political thought. According to some thinkers, democracy threatens to undermine and destabilize market processes by promoting political conflict in society and increasing levels of taxation. It may also promote corruption and lead individuals to pursue political power rather than affluence.

From Tocqueville to Schumpeter

An early contributor to this pessimistic view was Alexis de Tocqueville, who catalogued (in *Democracy in America*, 1835) several dangers of democracy. First, because "democratic institutions have a very strong tendency to promote the feeling of envy in the human heart," Tocqueville feared the despotism of the majority, which would use political power to tax the rich and increase public expenditure. Second, frequent changes of policy and leadership would waste resources and lead to long-term stagnation. Third, Tocqueville believed that democracy would promote centralization and state control over the economic activities of citizens.

Tocqueville hoped that America might set an example of how a democratic people could remain free. Economic progress would produce a large middle class, thereby moderating the effects of envy. The pace of technical change would also reduce the effects of regulation by undermining existing positions of privilege. A constitution with built-in checks and balances would also help. Especially important were the independent judiciary and the federal system, with its weak central government.

Much Victorian political thought was concerned with the possible corrupting effects of the rising tide of democracy. Later Victorian thinkers wrote with great immediacy about the effects of increasing the power of voters without property qualifications. In the 1890s the English philosopher Herbert Spencer, for example, foresaw a rise in the coercive power of government even though government spending in Britain and the United States was then less than 10 percent of the gross domestic product. Spencer and others feared that democracy would lead to interference with property rights and stifle initiative.

In the first half of the twentieth century, criticism of government and concern about its impact on economic and political democracy remained very much a minority view. The contrast with totalitarianism and the immediate concerns of war, depression, and postwar recovery led to a reduced interest in the blemishes of the few continuing democracies. Toward the end of World War II, economist Joseph Schumpeter (in *Capitalism, Socialism, and Democracy,* 1944) developed the thesis that capitalism would be the prisoner of its own success. Economic growth would lead to greater leisure and freedom to criticize, which would prepare the ground for new forms of collectivism. This thesis won few followers.

Friedman and Hayek

Milton Friedman revived many of the concerns of Victorian thinkers in *Capitalism and Freedom* (1962). Friedman's theme was that the market disperses power and makes it easier to make decisions, whereas the political process tends to concentrate power through charisma backed by organization. Friedman noted that although there might be many millionaires in one large economy there rarely was room for more than one "outstanding leader." The market is also essential for political freedom. Where the state is the only source of employment and income there can be no real freedom to dissent. The role of the market was clearly seen during the era of McCarthyism in the United States in the 1950s, when Sen. Joseph McCarthy led a witch hunt against communists. Most of those accused—the great majority of whom were later cleared—had to move into small business or farming to make their living.

In later work (*Free to Choose,* 1980), Friedman looked backward at the welfare and social security programs that had grown up during three decades of democracy. Pessimistic about the prospects of challenging the vested interests and giant bureaucracies that supported the programs, Friedman urged solutions that would bring market pressures to bear on the programs through privatization of pensions and use of vouchers to increase parent choice in schools.

The most powerful and influential criticism of the economic impact of democracy came from economist Friedrich A. von Hayek. In *The Constitution of Liberty* (1960) he stressed that democracy's limits must be determined in light of the purpose the polity wishes democracy to serve. A democratic society must include people with independent opinions, lest democracy degenerate into the tyranny of the majority. Democracy must also be constrained by limits on public monopoly. Markets depend on access to changing information, and society advances by making use of dispersed knowledge, which activates the price system and markets by stimulating innovation and the development of new products. Democracy, on the other hand, leads to central planning and regulation, which destroy the market mechanism.

Hayek subsequently became distinctly more pessimistic, fearing the imminent development of a totalitarian state and the weakening of independent opinion. His work no longer turned on the idea of conflict; he began to look apprehensively toward the inevitable decline of free markets. Where the legislature has unlimited powers, political parties become little more than coalitions of organized interests whose actions are determined by principles other than the general principles and ideals of the democratic polity. Hayek recommended a model constitution offering the legislature limited powers over day-to-day administration and limiting suffrage to people over the age of forty-five.

The theme of bias in voting systems was developed by James M. Buchanan and Gordon Tullock in *The Calculus of Consent* (1962). Buchanan and Tullock showed how majority voting was likely to lead to "logrolling" between intense minorities that would form coalitions, with the result of raising public expenditures to a level above that favored by the majority. Although he recognized that it would be difficult to devise voting systems without a bias toward higher public spending, Buchanan developed the case for fiscal constitutions that would impose limits on democratic action in order to avoid budget deficits.

The Post–Cold War View

The 1990s brought greater optimism about the fit between markets and democracy. New global perspectives tended to provide reminders about the unpleasant effects of totalitarianism. Countries as far apart as the United Kingdom, New Zealand, Colombia, Poland, and Mauritius showed signs that democratic governments were capable of carrying through market-oriented reform programs against strong opposition from organized interests. There were also some signs that increases in real income were related to economic and political freedom. The American economist Mancur Olson, who once demonstrated how democracy would increase the power of pressure groups, now argued that for all its defects democracy was more conducive to economic growth than dictatorship because property is more secure under democratic systems that protect individual rights.

Democracy, long portrayed as incompatible with the market, has come to be seen as the essential condition and complement for economic freedom. This view is bolstered by the poor political and economic results of years of dictatorship in Latin America and Africa.

One hundred and fifty years after Tocqueville the future of democracy seems neither threatened nor threatening. The new democratic consensus appears likely to gain support from the greater global mobility of people and capital, which tends to limit the power of national governments to raise taxes and public spending. The need to improve the state's effectiveness has also gained wide recognition. Programs for privatizing state monopolies, which had been highly controversial when first introduced in Britain in the 1980s, were spreading around the globe by the mid-1990s, as was the use of internal markets in the organization of public services. Internal markets divide funding from supply in public services and introduce contracting mechanisms that include much higher performance standards.

In general, the new consensus on the economic gains from democracy and on the proper economic role of the state offers some hope that stable democracy will become much more common in Central Europe and Asia in the early years of the twenty-first century.

See also *Development, Economic; Schumpeter, Joseph; Tocqueville, Alexis de.*

Nick Bosanquet

BIBLIOGRAPHY

Bosanquet, Nick. *After the New Right.* Aldershot: Gower, 1983.

Buchanan, James M., and Gordon Tullock. *The Calculus of Consent: Logical Foundations of Constitutional Democracy.* Ann Arbor: University of Michigan Press, 1962.

Friedman, Milton. *Capitalism and Freedom.* Chicago: University of Chicago Press, 1962.

———. *Free to Choose.* London: Secker and Warburg, 1980.

Hayek, Friedrich A. von. *The Constitution of Liberty.* London: Routledge, 1960.

Tocqueville, Alexis de. *Democracy in America.* 2 vols. Edited by Phillips Bradley. New York: Knopf, 1945.

Markets, Regulation of

Regulation of markets refers to the practices by which democratic governments intervene in the private sector to promote the public good. Democracy in economic thought has developed meanings distinct from those associated with political democracy. Philosophically akin to the Anglo-American ideal of parliamentarianism has been the liberal economic ideal of *laissez-faire,* or letting competitive markets work free from government regulation and allowing individuals to enrich themselves free from state interference. But as a consequence of the way markets have worked in practice, another set of almost diametrically opposite meanings has evolved, namely freedom through regulation from those oppressive market forces that deny individuals the right to work steadily and safely.

Economic Liberalism and Political Democracy

In Western Europe's postwar social democracies, where traditions of state intervention tended to be stronger than in England or the United States, this last sense of economic liberty reached its culmination in the "welfare state." As capitalism created unimaginable wealth, a citizen's democratic rights came to include not just a job but also public health care and other social services.

The regulation of markets took on still another meaning in countries that started industrializing after World War II, particularly the successful countries of East Asia. Instead of an American "regulatory state" or a West European "welfare state," the "developmental state" used industrial policies to interfere broadly with market forces in order to initiate capital accumulation and catch up with the world's technological leaders. Late industrializers altered the liberal equation of economic and political democracy. In Chile, for example, radical laissez-faire policies went hand in hand with brutal dictatorship under Gen. Augusto Pinochet, who held power from 1973 to 1989. The developmental state flourished under political repression in South Korea, Singapore, and Taiwan and under one-party democracy in postwar Japan. The dictatorial developmental state legitimized itself by providing "economic rights" in the form of sharply rising living standards.

Even in the United States, a stronghold of economic liberalism, the role of government expanded greatly during and immediately following World War II. This expansion of government led political economist Joseph Schumpeter to conclude that the American public had renounced capitalist values. Schumpeter also feared that the bureaucratic structures devised to manage the U.S. economy during the war years would not be dismantled, as they had been following World War I. Indeed, those structures did live on during the first decades of the cold war as the "military-industrial complex" grew to meet the perceived threat of the Soviet Union. By 1973, however, the end of a golden age of economic growth and the fraying of the welfare state reinforced American allegiance to the values

of economic liberalism. Military support for civilian technology came to be interpreted more and more narrowly. Hostility toward government increased around the world, nurtured in part by cracks in East Asia's managed economies and a crisis in Europe's welfare states.

The historical ups and downs of regulation illustrate the fragility in a market economy of economic definitions of democracy that include the right to employment and social-welfare protection. As the twenty-first century approached, and the Anglo-American regulatory state took aim at the East Asian developmental state, the costs of upholding those social democratic rights began to appear to be intolerably high to many.

The Age of Reform

Two opposing meanings of economic democracy have coexisted historically since two giant bureaucracies came to characterize capitalism in the 1890s: the modern industrial enterprise and the modern political state. Proponents of each bureaucracy viewed the other with antagonism. Those opposed to government regulation feared a powerful, interventionist state, while those in favor of regulation focused on the monopolistic practices of giant corporations. Alfred Chandler argued (in *Scale and Scope: The Dynamics of Industrial Capitalism,* 1990) that because big business arose in the United States before big government (the U.S. federal government remained small until the 1930s), and because the life of small-scale enterprise was threatened with the rise of the railroads, middle-class animus toward big business gave birth to the American regulatory state. In countries where big government came first, as in France and Japan, both the power and regulation of business were less.

It is debatable just how interventionist the American government ever really was, considering the country's commitment to private enterprise. The Progressives created an "age of reform," as the historian Richard Hofstadter called the period from 1890 to 1940. Following twenty-five years of explosive industrialization after the Civil War (1861–1865), the inequities engendered by industrial transformation led to a mass movement to police the big "trusts" responsible for much of the new industrial production in the United States.

Economic reform again dominated politics in the 1930s, in the United States as in Europe, but President Franklin D. Roosevelt's New Deal bore little resemblance to the Progressives' agenda. Unlike the Progressives, the architects of the New Deal accepted big business but aimed to redress the inability of the market to trigger economic recovery and reduce unemployment. Progressivism, which arose out of prosperity, was an expression of the middle class. The New Deal, on the other hand, was triggered by the Great Depression and was responsive to the demands of a large and growing labor movement. The Progressives elevated the principle of the state's neutrality in the struggle to restore popular democracy, whereas the New Deal was opportunistic: the state was neutral in endeavoring to provide benefits to everyone. New Deal democracy emphasized the right to work under a capitalist system which, as Charles Lindblom later articulated (in *Politics and Markets: The World's Political-Economic Systems*, 1977), privileged business and allowed private interests, through their investment decisions, to hold the economy at ransom.

There is still no entirely convincing explanation for why the Great Depression lasted so long (from 1929 to 1941 in the United States and in much of Europe) and proved so intractable. The depression ended only with the outbreak of World War II, as governments poured expenditures into armaments. Despite the wide variety of market-regulating medicine of the New Deal—ranging from measures to cut capacity and fix prices to attempts to increase government spending and so stimulate demand—unemployment in the United States in 1938 was comparable to its level in the early 1930s.

Most economists have come to believe that the Great Depression lasted so long because governments tried to halt it. In keeping with the long and deep tradition of laissez-faire thinking among Anglo-American economists, monetarists such as Milton Friedman blamed the origin of the depression on the fumbling of the Federal Reserve and the duration of high unemployment on activist measures to stimulate the economy in the early 1930s.

The Age of Counter-Reform

The U.S. government's stance toward reform has been principally determined by the prevailing political climate, but economists have been persuasive advisers and politically savvy handmaidens. Support among economists was widespread for the Keynesian revolution—shorn of its more radical elements—during the period of unprecedented global growth from 1945 to 1973. Domestic market regulation meant fine-tuning economic activity through fiscal policy and buoying effective demand through mushrooming military expenditures. In keeping with the rise of "big science" in the United States, economists emphasized abstract model building. With scientific principles to steer the economy, the infamous business cycle of boom and bust appeared to be dead.

Unfortunately, the golden age of postwar industrial growth faded, for reasons that are no more transparent than those behind the crash of the 1930s. For no obvious reason, productivity growth declined especially quickly in the United States. Simultaneously, a twelvefold increase in oil prices caused by the pricing decisions of a world oil cartel triggered inflation. Keynesian prescriptions were promptly abandoned in favor of cautious macroeconomic policies, which themselves dampened growth. In the United States tight monetary policies traditionally had been fought by inflationist senators from western states. By the 1970s almost all Americans had been convinced that inflation was worse than unemployment, although it turned out that the fight against inflation was accompanied by a steadily declining growth rate of real wages.

The political backlash that followed the breakdown of the golden age resulted in electoral victories of neoliberals in the United Kingdom and in the United States: Margaret Thatcher became prime minister in 1979, and Ronald Reagan was elected president in 1980. Economic ideology swung sharply back toward individualism and the liberalization, deregulation, and privatization of markets.

Ironically, economic theory at the time was discovering anew the theoretical limits of the competitive market model. New growth theories underscored the importance of state educational expenditures in promoting economic development. New trade theories warranted industrial policies to ensure competitiveness in international markets. New information theories demonstrated that imperfect knowledge on the part of consumers and investors invalidated key conclusions of free market theory. Yet the majority of economists vigorously opposed government intervention to counter stagnation. Even if a policy was good, the argument ran, it could not be well implemented because of conflicts among competing interest groups. Paul Krugman (in *The Age of Diminished Expectations*, 1992) reasoned that Americans had lowered their expectations about what their economy could do, and that economists could accordingly feel comfortable in accepting the status quo.

The New Deal had been conceived and executed in a spirit of "bold, persistent experimentation" according to Richard Hofstadter (in *The Age of Reform*, 1955). The reverse characterized the counter-reform of the 1970s and beyond. The approach of the year 2000 revealed a growing worldwide problem of joblessness but an abounding spirit of resignation on the part of policymakers.

The Age of Conformity

Without new technology to penetrate world markets, which had been the hallmark of the industrial revolutions of the eighteenth and nineteenth centuries, latecomers like Japan looked toward a developmental state to push industrialization forward. As first analyzed by Chalmers Johnson (in *MITI and the Japanese Miracle*, 1982), who studied Japan's Ministry of International Trade and Industry, late-industrializing states in the postwar period encouraged optimal rather than free competition and used subsidies to stimulate the growth of businesses that were radical in their pervasiveness even by nineteenth-century European standards.

Rapid rises in developing countries' per capita income were a pillar of the golden age. Growth, however, proved more sustained in some countries than in others. In all late-industrializing countries, governments had regulated labor. But latecomers that fared especially well, such as South Korea and Taiwan, also regulated capital, tying subsidies to performance standards, especially export targets. The United States subsidized business indirectly through the military and had regulated business since the Progressive Era. The difference was that in East Asia a centralized state coordinated support for and regulation of business for developmental purposes.

The slow-growth equilibrium of the last years of the twentieth century was disturbed by East Asia's soaring output and exports. As the U.S. trade deficit with Japan ballooned despite reductions in Japanese tariffs and quotas, Japan was pressured to eliminate its domestic "structural impediments" to U.S. exports and to organize its economy more in keeping with that of its major trading partner.

Meanwhile, the unilateral declaration of war against inflation by the industrialized countries in the 1980s had plunged many of the late-industrializing economies into a profound debt crisis. The measures taken to slow inflation in the industrialized world raised interest rates and thereby the costs of loan repayments. The generic medicine administered to the late-industrializing countries (as well as to the formerly socialist countries of Eastern Europe) by last-resort lenders such as the World Bank and International Monetary Fund was liberalization, deregulation, and privatization.

With the advent of "globalism"—defined as increased international trade and capital flows—countries that needed access to world markets were pressured to structure their domestic economies in conformance with an eighteenth-century free market model that had become thoroughly mythologized. The Age of Counter-Reform thus became an Age of Conformity, in which interventions designed to stimulate economic development began to take covert form.

See also *Capitalism; Complexity; Development, Economic; Economic planning; Globalization; Industrial democracy; Laissez-faire economic theory; Liberalism; Market theory; Progressivism; Roosevelt, Franklin D.; Social democracy; State growth and intervention; Welfare, Promotion of.*

Alice H. Amsden

BIBLIOGRAPHY

Addison, Argus. "Explaining the Economic Performance of Nations, 1820–1989." In *Convergence of Productivity: Cross-National Studies and Historical Evidence,* edited by William J. Baumol, Richard R. Nelson, and Edward N. Wolff. New York: Oxford University Press, 1994.
Amsden, Alice H. *Asia's Next Giant: South Korea and Late Industrialization.* New York: Oxford University Press, 1989.
Friedman, Milton, with Anna J. Schwartz. *A Monetary History of the United States, 1867–1960.* Princeton: Princeton University Press, 1963.
Hofstadter, Richard. *The Age of Reform: From Bryan to FDR.* New York: Vintage Books, 1955.
Johnson, Chalmers. *MITI and the Japanese Miracle: The Growth of Industrial Policy, 1925–1975.* Stanford, Calif.: Stanford University Press, 1982.
Krugman, Paul. *The Age of Diminished Expectations: U.S. Economic Policy in the 1990s.* Cambridge, Mass., and London: MIT Press, 1992.
Schumpeter, Joseph. "Capitalism in the Postwar World." In *Postwar Economic Problems,* edited by Seymour Harris. New York: McGraw-Hill, 1943.

Marshall, John

Chief justice of the United States (from 1801 to 1835), generally considered to have contributed more to the development of American constitutional law than any other person. Marshall (1755–1835) was born in Virginia and served in the Continental army during the American Revolution. He was an attorney in Richmond and active in Virginia politics; from 1799 to 1800 he served in the U.S.

John Marshall

House of Representatives, and from 1800 to 1801 he was secretary of state.

Although he considered himself no democrat, Marshall nonetheless influenced American democracy in three fundamental respects: the enunciation of the doctrine of judicial review, the strengthening of the authority and power of the United States in regard to the states, and the protection of vested property rights. In formulating the doctrine of judicial review in his opinion in *Marbury v. Madison* (1803), Marshall established the supremacy of the Constitution and the Supreme Court's interpretation of it over actions of the legislative and executive branches of the federal government. He positioned the Court as the guardian of the rule of law. As a result, the justices' decisions determine what the other branches of government constitutionally can and cannot do.

Although judicial review is commonly viewed as a limitation on the powers of government, Marshall used the principle most effectively to expand the powers of the federal government. In *McCulloch v. Maryland* (1819), he upheld the authority of Congress to establish a national

bank, notwithstanding the absence of any specific language empowering it to do so, by devising the doctrine of implied powers. This doctrine enables the federal courts to broadly construe the "necessary and proper" clause of Article I of the Constitution, thereby allowing Congress and the executive branch to address matters beyond those enumerated in the Constitution.

Marshall also established the policy of expansively defining the powers specifically delegated to the federal government. In *Gibbons v. Ogden* (1824), he defined the power to regulate interstate commerce as embracing all forms of intercourse, commercial or otherwise, that do not occur within the boundaries of a single state. The power also extends to activities within one state that affect other states. *McCulloch* and *Gibbons* both demonstrate that by broadening federal power Marshall concomitantly curbed state power. Incompatible local actions were voided by the supremacy clause, which gave federal law precedence over the laws of the states.

Thus, in *McCulloch,* Marshall ruled that the state of Maryland was without power to tax the Baltimore branch of the Bank of the United States. In *Gibbons* he said the force of the commerce clause prohibited state interference with federal regulations and the free flow of goods and services across state lines. Marshall coupled his antistate posture with unequivocal statements of the authority of the federal courts and the supremacy of their decisions on federal questions over those of the states. In *Martin v. Hunter's Lessee* (1816) and *Cohens v. Virginia* (1821), for example, he ruled that the Supreme Court not only had the authority to review and alter state court decisions involving the interpretation of federal law, treaties, or provisions of the Constitution but that the Supreme Court's—or other federal court's—interpretations superseded those of the states.

Marshall's support for vested economic rights derived from John Locke's view that property and individual liberty are closely intertwined. He applied this concept by invoking the contract clause of Article I, which forbids state abridgment of contracts. In *Fletcher v. Peck* (1810), the first decision to void a state law, he extended the clause's scope to include public, as well as private, contracts, even though the Constitution's Framers probably intended it to apply only to private agreements. Thus, in *Fletcher,* Marshall ruled that a huge land grant corruptly enacted by the Georgia legislature could not be repealed subsequently because innocent purchasers would lose their property and the land market would become unstable. In *Dartmouth*

College v. Woodward (1819), New Hampshire's effort to make Dartmouth a state university rather than a private college was declared unconstitutional on the basis that state charters as well as grants were contracts. Apart from enhancing private education, the Court's decision ensured the growth and development of business corporations, which require a state charter to operate.

Marshall's concern with individual freedom did not extend to civil rights and liberties, however. In his last constitutionally based decision, *Barron v. Baltimore* (1833), he adhered to the literal wording of the Constitution and ruled that the Bill of Rights binds only the federal government. The states, accordingly, were free to disregard any or all of its provisions, thereby forcing their citizens to rely on the very limited protections afforded under state law. In the case of racial and ethnic minorities, political and religious dissidents, women, and persons accused of a crime, this shield was flimsy indeed. *Barron* was nullified by the adoption of the Fourteenth Amendment (1868) and the Supreme Court's construction of its due process clause to encompass all major provisions of the Bill of Rights.

See also *Locke, John; United States Constitution.* In Documents section, see *Constitution of the United States (1787).*

Harold J. Spaeth

Karl Marx

BIBLIOGRAPHY

Dunham, Allison, and Philip B. Kurland, eds. *Mr. Justice.* Chicago: University of Chicago Press, 1964; London: Norton, 1991.

Kelly, Alfred H., Winfred A. Harbison, and Herman Belz. *The American Constitution: Its Origins and Development.* 7th ed. New York and London: Norton, 1991.

White, G. Edward. *The American Judicial Tradition: Profiles of Leading American Judges.* New York: Oxford University Press, 1976.

Witt, Elder. *Congressional Quarterly's Guide to the U.S. Supreme Court.* 2d ed. Washington, D.C.: Congressional Quarterly, 1990.

Marx, Karl

German social philosopher, social scientist, economist, and revolutionary activist, the most influential thinker in the history of socialism and the labor movement. Marx (1818–1883) was born in Trier in the German Rhineland, son of a liberal Jewish lawyer. He attended the University of Berlin, where he studied philosophy and was influenced by the thought of G. W. F. Hegel. Realizing that his radical views would prevent him from gaining a university position, Marx first became a newspaper writer and editor in the Rhineland and then emigrated to France in 1843. There he met international socialist exiles and embraced socialism.

Expelled from Paris in 1844, Marx moved to Brussels, together with his comrade-in-arms Friedrich Engels. There he elaborated the doctrine that would become known as Marxism. In 1849 he moved to London, where he spent most of his life working as a private scholar. However, he always endeavored to link his work to the emerging labor movement in continental Europe as well as in England.

Influenced by the Enlightenment philosophy of the eighteenth century, Marx also attempted to merge British classical economics, French utopian socialist thought, and, above all, the German philosophical tradition of Hegel. The core of Marxist doctrine was the assertion that humanity had evolved through various stages defined by modes of production; the mode of production determined social and cultural development. The stages through which all societies passed were primitive tribal communism, feudalism, and then capitalism, which had become dominant after the Industrial Revolution. Ultimately, capitalism would yield to communism.

In Marx's view, although capitalism had immensely increased the productive capacities of the Western world, it had also led to an unprecedented level of impoverishment and exploitation of the working class. Marx believed that workers would be able to free themselves from the capitalist yoke by banding together and developing a socialist labor movement. In the not too distant future, he believed, such a movement would overthrow the system of capitalist exploitation.

Marxist social thought attempted to link Marxist theory and revolutionary activity, socialist thinking and working-class action. Marx and his fellow thinkers saw Marxism as progress toward the universal reign of democracy. Eventually, however, one strain of Marxist thought led to the totalitarian views of Vladimir Ilich Lenin and Joseph Stalin. Marxism had a certain potential for nondemocratic thought and practice, but only in the context of Russian Bolshevism did it develop a totalitarian ideology and regime.

See also *Engels, Friedrich; Marxism.*

Lewis A. Coser

Marxism

A body of thought on economics, politics, and society created by Karl Marx (1818–1883) and Friedrich Engels (1820–1895). Neither Marx nor Engels left a cohesive critique or description of democracy from the Marxist perspective. Their written comments on democracy dealt not with how it could be used to constrain and tame the power of the state, but rather with how a society could use it to realize certain material goals. Marx and Engels never clearly separated the idea of the rule of the people from the prospect of achieving a just and equal society through the abolition of class division. What counted for Marx and Engels was what was to be achieved (social welfare and just distribution of resources), not how that goal was to be achieved and preserved (the political procedure used). At no time did Marx or Engels consider the possi-

bility that political procedures themselves might divert society from promoting the values "guaranteed" from class relations.

The Derivative Nature of Democracy in Marxist Theory

This curious neglect was caused in part by the structure of the Marxist theory of society. In this theory the state and politics in general were given no autonomous role to play; they were part of the "superstructure" that serves and is fully determined by the economic "base." Politics, therefore, is secondary and derivative, and the state is not considered to be an independent agency with its own impact on the shape and character of the society. The existing state, based on capitalist economics, was seen as an instrument in the hands of the exploiters, and it would be naïve to consider the possibility of the people ruling as long as the ownership structure remained unchanged.

The future communist society, on the other hand (which, Marx and Engels believed, was bound to result from the overthrow of the exploiters), would implement the rule of the people by the very fact of doing away with exploitation. Therefore, communist society would have no need for separate political institutions and elaborate, specialized instruments of state coercion. (This view was subsequently described as the Marxist theory of the "withering away of the state.") In any case it seemed redundant to consider democracy as a certain type of government and a certain code of political behavior—indeed, to think of it as an issue in its own right.

Marx addressed the question of the form that the self-government of emancipated producers might take only once, in an enthusiastic description of the political practices spontaneously improvised under the auspices of the short-lived Paris Commune in 1871, when workers rebelled against the government. Even in this case, however, the institutions invented by the *communards* were seen by Marx as temporary political means to promote the revolution. In an 1875 letter to German social democratic leader August Bebel on the party program, Engels demanded that there should be no more talk about the state, since the state as such ceases to exist as soon as true freedom arrives. Having reduced the state to an outgrowth of economic relations (and one emerging only from a certain type of economic relations, soon to be left behind), Marx and Engels saw no reason to dissect the effects of various procedures a state might use.

To be sure, this Marxist neglect of democracy had other causes beyond the structure of Marxist theory. Marx and Engels did not live long enough to witness the introduction of universal voting rights. While they were developing their political theory, the workers (whose exploiters were to be overturned by the communist revolution, which would do away with their misery) remained disenfranchised and for all practical purposes had no part in the body politic. The existing state did indeed look like the exclusive domain of the propertied classes—and in their calling it a "dictatorship of bourgeoisie," Marx and Engels were in tune with many progressive liberal thinkers of the time. Whatever democratic procedures were observed, they certainly did not include the lower classes, and it was hard to see how existing democratic practices could guarantee attention to the grievances of the dispossessed or offer fair representation of their interests. From the point of view of the disenfranchised, there was little to distinguish between "democracy" as it was practiced and the dictatorship of the rich and powerful.

The Expansion of Voting Rights and Marxist Revisionism

Radical change occurred at the end of the nineteenth century when voting rights were extended to include most of the working class. Just as the opponents of universal voting rights feared and warned, this expansion drastically altered the stakes of the political game. The sheer numbers of the newly enfranchised working-class voters meant that democratic mechanisms of government would force the questions of just distribution of wealth and influence onto the political agenda. In practical terms, that meant the creation and development of the welfare state—a state that uses political instruments to intervene in the economically determined distribution of wealth and one that guarantees basic necessities for those members of society incapable of securing them through their own individual efforts.

This change prompted enhanced interest in the daily workings of the state on the part of the political movements based on the Marxist theory and program, especially since unionized labor, the chief supporter of these movements, was unwilling to wait for the improvement of its lot until society and the state were thoroughly overhauled along Marxist lines. The forms of government could no longer be neglected by Marxists and related movements. Active involvement in politics, made possible by democratic procedure, seemed to promise visible and immediate social gains. Attempts to rethink the vision of the state as irredeemably an instrument of the exploiting classes—and as such beyond salvation—were soon undertaken. Initiated among German Marxists by Eduard Bernstein, these attempts at first encountered keen and angry resistance from orthodox Marxists as revisionist heresy, yet they soon became the practice, and eventually the official program, of the organized political movement inspired by Marxism.

Marx himself saw the passage from an exploitative capitalist society to a just socialist society as catastrophic. The revolution of the impoverished proletariat would abolish the system of private ownership, already—in Marx's view—hopelessly entangled in its own internal contradictions and nearing collapse, and would replace the state, the instrument of exploitation, with some association of free producers, the form of which would be determined by the newly emancipated people themselves. But this idea of catastrophic change gave way to an evolutionary perspective, with the old society of competing enterprises gradually becoming a regulated economy.

This was a fateful change. The traditional disdainful neglect of Marxists for the capitalist state as such, and their resulting refusal to evaluate the different ways in which that state's business was conducted, had to give way to an acute theoretical and practical interest in the existing state, in order to speed up and smooth the gradual socialist transformation of society. By the time of World War I (1914–1918), the sometimes vicious struggle in Western Europe between revisionist and orthodox tendencies had ended in favor of the former, and it had become clear that social democrats, the heirs to Marxism, should engage in practical politics as a party. This would enable them to strive to shorten working hours; protect workers against the most blatant and outrageous forms of exploitation; protect and enhance workers' bargaining power, to change the balance between profits and wages in their favor; and make sure the state provided a comprehensive network of insurance for unemployment, disability, illness, and other causes of poverty. In other words, social democrats would press for the creation of the welfare state, fight existing class inequality, and promote justice. Such an understanding of the role of the state forced Marxist-inspired political movements to become ardent and militant supporters of representative democracy, on which they now relied to protect the interests of the laboring majority.

The Failure of Evolutionary Marxism

By and large, there was little difference between the social democrats and other, non-Marxist theorists of the early twentieth century in what they thought the procedural aspects of representative democracy should be. However, Marxist analysts were particularly concerned by the lack of increased support for the socialist transformation of society. Their writings on democracy asked why democratic procedures alone had failed to secure the results predicted by Marxist theory and tended to explain the malfunctioning of democratic mechanisms by the active or passive resistance of capitalist interests. Hence, they emphasized the limits set on democracy by the economic and cultural domination of capitalists. The increasingly evident inability of democracy to produce a socialist transformation prompted orthodox Marxist writers (particularly the German Social Democrats) to seek causes in mainly economic factors—in the friction between formal equality of political rights and the lack of real power caused by class relations institutionalized by a capitalist economy.

But an increasing number of Western Marxists from the 1920s on stressed the role of ideological and cultural factors. Leaders of these theorists included György Lukács in Hungary and Antonio Gramsci in Italy. Lukács coined the concept of false consciousness to explain why workers did not vote so as to produce a socialist transformation of society: individual workers were too involved in their daily struggle for survival in a society biased against the workers' true long-term interests. Influenced by Gaetano Mosca, among others, Gramsci explained the power of the present class society over the minds of the oppressed by the cultural hegemony of the exploiting classes. It was the cultural folklore that prevented workers from even imagining an alternative to present reality.

Lukács's and Gramsci's insights were elaborated on by Louis Althusser, who was to have enormous influence on the thinking of Western Marxists in the 1960s and 1970s. Althusser argued that most of the institutions of capitalist society were designed to prevent workers from moving beyond the experience of deprivation to the desire for socialist change, brought about through democratic choice.

Still other Western Marxists remained suspicious of democratic procedures, as long as they were associated with the exploitative capitalist economy. According to this view, it would be foolish and unforgivable to invest the hopes of the impoverished and the exploited in parliamentary democracy, which would never go further toward improving the conditions of the oppressed than was absolutely necessary to stave off the immediate danger of rebellion. These theorists believed that the proletariat should seek freedom from capitalist domination through other means. Workers' involvement in collective, extraparliamentary, political actions would do the most to show the oppressed the nature of their oppression, to open the eyes of the masses to the true shape of social divisions and conflicts.

At the beginning of the twentieth century this view was upheld most conspicuously by the leaders of French syndicalism, a movement that preached direct action in the forms of a general strike or terrorism. Both general strikes and terrorism were seen as powerful means of simultaneously implementing socialist goals and educating the masses in socialist ideas. The syndicalists dismissed parliamentary democracy as a conspiracy to keep the capitalists in power.

The idea of the general strike figured prominently in Polish-German theorist Rosa Luxemburg's views of the socialist revolution, which she advanced in opposition to Vladimir Ilich Lenin's idea of revolution as the work of a small group of professional revolutionaries. However, Luxemburg's emphasis on the general strike did not stem from a concern with the limited revolutionary potential of parliamentary democracy. Rather, it stemmed from her premonition—later to be proved correct—that without the active involvement of the working class as a whole in the revolution allegedly accomplished in its name and for its sake, the resulting postrevolutionary regime could be only another form of dictatorship—over the proletariat, rather than of the proletariat.

Eventually, Western Marxists came to share the view that democratic procedures and freedoms were necessary to allow for unhampered socialist propaganda and the possibility of gaining popular support for the socialist transformation. But they believed that these procedures and freedoms alone were not sufficient, and certainly not a guarantee that the socialist society would ever be achieved. Democracy, in this view, was either a mixed blessing (the thought vividly expressed in Herbert Marcuse's memorable phrase of "repressive tolerance"), blocking the radical critique of existing society and the consideration of alternatives while ostensibly allowing and promoting them; or at best it was merely a formal condition of class struggle, with the results to be decided by factors located outside the political process. Whichever was the case, procedural democracy was seen as an instrument rather than the purpose of political struggle, and the theorists always distinguished between procedural and substantive democracy (the latter being seen as possible only after the abolition of capitalism).

The evolution of Marxist views on the role and significance of political democracy should be set against the background of Marxists' continued conviction that politics has no autonomy and is bound to play second fiddle to the maintenance or transformation of economic relations. But as electoral rights expanded in the West, Marxist-inspired movements increasingly participated in the daily life of democracy. This was not the case in Eastern Europe, which did not import democratic forms of government—unlike other modern inventions—from the West, and where democratic traditions were nonexistent or fragile.

Marxism in Russia

Czarist Russia, in particular, remained a police state into the twentieth century, with only rudimentary forms of political democracy and strictly limited electoral rights, shaped with a view toward protecting the advantages of the propertied classes. Russian political institutions came nowhere near the goal of majority rule. Moreover, the indispensable preconditions of democratic politics—such as habeas corpus and human rights in general—were systematically violated, and there was no well-developed and widely accepted liberal theory to promote them. In this context the incipient Marxist movements in Russia led a precarious existence, even when the movements were legally constituted. No wonder that Russian disciples of Marx believed that the possibility of social or economic change through democratic procedures was infinitely remote and not worthy of serious—or at any rate immediate—consideration.

Russian Marxists were divided on the best way to achieve change, however. The Mensheviks proposed to wait until capitalism developed and generated both a majority in favor of socialism and the democratic instruments necessary for the realization of that majority will. On the other hand, the Bolsheviks, of whom Lenin was by far the most energetic and important figure, concluded that world capitalism had already become irreversibly imperialist and that therefore it was too late for a democratic bourgeois state to develop. Thus the democratic road to

socialism, however plausible it might be in the West, was not possible in economically backward and politically underdeveloped Russia. There was no point in waiting for the state to become democratic, since politics simply reflected economic forces and interests, and a monopolistic capitalist economy, as in Russia, would neither create nor tolerate a democratic government. The only way to implement socialist goals was to have an elite group of professional revolutionaries use the various grievances of the population to mobilize the people and to show them that the socialist transformation of society was in their long-term interests.

Western options, so Lenin insisted, were not open to Russian socialists or to Marxists in other countries that were economically underdeveloped when they entered the monopolistic-imperialist stage of capitalism. In Russia the exploiting classes had to be dislodged from power by force, so that a new political elite, determined to bring about a Marxist future and capable of repelling the adversaries who sought to retain capitalism, could use the state to promote full economic development. Only once, in 1917, did Lenin try to explain how that government, destined to overthrow and replace czarist rule and to promote socialism, would be organized and conducted.

Lenin addressed this question in his unfinished book *The State and Revolution,* an extended, impassioned commentary on Marx's resounding endorsement of the 1871 experiments of the *communards* of Paris. In the book, Lenin described direct democracy, implemented through arming the people (that is, through the cancellation of the state monopoly of coercion) and characterized by rota (succession of officeholders), recall of the members of parliament by the voters, and remuneration of the members relative to the manual worker's wage. To Lenin, the "general will" (that is, the will one can deduce from an analysis of the proletariat's historical interests and mission) would be identical to the spontaneously expressed will of the masses, once they were free to express their opinions and to act on them.

In fact, Lenin's lofty goal of direct rule could not and did not stand up to the realities of postrevolutionary Russia. The almost total destruction of economic life brought about by the prolonged civil war between communist and anticommunist forces from 1918 to 1921 and the dissipation of Russia's small modern working class meant that the ruling Communist Party had to create virtually from scratch the class whose interests, purportedly, it took power to promote. The theoretically conceived "general will" proved to be jarringly at odds with the actual desires of virtually all classes of the population, and it was evident that true majority rule would not push postrevolutionary Russia toward socialism.

In addition, reconstructing ruined industries required an expert administration and stern labor discipline. By 1920 Leon Trotsky, then Lenin's first lieutenant and spokesman, openly declared the need to "militarize" labor, to reeducate the workers in order to increase productivity. The state was to hold power, and expert opinion would be preferred to the opinion of the working class. Lenin also believed that democracy must always be subordinated to revolutionary interest.

With ruthless determination, Joseph Stalin implemented Lenin's and Trotsky's ideas. The Communist Party had become virtually identical to the state and acted as the sole employer and the distributor of all scarce goods. Accordingly, politics turned into the administration of economic production. This role allegedly demanded, but at any rate justified, the suppression of interests characterized by the government as "sectional" and "short-term." No opinion different from that of the rulers and planners could be expressed freely.

The extinction of democratic rights and procedures in the Soviet Union necessarily led to a police state of unprecedented ruthlessness and to a degree of oppression rarely matched in history. Alongside the Nazi regime in Germany, the Stalinist state is the most conspicuous embodiment of the antidemocratic, totalitarian tendency of modern times. Nonetheless, Soviet Marxists depicted their society as the fullest embodiment of the democratic idea. Following Marx, they saw the proper role of the socialist state as doing what its essential being dictated, regardless of what the proletariat thought should be done.

Neither Marx nor Lenin ever acknowledged that variety of opinion or diversity of political standpoint within the working class was necessary or desirable. Both believed that if freed from oppression and faced with its historical mission, the working class could only speak with one voice. What mattered, therefore, was not so much that all opinions be expressed and defended but that the government act on the true voice of the working class, even if that voice was not expressed by the class itself. The interests of the working class could be determined through knowledge of the relentless laws of history, described in Marxist theory. Soviet Marxists identified democracy with action on that knowledge, regardless of the suppression of

individual and group rights and freedoms that accompanied it.

The important point is that suppression of human rights in the Soviet Union, the nation that best exemplified a Marxist state, did not generate much democratic freedom nor equality or justice.

See also *Bernstein, Eduard; Capitalism; Class; Communism; Engels, Friedrich; Gramsci, Antonio; Industrial democracy; Leninism; Luxemburg, Rosa; Marx, Karl; Mosca, Gaetano; Socialism; Theory, Twentieth-century European; Union of Soviet Socialist Republics; Welfare, Promotion of.*

Zygmunt Bauman

BIBLIOGRAPHY

Arendt, Hannah. *On Revolution.* New York: Viking, 1963.

Beilharz, Peter. *Labour's Utopias: Bolshevism, Fabianism, Social Democracy.* London: Routledge, 1992.

Harding, Neil. "The Marxist-Leninist Detour." In *Democracy, the Unfinished Journey,* edited by John Dunn. New York and Oxford: Oxford University Press, 1992.

Lenin, V. I. *Collected Works.* Moscow: Foreign Languages Publishing House, 1960–1970; London: Lawrence and Wishart, 1970.

Marx, Karl, and Friedrich Engels. *Collected Works.* New York: International Publishers, 1975.

Offe, Claus. *Der Tunnel am Ende des Lichts: Erkundungen der politische Transformation im neuen Osten.* Frankfurt: Campus Verlag, 1994.

Polan, A. J. *Lenin and the End of Politics.* Berkeley: University of California Press, 1984.

Trotsky, Leon. *Terrorism and Communism.* Ann Arbor: University of Michigan Press, 1961.

Weber, Max. "Socialism." In *Political Writings.* Edited by Peter Lassman and Ronald Speirs. Cambridge: Cambridge University Press, 1994.

Masaryk, Tomáš Garrigue

Czech statesman and intellectual who was instrumental in establishing the Czechoslovak Republic in 1918 and who served as its first president. Masaryk (1850–1937) was born in Hodonin to a Slovak father and Czech mother. Although his family circumstances were modest, he completed doctoral studies in philosophy at the University of Vienna. He continued his studies at Leipzig, where he met his wife, Charlotte Garrigue, an American. In 1882 he was appointed a professor of philosophy at the Czech university in Prague.

Tomáš Garrigue Masaryk

Modern Civilization (1881). Another book, *The Spirit of Russia: Studies in History, Literature and Philosophy* (1913), was a critical examination of religious, intellectual, and social problems in Russia. In this work, Masaryk emphasized the negative effect on Russian culture of the Orthodox Church and other conservative forces.

Masaryk quickly became engaged in the main public debates of the day. Writing in popular journals, including a political review he edited, he tackled controversial subjects, earning many enemies along the way. Among other things, he debunked forged Czech manuscripts that allegedly had demonstrated the superiority of Czech culture in medieval times, and he defended Jews accused of ritual murder. He also addressed issues related to Panslavism (a nineteenth-century movement for the unity of Slavic peoples) and promoted the ideals of the Protestant Czech Brethren.

Masaryk's principles were reflected in his politics. He attempted to link Czech culture and values to Western democratic ideals. He advocated a liberal, progressive, and pragmatic approach to politics. Masaryk served in the Austrian parliament from 1891 to 1893 as a member of the Young Czech Party and from 1907 to 1914 as a member of his own small Realist (Progressive) Party.

Originally a supporter of reform within the Austro-Hungarian Empire, Masaryk became an advocate of independence for the Czech Lands during the course of World War I. After leaving Austria in December 1914, he mounted a successful campaign abroad to persuade the great powers to create a Czechoslovak state.

Masaryk was elected the first president of the Czechoslovak Republic, which came into being October 28, 1918. For seventeen years he presided over the effort to create a progressive, democratic political system in Czechoslovakia. His devotion to the ideals of democracy and his ability to persuade the leaders of diverse political parties to cooperate were among the factors that contributed to the success of democracy in Czechoslovakia between the two world wars. Ill health forced Masaryk to resign in 1935. Czechoslovakia's first great statesman died at Lany, near Prague, on September 1, 1937.

See also *Czechoslovakia.*

Sharon L. Wolchik

BIBLIOGRAPHY

Masaryk, Tomáš G., and Karel Čapek. *Masaryk on Thought and Life (Conversations with Karel Čapek).* New York: Arno Press, 1971.

Masaryk's work as a scholar foreshadowed the causes he would champion as a political leader. Influenced by the philosophy of Plato, Masaryk also studied the writings of John Locke and David Hume. His work was affected as well by his conversion from Catholicism to Protestantism. His first major work was *Suicide as a Mass Phenomenon of*

Szporluk, Roman. *The Political Thought of Thomas G. Masaryk.* Boulder, Colo.: East European Monographs; New York: Columbia University Press, 1981.

Mass society

The form of society that results from the modern tendency to treat people as indistinguishable units or atoms, as undifferentiated parts of a mass. In a mass society, institutions deal with people in the aggregate. Transactions are uniform and impersonal. Large-scale activities replace communal relations. Rural communities, with their traditions, are absorbed into the cosmopolitan and standardized practices of the city. As social distinctions are leveled, bureaucratic regulations displace the rule of personal responsibility. This leveling produces and is supported by an egalitarian concept of justice.

The most obvious motivations for the emergence of mass society are economic and technological. First, large-scale organizations are more efficient than small ones. Second, a populace with uniform desires and opinions is predictable and manageable. Mass society is largely a consequence of the quest for prosperity that defines much of the modern world.

The liberation of the quest for prosperity was the work of the seventeenth- and eighteenth-century liberal political philosophers, including Thomas Hobbes, John Locke, and Adam Smith. These early modern thinkers thought that liberation must be justified by its improvement of the lot of the great mass of human beings. More generally, mass society is the consequence of the political choice of democracy or equality as the first principle of human effort. A mass society takes its bearings from the most powerful desires shared by most human beings.

It is unfair, however, to say that mass society was the intention of the liberal political philosophers. Their most effective disciples, the American Founders, thought the commercial society created by the Constitution of 1787 would be characterized primarily by diversity. They aimed to create a large society that would not be a mass society by creating a large democracy that would not be a mass democracy. They thought the key to this achievement was the mechanism of representation. Representation made possible a large, indirect democracy, which they called a republic. In a republic, a large number of citizens elect a small number of representatives, who make the law. A large republic might be called an elite, or aristocratic, democracy. The law is made by representatives distant enough from the people to be counted on to refine and enlarge public opinion by imposing their wisdom or at least their cleverness and virtue.

Mass democracy is a large, direct democracy that would seem to presuppose the conditions of mass society. The Founders saw that mass democracy could readily become rule by manipulative demagogues. The experience of the twentieth century with popular dictatorship has confirmed their perception. The Founders hoped that demagogic rule would be almost impossible in a large, diverse society. But large, direct democracy has become progressively more possible than ever before with the development of technology and the media of mass communications.

Alexis de Tocqueville (1805–1859), among others, saw that the idea of the desirability of both mass society and mass democracy was first found in the imagination of the extreme rationalists who provided the intellectual impetus for the French Revolution. Those thinkers opposed all human disorder or irrationality and sought to form human beings into a universal, homogeneous whole or mass. Because they came to prefer egalitarian consistency to human liberty, their ideal became mass society.

Since the French Revolution the tendency toward mass society has been subjected to two kinds of criticism. The American sociologist William Kornhauser has called these criticisms aristocratic and democratic. Aristocratic criticism defends the elite values of responsible political rule and personal liberty against the leveling impersonality that comes with the rise of mass society. Democratic criticism observes that mass society makes genuine or participatory democracy impossible.

Both kinds of criticism are found in the work of Tocqueville, who remains the most penetrating analyst of the democratic excesses of mass society. In Tocqueville's eyes, mass society is in one sense the perfection of democracy and in another sense a form of despotism. Mass society is, in its way, perfectly egalitarian. Human beings are reduced to an apathetic herd of docile animals that need not be ruled but only administered. Everyone appears to defer passively to a public opinion that seems beyond any individual's control or comprehension. From the perspective of the aristocrat's proud love of liberty for its own sake, this deference is a surrender of personal responsibility.

The truth about mass society is that egalitarian idealism, taken to an extreme, is misanthropic. Human beings will be perfectly equal only when they no longer have any distinctively human quality, when they have become nothing but indistinguishable atoms. Tocqueville believed that mass society was a manifestation of extreme individualism, the experience of oneself as isolated, contingent, and weightless, without particular qualities and attachments.

The diversity that the American Founders hoped would characterize the large republic is easily undermined by liberalism's individualistic premises. The progress of democracy tends to destroy the institutions and habits that enlarge the human heart in the direction of active citizenship. Tocqueville defended local government, religion, and the family, which he understood as America's fortunate aristocratic inheritances, in the name of a democracy full of free and responsible citizens.

Tocqueville's view that mass society is "soft," or apathetic, despotism might be taken as a criticism that anticipates certain tendencies in the contemporary welfare state. Hannah Arendt (1906–1975) added that such massification was also the precondition for, and the goal of, the "hard," or terror-filled, totalitarianism of the twentieth century. Totalitarian ideologies appeal to lonely, anxious, and despondent masses of atomized individuals by promising mass organizations in which individuals might lose their miserable experience of worthless individuality. The totalitarian view is that the cure for the miserable disorder of mass society is its perfection.

Human organization undeniably has moved in the direction of mass society, but that society is still far from reaching its perfection. Human beings also have shown, as Tocqueville hoped, the ability to resist massification on behalf of liberty and genuine democracy. Such resistance is especially clear in the thought of Aleksandr Solzhenitsyn, the Russian author and dissident, and Václav Havel, the Czech playwright, philosopher, and first president of the new Czech Republic in 1993. Their ideas profoundly animated and illuminated the 1989 revolution against totalitarianism.

See also *Egalitarianism; Media, Mass; Tocqueville, Alexis de.*

Peter A. Lawler

BIBLIOGRAPHY

Arendt, Hannah. *The Origins of Totalitarianism.* New York: Harcourt Brace Jovanovich, 1951.

Boesche, Roger. "Tocqueville and Arendt on the Novelty of Modern Tyranny." In *Tocqueville's Defense of Human Liberty,* edited by Peter A. Lawler and Joseph Alulis. New York: Garland Publishing, 1993.

Havel, Václav. "Address to the U.S. Congress." *Congressional Record—House.* Washington, D.C. February 21, 1990, H392-95.

Kornhauser, William. *The Politics of Mass Society.* Glencoe, Ill.: Free Press, 1959.

Mansfield, Harvey C., Jr. *America's Constitutional Soul.* Baltimore: Johns Hopkins University Press, 1991.

Tocqueville, Alexis de. *Democracy in America.* Translated by George Lawrence. New York: Harper, 1966.

———. *The Old Regime and the Revolution.* Translated by Stuart Gilbert. Garden City, N.Y.: Doubleday, 1955.

Mauritius

See *Africa, Subsaharan*

May Fourth Movement

An intellectual and nationalist movement that swept China in the wake of World War I. The May Fourth Movement takes its name from the demonstration in Beijing on May 4, 1919, that protested the outcome of the peace conference held at Versailles to bring an end to World War I. More broadly and significantly, however, it refers to a period of intellectual revolution, frequently described as the Chinese Renaissance, that reached maturity about 1917 and lasted until about 1921.

Intellectual and Political Roots

The May Fourth Movement in this broader sense marked a culmination of intellectual ferment and political frustration in China. A new intellectual elite was maturing in the postimperial order, most of them too young to have spent years preparing for the old examination system and many having had a chance to study abroad. The emergence of a more iconoclastic and cosmopolitan intellectual climate was marked by the founding of *Youth Magazine* (later renamed *New Youth*) in 1915. In his famous "Call to Youth," the magazine's founder, Chen Duxiu (who also helped found the Chinese Communist Party a few years later) exhorted the new generation to struggle against "old and rotten elements" in China's tradition and to create a new culture.

In January 1917, *New Youth* started a literary revolution by publishing an appeal to discard classical writing in favor of the vernacular. This literary revolution was inherently democratizing in that it was directed against the elitism of classical education and composition and thus invited wider participation in public debate. Hu Shi, author of this pathbreaking essay, later studied with John Dewey at Columbia University in New York and became China's leading exponent of pragmatism and liberalism.

The May Fourth Movement in general and the *New Youth* journal in particular were characterized by cosmopolitanism and liberalism, as Chinese writers drew eclectically on intellectual trends from throughout the world. In the pages of *New Youth,* Chen Duxiu presented "Mr. Science" and "Mr. Democracy" as patron saints of the new movement. Scientific skepticism would destroy the irrational beliefs held to be at the core of Chinese tradition, while the democratic spirit would shatter the authoritarianism of both the Chinese family and the Chinese political system. In 1917 Cai Yuanpei, the remarkable chancellor of Beijing University, brought the leading lights of this new culture movement—Hu Shi, Chen Duxiu, and Li Dazhao—to the university, thus marking a new stage in the intellectual revolution.

The May Fourth Movement captured the public's imagination because its iconoclasm and patriotism developed against a backdrop of warlord politics and imperialism. In 1915, Yuan Shikai, the first president of the Chinese Republic, revealed a scheme to make himself emperor and establish Confucianism as a state religion. While it evoked widespread opposition, Yuan's scheme also attracted the support of a number of prestigious intellectuals, including Kang Youwei, champion of an abortive reform movement in 1898, who never wavered in his goal of a constitutional monarchy and who came to advocate establishing Confucianism as a state religion.

These efforts to restore the monarchy and Confucianism came together again two years later, following Yuan's death, as the last emperor of the Qing dynasty, Pu Yi, was put back on the throne with the help of a loyal warlord—an effort that collapsed in ignominy after only seventeen days. The efforts of such egotistical and selfish leaders undermined Confucianism by linking it to a discredited monarchy and marking it as an atavistic remnant of a bygone era.

Nationalism and the May Fourth Demonstrations

At the same time that such conservative political movements were abusing and discrediting Confucianism, Japanese demands fueled a new tide of nationalistic fervor in China. In January 1915 Japan's minister to China presented Yuan Shikai with a list of twenty-one demands, which, if fully accepted, would have reduced China to a Japanese dependency. In an unusual appeal to public opinion, the Chinese government leaked the contents of the demands, provoking widespread protests in China's urban areas and unintentionally preparing the public for the much broader demonstrations to come in 1919.

The two elements behind the May Fourth Movement—intellectual revolution and nationalistic passion—came together in May 1919, when word arrived that the world leaders gathered in Versailles to forge a peace settlement had agreed to turn German concessions in China's Shandong province over to Japan. Japan's claim was based on a secret agreement in which the Chinese government had declared that it "gladly agreed" to transfer the areas to Japanese control. Learning both of the traitorous behavior of their own government and of the Western leaders' betrayal of the ideals of civilization and democracy that they had declared World War I to be about, more than 3,000 students from thirteen colleges and universities gathered in Tiananmen Square on May 4, 1919. Led by students from Beijing University, the demonstration culminated in the burning of the house of China's pro-Japanese minister of communications and the beating of the Chinese minister to Japan, who had signed the humiliating agreement with Japan.

The ensuing cycle of repression and agitation provoked China's first genuinely nationwide mass movement, as merchants and workers supported the demands of the students by launching their own strikes. The movement culminated in success when the government dismissed three pro-Japanese ministers and when, on June 28, the Chinese delegation to Versailles, without approval from Beijing, refused to sign the peace treaty.

Embedded in the May Fourth demonstration and the May Fourth Movement in general were elements of both enlightenment and national salvation. On the one hand, these elements gave the movement its dynamism and marked its significance in modern Chinese history. On the other hand, they were in such tension with each other that they could not easily coexist. As a movement of cultural enlightenment, the May Fourth Movement marked an effort to reflect critically on the Chinese past, assimilate foreign ideas, and build a new culture based on science, democracy, and rationality. It was this spirit of cultural reconstruction that had made Hu Shi, Chen Duxiu, and other collaborators on the *New Youth* journal abjure politics for twenty years.

Enlightenment vs. Political Realities

In the political currents of the day, however, it became difficult, and for many impossible, to hold firmly to the ideal of enlightenment. The patriotic passions unleashed by the May Fourth Movement reenergized the Chinese Nationalist Party (the Kuomintang, or Guomindang), which was reorganized with assistance from the Bolshevik-supported Comintern (Communist International) in 1923. These passions also led to the founding of the Chinese Communist Party in 1921. The cofounders of the Communist Party were Li Dazhao and Chen Duxiu, two leading May Fourth intellectuals. This turn away from the quest for cultural re-creation to political action is generally taken as marking the end of the May Fourth Movement. Nationalism and the goal of saving the nation had overwhelmed the mission of enlightenment.

Despite being overshadowed by the revolutionary politics of twentieth-century China, the goal of cultural enlightenment and the associated ideas of human rights and democracy have never disappeared. Although the Chinese Communist Party has always sought to identify the May Fourth Movement as a patriotic movement and itself as the embodiment of the May Fourth spirit, survivors of the movement have reminded others that the meaning of May Fourth was not limited to patriotism.

On the seventieth anniversary of the May Fourth demonstrations, in 1989, Chinese students several generations removed from the original event turned to it again for meaning and inspiration. Their hopes to carry out cultural regeneration in the spirit of May Fourth and to implement democracy—however different the Chinese concept of democracy may be from the Western concept—suggest that the goal of enlightenment and the democratic ideals of the May Fourth Movement will survive the nationalistic passions and revolutionary turmoil of the twentieth century and continue to inspire new generations.

See also *China; Confucianism; Dewey, John.*

Joseph Fewsmith

BIBLIOGRAPHY

Chow Tse-tsung. *The May Fourth Movement.* Cambridge: Harvard University Press, 1960.

Feigon, Lee. *Chen Duxiu: Founder of the Chinese Communist Party.* Princeton: Princeton University Press, 1983.

Goldman, Merle, ed. *Modern Chinese Literature in the May Fourth Era.* Cambridge, Mass., and London: Harvard University Press, 1977.

Grieder, Jerome B. *Hu Shi and the Chinese Renaissance.* Cambridge: Harvard University Press, 1970.

Meisner, Maurice. *Li Ta-chao and the Origins of Chinese Marxism.* Cambridge: Harvard University Press, 1967.

Schwarcz, Vera. *The Chinese Enlightenment: Intellectuals and the Legacy of the May Fourth Movement of 1919.* Berkeley: University of California Press, 1986.

Schwartz, Benjamin, ed. *Reflections on the May Fourth Movement: A Symposium.* Cambridge: Harvard University Press, 1973.

Measures of democracy

Attempts to gauge the political democracy of nations. It is nearly impossible to determine the first attempt at measuring democracy, though efforts date back at least to ancient Greece. Aristotle in the fourth century B.C. distinguished five varieties of democracy, which he ranked in a descending scale. Debate has always surrounded the measurement of democracy. Part of the disagreement consists of disputes over definitions. Thus a first step in examining how democracy is measured is to clarify the type of democracy in question.

This article examines some measures of political democracy—that is, the extent to which democratic rule and political liberties exist in a country. *Democratic rule* refers to the accountability of the governing elites and the openness of participation in the political system. *Political liberties* concern the freedom of expression and the freedom of association. The definition precludes some traits. For instance, the performance of democracies is separated from the meaning of democracy. Similarly, economic or social inequality have links to, but are distinct concepts from, political democracy. A political democracy can give rise to citizen satisfaction or discontent, apathy or involvement, but these are not defining components of the definition.

Any attempt to measure political democracy involves several major issues. Among them are categorical versus continuous measurement, objective versus subjective indicators, individual judge versus panel of judges, and single-time versus multiple-time measures.

Categorical vs. Continuous Measurement

In the earliest twentieth-century efforts at measuring political democracy, a country was either democratic or not. James Bryce's survey of democracy in the 1920s, for instance, listed only Argentina, Belgium, Chile, Denmark, France, Greece, Holland, Italy, Norway, Portugal, Sweden, the United States, the United Kingdom (and its self-governing dominions), and Uruguay as democracies. In 1959 Seymour Martin Lipset used one dichotomous classification of democracy for European and English-speaking countries and another for Latin American countries. Phillips Cutright, an early critic of this approach, proposed a continuous measure that would better reflect the gradations in democracy.

The issue of dichotomous versus continuous measures continues in contemporary research, though the difference between views may be less than it first appears. Analysts who use dichotomous measures often acknowledge that some cases fall between categories. For instance, where should Colombia, Malaysia, Mexico, Russia, Thailand, and Zimbabwe be placed (as of the early 1990s)? The acknowledged difficulty of placing countries into one of two categories supports the idea that political democracy is present in varying degrees. The treatment of democracy as a dichotomy seems to be based largely on the convenience and simplicity of such a measure. In addition, there is the belief that countries tend to cluster around the high end or low end of a continuum of democracy. Thus treating democracy as a dichotomy is a practical device for analysis.

Analysts who argue for continuous indicators suggest that measurement should correspond to the nature of the construct; a continuous construct should be measured on a continuous scale. The advocates of continuous measurement argue that categorical measures incorrectly treat countries within a category as homogeneous with respect to democracy. Broad categories also may lead analysts to miss real changes and trends in democracy within a country if the changes are not sufficient to shift the nation into a different category. Over a region, dichotomous measures of democracy might give the impression that the regional level of democracy is relatively homogeneous when in fact it varies widely. Africa and Asia in the early 1990s are cases in point. Using dichotomous measures would hide the diverse levels of democracy present in these regions. In addition, continuous measures often are more suitable for quantitative analysis because most quantitative techniques assume that continuous concepts are measured on continuous scales.

Thus the controversy seems to be less about whether democracy is present or absent than about whether it makes any practical difference to measure it as a dichotomy or as a continuous variable.

Objective vs. Subjective Indicators

To measure democracy, researchers have used either objective or subjective measures. In the twentieth century the earliest efforts used subjective indicators. For example, in the 1920s James Bryce, author of the two-volume work *Modern Democracies,* was the sole judge of which countries were classified as democracies. In the 1940s Russell H. Fitzgibbon organized a panel of judges to assess more than a dozen indicators of democracy for Latin American countries. From the late 1950s onward these pioneering studies stimulated the generation of expert ratings by other analysts. The measures derived from these studies were all formed from the judgment of one or more experts, so they are all considered to be subjective indicators.

In 1958 Daniel Lerner produced one of the earliest objective measures of democracy, using voter turnout statistics as an indicator. A few years later Phillips Cutright used party composition of the legislative body as an alternative. In his system, countries dominated by a single party were scored lower than countries with a greater mix of parties. Analysts have continued to rely on objective measures of political democracy. For instance, Tatu Vanhanen has measured democracy as a function of percentage of the population that votes and the percentage of the legislative seats held by the largest party in a nation's legislature.

Other indices of political democracy include both objective and subjective indicators. In 1973 Robert Jackman included an objective measure (voting turnout statistics) along with three other, largely subjective indicators. Kenneth Bollen's Political Democracy Index also combines objective indicators, such as whether the chief executive is elected, and subjective indicators, such as how free the press is and the effectiveness of the legislative body. A later version of the Political Democracy Index contains three subjective indicators (freedom of group opposition, political rights, and legislative effectiveness) and one objective indicator (legislature elected or not).

The objective indicators seem more likely than the subjective ones to be replicable across investigators. In addition, some allow finer gradations than do subjective indicators and therefore are more likely to allow continuous measurement. But objective measures have disadvantages as well. For example, the agencies reporting voter turnout may falsify statistics or may not record them accurately. And given the value placed on high turnout as a sign of government legitimacy, governments may be tempted to overreport voting. Countries that have political systems dominated by a single party or dictator are more likely to engage in such practices. In most countries, the national legislature is a public institution, so it is difficult for a state to hide the percentages of seats held by various political parties.

A key problem of the validity of many objective indicators is that they fall short of measuring political democracy as defined at the beginning of this article. Voter turnout, for instance, may reflect voter apathy or voter satisfaction, the existence of a law requiring citizens to vote, or even the weather on election day. An objective measure of whether the chief executive of a country comes to office by election only partly reveals the extent of the executive's democratic accountability. If the indicator is the party composition of the legislative body of a country, it is difficult to know what proportion of majority or minority parties best reflects the degree of democracy. A problem with indicators such as voter turnout, whether the chief executive is elected, and party composition is that the indicators do not always reflect the openness or fairness of the elections to which they correspond. For instance, the elections might be ridden with fraud, restrictions might inhibit candidates' ability to campaign, and limitations might be imposed on candidates for office. These factors all diminish the political democracy of a country, but they would not necessarily be revealed in statistics based on objective indicators.

The subjective indicators also have both advantages and disadvantages. On the positive side, subjective measures can gauge some of the key traits of political democracy that otherwise would escape detection. Freedom of expression, freedom of association, and fairness of national elections are important traits for which subjective ratings are available, while objective measures are lacking. In addition, judges are capable of incorporating many factors within a country when making their assessments. For instance, repressive practices often are not publicly recorded, though they may be widely known. These could be missed by objective indicators, yet they can be taken into account by expert judgments.

The main disadvantage of subjective measures is that they may reflect the judge's idiosyncrasies, which would lead to random or systematic errors in measurement. If these errors are large enough, they can render the subjective measures useless. On the other hand, provided the measurement errors are small, researchers are less likely to be misled in analyses that incorporate some subjective indicators.

Empirical evidence on the relative merits of subjective and objective indicators is limited. Voter turnout appears to have a weak (sometimes inverse) correlation with other subjective indicators of political democracy. Vanhanen found that his composite of objective measures was highly correlated with the subjective indicators developed by Raymond D. Gastil. Analyzing a mixture of subjective and objective indicators, Bollen found that subjective variables outperform the objective measure of whether the chief executive is elected.

Another strategy is to combine objective and subjective indicators. For example, the objective indicator of elected legislative body in the Political Democracy Index was multiplied by the subjective indicator of the effectiveness of the legislature. This helped give less weight to "puppet" elected legislatures that have essentially no power. Other such combinations of objective and subjective indicators are possible.

Individual Judge vs. Panel of Judges

An important issue concerning subjective indicators is whether an individual or a panel of experts should create the measure. Two of the earliest efforts at measuring democracy exemplify the problem. Bryce was the only judge developing his ratings, while Fitzgibbon's subjective democracy ratings came from a panel of experts on Latin America. The ratings now published by Freedom House, a nonprofit organization based in New York, offer another example of ratings that derive from a panel of judges. Single-judge ratings, however, also are still common.

A panel of judges has several positive features. One is that the pool of expertise is greater than when relying on a single judge. It is extremely difficult for an individual to be sufficiently familiar with all the countries that are to be rated; the task is more feasible if a group of judges are employed. Second, individual idiosyncrasies are less obtrusive when a study employs the weighted average of a pool of judges.

A single judge, however, is likely to be more consistent in the application of rating criteria. Individual members of a panel may have different standards for making their ratings. This raises the issue of how to weight the opinions of the different judges. This problem does not arise for a single judge.

Not much empirical evidence is available concerning the relative performance of panels versus individual judges. Fitzgibbon found considerable variance in the ratings of Latin American countries by his panel of experts. In the 1960s Raymond B. Nixon's panel of experts on freedom of the press also showed some divergence of ratings. Nonetheless, the Fitzgibbon measure correlates closely with the Political Democracy Index already mentioned, and Nixon's free press rating shows very high reliability.

Instead of a panel of judges, some analysts use multiple indicators from different sources to form a single measure of democracy. Thus freedom of the media might be rated by one judge, while the effectiveness of an elected legislative body is assessed by another. Each measure comes from a single source, either an individual or a panel of judges. Both measures then are incorporated into a democracy index. Collectively, this multiple indicator–multiple source measurement approach leads to a panel of judges even if each rating comes from a single judge.

Other Validity Issues

An indicator consists of three parts: validity, systematic error, and random error. Validity is the component of an indicator that truly measures the construct. Systematic errors are nonrandom and consistent errors that do not match the construct. Random error includes nonsystematic and unstable departures from the true variable. Few studies have estimated the relative contribution of these components, but those few suggest that some indicators of political democracy have large errors, whether systematic or random. For instance, the indicators in the Political Democracy Index generally have high validity. Considered individually, however, they show some evidence of systematic measurement error because of data source. In this case it was possible to combine the indicators into an index that minimized the systematic error and maximized validity.

Nearly all definitions of political democracy, including the one given at the beginning of this article, imply that democracy involves the largest possible proportion of the adult population of a country. But scholars often ignore the inclusiveness of the definition when constructing a measure. This omission may introduce systematic error into their measurements. For example, universal male suffrage is often used as a criterion for classifying coun-

tries as democratic, even though the definition of democracy implies that both males and females are included. Similarly, obstacles to voting or political participation of ethnic minorities often do not affect the ranking of countries.

Analysts who have collected information on suffrage have found that, except for a few countries, this indicator does not discriminate well between countries; most countries formally have universal suffrage. The problem is even more serious for studies that examine democracy in past years or those that focus on the few post–World War II countries that have had considerable periods with a restrictive franchise (such as Kuwait, South Africa, and Switzerland).

Another source of systematic error is found in indices that incorporate aspects of the political system that are related to, but conceptually distinct from, democracy. One common practice is to develop measures of political democracy that incorporate political stability. Lipset, for instance, looked for stable democracies in his classification of countries. In forming his measure, Cutright examined the party composition of legislative bodies and the nature of the executive-selection process over a twenty-one-year period.

Systematic error can also arise from confounding democracy with some of its possible causes and consequences. For example, Fitzgibbon included standard of living, national cohesion, and civil supremacy over the military among his measures of democracy. When a relation is found between one such indicator and another variable, it is difficult to know whether the association is due to democracy or to the other confounding variables contained within the democracy index. For instance, one study showed that a measure that incorporates stability tends to support the hypothesis that the timing of development influences the chances for democracy, while a measure that excludes stability does not support this hypothesis.

Virtually all studies treat measures of political democracy as if they were error-free. It is not known how far this approach has led to biased assessments of the causes and consequences of political democracy.

Single-time vs. Multiple-time Measurement

The temporal dimension is another way to classify measures of democracy. Single-time measures may cover a single year or a period of years. Cutright's measure, for instance, covers a single twenty-one-year period. J. S. Coleman's competitiveness measure is for a single time point (around 1959). Multiple-time measures range from two-time measures to annual measures for many years. Generally, analysts used single-time measures for one of two reasons: lack of data or the attempt to gauge democracy over a period of years. Most contemporary researchers prefer multiple-time measures because these measures allow more flexibility in analyzing trends and studying the dynamics of democratic development. In addition, analysts can group annual measures to produce period measures, while period measures often do not allow a return to the annual measures that went into them.

Conclusions

The measurement of political democracy is still at an early stage in its development. It has advanced further than the measurement of some other social-science constructs, such as national cohesion, openness of markets, or economic dependency. It is less developed, however, than the measurement of others, such as energy consumption or gross domestic product.

To agree on the measurement of political democracy, analysts will have to arrive at a consensus on the meaning of the term. Then they will have to resolve the issues outlined here. Some of the important tasks include (1) finding objective indicators to replace subjective measures, such as the fairness of elections and effectiveness of legislative bodies; (2) developing more precise measures than those currently available; (3) finding ways to incorporate aspects of inclusiveness into indices; and (4) gaining more knowledge of the validity and error in existing measures. Although perfect measures of political democracy will remain elusive, substantial improvements in measurement are feasible.

Kenneth A. Bollen

BIBLIOGRAPHY

Bollen, Kenneth A. "Issues in the Comparative Measurement of Political Democracy." *American Sociological Review* 45 (1980): 370–390.

———. "Liberal Democracy: Validity and Method Factors in Cross-National Measures." *American Journal of Political Science* 37 (November 1993): 1207–1230.

Bryce, James. *Modern Democracies.* 2 vols. New York: Macmillan, 1921.

Coleman, J. S. "Conclusion: The Political Systems of the Developing Areas." In *The Politics of Developing Areas,* edited by G. A. Almond and J. S. Coleman. Princeton: Princeton University Press, 1960.

Cutright, Phillips. "National Political Development: Its Measures and Analysis." *American Sociological Review* 28 (1963): 253–264.

Fitzgibbon, Russell H. "Measurement of Latin-American Political Phenomena: A Statistical Experiment." *American Political Science Review* 45 (1951): 517–523.

Gastil, Raymond D., and Freedom House. *Freedom in the World.* New York: Freedom House, annual.

Inkeles, Alex. *On Measuring Democracy.* New Brunswick, N.J.: Transaction, 1991.

Jackman, Robert. "On the Relation of Economic Development to Democratic Performance." *American Journal of Political Science* 17 (1973): 11–21.

Lerner, Daniel. *The Passing of Traditional Society.* Glencoe, Ill.: Free Press, 1958.

Lipset, Seymour Martin. "Some Social Requisites of Democracy." *American Political Science Review* 53 (1959): 69–105.

Nixon, Raymond B. "Freedom in the World's Press: A Fresh Appraisal with New Data." *Journalism Quarterly* 42 (1965): 3–5, 118–119.

Vanhanen, Tatu. *The Process of Democratization.* New York: Crane Russak, 1990.

Media, Mass

Mass media are means of communications in which one or more communicators transmit (or broadcast) messages to large numbers of receivers with whom they have no face-to-face contact. Communication is the transmission of meaning among persons by the use of symbols. Communications media are the means used to transmit the messages, which include spoken and written words, pictures, and facial and body movements. The term *mass media* is shorthand for media of mass communications.

Mass media are usually distinguished from interpersonal media, such as personal letters, conversations, and fistfights, in which the communications travel unmediated between communicators and receivers. Mass media include such devices as leaflets, posters, billboards, air raid sirens, and foghorns. But analysts of the mass media have focused mainly on the print media of newspapers, magazines, and books and on the electronic media of television, radio, and motion pictures.

Many social scientists believe that communication is the most basic of all social processes. They point out that if human beings were unable to exchange information and ideas with one another, each would live in total cognitive isolation from all others, and there could be no society. Similarly, mass communications are the vital ingredient of any large-scale society: it is impossible for each of the many millions of citizens of a modern nation to have interpersonal communications with each of the others, and so most of the meaningful exchanges that meld the individuals into a society are transmitted by the mass media.

The mass media also play a vital role in democratic government. Most of the attitudes and activities of citizens of modern democracies are rooted in information and explanations they get from the mass media, especially television, newspapers, and radio. To be sure, most people check that information against their understandings of the world gained from interpersonal communication with spouses, teachers, friends, work associates, and parents. If what the mass media tell them is strongly contradicted by what they hear from their families and friends, they are more likely to believe known and close associates than anonymous and distant broadcasters. Even so, much of what parents and peers tell children and friends is taken initially from the mass media. Thus the organization and regulation of the media are matters of the highest importance for modern democracy.

Ownership, Organization, and Regulation

The largest audiences for the mass media in modern democracies are (in order) those for television, newspapers, and radio. Audiences for magazines, books, and movies are far smaller. In almost all democracies, most newspapers are privately owned, operated for profit, and financed much more by revenues from selling advertising space than by subscription fees. The strong constitutional guarantees for freedom of the press in most democracies mean that there is little or no direct government regulation of the content of newspaper reports or editorial comments, although in many countries stringent libel and slander laws powerfully constrain what newspapers publish about political leaders and organizations.

For many years in many nations, television and radio were public monopolies, owned by governments and operated either by ministries of communication (as in many continental European and Scandinavian countries) or by independent public corporations (many modeled on the British Broadcasting Corporation). Only in the United States and a few other democracies were the electronic media largely owned and operated as private businesses. Since the 1980s, however, many nations (France and Sweden are notable recent examples) have followed Great Britain's change in policy in permitting private businesses

to own and operate television and radio stations supported by revenues from the sale of time for advertising. Hence in most democracies today private broadcasters compete with public broadcasters for audiences and influence.

In every democratic nation, television and radio operate under much stricter government regulation than do the print media. Broadcasting stations must obtain operating licenses from public authorities. The licenses generally assign a particular broadcasting frequency to each licensee, stipulate the power of the transmitter and the hours of broadcasting, and impose a ceiling on the number of stations one person or corporation may own. Other laws regulate such matters vital to democracy as the availability of air time for political parties, candidates, and interest groups to advocate their causes.

Public and private broadcasters in all democracies cover political events with news broadcasts, interview programs, discussions with "focus groups," call-in radio and television talk shows, and the like. The format and content of all such broadcasts are controlled by the broadcasters, not the participants.

Consequently, many political contestants are eager to buy air time to present their causes in ways that they control. Different democracies handle political advertising differently. The United States and Venezuela, for example, allow political organizations to buy television and radio time for advertisements, although in presidential elections the total amount they can spend for such purposes is limited. In Great Britain, on the other hand, no party or candidate can purchase air time for advertising from either public or private broadcasters. Each broadcaster is required to give the principal political parties some free air time to present their cases in any way they choose. The amount of time given to each party is roughly proportional to its share of the popular vote in the preceding general election. In Germany political parties are granted free television time to air several 150-second spot broadcasts. Italy also provides the parties with free time but requires that some of the time be used for press conferences.

Partisanship, Accuracy, and Fairness

The mass media play a critical role in modern democracies, for much of the information and understanding on which citizens base their decisions about leaders and policies comes from what they (and their families and friends) see on television, read in newspapers, and hear on radio. Hence most theorists of democracy hold that democracy can thrive only if the mass media both provide true accounts of each day's main politically relevant events in a way that gives them meaning for the general public and serve as forums for the exchange of political comment and criticism.

The general acceptance of these principles is relatively recent in most democracies. Until the 1920s most newspapers (the main mass medium until the advent of radio) were unabashed supporters of particular parties and candidates. Most people read only the newspaper identified with their party, and they expected the paper's reports and commentaries (little distinction was made between the two) to support the party's candidates and policies.

Since the 1920s, however, the idea has grown that all news organizations should keep their news reports accurate and unbiased by their policy preferences. It is permissible for a newspaper or broadcaster to advocate particular candidates and causes if that advocacy is confined entirely to "editorials" explicitly representing the views of the proprietor and to "columns" signed by other partisans. But it is not permissible to slant news reports so as to favor one candidate or cause over others.

Some critics of the media argue that the ideal of reportorial objectivity is merely a smokescreen to hide the naked realities of power—that all newspaper stories and news broadcasts inescapably promote the biases of their owners' gender, race, and social class. The evidence suggests, however, that most reporters and newscasters, like most readers and viewers, believe that objectivity is both right and achievable.

Perhaps the near universal acceptance of this principle explains why in most democracies political groups frequently charge that the presentation by the mass media of news and commentary is unfairly slanted against them. (It is hard to find a group criticizing the media for portraying its cause too favorably.) Moreover, such groups often charge that the slanting is due to deliberate decisions by media bosses who are determined to promote their personal political positions.

Other analysts argue that, while portrayals of political issues and events by the media are certainly biased, the bias is not political in the sense that it consciously seeks to promote certain parties and ideologies over others. Rather, they say, the bias is structural: it stems from communicators' concepts of their proper roles and of what readers and viewers want. For instance, most television newscasters and producers, like most newspaper reporters and editors, think of themselves primarily as professional journalists. They see themselves as the people's watchdogs, whose prime obligation is to inform citizens about what their government is doing. Journalists should, of course, duly note whatever good things government does; but their special obligation is to "blow the whistle" on government wrongdoing, for only thus can the citizens acquire the information they need to hold the government accountable. Journalists, then, believe that the proper role of the mass media is not to make it easier for the government to do good; it is to make it easier for ordinary citizens to keep the government from doing ill.

Several other constraints shape the workways of the mass media. For instance, the first goal of a privately owned newspaper or television station is to make a profit for its owners. Because such media depend on advertising for the bulk of their revenue, and because advertisers will pay high rates only for large audiences, the media must design their programs and newspaper features to attract and keep the most viewers and readers possible. Accordingly, communicators feel compelled to present what they think receivers want, not what the communicators think receivers ought to have.

Another constraint is imposed by the limited nonadvertising space in newspapers and the even more limited nonadvertising time on television and radio. No story or program can present all the facts relevant to a particular event or policy, let alone its entire historical and social context. The writers and producers must decide which facts are most relevant and present them as concisely and interestingly as they can.

Then, too, the technology of television, currently the most heeded of the mass media, compels broadcasters to present pictures as well as words. Although audiences want both, they are more interested in pictures than words; consequently, television newscasts and entertainment programs give high priority to "good visuals." As a result, television is much better at portraying individuals than groups. With color, motion, and sound, the screen shows individuals who look remarkably like people in real life. After viewing a candidate on television, most viewers feel that the candidate is a real person and that they know him or her—perhaps not as well as if they had met face to face but far better than if their information had come solely from the printed words and static photographs of newspapers.

On the other hand, television finds it difficult to portray a political party or any other organization. A party, after all, is an abstract aggregation of certain words and acts taken from all the words and acts of certain individuals. Television can show only the antics of delegates to party meetings and party leaders making speeches. Broadcasters have to depend on voice-over remarks by reporters and commentators to describe such abstractions as, for example, in the United States the Democratic Party's stand on abortion or the Republican Party's stand on prayer in the schools. Consequently, television makes parties less important than candidates—not because of any ideological bias against parties but because pictures are more important than words for the way television portrays reality. That expression is not a political bias; but neither is television, as some producers have claimed, an "electric mirror" that reflects political life exactly as it is.

Mass Media and Mass Publics

Most studies of the impact of the mass media on mass publics conceptualize the process as the interaction of several independent variables (communicator, message, medium, and receivers) and dependent variables (attitudes and behavior). Their findings may be summarized as follows.

Other things being equal, receivers are more likely to be influenced by messages from communicators they know personally and trust than from those they do not know or distrust. Consequently, messages from parents, siblings, spouses, friends, and work associates are likely to have a more powerful effect than messages from advertisers or newspaper publishers. By the same token, messages on television are likely to be more powerful than messages in newspaper stories: receivers see and hear what they identify as flesh-and-blood people delivering messages on television in a way that is far closer to real-life interpersonal communications than faceless voices on radio and faceless and voiceless print in newspapers.

Messages concerning issues about which receivers already have strong feelings (such as abortion) are less likely to change receivers' attitudes and behavior than are messages on issues about which they care little (such as the details of market access and environmental restrictions in trade agreements). Messages that state a conclusion after appearing to give fair consideration to different alternatives are more likely to convince than are messages in which the communicator's position is presented as one that only fools, knaves, and traitors could oppose.

Television is the most powerful of the mass media. Survey studies have reported that more than twice as many people say they get most of their information about the world from television as say they get most of their information from newspapers, radio, or magazines. Studies have also found that many more people trust television rather than newspapers to report accurately what is going on in the world. Moreover, in most modern democracies most people say they spend more time watching television than doing anything else except working and sleeping.

People who get their information mainly from a single medium (such as television) are more likely to be influenced by its messages than are people who get their information from several media (such as television, newspapers, magazines, and books). The better educated people are, the more media they pay attention to.

Many scholars believe that the main effect of the mass media on mass publics is not so much to shape what people think as to shape what they think about. That is, by paying attention to certain events, issues, and people rather than others, the mass media move them to the center of the receivers' attention. The media fall far short of absolute control over what people think about, however, as is shown by the different answers survey respondents give to two questions often asked in public opinion polls: What do you think are the most important problems facing the country? What problems facing the country concern you, personally, the most? Some items, such as jobs, crime, and taxes, are usually high on both lists of answers, but some items are high on the first list and low on or absent from the second. A leading example is environmental pollution, which often appears high on the first list and low on the second. Most analysts take this result to mean that people conclude that if the mass media show a lot of concern with pollution it must be important in some general sense, though it does not worry them personally. In other words, they see the issue and what to do about it as high on the public agenda but not on their personal agendas.

Teledemocracy?

Modern democracies are representative governments, some with a tincture of direct democracy supplied by occasional referendums. Most analysts agree that the mass communications media provide most of the information by which voters judge their representatives and the candidates and parties who seek to replace them. Some analysts, however, believe that new technologies, especially interactive television by coaxial cable, make it possible to bypass or replace representative institutions with "teledemocracy."

Coaxial cables enable communicators to send signals from central transmitters to receivers in homes and also allow signals to travel from homes to central stations. This technology has led to several experiments with electronic versions of Athenian-style direct democracy. For example, in the 1980s the Qube system in Columbus, Ohio, provided each of its cable subscribers with a device that enabled viewers to send signals back to the broadcaster. In one experiment, the station televised discussions of a proposed local political action and invited viewers to register their preferences by pressing the "yes" or "no" buttons on keypads connected to their receivers. The viewers' signals were transmitted to a central computer, which collated and reported the results. The British Prestel system used a similar device but had the advantage of transmissions by ordinary telephone lines. In 1993 the American billionaire and former presidential candidate Ross Perot purchased time on commercial broadcast television networks to present his criticisms of President Bill Clinton's administration; he invited viewers to express their opinions by calling a special telephone number.

Most commentators concerned with the health of modern democracy say that such teledemocracy is suited only for up-or-down plebiscites and eliminates deliberation and compromise from the lawmaking process. In *Democracy and Deliberation,* however, political scientist James S. Fishkin contends that, properly organized, teledemocracy can yield opinions by small representative samples of voters that emerge from mutual interchange and deliberation. His ideas were tested in an experiment performed in Manchester, England, in 1994. Four hundred residents of that city were chosen randomly as a representative sample of the city's electorate. They were tested on their opinions about possible causes of and cures for crime. Then for three days they studied together and discussed with each other the issues involved. Their discussions were recorded by television crews and newspaper reporters. At the end of the three days the respondents were tested again to find out whether their views had changed. The new test showed that quite a few people in the sample had changed their views on several issues. Fishkin concluded that people's opinions on policy questions are better informed and more worth knowing if they result from this kind of focused learning and discussion. He hoped to repeat the experiment in the early months of the American presidential selection process in 1996.

Even so, there is no reason to believe that interactive television will soon be used in making official democratic decisions. But there is every reason to believe that the mass communications media will play an even more important role in democratic government in the twenty-first century than ever before.

See also *Critiques of democracy.*

Austin Ranney

BIBLIOGRAPHY

Adler, Ronald B. *Understanding Human Communication.* 3d ed. New York: Holt, Rinehart and Winston, 1988.

Arterton, F. Christopher. *Teledemocracy: Can Technology Protect Democracy?* Newbury Park, Calif., and London: Sage Publications, 1987.

Berger, Charles R., and Steven H. Chaffee. *Handbook of Communication Science.* Beverly Hills, Calif., and London: Sage Publications, 1987.

Bryant, Jennings, and Dolf Zillmann. *Perspectives on Media Effects.* Hillsdale, N.J.: Erlbaum Associates, 1986.

Ernst, Josef. *The Structures of Political Communication in the United Kingdom, the United States, and the Federal Republic of Germany.* New York: P. Lang, 1988.

Fishkin, James S. *Democracy and Deliberation: New Directions for Democratic Reform.* New Haven and London: Yale University Press, 1991.

Hiebert, Ray Eldon, Donald F. Ungurait, and Thomas W. Bohn. *Mass Media V: An Introduction to Modern Communication.* New York: Longman, 1988.

McLean, Iain. *Democracy and the New Technology.* Cambridge: Polity Press, 1989.

Meadows, A. J. *Info-technology: Changing the Way We Communicate.* London: Cassell, 1989.

Ruben, Brent D. *Communication and Human Behavior.* 3d ed. Englewood Cliffs, N.J.: Prentice Hall, 1992.

Ward, Ken. *Mass Communications and the Modern World.* Basingstoke, England: Macmillan Education, 1989.

Mexico

A Latin American country marked by extensive poverty and highly concentrated wealth that shares a 2,000-mile border with the United States. Although Mexico shares several characteristics with other countries of Latin America, its differences explain its particular concept of democracy and route toward democratic government.

Unlike politics elsewhere in Latin America, politics in Mexico is highly institutionalized. Since political power was recentralized in the 1930s after almost two decades of civil war, political practices and expectations have become

highly routinized. The army, the Catholic Church, and the landed elites were virtually eliminated as significant actors. The Mexican political system is a form of "soft authoritarianism" in which a centralized, strong presidential system based on an official party controls the direction and pace of change and thus sets the terms of negotiation with opposition parties. Even so, opposition parties acquired enough force as a result of reforms beginning in the late 1970s and economic crises in the 1980s and 1990s that they exert significant influence over the government and the official party.

Historical Background

Like Bolivia, Ecuador, Guatemala, and Peru, Mexico was inhabited by highly developed indigenous civilizations centuries before the arrival of the Spanish conquerors in 1519. The three centuries of Spanish colonial rule that followed left deep legacies: Roman Catholicism as the established religion, Spanish as the common "high" language, a centralized political system with very limited popular participation, and a rigidly hierarchical caste society. The profound inequalities that continue to complicate Mexico's transition to democracy trace their roots to the colonial period.

Also like most countries of Latin America, Mexico experienced a period of prolonged instability, ushered in by the wars of independence from Spain in 1810–1821. This instability was even more acute in Mexico than elsewhere in the region: from 1846 to 1848 Mexico was involved in a devastating war with the United States in which it lost roughly half its territory, and from 1863 to 1867 it was under occupation by the French. Not until the onset of the prolonged dictatorship of Porfirio Díaz (1876–1910) did stability and economic growth return to the country.

It is the revolution of 1910 that marks Mexico as distinctive, if not unique, in Latin America, since Cuba can also claim a revolution. Mexico's revolution—passing through phases of liberal uprising (1910–1913) to bloody civil war (1913–1917) and religious war (1926–1929), and then to gradual consolidation of power in the mid-1920s by groups from the northern states of Sonora and Coahuila—ultimately claimed more than a million lives, or more than 10 percent of the population. The revolution destroyed or severely weakened established political actors—the Catholic Church, large landowners, the official army, and foreign interests. It brought important new powers into politics—labor unions, peasant groups, and a new middle class. And it forged new values—a strong, secular state, virulent nationalism, promotion of Indian rights, defense of workers and the lower classes, protection of individual liberties, and advocacy of democracy—as consecrated in the constitution of 1917.

Mexico is also distinguished by the fact that its experience with functioning democracy is virtually nonexistent.

The lack of a democratic tradition is due in part to Spanish colonialism, instability, and dictatorship, but much of the reason lies in the way a new political system was constructed in the 1930s after the period of civil and religious war.

The Impact of Populism on Modern Mexico

Anglo-American notions of democracy emphasize process: the role of legitimate opposition to government, periodic elections, extensive suffrage, and constitutional guarantees that make citizen participation effective. Although this liberal concept has historical roots in Mexico as well, a stronger influence is populism. The term *populism* encompasses a complex set of movements that arose in Latin America in response to the Great Depression, which began in 1929. This tradition added themes of social welfare and nationalism to the meaning of democracy. Populists generally criticized laissez-faire economics and "formal" democracy, advocating instead a strong state based on nationalism, anti-imperialism, social reform, and inward-looking economic policies.

Liberal notions of democratic procedures coexisted uneasily with the emphasis on ends that characterized populism. In many cases, populist goals were considered sufficiently important that leaders could invoke them to justify authoritarian practices. Liberal traditions in Latin America were rooted deeply enough, however, that populists generally felt obliged to recognize liberal democracy as the long-term legitimating goal of governance.

In Mexico the government of Lázaro Cárdenas (1934–1940)—like that of Franklin Roosevelt, whose New Deal program helped to promote economic recovery and social reform in the United States—legitimized an extensive role for government as an agent of economic development and social welfare. After a period of robust growth from the mid-1940s to the early 1980s, however, the economic policies of populism encountered increasing problems of stagnation and inflation. Beginning with the presidency of Miguel de la Madrid (1982–1988), and gaining momentum with the administration of Carlos Salinas de Gortari (1988–1994), the economic strategy was profoundly recast toward market-oriented, export-promotion policies.

The economy was substantially reformed by the early 1990s, but the debates about democracy nonetheless retained certain populist themes. Mexicans remained preoccupied with the questions of how democracy can reduce extreme inequality and reinforce national sovereignty.

Although the principal actors in Mexican politics agree on the need to move toward liberal democracy, they are often at odds on how to reconcile U.S.-style liberalism with their country's overwhelming problems of poverty and dependency. Radical democrats, for example, would hold that only by moving immediately to truly free elections can basic social ills be addressed. By contrast, moderates and conservatives, many allied with the government and the official party, often argue that an abrupt transition would create uncertainty, even instability. Finally, a neopopulist current holds that unfettered democracy would serve the interests of concentrated wealth and powerful foreign actors.

Political Institutions and Actors

Mexico's president serves a single six-year term and cannot be reelected. With eight uninterrupted presidencies since 1934, Mexican politics has taken on a distinctive sexennial rhythm. The peaceful successions make for stable expectations about behavior, policy adjustments, circulation of members of the elite through electoral and appointed posts, and renewal of public hopes for the future. Mexico is formally a federal system, with thirty-one states, a federal district, and more than 2,400 municipalities (similar to U.S. counties). The sexennial calendar is densely packed with elections of governors, state assemblies, city mayors, and city councils. These elections provide for significant turnover among the elite and policy adjustment throughout the country.

Mexico is one of the few remaining party-government systems. The Institutional Revolutionary Party (PRI) is closely integrated with government at all levels, as can be seen in the rotation of personnel between party and government bureaucracy and in the party's access to government resources and influence for strictly partisan purposes. From the 1930s to the 1980s the government could manipulate rules and outcomes, legally or otherwise, to preserve the party's power. The lead actor in this manipulation was the president, who could impose and remove the PRI leadership at will and who exercised virtually unchecked power over bureaucratic appointments.

At the elite level of party activists, the PRI can be divided roughly into two factions, one favoring the status quo and one promoting liberalization and reform. The status quo faction, whose leaders are often called *dinos* (dinosaurs), is based largely in organized labor, peasant organizations, and public employee unions. The reform faction, sometimes called *renos* (renovators), is a more heterogeneous group whose leadership comes predominantly from urban, middle-class groups, especially young professionals. An important debate within the PRI concerns the question of relative weight to give to the organized groups of the party, where the *dinos* hold sway, and to the local-level organizations, where the *renos* have tried to organize support. At stake is control over the PRI's nominations to elected office, as well as other aspects of the party's programs and practices. Another debate concerns how fast to reform the national polity and economy, with the *renos* generally pushing for rapid reform and the *dinos* resisting.

Among the opposition parties, the National Action Party (PAN) is the principal force on the center-right. Founded in 1939, the National Action Party is somewhat the conscience of the political system in its consistent advocacy of honest elections and politics. Three main currents coexist in the party: the traditional liberals, or anti-authoritarians, who work for the peaceful overthrow of the PRI; the Christian democrats, who promote Catholic views on matters of family, education, and state-society relations; and business leaders *(neopanistas)*, many of whom believe that real counterweights to authoritarian presidentialism must come through the electoral arena. Several recent government reforms coincide with the PAN's principles, thus creating a basis for loose policy coalitions. Diego Fernández de Cevallos—a leader in the pragmatic opposition bloc, the faction of PAN that has been willing to negotiate the terms of electoral and other reforms with the government—was the party's presidential nominee in the 1994 elections.

The main force on the center-left is the Party of the Democratic Revolution (PRD). Cuauhtémoc Cárdenas, the son of Lázaro Cárdenas, is the party's leader; he was the PRD's presidential candidate in 1994. The PRD is made up of a break-off faction from the PRI, led by Cárdenas; a Marxist faction that dates from the late 1920s; and an anti-PRI populist faction. Since the PRD's founding in 1989, the party's program has emphasized greater attention to protecting Mexican sovereignty and to softening the impact of economic restructuring on the lower classes. The main dynamic within the PRD today concerns what tactics to pursue to push the government toward electoral and other political reforms.

Several other parties have been active at the national level, but of these only the Labor Party received enough votes to preserve its registration after the 1994 election. At the grassroots level of the party, especially in rural areas, local bosses *(caciques)* exercise considerable influence over politics, including elections. They have aligned themselves with the PRI, especially its *dinos*. Although many of the bosses defected in the 1988 elections, especially to the center-left Cárdenas movement, most returned to the PRI fold.

Most Mexican citizens identify with one of the three main political parties. In an August 1994 opinion poll, 45 percent of those interviewed leaned toward the PRI, 19 percent favored the PAN, and 9 percent supported the PRD. Some 20 percent were undecided or favored none of these three parties. In the August 1994 presidential election, the PRI won 50 percent of the vote, followed by the PAN with 27 percent, and the PRD with 17 percent.

The Elections of 1994 and Reforms

The overriding issue in Mexico's August 1994 election was the credibility of the electoral process. The PRI regime had opened the electoral system to opposition parties in the late 1970s. In the midst of economic crisis in the early 1980s, however, the regime essentially shut down the electoral route through deliberate fraud. Throughout the 1980s and early 1990s, enormous pressure had built up to reopen the electoral option. Although the Salinas government had made some progress toward democratic reform, the important breakthrough came in the last year of Salinas's term in the wake of traumatic political violence—first a peasant insurgency in the southernmost state of Chiapas in early 1994 and then, in March, the assassination of the PRI's presidential candidate, Luis Donaldo Colosio, in Tijuana.

The violence and resulting public anxiety propelled the presidency and reform elements in the government to ally with reform currents in the PRI and principal opposition parties, especially in the PAN, to produce a negotiated transition. Such a transition was possible because the government retained enough power to set the terms of negotiation for electoral reform, taking opposition demands into account.

Reforms that were instituted included an updated voter registry, newly designed voter identification cards, an enhanced role for citizens in administering voting stations, official status for domestic and foreign observers, and speedy electoral tallying. Beyond these reforms, profound change at the grassroots level created the demand for more honest electoral procedures. The reforms and grassroots demands together contributed to a remarkable 78 percent voter turnout for the 1994 election, which was monitored by more than 80,000 independent observers.

The PRI still enjoys several key advantages as a result of its ties to government. It makes concessions to opposition parties, first, to create sufficient incentives for oppositions to continue to compete in elections and, second, to demonstrate that the general direction of reform continues toward democratic opening. At the same time, the government feels itself constrained by circumstances. The economic restructuring has created considerable short-term pain for the general population. Government officials had wanted the economic reforms to begin to produce improvements before they permitted open elections. Furthermore, many PRI members and government officials think it necessary not to alienate the party's *dinos* more than absolutely necessary. While the traditional forces might no longer deliver large voting blocs, they still represent strategic actors whose support is important to political and economic success. In particular, the cooperation of industrial and service unions is needed to make wage-price agreements work. In short, too much reform too fast can endanger the government's established base before new bases of support have coalesced.

The Challenge of the Political Agenda

The breakthrough of 1994 brought a new agenda to national politics. Winning candidate Ernesto Zedillo, who inherited the age-old tragedy of widespread poverty and enormous inequality of wealth and income, faced the daunting task of consolidating the economic reforms begun in the 1980s and creating conditions for sustainable growth. The Zedillo government also confronted growing pressures and dislocations caused in part by the North American Free Trade Agreement, which took effect in January 1994. For example, the third of Mexicans who work the land but produce less than 10 percent of the national product faced potentially devastating competition from U.S. and Canadian farmers.

The Zedillo administration's early performance was not encouraging. The important gains that President Zedillo and the Institutional Revolutionary Party won in the comparatively honest elections of August 1994 were squandered by the new government's inept handling of the devaluation of the peso in December. The government announced an unconvincing economic plan and followed this with a devaluation unaccompanied by such necessary measures as wage and price controls. Investors, already nervous about instability and Zedillo's inexperience, hur-

ried to protect their interests. Billions of dollars fled the country in a matter of weeks, and Mexico was again plunged into crisis. The impact of the devaluation was felt throughout other so-called emerging markets, as investors sought refuge in safer havens. Brazil was forced to devalue, and Argentina was put under extreme pressure. Mexico entered a period of economic austerity and slow growth.

Even in the face of economic austerity, however, the Zedillo administration attempted to hold to its ambitious agenda to promote decentralization, strengthen Congress and the judiciary, reform the police, and separate the electoral machinery from direct government control. And Zedillo has not renounced his plan to separate the official party from the government or his promise not to interfere in the party's internal procedures, including the way in which nominations to public office are decided. If actually carried out—and experience and the administration's early performance give cause for considerable skepticism—these reforms imply nothing less than the dismantling of Mexico's unique presidential system. In any case, Mexico has made important progress toward a democratic opening, and retreat toward a harder form of authoritarianism seems unlikely.

See also *Central America; Populism.*

John Bailey

BIBLIOGRAPHY

Camp, Roderic Ai. *Politics in Mexico.* New York: Oxford University Press, 1993.
Cornelius, Wayne A. "Politics in Mexico." In *Comparative Politics Today,* edited by Gabriel A. Almond and G. Bingham Powell. New York: HarperCollins, forthcoming.
Cothran, Dan A. *Political Stability and Democracy in Mexico: The "Perfect" Dictatorship.* Westport, Conn.: Praeger, 1994.
Huntington, Samuel P. "The Modest Meaning of Democracy." In *Democracy in the Americas: Stopping the Pendulum,* edited by Robert Pastor. New York: Holmes and Meier, 1989.
Meyer, Lorenzo. "Democracy from Three Latin American Perspectives." In *Democracy in the Americas: Stopping the Pendulum,* edited by Robert Pastor. New York: Holmes and Meier, 1989.
Middlebrook, Kevin J. *The Paradox of Revolution: Labor, the State, and Authoritarianism in Mexico.* Baltimore: Johns Hopkins University Press, 1995.
Paz, Octavio. *The Other Mexico: Critique of the Pyramid.* New York: Grove Press, 1972.
Sartori, Giovanni. *Parties and Political Systems.* Cambridge: Cambridge University Press, 1976.
Tutino, John. *From Insurrection to Revolution in Mexico: Social Bases of Agrarian Violence, 1750–1940.* Princeton: Princeton University Press, 1986.

Michels, Robert

German-born sociologist who wrote a classic study of political parties and democracy. Michels (1876–1936) was born in Cologne of a patrician Catholic family. He studied at the Universities of Munich, Leipzig, and Halle, completing a dissertation in history. He spent most of his adult life in Italy, where he died.

As a young assistant professor at the University of Marburg, Michels became a socialist and participated in several congresses of the German Social Democratic Party. His socialist views prevented a permanent academic appointment in Germany, however, in spite of the support of the well-known German sociologist Max Weber, who in 1913 asked him to become a coeditor of a famous social science journal, the *Archiv für Sozialwissenschaft und Sozialpolitik* (Archive of Social Science and Social Policy).

After receiving an appointment in Italy at the University of Turin, Michels became a member in 1907 of the Italian Socialist Party. Earlier, in Germany, he had been impressed by the contrast between the revolutionary rhetoric of the German socialist party and its leader, August Bebel, and the cautious policy it pursued, its emphasis on electoral success, and the pragmatic tendencies in the trade unions. This experience led to numerous publications and the writing of his classic work *Zur Soziologie des Parteiwesens in der modernen Demokratie* (1911), translated as *Political Parties: A Sociological Study of the Oligarchical Tendencies of Modern Democracy*. In those years he was in close contact with socialist intellectuals in Italy and France and was influenced by French syndicalism, a current of thought that was opposed to parliamentary democracy and advocated revolutionary trade unionism.

During World War I, Michels identified with Italy. This identification led to a break with Weber, his longtime friend and mentor. Michels continued living and teaching in Italy for the rest of his life, aside from a stint as visiting professor at the University of Chicago. He wrote extensively on imperialism, nationalism, the role of intellectuals, elites, social mobility, gender, and social morality. His *Psychologie der antikapitalistischen Massenbewegungen* (Psychology of Anticapitalist Mass Movements, 1925) remains one of the most interesting documented and systematic studies of working-class protest. He also wrote on the origins of fascism and Italy under fascism, which he viewed sympathetically.

Michels's study of political parties, particularly the internal politics of parties, and his "iron law" of oligarchy give him a central place in the development of the theory of democracy. According to the "iron law," organization gives rise to oligarchy. Organizations are oligarchic because they become divided between a minority of those who direct and a majority of those who are directed. Michels explained oligarchy not in terms of the psychology of leaders but in terms of organizational needs: the need to protect the organization, the division of labor, the complexity of tasks, the full-time activity of officials. Leaders committed to democracy, he believed, acted in ways that did not conform to their values in the interest of the organization. The tendency to put aside their democratic values was reinforced by the psychological predispositions not only of the leaders but also of the masses, who, because of their incompetence and emotionalism, put their trust in the leaders. Michels emphasized the responsiveness of leaders to the preferences of their constituents and thus did not regard electoral accountability as a criterion for democracy. The incompetence of the masses and the lack of effort on the part of the leaders to overcome it, he maintained, allowed leaders to give priority to the interests of the organization and sometimes to their own.

Michels was also concerned that the search for electoral majorities by the revolutionary party would preclude its commitment to revolutionary ideology. Because the ideological transformation of society was the goal of a socialist party and the realization of socialism was in the interest of the working class, only socialist parties, he contended, could be truly democratic, but even they would encounter difficulties. The assumption in that analysis was that the interests of the working class were not necessarily those expressed by the voters but those defined by the ideology.

Although the presumed "iron law" represents an overstatement that has been rightly criticized both on theoretical and empirical grounds, Michels's analysis has contributed much to the understanding of the limits of democracy in parties, trade unions, cooperatives, interest groups, churches, and voluntary associations. His focus on internal democracy in parties, particularly socialist parties, which for him were the only democratic ones, led him to miss the role of competition between parties in modern democracies. By focusing on dissent, debate, and competition for leadership within parties, he tended to neglect the fact that members and voters can vote with their feet—by resigning their membership, abstaining from voting, and joining and voting for other parties.

Michels's negative feelings about democracy within socialist parties prompted a critical stance that made him susceptible to the appeal of charismatic plebiscitary leadership, which he identified as an expression of a nonoligarchical democracy and which ultimately led him to sympathize with fascism. The theoretical mistakes, his sometimes inaccurate description of political reality, and his later political affinities should not, however, detract from his seminal contributions to political sociology. His book *Political Parties* is required reading for any student of democratic politics.

The work of Michels has stimulated research on the German Social Democratic Party and on trade unions, cooperative societies, religious institutions, and other organizations. The most important of these studies has been *Union Democracy: The Internal Politics of the International Typographic Union,* by Seymour Martin Lipset, Martin A. Trow, and James S. Coleman (1956), which analyzedthe conditions under which, contrary to Michels's "iron law," the International Typographic Union remained democratic when many American unions fitted Michels's analysis.

See also *Associations; Weber, Max.*

Juan J. Linz

BIBLIOGRAPHY

Linz, Juan J. "Michels e il suo contributo alla sociologia politica." Introduction to *La sociologia del partito politico nella democrazia moderna,* by Robert Michels. Bologna: Il Mulino, 1966.

Lipset, Seymour Martin. Introduction to *Political Parties: A Sociological Study of the Oligarchical Tendencies of Modern Democracy,* by Robert Michels. New York: Free Press, 1962.

———. "The Political Process in Trade Unions." In *Political Man: The Social Bases of Politics.* Garden City, N.Y.: Doubleday, 1960.

May, John D. "Democracy, Organization, Michels." *American Political Science Review* 59 (June 1965): 417–429.

Michels, Robert. *Political Parties: A Sociological Study of the Oligarchical Tendencies of Modern Democracy.* Translated by Eden and Cedar Paul. With an introduction by Seymour Martin Lipset. New York: Free Press, 1962.

———. *Sozialismus und Fascismus in Italien.* Munich: Meyer and Jensen, 1925.

———. "Eine syndikalistische Unterströmung im deutschen Sozialismus (1903–1907)." In *Festschrift zum 70 Geburtstag von Carl Grünberg.* Leipzig: C. I. Hirschfeld, 1932.

Röhrich, Wilfried. *Robert Michels—Vom Sozialistisch—syndikalistischen zum faschistischen Credo.* Berlin: Duncker and Humblot, 1972.

Roth, Guenther. *The Social Democrats in Imperial Germany: A Study in Working-Class Isolation and National Integration.* Totowa, N.J.: Bedminster Press, 1963.

Middle East

The countries that stretch from northeast Africa and the coast of the Mediterranean Sea down to the Persian Gulf, including Egypt, Iran, Iraq, Israel, Jordan, Lebanon, Saudi Arabia, Syria, Yemen, and the Gulf states of Bahrain, Kuwait, Oman, Qatar, and the United Arab Emirates. The political systems of the Middle East include monarchies (Jordan, Saudi Arabia, and the Gulf states), dominant, authoritarian party structures (Iraq, Syria), an Islamic republic (Iran), a reunified nation (Yemen), and an advanced multiparty pluralist state (Israel). With the exception of Israel, two features characterize the region: the powerful influence of Islam as a religious and political movement and the limited nature of democracy. This conjunction has inevitably led to an examination of the relationship between Islam and democracy.

On the one hand, Islam is regarded as an obstacle to the establishment of democracy mainly because of the incompatibility between the absolute rule of God (Allah) and the secular forms of political expression that rest on representation and accountability. One strand of Islamic thought associates democracy with secularism, with the consequence that democracy becomes a deliberate violation of God's law. Islam's total view contains social, political, and economic creeds enshrined in Islamic law and based on interpretations of the Quran. This view precludes the need for other political movements and militates against the full participation of Islamic groups in competitive multiparty politics.

On the other hand, some find within Islam an Islamic agenda for democracy. These ideas center on the notion of the wider Muslim community, the *umma,* and the need for consultation, *shura.* In large states, *shura* takes place in a form of national assembly, *majlis.* In this context, Islamic parties may stand for election to national assemblies, and they can deliberate, advise, discuss, and consult with individual leaders. Yet the central features of liberal representative democracy—freedoms of speech and association, accountability, legitimate opposition, rights of the individual, and adequate information and debate—are not included. The reasons that so few Islamic countries appear to be democratic are linked to the defining characteristics and demands of Islam, but other factors are also important.

The Middle East's diverse cultures—Jewish, Arab, Iranian (Persian), and Christian—have given rise to a num-

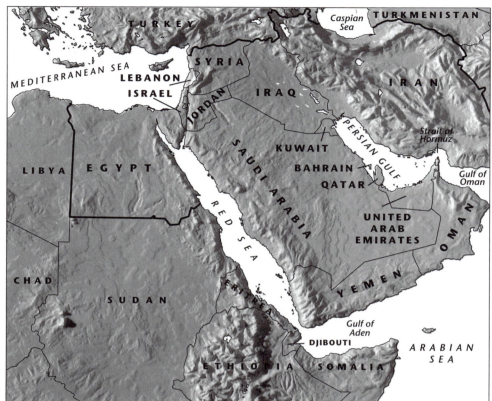

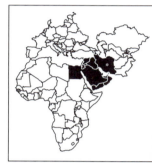

ber of political movements: Zionism, Pan-Arabism, Arab nationalism under Egyptian president Gamal Abdel Nasser (1918–1970), state socialism under the Baʿath parties, and Islamic revivalism. Conflicts since the end of World War II—including the Arab-Israeli wars of 1948–1949, 1967, 1973; the Iraq-Iran war of 1980–1988; the invasion of Kuwait by Iraq in August 1990 and the subsequent Persian Gulf war of 1991—contribute to a view, prevalent in the West, that political instability, tension, divisiveness, and military preparedness are endemic features of the area.

Impediments to Democracy

In spite of varying degrees of electoral activity in Iran, Jordan, Lebanon, Syria, and Yemen, lack of governmental accountability and full voter enfranchisement are major barriers to fully functioning democratic political systems. It can be argued that Middle Eastern states have rejected the liberal democratic option largely because of where it came from rather than what it contained. Certainly the impact of imperialism did much to foster anti-Western sentiments. Under a system of mandates established after World War I, France and Britain extended a system of

colonial rule over the area, arbitrarily dividing territory and stifling political development. The cold war, the post–World War II competition between the United States and the Soviet Union, further polarized opinion in the Middle East. Rivalry between the superpowers and political and military interference in the region exacerbated tensions.

Division and conflict between North and South Yemen was deepened by the institution of a Marxist government in South Yemen under the reorganized Yemen Socialist Party. South Yemen signed a twenty-year friendship pact with the Soviet Union in 1979 and declared the country a people's democratic republic. (North and South Yemen reunited in 1990.)

The decision of the United Nations in 1947 to recommend the partition of Palestine into two states, one Jewish, the other Arab, went against Palestinian wishes and caused much hostility. Israel was not recognized by members of the Arab community, who saw creation of the state as an act of imperialist intervention in land taken without their agreement. The creation of Israel set in motion a series of events that provoked some of the more enduring problems of the region: the plight of Palestinian refugees, the occupation of land, the recurrent conflicts and wars, and spiraling military expenditures.

The economic benefits of oil and its massive increase in price during the 1970s did little to encourage democratization. Rather, oil wealth led to increased power for regimes in Kuwait and the other Gulf states, which became benevolent autocracies, allocating the wealth through welfare schemes. In such *rentier* states, the nation accrues income not through traditional domestic taxation and economic programs, which often become associated with popular demands for political reform and legitimacy, but from such external sources as stocks, rents—or, in this case, oil exports. The oil-rich states are under no pressure to become democratic. State distribution of goods and services—that is, the allocation of oil wealth in the form of welfarism—meets societal needs, and the people therefore have no need to form trade unions, political parties, or any other economic or political organizations.

The Iranian Islamic revolution of 1979 introduced another dynamic into the region, that of theocratic politics—public affairs carried out in accordance with the belief that governance proceeds from divine authority. Under the stewardship of Ayatollah Ruhollah Khomeini (1901–1989), the popular revolt against the powerful Western-backed autocracy (1941–1979) of the shah, Mohammad Reza Pahlavi, contributed to the rise and importance of Islam as a strong political movement. The revolt also provided great momentum for anti-Western sentiment. Any possibility of introducing liberal democratic practices into the region seemed remote.

Indeed, Western countries did not want to see liberal democracies arise in the Middle East. Their dependence on oil, and the prevalence of strong communist parties in Iran, Iraq, South Yemen, and Syria, caused them to regard puppet regimes such as the shah's as preferable to, and potentially more stable than, democratic regimes. As the cold war was played out in the Middle East, the countries of the region became strategic assets. Coups engineered by the U.S. Central Intelligence Agency and military pacts with the Soviet Union were not the best ways of developing political structures and democratic processes. Furthermore, the Palestinian-Israeli conflict debilitated political advancement in the area as the ebbs and flows of stateless people affected the politics of surrounding states.

Iraq and Syria can both be described as authoritarian states, although they operate differently. In Iraq the president is the head of state with executive power and ap-

points the council of ministers. In Syria elections to the People's Assembly (parliament) are held every four years, and the president stands for reelection every seven years. Yet the controlling force and preeminent political organization in both countries has been the split, secular Ba'ath Party, one faction of which operates in Syria, the other in Iraq. Syria's constitution defines the country as a socialist popular democracy, while the Iraqi Ba'ath Party looks to a more powerful role at the vanguard of Pan-Arabism, an effort to achieve unity among Arab peoples beyond the constraints of national boundaries. One political feature that has differentiated Syria from Iraq is the National Progressive Front, an umbrella organization of various socialist parties that was formed in 1972 to broaden the Ba'ath Party's political base and to create an appearance of opposition.

Bahrain, Oman, Qatar, Saudi Arabia, and the United Arab Emirates have no political parties. In Saudi Arabia the king holds supreme power, and in Bahrain Sheik 'Isa ibn Salman Al Khalifa dissolved the National Assembly in 1975 for an indeterminate period on the grounds that it interfered with the administrative affairs of government. Oman has no constitution or modern judicial system. Final legal and administrative power is vested in the sultan, and all authority emanates from him. Qatar is an absolute monarchy. The emir is head of state, appoints the cabinet, and occupies the office of prime minister. There is an advisory council but no legislature. In these states, there is no semblance of contemporary democratic political institutions.

Citizenship

The concept of citizenship is crucial in any analysis of democratization processes within Middle Eastern countries. In liberal democratic theory, which emphasizes that the individual's rights and responsibilities lie within a legal framework, the citizen assumes a primary position. In the Middle East, citizens may be enfranchised and participate in the political process, but they are under a duty to accept being ruled. A pluralist society, which recognizes all interests, enables its citizenry to form pressure groups to petition the government, thereby permitting a structured form of participation.

The role of the citizenry can be both stable and responsible, but there are difficulties in regions that experience a high degree of population mobility for either political or economic reasons. The countries of the Middle East have high levels of population mobility partly because of the

Palestinian-Israeli dispute but also because of migrant labor, which reflects the uneven economies in the region. The support given to Iraq by the Palestine Liberation Organization during the 1991 Persian Gulf war resulted in the immediate expulsion of Palestinians working in Kuwait. Stateless Palestinians became as much of a security risk in Arab states as in the Jewish state of Israel.

Immediately before the invasion by Iraq, Kuwait had an estimated population of 2.2 million, of which approximately 70 percent was non-Kuwaiti. Population movement and citizenship affect the essential nature of nation-statehood and majority-minority apportionment within a society; both are vital elements in sustaining a democracy. In nations in which the majority of the population falls into noncitizen or semicitizen categories, democratization poses difficulties, in that political participation usually is confined to the minority. Palestinians living in Jordan are granted Jordanian citizenship and have participated in political procedures since 1950. The Jordanian constitution divides cabinet and parliamentary seats equally between Jordanians and Palestinians. In a sense the move toward the establishment of Palestinian autonomy, with the prospect of eventual statehood, presents a challenge to the region as well as to Palestinians living in the Diaspora. Palestinians who choose not to live in their sovereign territory may seek greater representation and influence in the political processes of their host states. For that reason or others, host countries may have to decide whether to grant citizenship and political rights to Palestinians.

Possibilities of Political Reform

Although some states felt internal pressure for democracy building during the 1980s, democratization was more widely discussed in the Middle East after the Persian Gulf war of 1991 and the end of the cold war. The changed global political environment, the disintegration of the Soviet Union, and the inefficiency of state-controlled economies led to some political reform, although not in every country of the region. Distinctions between the nation-states of the Middle East are such that a move toward democratization in one country may be symbolized by the removal of the ban on the formation of political parties or the introduction of a national assembly. In another country, it might be characterized by the establishment of a more equitable parliamentary system. A government decree passed in Jordan in 1992 permitted the formation of political parties, and elections were held for the National

Assembly in November 1993. In Lebanon elections were reintroduced in 1992 after a twenty-year absence, mainly because of that country's civil war.

By the end of the 1980s demonstrations, bread riots, and strikes had occurred in Iran and Jordan, and petitions calling for representative government appeared in Kuwait. In Jordan the population's grievances were twofold: a reaction against the dissolution of the parliament and changes in electoral laws and resentment of an economic reform plan that increased prices of basic foods and services. Government reforms that had aroused pleas for social justice and democracy had come in response to demands from the International Monetary Fund (IMF) that Jordan repay its foreign debt more quickly and effectively. In 1989 community leaders demanded changes in election law to provide democratic parliamentary representation, more political freedoms, a freer press, and formulation of a national economic program. Because it was bound to the IMF economic program, the government of Jordan had to create an atmosphere of confidence in the credibility of government policies by relaxing the curbs on freedom of expression and political rights.

The situation in Jordan showed that international organizations may exert pressure on a country to become democratic, but internal pressures may exist, too. The two elements are not mutually exclusive.

In Kuwait, beginning in 1989, three years after the dissolution of the National Assembly, a series of pro-democracy street rallies took place, and senior officials were involved in circulating secret petitions calling for a return to parliamentary life, or what passed as such. Suffrage had been confined to male citizens twenty-one and older who could prove Kuwaiti ancestry prior to 1920. Only 6.4 percent of the population was eligible to vote in the 1981 elections.

Although Kuwait is the only Gulf state in which a national assembly is elected entirely by popular vote, the restrictions on citizenship and enfranchisement make the term something of a misnomer. Nevertheless, the imprisonment of opposition leaders who demanded the reinstitution of the National Assembly and the glare of international publicity during the Persian Gulf war created a sensitivity about political processes. The emir announced that elections to a new parliament would be held, the question of women's participation in parliamentary life would be studied, and the status of naturalized "second category" citizens, previously denied the vote, would be reviewed. Kuwait learned from the war that the rights and responsibilities of citizens have as much to do with a nation's defense as with its maintenance of representative institutions. Denying the status of citizenship to people who have been residents in a country for decades undermines the fabric of a nation-state and renders it vulnerable both internally and externally.

Consociational Democracy

One promising model of democracy in countries with deep social cleavages and political or religious differences is consociational democracy. Consociationalism permits politicians representing sectional interests to govern at a national level in coalition with the leaders of other parties and groups. Through a system of proportional representation it is possible for leaders of all groups to participate at the decision-making level. This procedure permits all sectors of society to have a stake in the political institutions of the country. The political system of Lebanon between 1943 and 1975 fitted the consociational format.

Consociationalism can bring about a workable political system, but it does have disadvantages. The process may contribute to the continuing segregation of groups. Equally, it can allow an elite cartel to emerge that represents particular interests and exchanges favors for votes. In Lebanon it is estimated that twenty families have dominated the political arena since French colonial rule began after World War I.

The central difficulty with consociational forms of government is not necessarily that they are less democratic than conventional forms of liberal democracy but that decision making can be slow or can become immobilized. The larger the coalition, the more difficult it is to avoid stagnation and inefficiency.

Although the adversarial two-party system can be more decisive in policy making—largely because one party is in office at one time—animosity and suspicion may arise in parties excluded from government. The consociational model, even with its deficiencies, may create a climate more conducive to democracy. In the case of Lebanon, elections were held again in 1992 under a constitutional amendment that increased National Assembly membership and changed the division of seats from a 6:5 to 6:6 ratio—that is, an equal ratio—between Christians and Muslims. Of nine new seats available to Muslims in 1992, three were to be allocated for Shiʿites, and two each for the Sunni, Alawi, and Druze communities.

Lebanon's consociational electoral system may help ensure democracy and put an end to concerns about the participation of Islamic organizations in democratic exercises. Many fear the possible ulterior motives and ambitions of Islamic parties and doubt their true commitment to democracy. Consociationalism may offer a process of controlled democratic participation that will help preserve stability.

Economic Factors

The signing of the Declaration of Principles (the Oslo accord) between Israel and the Palestine Liberation Organization (PLO) on September 13, 1993, in which both parties agreed to end decades of confrontation and conflict and to recognize their mutual political rights, raised the prospect of peace in the Middle East. The agreement signed on May 4, 1994, finalizing plans for Israel to hand over the administration of Gaza and Jericho (the West Bank) to a Palestinian autonomous authority created an awareness in the region that economic advancement and cooperation may be the key to stability, peace, economic well-being, and political reform.

The Islamic Development Bank, the financial agency of the Islamic Conference Organization (the international body that coordinates and furthers the interests of Muslims), has called for an increased and more dynamic private sector and greater regional trade. The bank, however, does not connect economic change with political reform.

International experts agree that poor economic management and unpredictable governance are this region's chief liabilities. Influential bureaucracies, government control of production, a regulatory environment that stifles private initiative, public business sectors that are unresponsive to demand, and systems of governance that lack accountability and accessibility are seen as responsible for disappointing economic growth figures and high levels of unemployment. The World Bank, the German Development Agency, and Britain's Overseas Development Administration have all recommended that attention be focused on economic liberalization and cooperation between states in the region so that resources can be better utilized and greater efficiency and effectiveness can be promoted. Development of human resources through training, education, health care, and employment has been strongly emphasized. If these policies are implemented, pluralism can emerge in the form of economic, social, and labor groups that will be distanced from state structures.

In short, a civil society may develop in the Middle East that will demand political rights and freedoms. As the role of the state in the economy diminishes, businesses and organizations will be able to articulate their interests. Because competition is believed to be vital for the success of the private sector, a process of economic privatization, or *infitah* ("opening up"), was begun in Egypt. It is hoped that, through economic liberalization and increased trade and cooperation, greater bonds will develop between states in the region, hostilities will diminish, polities will stabilize, and political reform may be introduced.

Despite attempts at political reform in some states, it would be misleading to underestimate the formidable challenges confronting the successful introduction of liberal democracy in the area. Still, the ending of the cold war created a climate of opportunity for states in the Middle East to enjoy political autonomy. In a sense the onus is now on these states to become democratic. Some may follow a consociational pattern or reintroduce elections; others may remove bans on political parties and tinker with electoral processes; still others may resist reform altogether. The people of the region may make significantly greater demands on their governments. Increased participation is an important move toward democratization, but the next steps, if they are taken, must be in the direction of pluralism and accountability.

See also *Accountability of public officials; Egypt; Iran; Iraq; Islam; Israel; Jordan; Judaism; Kuwait; Lebanon; Marxism; Zionism.*

Heather Deegan

BIBLIOGRAPHY

Ayubi, Nazih. *Political Islam: Religion and Politics in the Arab World.* London and New York: Routledge, 1991.

Choueiri, Yousef M. *Islamic Fundamentalism.* Vol. 2 of *Twayne's Themes in Right-Wing Politics and Ideology.* London: Pinter; New York: Macmillan, 1990.

Deegan, Heather. *The Middle East and the Problems of Democracy.* Boulder, Colo.: Lynne Rienner; Buckingham: Open University Press, 1993.

Diamond, Larry, Juan J. Linz, and Seymour Martin Lipset, eds. *Democracy in Developing Countries: Asia.* Boulder, Colo.: Lynne Rienner, 1988; London: Adamantine Press, 1989.

Fischer, Stanley, Leonard J. Hausman, Anna D. Karasik, and Thomas C. Schelling. *Securing Peace in the Middle East: Project on Economic Transition.* Cambridge, Mass., and London: MIT Press, 1993.

Hudson, Michael C. *Arab Politics: The Search for Legitimacy.* New Haven and London: Yale University Press, 1977.

Lijphart, Arend. *Democracy in Plural Societies: A Comparative Exploration.* New Haven and London: Yale University Press, 1977.

Luciani, Giacomo. *The Arab State.* Berkeley: University of California Press, 1989; London: Routledge, 1990.

Owen, Roger. *State, Power and Politics in the Making of the Modern Middle East.* New York: Routledge, 1992.

Piscatori, James P., ed. *Islamic Fundamentalism and the Gulf Crisis: A Fundamentalism Project Report.* Chicago: University of Chicago Press, 1991.

Military rule and transition to democracy

Military rule has been endemic in many parts of the world, most prominently in Africa, Asia, and Latin America, where it has alternated with civilian administrations. The phenomenon is almost as old as recorded history. The accession of emperors in the Roman Empire was nearly always effected through an army coup d'état. As often happens in such cases, the ensuing regime was legitimated by its capacity to establish peace and organize an efficient administration. In time, however, the Roman Empire witnessed military intervention of an increasingly chaotic and illegitimate nature, associated with economic decadence and lack of success in international war. These experiences led to the coining of the term *praetorianism,* to describe the alternation of ephemeral governments based on the momentary support of the army units close to the head of state.

In the European successor states to the empire, continual warfare produced a close association between the upper classes and the armed forces. The violent politics of the time witnessed struggles between factions of armed citizens. It was difficult or impossible to differentiate either faction as "the military." In several Eastern societies, notably the Ottoman Empire, patterns similar to Roman praetorianism emerged. The civilian upper classes were only partially armed, and the military specialists were often former slaves and ethnic minorities, such as the Ottoman Janizaries, who as a consequence of their elevated status owed total loyalty to the authorities. The social isolation of the Janizaries from the majority of the civilian upper classes was a marked feature of the system. This social isolation is also a significant feature in modern cases, where the chasm is not so great. However, the fluidity of social interaction between the civilian and military sectors of the upper strata of society is still an important factor in the behavior of the armed forces.

Economic and social development in the West ushered in military professionalization, making for easier control by the civilian authorities. This control was first exerted by absolute monarchies and later by more constitutional systems of government. With the growth of industry and economic prosperity, the prospects for democracy increased, making military intervention and other forms of authoritarianism obsolete.

A notable exception was the wave of military coups in Brazil (1964), Argentina (1966 and 1976), Chile (1973), and Uruguay (1973)—some of the most advanced countries in Latin America. These coups were an attempt to establish new and permanent political systems, bent on intensifying the process of industrialization. Some scholars have suggested that unlike the economies of Western Europe, the United States, and Australasia, these dependent Latin American economies could not spare the resources to co-opt the working class into moderate channels, making a permanent or semipermanent repressive regime highly functional, if not inevitable, at that stage of economic development. In fact, what those countries experienced was a stop-and-go succession of military and civilian rule, with highly detrimental results in terms of both material growth and human rights. In East Asia, Hong Kong, Singapore, South Korea, and Taiwan made significant economic progress and yet escaped a similar sequence, perhaps because of their cultural traits and the support they received from the United States as bulwarks against a credible communist threat.

The Latin American Experience

In Latin America, Chile and Brazil provide two examples of the way in which what is perceived as a "popular menace" impinges on the dominant sectors, leading them to support an armed intervention. In Chile the challenge came from a highly organized working class that had extremely militant unions, with little bureaucratized leadership to act as a brake. Elements of pragmatism existed in the socialist and communist parties, but they were delegitimated by the success of the revolution in Cuba in 1959 and the May 1968 revolutionary upheavals among French students. During Salvador Allende's "Popular Unity" government (1970–1973), opposing party coalitions tended to reassert their militant ideology, trying to maintain the loyalty of their hard-core supporters rather than the sympathies of independents. Destabilization set in rather than the classic mechanism of competition for the center, which is typical of established democracies.

Even if the period of radicalization under President João Goulart (1961–1964) in Brazil bears some resemblance to that of the Popular Unity government in Chile,

the Brazilian situation was less predictable than the Chilean, because of the changing nature of its parties and the presence of a highly mobilized but mostly unorganized populace. The low degree of trade union or party organization made this popular mass less powerful than its Chilean counterparts, though more volatile and potentially more violent. The Brazilian masses hovered for a long time between a dormant state and various forms of populism, some quite conservative and others revolutionary. The exploitation of this revolutionary potential depended to a large extent on the work of elites.

The coup that took place in 1964 was a civilian, not just a military, reaction to Goulart's policies. The subsequent Brazilian military dictatorship was much more civilian oriented than were those in other parts of the continent. It never permanently closed the National Congress, though it purged it of some of its more radical elements.

Throughout its years in office, the Brazilian military regime held competitive (if tightly controlled) elections for the National Congress, which elected the president. There was press censorship and little freedom to organize for the opposition. The official candidates usually won a majority, because of the strong civilian support for the government among the middle and upper classes and the pliable nature of the rural and semirural electorate. This electorate tended to vote for local notables as long as it was not strongly stimulated by mobilizational tactics from above.

To understand the forces that led to a transition in Brazil, one must take into account the regime's success in implementing a program of industrialization and economic growth. The revolutionary menace, evident during Goulart's presidency, seemed to disappear. But a time bomb remains beneath the surface: a vast reservoir of rural poverty and a considerable number of poorly educated, unemployed youths who cannot be repressed forever.

An excessively harsh or protracted dictatorship may generate rebel forces and an overthrow not only of the regime but of the system of private property as well. Cuba and Nicaragua offer two examples. The details vary according to local circumstances and the degree of foreign interference. Hasty reform may not give time to either the regime or the dominant classes to create a credible successor structure. A hard-line faction within the dictatorship usually attempts to hold on. However, this tenacity increases the isolation of the military regime and makes a nonviolent, ordered transition more difficult.

In Nicaragua in the 1980s the Sandinistas attempted to

establish a variant of the Cuban regime, but they were forced by internal and external pressure to allow a competitive party system to function. They finally lost the elections to Violeta Chamorro in 1990. Chamorro was supported by most conservative forces and by disillusioned members of the early struggle against the Somoza regime, which was ended by the Sandinistas. The peculiarity of Nicaragua today is that the armed forces stand to the left of the bourgeois-oriented government, a totally unprecedented situation that may be repeated in Cuba if the regime there is forced to make concessions to pluralism and party competition.

Sometimes the armed forces become agents of radical transformation and thereby appropriate the ideological appeal of potential civilian revolutionaries. This is not an easy outcome because it antagonizes social groups that traditionally have been the armed forces' allies. The military in Peru came to power in 1968, with wide acclaim from the left and from progressives throughout the continent. The military takeover was planned not only to gain a freer hand against guerrilla forces but also to stop an almost certain Peruvian Aprista Party victory in the forthcoming presidential elections. The Apristas had long been unacceptable to the armed forces and to most of the upper classes, much more feared than the small communist party.

The military regime in Peru (1968–1980) introduced several radical reforms but, unlike the military regime in Brazil, it was incapable of generating a self-sustained process of growth. After an internal coup led by moderates in 1975, elections were promised in which all parties would participate freely. The Apristas were debilitated by the death of their leader, Víctor Raúl Haya de la Torre. The middle-of-the-road candidate, Fernando Belaúnde Terry, won the presidency in 1980, much to the relief of most people. Belaúnde was much more acceptable to the military and the upper classes than the Apristas. He paid a high price for the presidency; his party was practically dissolved at the end of his term in 1985. By then the prospect of an Aprista victory reappeared but did not generate excessive panic.

Another outcome for a military regime is exemplified by Colombia, where the transition to democracy took place as early as 1957. The dictatorship of Gen. Gustavo Rojas Pinilla (1953–1957) had been welcomed by many civilian sectors, which looked to him to stop the civil war between conservatives and liberals that had already cost some 300,000 lives. Inspired by Argentina's Juan Perón,

Rojas attempted to consolidate his rule by adopting a policy of social welfare and presidential largesse. His regime had some elements of the later Peruvian revolution, although the party system and the social structure in Colombia were quite different from those in Peru.

General Rojas attempted to form a following of his own, but in the process he antagonized the right and could not gather enough support elsewhere to remain in power. In 1957 he was toppled by a civil-military rebellion led by the two traditional parties, which had made a pact to share power between themselves after the return to constitutional rule. The resulting National Front involved an agreement for the two parties to alternate the presidency for sixteen years (later extended by another four) and to divide all major positions between themselves. General Rojas's attempt to form his own political party (the National Popular Alliance) to challenge this arrangement was unsuccessful.

In Argentina, which has the distinction of nurturing one of the stronger and more permanently rooted populist parties in the region, the transition was unique. Peronism was created in the mid-1940s by Juan Domingo Perón, one of the leaders of a military regime (1943–1946) who was bent on breaking the country's isolation from civil society through a policy of mass mobilization. The result, probably unintended by Perón himself, was the formation of a mass movement that came to be seen by the upper classes as a serious threat to their interests. Most of the time the dominant classes regarded Peronism as potentially more dangerous than the Marxist parties. The movement saw episodes of violence and radical antiestablishment confrontation, especially during its legal banishment (1955–1973). This led it to an alliance with guerrilla groups, partly originated from among its own rank and file, partly recruited from outside.

The principal purpose of the military regimes in Argentina since 1955 (1955–1958, 1962–1963, 1966–1973, and 1976–1983) was to topple or to forestall the installation of a Peronist government. Peronism, though threatening, was not revolutionary in intent, even if radical social change was the unintended result of its taking power after a violent struggle, especially in 1973. The complex nature of the highly organized Argentine pressure groups was the cause of the failure of all four military regimes to perpetuate themselves in a regular fashion, as occurred in Brazil and Chile. All four saw their prestige seriously eroded by internal coups. These were due not only to interservice rivalries and personal ambitions but also to the factions in the military that reflected the contentious nature of civil society with an intensity unparalleled in the other countries. The threat posed by the popular classes against the Argentine establishment was strong enough to alarm it but insufficient to dissuade aspiring politicians, both military and civilian, to use the masses as allies against their rivals. One such aspiring politician, Gen. Leopoldo Galtieri, resorted to the Falklands/Malvinas war as a way out of an already unbearable predicament.

The defeat of the Argentine dictatorship made it obvious that the military would not safeguard the interests of the dominant classes, even if in moments of crisis they might still be necessary. The Radical Civic Union victory of 1983 facilitated the transition to civilian rule. The Radical Civic Union, which was middle class and centrist, was less threatening to most sectors of Argentine society than Peronism—despite President Raúl Alfonsín's determination to make junta members pay for their misdeeds. It had become apparent that by themselves, without the support of any major social group, the military did not wield much power.

The Military in East European Transitions

In Eastern Europe the system had maintained itself since the end of World War II because of the Soviet presence. When that presence was withdrawn with the breakup of the Soviet Union, the national satellite governments could not resist internal opposition. They might conceivably have used the armed forces, but apart from the military's doubtful loyalty, the pressure from civil society was too great, especially when it was backed by groups in Western Europe and the United States that could exert economic pressure, support an eventual local uprising, or influence a faction of the armed forces.

Postwar Eastern Europe was no stranger to popular protests, several of which had been quelled only with Russian support. There was no way of telling, under conditions of crisis, what sectors of the establishment might join the rebels. Moreover, the disappearance of support seemed all the more likely because of the possibility for most of the upper classes to transform themselves into a private bourgeoisie, taking advantage of their positions of power and influence. There was no way out for the satellite governments but to yield to popular demands and thus avoid an armed uprising or coup.

In Poland the withdrawal of Soviet influence encouraged an increase in the role of the Polish army, which had never been happy under Soviet control. The potential rev-olutionary threat came not from the enlightened middle classes but from industrial workers, who held both resentments and traditional ideas. And, as in Latin America, such a threat brought in its wake military intervention aimed at repressing or co-opting it.

In Poland the legitimacy of the government was at a very low ebb. The Communist Party had been exceedingly small in prewar times, so it had to spread itself very thin to occupy the state apparatus. It was prepared to apply the usual doses of repression against dissidents, whether trade unionists or intellectuals. By October 1981, during an uncontrollable wave of strikes supported by the Catholic Church, the armed forces stepped in. Gen. Wojciech Jaruzelski, already prime minister since February, was made first secretary of the party, displacing the most intransigent faction from power.

Although he was an old party member, Jaruzelski was an independent actor, representing the more politically realist sectors of the armed forces and determined to integrate the more moderate members of the opposition into the system. In a smooth and bloodless coup, he removed the party hardliners in government, created a Military Council of National Salvation, and appointed some 2,000 officers as military commissars attached to enterprises and other major government institutions. One of Jaruzelski's first measures was to adopt martial law, but in the long run he followed a policy of normalization.

Once the process of liberalization had been set in motion, however, it could not easily be stopped. Partially free elections gave large majorities to the opposition, and power finally passed into the hands of Solidarity, a popular opposition movement. By this time, Solidarity had become a catch-all movement, but the moment of its victory was also the moment of its division. Polish politics has since evolved along multiparty channels, with a complex relationship between the presidency and the legislature and a role reserved for the armed forces, especially during the first stages of democratization. General Jaruzelski acted as guarantor of a smooth transition.

Romania took a different path. Nicolae Ceausescu's resistance to any significant reforms fostered a mood of popular revolt. To avert violence, the military stepped in and assassinated Ceausescu and his wife in 1989. Their example would be imprinted in the collective memory of Eastern Europe and throughout other communist or national popular systems. Romania's new government included a sector of the armed forces and the security apparatus as well as much of the old party leadership. It is capable of winning elections, though it does so by harassing the opposition and intimidating trade union groups. In Romania, in contrast with Poland, the Communist Party and its successor were able to don the mantle of nationalism and prevent the formation of a national popular opposition movement like Solidarity.

The transition in Russia did not involve the military directly, nor was there a sudden withdrawal of external support as in Eastern Europe. The military's inability to keep up in the arms race with the United States, and the high costs involved in the effort, eroded the economic capacity of the regime. Apparently, the armed forces played a conservative role in the process, with some of their numbers even trying to stage a coup in August 1991. It proved impossible to mobilize such a huge armed apparatus, which probably was also divided on the question of what policy to adopt in confronting the international situation. The possibility for bureaucrats and industrial managers to transform themselves into a bourgeoisie or remain as administrators of private businesses again helped to diminish resistance to change.

The Asian and African Patterns

In Asia two very different social systems—those of China and India—share a common trait: the relative passivity of the military regarding the political sphere. This situation in China today contrasts with the spread of warlordism during the 1920s and 1930s. Perhaps in this case it is totalitarianism that allows civilian control of the military. As the society becomes more liberal, however, and as leadership becomes less personalized and charismatic, the question of the future role of the army in internal politics is bound to arise. In India the lack of military intervention is more surprising, given the coup-ridden experience of other societies in Asia and Africa. Cultural traditions, especially the country's religious tradition, are often invoked by way of explanation. The extreme diversity of the country's regional composition—in terms of languages, ethnic groups, religions, and castes—makes elites realize that the absence of a strong and disciplined central government might lead to severe fragmentation. Economic and educational development is stimulating divisive tendencies, but the need to preserve national unity is paramount for the moment. Elites rely on the armed forces as an element of cohesion, without allowing the military to rule. Under the peaceful, or at least civilian, façade, however, a balance of terror is maintained between central and centrifugal forces.

In the Middle East and much of the Muslim world the armed forces took over after independence, replacing short-lived civilian regimes. A close association existed between the military and some modernizing intellectual and middle-class elites, who favored a strong regime capable of generating popular support while controlling the destabilizing features of mass mobilization. This type of system proved stable for decades but did not produce satisfactory economic results. As wider segments of the small-town and rural population were incorporated into the political system, discontent became widespread. In various countries this discontent has combined with a reaction from clerics and from traditional small traders and artisans, whose position was being eroded by forceful modernization. Thus the alliance between "the mosque and the bazaar" was established, and a powerful new force was generated, grounded in religious fundamentalism. This force has proved to be a good match for the military, although its main success has been in Iran, where it toppled a monarchical regime that was strongly bound to the armed forces but independent from them. In Algeria the Islamic Salvation Front has become a powerful challenger to the military and civilian modernizers who were trying to open up the system through free elections, though they soon backpedaled.

In Africa south of the Sahara, military rule is endemic. It does not usually have to cope with significant Muslim fundamentalism, although it does face serious ethnic cleavages. The armed forces espouse various ideologies. At the height of the cold war, those in Congo and Benin even embraced Marxism-Leninism.

The usual pattern is a succession of military and civilian regimes, the latter occasionally of a national popular variety, like Kwame Nkrumah's regime in Ghana. More solid civilian governments—like those of Léopold Sédar Senghor in Senegal, Jomo Kenyatta in Kenya, Félix Houphouët-Boigny in Côte d'Ivoire, or Julius Nyerere in Tanzania—have been quite stable. They have introduced elements of liberalization compatible with highly personalized rule and have kept the military under control. The more recent case of South Africa, which became a multiracial democracy in 1994 after centuries of white rule, represents a challenging case study for the role of the armed forces in a novel situation.

The Consolidation of a Democratic Polity

It is becoming increasingly obvious that although social structure and economic conditions may create a scenario for the consolidation of a democratic polity, they do not guarantee or preclude any result. Passages from military or civilian dictatorship to democracy can be violent or consensual. Violent transitions may involve a lost war, an armed popular uprising, or a coup by a military faction intent on opening up the system. Whether violent or more consensual processes are being planned, negotiation and coalition building between moderates in the government and the opposition often provide the basic strategy. The role of political parties becomes crucial.

A party system capable of channeling the tensions existing in any economically developed democracy needs at least two mechanisms to ensure that divergent views are expressed: first, a party with which the entrepreneurial classes will feel comfortable, assured that it will defend their points of view and occasionally win an election; and, second, a party linked to the trade unions and other popular sectors that can become a bulwark of social stability while retaining reformist aims and that is attuned to what is possible in terms of the current distribution of national and international power. In many cases the former can be called the "party of the right" and the latter, the "left" or "popular party." Regardless of the names chosen, the expression of the interests of both the entrepreneurs and the working class is necessary for the consolidation of democracy, once a certain level of economic and cultural development has been attained. In the absence of such channels of expression, the armed forces will remain a last resort for those momentarily out of power and will continue to interfere in the political process, with the support of some civilian faction.

See also *Civil-military relations; Europe, East Central; Populism.*

Torcuato S. Di Tella

BIBLIOGRAPHY

Chazan, Naomi, Robert Mortimer, John Ravenhill, and Donald Rothchild. *Politics and Society in Contemporary Africa.* Boulder, Colo.: Lynne Rienner, 1988.

Decalo, Samuel. *Coups and Army Rule in Africa: Motivations and Constraints.* New Haven and London: Yale University Press, 1975.

Diamond, Larry, Juan J. Linz, and Seymour Martin Lipset, eds. *Democracy in Developing Countries.* Vols. 2–3. Boulder, Colo.: Lynne Rienner; London: Adamantine Press, 1987–   . (Vol. 1 forthcoming).

Gutteridge, William. *Military Regimes in Africa.* London: Methuen, 1975.

Huntington, Samuel. *The Third Wave: Democratization in the Late Twentieth Century.* Norman: University of Oklahoma Press, 1991.

Linz, Juan, and Alfred Stepan, eds. *The Breakdown of Democratic Regimes.* Baltimore: Johns Hopkins University Press, 1978.

Lipset, Seymour Martin. *Political Man: The Social Bases of Politics.* Expanded and updated ed. Baltimore: Johns Hopkins University Press, 1981; Aldershot: Gower, 1983.

McClintock, Cynthia, and Abraham Lowenthal. *The Peruvian Experiment Reconsidered.* Princeton: Princeton University Press, 1983.

Abdel-Malek, Anouar. *Egypt: Military Society.* New York: Vintage Books, 1968.

O'Donnell, Guillermo, Philippe Schmitter, and Lawrence Whitehead, eds. *Transitions from Authoritarian Rule: Prospects for Democracy.* Baltimore: Johns Hopkins University Press, 1986.

Mill, John Stuart

English philosopher, economist, and political theorist. Mill (1806–1873) wrote frequently about democracy, and as a journalist and member of Parliament sought to promote democratic change over a period of five decades. He is widely recognized as a leading nineteenth-century spokesman for Anglo-American liberalism and remains one of the most important theorists of democracy in this political tradition.

Mill's initial views on democracy were adopted from those of the utilitarian legal philosopher Jeremy Bentham (1748–1832) and his father, James Mill (1773–1836), who was Bentham's leading disciple. At first Mill believed that universal suffrage, frequent elections, and the secret ballot would secure democracy. Agreeing with Bentham and his father, he recommended these devices as the democratic remedy for bad and corrupt government. Defective government was traced to a tendency among all who held public office to seek personal gain and pursue what Bentham called their sinister, or separate, interest. Mill followed Bentham in assuming that the sinister interest of the few would be countered by the universal interest of the entire populace and that corruption thus would be eliminated. In this perspective, democracy was useful, but it was not justified on the ground of natural rights or as being closer to a republican ideal than other forms of government or as promoting individualism and liberty.

After proselytizing in behalf of the utilitarian view for a decade, Mill developed doubts about it, influenced by the Saint-Simonians, who advocated a technocratic and socialist organization of society, and by the legal philosopher John Austin. Although he continued to approve of the creation of obstacles to corruption, Mill questioned whether democratically elected representatives had the special knowledge and highly developed intellectual capacities necessary for devising effective policies and making good laws. He likened politics to medicine. Patients know they have a problem, but they cannot devise the remedy. After consulting a physician, patients can decide whether to accept the recommendation of the medical experts, but they should not substitute their own remedy for that of the physician. Comparably, in politics, the democratic populace, exercising its sovereign power, can decide whether to adopt the policies recommended by political experts, but the people should not presume to diagnose problems or devise remedies. These responsibilities should be the function of the specially trained and qualified—the small group of truly knowledgeable persons Mill called the "instructed few."

The clearest analysis of the tension between the claims of the numerical majority and those of the best qualified intellectually is found in Mill's final statement on these matters. In *Considerations on Representative Government* (1861), Mill argued that democratically elected assemblies, because of the mediocre intellectual abilities of the representatives and of the public who elected them, are unfit to govern and legislate. He also warned that a democratically elected assembly would be responsive to the interests of a single class, thus creating class legislation. Yet, for all his criticism of the numerical majority, Mill remained convinced that popular control of government is essential. Therefore, wishing to combine representation of the majority, which would provide for popular control, with the knowledge and intelligence that would provide for skilled legislation and administration, he advocated that government draw in both the few and the many. Government was to be directed by the experienced and trained few while also being democratic.

In *Considerations on Representative Government*, Mill laid out the specific means required to bring about this combination. He proposed a commission of legislation, whose members were to be recruited from the intellectual elite; the commission's purpose was to devise laws but not to enact them. Because the commission's proposals were subject to approval by the democratically elected assembly, popular control was provided for. The same combination was to be promoted by universal suffrage, with extra votes for the well educated—a scheme Mill called "plural voting." He also proposed open voting (abandoning his earlier defense of the secret ballot), in order to subject voters to the social pressures arising from the fact that their votes were being scrutinized by their intellectual superiors. Most important to Mill, he recommended a plan of proportional representation in order to supplement majority representation with assured representation for minorities. He was enthusiastic about this device, considering it a way to give representation to the minority of those educated persons who formed the intellectual elite.

Mill was so convinced of the necessity of providing representation for knowledge and intelligence as well as for the numerical majority that he distinguished between true and false democracy. The true kind—he also called it "the pure idea of democracy"—included representation of the intellectual elite, and because it was government by this minority as well as by the majority, he regarded it as genuinely egalitarian. In contrast, the false kind was government of the whole people by a "mere majority." This form, moreover, was a government of privilege, not one of equality, for knowledge and intelligence, swamped by the majority, was denied a voice. False democracy was exemplified by government in the United States, where, Mill believed, the numerical majority ruled despotically.

Mill was uneasy about democratic majorities for another reason: their intolerance of those who do not comply with conventional norms of belief and conduct—that is, those with individuality. Such intolerance constitutes an infringement of individual liberty, a theme that occupied Mill in *On Liberty* (1859). He characterized the majority as a collective mediocrity consisting of persons who are passive, imitative, and slavish followers of custom. Using Alexis de Tocqueville's famous phrase "tyranny of the majority," he protested against attempts to impose conventional majoritarian tastes and norms of conduct on those with individuality.

Although an antimajoritarian theme runs through most of Mill's mature writings, his continued belief in the egalitarian ideal was evident in *The Subjection of Women* (1869). In this work he argued against claims that men are intellectually superior and deserving of patriarchal authority. His belief that majoritarian democracy should be tempered by provision for intellectually enlightened leadership has influenced much twentieth-century debate about democracy.

See also *Tocqueville, Alexis de; Utilitarianism.*

Joseph Hamburger

BIBLIOGRAPHY

Anschutz, R. P. *The Philosophy of J. S. Mill.* Oxford: Oxford University Press, 1953.
Burns, J. H. "J. S. Mill and Democracy, 1829–61." In *Mill: A Collection of Critical Essays,* edited by J. B. Schneewind. Garden City, N.Y.: Anchor Books, 1968.
Robson, John M. *The Improvement of Mankind: The Social and Political Thought of John Stuart Mill.* Toronto: University of Toronto Press, 1968.
Stephen, Leslie. *John Stuart Mill.* Vol. 3 of *The English Utilitarians.* London: Duckworth, 1900.

Monarchy, Constitutional

Constitutional monarchy is government under a constitutional monarch, a hereditary head of state with ceremonial responsibility and sometimes with a few political functions limited by law. Until the twentieth century the great majority of modern states were monarchies but not democracies. By the early 1990s the majority of modern states were democracies and republics headed by a ceremonial president politically subordinate to the prime minister and the parliament.

Origins of Constitutional Monarchy

The idea of kingship is as old as recorded history; its origins are lost in myths. Early kings were often heroic leaders in battle, inspiring confidence as well as fear in their subjects. They could claim office by popular acclaim, by choice of elders, or by force. The role of heredity in determining who was to be king came much later. This practice was adopted to end disputes and intrigues about leadership. In many countries only a male could inherit the monarchy, and the throne would pass to a more distant relative if a king had only daughters or was childless. In England, however, a woman could inherit the throne, and several did: Elizabeth I (ruled 1558–1603), Victoria (reigned 1837–1901), and Elizabeth II (reigned 1952–).

The development of constitutional monarchy followed from the creation of the modern state—that is, a central authority governing a well-defined territory by the rule of law. The feudal systems of the Middle Ages did not meet this standard because much power was in the hands of barons and other territorial lords. The first modern states centralized authority in an absolute monarchy. France under Louis XIV (ruled 1643–1715) is an early example of an absolute monarchy. Frederick the Great of Prussia (ruled 1740–1786) developed the central institutions of an absolute monarchy. Absolute monarchies were intended to maintain order and build up the military strength and wealth of the state. They were also designed to defend the state against the "excesses" of democracy, which since the time of Athens in the fifth century B.C. had been regarded as equivalent to mob rule.

By the nineteenth century the idea of constitutional monarchy was so taken for granted in Europe that when a new country was established it would import a king if it did not have a ruling family at hand. For example, when Italy achieved unification in 1861, the house of Savoy provided the royal family. Norway adopted a Danish prince as its first king on becoming fully independent in 1905. The Greeks declared independence from rule by the Ottoman Turks in 1821, and independence was guaranteed by their allies. In 1833 a new "Greek" king was imported from Bavaria; he was succeeded in 1862 by a Danish prince.

At the outbreak of World War I in 1914 the great majority of European states were monarchies; only France, Portugal, and Switzerland were republics. Furthermore, leading monarchies were usually not nation-states but multinational empires created by intermarriage and inheritance among royal families and sometimes by conquest. For example, England and Scotland were joined in 1603, when

Elizabeth I of England died unmarried and childless and the nearest relative to inherit the crown was the king of Scotland. He reigned as James VI in Scotland and as James I in England until his death in 1625. The two kingdoms, however, were governed as separate countries until 1707, when an act of union created a single Parliament of Great Britain in London. The Austro-Hungarian Empire consisted of territories of the Hapsburgs, a royal family based in Vienna. The subjects of this empire had no common language or shared national identity; the only thing they had in common was their status as subjects of the same monarch.

Response to the Challenge of Democracy

Because constitutional monarchy originated in absolutism, nineteenth-century democrats usually regarded royalty as enemies. They also regarded as enemies the aristocrats, court servants, and state officials who advised or depended upon royalty. The French Revolution of 1789 took as its motto "liberty, equality, and fraternity." Its leaders deposed Louis XVI and proclaimed a republic. In 1793 the king was executed. Monarchs willing to grant popular demands, however, could do much to facilitate the introduction of democracy. They could endorse change and influence potential opponents, such as aristocrats, the church, and civil servants, to do the same. In practice, monarchies were altered in three very different ways: through evolution, revolution, and the dissolution of empire.

Seven European states preserved their monarchies through an evolutionary process in which royalty withdrew from politics: the United Kingdom, Sweden, Norway, Denmark, Belgium, the Netherlands, and Luxembourg. The withdrawal typically occurred as the result of pressures from aristocrats and notables to place restraints on an absolute monarch.

This was the case in seventeenth-century England when Parliament, then elected by only a small percentage of English males, successfully revolted against the Crown and beheaded Charles I. A king was restored later but with weaker powers than before. By the end of the eighteenth century Parliament had established its domination of the king, who now had to act on the advice of ministers. Parliament could vote confidence (or lack of confidence) in the ministers and also had the power to refuse the annual appropriation of money to run the government if the monarch refused to act as it advised. The movement for democracy in Great Britain that took place in the nineteenth century was thus a struggle between representatives of people seeking the right to vote and protectors of a Parliament elected by a small minority of the population. It was not a struggle between the monarch and the people, and Queen Victoria thus avoided being caught up in the politics of democratization.

As the example of Great Britain shows, a monarch who was not an absolute ruler was better able to negotiate a withdrawal from politics. In the nineteenth century such monarchs shared power with the nobility, landed interests, the church, and related groups in predemocratic parliaments. They also shared power with expert advisers and civil servants who had technical knowledge and interests that they lacked. The claims of democrats often involved a loss of power by notables, while the monarch could choose to remain above the conflict.

Sweden also preserved its monarchy through an evolutionary process. Here the process involved claims to power from popular representatives and also from estates of the realm whose authority rested on preindustrial and predemocratic practices. The Swedish king did not resist change and did not allow opponents of change to use the monarchy as a symbol of resistance. Instead, he endorsed compromises negotiated between conservative and democratic leaders; these agreements effectively turned the monarch into a symbolic head of state.

Japan is a distinctive case. The Japanese emperor maintained his position without interruption during an abrupt shift from a military dictatorship to democracy following Japan's defeat in World War II. Emperor Hirohito ascended the throne in 1926 as a monarch with very limited influence on government, although the office had great symbolic value. The country's involvement in war was the responsibility of a military government. Therefore, the emperor was allowed to remain as a symbol of national unity. Allied occupation forces ensured, however, that the 1947 Japanese constitution was democratic in form and that free and competitive elections then institutionalized democracy in practice.

Another distinctive case is that of Thailand. The institution of a traditional and absolute monarchy played a critical role in keeping Thailand free from Western colonial domination. It was the only country in South Asia and Southeast Asia that remained independent. In 1937, however, a military coup, inspired in part by students who had returned from Great Britain, forced the king to become a constitutional monarch. Since then the Thai kings have played a positive role in liberalizing Thai politics and in encouraging democratic tendencies.

In Europe the abrupt removal of the monarchy by revolution or military defeat did not guarantee the introduction of democracy. Most East European states created in the aftermath of World War I were republics. Of these, only Czechoslovakia remained a democracy until it was occupied by the armies of Adolf Hitler in 1939. The process of creating republics in Eastern Europe was completed by Soviet occupation at the end of World War II. The Soviets turned undemocratic monarchies, such as Bulgaria, Romania, and Yugoslavia, into republics. In most post-communist societies of the early 1990s there was no royal family that could claim to inherit the throne and no significant popular demand for the creation of a monarchy.

An individual monarch can momentarily gain influence through involvement in politics, but political involvement creates opponents as well as allies. By taking sides in a major political conflict, a reigning monarch puts the future of monarchy at risk. When political fortunes change, an individual monarch may be forced to abdicate by the new government, or the monarchy itself may be abolished. Leopold III of Belgium chose to remain in the country when it was conquered by Hitler's army in 1940. His decision had important political consequences. In 1950 a referendum on the king resulted in 58 percent in favor of his remaining on the throne and 42 percent against. The country was so divided in its views of the king's wartime behavior that he was forced to abdicate in favor of his son, Baudouin. In Italy, Victor Emmanuel III was head of state for two decades of the fascist regime of Benito Mussolini. In 1946 a referendum in Italy voted to abolish the monarchy and create a democratic republic. Of the last six Greek sovereigns, one was assassinated and three were exiled because of their involvement in national politics. Greece became a republic in 1974.

The example of France demonstrates that republican revolutions can fail, leading to the return of a dictator or monarch. After the revolution of 1789 the country was ruled successively by a first consul (Napoleon Bonaparte), an emperor (Napoleon, crowned in 1804), a king, a republican head of state, and another Napoleon as president and emperor (Napoleon III). France has been a republic since 1871.

Spain is unique among contemporary European states in promoting democracy through the restoration of a monarchy in 1975. The circumstances were exceptional. The Spanish civil war of 1936 was begun by a military revolt under General Francisco Franco against the government of a republic. Franco's side won, and he became chief of state in a regime that was nominally a monarchy but lacked a king. The grandson of the last Spanish king was groomed to become a symbolic head of state and did so after Franco's death in 1975. This step was meant to calm conservative antidemocrats, who feared that democracy would lead to communism. Former republicans accepted the monarchy as a bulwark against the return of civil war. When colonels attempted a military coup in the name of the king in 1981, their efforts collapsed after being publicly repudiated by King Juan Carlos.

The breakup of empires in the wake of World War I brought an end to many monarchies. The empire of the Russian czar was replaced by a republican state, the Union of Soviet Socialist Republics. The Communist Party controlled the state, using the doctrines of Marxism-Leninism as the unifying force. The Austro-Hungarian Empire was replaced by a series of nation-states that were mostly republican in form. At the moment of military defeat in 1918 the German kaiser resigned the throne, and Germany became a republic based on a constitution prepared at Weimar. The Ottoman Empire was ruled by a sultan. The Young Turks, who sought to create an independent and modern Turkish nation-state, succeeded in abolishing the sultanate in 1922.

The breakup of empires outside Europe commenced in the Western Hemisphere with the revolt of colonies against the British, Spanish, and Portuguese crowns. Article I of the U.S. Constitution contains an explicit prohibition against the grant of titles of nobility. In the nineteenth century a few Latin American countries briefly had kings imported from or imposed by Europe, but they were soon deposed. Latin American countries have consistently been republics, whether democratic or nondemocratic.

The British Empire continued until after World War II, with the British monarch as its nominal head. The colonies were governed under constitutions subject to the rule of law as determined by the British Parliament. Successive kings and queens of England were also emperors of India and heads of state in old dominions, such as Australia and Canada. Anticolonial movements after 1945 demanded and received independence, with the result that the former British Empire became a commonwealth—a

Queen Elizabeth II, accompanied by the Duke of Edinburgh, reads her government's statement during the opening of Parliament in the House of Lords. In Britain's constitutional monarchy the queen is head of state while the prime minister is head of government.

free association of independent states, many of them republics. The titular head of the commonwealth is Elizabeth II of England, but she holds this symbolic post by decision of the commonwealth and not by heredity.

A comparative analysis of the role of monarchies by Richard Rose and Dennis Kavanagh supports two major conclusions. First, the survival of a monarchy depends upon the readiness of the reigning family to withdraw from a politically active role. Second, the repudiation of a monarchy results from the involvement of the monarchy in politics.

Monarchy in Contemporary Democracy

In democratic political systems with a hereditary monarch, the primary role of the head of state is nonpolitical.

Formally, a monarch may be asked to choose the head of government, and in Britain the government is technically referred to as Her Majesty's government. Elected politicians, however, have taken pains to specify procedures that reduce the discretion of the head of state, whether a monarch or a figurehead president. These procedures also maximize the room for the maneuvering of party leaders after a general election. In Britain, one party normally wins a majority of seats in the House of Commons and thus gains the right to form a government. In many European countries no party wins a majority of seats, and a coalition is necessary. In the Netherlands the monarch appoints an elder politician to identify which politician is to be given the first opportunity to form a coalition government. In republican Greece the law prescribes an automatic procedure in which the leader of the party with the largest number of seats in the parliament is the first choice to form a coalition.

By virtue of many years in office, a monarch can claim to be experienced in the ways of government. Elizabeth II has been in office far longer than any of the cabinet ministers now governing Great Britain, and she has seen the occupant of the prime minister's office change nine times since her coronation. The queen is kept informed of major public business, especially foreign affairs, and normally meets with the prime minister once a week to discuss affairs of state. This is an opportunity for the prime minister to think aloud in the presence of a person who is not a competitor for that office. A monarch may focus attention on a problem through comments or questions. In Great Britain any attempt by a queen or king to give unwanted counsel can be rejected by a popularly elected prime minister, and any public hint of royal influence would risk the political neutrality of the monarchy.

The primary function of a monarchy in a democracy is symbolic: the monarch represents the unity of the country. This is an easy task in Scandinavian countries, where societies are extremely homogeneous. In Northern Ireland, however, there is a longstanding conflict about whether the country should be united with Great Britain or with the Republic of Ireland. In Northern Ireland the British crown represents one party to a conflict between nationalists, just as the Irish flag represents another party. The existence of a president of the Republic of Ireland symbolizes that country's rejection of everything British, including its monarch.

Members of a royal family have celebrity status. In earlier times they were treated respectfully, even reverently, by the press, whatever their behavior in private life. That situation changed with the advent of television. The increase in celebrity can make some members more popular, but it also creates far more embarrassment when members of a royal family lose their temper, become involved in extramarital affairs, or associate with people of dubious habits or morals.

Traditional royal pomp, financed by public funds, is under challenge in an era in which very few people inherit a job or enough wealth to live on all their lives. This is the case especially when the royal income is deemed to come from public funds. Scandinavian monarchs responded to the rise in egalitarianism by abandoning many of the ancient symbols of authority and wealth. They have fre-

quently been described as "bicycling" monarchs, because they do not go everywhere in a limousine. By contrast, the British queen retains a lifestyle from an earlier, aristocratic era, which has attracted criticism from members of Parliament and the media.

As long as the monarch remains above party politics, his or her position is normally unchallenged. Still, the decision whether to make the monarchy controversial rests with the parties. A republican pressure group can stir up controversy about the monarchy. This has occurred in Australia, where Labor leaders decry having an English queen as their nominal head of state.

Any effort to abolish a monarchy faces problems, for every country requires a head of state. France and the United States are unique among democracies in having a head of state who is also the effective head of government. Everywhere else the role of the head of state is symbolic, whether it is filled by a hereditary monarch or by an elder politician holding the ceremonial office of president. The fact that a monarch holds office by virtue of birth may be inconsistent with democratic norms, but it offers one consolation to the country's prime minister: the head of state is in no position to challenge decisions taken by a national leader who can claim the legitimacy of popular election.

See also *Leadership; Revolutions.* In Documents section, see *Constitution of the United States (1787); Constitution of Japan (1947).*

Richard Rose

BIBLIOGRAPHY

Bogdanor, Vernon, ed. *Coalition Government in Western Europe.* London: Heinemann, 1983.

———. *Constitutions in Democratic Politics.* Aldershot: Gower, 1988.

da Graca, John V. *Heads of State and Government.* London: Macmillan, 1985.

Lipset, Seymour Martin. *Political Man: The Social Bases of Politics.* Expanded and updated ed. Baltimore: Johns Hopkins University Press, 1981; Aldershot: Gower, 1983.

Rose, Richard, and Dennis Kavanagh. "The Monarchy in Contemporary Political Culture." *Comparative Politics* 8 (1976): 548–576.

Monnet, Jean

French diplomat and civil servant, who was the principal founder and intellectual author of the movement toward European integration after World War II. Monnet

Jean Monnet

(1888–1979) was the best known and most successful of a new type of actor that emerged in European democracies during the twentieth century: the technocrat. Although he was never elected to a single office during his entire career, he profoundly influenced public policy in France and in Europe as a whole. Ironically, given the number of expert positions he occupied, he left school at sixteen, never having attended either university or one of the French *Grandes Ecoles*.

Monnet was born in southwest France to a family of cognac producers. At an early age, he traveled to Great Britain as a commercial representative. During World War I, he lived in London and participated in the first large-scale effort at international functional cooperation: the Inter-Allied Maritime Commission. After the hostilities ended in 1918, he became the deputy secretary general of the League of Nations, the first organization for global security.

In 1939, when World War II was imminent, Monnet moved to Great Britain to lead the effort at Franco-British logistical coordination. He was also the inspiration behind the abortive effort in June 1940 to federate the two countries after France was defeated by Germany.

During the war years Monnet lived in Washington, D.C., where he joined the British purchasing mission and became a close associate of President Franklin D. Roosevelt and of many officials in Roosevelt's New Deal administration. After the war, he led the newly created French Planning Commission (1945–1955) and played a leading role in the country's industrial recovery.

Monnet's unusually cosmopolitan career was dominated by international war and its consequences. He turned his extensive personal contacts with leading European and American politicians to an effort to remove all possibility of future conflict between France and Germany. After the French parliament rejected a proposed European Defense Community in 1952, Monnet developed a novel "functionalist" approach to regional integration (the "Monnet method"). By focusing narrowly on a key strategic industry, coal and steel, by placing it under an organization with limited supranational authority, and by persuading France and Germany, along with Belgium, Luxembourg, the Netherlands, and Italy, to join, Monnet succeeded in making war virtually impossible in Western Europe. Monnet served as the first president of the High Authority of the European Coal and Steel Community (1952–1955), the antecedent of the European Union.

After resigning that position, Monnet founded a new type of political organization, the Action Committee for the United States of Europe, which brought together a select group of top-level civil servants from member countries. Thanks to its activities, and to Monnet's personal contacts with leading politicians, businesspeople, and trade union officials, the committee played an important role in expanding the integration effort into the fields of atomic energy (the European Atomic Energy Community, or Euratom) and trade liberalization (the European Economic Community).

Monnet was never a politician publicly accountable to the citizenry, nor did he ever appeal for mass support for his many policy initiatives. Nevertheless, his success in working behind the scenes with a vast transatlantic network of elected politicians and selected administrators profoundly influenced postwar democracy in Western Europe.

See also *European Union; League of Nations.*

Philippe C. Schmitter

BIBLIOGRAPHY

Duchene, François. *Jean Monnet: The First Statesman of Interdependence.* New York: Norton: 1994.
Monnet, Jean. *Memoirs.* New York: Doubleday, 1978.

Montenegro

See *Europe, East Central*

Montesquieu

Montesquieu, Charles-Louis de Secondat, Baron de

French political theorist who formulated the idea of separation of powers. Charles-Louis de Secondat, baron de La Brède et de Montesquieu (1689–1755), was educated in the law at the University of Bordeaux. After inheriting his uncle's estate in 1716, he had sufficient wealth and leisure to study Roman law and pursue research in the natural sciences. He traveled extensively in Europe and spent time in England before settling down to serious writing.

Montesquieu's paramount work is *The Spirit of the Laws* (1748). Like his seventeenth-century predecessors Thomas Hobbes and John Locke, Montesquieu was dissatisfied with the ineffectiveness of a classical political science centered on the idea of a perfect regime. Examining various political arrangements and historical conditions from the perspective of modern science, he recommended principles that would ensure greater justice than those of previous regimes.

The Spirit of the Laws made three important arguments. First, Montesquieu replaced the classic taxonomy of regimes—monarchy, aristocracy, and democracy—with his own classification—republic (democratic or aristocratic), monarchy, and despotism. Each regime has a fundamental principle: virtue, honor, and fear, respectively. A prudent legislator will rule in such a way as to maintain and strengthen the regime's distinctive principle. The principle will determine whether certain tools of governance are appropriate. In a republic, for example, where the principle is virtue, censorship is necessary because attention must be paid to the practices subverting virtue. In monarchies, though, where honor acts as a omnipresent censor, there is no need for additional censors.

Montesquieu's second major argument was that moderate governments should divide governing authority among three branches: executive, legislative, and judicial. Only when each of these powers is held by independent bodies, each exercising authority in its own area of competence, and preferably each representing a different social group, can liberty thrive. The idea of separating powers also allowed for a diversity of classes. The great, Montesquieu argued, by virtue of their honor, wealth, or birth, should have the power to check the enterprises of the people as the people should have the power to check the great. Equally important for the balance of power are intermediary institutions—the church, local and provincial parliaments and courts, professional associations and guilds—as well as political parties. Freedom of expression promotes a healthy plurality that also serves to check power. The balance of power ensures security as well as liberty. For example, the effect of mutual correction and moderation separate states can have on one another will play a major role in ensuring their collective security.

Finally, Montesquieu argued that laws alone do not determine how individuals act or whether legislation will be successful. In each society a general spirit is operating. This inner logic of human conduct is formed by religion, laws, customs, manners, economics, and geography and climate. Effective rulers must understand the causes that form national character. The general spirit is one more variable rulers must account for in attempting to foster freedom and security. It requires that they exercise a Machiavellian prudence, sometimes adapting to the general spirit, other times resisting that spirit. Religion, for example, must be judiciously deployed by rulers for its political effects.

Montesquieu also considered which regime was best able to ensure the security and freedom of its members and the possibility for free self-government. Monarchy, he believed, was best suited to modern Europe and most capable of governing human passions. Moreover, it granted individuals the most freedom. Yet the honor system in a monarchy, insofar as it is based on preferment and social distinction, is unstable, for it is subject to the irregularity of capricious pride. In addition, in a monarchy political participation and self-rule are not open to all citizens. Democracy satisfies the need for the people to hold sovereign power in making law, and its citizens are the least corruptible. But, unless tempered, the spirit of equality will grow beyond the desire of equal protection before the law to the people's demand for a right to manage all political offices. Liberty can degenerate to license. The best choice is a mixed government, in which some guide and command, but the people have the power to choose and recall them.

English society, to Montesquieu, was a model of a mixed government. It effectively converted private interest to public good and ensured peace and natural humanity; in short, it was a modern commercial republic. Montesquieu praised the English system because he saw it as an alternative to the virtuous republics of antiquity, whose ideals he considered to be a threat to security and free-

dom. English commercial society and its monarch were constrained by a balance of powers. Humanity and tolerance prevented the harshness associated with regimes based on virtue. The moderation of the English system inclined people to think of the common good. Montesquieu saw the dangers of a society based on selfish passions from which avarice and ambition could easily grow. But the strength of the English system was that its institutions were the most effective in guaranteeing political liberty and civic virtue because they moderated the most powerful passions of the people. Social and political plurality were used to preserve liberty.

Moreover, in England education was used to moderate private desire and to produce love of country and of the law. Montesquieu believed that the political virtue education fostered could evolve only if the regime could prevent excesses of equality and inequality. Sumptuary laws regulating luxury, as well as controls on property accumulation and the judicious use of taxation, were necessary to prevent the corruption of morals. Only if these conditions were met would the spirit of commerce produce frugality, tranquility, and self-rule. The English commercial republic would be a regime in which people would experience freedom as security from fear.

Montesquieu sharply distinguished between a state based on security and a despotism based on fear. In a despotism, people's lives are like those of beasts. Life under despotism is one of isolation, timidity, fear of violence, blind obedience, ignorance, suspicion, and lack of spirit. Montesquieu also warned that the predominance of these characteristics, as well as excess equality, can tip a free, self-governing society toward despotism. The moderate regime Montesquieu favored had some potent tendencies inclining toward its corruption: a mediocrity of talents, the prevalence of destabilizing passions, unrelenting mobility, and inconstancy. But he still preferred it to virtuous republics whose ardor was usually irascible, and he believed its weaknesses could be counteracted by prudent rulers.

Montesquieu's work has particular significance for liberal democracies, providing lessons that were not lost on the American Founders and Alexis de Tocqueville. More than anything, Montesquieu taught the need for moderation, especially in regimes where the people are self-governing.

See also *Censorship; Nationalism; Republics, Commercial; Separation of powers; Virtue, Civic.*

Peter C. Emberley

BIBLIOGRAPHY

Althusser, Louis. *Politics and History: Montesquieu, Rousseau, Hegel, and Marx.* Translated by Ben Brewster. London: NLB, 1972.

Cohler, Anne M. *Montesquieu's Comparative Politics and the Spirit of American Constitutionalism.* Lawrence: University Press of Kansas, 1988.

Destutt de Tracy, Antoine-Louise-Claude, Comte. *Commentary and Review of Montesquieu's Spirit of the Laws.* Translated by Thomas Jefferson. Philadelphia: Burt Franklin, 1969.

Durkheim, Emile. *Montesquieu and Rousseau: Forerunners of Sociology.* Ann Arbor: University of Michigan Press, 1965.

Hulliung, Mark. *Montesquieu and the Old Regime.* Berkeley: University of California Press, 1976.

Pangle, Thomas L. *Montesquieu's Philosophy of Liberalism: A Commentary on The Spirit of the Laws.* Chicago: University of Chicago Press, 1973.

Richter, Melvin. *The Political Theory of Montesquieu.* Cambridge: Cambridge University Press, 1977.

Waddicor, Mark. *Montesquieu and the Philosophy of Natural Law.* The Hague: M. Nijhoff, 1970.

Morocco

A constitutional monarchy situated on the northwest coast of Africa, where the effective political authority remains in the hands of a monarch. King Hassan II combines political power with authority derived from religion. (He is known as the supreme religious ruler or "commander of the faithful.") The monarch is skilled at playing off competing elites, manipulating electoral politics to ensure that only representatives of political parties loyal to the throne serve in government, and, after abortive military coups in 1971 and 1972, maintaining tight control of the military. Periodically, the king uses repression and imprisonment to silence critics.

The centrality of the monarchy in politics reflects Morocco's unique position at the crossroads between the West, Middle East, and Subsaharan Africa. From its position in the northwest corner of Africa, Morocco is separated from Europe only by the Straits of Gibraltar. Historically, Morocco was settled by Berbers, colonized by Rome, and conquered by Arabs, before being incorporated as an autonomous province of the Ottoman Empire in the early nineteenth century. King Hassan II uses these linkages to play a key role in international relations among Western, Middle Eastern, and African countries, while seeking increased economic integration with the European Union.

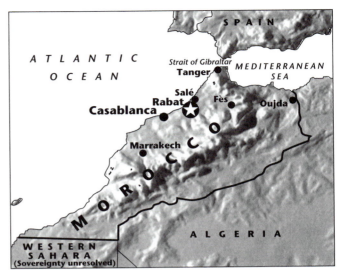

Economically, Morocco relies heavily on remittances from workers abroad, including more than a million in Europe, and/or Western trade and tourism.

Morocco was partitioned by France and Spain into formal protectorates in 1912, commencing forty-four years of colonial rule. But political traditions were preserved throughout the colonial era, and the local monarchy reemerged after independence in 1956. Hassan's father, who assumed the title of King Mohammed V in 1957, reigned until his death in 1961.

After Spain withdrew from the Western Sahara in the mid-1970s, Morocco fought a nationalist movement, popularly known as the Polisario Front, for control of the territory. Although the Polisario Front won recognition from more than sixty nation-states as the Saharan Arab Democratic Republic, by the mid-1980s Morocco had gained effective control over most of the territory. Morocco's campaign to annex the Western Sahara was costly (military costs ran $1 billion annually), but it enjoyed widespread popularity at home. The king repeatedly used this support and the international stalemate to his political advantage. For example, in the 1970s, when the monarchy faced social and labor unrest, it used the idea of a "Sahara consensus" to postpone parliamentary elections until 1977. When parliamentary elections were postponed again in 1989, the need to allow King Hassan to settle the Sahara conflict was cited.

The king also uses his constitutional authority to maintain power. The first constitution, ratified in a national referendum in 1962, codified the constitutional monarchy, guaranteed personal and political freedoms, and recognized Islam as the official state religion. Although opposition leaders participated in the first postindependence government, King Hassan II, after assuming the throne in 1961, moved quickly to consolidate his power. In 1962, while removing critical opposition party members from government, he outlawed single-party rule in Morocco. He instituted a state of emergency and direct rule in 1965, permitting normal political activities to resume only gradually in the late 1960s. Throughout the 1970s no major political parties participated in the government.

The current constitution was approved in a national referendum in 1970 over the objections of the major political parties, trade unions, and student organizations. This constitution reaffirmed the king's role as chief executive, the supreme civil and religious authority, and commander in chief of the armed forces. The king appoints all important officials, including the prime minister and cabinet, the governors of the forty-three provinces (including four in the Western Sahara), and the two urban prefectures of Casablanca and Rabat-Salé. The king also dominates the legislative process in the unicameral (one-chamber) legislature, the Chamber of Representatives, and retains broad powers, including the power to amend the constitution, to pass laws subject to ratification in national referendums, and to declare a state of emergency during which the king rules by decree.

The majority of representatives elected to the parliament in 1977 and 1984 represented center-right parties willing to support strong monarchical rule. In June 1993, after acrimonious local elections and voter registration campaigns, parliamentary elections were held once again. Representatives from center-right parties again won a slight majority. The opposition made its strongest showing to date, winning ninety-nine seats compared with eighty seats in the 1984 elections. Two socialist opposition parties, the Socialist Union of Popular Forces and the Independence Party, together hold the largest bloc of seats in the parliament. These parties are expected to use their increased electoral strength to press for improvements in the country's observance of human rights and, eventually perhaps, to participate in the government after a thirty-year absence. The elections also were notable in that the victorious candidates included the first two women to serve in the parliament.

In the early 1990s the king promised a series of political changes that he claimed would make Morocco the boldest democratic experiment in the Arab world. He sponsored a series of legislative changes, including the requirement that the government submit its program to a vote by the Chamber of Representatives and seek legislative approvals to extend states of emergency beyond the first thirty days. The king also sponsored constitutional changes, including amendments to enhance basic political rights and the creation of a constitutional council to review new laws. These constitutional changes were approved in a national referendum in 1992. The official results, however, raised doubts about the integrity of the process: 99.96 percent of all voters, including 100 percent of all voters in the main cities and in three of the Western Sahara provinces, approved the king's proposals.

Critics of recent reforms, including leaders of the main opposition political parties, remain skeptical about whether top-down multiparty system reforms can lead to meaningful democracy. Some observers predict major political changes after Crown Prince Sidi Mohammed, who is reported to favor a more ceremonial role for the monarchy, assumes the throne. But the status quo is also threatened by the fundamental economic, social, and political trends evident throughout North Africa today: high unemployment in an increasingly youthful population (two-thirds of Moroccans are under twenty-five), declining standards of living for laborers, growing awareness of elite corruption and mismanagement, an increasing gap between the wealthy urban elite and the three-quarters of Moroccans who still earn their living by farming, and rising expectations fueled by comparisons with European living standards. These trends will continue to foster demands for political freedoms and support for Islamic fundamentalism.

See also *Colonialism; Islam.*

Helen E. Purkitt

BIBLIOGRAPHY

Amin, Samir. *The Maghreb in the Modern World.* Harmondsworth, England: Penguin Books, 1971.

Hodges, Tony. *Western Sahara: The Roots of a Desert War.* London: Croom Helm, 1983.

"Morocco." In *The Middle East and North Africa.* 39th ed. London: Europa Publications, 1993.

Munson, Henry, Jr. "Morocco's Fundamentalists." *Government and Opposition* 26 (summer 1991): 331–344.

Nelson, Harold D. *Morocco: A Country Study.* Washington, D.C.: Library of Congress, 1986.

Zartman, I. William, ed. *The Political Economy of Morocco.* New York: Praeger, 1987.

———, and William Mark Habeeb, eds. *Polity and Society in Contemporary North Africa.* Boulder, Colo.: Westview Press, 1993.

Mosca, Gaetano

Italian political scientist and politician identified with elite theory. Born in Sicily and educated as a lawyer, Mosca (1858–1941) later taught constitutional and administrative law at the Universities of Turin and Rome. During the critical years surrounding World War I, he was a member of the Chamber of Deputies and then a senator. Mosca thus wrote as an insider in Italian politics and as a close observer of the downfall of Italian democracy during the 1920s.

His ground-breaking *Elementi di scienza politica* (1896, rev. ed. 1923), translated as *The Ruling Class* (1939), emphasized the ability of small minorities to dominate large majorities in political matters. Through electoral collusion, policy trade-offs, and manipulation of some "political formula" or collective illusion, such as the idea of popular sovereignty, a political class consisting of those who wield government power perpetuates itself. In his later writing Mosca situated the political class in a wider ruling class consisting of all economic, religious, intellectual, technological, and military minorities or elites. He contended that these disproportionately powerful minorities are unavoidable in modern societies and that they limit democratic possibilities.

Mosca nevertheless developed a concept of democracy that anticipated the work of Joseph Schumpeter and other exponents of democratic elite theory. He believed that there must be an equilibrium among elites so that no single group or approach to governing predominates. Crucial to this equilibrium is a process of "juridical defense," whereby elites govern through laws and due process while adhering to a code of political and ethical conduct that restrains their competitions and conflicts, avoids sudden or radical changes, and puts the requirements of social order uppermost. Continual recruitment of persons from a prosperous and diversified middle class, or "second stratum," to ruling-class positions is vital for the equilibrium. Mosca held, in sum, that any lasting, robust democracy must have an open, balanced, and wise constellation of elites that are well rooted in the rest of society.

See also *Elite theory; Schumpeter, Joseph.*

John Higley

Mozambique

See *Africa, Lusophone*

Multiethnic democracy

An independent, sovereign political system that is characterized both by democratic decision-making institutions and by the presence of two or more ethnic groups. An ethnic group can be defined as a group of people who see themselves as a distinct cultural community; who often share a common language, religion, kinship, and/or physical characteristics (such as skin color); and who tend to harbor negative and hostile feelings toward members of other ethnic groups.

Ethnic group used to be defined more narrowly, since the possession of a common language used to be considered almost a necessary criterion. Nowadays, however, the term has become virtually synonymous with *communal group*. For instance, the major groups in the former Yugoslavia—Serbs, Croats, and Bosnian Muslims—as well as the Christian and Muslim sects in Lebanon are commonly referred to as ethnic groups. They differ from each other in religion but not (or only barely) in language.

Since the middle of the nineteenth century there has been broad agreement among social scientists that the division of a society into different ethnic groups constitutes a formidable obstacle to stable and viable democracy. For instance, political theorist John Stuart Mill argued that democracy was next to impossible in multiethnic societies, especially if the ethnic groups were linguistically differentiated from each other. (This argument was made in his *Considerations on Representative Government,* first published in 1861, one of the first book-length studies of the operation of democratic institutions.)

Later thinkers have generally supported both Mill's conclusion and the basic argument that underlies it. Democratic decision making, according to Mill, can work well only if the differences to be resolved with regard to preferred public policies are not too great. Therefore, although democracy does not require a completely homogeneous society, it does require a minimum of social and political unity and consensus. The degree of unity and consensus in multiethnic societies is generally below this necessary minimum.

The most extreme interpretation of Mill's proposition—that multiethnic democracy is impossible—leads to the conclusion that the only way for people in a multiethnic society to enjoy democracy is to eliminate their ethnic differences. Logically, there are four possibilities for doing so: genocide, expulsion, partition, and assimilation. Social scientists who have regarded multiethnic democracy as a difficult, but not impossible, objective have identified four principal models of democracy that may be able to manage ethnic differences and conflict: power sharing, crosscutting cleavages, vote pooling, and majority control.

Eliminating Ethnic Differences

Of the four possibilities of eliminating ethnic differences, genocide and expulsion are not without historical precedent, but they are morally unacceptable policies. Partition and assimilation can be regarded, at least in principle, as acceptable solutions.

Partition entails the geographical division of a multiethnic society into two or more sovereign states, each of which is ethnically homogeneous—and each of which can therefore more easily sustain a democratic system. The major problem with partition is that ethnic groups are almost never perfectly concentrated in particular geographical areas. The usual intermixture of ethnic groups makes it impossible to divide a multiethnic society in such a way that perfectly homogeneous separate states are created. The breakup of the Soviet Union and Yugoslavia into a large number of independent states in the early 1990s provides telling examples. Although the successor states are often thought of as ethnic states, and although most of them carry ethnic names (such as Russia, Armenia, and Croatia), all harbor large minority ethnic groups within their borders.

Thus, to reach the objective of creating homogeneous states, partition must be accompanied by population transfers. Even if such transfers are voluntary and take place under peaceful circumstances, they involve painful changes for the individuals who must leave their residences and resettle in different areas. And if they are involuntary and take place under conditions of widespread violence and civil war, they are tantamount to morally unacceptable "ethnic cleansing."

Many states have opposed partition out of fear that it may have a domino effect. Because so many countries are multiethnic in character, allowing one state to divide into two or more separate monoethnic, or at least ethnically more homogeneous, states may encourage ethnic minorities in other states to seek the same goal. The trend has the potential to trigger conflict and instability within states as well as the fragmentation of the international system of states.

Although international opposition to partition and secession has been far from unanimous in the post–World War II era, attempts at partition and secession have rarely been successful. The primary examples before 1990 are the creation of Bangladesh in 1971 and Singapore in 1965. The hostility toward partition may be softening in the 1990s, however, as evidenced by the international acceptance of the partition of the former Soviet Union and Yugoslavia, as well as the breakup of Czechoslovakia and the secession of Eritrea from Ethiopia.

The fourth method of eliminating ethnic differences is

cultural assimilation—that is, the blending of different ethnic groups into one ethnically homogeneous group. This approach has been widely used under the rubric "nation building" in developing countries after decolonization. It has sometimes involved the encouragement or requirement that ethnic minorities adopt the ways and customs, and especially the language, of another ethnic group, usually the majority or dominant ethnic group. But it also sometimes involves the imposition of a lingua franca that is not the native language of any ethnic group, such as Malay in Indonesia and Swahili in East African states.

Primordialism vs. Instrumentalism

Nation-building policies are based on the premise that ethnicity is flexible, adaptable, and manipulable. Whether this view is correct is the subject of much controversy in the social sciences between the so-called primordialists and their critics, who espouse what is variously called the instrumental or situational approach to ethnicity.

Primordialist theory assumes that ethnic identity is an inherited characteristic and, if not permanently fixed, at least very difficult to change. The opposite perspective is that ethnicity is fluid and manipulable, and that it does not become politically salient unless and until politicians use it to mobilize political support. In contrast with a primordial "given," it is an instrumental "made" or "taken" created by political leaders.

A third approach, which can be thought of as steering a middle course between the primordialists and the instrumentalists, is that of the constructivists. Constructivists share with the instrumentalists the assumption that ethnicity is made rather than given, but they emphasize the imaginative creation of ethnicity to satisfy the social needs of groups in the process of profound political, social, and economic change. In this view the constructors of ethnicity are social-cultural brokers rather than political entrepreneurs.

Both the primordial and the instrumental approaches can be criticized. There is much empirical evidence, especially in Africa, of the fluidity of ethnic boundaries. Yet it is unrealistic to assume that politicians can make successful ethnic appeals where such appeals do not resonate with basic cultural differences among people. Moreover, where such differences do exist, it is equally unrealistic to think of politicians as completely free agents who can decide either to use or to ignore these divisions. On the contrary, they often have a strong incentive to mobilize support on the basis of ethnic divisions and can ignore them only at their own peril. Most important for the purpose of this article, efforts at manipulating ethnic identities in order to build culturally unified nations have had very limited success, and attempts to discourage or suppress ethnic differences have often backfired, strengthening ethnic feelings and exacerbating ethnic conflict.

Modernization Theory

The 1950s and 1960s were characterized by an exaggerated faith in the possibilities of nation building. One reason is the popularity of modernization theory, which held that the various processes of modernization—industrialization, urbanization, increases in transportation, improvements in communication, the growth of mass education, and so on—would inevitably undermine the "premodern" forces of ethnicity and lead to national and even worldwide integration. The industrialized Western world was seen as already largely devoid of ethnic conflicts, and the developing countries were seen as moving to the same end.

From the 1970s on, however, it has become clear that modernization and ethnic assimilation do not necessarily develop in tandem. There has been a remarkable resurgence of ethnic demands and conflict in the most modern parts of the world. Outstanding examples are English-French tensions in Canada, racial conflict in the United States, the linguistic struggle in Belgium, the Jura separatist problem in Switzerland, and Catalan and Basque nationalism in Spain. Furthermore, ethnic loyalties in most developing countries have persisted in spite of strong nation-building efforts. Similarly, ethnic divisions have survived in the former Soviet Union and other communist countries through the years of communist efforts to "solve" the nationality problem.

The other reason for the confidence in nation building in the 1950s and early 1960s was the prominence of the U.S. "melting pot" model of ethnic and cultural assimilation and the worldwide prominence of American political and social scientists. Since then, however, the melting-pot model has come under attack as an idealized depiction of only partially successful assimilation. Correspondingly, public policy in the United States has shifted to the recognition of cultural diversity and the introduction of programs of affirmative action for the benefit of explicitly defined ethnic and racial groups. Another weakness of the melting-pot model was the failure to recognize the difference in the strength of ethnic loyalties in immigrant and nonimmigrant societies. Immigrants, having voluntarily uprooted and resettled themselves, have shown a greater willingness and aptitude to assimilate culturally than have nonimmigrants, although even here there are the major exceptions of the French speakers in Canada and the Afrikaners in South Africa.

If ethnic differences cannot be eliminated, can they be successfully managed and accommodated in multiethnic democracies? Three of the four models of democracy that answer this question in the affirmative (cross-cutting cleavages, vote pooling, and majority control) can be grouped together in the broad category of majoritarian models, and they stand in sharp contrast to the fourth model of power sharing.

Joint Decision Making in Power Sharing

Power-sharing democracy—often called consociational democracy—can be defined in terms of four characteristics. The two primary characteristics are the participation of the representatives of all significant ethnic groups in political decision making and a high degree of autonomy for these groups to run their own internal affairs. The secondary characteristics are proportionality and the minority veto. The major aim of these four devices is to increase each group's sense of security by maximizing its control of its own destiny, without increasing the insecurity of other groups.

The joint exercise of governmental, especially executive, decision-making power may take a variety of institutional forms. The most straightforward and common form is that of a grand coalition cabinet in a parliamentary system, as in Belgium and Malaysia. The Swiss seven-member executive provides another example: the seven members are selected in such a way that all major religious and linguistic groups as well as the four largest political parties are given representation.

In presidential systems of government, a grand coalition is more difficult, but not impossible, to arrange. In the Lebanese presidential system (with a powerful although not popularly elected president), power sharing is organized by distributing the presidency and other high offices to the different groups: the presidency is reserved for a Maronite Christian, the prime ministership for a Sunni Muslim, the speakership of the legislature for a Shiʿite Muslim, and so on. In addition, the Lebanese cabi-

net is a broadly representative power-sharing body. In both parliamentary and presidential systems, power sharing may be strengthened by broadly representative councils or committees with important advisory or coordinating functions.

Nevertheless, a presidential form of government is not optimal for power sharing in multiethnic societies. Presidentialism usually entails the concentration of executive power in the hands of one person, who, in an ethnically divided country, is almost inevitably a member of one of the major ethnic groups. Power sharing requires joint decision making by the representatives of the different ethnic groups; the best vehicle for this is a multimember collegial body. The Lebanese power-sharing arrangement alleviated this problem but did not solve it completely because, until the constitutional changes of 1989, the presidency was by far the most powerful of the offices distributed among the ethnic groups.

Group Autonomy in Power Sharing

The second characteristic of power-sharing democracy is group autonomy. On all issues of common concern, decisions are made jointly by the representatives of the different ethnic groups; on all other matters, decision-making power is delegated to the separate ethnic groups to be exercised by and for each group. If the ethnic groups are geographically concentrated, group autonomy can take the form of a federal system in which federal boundaries coincide with ethnic boundaries so as to create ethnically homogeneous or largely homogeneous territorial units. Examples are multilingual Switzerland, in which most of the cantons are monolingual, and Canada, where the majority of French speakers are concentrated in the province of Quebec.

If the ethnic groups are geographically intermixed, autonomy must assume a nonterritorial form. For instance, the 1960 constitution of Cyprus set up separate Greek Cypriot and Turkish Cypriot communal chambers with exclusive legislative powers over religious, cultural, and educational matters. These chambers were separately elected by Greek and Turkish Cypriot voters, respectively, regardless of where on the island they lived. In addition, the constitution prescribed similar separately elected municipal councils in the five largest towns in the island.

Another example of power sharing without regard to geography is the Law of Cultural Autonomy adopted by Estonia in 1925, which gave each minority ethnic group with more than 3,000 formally registered members the right to establish autonomous institutions under the authority of a cultural council elected by the members of the ethnic group. The council could organize and administer minority schools and other cultural institutions such as libraries and theaters. The German and Jewish minorities took advantage of this law to establish their own autonomous institutions.

Territorial and nonterritorial autonomy may be used in the same system, as in the case of Belgium, which has experimented with the delegation of political authority both to geographically defined areas that are ethnically homogeneous (Dutch-speaking Flanders and French-speaking Wallonia) and to communities defined in nonterritorial terms (French speakers and Dutch speakers in bilingual Brussels).

Proportionality and Minority Veto

Proportionality, the third characteristic of power-sharing democracy, serves as the basic standard of political representation, civil service appointments, and the allocation of public funds. Proportionality is especially important as a guarantee for the fair representation of minority groups. The most common and straightforward method for achieving proportionality of political representation is to use a proportional representation electoral system, as in Belgium and Switzerland. Reasonable proportionality can also be achieved by other partly proportional methods that guarantee minority representation (as in Lebanon), or by single-member district electoral systems when the ethnic groups are geographically concentrated (as in Canada), and when, in addition, the ethnic groups make informal agreements about the distribution of seats (as in Malaysia).

Two extensions of the proportionality rule entail even greater minority protection: overrepresentation of small groups and parity of representation. An example of the former is the allotment in Cyprus's 1960 constitution of 30 percent of the seats in the national legislature to the Turkish Cypriot minority, which made up less than 20 percent of the total population. The Belgian constitution prescribes parity of representation in the national cabinet for the Dutch-speaking majority and the French-speaking minority.

The fourth characteristic of power-sharing democracy is the minority veto. This device is usually restricted to the most vital and fundamental matters, and it is usually based on informal understandings rather than formal legal or constitutional rules. Examples of the latter, however, are the requirements of concurrent majorities (that is, a majority not only of the total legislature but also majorities within each of the ethnic groups represented in the legislature) for the passage of legislation with regard to taxes, the municipalities, and the electoral system in the 1960 constitution of Cyprus and for the adoption of laws on cultural and educational matters in the Belgian constitution.

Power Sharing vs. Majority Rule

All four characteristics of power-sharing democracy contrast sharply with the basic features of majority-rule or majoritarian democracy, exemplified most clearly by the British Westminster model of parliamentary government. The essence of majoritarianism is the concentration of political power in the hands of the majority. Instead of concentrating power, the power-sharing model's basic approach is to share power, to diffuse and decentralize power, to divide power proportionally, and to limit power.

First, the grand coalitions and joint decision making characteristic of power sharing contrast with the concentration of power in a one-party, bare-majority, noncoalition cabinet typical of the Westminster model. Second, group autonomy on a territorial or nonterritorial basis contrasts with the unitary and centralized nature of the Westminster model, which does not allow for geographical or functional areas from which the parliamentary majority at the center is barred. Third, the Westminster model's basic election rule is plurality, or winner-take-all: the candidate with the most votes wins, and all other candidates lose. In proportional systems both majorities and minorities can be winners in the sense of being able to elect their candidates in proportion to each group's electoral support. In practice, the plurality rule tends to exaggerate the representation and power of the majority and therefore entails disproportional representation. The two extensions of proportionality—minority overrepresentation and parity—are also methods of disproportional representation but in this case the disproportionality works in favor of minorities and small groups. And, fourth, the minority veto on constitutional or other vital matters contrasts sharply with the unwritten constitution in the Westminster model of democracy, which gives the majority the right to change even the most fundamental rules of government, limited only by morality and common sense.

Examples of Power Sharing

Power-sharing democracies can be found in all parts of the world. The Netherlands in 1917 accommodated the conflicts between the country's religious-communal groups by instituting proportional representation elections, granting far-reaching autonomy in the field of education, and cementing informal agreements to pursue government by broad coalitions and to accord minorities veto rights on the most sensitive political issues.

Switzerland's arrangement, worked out in 1943, stipulated a permanent grand coalition of the four largest parties, representing more than 80 percent of the Swiss voters, as well as a grand coalition of the major religious and linguistic groups. These were added to existing proportional representation and a decentralized federation that provided strong linguistic autonomy.

In Lebanon, also in 1943, the several Christian and Muslim sects agreed to govern the country, which had declared its independence from France, according to a complex system of the distribution of the top political offices to the different sects. They guaranteed representation in the parliament for each sect according to a predetermined, roughly proportional, ratio. They set up separate and autonomous sectarian schools as well as autonomous sectarian courts to administer the personal status laws (concerning such matters as marriage, divorce, and inheritance) that tend to differ from sect to sect. And, finally, they established an informal veto power.

Austria had experienced a civil war in the early 1930s between Catholics and Socialists. In 1945, at the end of World War II, the groups decided to govern together rather than to compete. Their agreement was complemented by strict adherence to proportionality, respect for each other's autonomy, and an informal but firm agreement on a mutual veto power.

In 1955 a broad and inclusive coalition of ethnic (Malay, Chinese, and Indian) political parties was formed in Malaya. The arrangement continued after independence in 1957 and also after the addition of the Bornean states of Sabah and Sarawak (and, briefly, Singapore) to the federation, renamed Malaysia, in 1963. This coalition was originally called the Alliance and later, when additional parties joined the coalition, the National Front. The coalition partners negotiate the nomination of joint candidates in the single-member districts used for parliamentary elections, thereby achieving a rough proportionality of representation for each ethnic party.

A 1958 accord ended a long and bloody civil war in Colombia, in which the formerly feuding Conservative and Liberal Parties, representing the country's main communal groups, agreed to collaborate according to the rules of parity and coparticipation and to take turns in occupying the country's powerful presidency. The Cyprus constitution of 1960 has been mentioned. It provided for a Greek Cypriot president and a Turkish Cypriot vice president with virtually coequal powers, far-reaching educational and cultural autonomy for the two groups, a strong veto power for the Turkish Cypriot minority, and overrepresentation of this minority in the legislature and the cabinet. Another previously discussed example is Belgium. The 1970 amendments to the constitution required equal representation of Dutch speakers and French speakers in the cabinet, established a veto power for the French-speaking minority over proposed legislation concerning culture and education, and granted regional decentralization and autonomy for the linguistic communities.

All of these power-sharing democracies are characterized by both thorough power sharing and full democracy. In addition, many instances can be cited of predemocratic power sharing (such as the United Province of Canada from 1840 to 1867 and Belgium during the first decades of its independence after 1831) and of partial power sharing (especially the use of federal or highly decentralized systems to give autonomy to minority linguistic groups, as in India, Canada, and Spain).

The first modern scholar to identify the power-sharing model of democracy was the economist and Nobel laureate W. Arthur Lewis. In *Politics in West Africa* (1965), he proposed broad interethnic coalitions, proportional representation elections, and ethnic group autonomy by means of federalism for the ethnically divided countries of West Africa. Although Lewis did not attach a comprehensive label to these proposals, they clearly add up to power sharing. He developed his proposals as a solution to the failures of majoritarian democracies in the West African countries, which, as an economic adviser to several of their governments, he observed and deplored.

Criticisms of Power Sharing

Power-sharing theory has been criticized on a variety of grounds. Because it recommends power sharing as a model of stable and effective democracy that multiethnic countries ought to follow, these criticisms deserve careful examination. The most serious charge is that power sharing cannot work well because of its inherent problems of immobilism and deadlock and its tendency to encourage rather than to discourage political mobilization along ethnic lines. Critics have also placed great emphasis on the failure of power-sharing democracy in two of its major examples—Cyprus and Lebanon—as well as the British government's lack of success in its efforts to solve the Northern Ireland problem by power sharing.

Power-sharing theorists respond that the theory does not claim that power sharing will be successful in every case. In fact, they have tried to refine and strengthen power-sharing theory by defining the conditions in which power sharing is more or less likely to be instituted and maintained. The two most important favorable conditions are the absence of a majority group—majority groups understandably prefer majoritarian to power-sharing solutions—and the absence of large socioeconomic inequalities among the groups. Both of these factors have been major obstacles to power sharing in Cyprus and Northern Ireland, particularly the presence of strong and uncompromising majorities—an almost 80 percent Greek Cypriot majority and a two-thirds Irish Protestant majority, respectively. Other favorable conditions are as follows: the groups do not differ greatly in size, the country has a relatively small population, internal unity is strengthened by external dangers, countrywide loyalties counteract ethnic loyalties, and traditions of compromise and consensus already exist when power sharing is instituted.

The collapse of the Lebanese power-sharing system in 1975 presents a special problem for power-sharing theory because most of the favorable conditions were present in this case. It should be pointed out, first, however, that several of the background conditions were not favorable in Lebanon: foreign threats reinforced rather than weakened internal divisions, there were substantial socioeconomic inequalities among the Christian and Muslim sects, and the country was fragmented into a relatively large number of sects. Second, the outbreak of the civil war in 1975 should not obscure the fact that power sharing worked quite well in this severely divided country from 1943 to 1975. Third, a major part of the blame for the collapse of power sharing belongs not to internal problems caused by the power-sharing system itself but to Lebanon's precarious position in the international arena of the Middle East

and, in particular, to repeated Palestinian, Syrian, and Israeli interventions. In this sense, the civil war that broke out in 1975 was not an ordinary civil war but an international conflict fought on Lebanese soil. Finally, it must be admitted that Lebanon's power-sharing system had some weak spots. The fixed 6:5 ratio for parliamentary elections continued to give the Christian sects the majority of the seats despite the fact that the Muslims gradually had become the majority of the population. Furthermore, the most powerful political office, the presidency, was permanently assigned to the Maronite Christians. But the Lebanese themselves have recognized these problems and have tried to solve them. The 1989 Ta'if Accord changed the 6:5 ratio to equal parliamentary representation for Christians and Muslims, and it also roughly equalized the powers of the Maronite president and the Sunni Muslim prime minister.

The most important lesson of the Lebanese case is that power sharing needed to be repaired and improved rather than replaced. In the eyes of most Lebanese and knowledgeable foreign observers, a switch to a majoritarian form of democracy has not been regarded as a realistic option. It is even more significant that the same conclusion applies to Cyprus, where, admittedly, power sharing never worked well. Instituted in 1960, it was ended by the 1963 civil war, and it appeared to be permanently doomed by the Turkish invasion in 1974 and the subsequent de facto partition of the island into a Greek Cypriot southern state and a Turkish Cypriot northern state. Nevertheless, since 1985 Javier Pérez de Cuéllar, then UN secretary general, and his successor, Boutros Boutros-Ghali, have made several proposals for a unified Cyprus that strikingly resemble the basic power-sharing features of the 1960 constitution. Their efforts demonstrate their recognition of the fact that power sharing, although it may not succeed, represents the optimal chance for a successful solution. Similarly, the British government's failure to have its power-sharing proposals accepted in Northern Ireland has not budged it from its basic conviction that power sharing is the only possible and acceptable solution there.

One weakness the critics of power sharing have focused on is its alleged tendency to immobilism and deadlock. In particular, executive power sharing and the minority veto are seen as threats to effective decision making; majority rule appears to be much more decisive and efficient. Short-term efficiency under majority rule, however, is likely to cause antagonism and frustration on the part of the losing groups. In the long run, tensions and instability result. Conversely, the slower operation of power sharing in the short run is more likely to be effective over time.

The other characteristics of power sharing also appear to have negative consequences. If proportionality, in addition to individual merit, is a standard for appointment to the civil service, some administrative inefficiency may result. And group autonomy may require an increase in the number of governmental units and the duplication of schools and other facilities to serve the different groups, both of which may entail additional costs. These, however, are relatively minor problems rather than system-threatening ones. They are offset by other aspects of the same rules: proportionality is a valuable time-saving formula for allocating resources and appointments, and group autonomy distributes the total decision-making load among several bodies and hence alleviates the burdens on each of them.

Ethnic Group Cohesion Under Power Sharing

Another alleged weakness of power sharing is that it strengthens rather than weakens the cohesion and distinctiveness of ethnic groups. By explicitly recognizing the legitimacy of these groups, by giving group organizations a vital function in the political system, by subsidizing them on a proportional basis, and by encouraging ethnic parties through the use of proportional representation, power-sharing democracy undoubtedly increases the organizational strength of ethnic groups. The existence of strong and autonomous ethnic groups, however, does not necessarily translate into serious conflict among them. Under power sharing, the strengthened ethnic groups are designed to play a constructive role in conflict resolution.

A variant of this criticism is that power sharing, by recognizing particular groups as the constituent units of the political system, rigidifies ethnic differences that may be fluid and changing and discriminates against groups that otherwise might have formed by splits and mergers. This criticism is to some extent valid. Many power-sharing systems, notably those of Belgium, Lebanon, and Cyprus, have been based on formally predetermined groups. For instance, the Belgian constitution explicitly names Dutch speakers and French speakers (and, for some purposes, the small group of German speakers) as the officially recognized communities that make up the Belgian political system. On the other hand, power-sharing systems based

on broad coalitions of communal parties, as in Malaysia, Colombia, Austria, and the Netherlands, have been much more flexible.

Power sharing does not require the predetermination of specific groups. In fact, for any group that wishes to make use of it, there are major advantages to allowing the groups to be self-determined by such means as proportional representation (which does not rigidify ethnic groups or discriminate in favor of or against any groups) and Estonian-style cultural autonomy.

Because power sharing has been studied more extensively in the European cases and by European scholars, it is sometimes alleged to be a European or Western model that is foreign and unsuitable for multiethnic societies in other parts of the world. This criticism is clearly erroneous because it ignores such major examples as Lebanon, Malaysia, and Colombia, where power sharing was developed by indigenous leaders without external influence or assistance. It is also worth pointing out that Lewis, the first power-sharing theorist, was not a European or a student of European politics but a native of the Caribbean island of St. Lucia, a black scholar whose interest was in African politics. Finally, Lewis and numerous other non-Western scholars and political leaders have emphasized that majority rule violates their native traditions of trying to arrive at consensus through lengthy deliberations—traditions that correspond closely to the power-sharing idea.

The Democratic Nature of Power Sharing

As serious as the criticism that power sharing cannot work well is the charge that it is not sufficiently democratic. This charge is based on the importance of compromises negotiated, often behind closed doors, by the leaders of the various groups in power-sharing systems. Moreover, power-sharing systems often use list forms of proportional representation, in which party leaders have a great deal of influence on the composition of the lists and hence on who can get elected. These observations are not wrong, but it is wrong to imply a stark contrast with majority-rule democracy.

For instance, in the United Kingdom, the flagship of majoritarian democracy, all important decisions are typically prepared by bureaucrats, adopted in the cabinet in complete secrecy, and, after being announced, hardly ever changed under parliamentary or public pressure. And, in spite of Britain's plurality electoral system, party leaders have usually been able to reserve safe seats for themselves and to oppose the nomination of undesirable candidates by constituency organizations. Elite domination does not vary a great deal among democracies. The difference between majority rule and power sharing is not whether leaders do or do not predominate but whether they tend to be competitive or cooperative.

Opponents of proportional representation concentrate their criticism on its tendency to encourage multiparty systems and multiparty coalition governments, which allegedly make government less decisive and effective. Friends and foes of proportional representation largely agree that, purely in terms of the quality of democratic representation, proportional representation is superior to majoritarian election systems. Finally, the criticism of insufficient democracy is difficult to maintain when one looks at actual cases. Switzerland, Belgium, and the Netherlands, for instance, are usually and correctly considered to be not just unambiguously democratic but among the most decent and humane of the world's democracies.

The three theories that argue that majoritarian democracy can deal more effectively with the problem of ethnic divisions than power sharing are the theories of cross-cutting cleavages, vote pooling, and majority control.

Cross-Cutting Cleavages

The theory of cross-cutting cleavages is the leading interpretation of how democracy in the multiethnic United States works. It has found its clearest articulation in the work of Seymour Martin Lipset, especially in his classic 1960 volume, *Political Man.*

Lipset's theoretical point of departure is the notion that in any society, but especially in divided societies, political moderation and tolerance, and hence the chances for stable democracy, are enhanced if individuals have cross-cutting affiliations to a variety of groups that pull them in different directions. If, on the other hand, a person's affiliations are to groups with the same outlook and/or within the same ethnic or cultural community, they are mutually reinforcing and are likely to lead to intolerance and hostility.

If cross-cutting loyalties moderate voters' politics, as voting behavior studies imply, two-party systems, majoritarian elections in single-member districts, and federalism may be preferable to, respectively, multiparty systems, proportional representation, and unitary government. Both parties in a two-party system will seek to win majorities of the voters; this objective forces them to try to appeal to a variety of groups, which in turn forces them to be moderate. On the other hand, the many smaller parties in multiparty systems have a stronger incentive to seek support from a limited base and to target their appeals narrowly to this base; this aim rewards immoderate rather than moderate positions and promises. Consequently, in a multiethnic society with a large number of ethnic minorities, a two-party system entails moderate competition between two large multiethnic parties, whereas a multiparty system is likely to be characterized by more extreme confrontation among many ethnically exclusive parties.

Lipset's preference for majoritarian electoral systems rests on their discrimination against small parties and their consequent tendency to encourage two-party systems, in contrast with the tendency of proportional representation to allow and encourage a multiparty system. Federalism has the advantage of enhancing the cross-cutting of cleavages by adding regional divisions to ethnic and other divisions. But Lipset adds the crucial qualification that such beneficial cross-cutting occurs only when federal boundaries cut across ethnic boundaries. When federal and ethnic boundaries tend to coincide, federalism becomes a disadvantage, as in the cases of India and Canada.

Criticisms of Cross-Cutting Theory

Just as power-sharing theory has been criticized mainly by majoritarians, the cross-cutting cleavage approach has been criticized by power-sharing theorists. The latter have argued that, although plurality elections entail strong pressures toward a two-party system, these pressures work only imperfectly in multiethnic societies. The reason is that ethnic loyalties are usually strong and that ethnically motivated voters will often vote for small ethnic parties despite the low probability that these parties will be elected or, if elected, will be able to exert much influence. Plurality elections have usually yielded a three-party or four-party system in Canada, a multiparty system (with one dominant party) in India, and a multiparty system in Nigeria (except in the 1993 elections, when the military government imposed a strict two-party system). Even in the mainly two-party British Parliament elected by plurality, Scottish, Welsh, and various Northern Irish ethnic parties have almost always been represented, albeit in small numbers.

A more serious criticism of the cross-cutting approach, forcefully articulated by Lewis, is that even when plurality elections do lead to two-party systems, or at least to limited multiparty or dominant-party systems in which one party is likely to win election victories, such an outcome is undesirable. Again because of the rigidity of voters' loyalties in ethnically divided societies, such a system lacks the floating vote that makes alternation in exercising governmental power possible. Winning parties are likely to be permanent winners—which, Lewis argues, is both undemocratic and destabilizing.

Dominant-party systems are undemocratic because the primary meaning of democracy is participation in decision making, either directly or through elected representatives, and the permanent exclusion of the losing minority or minorities violates this fundamental principle. Moreover, permanent majorities are dangerous because minorities that are permanently excluded from power feel discriminated against and tend to lose their allegiance to the regime. This danger is especially serious when the winning party represents not a coalition of ethnic groups but one ethnic group, as was the case in Northern Ireland for many decades. Of course, proportional representation cannot reduce a popular majority to a parliamentary minority either—this is one reason why the power-sharing approach does not rely exclusively on proportional representation—but it gives at least some encouragement for a majority ethnic party to split into two or more parties along intraethnic dividing lines.

A further criticism of the cross-cutting approach is that it favors incentives toward political moderation at the expense of allowing voters to elect representatives belonging to their own ethnic group. More important, this approach ignores the potential for moderation that multiparty systems consisting of several ethnic parties can have for a different reason: having its own representative in government can give a group a sense of security that limits antagonism between ethnic factions.

The historical evidence concerning the adoption of proportional representation in Western Europe about 1900 and in the early decades of the twentieth century shows that one of the main motivations for this change was to ameliorate linguistic and religious tensions. The previous majoritarian systems had proved unable to foster the kind of moderation that the theory of cross-cutting cleavages credits them with.

The evidence of the use of federalism in multiethnic countries demonstrates that the goal of creating autonomy for ethnic groups by drawing federal boundaries that coincide with ethnic dividing lines has won out over the idea of fostering moderation by designing cross-cutting federal arrangements. In addition to the examples of India and Canada, the Nigerian case is instructive. The government started out in 1960 as a three-unit federation with heterogeneous units, but it has gradually increased this number to about thirty states that have a much higher degree of ethnic homogeneity. Belgium has found its unitary system of government, established upon independence in 1831, incapable of managing interethnic tensions. It moved via a strongly decentralized but still formally unitary system in 1970 to a fully federal system in 1993—maximizing autonomy for the ethnic groups and minimizing the cross-cutting of federal and ethnic boundaries. And in the universally admired Swiss federal system, most of the cantons are monolingual and cross-cutting is limited to a handful of linguistically more heterogeneous cantons.

Vote Pooling

The vote-pooling approach was launched by Donald L. Horowitz in his influential book *Ethnic Groups in Conflict* (1985). It was elaborated further in his 1991 book on South Africa, which contained detailed proposals for the structure of a democratic system there. Horowitz uses the term *vote pooling* specifically for the kind of electoral system he advocates, but the expression can be used aptly and conveniently for his entire set of proposals. Although he agrees with Lewis's critique of plurality elections in multiethnic societies, he disagrees with Lewis's preferred alternative of proportional representation and broad power-sharing cabinets. Horowitz argues that the formation of a power-sharing coalition by seat pooling (the pooling of parliamentary seats in order to build majority, or larger than majority, support for a cabinet) does not necessarily produce compromise. If compromise is to be achieved, there must be additional incentives for it; without such incentives, coalitions will quickly fall apart. Incentives for vote pooling can be interpreted as refinements of the cross-cutting cleavage approach.

The two major examples of electoral systems that can foster moderation by vote pooling are the special vote distribution requirement used in the Second Nigerian Republic (1979–1983) for presidential elections and the alternative vote used in Sri Lanka and a few other countries. The Nigerian system required the winning candidate to obtain not only the largest number of votes nationwide but also at least 25 percent of the vote in no less than two-thirds of the nineteen states. The second requirement made it impossible for a candidate to be elected by the ethnic groups of one major area of the country. All candidates were forced to appeal widely to different ethnic groups and different parts of the country.

In alternative vote systems, voters are asked to rank order the candidates. If a candidate receives an absolute majority of first preferences, he or she is elected; if not, the weakest candidate is eliminated, and the ballots with that candidate as first preference are redistributed according to second preferences. This process continues until one of the candidates has reached a majority of the votes. For instance, if there are three candidates who receive 45, 40, and 15 percent of the first preferences, the third candidate is eliminated and the 15 percent of the ballots with the third candidate as first preference will be redistributed according to second preferences. In this hypothetical situation, the two major candidates will have to bid for the second preferences of the third candidate's supporters in order to win—which, according to Horowitz, has the major advantage of rewarding moderation.

Horowitz advocates a presidential system of government with the proviso that the president be elected by the alternative vote. The main reason for this proposal is that it provides another chance for vote pooling to be applied. In contrast, power-sharing theory sees presidentialism as inherently majoritarian and prefers the collegial executives that cabinets in parliamentary systems can provide. Moreover, while the alternative vote is an unusual voting system, it is clearly a majoritarian system; in fact, any method for the election of one top officeholder must logically be a majoritarian method.

Like the cross-cutting cleavage advocates, Horowitz favors heterogeneous federal units. But the federal boundaries must be drawn in such a way that large ethnic groups are divided over several states in order to reduce their political power compared with that of smaller ethnic groups. He therefore approvingly cites the Nigerian example of creating a large number of states. Increasing the number of states also entails increasing the homogeneity of these states.

Criticisms of Vote-Pooling Theory

Vote-pooling theory can be criticized, first, for disregarding the incentives for compromise that are inherent in the process of coalition building. There are indeed many examples of multiethnic coalitions that have fallen apart, but also there are many contrary examples of broad coalitions that have worked effectively, as in most of the major cases of power sharing. Coalescence and compromise are analytically distinct, but the desire to coalesce implies a need to compromise: if parties are interested in gaining power (which is a basic assumption in political science), they will, in multiparty situations, want to enter and remain in coalition cabinets. To do so, they must reach compromises with their coalition partners.

A problem with the distribution rule is that it may fail to produce any winner. The very first application of the method, in the 1979 presidential election in Nigeria, provides a telling example: the nationwide plurality winner gained a minimum of 25 percent support in twelve of the nineteen states—falling just short of the two-thirds of the states needed. (However, the electoral commission expediently decided that he had come close enough to be declared duly elected.)

The weakness of the alternative vote as a moderation-inducing mechanism is that bidding for the second preferences of other ethnic groups is likely to decrease the number of first preferences from the candidate's own group. The only two examples of the use of the alternative vote in an ethnically divided society—in Sri Lanka's 1982 and 1988 presidential elections—yielded victories on the basis of first preferences, and therefore they do not lend empirical support to Horowitz's proposal.

There is also some doubt that the incentives for moderation inherent in the alternative vote are much greater than incentives in other majoritarian systems. For instance, if the plurality method were used in the hypothetical situation of three candidates with 45, 40, and 15 percent support, respectively, many of the weakest candidate's supporters would not want to waste their votes on a hopeless candidacy, or the candidate might decide to drop out of the race. The two major candidates would have to appeal to the third candidate's supporters in order to win. If there is a difference between plurality and the alternative vote with regard to the inducement of moderation, it is a difference only of degree.

The alternative vote resembles the third principal majoritarian electoral method, the majority runoff, even more closely. As in plurality, the voters cast their ballots for one candidate only. If no candidate wins an absolute majority of the votes, a runoff election is held between the top two candidates. In the hypothetical example mentioned above, the third candidate is eliminated in the first round, and the two major candidates have to compete for the votes of the third candidate's supporters in the runoff. The alternative vote merely accomplishes in one round of voting what requires two ballots in the majority-runoff system. The incentives for moderation do not differ much. The introduction of proportional representation in Western Europe gives rise to doubt about the merits of the alternative vote: most of the failed majoritarian election systems were majority-runoff systems.

Control Theory

Ian Lustick formulated his control model as an alternative to the power-sharing model. His main point is that power sharing is not the only method for achieving civil peace and political stability in ethnically divided societies. Control entails an asymmetrical relationship in which the superior power of one group is used to impose stability by constraining other groups. Lustick concedes that control is not an attractive alternative to power sharing, but it is preferable to civil war, extermination, and deportation. Control usually entails a political system that is not democratic and hence cannot be a model for multiethnic democracy.

The only exception is the case of a majority group that controls one or more minority groups in a majoritarian democracy. A clear example is Northern Ireland, where Protestant majority control was relatively successful in preserving both peace and democratic institutions from the 1920s to the 1960s. This example also shows the two major drawbacks of majority control: the "peace" and "democracy" that it can achieve are both questionable. Majority control in Northern Ireland meant the permanent exclusion from power of Roman Catholics and widespread discrimination against them. Majority control therefore spells majority dictatorship rather than majoritarian democracy. Moreover, while majority control may endure in the short and medium run, in the long run it tends to cause much frustration on the part of the excluded minority. Northern Ireland's four decades of civil peace turned into civil war in the late 1960s.

Lustick's control model, however, can serve as a useful refinement of the power-sharing model. Perfect power sharing means completely equal influence (when the groups are equal in size) or proportional influence (when the groups are unequal) in decision making. In practice, the groups' relative powers are usually not perfectly equal or proportional.

Perfect power sharing and perfect majority control can therefore be seen as opposite ends of a continuum. For instance, Malaysian multiethnic democracy—which is based on broad interethnic power sharing but with a predominant and disproportionately strong Malay share of power—can be placed on this continuum at a spot that is some distance removed from perfect power sharing but still considerably closer to the power-sharing end than to the majority-control end of the continuum.

Abstract Models and Concrete Cases

The example of Malaysia shows that concrete cases do not always fit perfectly with abstract models. In fact, Malaysia can also be used to exemplify vote pooling since the nomination by the National Front of one joint candidate in each single-member district means that this candidate must seek voter support across ethnic divisions. The same can be said of just about all the cases mentioned in this article. Even the United States does not fit the cross-cutting model perfectly: the drawing of election districts in such a way as virtually to guarantee the election of ethnic and racial minority representatives, as well as affirmative action in civil appointments and college admissions, clearly follows the power-sharing principle of proportionality.

Similar mixes of cross-cutting and power sharing may be used in the design of democratic constitutions for multiethnic countries. For countries with relatively shallow and fluid ethnic cleavages, such as the immigrant multiethnic society of the United States, the mixture may be weighted toward cross-cutting. For the most deeply divided societies, however, power sharing must be the main component of the democratic prescription.

See also *Affirmative action; Althusius, Johannes; Electoral systems; Federalism; Furnivall, John Sydenham; Historicism; Lipset, Seymour Martin; Majority rule, minority rights; Mill, John Stuart; Pragmatism; Proportional representation; Secession; Theory, Postwar Anglo-American.*

Arend Lijphart

BIBLIOGRAPHY

Daalder, Hans. "The Consociational Democracy Theme." *World Politics* 26 (July 1974): 604–621.

Dix, Robert H. "Consociational Democracy: The Case of Colombia." *Comparative Politics* 12 (April 1980): 303–321.

Hanf, Theodor, Heribert Weiland, and Gerda Vierdag. *South Africa: The Prospects of Peaceful Change.* London: Rex Collings, 1981.

Horowitz, Donald L. *A Democratic South Africa? Constitutional Engineering in a Divided Society.* Berkeley: University of California Press, 1991.

———. *Ethnic Groups in Conflict.* Berkeley: University of California Press, 1985.

Lehmbruch, Gerhard. *Proporzdemokratie: Politisches System und politische Kultur in der Schweiz und in Österreich.* Tübingen: Mohr, 1967.

Lewis, W. Arthur. *Politics in West Africa.* London: Allen and Unwin, 1965.

Lijphart, Arend. *Democracy in Plural Societies: A Comparative Exploration.* New Haven and London: Yale University Press, 1977.

Lipset, Seymour Martin. *Political Man: The Social Bases of Politics.* Expanded and updated ed. Baltimore: Johns Hopkins University Press, 1981; Aldershot: Gower, 1983.

Lustick, Ian. "Stability in Deeply Divided Societies: Consociationalism versus Control." *World Politics* 31 (April 1979): 325–344.

McRae, Kenneth D., ed. *Consociational Democracy: Political Accommodation in Segmented Societies.* Toronto: McClelland and Stewart, 1974.

Messarra, Antoine Nasri. *Le modèle politique libanais et sa survie: Essai sur la classification et l'aménagement d'un système consociatif.* Beirut: Librairie Orientale, 1983.

Montville, Joseph V., ed. *Conflict and Peacemaking in Multiethnic Societies.* Lexington, Mass.: Lexington Books, 1990.

Steiner, Jürg. *Amicable Agreement versus Majority Rule: Conflict Resolution in Switzerland.* Chapel Hill: University of North Carolina Press, 1974.

Von Vorys, Karl. *Democracy without Consensus: Communalism and Political Stability in Malaysia.* Princeton: Princeton University Press, 1975.

Myanmar

See *Burma*

N

Namibia

An African country that has overcome more than one hundred years of authoritarian colonial rule to establish a democratic system of government. Called South West Africa prior to its independence from South Africa in 1990, Namibia now has free elections and an independent judiciary.

Historical Background

Before the creation of South West Africa as a colony in the late nineteenth century, indigenous political systems predominated, including seven powerful Ovambo kingships in the far north-central regions, the Kavango in the northeast, and the highly centralized authority systems of the Mafwe and Basubia in the far northeast. A number of important Nama clans ruled over the southern regions, while a dozen pastoral Herero chieftainships dominated the eastern regions and competed with Nama groups for control of central areas.

Smaller groups had already been dispersed to isolated regions before the eighteenth century. German colonial rule (1884–1915) and South African colonial rule (1915–1989) destroyed most of the indigenous political systems and perpetrated relentless violence against the Namibian people as a whole. South Africa had been granted control over South West Africa in 1919, when the League of Nations accorded political rule of the country to Britain after Germany's defeat in World War I, and Britain passed on this responsibility to South Africa.

The Germans initiated and the South Africans consolidated a rigid division of the country along racial and ethnic lines for the benefit of the white settlers. The far northern and eastern regions were called "communal" areas, and they remained politically divided from the rest of the country, although the Ovambo-dominated northern areas were exploited as labor reserves for the mining industry. Meanwhile, an immense police zone was established, comprising the central and southern regions, within which blacks were forced off their land to make room for large, white-owned farms that raised livestock. South African authorities imposed strict military and police rule over the black populace in this zone, where serf-like conditions prevailed for farm workers. Pass laws curtailed the mobility of urban and rural blacks. In the populous northern regions outside the police zone, traditional black leaders became subservient to South African officials. The black majority, comprising 94 percent of the populace, enjoyed no political or human rights.

End of Colonial Rule

In 1960 an anticolonial political party was established—the South West Africa People's Organization (SWAPO). Six years later it began an armed struggle to liberate the colony. South Africa's modern military forces, however, easily held SWAPO's tiny guerrilla army at bay and terrorized the peoples of the northern regions in an effort to force them to curtail their support of SWAPO. Also during the 1960s and 1970s puppet governments were erected in all communal areas to represent the different ethnic groups. This ethnically based political division of the country gave rise to a political party, the Democratic Turnhalle Alliance (DTA).

South Africa now sought to construct a democratic façade in South West Africa in response to SWAPO's anti-colonial political movement. National elections in 1978 were boycotted by SWAPO and manipulated by the South African authorities. These elections resulted in the creation of a DTA-dominated, ethnically constituted National Assembly that remained under the authority of the South

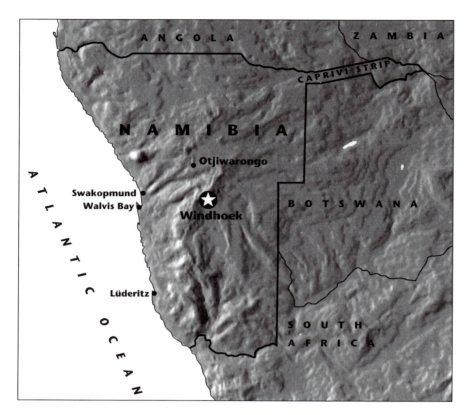

African–appointed administrator general. The legislature, temporarily abolished in 1983, was reconstituted in 1985 as the Transitional Government of National Unity—a non-elected body with circumscribed legislative powers.

Meanwhile, international factors played an increasingly important role in pushing South West Africa toward a genuinely democratic future. The United Nations in 1966 revoked South Africa's right to rule South West Africa and in 1978 passed a resolution urging free and fair elections and full independence. After a decade of international negotiations aimed at resolving both the Angolan civil war and the anticolonial struggle in Namibia, South Africa agreed in 1988 to United Nations–supervised elections in Namibia in preparation for full Namibian independence (while Cuba agreed to withdraw its troops from Angola). As a result, 1989 witnessed the ending of SWAPO's armed rebellion, the return from abroad of the SWAPO leadership, and an active electoral campaign on the part of SWAPO, the DTA, and eight minor political parties.

Independence

National elections, administered by South Africa and tightly monitored by the United Nations, were held in November 1989. Ninety-seven percent of the eligible voters (totaling about 700,000 people) selected the party of their preference in the balloting. There was some violence and intimidation, purportedly by the South African military (which supported the DTA) and SWAPO supporters, but the elections as a whole were declared free and fair by a wide range of observers. A party list system of proportional representation was used. SWAPO, with 57 percent of the national vote, received 57 percent of the seventy-two seats in the Constituent Assembly (that is, forty-one seats). SWAPO's chief rival, the DTA, won 28 percent of the vote and thereby twenty-one seats. Five minor parties also won legislative representation: the United Democratic Front (four seats), National Christian Action (three seats), the National Patriotic Front (one seat), the Federal Convention of Namibia (one seat), and the Namibia National Front (one seat).

This first free and fair election marked the country's historic passage to democratic rule. The resultant Constituent Assembly negotiated a constitution that is among the most democratic in the world, codifying a large number of political rights and human rights. The bargaining that took place among SWAPO, the DTA, and minority party members of the Parliament from November 1989 to February 1990 set the stage for a political culture of compromise and tolerance that has characterized both the Parliament and Namibian politics more generally since that time. This is remarkable in light of the brutal oppression and racial intolerance that characterized Namibia's colonial experience. Moreover, SWAPO has demonstrated an impressive capacity to shift roles from that of a liberation party directing a guerrilla war to that of a parliamentary party overseeing a democratic republic. Similarly impressive is the DTA's willingness to step peacefully out of its former role as ruler of the Parliament into its new role as the official parliamentary opposition.

From among its members the Constituent Assembly elected SWAPO leader Sam Nujoma as president in February 1990. Then on the day of independence, March 21, 1990, South West Africa became Namibia. The Constituent Assembly, reconstituted as the National Assembly, expanded to seventy-eight members to accommodate six nonvoting members appointed by the president, as stipulated by the constitution. Between April 1990 and November 1994 the National Assembly held eight full sessions, lasting three to four months each. The Assembly continues to serve as a forum for intensive political debate.

Consolidation of Democratic Institutions

Democratic institutions in Namibia were further strengthened by direct popular elections from November 30 to December 3, 1992. These elections, the first carried out by the SWAPO-run government, established fifty new local authorities (mostly town councils) and thirteen regional councils. Despite some organizational problems with registration, almost all eligible voters were able to participate. The councils preside over a redistricted nation with the new constituencies based on geographic and economic factors (rather than on ethnicity, as was the case under South African rule).

The election of the new regional councils made possible the creation of Namibia's second house of Parliament, the National Council, as mandated by the constitution. In December 1992 each of the regional councils elected two members to form a twenty-six–member National Council, which was officially inaugurated in February 1993. The principal function of the National Council is to review bills passed by the National Assembly and to recommend revisions where necessary.

The National Council is the weaker house of Parliament, but it can influence national decisions. Its regional

bases provide it with a grassroots linkage that the National Assembly lacks. With a two-thirds majority vote, the National Council can force the National Assembly to reconsider a bill that it has passed.

The democratic principles and tolerance that have predominated in the legislature are also reflected in Namibian society as a whole. The half-dozen daily and weekly newspapers are intensely critical of government policies much of the time. Political interest groups, several minor opposition political parties, and influential church groups are essentially unrestricted in their activities, and basic democratic rights have been upheld. The judicial system is independent from the legislative and executive institutions, and its decisions have been respected (if not always appreciated) by both ruling and opposition political parties.

Many divisions and inequities created by colonial rule persist, however, despite an official government policy of national reconciliation. Most land in southern and central Namibia remains in the hands of a few thousand white farmers, and black Namibians await a clear land reform policy by the government. Although the ethnic communal area governments were abolished at independence, ethnic divisions could become more prominent if the economy fails to improve. In the long run such problems, if unattended, could threaten the stability of Namibia's new democratic institutions.

The national elections held December 7–9, 1994, however, strengthened the country's democratic promise. The president was chosen through direct suffrage on separate balloting for the first time (henceforth the election will be every five years). Incumbent president Sam Nujoma defeated DTA leader Mishake Muyongo, with Nujoma receiving 74.46 percent of the vote and Muyongo received 23.08 percent. Balloting for the National Assembly was again held according to the party list system (as it will be henceforth). SWAPO received 72.72 percent of the vote, augmenting its majority to fifty-three seats, and the DTA received 20.45 percent of the vote total, with its preliminary seat total declining to fifteen. Also winning National Assembly seats were the United Democratic Front (two seats), the Democratic Coalition of Namibia (one seat), and the Monitor Action Group (one seat). This election provided SWAPO with a two-thirds majority in the National Assembly, enabling it to revise the constitution with a straight party vote.

These national elections represented an impressive step toward the consolidation of Namibian democracy. Continuing progress, however, will depend in large part on the new government's ability to moderate lingering socioeconomic inequities.

See also *South Africa*.

Joshua Bernard Forrest

BIBLIOGRAPHY

Bley, Helmut. *South West Africa under German Rule*. London: Heinemann, 1971.

Cooper, Allan D. *The Occupation of Namibia: Afrikanderdom's Attack on the British Empire*. Lanham, Md.: University Press of America, 1991.

Drechsler, Horst. *Let Us Die Fighting: Namibia under the Germans*. Berlin: Academie Verlag, 1966; London: Zed Books, 1980.

Du Pisani, André. *SWA/Namibia: The Politics of Continuity and Change*. Johannesburg: Jonathan Ball, 1986.

Forrest, Joshua Bernard. "Namibia: The First Postapartheid Democracy." In *Journal of Democracy* 5 (July 1994): 88–100.

Goldblatt, I. *History of South West Africa from the Beginning of the Nineteenth Century*. Cape Town: Juta, 1971.

Katjavivi, Peter H. *A History of Resistance in Namibia*. London: James Currey, 1988.

Sparks, Donald L., and December Green. *Namibia: The Nation after Independence*. Boulder, Colo.: Westview Press, 1992.

National security

The policy area in which an independent country protects itself against foreign military attack or against intimidation by the prospect of such an attack. Provisions for national security include the maintenance of armed forces but, more broadly, national security involves anything related to the possibility of war.

The Problem of National Security in Democracies

The maintenance of national security confronts any democracy with the most difficult of problems. No democratic nation wants to be governed against its will by a foreign army. But neither does any democratic nation want to have its freedom suppressed by the army it created. If all the world were governed by democratic processes, and if the assumption were truly correct that democracies do not fight wars with one another, this problem might fairly readily solve itself: military forces could be dispensed with.

That practice is already followed in Iceland, one of the world's oldest democracies, and in Costa Rica, the long-standing exception to the pessimistic generalization that democracy does not work in Latin America. Iceland has never had armed forces of its own. It was occupied by British and American armed forces during World War II at the moment it declared its independence from Denmark. Costa Rica, which has not faced any recent threat of invasion, disbanded its army precisely to avoid the threat to democratic rule that such armies had posed so often in other Latin American countries.

Yet if even one state in the world is imperialistic and power minded, the problem reappears of how the citizens of other self-governing states can avoid domination by this power. And if they prepare an army to hold back foreign dictators, how do they keep that army from itself becoming a threat to domestic democratic rule? Iceland and Costa Rica have been exceptional; virtually every other sovereign entity maintains a national army.

If peace spreads as democracy spreads, a basic paradox arises. The liberal who believes in democracy believes in peace. But this belief may tempt others, lusting after power, to try to exploit the situation—as illustrated quite well in the post–World War I gambits of Benito Mussolini and his allies in Italy and in the post–cold war foray of Iraq's Saddam Hussein into Kuwait.

The atmosphere at the founding of the League of Nations in 1919 was similar to the mood at the sudden end of the cold war in 1989. In 1919 tired of the trench slaughter, and in 1989 fearful of the prospect of nuclear holocaust, the world welcomed peace with great enthusiasm, expecting a "peace dividend." In each instance this optimism was matched with an anticipation that democracy in domestic politics would spread. But in each case this was also an opening for someone less democratic and less peace loving to try to exploit the democracies' commitment to peace.

Karl von Clausewitz, the great nineteenth-century Prussian analyst of military and political affairs, alluded to the basic paradox by an aphorism: "the aggressor always loves peace." As Clausewitz pointed out, it is not the aggressor who starts a war, but the side that resists. Thus we remember World War II in Europe as beginning in September 1939, when Adolf Hitler's forces crossed into Poland, and not in March of that year, when the same forces had crossed into what was left of Czechoslovakia. The reason for this is simply that the Czechs did not resist, whereas the Poles did.

Believers in democracy and in international peace may look forward to a world in which there are no such paradoxes. But it takes only one Mussolini or Hitler or Saddam Hussein to force the democracies to arm themselves as well. This process necessarily entails domestic threats to democracy, a willingness to impose secrecy and censorship, and some willingness to suppress dissent, at least among those in uniform.

Naval Forces Versus Ground Forces

One solution to this dilemma, but only where geography cooperates, is to be surrounded by water, so that naval rather than ground forces are the appropriate means to national security. Navies are good at holding back potential invaders, but they are far less useful than armies for overthrowing a parliament. As we try to explain why the democratic tradition has thrived, even if it emerged slowly, in England and then in the rest of the English-speaking world, the safety provided to Britain by the English Channel must be considered an important contributing factor.

Navies might tempt a nation to engage in imperialism and gunboat diplomacy far from the homeland and thus to become a threat to the self-government of others. But unless imperialism generated large armies of conquest that could be brought home to topple governments whenever their commanders became dissatisfied or ambitious, the result would be as before: the home country would remain pluralistic and free enough to keep democracy alive.

Similarly, in the twentieth century there might be somewhat less of a problem with the existence of an air force than with an army. As we shall discuss further, when an air force is coupled with the threat of destroying densely populated cities (a possibility established in particular by the atomic bomb), the links to democratic theory become much more complicated.

Yet military reliance on air power alone, or even on sea power alone, has for most geopolitical situations been inadequate. Skeptics about sea power or air power contend that only an army can take possession of the enemy's territory to control and govern it. And just as naval power cannot conquer an adversary by itself, so an air force cannot conquer territory by itself. If this proposition is true, it follows that air forces also cannot take charge of one's own country any more readily than a navy could. In the juntas assembled after coups deposing elected presidents in Latin America, the navy and air force are often represented, but the ground forces are always represented and are almost always predominant.

The maintenance of armies thus is a threat to democratic government in a variety of ways. Armies have heavier weapons than do the police or ordinary citizens, and they can inflict violence on the capital city and its inhabitants. Armies, by reason of their need to be ready for conflict with other countries' armies, can impose requirements for discipline and secrecy, both of which run counter to democracy's need for openness and disagreement. An army that questions orders will not do well in combat. An army that feels free to discuss its possible operations openly before they are launched will never surprise an enemy but instead will lay itself open to being surprised. An effective army must indeed engage in espionage to try to learn the plans of possible enemies, and perhaps even engage in sabotage, to frustrate such plans. It must also engage in extensive efforts to prevent the adversary's ventures into espionage and sabotage.

Yet these same activities and capabilities can also be used to eliminate elections or to distort the outcomes of elections. Incumbents will mint slogans such as "don't change horses in midstream," and they may cite, as ammunition for their own reelection, the external dangers that they are so ably managing as civilian or military commanders in chief. Even if soldiers are able to vote freely, they may still feel guided to vote for their existing commander because they have to obey that commander on other issues as long as they are in uniform.

Secrecy can be abused to hide developments that would be embarrassing to the incumbent; in an open discussion these developments could give votes to the opposition. Secrecy can be justified on the ground (perhaps specious, perhaps genuine) that "the enemy" would benefit from such information. An example arose during the U.S. election of 1944. The Republican candidate, Thomas E. Dewey, was preparing to make an issue of Franklin D. Roosevelt's administration's alleged lack of readiness for the Japanese attack at Pearl Harbor in 1941. Dewey was dissuaded from exploiting this issue, which might have helped him prevent Roosevelt's reelection, by a warning conveyed by Gen. George C. Marshall, the U.S. Army chief of staff, that his electioneering would give away the fact that the United States had successfully broken the Japanese codes. If Japan became aware of this espionage success, it would change the codes, the American advantage would have been compromised, and additional American soldiers and sailors would have been killed in combat.

To support democracy is almost by definition to oppose secrecy and authority. And, generally, to be distrustful of government is to be averse to violence, since what government brings to bear in human situations is an organized capacity for violence. If geography does not provide a watery moat against outside threats, the supporter of democracy faces a dilemma: fending off foreign threats requires the maintenance of ground forces, which can impose domestic threats.

Attempts to Restrict Armies

The drafters of the U.S. Constitution were very aware of these dilemmas and attempted to address them, but they did so in ways that have proved to be imperfectly effective. To avoid excessive buildup of the kind of power that is particularly threatening to democracy, the Constitution limits appropriations for the army to two years. It places no time limits on appropriations for the navy (thus showing an early awareness of the distinction between types of military force).

The elected president was specifically designated the commander in chief of all the armed forces, but Congress retained the prerogative of declaring war. As noted earlier, the determination of when wars begin is always somewhat more complicated than legal declarations can settle. Did World War II with Japan begin on December 8, 1941, when Congress declared war, or on December 7, when the Japanese launched their surprise attack on Pearl Harbor?

In keeping with the United Nations charter, which commits all member states to avoid war, no member states have declared war since World War II. The U.S. involvements in fighting since 1945 have all come without a declaration of war by Congress, thus supporting the fear that the national security function can be a threat to the constitutional checks and balances intended to preserve representative government.

Yet it would be historically inaccurate to conclude that such undeclared wars, undertaken by the executive branch without formal action of Congress, occurred only in the cold war era. The U.S. navy fought an undeclared war with the French navy at the end of the eighteenth century and chased after Barbary pirates in the Mediterranean in the same years. And American army units entered Mexico in 1916 in pursuit of Pancho Villa.

Whenever the military forces of democracies become engaged in international interactions, they can come under attack by other armed forces and may have to defend themselves immediately, regardless of the provisions of any carefully crafted constitutions intended to circumscribe executive authority. When a government fighting against domestic bandits or insurgents asks for help, there is no opposing government to declare war against.

The War Powers Act of 1973, passed over President Richard Nixon's veto during the depths of American dissatisfaction with the Vietnam War, attempted in various ways to circumscribe executive authority over the use of military force and to reinforce the authority of the elected legislature. It is too early to conclude that such an effort can succeed, when the dynamics of international military confrontations and initiatives place such a premium on centralized command authority.

No matter how carefully one tries to circumscribe a government, as is the intention of the U.S. Constitution and many other written constitutions, the international threats to national security generate a countervailing logic.

Citizen Armies Versus Professional Armies

In the United States at the time of the Vietnam War a debate broke out about an all-volunteer armed force versus a compulsory draft. People to the left of center generally opposed the draft, while those to the right of center supported it. A student of the history of political democracy in Europe might have found this situation bizarre, for the pattern of the nineteenth century was the reverse: the defenders of hereditary rule and traditional privilege, after their experience with the French Revolution and Napoleon Bonaparte, typically favored small, professional "mercenary" military forces, while the liberal and radical political elements called instead for "a nation in arms," a nation in which all young men would receive military training.

The aristocrats supporting the old regime preferred an armed force that would support the king unquestioningly, even if it were called upon to fire on a protesting people. They favored an armed force whose officers were all nobles, perhaps distantly related to the monarch, and were in any event wedded to the hereditary principle. The radicals, by contrast, wanted larger armies that, by including all the people, would be more loyal to the people at large. The officers would be drawn from the middle class and perhaps even the poorer classes.

One can find contemporary situations where "militarism" does not seem to conflict very much with "democracy." Israel, Switzerland, Sweden, and Finland, for example, all have maintained systems of universal military training because of the external enemies they fear, without concerns about what military preparations can do to their democracies.

The Swiss tell a joke about a tourist who says, "I didn't

know Switzerland had an army." The Swiss guide replies, "Switzerland doesn't have an army; Switzerland is an army." No one speculates about the military overthrowing the government in Israel, Finland, Sweden, or Switzerland because the entire country (at least all the males between ages eighteen and fifty) is in arms.

When the French army tried to overthrow President Charles de Gaulle in 1961, the best combat units in the army, the all-volunteer paratroopers, were enthusiastic for the overthrow, feeling (in a "them or us" mentality) that French governments had underappreciated and betrayed their combat efforts since the end of World War II. What kept this coup against French democracy from succeeding was the presence in uniform of large numbers of French draftees, not nearly as good soldiers as the professionals but able to outnumber the rebels and keep democratic government alive.

The American debate of the 1960s, which resulted in the termination of the draft and a reliance instead on an all-volunteer force, pitted two liberal principles against each other: voluntarism and representativeness. Distrustful of force and of government in general, those who desire free elections may feel an aversion to compulsory military service, for themselves or for anyone else.

Yet the result of a reliance on volunteers, as was the case in nineteenth-century Europe and was sometimes the case in France after World War II, might then be a military force unrepresentative of the country as a whole, a force that sees itself as doing more than its share of the dangerous and unpleasant work of national security, a force that begins thinking in terms of "them" versus "us."

Aside from compulsory military service, there is only one example of compulsory activity in a democratic country: jury duty. The analogy raises some important questions. Would an all-volunteer jury system be preferable, or would it draw in people who enjoy judging the guilt or innocence of others? Just as an army raised on a volunteer basis will often not be representative of the varying ethnic groups or geographical regions or economic classes of a country, so an all-volunteer jury would be unrepresentative.

Indeed, the parallel between jury duty and military service is not so tenuous, for they share an important potential role. In the American and British systems, only two kinds of people can put a citizen into prison: jurors or soldiers. If the army overthrew the constitutional order, it could well suspend the right of trial by jury.

Another consideration is that after several decades, all-volunteer ground forces of a democratic country might view themselves as "different" from the civilians of the country and perhaps alienated from them. Thus they might be prone to use force to overthrow an elected government.

In addition to the concern about representativeness, another liberal principle to consider is the fairness of burden sharing. Military service is dangerous and can be unpleasant. If recruitment is handled entirely on a volunteer basis, those who have not been successful in life will be more willing to sign on for military service than their more successful counterparts, and thus they may be overrepresented. Even if this possibility never raised the specter of a military coup, it is upsetting to those who see minorities or the economically disadvantaged drawing more than their fair share of casualties in combat. It also could draw foreign propaganda attacks, if the forces dispatched by a democratic country were to seem exploitative of its economically less well off minorities.

The suggestion is sometimes advanced that the unfairness of a military burden can be compensated for by making military service a great learning experience. There are at least two inherent problems with this idea. First, an army that excels as a remedial school, making up for the unfairness and inequities of civilian society, may not excel as a combat force supporting national security. Second, enhancing the teaching role of the military could condition those in this "school" to an authoritarian outlook, at variance with the pluralistic and democratic world view that civilian schools teach.

Another argument for universal military training, illustrated by the Finnish, Swedish, and Swiss examples (but not so much by the Israeli), is that citizen armies in which every male has to serve have tended to be more inclined to military defense and less to invasion of neighboring countries. Territorially based militia, who are part-time soldiers, may not be adept at the maneuver warfare of a grand armored offensive, but they may be expert at defending the particular mountain passes and turns of the road of the region in which they live.

The system of "a nation in arms" has thus at times been put forward as a way to take care of two very different problems in relating national security to democracy: protecting oneself without looking threatening to a neighbor (restoring real meaning to the old and often blurred or abused distinction between "defense" and "offense") and mustering military competence without generating a domestic threat to free elections.

International Peace Versus Democracy

Coups in which a professional military overthrows a democratic government seldom occur in the face of outside military threats to national security; rather, they occur in the absence of such threats. Before becoming too pessimistic about conflicts between genuine national defense and the maintenance of democracy, one might find some solace in comparing the patterns common to Latin America with those common to Europe and North America.

Latin American armed forces, despite what they may claim as their reason for existence, do not have to be constantly ready for war with one another. Latin America is a part of the world that has been relatively free of warfare and of burdensome arms races, a part of the world that has taken international law more seriously than other continents. In short, there is much to admire here, much that the rest of the world could learn from in the management and moderation of international disputes. For whatever reason—high mountains separating countries, a greater international reasonableness, or the influence of the United States—Latin America has seen few wars. But it has witnessed a great many coups deposing democracies. In effect, there has been no real national security problem.

Paradoxically, the absence of a national security problem seemingly has resulted in the armed forces of these countries being inclined to depose elected presidents and generally to interfere with democracy. Cynics have sometimes suggested that fear of an opposing army is the most important tool for making an army responsive to duly constituted authority. Civilian authority is much more in danger of being challenged where this fear is absent, as in Latin America, than where it is present. Where the national security issue is real—where wars are already being fought or where conflicts continually threaten—the military is a threat to democracy as well, but it has to think twice before plunging its own country into the confusion of a coup d'état.

Looking at Nazi Germany, any supporter of democracy and liberal humane values would have welcomed a military coup against Hitler's dictatorship. What made Gen. Claus Schenk von Stauffenberg's assassination attempt so difficult was that most Germans believed that it was supremely important to stay united against the enemy.

Of course, one does not welcome the kind of military insubordination carried out by the German officers against Hitler where a democratic government is in place, but the causal point remains the same. If threats of foreign armies are what bring armies into being, the same threats may keep armies subordinated to proper civilian authority. The most severe threat to civilian democratic authority may come when a nation maintains an army without a plausible enemy, when a nation invests in soldiers and firearms and officer corps that never see combat.

Bureaucratic Politics

A different kind of threat to democracy involves no violence or suspension of civil liberties and no coups or tanks rolling in the streets. This kind of threat comes from the lower-level government bureaucrats who misinterpret their orders so as to advance their own careers, regardless of what the voters want and regardless of who is elected to executive and legislative positions.

Such an interpretation of how governmental decisions are made and how budgets and priorities are shaped became fashionable among American political scientists in the 1960s and 1970s. What makes theories of "bureaucratic politics" particularly relevant to a discussion of democracy and national security is that most of the examples offered to support such theories were drawn initially from the U.S. defense policy process.

According to proponents of this theory, lower-level officials seek to increase their budgets because higher budgets lead to more rapid promotion. They seek to expand their mandates because broader authority makes it easier to pursue activities in accordance with their organizational traditions. Regardless of what elected government officials ask for in policy options, the only options offered back will be those serving these bureaucratic goals. The result, so the allegation goes, was a policy that wasted funds and committed the United States to needless arms races and international confrontation. Lower-level bureaucrats, both military and civilian, would be adept at embarrassing or confusing any superior who attempted to thwart such tendencies and give the voters what they really wanted.

To tie such theories to national security, one would have to look for any particular advantages the armed services would have in competition with the civilian bureaucracies of the rest of the government (which presumably are also intent on getting promoted and on continuing with their organizational hobbyhorses) that would enable them to obtain an inappropriately larger share of the budget. One might return to the generic problems that national security has always posed for democracy.

Three characteristics peculiar to military organizations may enhance the military's ability to play "bureaucratic politics" better than other government structures: (1) a need for and ability to maintain secrecy may enable the military to hide from Congress and the taxpayers some of the operational shortfalls of weapons systems that it is intent on acquiring; (2) the size of military organizations may enable them to lobby more effectively for increased budgets; and (3) they may have a greater capacity for alarming the public.

Yet the emphasis of the bureaucratic politics literature on defense policy models has been accused of being exaggerated. Some political scientists argue that such obstruction of the public interest can be found in every corner of government.

The Military-Industrial Complex

The bureaucratic politics theories often depict a coalition of in-government military managers and out-of-government suppliers of weapons—what Dwight D. Eisenhower called the military-industrial complex. The allegation is that this combination sells a country more weapons than it needs because large purchases suit the career advancement interests of generals and admirals and increase the profits of the corporations building military equipment.

A skeptic might question whether heads of government and legislatures are powerless to scrutinize and veto such projects and whether the military officers and civilian defense officials involved lack in patriotism and concern for the national interest. Moreover, one can ask whether there would not be comparable coalitions of government officials and out-of-government suppliers of equipment in other areas of public policy—in education or agriculture or highways, for example—using the same tricks to sell their pet projects to the taxpayers and their elected representatives, thus making for a balance of competing sales efforts.

The Issue of Expertise

There is yet a broader problem: is democracy compatible with foreign policy in general, as well as with national security policy in particular? Specifically, is the public able to learn enough and know enough to participate meaningfully in the decision process?

Poll surveys have shown that the average American knows little about international events, since most American newspapers assign little coverage to the evolution of foreign disputes or to arcane details of military weapons and strategy. Although Europeans and their newspapers

do slightly better by the same measure, the general concern remains the same: the details of sorting out international conflicts can be handled only by an elite, not by the masses of ordinary voters.

In the past the general public's lack of knowledge has been an argument for allowing professional military officers, who are graduates of military and naval academies, to make wartime decisions. The reasoning is that only they have the necessary expertise, just as only the graduates of medical schools should make decisions about epidemics and public health. Some have proposed that the ends of foreign and defense policy should be determined by the people as a whole but that the application of means to these ends should be handled by professionals. They would distinguish between political and military decisions, asserting that the latter are inherently beyond the effective working of a normal democratic process.

After the end of World War II, however, as nuclear weapons became the central issue, the trend in the United States and in other democracies has been the opposite. The distinction between "military" and "political" decisions was hardly so clear anymore, and much of the development of nuclear strategy was undertaken by civilians.

The greater involvement of civilians in nuclear strategy came about for several reasons. First, nuclear weapons had been invented by civilian nuclear physicists and engineers. They felt a strong moral commitment to staying involved in the deliberations about how such weapons would be used. Furthermore, the target of these massively destructive weapons would be the civilian populations of both sides. If "total war" was going to include all the people as targets, all the people had a right to demand participation in decision making. Finally, "strategy" would be as much about the nonuse of nuclear weapons as about their use. This fact brought into play the logic that psychologists, economists, and political scientists had developed from the experiences of domestic conflict. Now that the "military" question was about what made nuclear deterrence work, it was unclear who would be a professional expert.

In cases where the likely adversary was a nondemocracy—for example, the Soviet Union—relating national security policy to morality created yet another problem. The question raised in the Roman Catholic bishops' statement of 1983 on the immorality of nuclear deterrence was whether one could morally aim at Soviet civilians as a way of deterring Soviet aggression against Western Europe or the United States when those civilians had no voice in these acts of aggression and had not been allowed to vote on the government that might launch them. The problem has rounded upon itself. With nuclear weapons in Russia in the possession of a democratically elected government, would it now be more moral to aim at the Russian civilian population, since they could be considered truly responsible for whatever aggression their country might initiate?

It is an article of faith that wars will not occur between democracies. Would it be a logically tenable proposition that mutual nuclear deterrence and mutual assured destruction would be morally acceptable only between democracies? Such moral questions may be too arcane ever to become politically real, but the general point is that the introduction of nuclear weapons has eroded the antidemocratic distinctions by which "military" questions were considered to be out of reach of the voters and their elected representatives, to be handled only by "experts."

See also *Foreign policy; Nationalism.*

George H. Quester

BIBLIOGRAPHY

Allison, Graham. *Essence of Decision: Explaining the Cuban Missile Crisis.* Boston: Little, Brown, 1971.

Blechman, Barry. *The Politics of National Security: Congress and U.S. Defense Policy.* New York: Oxford University Press, 1990.

Bowman, William. *The All-Volunteer Force after a Decade.* New York: Pergamon-Brassey's, 1986.

Clausewitz, Karl von. *On War.* Princeton: Princeton University Press, 1975.

Crabb, Cecil, and Pat Holt. *Invitation to Struggle.* Washington, D.C.: CQ Press, 1989.

Edwards, George, and Wallace E. Walker, eds. *National Security and the U.S. Constitution.* Baltimore: Johns Hopkins University Press, 1986.

Halperin, Morton. *Bureaucratic Politics and Foreign Policy.* Washington, D.C.: Brookings Institution, 1974.

Hilsman, Roger. *The Politics of Policy-Making in Defense and Foreign Affairs.* New York: Harper, 1971; Hertfordshire: Prentice-Hall, 1990.

Huntington, Samuel. *The Soldier and the State.* Cambridge and London: Harvard University Press, 1957.

Janowitz, Morris. *The Professional Soldier.* New York: Free Press, 1960.

Murray, Douglas, and Paul Viotti, eds. *The Defense Policies of Nations.* Baltimore: Johns Hopkins University Press, 1989.

National Conference of Catholic Bishops. *The Challenge of Peace: God's Promise and Our Response.* Washington, D.C.: United States Catholic Conference, 1983.

National Socialism

See *Fascism*

Nationalism

A political doctrine that regards the nation as the primary object of loyalty and advances a cultural, social, political, and moral point of view in which nations play a central role. Semantically, the term *nationalism* comes from the Latin word *natio*, which is derived from the verb *nasci*—"to be born." The term came to be used to define a group of individuals born in the same area. In medieval universities, for example, communities of students coming from particular regions were defined as *nations*.

There is a debate as to when the term acquired political significance. Some argue that as early as the beginning of the sixteenth century the term *nation* was applied to the population of a particular state, thus becoming synonymous with the term *people*. Others trace this development to the American and French Revolutions. It is widely accepted, however, that by the end of the eighteenth century the term *nation* referred to a sovereign people or, alternatively, to the government of a sovereign state.

The tendency to identify *nation* with *state* resulted from a shift in the type of legitimacy sought and claimed by political institutions. In his philosophical writings, Jean-Jacques Rousseau (1712–1778) rejected the legitimacy of divinely or historically appointed rulers in favor of a new source of legitimacy—popular sovereignty. This ideal, which lies at the heart of democratic theory, turned into a nationalist one as the body of citizens came to be identified with the nation. The doctrine of self-rule was thus bound up with the ideal of national self-determination. It therefore became widely accepted that sovereignty resides essentially in the nation. The state, previously identified with the ruler, came to be seen as the institutional representation of the nation's will. The nation thus became the symbol of fellowship among all members of the political framework as well as the tie between the ruled and the ruler. Hence a new political norm was established that fostered the belief that the legitimating principle of politics and state making is nationalism.

This norm found its best expression in the nation-state, which evolved in the nineteenth century. The nation-state was supposed to allow for the development of the most stable and advanced form of democratic life. National homogeneity was to lead to internal harmony and solidarity as well as to patriotic feelings and readiness to defend the state from external threats.

How deep is the link between nationalist and democratic ideals? Some argue that democracy and nationalism are inherently linked because they share two basic tenets: the belief that members of the various social-economic classes are political equals and that sovereignty lies with the people. This claim is, however, somewhat misleading. The equality that membership in a nation accords is not necessarily a democratic one. Nationhood may grant individuals a feeling of belonging and a certain sense of mutuality, but it does not necessarily imply either political equality or democratic structures. The kind of equality that nationalism grants fellow nationals is not necessarily political but communal. If nationalism was necessary for the development of democracy, it was not because it justified political equality but because it gave a rationale for the division of the world into distinct political units in which democratic principles could be implemented. The belief in liberal democratic values may be fundamental to the culture of some nations—to the English, American, and French national cultures, for example—yet these values are not nationalist values in that they are not inherent to the national way of thinking. Nationalist movements have indeed been invariably populist in outlook, and their emergence, in a modern sense, has been tied to the political baptism of the lower classes. They often have been characterized by attempts of the middle classes and intellectual leadership to induct members of the lower classes into political life and to channel popular energies into support for new states. Nonetheless, many of these movements were hostile to democracy and entertained totalitarian, fascist, and racist ideologies.

The growing rift between contemporary nationalist movements and democratic ideals does not indicate that these movements are illiberal and undemocratic by nature; rather, it follows a change in political circumstances that has not been met by appropriate theoretical and political developments. The identification between the citizens of a state and members of a nation has been frustrated as new states inhabited by more than one nation have been established, massive waves of immigration have taken place, and groups previously excluded from the political process have been included.

At the end of the twentieth century, hardly any state is homogeneous from a national point of view. Yet the idea that the nation is the only valid source of state legitimacy is still widely accepted. Consequently, every group of individuals who consider themselves a nation wants to establish their own independent state—a desire that leads to separatist and secessionist policies. Existing governments are also pressured to prove that they represent a nation rather than a mere gathering of individuals. Nation-states are therefore interested in homogenizing their population: they intervene in their population's language, interpretation of history, myths and symbols, or—to put it more broadly—in their culture. Modern nation-states thus are agents for cultural, linguistic, and sometimes religious unification. Their attempts to build a nation lead to the oppression of national minorities and, in extreme cases, to ethnic cleansing and genocide.

In a world of nationally heterogeneous states, nationalism and democracy can coexist only if the nationalist ideal is moderated and reshaped. This calls for a redefinition of the terms *state* and *nation* that will draw a sharp distinction between the two, with the former seen as a political organization and the latter as a cultural group that shares a common history, tradition, language, sometimes religion, and national consciousness. This conceptual redefinition will imply that the democratic ideal of self-rule, seen as the right of individuals to participate in decision-making processes, and the nationalist ideal of national self-determination, seen as a desire to retain an active and lively national life, should not be used synonymously. Divorcing the nationalist ideal from the demand for independent statehood and acknowledging the multinational nature of most states might allow nationalism to retain its alliance with democratic ideals and play a role in a world in which the need for cross-national cooperation on a variety of economic, ecological, and strategic questions cannot be ignored.

See also *Fascism; Immigration; Locke, John; Majority rule, minority rights; National security; Popular sovereignty; Racism; Revolution, American; Revolution, French; Rousseau, Jean-Jacques.*

Yael Tamir

BIBLIOGRAPHY

Anderson, Benedict R. *Imagined Communities: Reflections on the Origin and Spread of Nationalism.* London and New York: Verso, 1983.

Barry, Brian M. "Self-Government Revisited." In *Democracy and Power: Essays in Political Theory,* edited by Brian M. Barry. Oxford: Clarendon Press; New York: Oxford University Press, 1991.

Gellner, Ernest. *Nations and Nationalism.* Oxford: Blackwell; Ithaca, N.Y.: Cornell University Press, 1983.

Greenfeld, Liah. *Nationalism: Five Roads to Modernity.* Cambridge, Mass., and London: Harvard University Press, 1992.

Smith, Anthony D. *National Identity.* Las Vegas: University of Nevada Press, 1991.

———. *Theories of Nationalism.* 2d ed. London: Duckworth; New York: Holmes and Meier, 1983.

Tamir, Yael. "The Enigma of Nationalism." *World Politics* 47 (spring 1995): 418–440.

———. *Liberal Nationalism.* Princeton: Princeton University Press, 1993.

Natural law

A two-thousand-year-old ethical, political, and legal theory that, in its later forms, supplied the philosophical foundations of modern liberal democracy. The term *natural law* is often loosely applied to any theory that adheres to objective standards of morality. In its proper sense it designates a moral law that exists by nature and is known by nature to be binding on everyone. Thus defined, natural law is distinguished from civil law, whose statutes are enacted and enforced by some human legislator, and from divine law, which is communicated through sacred scriptures. Natural law is also distinguished from Immanuel Kant's moral law, which presents itself as a law of reason rather than a law of nature.

Natural law was for centuries the cornerstone of Western ethical and political thought. It inspired some of the most famous documents of modern liberalism, including the American Declaration of Independence (1776) and the various versions of the French Declaration of the Rights of Man and the Citizen (1789, 1793, 1795). Today it is for the most part an object of historical study rather than a source of authoritative moral judgment. Although efforts to revive it have not been lacking, nothing indicates that it is about to regain the prominence it once occupied in the Western tradition. Even the Roman Catholic Church, where until recently it continued to hold sway, now appeals less and less frequently to natural law in its official documents.

The doctrine of natural law that informs modern constitutions is the dynamic and reformist doctrine of the seventeenth- and eighteenth-century Enlightenment. The original theory of natural law was considerably more conservative than that of the Enlightenment. The theory emerged by way of transformation of Plato's and Aristotle's teaching of natural right. Its most conspicuous departure from the classical teaching is that it not only points to what is intrinsically right or wrong but commands the performance of the one and the avoidance of the other under threat of sanction.

Classical and Medieval Background

Modern scholars usually attribute the invention of natural law to the Stoic philosophers. There is no solid evidence, however, that the old Stoics ever used the term *natural law.* Stoicism nevertheless furnished one of the fundamental premises of that theory: the notion of a providential god who guarantees the moral consistency of the universe by ensuring that the just are rewarded and the wicked punished, if not in this life at least in the next. The mode and severity of the punishments in question are not specified by the natural law itself. They are left to be determined by the civil law and may vary according to circumstances. Capital punishment, for example, is neither imposed nor forbidden by natural law.

The earliest extant accounts of natural law are found in the *Republic* and *Laws* of the Roman statesman and philosopher Marcus Tullius Cicero (106–43 B.C.). In the *Republic* the jurist Laelius, one of the dialogue's main characters, uses natural law to defend the justice of Rome's conquest of the civilized world. It is doubtful whether Cicero, a critic of the Stoic notion of divine providence, personally subscribed to Laelius's theory. Cicero seems to have endorsed it less as a true doctrine than as a rhetorical tool with which to curb the excesses of Roman imperialism.

From Cicero, the natural law was absorbed into the Roman legal tradition, and soon thereafter it became a standard feature of the theological tradition of the Christian West. St. Augustine (354–430 A.D.) invoked it to defend his own just-war theory (*Contra Faustum*) and also to absolve God of the blame that he would have incurred for the sins of his creatures had he left them invincibly ignorant of the basic principles of moral behavior. For Augustine, compliance with the natural law, which requires the subordination of the lower to the higher both within the individual and in society at large, is synonymous with the whole of human perfection.

The premodern doctrine of natural law achieved its classic formulation in the works of Thomas Aquinas (1225–1274). Thomas distinguishes between the primary principles of the natural law, which are immutable, and its secondary principles, which are subject to change. The primary principles are said to be self-evident and form the object of a special virtue that the Christian tradition called *synderesis,* the storehouse of the most general principles of the moral order. These principles are intimated to human beings through the natural inclinations by which they are directed to the most general ends of human existence, the highest of which are the knowledge of the truth and life in society. Nowhere are we given an exhaustive list of these principles, although Thomas does say that the moral law of the Old Testament, which is summed up in the Ten Commandments, belongs to the natural law.

Thomas's teaching met with much resistance on the part of later medieval philosophers and theologians. Marsilius of Padua (c.1280–c.1343) rejected it on the Aristotelian ground that human reason alone is unable to prove that God is a legislator. Duns Scotus (1266?–1308) and William of Ockham (c.1285–1349?) objected to it, asserting that by binding God to its precepts natural law conflicted with the biblical notions of divine freedom and omnipotence. Accordingly, Scotus reduced the natural law to a single negative precept, the one that prohibits the hatred of God. Ockham went even further, asserting that God could command us to hate him if he so desired.

The sixteenth and seventeenth centuries witnessed a return to the Thomist teaching, spearheaded by a number of influential commentators among whom Francisco de Vitoria and Francisco Suárez stand out, along with Hugo Grotius. The motivation for this revival was furnished by the wars of religion that were ravaging Europe and by the cruelties inflicted on the American Indians by the Spanish conquistadors. The rules of just warfare were spelled out in ever greater detail, and the old Roman notion of the "law of nations" was transformed into what became known as international law.

Modern Theory

A milestone in the development of modern democratic theory was the appearance of the natural law teachings propounded by the seventeenth-century founders of modern liberalism, especially the teachings of Thomas Hobbes and John Locke. Breaking decisively with tradition, Hobbes and Locke sought to establish political thought on a new, more solid foundation. Human beings no longer were said to be political and social by nature. They were seen as solitary individuals who once existed in

a prepolitical "state of nature" and were actuated, not by a desire for some preexisting end in the attainment of which they achieved their perfection, but by a premoral passion, the desire for self-preservation, from which the "right" of self-preservation arises. In the thinking of Hobbes and Locke, individual rights, conferred by nature, replace duties as the primordial moral phenomenon. Civil society is not something natural and desirable for its own sake. It comes into being by way of a contract made by human beings who enter freely into it for no reason other than to escape the dangers that threaten them in the state of nature. As for the natural law, it has nothing to do with the self-evident principles of which the medieval philosophers spoke, but it is identified with the sum of the conclusions that human reason arrives at by a process of deduction from the right of self-preservation. In the *Leviathan* (1651), Hobbes lists nineteen such principles, all of them calculated to ensure the individual's security and physical well-being.

Unlike the old doctrine of natural law, which was not essentially egalitarian and whose compatibility with any decent regime, whether democratic or aristocratic, was never doubted, the new doctrine held that there was but one just and legitimate regime—that is, liberal democracy or popular sovereignty—in the name of which authoritarian or nondemocratic regimes could rightfully be overthrown (as in fact they were in America and France during the last quarter of the eighteenth century).

The last and the most radical of the modern theorists of natural law was Jean-Jacques Rousseau, who criticized the Hobbesian and Lockean schemes for fostering a bourgeois mentality that undermines civic virtue and therewith the freedom and equality for the protection of which civil society was established. The solution to the problem, Rousseau thought, lay in forming small societies in which all citizens would participate on an equal basis in accordance with the principle of "one man, one vote."

The Demise of Natural Law

Rousseau argued that neither Hobbes nor Locke had found the true state of nature for the simple reason that they took as their standard a human nature that was already corrupted by society. Rousseau's search led him backward in time to a stage that antedates not only the formation of civil society but the emergence of rationality and, indeed, of humanity itself. But if the state of nature is not a properly human state, one fails to see how it could serve as a reliable guide to human behavior. The critical next step was taken by Immanuel Kant, who abandoned nature as the touchstone of the moral rightness of human actions and replaced it with the categorical imperative, or the laws of universal reason.

Further challenges to natural law came from two of the most powerful intellectual forces of modern times, historicism, or historical relativism, and social science positivism. Historicism originated as a reaction against the atrocities spawned by the French Revolution. It tried to forestall the possibility of such revolutions in the future by rejecting the notion of a permanently valid natural or higher law to which a direct appeal could be made from existing civil laws. Social science positivism denies scientific status to any proposition that is not empirically verifiable and relegates all principles of natural law—none of which is subject to this kind of empirical verification—to the subjective realm of "value judgments."

This is not to say that the idea of natural law has simply vanished from our midst. The Neo-Thomist movement of the nineteenth and twentieth centuries did much to keep its memory alive, even though the literature that it produced is more notable for its abundance than for its originality. Some scholars, such as R. W. and A. J. Carlyle and Edward S. Corwin, have argued that the tradition of natural law continued unbroken from its inception in pre-Christian antiquity to the end of the eighteenth century. Jacques Maritain and John Finnis have since offered revised versions of both the medieval doctrine of natural law and the initially antithetical doctrine of modern rights in a valiant attempt to reconcile the two streams of thought, though with limited effect. Rightly or wrongly, most contemporary thinkers remain suspicious of natural law, finding it either too vague to be of any real use, too inflexible for the proper conduct of the affairs of state, or potentially subversive.

Yet experience has shown that dispensing with natural law altogether is not an easy matter: without it one is deprived of a valuable moral argument against the blatantly unjust laws under which people often are made to live. Some Germans resorted to natural law in the 1940s to justify their resistance to the Nazi regime and the assassination attempt on Hitler's life. After the war the same argument was pressed into service at the trials of Nazi war criminals at Nuremberg, the legality of which could not be established on the basis of existing national and international laws. Martin Luther King, Jr., referred to natural law in his famous letter from the Birmingham City Jail, citing Thomas Aquinas in support of the view that a hu-

man law not rooted in eternal and natural law is an unjust law. Similar problems arise when a country, either alone or with the help of others, intervenes in the domestic affairs of another country to prevent crimes against humanity. Finally, a serious question arises as to whether judges, in upholding or striking down civil laws, can consistently avoid being drawn into some kind of reasoning based implicitly on natural law.

See also *Aristotle; Catholicism, Roman; Christian democracy; Contractarianism; Historicism; Hobbes, Thomas; Human rights; Kant, Immanuel; King, Martin Luther, Jr.; Liberalism; Locke, John; Maritain, Jacques; Obligation; Plato; Revolution, French; Rousseau, Jean-Jacques.*

Ernest L. Fortin

BIBLIOGRAPHY

Carlyle, A. J., and R. W. *A History of Mediaeval Political Theory in the West.* 6 vols. 2d ed. New York: Barnes and Noble, 1950.

Corwin, Edward S. *The "Higher Law" Background of American Constitutional Law.* Ithaca, N.Y.: Cornell University Press, 1955.

Crowe, Michael B. *The Changing Profile of the Natural Law.* The Hague: M. Nijhoff, 1977.

Jaffa, Harry V. *Thomism and Aristotelianism: A Study of the Commentary by Thomas Aquinas on the Nicomachean Ethics.* Chicago: University of Chicago Press, 1952.

Maritain, Jacques. *The Rights of Man and Natural Law.* New York: Scribner's, 1943.

Nussbaum, Arthur. *A Concise History of the Law of Nations.* New York: Macmillan, 1954.

Sigmund, Paul E. *Natural Law in Political Thought.* Cambridge, Mass.: Winthrop, 1971.

Strauss, Leo. "Natural Law." In *International Encyclopedia of the Social Sciences.* New York: Macmillan, 1968.

Nazism

See *Fascism*

Nehru, Jawaharlal

Prime minister of India from the country's independence in 1947 until his death. Nehru (1889–1964) was born into a family of substantial wealth in the northern Indian town of Allahabad. His father, Motilal, was among the

Jawaharlal Nehru

leading lawyers of India and played an important role in Indian politics in the 1910s and 1920s. In 1912 Nehru returned to India after seven years of education in England at Harrow and Cambridge University. Upon his return, he took to his father's profession, practicing until 1920.

Law as a profession, however, did not excite him, and Nehru eventually found a meaningful vocation in politics. Meanwhile, his marriage in 1916 led to the birth of a daughter, Indira, who became India's prime minister in 1966, two years after Nehru's death. (Indira Nehru became Indira Gandhi, dropping her maiden name after marrying Feroze Gandhi.)

Political Influences and Beliefs

Exposure to the West during his student days had an enduring influence on Nehru's life, but it did not directly motivate him to political action. By his own testimony and that of his contemporaries, three events during 1919 and 1920 marked a turning point in his life. The first was the massacre that took place at a public park in Punjab in April 1919, when a British general ordered his troops to fire on an unarmed crowd of Indians gathered for an anti-British political meeting. By the time the ammunition ran out, 379 Indians were dead and 1,200 wounded. The massacre shook Nehru's faith in the reformability of British rule; independence became his slogan after that.

The second experience was Nehru's feeling of shame and guilt about his aristocratic background that arose when, in 1920, he traveled through the countryside for the first time and saw India's poverty at firsthand. His desire to eliminate poverty in India sprang from his travels among the peasants. The third event was the emergence of Mahatma Gandhi on the scene during 1919–1920, with his call for nonviolent civil disobedience. Gandhi's use of nonviolence struck Nehru deeply, although Nehru's perspective on it was different. Gandhi's nonviolence stemmed from his religious convictions; an unreligious Nehru came upon it through a liberal conception of ethics. He disagreed with Gandhi on many issues—especially on the role of religion in public life—but shared with him a passion for nonviolence in politics and a commitment to liberate and rebuild India. Nehru accepted Gandhi, twenty years his senior, as a mentor.

Gandhi and Nehru also disagreed on whether representative democracy was the best way to run India's polity. Gandhi believed in a moral transformation of individuals through politics. Representative democracy or constitutions, Gandhi thought, were not the best means to achieve such a transformation. Power, according to Gandhi, corrupted politicians, who should instead be engaged in social upliftment and direct democracy at the village level. Nehru did not share this view. He believed that representative institutions could be used either positively or negatively. Such institutions, he thought, could be built all the way up from village-level elected institutions to the highest levels of the polity, each level doing what it could do best. Some governmental functions—for example, planning for industrialization—could be performed only at the highest level.

Moreover, Nehru argued, if the poorer classes—by making use of their numbers—came to dominate the elected institutions, the representative institutions could be used for bringing about social justice in an inegalitarian India. Gandhi would depend on moral suasion to convince the rich that they should share with the poor; Nehru would give the poor the opportunity to capture institutions through elections. Using democratic institutions, the poorer members of society could subdue the privileged.

The democratic empowerment of the poorer and lower castes is taking place in India today, but it was not a dream Nehru could realize in his lifetime. The first occupiers of democratic power were predominantly the privileged. Still, Nehru did not give up his insistence on democratic institutions. If democracy could not quickly deliver social justice, argued Nehru, more effort had to be put into educating the masses about how they could use democracy to express and realize their interests.

Nehru abhorred the idea of suspending democracy for the sake of social justice, a solution chosen in many other developing countries. Violence or force, he argued, would not produce honorable leaders; social justice brought about by dishonorable men was not worth having; and respectable means were as important as laudable ends. He was a democratic socialist, not a socialist per se.

Nehru the Prime Minister

These ideas led to some remarkable institutional initiatives as well as considerable ideological frustrations. India held its first free elections based on universal adult franchise in 1952. It was a "leap of democratic faith." Universal franchise, after all, had yielded 173 million voters. Because three-fourths of the new voters were unable to read and write, symbols were used on the ballot to identify parties and contestants. It took a million supervisory officials and six months to conduct the elections. The 1952 elections were the biggest free and peaceful elections in human history. After two more elections under Nehru—in 1957 and 1962—elections had become part of India's political consciousness.

Nehru also nurtured a free press, a free judiciary, and a spirit of debate in parliament and in the Congress Party. Moreover, he respected the autonomy offered to the state governments by India's federal constitution. Several of his programs were defeated in parliament or overturned by the judiciary. Yet he did not undermine institutions, accepting their constraints on his functioning. His response to defeat was to make a greater effort at persuasion or to accept failure with stoic grace.

It is possible to distinguish between Nehru the prime minister and Nehru the democrat while assessing his record. Prime Minister Nehru, though a towering figure, had two remarkable failures: his inability to transform India's agriculture during his lifetime (it happened after his death) and India's defeat in a war with China in 1963. The latter was a profound shock, and Nehru died not long thereafter. Before 1963 his energies for Indian and world politics always seemed youthful, boundless, and inexhaustible. Exercising remarkable charisma, he inspired many to high political standards and held India together at a difficult time.

Nehru as a democrat was even more successful. India's democracy, in its troubled childhood, drew much of its vitality from Nehru's unshakable liberalism. The only big compromise he made was with respect to secessions. It is said that he used to keep two statuettes, one of Mahatma Gandhi and one of Abraham Lincoln, on his office desk. From Gandhi, he grasped the art of nonviolence and persuasion; from Lincoln, the utility of force in keeping the union alive. After partition in 1947, when Pakistan became a separate state, Nehru ruled out secession as an available option to disaffected groups. He used force to defeat secession in northeastern India and secessionist leaders in Kashmir. Democracy was not more important than the nation, he said. It is not clear whether this stance was Nehru's personal failure or a reflection of the generic inability of political liberalism to deal with secession in purely democratic terms.

If Gandhi was the father of India, Nehru was the principal architect of India's democracy. In and of themselves, leaders do not create a nation or a democracy. Yet there is no doubt that charismatic leaders can exercise enormous influence in the history of nations. Second in stature only to Mahatma Gandhi in twentieth-century India, Nehru inspired an entire generation of Indians to participate in, and value, the democratic process.

See also *Gandhi, Mohandas Karamchand; India.*

Ashutosh Varshney

BIBLIOGRAPHY

Akbar, M. J. *Nehru: The Making of India.* London: Penguin Books, 1988.

Brecher, Michael. *Nehru: A Political Biography.* London: Oxford University Press, 1959.

Gopal, S. *Jawaharlal Nehru: A Biography.* 3 vols. Cambridge: Harvard University Press, 1984.

Nehru, Jawaharlal. *The Discovery of India.* Delhi: Oxford University Press, 1989.

Varshney, Ashutosh. "India: Liberalism versus Nationalism." *Journal of Democracy* 3 (July 1992): 147–153.

Netherlands

See Low Countries

New Zealand

See *Australia and New Zealand*

Nietzsche, Friedrich

German philosopher of aristocratic radicalism and advocate of militant atheism. Descended from a family of Lutheran pastors, Nietzsche (1844–1900) was educated at the University of Leipzig and in 1869 became a professor of classical philology at Basel, Switzerland. After resigning in 1876, he wrote in sickly solitude until a nervous breakdown in 1889 ended his career as a writer and thinker.

Nietzsche's work can be divided into three phases. In his youth, as a romantic disciple of Richard Wagner, he fought for a revival of German culture and, inspired by the pagan poetry of the Greeks, wrote such books as *The Birth of Tragedy* (1872). A middle period of disillusioned positivism was expressed in *Human, All Too Human* (1878–1879) and similar works. And the mature Nietzsche produced *Thus Spoke Zarathustra* (1883–1885) and the works following it.

The hero of *Thus Spoke Zarathustra* utters Nietzsche's most famous sentence, the basis and core of all his philosophical labors: "God is dead." By this statement, Nietzsche means primarily that belief in the Christian God has lost its efficacy and thus has plunged humanity into an all-encompassing crisis. Ultimately he means that all transcendent and objective standards by which human beings have taken their bearings have crumbled to reveal a chaotic world of meaninglessness.

Nietzsche finds signs of that loss of meaning wherever he looks. Hitherto human beings have been constituted by their reverence, their aspirations; now all yearnings are revealed as arbitrary, all preferences and longings as capricious in a world deprived of meaning and standards— whether one calls them God or nature or goodness—and human beings confront an abyss.

They can react in various ways. They may take refuge in the petty pursuit of comfortable self-preservation. Nietzsche calls such people, whose lives lack all poetry and grandeur, "last men." They may lash out against a world that is indifferent at best and malignant at worst by becoming nihilists, seeking the destruction of all they en-

Friedrich Nietzsche

counter. Or they may seek to reinterpret the catastrophic death of God as the discovery of human creativity, a new realm of possibility in which human beings create their own meaning, believing themselves to be liberated from ordinary responsibilities and morality. They will attain a cosmic innocence of becoming, ridding themselves of the resentment that has plagued humanity throughout history by affirming as necessary and good all that exists. Nietzsche refers to these creatures as "supermen." They will be a synthesis and a surpassing of the highest human types of the past: poets, philosophers, rulers, saints.

Nietzsche constructs a new philosophical doctrine to buttress his analysis of the crisis of his and our time, a teaching to explain the world's flux and humanity's way of overcoming it. He calls that doctrine "the will to power": human beings are motivated by a ceaseless desire to overcome and possess, a desire that at its peak can become self-overcoming. Human beings are not fundamentally characterized by their rationality but by their instinctive yearning for domination. Nietzsche seeks to understand all reality as will to power, positing the world as energy rather than as matter, a vast field of conflicting wills.

According to Nietzsche, the doctrine of the will to power explains how beasts overcame their beastliness to become human, even as it explains how human beings can overcome their humanity to become supermen. He struggles to resolve the difficulties of his own teachings: Is his doctrine of the will to power the result of his own will power or is it true? If everything can and will be overcome, will not a humanity no longer faced by challenges decline into last men? Can one overcome the past? His final and most enigmatic teaching of the eternal return of the same describes a world in which the future will become a past that human beings can will.

Nietzsche's influence is pervasive in the twentieth century, but the implications of his thought for politics in general and for democracy in particular remain ambiguous, above all because of the tensions in his thought. One strand of his philosophy is apolitical: Nietzsche celebrates the creative individual for whom society is at best a necessary evil. He counsels superior people to flee into solitude. At the same time, he conceives of the superman as the molder of the human future, a legislator on the grandest scale. He praises war for its energizing effects and writes vaguely but enthusiastically of a great politics of the future that will undo the legacy of the petty politics afflicting the present.

At rare intervals Nietzsche comments benignly on democracy, mostly because it counterbalances the corruptions of authoritarian regimes. More often, however, his attitudes range from contemptuous indifference to vehement hostility. He frequently holds democracy responsible for the mediocrity that softens modern life and the egalitarianism that endangers human greatness. He faults it for being little but a prelude to communism, for being the decadent inheritor of a Christian morality that can no longer function, for inculcating people with softness at a time when they need to be hard, and for denying the imperatives of human cruelty. Nietzsche tends to equate democratic rule with the rule of the last men.

Such views necessarily raise the problem of Nietzsche's influence on and responsibility for fascism. He was not a conservative in any conventional sense because he thought a return of any kind to former times impossible. Instead, he dreamed of a new planetary nobility. His image of the radical individuals fit to preside over human regeneration is that of a genuine nobility gifted with artistic productivity and moral sensitivity. It thus bears no resemblance to the reality of Adolf Hitler. Nevertheless, Nietzsche is responsible for making extremism seem more de-sirable than moderation, for deriding rationality, and for mocking the common decencies. Moreover, his general aversion to Western civilization played into the hands of a feeling in Germany that it was not properly part of the West.

See also *Fascism*.

Werner J. Dannhauser

BIBLIOGRAPHY

Detwiler, Bruce. *Nietzsche and the Politics of Aristocratic Radicalism.* Chicago: University of Chicago Press, 1990.

Jaspers, Karl. *Nietzsche: An Introduction to the Understanding of His Philosophy.* Translated by Charles F. Wallraft and Frederick J. Schmitz. Tucson: University of Arizona Press, 1965.

Kaufmann, Walter. *Nietzsche: Philosopher, Psychologist, Antichrist.* Princeton: Princeton University Press, 1974.

Löwith, Karl. *From Hegel to Nietzsche.* Translated by David Green. Garden City, N.Y.: Anchor Books, 1956.

Warren, Mark. *Nietzsche and Political Thought.* Cambridge: MIT Press, 1988.

Niger

See *Africa, Subsaharan*

Nigeria

The most populous country on the African continent, and one of the wealthiest in natural resources, lying at the inner corner of the Gulf of Guinea in West Africa. The Nigerian experience with democracy has been paradoxical and ambiguous.

Three times the country has undertaken to govern itself under liberal democratic constitutions, and each time it has failed. The first two republics (1960–1966 and 1979–1983) were overthrown by military coups after they were widely discredited by corruption, election rigging, and undemocratic conduct. The transition to a third republic (1986–1993), also characterized by extensive corruption and controversy, was never completed: a cynical military regime kept extending the deadline and changing the rules, until it finally annulled an otherwise successful presidential election and was forced out of power. Another military coup displaced the transition process altogether on November 17, 1993, leaving the country in a quagmire of political illegitimacy and ethnic tension.

Although the military controlled the government for twenty-four of the first thirty-four years of independence, Nigeria has never accepted indefinite authoritarian rule, and no military regime that has not committed itself to a transition to democracy has been able to survive. Through ten national governments, six successful military coups, a civil war, and a dizzying economic boom followed by a crushing depression—not to mention repeated assaults by military regimes on human rights and associational life—Nigerians have maintained a passionate commitment to personal freedom and political participation. Pressure for democratization continues to emanate from the country's many ethnic groups and from a battered but still vigorous civil society. Nigeria boasts the largest, most pluralistic, and most resourceful independent press in black Africa, as well as a wide array of human rights groups, trade unions, business groups, student and professional associations, women's groups, and other organized interests.

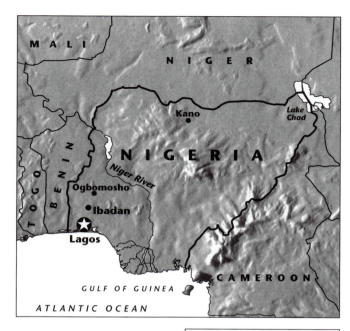

The Ethnic and Regional Setting

Home to some 250 distinct linguistic groups, Nigeria has been prone to the intense politicization of ethnic differences. Although most of its ethnic groups are relatively tiny, three groups constitute somewhere between 60 and 67 percent of the population. (No authoritative population figures exist because there has been no reliable and broadly accepted census since independence in 1960.) These are the Yoruba (whom different censuses have placed at anywhere from 16.6 to 20 percent), the Igbo (16.6 to 18 percent), and the Hausa-Fulani (28 to 30 percent).

Regional location and religion have served to reinforce this tripartite cleavage. The Hausa-Fulani, located in the north, are predominantly Muslim. They have a history of centralized, theocratic kingdoms, or emirates, owing political and religious allegiance to the Caliph at Sokoto. The Igbo, who attempted to secede in 1967 as the Republic of Biafra, occupy the east and are almost exclusively Christian; their political traditions are very egalitarian. The Yoruba, in the west, have an extensive tradition of monarchical but more limited political authority. They are roughly evenly divided between Muslims and Christians and generally are more tolerant in religious matters than are other ethnic groups.

Numerous ethnic minority groups make up the remaining one-third of the population. These are concentrated in the oil-producing areas of the midwest (the largest group here being the Edo) and southeast (the Ibibio, Efik, and Ijaw), in the "Middle Belt" of the country

(the Tiv), and in the northeast corner, just below Chad (the Kanuri, who are Muslim and the largest single minority group). The Middle Belt has been a zone of particularly keen political rivalry, where Christians have resisted the domination of the Muslim emirates of the far north.

British colonial rule reinforced these regional and cultural differences. To be sure, precolonial history did feature warfare among rival Hausa states and rival Yoruba kingdoms; an Islamic jihad (1804–1830) that extended the Fulani empire, or Sokoto caliphate, over the Hausa states and most of the rest of the north; and myriad other conflicts. However, trade and peaceful interchange also featured prominently in the contacts between peoples.

The British initially established separate protectorates for Northern and Southern Nigeria in 1900; they continued to rule the two parts separately even after formal amalgamation in 1914. In the north, a Native Authority system was constructed to rule indirectly through the centralized structures of traditional authority in the emirates. In the south, indirect rule was less successful. Western commerce, religion, and education spread much more rapidly there than in the north (particularly the emirates), where Western practices were severely restricted. This unequal exposure to Western influences and resources under colonial rule gave rise to enormous and enduring disparities in income, education, and entrepreneurship between north and south. These disparities have been a source of political tension and instability ever since.

Early Democratic Steps

Democratic politics began in Nigeria during the final decade of colonial rule. The 1951 constitution designated the western, eastern, and northern provinces as regions in a quasi-federal system and provided for indirectly elected assemblies in each to participate in governance. This decade of pre-independence electoral politics further crystallized the tripartite ethnic cleavage, as ethnically based political parties rose to dominance in each region. These were the Northern Peoples' Congress (led by Sir Ahmadu Bello, holder of the powerful traditional title, sardauna of Sokoto), the Action Group (led by Chief Obafemi Awolowo), and the National Council of Nigeria and the Cameroons (NCNC, led by Dr. Nnamdi Azikiwe, a major nationalist leader).

The NCNC (which was renamed the National Convention of Nigerian Citizens in 1961) sought with some success to reach out nationally beyond its Igbo base, and the Action Group later also campaigned aggressively in other parts of the country (particularly the minority areas). In contrast, the Northern Peoples' Congress presented itself as strictly a northern party and was mobilized hurriedly in defense of the class and ethnic interests of the traditional ruling class of the emirates. Challenging it on its own turf was the Northern Elements Progressive Union (led by Mallam Aminu Kano), a party of radical young northern commoners who sought to dismantle the "feudalistic" structures of the emirates. Several parties representing ethnic minority groups also ran candidates in local elections within each region.

Although political alignments were to shift constantly thereafter, the basic ethnic and political axes of party competition for the next four decades can be traced to this initial configuration of electoral politics in 1951. This structure consisted of a party of the traditional northern establishment, which sought to extend its hegemony throughout the north and (beginning in the First Republic) to pick up some allies among minority groups in the southeast opposed to Igbo domination; a political party dominated by the Yoruba and seeking to mobilize a national coalition of "progressive" forces opposed to political domination by the northern establishment; and an Ig-

bo party oriented to the "progressive" cause but shifting pragmatically in its alliances.

The identity between region, party, and ethnicity deepened in 1954 with a constitutional change that created a fully federal system: it devolved enormous autonomy and control over resources to each of the three regions. Intense struggle ensued along the cumulative fault line of region, party, and ethnicity, over such issues as the distribution of socioeconomic resources, the timing of self-government, and efforts by the Northern Peoples' Congress to purge southerners from the northern bureaucracy and economy. Most intense of all was electoral competition, which progressively tightened the grip of each ruling party over its region, and which was marred by considerable violence, repression, intimidation, fraud, intolerance, and blatant appeals to ethnic prejudice.

Abuses reached new levels in the federal election of 1959, called to select the national government for the forthcoming independence. The northern region was to have half the seats in parliament. The Northern Peoples' Congress won an enormous plurality and formed the new government in coalition with the NCNC. The prime minister was Abubakar Tafawa Balewa, the Northern Peoples' Congress vice president who had headed a broad coalition cabinet since 1957.

Although British colonial rule had produced constitutional reform and a brief but staged transition to self-rule with significant indigenous participation, it left behind deep contradictions that would devour constitutional democracy within a few years. Most seriously, the colonial authorities steadfastly resisted eloquent Nigerian appeals to scrap the awkward and unstable three-region system in favor of a more balanced federal system with more constituent units and autonomy for minority groups. This type of system would have been more fluid and competitive, with better protection for minority rights and interests. With the breakup of the huge Northern Region, it would have been impossible for the northern elite simply to convert hegemonic control of their own region into control of the entire federation.

The British also bequeathed a political economy in which the indigenous capitalist producers were few and weak, while the state controlled the most important sources of capital accumulation: the marketing of cash crops, mineral production, numerous industries, and a sizable bureaucracy. Through corruption and clientelism, which grew rapidly in scope and scale, the state quickly became the principal means for the accumulation of personal wealth and the achievement or consolidation of dominant class status. Few avenues of upward social mobility existed independent from politics. With so high a premium resting on control of the state, no party was willing to tolerate opposition or accept defeat.

The First Republic

Nigeria achieved independence on October 1, 1960, under a formally democratic parliamentary system that was the object of high hopes domestically and internationally. As part of the coalition arrangement, NCNC leader Azikiwe became the first head of state (initially, governor general and then president after Nigeria became a republic on October 1, 1963). Constitutionally, power was separated and rights were protected. A partisan but vigorous and diverse press assured pluralism outside the party system as well.

Democracy in the First Republic, however, quickly fell victim to its own contradictions. Political competition was increasingly restricted to the federal arena as one-party states emerged in each region. The center was rocked by five successive crises that progressively deepened ethnic and regional polarization.

The first crisis began in 1962, when a political split developed within the Action Group between Chief Awolowo, now opposition leader in the Federal House, and his successor as western premier, Chief S. L. Akintola. Although the latter was voted out of power by Awolowo's larger faction, the ruling federal coalition of the Northern Peoples' Congress and NCNC seized upon the conflict to declare emergency rule in the Western Region; they restored Akintola to power and destroyed their mutual rival, Chief Awolowo, through the dubious device of a treason conviction.

The second crisis, over the 1962 national census, underscored the determination of the north to preserve its political power. When the census showed a southern population majority, a subsequent "verification check" found 8 million more northerners (thus restoring the north's population majority). A fresh census conducted in 1963 reconfirmed the northern population majority, and its results were accepted over bitter protests from the Eastern Region's NCNC government.

Highlighting widespread public disillusionment with the political class, a general strike brought the country to a standstill for thirteen days in June 1964. Although the strike was resolved by government concessions, a fourth crisis, the 1964 general elections, soon arose. In what

would become the principal, enduring bifurcation of Nigerian politics, the NCNC joined in alliance with the politically devastated Action Group, the Northern Elements Progressive Union, and the ethnic minority party of the Middle Belt to form the United Progressive Grand Alliance. The Northern Peoples' Congress drew in the accommodationist political party of the Yorubas, under Chief Akintola, and a few southern minority parties to form the Nigerian National Alliance.

With the consolidation of the parties, politics was reduced to a bipolar struggle, dominated then by the Igbos of the east and the Hausa-Fulani of the north. The election campaign was disfigured by unprecedented levels of political thuggery and by official obstruction and repression. A United Progressive Grand Alliance boycott provoked a tense showdown between the Northern Peoples' Congress prime minister and the NCNC president during which, for several days, the country seemed close to civil war. Unable to rally military and police support to his side, President Azikiwe finally yielded and the NCNC took a diminished role in a new coalition government more than ever dominated by the Northern Peoples' Congress.

The fifth and final crisis was triggered by the Akintola government's resort to massive, wholesale electoral fraud to award itself victory in the October 1965 Western Regional election. With the party's victory announcement, the region erupted into popular rebellion. Public disgust was intensified by a spate of corruption scandals during the year and the growing arrogance, pomposity, waste, and incessant political crisis associated with the politicians as a class. When a group of young army majors and captains seized power on January 15, 1966, assassinating Prime Minister Balewa and Premiers Ahmadu Bello and Akintola, the public welcomed their coup in an outpouring of joy and relief.

The First Military Interregnum

As would prove to be the case repeatedly in the future, the military was even less capable than the politicians of managing the country's ethnic and political tensions. The perception of the coup as being an Igbo affair (no leading Igbo politician was killed) and the insensitive handling of ethnic concerns by the Igbo major general (Johnson Aguiyi-Ironsi) who took control of government prompted a countercoup six months later. Aguiyi-Ironsi and other Igbo officers were killed and a compromise choice, Lt. Col. Yakubu Gowon (a northern Christian from a minority group), became head of state.

Although Gowon sought constitutional dialogue and reform, ethnic tension spun out of control later in 1966, with a wave of Igbo massacres in the north and a massive migration of Igbo settlers back to the east. In May 1967 the Eastern Region, under the leadership of Col. Odumwegwu Ojukwu, seceded, declaring itself the Republic of Biafra. Thirty months of civil war began in July, claiming perhaps a million lives and devastating the Eastern Region.

Nigeria emerged from the war in January 1970 with a hopeful future, as large-scale oil production was commencing and Gowon pursued a policy of reconciliation with the defeated Eastern Region. His earlier division of the country into twelve states now took full effect. With the quadrupling of oil prices in 1973–1974, an economic boom began, but corruption, another census debacle, and Gowon's indefinite postponement (on October 1, 1974) of the promised return to civilian rule produced broad disaffection. Nine years after he had assumed power, on July 29, 1975, Gowon was toppled by a coup of senior officers led by Brigadier Murtala Muhammad.

Muhammad purged the army and bureaucracy in an anticorruption campaign. On October 1, 1975, he launched a detailed and imaginatively staged four-year timetable for democratic transition. At the peak of his popularity, he was assassinated in an abortive coup attempt on February 13, 1976. However, his successor, Gen. Olusegun Obasanjo, implemented the transition timetable with skill and efficiency. Under Obasanjo's rule, the federal system was developed into nineteen states, new local governments were elected, an elected Constituent Assembly debated and adopted a new constitution (with an American-style presidential system), and civilian legislatures and executives were elected at the state and federal levels.

The Second Republic

Although many thought the Second Republic largely reproduced the party system of the First Republic, there were significant differences. The presumed successor to the Northern Peoples' Congress, the National Party of Nigeria, was still dominated by the northern Muslim elite, but it had the broadest national base of any Nigerian party to date, having won control of several ethnic minority states. The Unity Party of Nigeria, led again by Awolowo, was viewed as a successor to the (mainly Yoruba) Action Group; the Nigeria Peoples Party, led again by Azikiwe, as successor to the NCNC; and the Peoples Redemption Party, led by Aminu Kano, as successor to the radical North-

ern Elements Progressive Union. In addition, there was a Kanuri-based party, the Great Nigeria Peoples Party, which resulted from a split in the Nigeria Peoples Party.

Each of these five parties became dominant in its ethnic base, winning at least two of the nineteen states. But there was more cross-cutting support than in the First Republic and less partisan solidarity than before in the Hausa and Igbo heartlands in particular. The nineteen-state system and other provisions of the new system (such as the requirement that parties eschew ethnic symbols and have national political bases) seemed to be generating a more complicated politics. Although the National Party of Nigeria candidate, Alhaji Shehu Shagari, won a clear plurality of the vote over runner-up Awolowo, the legitimacy of his election was tarnished by a dispute over whether he had satisfied the requirement that a presidential candidate win 25 percent of the vote in at least two-thirds of the states.

There were other echoes of the First Republic. A working alliance developed between the Hausa-led National Party of Nigeria and the Igbo-led Nigeria Peoples Party within the National Assembly. Gradually, a "progressive" alliance emerged against the National Party of Nigeria, involving first the nine state governors from the Unity Party of Nigeria, Peoples Redemption Party, and Great Nigeria Peoples Party, and then eventually the three Nigeria Peoples Party governors as well.

Gradually, this transethnic and somewhat ideological cleavage between self-styled progressive and more conservative, traditionalist forces seemed to be reorganizing politics and bridging multiple ethnic divisions. Advanced by a number of events—including the controversial impeachment of a militant Peoples Redemption Party governor in June 1981 and an orchestrated riot against the other Peoples Redemption Party government the following month—this political division held promise of maturing into another "grand alliance" or even a party merger for the 1983 presidential elections.

The progressives, however, were unable to unite behind a single candidate (both Awolowo and Azikiwe ran again). An effort of the dominant factions of the Nigeria Peoples Party and Peoples Redemption Party to unite with the Great Nigeria Peoples Party in a new, broad party was refused in a baldly partisan ruling of the electoral commission. The five weeks of state and national elections in August and September 1983 witnessed the most blatant election rigging since the 1965 Western Regional election, as the National Party of Nigeria entrenched its political control with margins of victory that grew more incredible by the week.

By 1983 public disillusionment with the Second Republic was intense and pervasive, fed by an unending succession of breathtaking financial scandals, endemic political corruption, rising levels of political violence and intolerance, increasing disarray within the political parties, and a broad economic collapse. A second oil boom went bust, cutting the country's peak oil earnings of $24 billion in 1980 by more than half. Schools, clinics, and other government services ceased functioning.

Blocked from achieving change by legal means, the Yoruba areas in particular erupted in violence, and the country seethed. Once again when the soldiers seized control of government, on December 31, 1983, the people celebrated.

The Second Military Interregnum

In avoiding the polarization of ethnic conflict and generating broader forms of political cleavage and identity, the Second Republic made significant progress over the first. The major reasons for its collapse were corruption, abuse of power, and electoral fraud, rather than ethnic conflict. Many saw bad politicians as the problem and hoped the military might purge the system and quickly withdraw. The government of Maj. Gen. Muhammadu Buhari and Maj. Gen. Tunde Idiagbon moved quickly to punish corruption and eliminate waste, detaining hundreds of former politicians and seizing huge sums of cash from their homes. Their popularity from these moves abruptly waned, however, as the regime acted with unprecedented harshness and impunity to silence criticism and dissent. Journalists were arrested and prominent associations banned (along with any discussion of the country's political future). In response to the new cycle of bitter public disaffection, deepened by the inability of the Buhari government to come to grips with the economic crisis it inherited, high-ranking officers, led by Maj. Gen. Ibrahim Babangida, seized power in a bloodless coup on August 27, 1985.

Rejecting the authoritarian tactics of his predecessors in power, Babangida was enthusiastically welcomed by Nigerians. His popularity rose when he repealed repressive decrees and released from jail detained journalists and many civilian politicians. In a brilliant political maneuver, he even managed to launch a far-reaching structural adjustment program while neutralizing public opposition by rejecting the International Monetary Fund loan that was to have accompanied the program.

The most skillful, corrupt, wily, and manipulative military politician in the country's history, Babangida managed to rule for eight years through three tactics: co-optation of prominent civilians and military officers (through the prodigious dispensation of cash and other favors), repression and intimidation of opposition (repeatedly closing down publications and associations and arresting critics), and constant manipulation of the political game. By continuously holding out the prospect of a return to civilian rule, and by leading a wide range of politicians to believe they enjoyed his secret support, Babangida managed to prevail through a period of enormous political turbulence and economic suffering.

At the beginning of 1986 Babangida promised a return to civilian democratic rule in 1990. But when he announced a formal timetable for the transition in 1987, the return was deferred until 1992. The transition plan called for a sequential phasing in of democratic politics, beginning with local elections in 1987, formation of parties in 1989, state elections in 1990, and national elections in 1992. Babangida revised the timetable repeatedly, first in 1989, then in 1990, after the regime announced that it would establish the two political parties called for in the new constitution, rather than register any of the thirteen parties that applied.

The two parties were to be "a little to the left" (the Social Democratic Party) and "a little to the right" (the National Republican Convention). When they took shape in 1990 they reproduced to a considerable degree the progressive-conservative fault line that had been developing through the previous two republics. For the first time, however, the progressive and more southern-based party, the Social Democratic Party, emerged as the stronger political force, controlling a majority of states and local government areas.

Protest against official manipulation of the transition deepened in November 1992, when the regime seized upon chaos and fraud in the presidential primary elections of both parties to disqualify all presidential candidates, dissolve the party structures, and postpone the hand over of power yet again, from January 2 to August 8, 1993. To rally support from segments of the political class, Babangida reversed his policy of banning the old politicians from competing during the transition. The lift of the ban generated a new rush of presidential candidates.

By then there was general skepticism that Babangida intended to hand over power at all. As the first Nigerian to establish a personal dictatorship, Babangida was the object of increasing scorn for his brazen mismanagement of public funds, his repression of dissent, his inability to reverse the economic crisis, and his costly concessions to the demands of various interest groups. These included swelling the federal system to thirty states and doubling the number of local governments. Christian political militancy rose in reaction to the perception that he was favoring Muslim interests, and religious conflict reached unprecedented levels of intensity and violence.

The 1993 Elections

Surprisingly, to many skeptics, the presidential election process did go forward in early 1993. At the two party conventions one of the country's wealthiest industrialists, Moshood Abiola, emerged as the Social Democratic Party presidential candidate. A relatively young and unknown banker, Bashir Tofa, became the National Republican Convention nominee. Like Shehu Shagari of the Second Republic, Tofa was a Hausa Muslim from the far north. By contrast, as a Yoruba Muslim (and generous philanthropist) whose name was known around the country, Abiola was able to mobilize political support of an ethnic and regional breadth never before seen in Nigeria.

In the June 12, 1993, presidential election, Abiola won a decisive victory, capturing nineteen of the thirty states (including Tofa's home state of Kano) and scoring well in virtually every section of the country. The election was considered the freest, fairest, and most peaceful since independence, perhaps partly because of the light turnout and the doubts about whether its results would count. (Babangida supporters had filed in court to halt the election.)

Abiola became the first southerner (and the first Yoruba) ever elected to head a Nigerian government. But before the results were officially announced, the military embargoed their release and annulled the election. Southerners (in particular Yorubas) were outraged—noting the continuous control of government by northern Muslims since 1979—and intense, sometimes violent, public protest ensued. The National Republican Convention and a faction of Abiola's own Social Democratic Party, however, accepted the annulment in pursuit of their own political interest in new elections.

Fearing arrest, Abiola fled the country. Tension mounted. After weeks of controversy and extensive negotiations among the military and several political factions, President Babangida was forced to resign on August 25, 1993, handing over power to an interim national government headed by a Yoruba businessman, Ernest Shonekan, who had been the figurehead chairman of the Transitional Council since January. All previously elected officials (including the National Assembly) remained in place. But real power remained with the military, now commanded by the longtime defense minister, Gen. Sani Abacha (another northern Muslim).

Once again, as in the first and second republics, the politicians proved unable to bridge their political differences in response to a national crisis. With the country deadlocked over the legitimacy of the June 12 election and the economy reeling from protracted strikes, financial mismanagement, swelling debt, and 90 percent inflation, the Shonekan government floundered. On November 17, 1993, the military reclaimed total power, dismissing all elected officials, suspending the 1989 constitution, and liquidating the transition process.

Although the new military dictator, General Abacha, promised a new democratic transition process and filled his cabinet with civilian politicians from across the political (and regional) spectrum, he seemed intent on trying to prolong his stay in office. A promised Constitutional Conference commenced months later than promised and quickly adjourned in June 1994 because of inadequate housing for delegates. During that June and July the political crisis deepened as disaffected Yorubas and other southerners warned of a breakup of the federation if power was not allowed to rotate among ethnic groups.

On the first anniversary of his election, Abiola was about to declare himself president when he was arrested and charged with treason. Workers in the strategic oil sector went out on strike in support of his claim, and protests spread around the country. The strike was broken after several weeks, but popular discontent with the regime intensified.

This volatile political impasse underscored the deterioration of the country's democratic prospects. Although the military was more discredited and hated than ever—unable to legitimate its rule even with broad civilian participation—it was also reluctant to surrender control over the nation's oil wealth. And the politicians, driven by the same corrupt ambitions as ever, were unable to unite behind a clear alternative. Despite the courageous mobilization for democracy by human rights organizations and other groups in civil society, and the vigorous coverage and commentary by the press, the country remained adrift politically. It was less and less capable of managing its profound ethnic, regional, and religious divisions.

See also *Africa, Subsaharan; African transitions to democracy; Azikiwe, Nnamdi; Civil-military relations; Colonialism; Multiethnic democracy.*

Larry Diamond

BIBLIOGRAPHY

Coleman, James S. *Nigeria: Background to Nationalism.* Berkeley: University of California Press, 1958.

Diamond, Larry. *Class, Ethnicity, and Democracy in Nigeria: The Failure of the First Republic.* London: Macmillan; Syracuse: Syracuse University Press, 1988.

———. "Nigeria: Pluralism, Statism, and the Struggle for Democracy." In *Democracy in Developing Countries: Africa,* edited by Larry Diamond, Juan J. Linz, and Seymour Martin Lipset. Boulder, Colo.: Lynne Rienner; London: Adamantine Press, 1988.

———, and Oyeleye Oyediran. "Military Authoritarianism and Democratic Transition in Nigeria." *National Political Science Review* 4 (1994): 221–244.

Ekeh, Peter P., and Eghosa E. Osaghae, eds. *Federal Character and Federalism in Nigeria.* Ibadan, Nigeria: Heinemann, 1989.

Ekeh, Peter P., Patrick Dele Cole, and Gabriel O. Olusanya. *Politics and Constitutions.* Vol. 5 of *Nigeria since Independence: The First Twenty-Five Years.* Ibadan, Nigeria: Heinemann, 1988.

Joseph, Richard A. *Democracy and Prebendal Politics in Nigeria: The Rise and Fall of the Second Republic.* London: Cambridge University Press, 1987.

Kirk-Greene, Anthony, and Douglas Rimmer. *Nigeria since 1970: A Political and Economic Outline.* New York: Holmes and Meier, 1981.

Lewis, Peter. "Endgame in Nigeria? The Politics of a Failed Democratic Transition." *African Affairs* 372 (July 1994): 323–340.

Sklar, Richard L. *Nigerian Political Parties: Power in an Emergent African Nation.* Princeton: Princeton University Press, 1963.

Suberu, Rotimi. "The Democratic Recession in Nigeria." *Current History* 93 (May 1994): 213–218.

Kwame Nkrumah

Nkrumah, Kwame

First prime minister and president of Ghana. After studying at various American universities for ten years, Nkrumah (1909–1972) left for London and became immersed in anticolonial politics. He was an active member of the West African Students' Union, and he helped to organize the Fifth Pan-African Congress. Subsequently appointed general secretary of the United Gold Coast Convention, Nkrumah returned home. Dissatisfied with the conservatism of the convention's leadership, he broke with the organization and formed his own, more militant Convention People's Party, the vehicle for his rapid rise to political power in Ghana.

As the first prime minister of an independent Ghana (March 6, 1957), Nkrumah was ambivalent about democracy as a process, even though he had an ardent commitment to the political expression of popular will. For Nkrumah, democracy was best served by direct cooperation between himself and "the people," something he felt that he had achieved during his rule.

Nkrumah's reservations about the democratic process are evident in the tensions between his writing and his practices while in office. He spoke of his attachment to parliamentary democracy in Ghana and, in a speech to the United Nations Security Council on February 25, 1961, urged that the Congolese people be allowed to choose their own government in a free manner. At the same time, under his leadership, Ghana moved steadily toward a one-party, unitary state with powerful military and secret police organizations. Nkrumah warned in his autobiography that even in a democratic system the use of totalitarian measures may be warranted during the period following independence.

It is the other side of Nkrumah's approach to democracy, his championship of deeply held public aspirations in Ghana and in Africa at large, that continues to be venerated in many quarters. Perceiving a mandate for activism, he sought to use the power bestowed on him by the majority of Ghanaians to promote the public's will on such issues as equality, self-determination, social opportunity, rapid economic development, and African unity. In his view the increased authority that he secured while in office was justified because it enabled him to offer the positive leadership that a developing country and continent vitally needed.

Donald Rothchild

Norway

See *Scandinavia*

Julius Nyerere

Nyerere, Julius

President of the United Republic of Tanzania from 1964 to 1985. Nyerere (1922–   ) was responsible for a historic attempt to create a socialist economy in a society of rural dwellers without deferring significant improvements in the cultural quality and economic conditions of rural life. His steadfast pursuit of that goal for nearly two decades entitles him to recognition as the most influential communitarian socialist of his time in Africa, if not in the world.

Brought up in the Roman Catholic religion, Nyerere qualified for a teaching diploma at the University of East Africa in Uganda; subsequently, he taught at a mission school and studied for a master's degree in economics and history at Edinburgh University. At the age of thirty, he became the first Tanganyikan student to earn a degree at a

university in Great Britain. In 1954 he participated in founding the Tanganyikan African National Union, serving as its president during the transition to independence, which was attained in 1961. Shortly after independence he resigned from his governmental office of prime minister and devoted a year to reorganizing the Tanganyikan African National Union in preparation for the tasks ahead. With the adoption of a republican form of government in 1962, he returned to public office as the country's first president.

Nyerere's policies for Tanzania (so named in 1964 following the unification of Tanganyika and Zanzibar) were based on his conception of *ujamaa* ("familyhood" in Swahili). *Ujamaa* connotes Africa's tradition of egalitarian village life, implying both material security for all and the formulation of community decisions by means of community-wide discussion. In the absence of fundamental, socially divisive issues, Nyerere reasoned, competition between rival political parties is not only incompatible with the *ujamaa* tradition but also artificial, tending to create factions that would not otherwise exist. Nyerere applied this argument to the entire republic in 1965 on the empirical ground that competitive elections had deteriorated into ritualistic charades because the Tanganyikan African National Union enjoyed near-universal support. He concluded that competition within a legal one-party state would be more democratic than competition between parties.

Nyerere also believed that Africa's communitarian tradition would enhance the feasibility of rural socialism as a mode of economic development. However, the bulk of the peasantry refused to relocate voluntarily from their villages to larger, collectivized settlements. Between 1974 and 1976, 70 percent of the population, some 12 million people, were required to move their homes into new *ujamaa* villages. While this resettling enabled the government to provide most of the people with rudimentary services (health care, education, clean water, and agricultural advice), the related aim of collective farming eventually had to be abandoned in the face of peasant resistance, manifest in an intractable food crisis.

In 1985 Nyerere retired as president; in 1990 he relinquished his chairmanship of the Tanganyikan African National Union. Rural socialism was abandoned. With Nyerere's stoic approval, multiparty politics was restored. The record of his great experiment demonstrates the limitations of rural socialism and the dangers of communitarian ideology when it is used to undermine dissent, thereby minimizing opportunities for timely corrective changes in public policies. These lessons are all the more lasting for having been taught by the bitter experience of a sincere humanitarian.

Richard L. Sklar

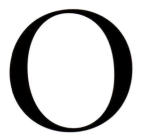

Obligation

The sense of moral responsibility that enjoins individuals to give others their due. In discussing the nature and problems of obligation, we shall seek to clarify such questions as, What are obligations and why do people fulfill them? Why do people shirk them? What is the connection between personal and political obligations? Why do individuals subordinate and even sacrifice themselves to the common good by obeying the laws and injunctions of political society? And how does American liberal democracy resolve the problems of political obligation?

Human beings in all societies generally admit that they have obligations and tend to act accordingly. Growing from our affections and associations, our sense of obligation helps bind us to our families, friends, communities, and countries even when we would rather not be bound. Parents accept the burdens of rearing their children; friends stand by friends and patriots stand by their country even in the face of danger. Obligation thus implies that individuals know what should be done and requires that they voluntarily subordinate their own immediate desire or good to that end. Responsible persons fulfill obligations.

Obligation rests upon justice. In saying that people should fulfill their obligations, we imply that doing so is just and that justice, being a greater end than personal satisfaction, requires and justifies sacrifice. Obligations entail justice in two reinforcing senses: First, they enjoin particular just acts, such as doing good to family and friends, and, second, they assume that the act of fulfilling obligations, such as keeping promises, in itself is just. Obligations help to order and unite our associations into a political society that aims at justice. The vitality of our sense of obligation demonstrates the authority of justice over human affairs.

The problems of obligation are inherent in its nature. People in all societies shirk their obligations. This avoidance stems from the voluntary nature of obligations. We should do our duty, but we can choose not to. Injustice in this sense is done knowingly. We shirk our obligations when some apparent good outweighs them. Parents might choose independence rather than support their children; soldiers might save themselves at the expense of their friends and country. Because those who make such choices must justify their actions, if only to themselves, they see some justice in choosing the apparent good. Obligation thus entails tensions in our sense of what is good and just that manifest themselves in the ongoing struggle between our own apparent good and the call of the common good. We can summarize the nature and problem of obligation as follows: Most people act justly because they are constrained by their obligations, and they can be so constrained because they respect justice. Constraint is required, however, because most people can and sometimes will choose injustice. The order imposed by obligations is fragile.

Political societies everywhere subordinate and sacrifice their members to the common good as expressed by laws and injunctions. Why do governments have such power and authority? Why, as the call to arms and its attendant loss of blood and treasure demonstrate, do individuals customarily obey? Ordinary associations most often depend upon political power and laws for definition, promotion, and preservation. This dependence bonds our own good and personal obligations to the common political good in a way that gives political obligations force. For example, if our family structure is generated and enforced by laws, the common good of parents and children is bound to the laws of our country. Our families and ourselves are political beings with the particular status of being members of one nation. We are Athenian or Japanese. Political society traditionally is seen as an organic whole that precedes and produces its members, and its laws and injunctions authoritatively preside over all internal affairs: law is justice, religion guards law, freedom is noble and worth dying for, and freedom entails allegiance to the nation's laws. Absorbing individuals into a corporate polity, which they feel obliged to defend as their own, greatly eases and arrests tensions between individual interests and the common good.

This traditional account of political obligation raises questions. All societies may require and often secure their members' obedience, but are all societies equally just? During World War II the soldiers of Nazi Germany and those of liberal democratic America may have done their duty, but were these opposing regimes both worthy of obedience? Can we be content to answer that the psychology and phenomenon of obligation is universal, but justice is relative to the laws of particular historical regimes? If not, by what standard can all regimes be judged?

Liberal democracy as expressed by the Declaration of Independence and the U.S. Constitution stands upon its claim to justice. The laws of nature evince the self-evident truth that all human beings have equal and inalienable rights to life, liberty, and the pursuit of happiness. Individuals consent to form a people and institute government to secure those ends. Government is obliged to serve the people's safety and happiness, and the people's consent obliges them to obey its laws as their own. But the people reserve the right to alter and abolish their government and to decide upon what principles their new government will stand. When government oppresses, it is the people's right, indeed their duty, forcefully to resist. Liberal democracy eases the tensions between individual interests and the public good by liberating the individual and by showing that liberty itself obliges dedication to the public good.

Liberal principles and political practices constitute a radical departure from traditional experiences and conceptions of political obligations. To understand liberal principles, one must turn to the writings of Thomas Hobbes and John Locke. The relation between liberal principles and democratic government is clarified in the writings and acts of the American Founders, who saw the American Republic as the first to be founded on the basis of liberal principles.

Liberal democracy may justify political obligation but not without presenting problems. Can the aggregate of private rights amount to a compelling common good? Because democracy entails majority rule, are opposed minorities obliged to obey? If government serves private ends, is anyone really obliged to obey? Liberal democrats are justly devoted to their regime, but they must always confront the paradox of being obligated to sacrifice for their own good.

See also *Consent; Declaration of Independence; Hobbes, Thomas; Locke, John; Majority rule, minority rights; United States Constitution.*

Michael Rosano

BIBLIOGRAPHY

The Federalist Papers. Edited by Clinton Rossiter. New York: New American Library, 1961.

Hobbes, Thomas. *Leviathan.* Edited by C. B. Macpherson. New York: Viking Penguin, 1982.

Locke, John. *Two Treatises of Government.* Edited by Peter Laslett. Cambridge: Cambridge University Press, 1967.

Pangle, Thomas L. *The Ennobling of Democracy.* Baltimore: Johns Hopkins University Press, 1991.

Plato. *The Apology of Socrates* and *Crito.* In *Four Texts on Socrates.* Translated with notes by Thomas G. West and Grace Starry West. Ithaca, N.Y.: Cornell University Press, 1984.

Rawls, John. *A Theory of Justice.* Cambridge: Harvard University Press, Belknap Press, 1971; Oxford: Oxford University Press, 1973.

Ortega y Gasset, José

Widely considered the greatest Spanish philosopher of the twentieth century and a major Spanish political figure. Ortega y Gasset (1883–1955) was born in Madrid and educated in the Jesuit tradition. After earning a doctorate at the University of Madrid, he studied at the University of Marburg, where he perfected his knowledge of classic German philosophy.

Having obtained the chair in metaphysics at the University of Madrid, Ortega made his mark in Spanish politics as an editorial writer for the newspapers *El Imparcial* and *El Sol,* as founder of the Liga de Educación Política Española (1914) and Agrupación al Servicio de la República (1931), and as a member of the Cortes Constituyentes (parliament) of the Second Republic. He gained international renown with his work *The Revolt of the Masses,* published in 1930. In this book he analyzed the crisis of Europe in the years following World War I and what he saw as the moral disease corroding the institutions and values of liberal civilization.

Ortega went into voluntary exile at the outbreak of the Spanish civil war in 1936. He returned to Spain in 1948 and spent the rest of his life in what he called internal exile. Under the dictatorship of Francisco Franco, Ortega was viewed with suspicion, but he still enjoyed enormous prestige as founder of the philosophical school of Madrid.

Ortega made his debut on the Spanish political scene as a journalist and liberal theorist who was particularly sensitive to the values of the socialist tradition. He believed that socialist liberalism is the only morally acceptable form of liberalism, because only through it could liberty become a universal good, enjoyed by all social classes.

Before 1919 Ortega had considered himself (and was viewed by others) as a companion of the Spanish Socialist Workers' Party, which he believed had a fundamental role to play in the construction of the "new" democratic, European Spain. After the publication of *Invertebrate Spain* in 1920, Ortega's attitude became more elitist, though he remained within the liberal-democratic tradition. He came to believe that the historical dynamics of civilization could be understood only from the starting point of the dialectic between creative minorities and imitative masses. Socialism therefore must strive not for the attainment of social justice but for a form of societal organization that guarantees the selection and formation of an "aristocracy of the spirit." Such a society would no longer be tyrannized by the logic of either economic profit and success or what Ortega called "morbid democracy," aimed at leveling all people.

The fundamental issue for every society, Ortega believed, was to produce an elite of leaders of high intellectual and moral worth. Thus it was necessary to distinguish between incoming and outgoing democracy—that is, between equal opportunity and equal results. Ortega's view rejected the latter for the former. Democracy was a system for the recruitment of "open aristocracies" and not for the destruction of all forms of hierarchy. Society had to consist of a hierarchy of functions, and equal results could only be an illusion.

Ortega also saw a division between liberalism and democracy. Western civilization, he believed, had mistakenly tried to join them, when in reality democracy and liberalism respond to two different issues of public law. Democracy answers the question of who is responsible for exercising the power of command. It holds that every citizen has the sovereign right to intervene in the decision-

José Ortega y Gasset

making processes that invest the political community. Liberalism answers the question of the limits of public power. It holds that the exercise of public power can never be absolute, because citizens have basic rights that the state is obliged to respect and protect. Thus liberalism is the theory and practice of individual rights based on the institutionalization of the constitutional state—that is, a form of limited domination rigidly regulated by law. In Ortega's view, liberalism can be oligarchic, and democracy can be totalitarian. Earlier, he had refuted both possibilities because of his conviction that the mission of modern industrial civilization was to join liberalism and mass democracy, stressing liberty over equality.

The emergence of disturbing political and cultural issues after World War I was evidence of a trend against liberalism in European society. The Industrial Revolution and the prodigious increase of material wealth had produced a new being: mass man. Ortega believed that this all-pervasive presence in every class of society was responsible for a new, direct style of political action and for the birth of a new idol: state providence. State providence satisfied every need of the masses with its bureaucracy and kept the masses in a state of permanent military mobilization. This situation brought about an upheaval of society, in which the main actor was not the worker, as prophesied by Karl Marx, but rather an "internal barbarian." This being wandered among the goods and institutions of industrial society to bring about the final demise of the two elements responsible for the historical grandeur of Western civilization: reason and individual liberty.

To halt the disastrous "rebellion of the masses," Ortega advocated a new democracy centered on the work principle. He also advocated ending the laissez-faire economic system, while still respecting liberty. Ortega criticized "statism" in its dual form of fascist and communist revolution. Both fascism and communism, he believed, attempted to destroy social spontaneity and political and cultural pluralism in the name of revolutionary ideologies.

Luciano Pellicani

BIBLIOGRAPHY

Ferrater Mora, José. *Ortega y Gasset.* New Haven: Yale University Press, 1957.
Guy, Alain. *Ortega y Gasset.* Paris: Gallimard, 1969.
McClintock, Robert. *Man and His Circumstances.* New York: Philosophical Library, 1973.
Ortega y Gasset, José. *Obras completas.* 12 vols. Madrid: Revista de Occidente, 1983.
Pellicani, Luciano. *Introduzione a Ortega y Gasset.* Naples: Liguori, 1977.
Raley, Harold C. *José Ortega y Gasset.* Montgomery: University of Alabama Press, 1971.
Redondo, Gonzalo. *Las empresas políticas de Ortega y Gasset.* Madrid: Aliaza Editorial, 1967.
Ripepe, Eugenio. *Il pensiero politico di José Ortega y Gasset.* Milan: Giuffrè, 1967.

Orthodoxy, Greek and Russian

The beliefs and customs followed by the Greek and Russian Orthodox Churches, which are branches of the larger Christian Orthodox Church. In the eleventh century A.D., after several centuries of estrangement, the Orthodox Church, dominant in eastern Europe and western Asia, and the Roman Catholic Church, dominant in western Europe, broke communion. Although this severance of relations was conditioned by cultural, political, and economic factors, the two churches ultimately quarreled over key issues of doctrine: the pope's claims of universal jurisdiction over the church and the differing views of whether the Holy Spirit proceeded simply from the Father (the Eastern view) or from the Father and Son (the Western view). The Orthodox Church today is a family of self-governing churches held together by the bonds of unity in the faith and of communion in the sacraments.

The Greek Orthodox Church

The Greek Orthodox Church's vision of politics and of church-state relations harks back to the 1,100-year history of the Byzantine Empire (A.D. 324–1453). During that millennium of historical development, the relationship of the church to the state was conceived of as one of harmony and mutuality, under which the emperor and the church cooperated closely as parts of an organic whole. The Byzantine emperor, according to this view, was to fashion his government after the original model of Christian civilization sketched out in the New Testament, and it was believed—wrongly, it turned out—that the state could be transformed into a Christian organism.

Although manifestly dependent on the good will of the emperor, the Byzantine church was prepared to challenge the state if its vital interests—especially in the area of doctrine—were perceived to be at stake. The church also sought actively to humanize and to Christianize the state by whispering in the ear of the emperor and other notables, and to obtain charitable aid for the poor and underprivileged.

The fall of Byzantium to the Turks in 1453 brought this lengthy era of church-state harmony to an abrupt end. Greek independence from the Ottoman yoke in 1821 did not bring its return. Following a model established a century earlier by Peter the Great in Russia, Greece set up a Protestant-style system under which the church became merely a department of state. Although the subjection of the church to the state was later softened, the Greek church today remains an established, or state, church. And the state—particularly during the rule of the Greek colonels (1967–1974)—has often intruded heavy-handedly into church affairs.

As for the future of the church and its relationship to the state, two schools of thought have formed. Nearly all Greek Orthodox commentators believe that Byzantine harmony remains an ideal to be pursued, but some, citing statements by the founders of the Greek church, advocate the restoration of the absolute monarchy as the sole feasible way to reclaim the Byzantine heritage. Such traditionalists reject democracy as the path toward disharmony, division, greed, and discord, which are incompatible with the Orthodox vision of society as a harmonious whole.

Stanley Harakas, an American professor of Christian ethics, belongs to the other school. Drawing on the insights of leading Orthodox thinkers in twentieth-century Greece, he insists that the harmony theory can successfully be reinterpreted in a way that will provide ethical guidance for Orthodox citizens living in democracies. There is, he points out, no essential connection between the Orthodox Church and any specific political form, including monarchy, because, simply put, the message of the church does not change, unlike the world that it seeks to sanctify. Moreover, in a democracy the function of the Byzantine emperor is exercised by the people, who rule through their elected representatives. The church thus can speak directly to the political authority through its membership. The separation of church and state, when both these institutions are truly free, is no obstacle, then, to the church's attempts to infuse the state with Christian principles. In fact, because Orthodox Christians are enjoined by Christ to render unto Caesar that which is Caesar's, the fate of the state and the spiritual and physical health of society are of direct concern to Christians. Indeed, in actively participating in democratic politics, Harakas notes, Christians also seek to defend and to inculcate basic human rights based on the theological truth that all persons are created in the image and likeness of God and thus have inviolable dignity as the children of God.

Finally, Harakas points out that in the legal sphere a democratic state is dependent for its very survival on the quality and level of the common morality. The state needs the church to bolster this common morality, even though it cannot directly appeal to the church in support of its legal judgments and sanctions. Thus, indirectly, a kind of harmony is reestablished.

A bishop of the Greek church and another leading Orthodox theologian, Kallistos Ware of Oxford University, has concurred with many of the points made by Harakas. As Ware sees it, the Greek church should actively seek its own gradual disestablishment; in particular, it should become independent of the state in financial matters. In this way it can once again become a church that is genuinely alive and free.

The Russian Orthodox Church

Like the Greek church, the Russian Orthodox Church is being required by historical circumstance to reevaluate its traditional views of democracy and the separation of church and state. If the 1,100 years of the Byzantine Empire represent a kind of "golden age" for the Greek church, the much briefer Kievan interlude (from the tenth to the thirteenth centuries), when something similar to the Byzantine harmony was achieved, is such an era for the Russian church (as well as for the Ukrainian and Belarusian Orthodox Churches, which also derive from Kievan Christianity). After the thirteenth-century Mongol invasion, however, the Russian church was gradually subordinated to the state.

The effective transformation of the Russian Orthodox Church into a department of the state under Peter the Great, who reigned from 1682 to 1725, had a deleterious effect on church life. Later, under the rule of Emperor Nicholas I (1825–1855), the state achieved a greater degree of control over the church than in any previous period of Russian history. Indeed, in his doctrine of "Official Nationality," Count Sergei Uvarov, Nicholas's minister of education, described the state as firmly bolstered by three supports: Orthodoxy, autocracy, and nationality.

By the early twentieth century, parish life seemed to have lost its vitality and the clergy had largely become a closed caste. The brief interval of semidemocracy (the so-called Duma period) between 1905 and 1917 required Orthodox churchmen to begin contemplating the advantages and disadvantages of a parliamentary system of government. Clergy were elected as deputies to all four Dumas (legislative assemblies).

In 1917–1918, just as the church was in the process of gaining its independence from the state, the militantly antireligious Bolsheviks seized power and subjected the church to one of the severest persecutions of the Christian era. What survived of the church came to be dominated and controlled, especially in its foreign activities, by two powerful bodies: the ideological department of the Communist Party of the Soviet Union and the Committee of State Security, the KGB.

In 1991 the Soviet Union collapsed and the Communist Party was forced to surrender its power. The Russian church, which on the surface had regained its freedom, remained hobbled by the reality that almost all of its approximately 120 bishops had passed through the tight filter maintained by the party and the KGB.

From the beginning of the Brezhnev period (1964–1982), Russian religious rights activists struggled to free the church from the grip of the Communist Party and the state. For example, in late 1965 Orthodox priests Gleb

Yakunin and Nikolai Eshliman coauthored letters to the head of the Russian church and to the chairman of the USSR Supreme Soviet that chronicled in detail the repressive measures used by the state against the church and the connivance of the church leadership in that persecution. As punishment, Yakunin and Eshliman were banned by the Moscow Holy Synod from serving the sacraments, perhaps confirming the perception of many educated Russians that the church leadership had compromised itself by its acquiescence in and collaboration with totalitarian rule.

In 1976 Yakunin emerged as cofounder of the Christian Committee for the Defense of Believers' Rights in the USSR. The new committee pointed out that, even though the constitution of the Soviet Union proclaimed freedom of conscience, there was an inevitable conflict between believers and a government whose declared aim was the construction of a nonreligious society. Moreover, the committee noted, the bishops of the Russian Orthodox Church did not concern themselves with the defense of believers' rights. Yakunin was arrested by the KGB in 1979 and sentenced to five years in a concentration camp. In late 1993 he was defrocked by the Holy Synod for his announced intention to run for election to the new Russian parliament.

Notable among modern-day Russian Orthodox writers who began to rethink the relationship of the church to democracy and the question of the separation of church and state was the late Anton Kartashev, who served as minister for Orthodox affairs in the short-lived 1917 provisional government and as a delegate to the 1917–1918 Church Council, which reestablished the patriarchate. In a pathbreaking essay on the church's relationship to the state published in the early 1950s, Kartashev arrived at many of the same conclusions reached later by Harakas. According to Kartashev, the church is able to "harmonize" with most political systems—be they absolute monarchies, authoritarian regimes, or democracies—with the sole exception of totalitarian regimes, such as those of the Soviet Union and Nazi Germany. Under such savage antihuman regimes, the church can only choose martyrdom.

Kartashev showed strong sympathy for modern Western-style democracy, which provides rich soil for the flourishing of religious life. Moreover, he recognized that democracies are seen as a growing present-day reality, the predominant political tendency of modern times. Thus it would be foolish and counterproductive for Orthodox Christians to seek to return to a vanished absolutist past.

Orthodoxy and Politics

Greek Orthodoxy may have no tradition of religious-based political parties, but since 1989 some Russian Orthodox activists such as Gleb Yakunin have been attempting to create European-style Christian democratic parties in order to influence more directly the future direction of Russian political life. Such efforts have met with only limited success. The encounter of Greek and Russian Orthodoxy with democracy, although largely a recent phenomenon, promises to yield new fruit over the coming decades.

John B. Dunlop

BIBLIOGRAPHY

Azkoul, Michael. *Sacred Monarchy and the Modern Secular State.* Montreal: Monastery Press, 1980.
Ellis, Jane. *The Russian Orthodox Church: A Contemporary History.* Bloomington: Indiana University Press, 1986.
Harakas, Stanley S. *Contemporary Moral Issues Facing the Orthodox Christian.* Minneapolis: Light and Life Publishing, 1982.
———. "Orthodox Church-State Theory and American Democracy." *The Greek Orthodox Theological Review.* Bicentennial Issue (winter 1976): 399–421.
Kartashev, Anton. "The Church and the State." In *Orthodoxy in Life* (in Russian), edited by S. Verkhovskoi. New York: Chekhov Publishing, 1953.
Ramet, Pedro, ed. *Eastern Christianity and Politics in the Twentieth Century.* Durham, N.C.: Duke University Press, 1988.
Runciman, Steven. *The Orthodox Churches and the Secular State.* Auckland, New Zealand: Auckland University Press and Oxford University Press, 1971.
Ware, Kallistos. "The Church: A Time of Transition." In *Greece in the 1980s,* edited by Richard Clogg. New York: St. Martin's, 1983.

Ostrogorski, Moisei Yakovlevich

Russian lawyer, political scientist, and student of English and American political parties. Ostrogorski (1854–1919) was born into a well-off Jewish family in Grodno, Russia. He earned a degree in law from the University of St. Petersburg and in 1882 became head of the legal department of the Russian Ministry of Justice. With the establishment of a reactionary regime after the assassination of Alexander II, he emigrated to France, where he began his study of political parties at the Ecole Libre des Sciences Politiques.

Strongly influenced by Alexis de Tocqueville's description of "great" (principled) and "minor" (factional) parties in *Democracy in America* (1835–1840), Ostrogorski expressly set out to reinterpret Tocqueville's conclusions in the light of the development and decline of party in the late nineteenth century. His early work on American parties (1888) was highly critical, describing them as the cause of a split between liberalism and democracy.

In 1889 Ostrogorski decided to write a book on parties and democracy, which would focus on comparing the development of American and English parties. He made frequent visits to England to observe political developments there, and in 1896 he traveled to the United States to reassess his study of American parties. This long research resulted in the publication of *Democracy and the Organization of Political Parties* (1902), his most important work published in English.

Although the British historian James Bryce had suggested the study, Ostrogorski's conclusions were not what Bryce had expected. Instead of distinguishing between English and American parties, Ostrogorski concluded that the same trend toward corruption was inscribed in English as in American parties. If the reputation of liberal democracy was to be saved, parties would have to be replaced by single-issue leagues, limited to particular goals and for a specific period of time. This type of organization, according to Ostrogorski, would be instrumental in reconciling the theory and practice of liberalism with those of democracy.

After the publication of *Democracy and the Organization of Political Parties,* Ostrogorski returned to Russia. In 1906 he was elected to the first Duma (an elected legislative assembly created in response to the revolution of 1905) as a representative of the Jewish lobby. After the Duma was dissolved by the czar later that year, Ostrogorski returned to his studies.

In 1916 Ostrogorski's *Development of the English Constitution* was published in Russian. In this work he criticized the English political model, which was widely admired by nineteenth-century European liberals. In his opinion the main characteristics of the English model—cabinet government, a two-party system, and government by party leaders—were compatible with liberalism only in an oligarchic regime. The emergence of the mass party and the transition to democracy caused a radical transformation of the English model, making it incompatible with liberalism. If democracy and liberalism were to be reconciled, a new political model had to be devised, in which there would be no room left for the party.

In this case Ostrogorski was wrong: subsequent developments in Western politics proved the mass party to be compatible with both liberalism and democracy. Yet Ostrogorski's fears about parties were widespread among European scholars and politicians of his time; it is to this attunement with his intellectual environment that Ostrogorski owed most of his success. *The Development of the English Constitution* was the culmination of his thinking on parties and democracy.

In his last years Ostrogorski suffered from a progressive nervous illness. He died in St. Petersburg in 1919.

See also *Bryce, James; Liberalism; Parties, Political; Politics, Machine; Spoils system.*

Gaetano Quagliariello

BIBLIOGRAPHY

Ostrogorski, Moisei. *Democracy and the Organization of Political Parties.* Introduction by Seymour Martin Lipset. 2 vols. Chicago: Anchor Books, 1964.

Pombeni, Paolo. "Starting in Reason, Ending in Passion: Bryce, Lowell, Ostrogorski and the Problem of Democracy." *Historical Journal* 37 (1994): 319–341.

Quagliariello, Gaetano. *La politica senza partiti. Ostrogorski e l'organizzazione dei partiti politici tra ottacento e novacento.* Bari-Roma: Laterza, 1993. English translation forthcoming: *Politics without Parties: Ostrogorski and the Political Party Debate between the Nineteenth and Twentieth Centuries.*

P

Paine, Thomas

British-born pamphleteer, agitator, and writer on political and religious subjects. Paine (1737–1809) is known as a popularizer of radical ideas attacking the old order of feudalism, hereditary monarchy, and orthodox Christianity. His major works are *The Rights of Man* (1791–1792) and *The Age of Reason* (1794).

Paine was born in Thetford, England, to a poor Quaker family. He received little formal education, beginning work at the age of thirteen. He emigrated to America in 1775 on the advice of Benjamin Franklin and soon began working for the cause of American independence. His pamphlets *Common Sense* (1776) and *The Crisis,* which eloquently argued the cause of American independence and republicanism, greatly aided the Revolution. He traveled to France, where he supported the French Revolution, in 1787 and 1792; he was imprisoned during the Terror and narrowly escaped execution. When he returned to the United States in 1802, he was widely denounced for his unorthodox religious views. He died in poverty in New York.

Paine drew from John Locke the ideas that individuals have innate natural rights to life, liberty, and possessions and that they institute governments to secure those rights (and may abolish states that do not ensure them). From this perspective, he ridiculed monarchical and aristocratic Europe as a system based on fraud, ignorance, and superstition. Only a representative democracy, such as that of the United States, could reform the abuses, corruption, and tyranny of the old order.

Paine's libertarian political views corresponded with his free market capitalist ideology. Still, in his last book, *Agrarian Justice* (1796), Paine advocated a welfare state

Thomas Paine

with a redistributive tax structure, old age pensions, and public assistance to the blind and lame. He maintained that private property is largely obtained by social advantages rather than by personal labor; therefore all owe a portion of their wealth to society.

Thomas Paine is remembered as a radical democrat whose extreme egalitarian views caused considerable discomfort among the traditional political and religious orders of his time.

Garrett Ward Sheldon

Pakistan

A constitutionally Islamic country of South Asia, founded in 1947, and a test case for Islamic democracy. In its experience with democracy, Pakistan compares well with other constitutionally Islamic states. But when measured by the extent of popular participation, the effectiveness of representative institutions, and commitment to a constitutional order, democratic rule in Pakistan has been inconsistent and shallow.

For more than half the time since its founding, Pakistan has experienced military rule. A parliamentary vote in 1970 was the first conducted under universal suffrage, and the election of 1988 was the first in which a transfer of power occurred smoothly, without military interference. As of the mid-1990s, no government had completed its term of office since the lifting of martial law in 1985. In 1990 a popularly chosen prime minister was dismissed, and the federal legislature was dissolved, by a president who had been chosen indirectly. When, in 1993, the same president again attempted to remove a government, his action was overturned by Pakistan's Supreme Court.

This very mixed picture of democracy in Pakistan raises two questions, which may be related: Why has Pakistan failed to emulate its neighbor India in that country's relative success with democratic institutions? And how instructive are Pakistan's problems in understanding the transition to democracy, especially the compatibility of an Islamic state with liberal democratic institutions?

The Partition and Later Divisions

Pakistan was created in August 1947 as the British, hurriedly departing, partitioned colonial India. The accession to Pakistan of the provinces and districts with the largest concentrations of Muslims met the demands of Muslim nationalists seeking self-determination apart from India's Hindu majority. The two-nation solution left Pakistan itself divided geographically into east and west wings, more than a thousand miles apart. The west encompassed the ethnically distinct provinces of Punjab, Sindh, Baluchistan, and North-West Frontier. The more populous eastern province was dominated by Bengali Muslims.

The two wings were culturally and linguistically distinct and marked by wide economic disparity. For nearly twenty-five years they struggled for political ascendance. After the 1970 elections the eastern wing, led by Mujibur Rahman, was denied the parliamentary control it had won. East Pakistan agitated for sovereignty, only to be brutally suppressed by Pakistan's army. Indian military intervention late in 1971 defeated Pakistani forces and paved the way for Bengali independence as Bangladesh. Still unresolved in Pakistani eyes, however, has been the status of Kashmir. Although predominantly Muslim, at the time of independence Kashmir had a Hindu ruler who brought the state into the Indian union. Three wars later, the issue continues to poison relations between India and Pakistan.

The Decades After Independence

The mass movement that resulted in a separate Islamic state was led by Mohammad Ali Jinnah, who became Pakistan's first head of state. A charismatic leader who had earlier expressed misgivings about parliamentary government, Jinnah was nonetheless committed to free and open elections and to the rule of law in Pakistan. He died in September 1948, just thirteen months after independence. The country's only other political figure of national stature, Liaquat Ali Khan, was assassinated in October 1951. The deaths of these leaders dimmed hopes for legitimizing participatory institutions and building a political consensus through a national party.

For at least the first twenty years of the republic, none of Pakistan's leaders saw a need to cultivate popular support. The people, in turn, had little understanding of the kind of vigilance necessary for citizens to hold political leaders accountable. Little attention was given to educating the people to practice democracy through meaningful participation in their political affairs. In the absence of effective public opinion, the political system was open to ambitious, corrupt leaders. Power was concentrated in the hands of an elitist bureaucracy and an overbearing military. The semifeudal system on which so much of the country's politics was based was not conducive to building a democracy. Large, wealthy landowning families remained the traditional power brokers, prepared to lend support to any leader who promised to protect their interests.

Jinnah's successors were unable to resolve several basic

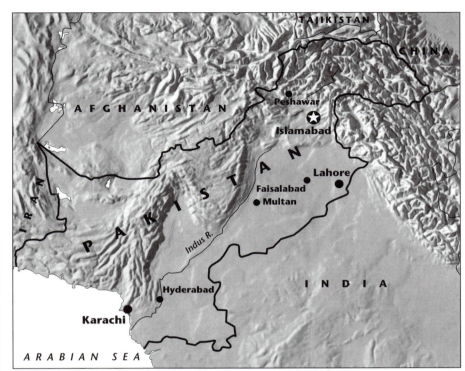

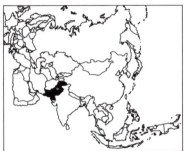

constitutional issues, the most important of which was provincial autonomy. For example, much dissension followed the decision to impose the Urdu language on the mainly Bengali-speaking population of the eastern province. Politicians from East Pakistan also argued for a proportional system of representation to ensure that Bengali interests would be heard in a future federal legislature. Since Pakistan lacked a formal, written constitution until 1956, precedents were created in the meantime that rapidly undermined parliamentary and democratic norms. For example, in the early years there was a practice of appointing nonparty prime ministers who owed their position to the head of state rather than to a constituency of voters. This contributed to the country's political instability and the failure of its parliamentary system.

Heads of state after Jinnah came from the ranks of the bureaucracy rather than from the Parliament. Having little feel for democratic politics, they often governed in an arbitrary fashion. The concept of impartiality that Jinnah had tried to instill was damaged by the appointments and dismissals of Ghulam Mohammad as governor general. Ghulam Mohammad, a former civil servant and a Punjabi, had replaced a Bengali, Khwaja Nazimuddin, who became prime minister in 1951. Ghulam Mohammad's removal of Nazimuddin from that position in 1953, while

the prime minister still commanded a majority in the Constituent Assembly, revealed the governor general's disdain for parliamentary procedures and his determination to expand the powers of his office. Ghulam Mohammad's decision the following year to dissolve the Assembly and impose central rule, or governor's rule, in the provinces further undercut democratic practice.

As a consequence, lines of authority became increasingly vague. With legislators locked in constitutional debate, the running of the country fell to the permanent bureaucracy. Meanwhile, the Muslim League, which had spearheaded the independence movement, degenerated in the public's eyes from a body of men speaking for the whole nation to a collection of squabbling, self-aggrandizing politicians.

Martial Law

Pakistan, like India, inherited a tradition of the military's detachment from active involvement in politics. Within a decade after partition, however, civil-military relations in the two countries sharply diverged. In India, the practice of having regular elections took deep root in the political culture. India also had the benefit of retaining the leadership of Jawaharlal Nehru for sixteen years after independence. Over those years democratic practices became institutionalized, and India was able to avoid a highly personalized system of government. The supremacy of the civil authority established under India's constitution of 1950 contrasts with Pakistan's constant struggle to head off military rule and revive disintegrating political institutions.

In 1958 weak parties and unelected, ineffective governments gave way to the martial law regime of Gen. Mohammad Ayub Khan. As president, Ayub Khan in 1962 offered a constitution that called for a system of "Basic Democracies." The constitution, adopted that same year, centralized national political power in the presidency, leaving the legislature little control over finances and legislation. It established a pyramidal, four-tiered system, providing for administrative responsibilities and local government, as well as national development. Local bodies acted as electoral units in contests for the presidency and National Assembly. In Ayub Khan's view, the only sound political system was one that was home-grown. The system supposedly had older roots in the *panchayats,* or local governing bodies, of historic India. Democracy's failures in Pakistan were seen as resulting from the importation of alien institutions from the West. Parliamentary democracy, Ayub Khan believed, tended to divide people when Pakistan needed unity and singleness of purpose.

Besides serving to legitimize Ayub Khan's regime, the system of Basic Democracies was expected to help mobilize people and educate them to participate in local affairs. Its localized, indirect system of elections was said to be particularly well suited to largely illiterate rural populations, making the government process more meaningful to them. In practice, the system severely limited popular participation. Eighty thousand "Basic Democrats" were designated to elect the National Assembly. Local units fell under the influence of government officials and council chairmen, and ordinary citizens were kept out of politics.

Ayub Khan's constitution, and with it his regime, came to a turbulent end in March 1969. Student-led demonstrations, backed by a new political organization headed by former government official, Zulfikar Ali Bhutto, spread from West Pakistan to East Pakistan. The protests against restrictions on political activity and the press and against the government's educational policies led Ayub Khan to resign in favor of Gen. Agha Mohammad Yahya Khan. As president, Yahya Khan reimposed martial law and

promised a new constitution. He also scheduled for December 1970 Pakistan's first general election among the entire adult population. In contests for a National Assembly, Bhutto's Pakistan People's Party was dominant in the western provinces, but Mujibur Rahman's Awami League held a clear majority of legislative seats and moved into a position to draft the new constitution. Bhutto and his supporters, however, prevented the convening of the Assembly the following March. This failure to honor the election led to a general strike and administrative paralysis in East Pakistan, which provoked the army's crackdown against a fast-growing independence movement. After the Indian army's invasion and quick defeat of Pakistan in December 1971, Yahya Khan was forced to quit. He transferred the presidency of the now truncated country to its most popular politician, Zulfikar Ali Bhutto.

Bhutto and Zia

The 1970 election did more than legitimize Bhutto's ascension to power. It marked the first time that a party in Pakistan could claim to reflect the will of a majority of the people, at least in the western provinces. Offering a quasi-socialist program, Bhutto's Pakistan People's Party achieved the mass mobilization of the electorate, communicating effectively with rural voters for the first time. The election set the standard in Pakistan for orderly and honest balloting.

In 1973 legislators, under Bhutto's leadership, approved Pakistan's most democratic constitution, which contained guarantees for fundamental rights. Although Bhutto initially emphasized the supremacy of the people and asserted civilian control of the military, in time he abandoned this populist ideology. Rather than work through participatory institutions, he strongly personalized his power. To deal with his enemies, Bhutto resorted to constitutional changes, and he came to rely on military and paramilitary forces. In maneuvering for the March 1977 elections, he restored ties with the landed families that were still locally powerful. Pakistan had made some progress toward increased participation, but Bhutto had failed to deliver a liberal state, one that was able to tolerate a legitimate political opposition. At the same time, the regime's opponents were never fully willing to trust the system.

The parliamentary elections of March 1977 that officially returned Bhutto to office as prime minister were delegitimized by evidence of widespread fraud. Demonstrations organized by a coalition of opposition parties nearly brought the country to a standstill. As a result, Bhutto's handpicked army chief, Gen. Mohammad Zia ul-Haq, was able to seize power in July 1977 with claims of restoring order and instituting truly Islamic rule. As president, Zia repeatedly refused to hold promised elections. Not until 1985 did he agree to share power with an appointed civilian government and allow a nonparty election for the legislature. Zia had legitimized his continued hold on the presidency with a national referendum in December 1984 and through revisions of the 1973 constitution. Most important was the eighth amendment, which he pressed on legislators in 1985. This amendment assured wide discretionary powers for the president in post–martial-law governments. Zia was then able to dissolve the federal legislature and call fresh elections as well as to make senior government and military appointments. Critics charge that the eighth amendment perpetuates the kind of arbitrary rule that undercuts the authority of elected officials and renders a democratic mandate nearly meaningless.

Contemporary Politics

Zia ul-Haq's death in an airplane crash in August 1988 paved the way for a party-based election in which the Pakistan People's Party under Benazir Bhutto assumed power. Bhutto is the daughter of the former prime minister. The Zia regime, fearing her father's return to power, had had him executed in 1979 for complicity in the murder of an opposition politician some years earlier.

Benazir Bhutto promised to strengthen constitutionally protected liberties, notably for women. Once in office as prime minister, however, she found her policies constrained by military and religious leaders. After just twenty-one months, she was dismissed by President Ghulam Ishaq Khan and replaced by a caretaker government. Initially, it seemed that democracy had been dealt a severe blow. These concerns were eased, however, when elections were held as promised in October 1990, and Bhutto and her party were allowed to compete in a reasonably honest contest. Bhutto's party lost the election.

Although marked by some demagoguery and violence, the elections of 1988 and 1990 had seemed to signal a gradual strengthening of the democratic system. This was again cast in doubt by President Ishaq Khan's attempt to oust Prime Minister Mian Mohammad Nawaz Sharif in April 1993, followed nearly three months later by the resig-

nation of both men, under pressure by the military. Military leaders were impatient with the political struggle and resolved to hold army-supervised parliamentary elections.

Rather than instituting a martial-law regime leading up to new elections, the military supported an interim civilian government headed by Moeen Qureshi, a former senior vice-president of the World Bank. An outsider without political debts to pay, Qureshi implemented bold economic and anticorruption measures, although not all his ordinances survived the necessary parliamentary approval. In national elections on October 6, 1993, Benazir Bhutto's People's Party captured eighty-five seats. With the support of thirty-six other legislators, Bhutto formed a coalition government in the National Assembly. Soon after, in provincial assembly elections, and in a combined vote of national and provincial legislators that chose the country's new president, her followers tightened their political control. Although the results appeared to leave Prime Minister Bhutto with a freer hand than she had had in her earlier term to chart policy and stabilize Pakistan's democracy, she has thus far disappointed many. She has tolerated corruption, permitted abuse of political opponents, and acquiesced in discrimination against minorities.

The Issue of Islamic Democracy

A history of weak democratic accountability in Pakistan raises the question of who or what is to blame. Many observers cite a poor quality of leadership and failures of institutional design, while others point to the absence of a supportive, participatory political culture. Ayub Khan claimed that because Muslims historically had never known real sovereignty in the predominantly Hindu subcontinent, they had difficulty adjusting psychologically to their new freedom as Pakistanis.

Still others trace the problem specifically to education and the Islamic religion. The most common assertion is that Islam, by basing ultimate authority in God's word, must reject the principle that sovereignty lies in the will of the people. The Sunni branch of Islam recognizes the concept of elevating rulers by election. Nonetheless, regimes in the Islamic world have so far derived little of their legitimacy from authentic popular forces expressed through representative institutions. Likewise, they have not tempered their authority with tolerance for those who disagree with them. To many critics, Islam fails to support democratic values because it makes no provision for legitimate opposition and allows only second-class citizenship to non-Muslims. Islam is also said to have a particular reverence for the military. The concept of holy war gives the military the kind of prestige that inevitably leaves civilian-run democratic rule vulnerable.

At a minimum, a religiously prescribed constitution for Pakistan would place certain prohibitions on the majority's lawmaking powers. Whether such restrictions, along with limits on the civil rights of minorities, would fatally compromise a modern democratic system is debatable. It is notable that Pakistan's radical Islamic parties have never gained wide popular support. Pakistan could in fact be a test case for determining whether extensions of democratic practice can accommodate and moderate militant Islamic political movements.

Elected officials in Pakistan have had difficulty competing with a military that is integrated, disciplined, and respected. Pakistan's institutions are sufficiently weak and discredited, and its politicians are held in enough contempt, that the military has easily dislodged them. Civilian regimes were subject to military dominance from 1962 to 1968 and from 1985 to 1988, and the country came under complete martial law during 1958–1962, 1969–1971, and 1977–1985. From the mid-1950s on, the influence of the military was bolstered by assistance from China, Saudi Arabia, the United States, and other nations. Especially during the Afghan conflict, from 1979 to 1989—when Pakistan acted as host to about 3.2 million Afghan refugees and largely orchestrated the activities of exiled party leaders—the weapons and training received strengthened the military's confidence and status. When in power, military regimes—most effectively the Zia government—contained political activity while scoring some economic successes. Full legitimacy has continued to elude the military, however, when it has grasped a governing role in Pakistan's politics.

The military's restraint after Zia's death, as seen in its willingness to abide by the constitution, appeared to be a serious attempt to respect elected governments. In the ongoing power struggle between feudal families and bureaucrats, on the one hand, and industrialists and the middle class, on the other, the military became an arbiter. But not all military leaders are reconciled to losing direct management. The military carved out for itself areas of policy dominance—management of the Afghan war, nuclear development, and the conflict over Kashmir. Civilian governments faced with ethnic crises in the provinces found themselves dependent on military forces to restore law and order. To keep the loyalty of the military, governments have had to allocate a large segment of the country's resources to defense expenditures.

For democracy to prosper in Pakistan, it must survive the elites that subvert it in pursuit of economic interests, ideologies, and personal ambitions. Democracy must also ensure reasonable security from external enemies who are widely perceived as threatening the state, especially now, in the region's nuclear age. The tensions that threaten a major war between Pakistan and India may severely test the proposition that democracies do not fight one another. Over the long haul, liberal civilian governments must demonstrate their ability to function as well as or better than authoritarian ones. They will have to overcome wide economic disparities, allow for sustained development, and avoid corruption and mismanagement.

Pakistan's democratic institutions and elected leaders may be judged most of all by their solutions to the country's disruptive ethnic and regional problems. Despite the common religious identity that justified the state's creation, its varied population—Punjabi, Sindhi, Pathan, and Baluchi—has yet to shed the resentments and distrust that deny Pakistan its full nationhood.

See also *India; Islam; Jinnah, Mohammad Ali.*

Marvin G. Weinbaum

BIBLIOGRAPHY

Callard, Keith. *Pakistan: A Political Study.* London: Allen and Unwin, 1957.

Khan, Mohammad Ayub. *Friends Not Masters.* London: Oxford University Press, 1967.

Richter, William. "The 1990 General Elections in Pakistan." In *Pakistan 1992,* edited by Charles H. Kennedy. Boulder, Colo.: Westview Press, 1992.

Rizvi, Hasan-Askari. "The Legacy of Military Rule in Pakistan." *Survival* 31 (May–June 1989): 255–268.

Rounaq, Jahan. *Pakistan: Failure in National Integration.* New York and London: Columbia University Press, 1972.

Safdar, Mahmood. *A Political Study of Pakistan.* Lahore: Sh. Muhammad Ashraf, 1975.

Wriggins, Howard W., ed. *Pakistan in Transition.* Islamabad: University of Islamabad Press, 1975.

Ziring, Lawrence, Ralph Braibanti, and Howard W. Wriggins, eds. *Pakistan: The Long View.* Durham, N.C.: Duke University Press, 1977.

Pankhurst, Emmeline

Militant leader of the English women's suffrage movement. Pankhurst (1858–1928) was born in Manchester, England. She was associated with the socialist movement and was committed to social and economic reform. In 1879 she married Richard Marsden Pankhurst, a barrister who shared her interests in reform.

Pankhurst served on the Married Women's Property Act Committee. The committee's efforts led to the 1882 passage of the act, which granted married women control of their income. She campaigned for passage of the Local Government Act, which became law in 1894 and guaranteed women the vote in local elections. In 1889 the Pankhursts founded the Women's Franchise League to promote political and social equality for women. Advocating local political participation to bring about social change, Pankhurst won a seat on the Chorlton Board of Guardians in 1894 and on the Manchester School Board in 1900.

Pankhurst was an early member of the Independent Labour Party. In the 1890s she worked to alleviate pressing social problems—especially poverty, hunger, and unemployment. She supported freedom for the Boer Republics in Africa and resigned from the Fabian Society, which sought gradual and peaceful change in society, because it refused to oppose the Boer War.

In 1903 Pankhurst organized the Women's Social and Political Union and pressed the Independent Labour Party to adopt women's suffrage and parliamentary enfranchisement in its platform. The party, later known as the Labour Party, appointed Pankhurst to its National Administrative Council and supported the women's enfranchisement bill.

The Women's Social and Political Union demonstrations became increasingly militant. Members heckled parliamentary leaders and disrupted speeches. During direct-action campaigns, demonstrators rioted, committed arson, and destroyed property; consequently, Pankhurst and other suffragists were imprisoned. In protest, they participated in prolonged hunger strikes that prison authorities ended by forced feeding. At the end of World War I, Pankhurst saw her efforts to secure women's suffrage succeed.

Pankhurst, who had contracted bronchitis in prison, died of the illness in a nursing home shortly before her seventieth birthday. Her daughters also were suffragists.

See also *Anthony, Susan B.; Stanton, Elizabeth Cady; Women and democracy; Women's suffrage in the United States.*

Susan Gluck Mezey

Pareto, Vilfredo

Italian economist and sociologist identified with elite theory. An engineer by training, Pareto (1848–1923) made important mathematical contributions as professor of political economy at the University of Lausanne. Disillusioned by the corruption of the fledgling Italian and French democracies in the late nineteenth and early twentieth centuries, he turned to sociology and constructed a theory noted for its bleak assessment of social and political possibilities.

In the *Trattato di sociologia generale* (1916), published in English as *The Mind and Society* (1935), Pareto advanced the idea that elites are inevitable in society. If social mobility were unrestricted, elites would be the most talented. Short of that ideal condition, however, they are persons adept at using force and persuasion, the two bases of rulership. Pareto believed that the behavior of elites and mass populations alike can be explained in terms of economic interests and basic human propensities. But the mix of interests and propensities among elites differs from that among the masses. Because of this difference, and because their cleverness or fortitude gradually weakens, elites sooner or later are displaced by new elites whose interests and propensities for a time are more in step with those of the masses. This circulation of elites is inescapable.

Pareto believed that all political regimes, including democracies, are created and dominated by elites. Democratic regimes are distinctive because they involve unusually broad alliances, approximating cartels, among the most important elite groups. The task of cabinets and other government authorities is to sustain these alliances by distributing public goods in ways that mollify elite groups and their supporters. This undertaking requires a high order of political shrewdness and skill that governments often lack; consequently, they are replaced.

While acknowledging the resilience of democratic regimes, Pareto concluded that the ones he knew best were increasingly unstable and that a swing toward militaristic regimes was imminent. To this extent, he foresaw Benito Mussolini's fascist takeover in Italy, which occurred when Pareto was on his deathbed. Although Mussolini later sought to gain intellectual respectability by invoking Pareto's theory, Pareto never endorsed fascism. Had he lived longer, he surely would have seen it as another instance of the endless circulation of elites.

See also *Elite theory*.

John Higley

Parliamentarism and presidentialism

Parliamentarism and presidentialism are the two dominant forms of democratic governmental systems. In presidential systems the head of government (called the president) and the legislature (often called the Congress) are elected for terms of office prescribed by the constitution. Except under exceptional circumstances the Congress cannot force the president to resign, although it can remove him or her by the highly unusual process of impeachment. In most presidential systems the president cannot dissolve Congress. In parliamentary systems, on the contrary, the head of government (who may be called prime minister, premier, chancellor, president of the government, or—in Ireland—*taoiseach)* can be dismissed from office by a vote of no confidence in the legislature. Normally, the prime minister can also dissolve the legislature and call for new elections. Presidentialism is based on a stricter separation of powers, whereas parliamentarism, although distinguishing between the powers of the executive and legislature, is based on cooperation between the two branches of government.

A basic characteristic of presidentialism is that the president is popularly elected, either directly or through an electoral college, which is elected for that sole purpose. In parliamentary systems the people elect only their own representatives—the members of parliament—who in turn select the head of the government.

In parliamentary systems there is a distinction between the head of state, who represents the nation symbolically, and the chief executive, or prime minister, who governs. The head of state, who can be a monarch or a president of the republic, is generally not popularly elected and has no power to govern, although he or she exercises some influence, offers advice, and often acts as a moderator by working with political leaders to craft an agreement or, occasionally, trying to influence public opinion. Japan, Spain, the United Kingdom, the countries of Scandinavia, and the Benelux countries are parliamentary monarchies. Among the parliamentary republics are Hungary, Italy, the Czech Republic, the Federal Republic of Germany, and the French Third and Fourth Republics.

Terms of Office for Presidents and Prime Ministers

In many presidential systems, presidents cannot be reelected at all, or they cannot be reelected for more than a certain number of terms or without a period of time elapsing after the end of the first term. In parliamentary systems the prime minister can stay in office as long as his or her party, or the coalition supporting the government, has a majority in the parliament.

One disadvantage of the presidential system is that a successful and competent politician who has the trust of the people often cannot continue in office. A "lame duck" president, who cannot run again, has limited power. A former president is not likely to be the leader of his or her

party in the Congress and may not be able to use the experience and knowledge acquired in office. Another problem is that an incompetent president has to finish his or her term unless there are grounds for impeachment; such a president is often unable to govern effectively. Similarly, if a president faces a hostile Congress, the president may be unable to govern, however competent or popular he or she is. Unlike a prime minister, a president cannot dissolve the legislature and call for new elections.

In parliamentary systems the legislators can dismiss the prime minister through a vote of no confidence. The disadvantage, however, is that the parliament can be too powerful and replace prime ministers too often. In multiparty systems or cases with little party discipline, coalitions of parties can realign themselves continuously, causing many changes in leadership in a short time. This has been the situation in the Third and Fourth Republics of France and in Italy.

Some modern constitutions, like those of Germany and Spain, have introduced mechanisms to ensure government stability. In Germany, for example, electoral laws establish a threshold of representation to keep small, often extremist parties out of the parliament. Or the parliament may be allowed to vote no confidence only by electing a successor to the current prime minister.

Other Members of the Executive Branch

Many presidential systems have a vice president. Sometimes the vice president and the president are elected separately. If they are elected separately, they may be of different parties and the vice president may try to undermine the president. Normally, however, they are elected on the same ticket, with the president playing a large role in choosing a vice presidential running mate. This practice may result in a vice president who would not have been chosen on the basis of qualifications. For example, María Estela (Isabel) Martínez de Perón, the wife of Juan Domingo Perón, succeeded him to the presidency of Argentina in July 1974. Or it may result in a vice president who is selected mainly to balance the ticket in one way or another—perhaps geographically or in terms of political appeal to the voters. An example is Boris Yeltsin's selection of Aleksandr Rutskoi as his running mate in 1993. In the fall of 1993 Rutskoi, together with Ruslan Khasbulatov, president of the legislature, led a revolt against Yeltsin.

The automatic succession of the vice president to the presidency if the president is unable to complete the term of office can therefore bring to the highest office someone who never could have won election independently, as happened in Brazil in the cases of both José Sarney in 1985 and Itamar Franco in 1990. In parliamentary systems the death or resignation of a prime minister does not necessarily involve discontinuity or even new elections. The ruling party or coalition can simply elect a new prime minister, as happened when John Major replaced Margaret Thatcher in the United Kingdom in 1991.

The cabinet, which helps the president or prime minister govern, is much more independent in a parliamentary system than in a presidential system. In a parliamentary system the prime minister is merely one among equals. Many cabinet members will serve under more than one prime minister, since they are likely to be important leaders in their party and members of parliament with experience in preparing legislation. In a presidential system, on the other hand, the president usually has considerable freedom to appoint members of the cabinet. This means that few cabinet members will have served another president, and they may lack experience in government.

Choosing a President or Prime Minister

In presidential systems, many voters focus on the personalities of the presidential candidates more than on their parties and programs. It is possible for someone who has never held any elective office, or only a local office, to win a substantial number of votes for president (like Ross Perot in the United States in 1992 and Stanislaw Tyminski in Poland in 1990). If such a candidate is elected (as was Alberto Fujimori in Peru in 1990), he or she is likely to come into office without the support of any party in the legislature and may be unable to govern effectively. In parliamentary systems, on the other hand, a politician who wants to become prime minister must build support within a party or coalition of parties, which will share the responsibility of governing.

Unsuccessful candidates for the presidency may leave politics, and their parties may be left largely leaderless. In parliamentary systems, however, defeated candidates become the leaders of the opposition.

An elected prime minister knows he or she has the support only of those who voted for the governing party or coalition of parties and of the members of parliament who supported his or her candidacy. An elected president, by contrast, represents all the people, even if he or she may not have obtained a majority of the votes cast. Bolivia

is an exception here. When no presidential candidate receives an absolute majority of the popular vote, the legislature decides between the two front-runners.

Governing

In a parliamentary system, only the parliament has democratic legitimacy, and it supports the prime minister or withdraws that support by a vote of no confidence. In a presidential system the president and the legislature both have democratic legitimacy, and it is not possible to say which more accurately represents the will of the people. If they conflict, the only solution is to turn to the judicial power—the constitutional or supreme court. In Latin America, where the judicial power does not always enjoy high prestige, such conflicts have often been resolved by the armed forces. The armed forces sometimes support the president and close the legislature, sometimes dismiss both the president and the legislature and install an interim government, or sometimes assume dictatorial power for a long period of time.

The separation of powers in the United States is designed to weaken the power of presidents. If a president has only minority support in Congress, his or her power to implement policies can be severely limited. This inability to implement policies can be an important source of frustration among voters and a cause of political instability.

On the other hand, the greater independence of Congress means that many special or regional interests are better represented than in a parliamentary system, since members of Congress can vote against their party and president to win favor with constituents. In parliamentary systems, party discipline is enforced to support governments, thus weakening the "representative" function and causing voters to feel ignored. This problem may be magnified in cases where no party has a majority and the government relies on a coalition of parties.

Other Forms of Democratic Institutions

Although presidentialism and parliamentarism are the dominant forms of democratic government, a few other forms can be mentioned. In some systems, voters elect more than one person to executive office. In Crete between 1960 and 1963 a Greek Cypriot was president and a Turkish Cypriot was vice president. In Uruguay from 1952 to 1967 a nine-member body called the *Colegiado* governed. There are also executives elected by the legislature who have a fixed term of office and thus cannot be dismissed by a vote of no confidence; examples are the president of Lebanon and the seven-member Swiss Federal Council.

Another form of government has been called dual-executive, premier-presidential, or semipresidential. In this type of system there is both a popularly elected president and a prime minister selected and supported by a majority in the legislature. The president assumes a major role in foreign affairs and defense, while the prime minister deals with other matters. In this system the president may belong to one party and the prime minister to another, as happened in France between 1986 and 1988 and again from 1993 to 1995, with socialist President François Mitterrand and conservative prime ministers Jacques Chirac and Edouard Balladur. This arrangement is called *cohabitation.* Some argue that when the two offices are held by the same party, the system is like presidentialism, whereas if the two offices represent different parties, it is more like parliamentarism. In either case the system requires considerable flexibility on the part of both leaders.

The semipresidential system was originally introduced in Germany in 1918, but it began to fail as the parties abdicated their responsibility to govern and let the president use emergency powers—a situation that led to the Nazis' rise to power. Other semipresidential regimes—such as those in Austria, Finland, France, Greece, Iceland, and Ireland—were more successful. It is perhaps no accident that a number of these regimes were founded in moments of national crisis and that quite a few of the first presidents were military men (like Carl Gustav Mannerheim in Finland, Charles de Gaulle in France, and António Ramalho Eanes in Portugal).

There is considerable debate about which type of government is more stable. Some argue that presidential and parliamentary systems are equally stable, while others say that presidential systems have a greater risk of instability. Research on the question is only beginning, though a recent study reveals a better performance by parliamentary systems. It will be interesting to see how successful presidential or semipresidential systems are in the successor states of the Soviet Union.

See also *Checks and balances; Legislatures and parliaments; Presidential government; Separation of powers.* In Documents section, see *Constitution of the Federal Republic of Germany (1949).*

Juan J. Linz

BIBLIOGRAPHY

Beyme, Klaus von. *Die parlamentarischen Regierungsysteme in Europa.* Munich: R. Piper, 1970.
Cronin, T. E. *The State of the Presidency.* Boston: Little, Brown, 1980.
Duverger, Maurice, ed. *Les regimes semi-presidentiels.* Paris: Presses Universitaires de France, 1986.
Jennings, Ivor. *Cabinet Government.* 3d ed. Cambridge: Cambridge University Press, 1959.
Linz, Juan J., and Arturo Valenzuela, eds. *The Failure of Presidential Democracy: Comparative Perspectives.* Vol. 1. Baltimore: Johns Hopkins University Press, 1994.
Mainwaring, Scott. "Presidentialism in Latin America." *Latin American Research Review* 25 (1990): 157–179.
Neustadt, Richard. *Presidential Power: The Politics of Leadership.* New York: Wiley, 1960.
The Postcommunist Presidency. Special issue of *East European Constitutional Review* 2–3 (fall 1993–winter 1994).
Riggs, Fred W. "The Survival of Presidentialism in America: Paraconstitutional Practices." *International Political Science Review* 9 (October 1988): 247–278.
Rose, Richard, and Ezra N. Suleiman, eds. *Presidents and Prime Ministers.* Washington, D.C.: American Enterprise Institute, 1980.
Shugart, Matthew Soberg, and John M. Carey. *Presidents and Assemblies: Constitutional Design and Electoral Dynamics.* Cambridge: Cambridge University Press, 1992.
Verney, Douglas V. *The Analysis of Political Systems.* London: Routledge and Kegan Paul, 1979.

Participation, Political

Political participation is the opportunity for large numbers of citizens to engage in politics and is a prerequisite for democracy. In the fourth century B.C. Aristotle, in his *Politics,* classified political systems according to two principles: the number of people who participated in making political decisions and whether the system was guided by good or by perverted ends. A perverted system in which many ruled was a democracy—literally, "rule by the people."

Although popular participation does not by itself make a democracy, the opportunity for the average citizen to participate in the political process is essential for any democracy, and participation is often included in the definition of democracy. Voting is the most common form of political participation in a democracy, but it is not the only form. We can distinguish between conventional forms of political participation, which are legal in all democracies, and unconventional forms of political participation, such as boycotts and demonstrations, which may sometimes be illegal.

In addition to voting, conventional forms of political participation include working in a political campaign, joining with others to solve local problems, and attempting to influence political leaders on matters of personal concern. Political scientists have attempted to measure various modes of participation. Sidney Verba, Norman H. Nie, and Jae-on Kim, as they reported in *Participation and Political Equality* (1978), used surveys conducted in the late 1960s and early 1970s to compare modes of participation in Austria, India, Japan, the Netherlands, Nigeria, the United States, and Yugoslavia. Their analysis identified similar modes of participation in all seven countries, and their more recent analyses have found them in other countries as well.

It is more difficult to study unconventional political acts, if only because surveys designed to evaluate them may in some cases have to ask respondents whether they have engaged in certain illegal activities. To overcome this problem, Samuel H. Barnes, Max Kaase, and their colleagues developed a measure of what they called *protest potential*. In the mid-1970s they conducted surveys in Austria, Great Britain, West Germany, the Netherlands, and the United States. In all five countries, high levels of protest potential were found most often among the young. Follow-up studies were conducted between 1979 and 1981 in the Netherlands, West Germany, and the United States; some of the same respondents were interviewed again. Most of the findings based on the earlier study were confirmed by the more recent analysis, including the tendency of young adults to have higher levels of protest potential.

Another basic finding by Barnes, Kaase, and their colleagues was that a belief in certain values contributes to unconventional forms of political participation. They found that persons who value economic stability and physical security (whom they, following Ronald Inglehart, called *materialists)* are less likely to approve of unconventional political participation than those who value freedom and self-expression *(postmaterialists)*. Europeans who were identified as having materialist values had low levels of protest potential, whereas those who were labeled postmaterialists had relatively high levels. Moreover, because postmaterialists were generally better educated than

materialists, they were more likely to have the political skills to use new forms of political participation.

Suffrage

Suffrage, or the right to vote, is the most basic form of democratic participation. In the ancient Greek city-states, the right to participate in any form of political activity was limited to adult male citizens, always a minority of the population, since many residents were foreigners or slaves. Likewise, the right to vote in the Roman Republic was limited to male citizens.

Widespread male suffrage was rare until the late nineteenth and early twentieth centuries. In the United States most white adult men had the right to vote by the end of the 1830s. In France and Switzerland universal male suffrage was granted in 1848, although in France the right to vote in free elections was not firmly established until the constitution of the Third Republic in 1875. In Britain the majority of the male working class won the right to vote with the Reform Act of 1884, but universal male suffrage was not granted until 1918. In Prussia universal male suffrage was undermined by a system of unequal representation during the Wilhelmine empire (1871–1918) and was not actually ensured until the German Weimar Republic was founded in 1919.

In most countries the right of women to vote came even later. Women earned the right to vote in Britain in 1918, although there were restrictions on female suffrage that did not apply to men, and in the United States women won the right to vote in all states when the Nineteenth Amendment to the Constitution was ratified in 1920. In Germany women were granted the franchise with the Weimar Republic in 1919, but in France they did not win the right to vote until 1946. In many respects Switzerland is a model democracy, but women did not gain the right to vote in national elections there until 1971.

The vast majority of social scientists view attempts to limit political participation as inherently undemocratic, although the point is not always evident in their writings. About half of the African Americans in the United States could not exercise their constitutional right to vote until the Voting Rights Act of 1965 placed the power of the federal government behind attempts to register southern blacks. Despite this blight on the American political system, most Western social scientists viewed the United States as a democracy. Seymour Martin Lipset's study *Political Man* (1960) reflected this view. Likewise, in *The*

Civic Culture (1963), a major study of values in five democracies, Gabriel A. Almond and Sidney Verba concluded that the United States and Great Britain were established democracies, whereas West Germany, Italy, and Mexico were not. Indeed, even a discussion of group differences in participation and values by Almond and Verba does not refer to racial differences in the United States. Apparently, most social scientists viewed the suppression of political rights for southern blacks as an aberration that should not lead scholars to view the United States as a whole as undemocratic.

Once the right to vote is extended to more and more classes of the people, it is extremely difficult to take this right away. In fact, democracy is more at risk than the right to vote itself. Most Germans did not lose the right to vote when Hitler came to power, and Hitler conducted several referendums to create the appearance of popular support. In the former Soviet Union more than 99 percent of the adult population voted, but since voters did not actually choose among competing political elites, few Western observers viewed these elections as democratic.

If political parties are not free to compete, few consider a country to be democratic, regardless of how many citizens participate in the political process. Some Eastern European countries had nominally multiparty systems, but the Communist Party ruled. For example, in the German Democratic Republic (East Germany) there were nominally competing political parties, but the Socialist Unity Party (the East German communist party) monopolized political power. Even so, participation in the Volkshammer ("People's Chamber") elections was strongly encouraged, and more than 90 percent of those who were eligible to vote went to the polls; most of the votes went to the Socialist Unity Party. But in the free elections held in 1990, the Party of Democratic Socialism (the successor to the disbanded Socialist Unity Party) won only 11 percent of the vote in the newly created *Länder* (states) located in the territory of the former East Germany.

National Differences in Turnout

Voting is easier to study than other types of political participation because one can gain a great deal of information from official voting statistics. The proportion of adults who vote (referred to as turnout) varies substantially from democracy to democracy. In parliamentary democracies the numerator of the fraction used to calculate the percentage figure for turnout is the number of votes cast in the legislative election. In the United States the turnout numerator in presidential years is the number of votes cast for president. The turnout denominator in most democracies is the voting-age population.

Not all voting-age residents of a country are eligible to vote. In most democracies only citizens can vote, and the difficulty of obtaining citizenship varies greatly from one country to another. For example, Jews who immigrate to Israel can obtain automatic citizenship under the Law of Return, and new citizens can vote within a few months of their arrival. By contrast, it is very difficult for non-Germans to attain citizenship in Germany, even if they were born there.

In the United States citizenship is not a constitutional requirement for voting, but all states and the District of Columbia require it. Thus, of the 189 million voting-age adults living in the United States in 1992, about 10 million were not legally eligible to register to vote. If these figures are used, turnout in the 1992 presidential election can be counted either at 55 percent (based on the voting-age population) or at 58 percent (based on the politically eligible population).

Table 1 presents the percentage of the adult population of twenty democracies that voted during the 1980s. With the exception of Spain, all these democracies have a long history of democratic elections, at least since the end of World War II. Very few citizens are denied the right to vote in any of these democracies. Yet the extent to which citizens actually vote varies greatly. It is apparent that the United States has relatively low levels of turnout. Among the democracies listed in Table 1, only Switzerland has lower voter turnout.

Swiss turnout is low despite several conditions that should contribute to high levels of political participation. Swiss adults are automatically registered on the voting rolls, and four cantons have compulsory voting. Nevertheless, Swiss turnout has been declining steadily since World War II. The most plausible explanation is that the major political parties have set out to discourage voter participation. The four major parties have agreed to share the Swiss collective leadership among themselves. The voters have little reason to participate, and the parties have little reason to try to get them to do so.

It is useful to distinguish between the right to participate and the range of participation. The range of political participation depends on four factors: the type of offices that are directly elected; the levels of government; the fre-

TABLE 1. Turnout and institutional characteristics in twenty democracies during the 1980s

Country	Average turnout (percent)	Voting compulsory?	Registration mandatory?
Australia	91	Yes	Yes
Austria	90	No	Automatic
Belgium	87	Yes	Automatic
Canada	73	No	Automatic
Denmark	86	No	Automatic
Finland	75	No	Automatic
France	83	No	No
West Germany	86	No	Automatic
Ireland	74	No	Automatic
Israel	78	No	Automatic
Italy	84	Yes	Automatic
Japan	78	No	Automatic
Netherlands	84	No	Automatic
New Zealand	89	No	Yes
Norway	83	No	Automatic
Spain	75	No	Automatic
Sweden	90	No	Automatic
Switzerland	47	No	Automatic
United Kingdom	74	No	Automatic
United States	52	No	No

SOURCES: Based upon G. Gingham Powell, Jr., "American Voter Turnout in Comparative Perspective," *American Political Science Review* 80 (March 1986): 17–43; Russell J. Dalton and Martin P. Wattenberg, "The Not So Simple Act of Voting," in *Political Science: The State of the Discipline II,* ed. Ada W. Finifter (Washington, D.C.: American Political Science Association, 1993), 193–218; and Thomas T. Mackie and Richard Rose, *International Handbook of Electoral Statistics,* 3d ed. (Washington, D.C.: Congressional Quarterly, 1991).

NOTE: The elections in France and the United States are presidential elections.

quency of elections; and the number of votes that the ballot gives the voter at any one election. The Swiss, like Americans, have many opportunities to participate. As in most democracies the head of government in Switzerland is not directly elected. But because Switzerland is a federal system, voters can vote for different levels of government. Moreover, the Swiss make widespread use of the referendum in both national and cantonal elections, so Swiss citizens have many opportunities to vote. Between the end of World War II and 1980 the Swiss held more than 160 national referendums, far more than any other democratic country.

One reason that turnout is low in the United States is the relative difficulty of registering to vote. As Table 1 shows, in most democracies either registration is automatic or all eligible persons are required by law to register. In every U.S. state except North Dakota, registration to vote is a precondition for voting; in a few states residents can register to vote on election day. Moreover, registering is the individual's responsibility. Some scholars have estimated that turnout in U.S. presidential elections would rise by about 15 percentage points if voter registration requirements were eased dramatically. France is the only other democracy in Table 1 that does not require eligible persons to register to vote. However, French citizens are required to register in their communities to obtain identity cards, and they can register to vote at the same time.

Although turnout is low in the United States, the range of elections is wide. When they went to the polls for the 1992 presidential election, for example, voters in twelve states chose the state's governor, and in thirty-three states they elected a U.S. senator. Except for voters in the District of Columbia, all voters have the opportunity to choose representatives for the U.S. House of Representatives in presidential election years (although in a handful of races the choice has already been made before the presidential election). In addition, voters choose state representatives and dozens of lesser offices. In many states they may also vote on proposals for amending the state constitution or enacting legislation. Most states allow voters to vote a straight ticket, that is, for all candidates of a particular party at once. All states allow voters to pick and choose among the parties. A large number of U.S. voters generally split their ticket, voting Republican for some offices and Democratic for others.

In its wide variety of choices, the United States contrasts dramatically with most parliamentary democracies, in which the voter makes a single ballot choice. In Great Britain, for example, voters choose a single candidate in their district ("constituency"). In Israel voters are offered lists of candidates, and they can make no alterations to the lists. German voters cast one vote for a district representative to the parliament (Bundestag) and one for a party.

The U.S. voter is also faced with a large number of elections, especially in those states in which propositions to enact legislation or to amend the state constitution are placed on the ballot. In some states and cities, voters can remove elected officials during their terms, through a process called *recall.* Successful recalls are rare, but even unsuccessful recall efforts create an additional opportunity to participate. On balance, Americans have far more opportunities to vote than do the citizens of any other democracy. Indeed, some scholars argue that the large number of elections in the United States contributes to low turnout in presidential elections. Likewise, frequent elections on ballot propositions are thought to contribute to low turnout in Swiss parliamentary elections. Citizens, some argue, are simply overloaded by frequent elections.

As Table 1 shows, in a few democracies adults are required to vote, or at the very least they are penalized for failing to go to the polls. Australians and Belgians who do not vote are subject to fines. Italians who do not vote can have "nonvoter" stamped in their identity papers, a label that many believe leads to discrimination in employment and makes it more difficult to obtain government benefits. The Netherlands had compulsory voting until 1971. When penalties were imposed for not voting, turnout was more than 90 percent; when compulsory voting ended, turnout fell to just over 80 percent.

Electoral System Effects on Turnout

The level of competition among political parties also affects turnout. Where parties are competitive, participation tends to increase; where a single party consistently wins elections, turnout tends to be lower. In the United States between the end of Reconstruction after the Civil War and the end of World War II, the Democratic Party dominated southern politics, and the absence of party competition helped keep turnout low. Differing election rules also affect the likelihood that citizens will go to the polls. In most congressional districts in the United States, the winner is selected by plurality vote. The candidate with the most votes wins, even if he or she does not win a majority of the votes. A system in which a plurality vote wins is used to select presidential electors in every state except Maine and Nebraska. As a result of these rules, there is often very little political competition within a congressional district, and even in a close presidential election the results are often a foregone conclusion in many states.

In Great Britain, where a plurality vote winner in each district is elected to Parliament, most legislative districts have been safely held by either the Conservative Party or the Labour Party. Potential voters recognize this fact, and turnout in noncompetitive districts tends to be low. On the other hand, in countries like the Netherlands and Israel, where the legislature is chosen by proportional representation, each additional vote cast may increase a party's representation in the national legislature.

Even such apparently minor factors as the day of the week on which an election is held may affect participation. In the United States and Israel, for example, national elections always take place on Tuesdays, whereas in Britain they take place on Thursdays. Election day in these three countries is not a holiday, and—even if the polls open early and close late—many potential voters find it difficult to get to the polls. In France and Germany, on the other hand, elections are held on Sundays, when most people are not working and are free to go to the polls; the timing facilitates turnout.

Provisions may be made for citizens who are unable to go to their polling place to vote by some other means. In some countries, such as the United States, absentee ballots are relatively easy to obtain. Even the several million Americans who live overseas can vote by mail, although making the arrangements may be time consuming. In other countries, provisions may be made for voting by post, and special voting stations may even be set up for citizens who are away from home. In Israel soldiers posted away from home and prisoners in jail are allowed to vote. But it is very difficult for Israelis who live outside Israel to vote. The only exception is made for Israeli seamen on Israeli-flagged vessels. Several hundred thousand Israelis live outside Israel, and they can vote only if they return to Israel for the election.

In a study of nineteen democracies (all of the democracies listed in Table 1 except Spain), Robert W. Jackman found that a high level of proportionality in the representation of parties in the national legislature tends to encourage turnout. The presence of a large number of political parties tends to discourage turnout because voters realize that the actual struggle for power occurs among parties as they bargain in the legislature after the election. Moreover, countries with unicameral systems often have higher turnout than do democracies that have a strong upper house: in a unicameral system the election results are more likely to lead to decisive and important outcomes. For example, the victory of the Labor Party over Likud in the 1992 Israeli election led to breakthroughs in the Arab-Israeli peace process that no upper chamber could delay.

Group Differences in Turnout

Within democracies, turnout generally varies among social and political groups. The differing levels of voter participation among social groups have been studied more extensively in the United States than in any other country.

The reason is that turnout in the United States is very low, and many scholars view low turnout as a problem for a democracy. By studying the reasons for low voter turnout, some scholars hope to learn how participation might be increased. Moreover, it is easier to study turnout when many people fail to vote. When overall turnout is very high, there can be little difference in turnout among social groups. If turnout approached 100 percent, it would be logically impossible for any sizable group to have low turnout; in countries like Australia, Austria, and Sweden, where nine out of ten adults vote, turnout variation among social groups is very low.

In the United States several patterns have become well established. Until about 1980 men were more likely to vote than women, but by the 1980s this relationship had been eliminated or even reversed. Before the Voting Rights Act of 1965, turnout was much lower in the South than in the rest of the United States. Since then, turnout in the South has increased substantially, whereas turnout outside the South declined between 1960 and 1988. Even so, the American South remains a low turnout region. African Americans are less likely to vote than are whites, although the low turnout of blacks is in part due to their relatively low socioeconomic status and the fact that blacks are more likely than whites to live in the South, where turnout is generally low. High-income Americans are more likely to vote than are low-income Americans. Young Americans have very low turnout, but their turnout tends to increase as they grow older, marry, have children, and develop ties to their communities.

Education appears to be the most important factor in explaining turnout differences. Americans with high levels of formal education are much more likely to vote than are those with low levels of formal education. There are two main reasons for this relationship. First, voting in the United States is a complicated process; it is far easier for better educated Americans to find out how to register than for less educated citizens. Second, education appears to contribute to the belief that citizens should participate in politics.

In addition to these social characteristics, turnout is also affected by political attitudes. Americans who believe that citizens have a duty to vote are much more likely to vote than are those who have a lower sense of duty. Likewise, Americans with strong feelings of political effectiveness, that is to say, those who believe that political leaders respond to citizens, are more likely to vote than are those with low feelings of political effectiveness. And Americans who feel a strong attachment to either the Republican Party or the Democratic Party are more likely to vote than are those who do not have a strong party attachment.

The attitudinal factors that contribute to voting have not been as systematically researched outside the United States. It does appear, however, that feelings of political effectiveness contribute to voter participation. Moreover, as Russell J. Dalton reported in *Citizen Politics* (1988), in Britain and Germany persons with strong feelings of party identification are much more likely to vote than are those with weak partisan loyalties.

Outside the United States the better educated are only slightly more likely to vote than those with relatively little formal education. That the government is responsible for maintaining the registration rolls substantially reduces the effort of voting for the less well educated. Moreover, most countries have parties that attempt to mobilize the lower social classes, whereas the U.S. party that would benefit most from doing so, the Democratic Party, makes relatively little effort to get disadvantaged Americans to the polls.

Although turnout differences between social groups are relatively small outside the United States, there are probably substantially greater differences in other forms of political participation. In all societies the better educated have greater organizational skills, which means that they can more effectively launch petition drives, contact political leaders, and organize groups to exert pressure on the political system. On the other hand, in countries with strong labor unions there may be some efforts to present the demands of manual workers.

In most democracies, women are less likely to vote than are men, but gender differences have been eroding during the past two decades. Turnout is somewhat lower among the young in most democracies, but, as in the United States, the reason apparently is that young adults are less well established than older adults. The phenomenon does not presage a future decline in participation rates.

Most studies of electoral participation rely on surveys conducted after elections that ask respondents whether they voted; the resulting data are then related to the social background and attitudes of the respondents. The same surveys are also used to study voting behavior, which includes both whether and how respondents voted. In the United States more survey respondents report having voted than actually do: the percentage of respondents who say they voted is substantially larger than the percentage of citizens who actually voted. If members of some social groups are more likely to falsely report voting than others, or if overreporting is systematically related to the political attitudes of respondents, researchers who rely on reported turnout may reach the wrong conclusions about voting.

To minimize the effects of overreporting in the 1964, 1976, 1980, 1984, and 1988 presidential elections and in the 1978, 1986, and 1990 midterm congressional elections, the National Election Studies surveys conducted by the Survey Research Center and the Center for Political Studies of the University of Michigan have carried out vote validation studies, checking actual voting records to determine whether survey respondents were registered to vote and whether they voted. The validation studies suggest that in general self-reported participation can be used to study turnout, although African American turnout was somewhat overreported in all eight of the elections studied. Similar vote validation studies have been conducted in Great Britain and in Sweden. Where turnout is very high, as in Sweden, we can safely conclude that most people accurately report having voted.

Is High Turnout Desirable?

Many scholars view with dismay the low levels of political participation in the United States. Furthermore, most agree that the right to participate is a fundamental aspect of democracy. Yet it is not clear that high turnout is in itself desirable.

Increased turnout brings those who generally do not vote to the polls. Habitual voters vote in part because they believe that they should participate politically—that participation is essential to democracy. They often support the established political parties, which in turn usually support democratic principles. Many studies have revealed that nonvoters are less likely to express a commitment to democratic values and also are less likely to identify with the established political parties. The mobilization of nonvoters is likely to bring citizens who are less committed to democratic values to the ballot box.

In one important case, high turnout accompanied the destruction of a democracy. That happened in the German Weimar Republic, a democracy that came into existence in 1919, after the Wilhelmine empire was defeated in World War I. The Weimar Republic ended in January 1933, when Adolf Hitler and the Nazis came to power.

The Weimar Republic faced devastating economic problems. During 1922 Germany suffered through a period of hyperinflation that destroyed the savings of millions of middle-class Germans. Later in the decade, with the beginning of the Great Depression, Germany suffered massive unemployment. The civilian leaders of the Weimar Republic lived with the liability of having surrendered to the Allied forces, even though Germany had not actually been defeated on the battlefield. Most of the German military leaders were hostile toward the republic, as were most of the judges and bureaucrats who were holdovers from Wilhelmine empire. Hitler and the Nazis would eventually emerge victorious. Table 2 tells some of

TABLE 2. Reichstag Elections in the Weimar Republic: Nazi Vote, Communist Party Vote, and Turnout (in percentages)

Party	June 1920	May 1924	Dec. 1924	May 1928	Sept. 1930	July 1932	Nov. 1932
National Socialists[a] (Nazis)	——	6.5	3.0	2.6	18.3	37.3	33.1
Communists[b]	2.1	12.6	9.0	10.6	13.1	14.3	16.9
National Socialists and Communists	2.1	19.1	12.0	13.2	31.4	51.6	50.0
Turnout[c]	79.2	77.4	78.8	75.6	82.0	84.1	80.6

SOURCE: Based upon election results reported in Eberhard Kolb, *The Weimar Republic*, trans. P. S. Falla (London: Unwin Hyman, 1988), 194–195.

a. NSDAP (German National Socialist Workers' Party); in 1924, NS-Freiheitsbewegung.

b. KDP (German Communist Party).

c. Number of votes cast divided by the number eligible to vote.

the story of the seven elections for seats in the lower house of the legislature (Reichstag) during the Weimar Republic.

During the first Reichstag election (June 1920), the Nazis did not yet exist, and the Communists won only one vote in fifty. Even in May 1924, after the hyperinflation had ended, the Nazis won only 6.5 percent of the vote, although the Communists won 12.6 percent. But support for both these parties increased in the 1930 election, which was held after the Great Depression began. Turnout rose more than 5 percentage points, while support for the Nazis increased more than 15 percentage points and support for the Communists rose by 2.5 percentage points.

In the July 1932 election turnout rose 2 more percentage points, reaching 84.1 percent, the highest level attained in this short-lived republic. Support for the Nazis doubled, and support for the Communists rose slightly. Together, these two parties, both of which were committed to destroying the democratic political institutions of the Weimar Republic, won a majority of the popular vote and held a slight majority of the seats in the Reichstag. Turnout dropped nearly 4 percentage points in the November 1932 election, as did support for the Nazis, although support for the Communists increased. With parties opposed to its continued existence holding half the seats in the Reichstag, the Weimar Republic was doomed. Less than three months after the election, President Paul von Hindenburg appointed Hitler as chancellor, and for all intents and purposes the Weimar Republic ended.

The demise of the Weimar Republic provides an example of the dangers of rapid increases in political participation, as Lipset has pointed out, but the evidence is ambiguous. It is easy to demonstrate statistically a clear association between the increase in turnout and increasing support for the Nazis and a weaker relationship between increased turnout and support for the Communists. But these relationships do not prove that new voters, with a weak commitment to democratic norms and weak attachments to the democratic parties, were responsible for the growing vote for antidemocratic parties. The Nazi vote increased far more than turnout did, and presumably many voters who had previously supported other political parties turned to the Nazis after the Great Depression began.

Despite its ambiguity, the Weimar example is a useful one for those who study participation. The episode shows that high turnout in itself is not necessarily desirable. As a result of the increase in turnout, more than 4 million more Germans voted in July 1932 than had voted in May 1928. As important as participation is for democracy, it can also work against democracy. In 1928 fewer than 1 million Germans voted for the Nazis; in July 1932 nearly 14 million did.

Other things being equal, high levels of political participation are desirable, but other things are rarely equal. In established democracies, high levels of political participation often indicate high levels of interest in politics and commitment to democratic institutions. But high levels of political participation can also result from disaffection, distrust, and a desire for radical change, as was apparently true in Weimar Germany.

In democratizing societies, which have little experience with voting or with democratic institutions, the effects of high levels of political participation are even more difficult to evaluate. The collapse of the Weimar Republic was unique, but many analysts saw parallels between the Russian legislative election of December 1993, in which antidemocratic parties fared well, and the turmoil of the Weimar Republic. In many new democracies, overall levels of education are much lower than in Russia, and in some many adults cannot read. In these fledgling democracies, high levels of participation may create problems for maintaining democracies, even if many political leaders want to build democratic institutions.

See also *Ballots; Election campaigns; Electoral systems; Federalism; Hermens, Ferdinand A.; Political alienation; Political culture; Proportional representation; Protest movements; Referendum and initiative; Voting behavior.*

Paul R. Abramson

BIBLIOGRAPHY

Abramson, Paul R., John H. Aldrich, and David W. Rohde. *Change and Continuity in the 1992 Elections.* Washington, D.C.: CQ Press, 1994.

Almond, Gabriel A., and Sidney Verba. *The Civic Culture: Political Attitudes and Democracy in Five Nations.* Princeton: Princeton University Press, 1963.

Barnes, Samuel H., et al. *Political Action: Mass Participation in Five Western Democracies.* Beverly Hills, Calif.: Sage Publications, 1979.

Crewe, Ivor. "Electoral Participation." In *Democracy at the Polls: A Comparative Study of National Elections,* edited by David Butler, Howard R. Penniman, and Austin Ranney. Washington, D.C.: American Enterprise Institute, 1981.

Dalton, Russell J. *Citizen Politics in Western Democracies: Public Opinion and Political Parties in the United States, Great Britain, West Germany, and France.* Chatham, N.J.: Chatham House, 1988.

———, and Martin P. Wattenberg. "The Not So Simple Act of Voting." In *Political Science: The State of the Discipline II,* edited by Ada W. Finifter. Washington, D.C.: American Political Science Association, 1993.

Hamilton, Richard F. *Who Voted for Hitler?* Princeton: Princeton University Press, 1982.

Inglehart, Ronald. *Culture Shift in Advanced Industrial Society.* Princeton: Princeton University Press, 1990.

Jackman, Robert W. "Political Institutions and Voter Turnout in the Industrial Democracies." *American Political Science Review* 81 (June 1987): 405–423.

Jennings, M. Kent, et al. *Continuities in Political Action: A Longitudinal Study of Political Orientations in Three Western Democracies.* Berlin: Walter de Gruyter, 1989.

Lipset, Seymour Martin. *Political Man: The Social Bases of Politics.* Expanded and updated ed. Baltimore: Johns Hopkins University Press, 1981; Aldershot: Gower, 1983.

Powell, G. Bingham, Jr. "American Voter Turnout in Comparative Perspective." *American Political Science Review* 80 (March 1986): 17–43.

———. *Contemporary Democracies: Participation, Stability, and Violence.* Cambridge, Mass., and London: Harvard University Press, 1982.

Riker, William H. *Liberalism against Populism: A Confrontation between the Theory of Democracy and the Theory of Social Choice.* San Francisco: Freeman, 1982.

Verba, Sidney, Norman H. Nie, and Jae-on Kim. *Participation and Political Equality: A Seven-Nation Comparison.* New York: Cambridge University Press, 1978.

Participatory democracy

Participatory democracy has also been called direct or pure or strong democracy. It can be understood in two ways: as a variation on the democratic form of regime or as the essential form. Democracy, which means government by the people (the *demos* in classical Athens), refers to popular rule (or popular sovereignty) in a broad and general sense. Participatory democracy, however, denotes the form in which the people literally rule themselves, directly and participatorily, day in and day out, in all matters that affect them in their common lives.

All democracy is of course to some degree participatory. Even minimally democratic governments are rooted in an act of original consent—a popularly ratified social contract or constitution, for example—and in periodic popular elections. To its advocates, however, participatory democracy involves extensive and active engagement of citizens in the self-governing process; it means government not just for but by and of the people. From this per-

spective, direct or participatory democracy is democracy itself, properly understood.

Representative Versus Participatory Democracy

The distinctiveness of participatory democracy can be seen clearly in the contrast with representative democracy. In representative systems, popular sovereignty—once it has been manifested in a founding document, a constitution, and a set of working political institutions—is delegated to chosen representatives who do the actual work of government. These representatives remain accountable to the people through elections; the people retain their sovereignty only in a passive or potential sense. Representative democracy thus relegates citizens to the role of watchdogs, and democracy comes to mean periodic legitimation of representative governors through elections. From the point of view of participatory democrats, representative democracy is weak or thin democracy. In the words of Robert Michels, the German sociologist and economist, liberty disappears with the ballot into the polling box.

Historically, the earliest forms of democracy—in ancient Athens or the town republics of early modern Europe or the Alpine communes of the Helvetic confederation (Switzerland), for example—were participatory. Representation came later, as the scale of society increased. In Athens in the fifth century B.C. the entire body of citizens met every seven to ten days in assembly to deliberate and pass laws, regulate trade, and make war and peace. Citizens sat on large juries of 500 to 1,000 or more to adjudicate legal and policy disputes. Citizens, selected by lot, also occupied nearly one-half of the public magistracies on a regular basis. In the classical scheme of classifying regimes (in the manner of Polybius, Aristotle, and Cicero, for example), democracy meant participatory democracy, rule by the many in contrast with aristocracy (literally "rule by the best") and monarchy (the rule of one). In the same way that monarchy's corrupt form was tyranny and aristocracy's corrupt form was oligarchy (rule by the few), so democracy's corrupt form was ochlocracy, or rule by the mob. Aristocratic critics of democracy argued that democracy was always likely to be corrupt—that democracy and mob rule were identical.

In the ancient world, participatory democracy required the participation of every citizen, but not everyone was a citizen. In Athens only those qualified by birth and talent (civic virtue or excellence) could participate: only Athenian-born males—who made up approximately one-fifth of the total population of men, women, resident foreigners, and slaves—qualified as citizens. Aristotle regarded women and non-Greeks ("barbarians") as unfit for self-rule and suggested that, slaves by nature, they were perpetually unfit to be citizens. Many later participatory democracies, including the Swiss Confederation and the American Republic in its first century and a half, limited citizenship to males. One of the great ironies of Western political history is that as democracies became more inclusive they became less participatory. The ancients permitted only a few to be citizens but asked much of them, while the moderns extend citizenship to everyone but ask almost nothing of them.

This irony arises in part from the fact that robust participation is possible only in small states with limited, but virtuous, citizen bodies of the kind found in the town governments and rustic republics of the Swiss, the Dutch, the Italians, and the Germans. In the eighteenth century the French philosopher Montesquieu believed that democracy was appropriate only to very small political entities, while empire was appropriate for large ones. This belief was widely shared throughout the eighteenth century. Indeed, the American Founders understood their challenge to be how to devise a form of democracy that could function in a compound and extended republic of potentially continental proportions. The device of representation was introduced in part to salvage the idea of democracy in polities too large to afford regular participation by all citizens and too diversified, heterogeneous, and commercial to support classical civic virtue in the entire citizen body. Popular accountability was maintained through elections nominally open to all (in reality, only to propertied males). But the actual tasks of government were delegated to elected officials who were (in John Locke's term) fiduciary representatives, entrusted to rule on behalf of the sovereign people.

Representative government was in part intended to preserve the spirit of democracy in large-scale societies where the cumbersome institutions of participatory democracy could no longer function. But it also reflected a certain antidemocratic impulse in that it provided a remedy to the excesses of popular government, which many eighteenth-century constitution makers distrusted. In the new American Republic there were those, especially among the Federalists, who disdained ancient democratic republics as sources of contention and petty jealousy. American Founders such as James Madison and Alexander Hamilton believed that representation was a filter by which prudent government might be screened from popular prejudices and demagogic individuals. Civic virtue was not a property of everyman and everywoman, but elections, especially indirect elections, might put those who were virtuous in office. To a considerable extent, this distrust of direct, or pure, democracy has been retained by modern social scientists who express suspicion of too much direct democracy. Samuel Huntington, for example, has suggested that an overactive populace can create a democratic overload that paralyzes a representative democracy.

Modern Accommodations

Given the larger scale of modern societies, participatory democracy as a political reality has in any case been reserved mostly to local and municipal government. The Swiss-born philosopher Jean-Jacques Rousseau observed in the eighteenth century that for a people to discover or forge a common will (the general will) they had to share common customs, simple beliefs, and local institutions. Participatory democracy worked best on a modest scale where institutions like the town meeting or the cantonal or state initiative and referendum could facilitate consensus and common willing in a face-to-face society.

Arguments about scale, however, have been challenged in recent decades. In many Western democracies, cynicism about the professional ruling classes has given a new appeal to referendums and to such antigovernmental devices as term limits for elected officials and recall mechanisms for corrupt representatives. Moreover, new telecommunications technologies have offered the possibility of interaction among widely dispersed citizens across space and time in a fashion that encourages new experiments with participation. Aristotle had argued that the ideal republic was small enough that a man could walk across it in a single day, thus ensuring regular participation in the assembly by all citizens. Interactive telecommunications technologies, which in effect permit the hundreds of millions of citizens of a mass society to be in touch without leaving their television screens, raise the possibility of "teledemocracy" and "virtual communities." These new forms look far more participatory (if also potentially more demagogic) than older representative models. Experiments in deliberative teledemocracy currently are under way in which citizens participate in debates and vote on several readings of a bill before reaching a final decision.

At the same time that technology has enhanced the feasibility of new forms of participation, communitarian political theory emphasizing obligation and responsibility rather than personal liberty and rights has asserted the desirability of more participatory forms of democracy. Communitarians use both the language of civic virtue of the ancients and the new rhetoric of community and national service to argue for a more vigorous form of democracy. Critics of communitarianism fear that too much emphasis on participation and community, especially when reinforced by new interactive technologies, increases democratic overload and imperils individual liberty. From Alexis de Tocqueville to Robert Nozick, liberals have worried that excessive participation will lower the level of rationality in politics and nurture majoritarian tyranny and a disregard for the rights of private persons and private property. Now, as in ancient times, critics of pure democracy see in it merely a rationalization of demagoguery and mob rule: the government of opinion and prejudice.

Education for Deliberative Government

Proponents of participatory democracy sometimes dismiss their liberal critics as privileged defenders of property who attack democracy because it undermines their hegemony. Yet they also acknowledge the powerful liberal line of criticism that worries about majority tyranny. Their response is to defend not mob rule but the distinction between it and deliberative democracy. Direct democracy requires not simply participation but the civic skills and civic virtues necessary for effective participatory deliberation and decision making. Participatory democracy is thus understood as direct government by a well-educated citizenry. Citizens are not simply private individuals operating in the civil sphere but informed public citizens as distanced from their wholly private selves as the public is from the private sphere. Democracy is less the government of the people or the masses than the government of educated citizens.

From Thomas Jefferson's time in the early days of the American Republic to our own, an enthusiasm for participatory democracy has thus been coupled with a zeal for public and civic education: the training of competent and responsible citizens. With Jefferson, participatory democrats enjoin those anxious about the indiscriminate public abuse of power not to take away the public's power but to inform the public's discretion. Democracy demands a public well educated in the liberal arts, which also are the arts of liberty. Jefferson, like his Massachusetts colleague John Adams, saw education as indispensable to democracy and showed more pride in his role as father of the University of Virginia than in his role as the two-term third president of the United States—having the former office but not the latter inscribed on his tombstone.

The argument today for participatory, or strong, democracy, consistent with Jefferson, is thus an argument for civic education as well as for participation, for the cultivation of civic virtue as well as for the nurturing of popular sovereignty, and for an emphasis on community responsibility as well as for a focus on individual engagement. The debate among advocates and critics continues to be about the nature of the deliberative process (can average men and women be educated to be as prudent and deliberative as experienced representatives?), the character of civic education (will civics courses, community and national service, or direct political engagement successfully train individuals for responsible citizenship?), and the attributes required by diligent citizens (should public citizens merely give public expression to their private interests, or do they need to develop new public ways of thinking about policy—"we" thinking rather than "me" thinking?).

Theoretical Bases

The political philosophy of participatory democracy has roots in the early modern theorists who extrapolated a defense of democracy from the practices of the ancient Greeks. Rousseau is perhaps the authoritative source, although elements of his theory can be found in the writings of the sixteenth-century Florentine political philosopher Niccolò Machiavelli and in Montesquieu. In his *Social Contract* (1762), Rousseau argues that a communal authority can be legitimate only when it leaves individuals who obey it as free as they were before. Direct democracy affords individuals the opportunity to participate in making the laws they must obey, thus guaranteeing that in obeying the law they will obey only themselves. Freedom to do anything at all is a kind of license, Rousseau concludes, while obedience to a law we prescribe to ourselves is true freedom.

Immanuel Kant, the eighteenth-century German philosopher, and other modern advocates of positive liberty concur with Rousseau in seeing in liberty a positive power for action rather than a negative liberty from interference. Negative liberty turns out to be incompatible with active government and underlies liberal political philosophies that distrust all government. Positive liberty is in harmony with democratically enacted laws and thus is compatible with a more forceful understanding of a democratic welfare state or a democratic socialist society. While negative liberty is associated with theories of limited government and representative democracy, positive liberty is associated with participatory democracy. Only laws we make for ourselves leave us with freedom. Democracy requires self-legislation: for Rousseau, it must be participatory.

Although Jefferson was not a theorist, the author of the Declaration of Independence and the Virginia Statute on Religious Freedom (as well as president of the United States) was in many ways America's founding participatory democrat. He argued on behalf of the involvement of citizens in every aspect of their local affairs and suggested that ward government in which all citizens might participate regularly could alone secure American democracy. Not among those who feared the people (as he boasted), he insisted that only popular participation could prevent government from becoming tyrannical. To critics who preferred to insulate the people from government through representative institutions, Jefferson replied that it was absurd to think that citizens who could not even be trusted to govern themselves might somehow be trusted to govern others.

In the late nineteenth and early twentieth centuries American Progressive and Populist politicians and pragmatic philosophers argued the virtues of participatory democracy. John Dewey, the American philosopher and educator, saw in democracy not merely a form of government but a way of life; he was convinced that only participating citizens could make free government function. The debate continues today, with many social scientists and professional politicians still distrustful of what they think of as too much democracy. Participatory and strong democrats prefer to think that real democracy has never been tried and that the demagogic excesses visible in today's political arena are precisely the consequence of the professionalization of politics and the exclusion of an alienated public from any real civic responsibility.

As in ancient Greece, the real question remains whether a regime that is not genuinely participatory can be regarded as a democracy at all, or whether democracy, to be safe, must be coupled with limited government and the indirect popular accountability of representative government. Because democracy is in part the debate about what democracy is, this argument can be expected to continue as long as citizens argue about how they best can rule themselves.

See also *Communitarianism; Education; Education,* *Civic; Federalists; Popular sovereignty; Representation; Rhetoric; Theory, Ancient; Types of democracy; Virtue, Civic.* In Documents section, see *American Declaration of Independence (1776).*

Benjamin R. Barber

BIBLIOGRAPHY

Arendt, Hannah. *The Human Condition.* Chicago: University of Chicago Press, 1958.
Barber, Benjamin R. *Strong Democracy: Participatory Politics for a New Age.* Berkeley: University of California Press, 1984.
Cronin, Thomas E. *Direct Democracy: The Politics of Initiative, Referendum, and Recall.* Cambridge, Mass., and London: Harvard University Press, 1989.
Dewey, John. *The Public and Its Problems.* Chicago: Swallow Press, 1954.
Fishkin, James S. *Democracy and Deliberation: New Directions for Democratic Reform.* New Haven and London: Yale University Press, 1991.
Mansbridge, Jane J. *Beyond Adversary Democracy.* New York: Basic Books, 1980.
Matthews, Richard K. *The Radical Politics of Thomas Jefferson: A Revisionist View.* Lawrence: University Press of Kansas, 1984.
Pateman, Carole. *Participation and Democratic Theory.* Cambridge: Cambridge University Press, 1970.
Rousseau, Jean-Jacques. *The Social Contract.* Harmondsworth, England: Penguin Books, 1968.
Tocqueville, Alexis de. *Democracy in America.* Edited by J. P. Mayer. Translated by George Lawrence. Garden City, N.Y.: Anchor, 1969.

Parties, Political

Political parties are groups or organizations that seek to place candidates in office under a specific label. Parties are among the most important organizations in modern politics. In the contemporary world, they are nearly ubiquitous: only a small percentage of states do without them.

Students of political parties have commonly associated them with democracy itself. Democracy, it is argued, is a system of competitive political parties. The competitive electoral context, in which several political parties organize the alternatives that face the voters, is what identifies contemporary democracy. Nonparty states are predominantly traditional dynasties (such as Saudi Arabia) and a few military regimes; their numbers have declined in recent years.

In the many states where parties exist, however, their numbers vary. One-party systems are particularly common in authoritarian socialist societies and in parts of the developing world, especially Africa. Two-party systems are found almost exclusively in states that have at one point been under British rule. Multiparty states (those with three or more significant parties) form the largest category of party states.

Development of Parties

The word *party*, which is derived from *part* and refers to division or opposition within a body politic, first appeared in political discourse in the late Middle Ages. The German social scientist Max Weber (1864–1920) thus referred to the Florentine Guelphs as a party. For centuries, however, parties, like factions, were regarded with suspicion, a sentiment shared by the Framers of the U.S. Constitution near the end of the eighteenth century. Yet the first modern parties developed in the United States in the early decades of the nineteenth century.

Modern parties such as the Jacksonian Democrats in the United States emerged when legislatures were institutionalized and, most important, when broad segments of the adult population gained the suffrage. Similarly, the breakthrough of British parties is associated with the Voting Reform Acts of 1832 and 1867. The modern parties that emerged had permanent extraparliamentary organizations and mass memberships.

Early modern parties, such as the American parties and the British Conservatives and Liberals, were internally created, which is to say that they evolved gradually from the activities of the legislators themselves. With the adoption of universal adult male suffrage and the advance of the Industrial Revolution, externally created parties gained strength about the turn of the century. Externally created parties originate outside the legislature and invariably involve some challenge to the ruling groups, as well as demands for representation. The most important externally created parties to emerge at this time were socialist working-class parties, such as Labour in Britain and the Social Democrats in Germany, and, later, Christian democratic parties, particularly in Roman Catholic countries.

The early days of the twentieth century marked the breakthrough of political parties as the democratic organization par excellence. Parties attained this position both because they were unrivaled in their functions and, in particular, because they represented previously unenfranchised groups.

Across the democracies of the world, political parties tend to fall into a number of different families, which are identified by ideologies and policy programs. No two political parties are exactly the same. But many were formed in similar circumstances, with the aim of mobilizing the same constituencies—and sometimes with the help of explicit bonds across national boundaries.

Roughly from left to right, the most important such families are communists, social democrats, greens, liberals, Christian democrats, agrarians, conservatives, nationalists, and the authoritarian right (for example, fascists). The families of the left show the greatest similarities and the closest international ties, whereas nationalism, on the right, obviously does not travel well across boundaries. Christian democrats are internally divided among those representing mainly Catholics (in Austria, Belgium, and Italy), those representing mainly Protestants (in the Scandinavian countries), and those representing a mixture of Catholic and Protestant voters (in Germany and the Netherlands). Parties on either extreme (communists and fascists), as well as some irredentists or anticonstitutional parties, are commonly referred to as antisystem parties. The strong presence of such parties is generally inauspicious for democratic stability.

Studies of political parties commonly distinguish among three aspects. The first is the party as an organization of public officials (party in government). The second is the party as an extraparliamentary organization designed in large part to contest elections (party organization). The third is the party as a collection of voters, members, and activists (party in the electorate).

Party in Government

The first modern parties in democratic societies were loose cliques or clubs of legislators in the national government. The British Tories and Whigs of the eighteenth century exemplify this early stage of party development. Many contemporary parties, such as the British Conservatives, that originated in these embryonic parties continue to feature a party organization in which the legislative party, the caucus, dominates other segments of the organization.

Why did modern legislative parties emerge? Such organizations can be viewed as solutions to collective dilemmas faced by individual legislators. If parties did not exist, members might engage in redundant and collectively self-defeating efforts to get reelected. While each legislator may act rationally in the interest of securing reelection, the product of their joint efforts may be collectively irrational. Bribing the voters in one's district, for example, may be rational for the individual representative, but such behavior is collectively self-defeating when all candidates do so.

Political parties have emerged as a way for legislators to coordinate their efforts for mutual gain, to monitor compliance, and to discipline those who violate the group's norms. Party organizations may also help legislators avoid other problems, such as excessive constituency orientation or having to be knowledgeable in too many issue areas. Parties have come to take on such functions despite the neglect or active resistance they have met among the framers of most older political constitutions. The perceived "evils of faction" were such that political parties were rarely recognized and occasionally actively discouraged by those who crafted these documents.

Representative democracy has long been associated with, or even equated with, party government, which involves the following conditions. First, government decisions are made by elected party officials or by those under their control. Second, government policy is decided within political parties. Third, these parties act cohesively to enact and implement government policy. Fourth, public officials are recruited through political parties. And, finally, public officials are held accountable through political parties. Party government is not an all-or-nothing proposition. No contemporary democracy satisfies these conditions fully, and none violates all of them consistently. The first condition is met in most modern democracies in the sense that members of the cabinet are almost always party members and indeed representatives of their parties. Although nonpartisan governments occasionally occur, for example, in Finland, they are normally short-lived caretakers. Party government is everywhere the norm.

Government policy making has also in large measure been displaced to political parties, as indicated in the second condition of party government. This feature of party government has contributed to the decline of legislatures and cabinets as policy-making bodies. Political parties contest elections on the basis of more or less specific programs or platforms. These are commonly adopted at party conventions, as in the United States, or simply drafted by the party leadership in more oligarchical parties such as the British Conservatives. Although party platforms are not binding and parties occasionally renege on their promises, empirical studies have shown that parties on the whole make efforts to fulfill explicit promises and that the contents of party programs are a good guide to subsequent party policies.

One major purpose of political parties, particularly internally created ones, is to facilitate joint voting in legislatures (an aspect of the third condition). In most democratic states, parties indeed serve this purpose in the sense that two members of the same party are much more likely to vote together than are any random sample of two representatives. Yet the degree of party cohesiveness in legislative voting varies a great deal. American parties are less cohesive than most, particularly in the U.S. Senate. European parties in parliamentary systems tend to be highly cohesive. Party cohesion is facilitated by tight party discipline enforced by an elaborate system of parliamentary whips, as in the British House of Commons.

Political parties beset with factionalism exhibit a particular form of incohesion. Factions, or fractions, are distinct subunits within parties. Although usage is inconsistent, it is customary to distinguish between well-organized factions and less well organized tendencies. Tendencies may operate in a very casual way in the parliamentary party, whereas factions typically extend to the extraparliamentary party and often to society at large. While tendencies commonly are ideologically based, factions are often portrayed as concerned with patronage and personalistic politics.

Factions have generally been neglected within the study of political parties, in part because they often deliberately seek to escape attention. Yet in some countries factions enjoy a well-publicized existence and are even recognized by the parties themselves. Students of Italian and Japanese politics especially have noted the important role of factions in previously dominant parties such as the Italian Christian Democrats and the Japanese Liberal Democrats. The factionalism of these parties seems to have been promoted by electoral systems that allow voters to align themselves with particular candidates. Japanese factionalism is sustained by the unique system of the single nontransferable vote, whereas Italian factions sustain themselves through the intraparty preference vote, which allows voters to lend their support to particular candidates on the party's list.

Finally, party government implies an active role for political parties in the recruitment and accountability of political leaders. Here, again, American parties are less instrumental than their opposite numbers in most other western democracies, and particularly in Europe. In Great Britain, for example, all members of the cabinet must simultaneously hold parliamentary office, the great majority in the House of Commons.

Party Organization

Political parties take many different organizational forms. Traditionally, many parties were little more than loose groupings of parliamentarians and notables, with no extensive extraparliamentary membership organization. This form of organization is commonly referred to as a cadre party. Other parties (mass parties) have much more encompassing organizations, with a considerably stronger role for members and extraparliamentary activists.

The most ambitious of such organizations, known as parties of social integration, have attempted to provide "cradle to grave" services for their members, in the form of auxiliary organizations for sports, cultural activities, religious observance, publishing, travel, insurance, adult education, and even hiking and stamp collecting. Social democratic parties in such countries as Austria and Sweden, as well as Communists and Christian Democrats in Italy, are among the best examples of parties of social integration. Such parties have been most successful where they have been able to appeal to well-defined and relatively insulated social subcultures. Their vitality has tended to decline in recent decades as advanced democratic societies have become more open and their populations more mobile socially.

Organizational features are closely tied to the origins of political parties and the circumstances of their formation. Externally created parties have tended to retain an organizational center of gravity outside the legislative arena. Since the advent of mass suffrage, many of them have developed large extraparliamentary organizations. The largest of these organizations, such as the British Labour Party and even the Swedish Social Democrats, have been able to claim millions of members. The Labour Party and other social democratic parties have built up their organizations in large part by obtaining collective memberships through union affiliations. Parties without such ties to organized labor, such as the Conservatives, have achieved impressive numbers relying exclusively on individual memberships.

Extraparliamentary parties have grown strong because party leaders have relied on such organizations for funding, information collection (for example, canvassing), education, communication, mobilization, and transportation, all of which are typically required in political campaigns. Campaigning is a purpose for which a large membership organization may be very useful. Parties without large membership organizations may, of course, be able to conduct campaigns successfully by relying on patronage machines—once common in most large U.S. cities—or through capital-intensive campaigns focused on the electronic media.

Membership organizations, however, have advantages, particularly where elections can be called at short notice, as is the case in Great Britain and many other European and Commonwealth countries. The volunteers who staff these organizations can be of particular value in door-to-door canvassing in marginal districts. They are also critical to ongoing party activities between election campaigns.

Mass membership parties, and especially socialist working-class parties, historically have also relied on their members for a major part of their funding, through modest membership dues. In recent years the financial importance of membership dues has declined for most parties, as public subsidies to political parties have become widespread. Public party finance was first introduced in Argentina, Costa Rica, and Germany in the 1950s and has since spread to most of the democratic world. Moreover, such aid has generally been expanded where it has been introduced. In many modern democracies, parties now rely on taxpayers for the major part of their revenues.

Large and complex party organizations depend on activists for a variety of organizational tasks. One of the most important challenges facing mass membership parties, therefore, is how to attract effective activists at the lowest possible cost in terms of resources and policy commitments. The literature on political organizations distinguishes among three types of incentives for activists: material, solidary, and purposive.

Material incentives are such tangible rewards as wages, gifts, tax or fringe benefits, and other private goods and services. Private or collective solidary incentives are intangible rewards such as honor, deference, camaraderie, or conviviality. Purposive incentives pertain to the goals of the organization itself, such as the policy program of the political party. Party leaders often like to employ solidary and purposive incentives to attract activists. Such incentives are cheap because they do not drain the financial resources of those who seek power. But activists driven by purposive or solidary incentives have their costs in other currencies. Ideological activists motivated by purposive incentives constrain parties to be, or at least to appear to be, true and consistent in their pursuit of policy objectives. Activists motivated by solidary incentives, on the other hand, can be fickle and ineffective laborers in the vineyards of electoral politics.

Party in the Electorate

The overriding objective of democratic parties is to gain votes. Research on American voting has long focused on party identification as a key to traditional electoral behavior. Party identification refers to long-term psychological attachments that voters make to political parties and that influence their voting behavior. Party identification may be an effective shortcut to the information voters need in order to make sensible choices, particularly where parties are perceived as reliable and responsive. Such attachments are often related to social cleavages or divisions, such as class, religion, or language, which have structured popular attitudes toward the parties.

New political parties typically form among population groups opposed to existing rulers and policies, and the politicization of new cleavages has tended to lead to the formation of new parties. Two major historical developments have been particularly important for social cleavage patterns and party formation in Western democracies: the national revolution (especially in Western Europe) and the Industrial Revolution. The national revolution, beginning with the Protestant Reformation in the sixteenth century and the emergence of national languages and cultures, led to political conflicts between church and state, as well as between center and periphery in the emerging nation-states. In many countries, parties formed along these cleavages, which retained a significant impact on popular voting patterns. The Industrial Revolution introduced social cleavages between the growing urban population and the countryside, reflected in such issues as corn laws and tariffs, as well as conflicts between the owners of capital and the new industrial working class. The latter cleavage, of course, set a particularly profound mark on the politics of just about every industrialized democracy in the late nineteenth and early twentieth centuries.

By the 1920s most Western democracies had adopted more or less universal adult suffrage, although in some countries women still had to wait several decades for the right to vote. At the same time, institutional reforms such as parliamentary government and proportional representation had reached most European democracies. New parties multiplied in the wake of these reforms. After the 1920s, however, fewer new parties appeared on the scene.

Voter attachments stabilized, and the party systems of Western Europe in particular appeared "frozen."

This situation persisted well beyond World War II. In most industrialized states, postwar party politics resembled prewar patterns. Even in former fascist states, such as Germany, Italy, and Austria, most of the democratic parties that appeared after the war had clear roots in the prefascist past. Over time, the established parties formed fairly stable "cartels." Voters tended to identify strongly with their respective parties, and electoral participation was high.

Eventually, this stability of party politics eroded. In many countries, change came in the 1960s or 1970s. In some cases, such as Denmark, the Netherlands, and even Britain, electoral change was abrupt once it arrived. Elsewhere, as in Italy and Japan, significant new parties emerged much later, but the changes they brought were no less profound.

Electoral change came in the form of new parties, or in the rapid growth of existing parties, that previously had been little more than nuisances. Many of the new parties that have emerged since the 1960s can be understood as champions of beleaguered groups or values. Particularly in Protestant nations, new religious parties have risen to the defense of traditional Christian and family values that have seemed threatened by secularization and social permissiveness. In many countries, including Canada, Britain, and Spain, regionalist or separatist parties have mobilized the voters of culturally distinct regions against the ambitions of central governments. During the 1980s and the 1990s, anti-immigration parties have surfaced in response to the growing flow of migrants into Western Europe. Some new parties on the right direct much of their fire toward the encroachments of governments into the market or into the traditionally private sphere of life. Some analysts even view the green parties of Germany and other nations as defenders of a generation of highly educated young people threatened by unemployment.

Yet the rise of new political parties also reflects dramatic changes in popular values. The generations born into relative affluence in Europe and North America after World War II have put new issues, such as ecology and gender equality, on the political agenda. They are markedly less supportive of traditional authority and institutions, including government as well as business, than their elders were. They are much more inclined to support alternative lifestyles and to be concerned about the rights of minorities and women. In some countries, though not in the United States, religious observance has declined dramatically, particularly among younger voters. All these changes have paved the way for a variety of new parties. The parties that have suffered the most substantial losses as these new organizations have emerged on the scene have been traditional communists, social democrats, and Christian democrats.

Political Parties in Decline?

In recent years the conventionally sanguine view of the role of democratic political parties has been subject to considerable skepticism and attack, most notably among students of American parties. Decline in party identification and membership and increased voter volatility and split-ticket voting are seen as symptoms of declining parties. It has also been claimed that there is a general decline in the trust in the political institutions within which parties operate—and indeed in the parties themselves.

Yet this gloomy picture of contemporary parties is far from complete. The recent democratization of most of Eastern Europe and Latin America, as well as parts of Asia and Africa, has everywhere been effected in large part through new or reborn democratic parties. The alleged demise of political parties in the United States and Western Europe has in no way dissuaded elites in nascent democracies from developing such vehicles of mass representation. And even among students of American parties, dissenting voices have insisted that political parties are alive and well.

Many current challenges to political parties lie specifically in large-scale changes in society and polity. Perhaps most significant, the resources of citizens have grown dramatically, fueled by such broad social changes as growing prosperity, urbanization, the entry of women into the labor force, and improved educational standards. The average Western citizen of the 1990s enjoys educational standards, leisure opportunities, financial security, and access to information that were unthinkable even a few decades ago.

These changes in resources have had substantial effects on partisan attachments. With much greater access to independent information, voters no longer depend on political parties for their political socialization and information. The material incentives that party organizations have traditionally offered their followers have lost their attractiveness with rising standards of living, especially where

political patronage is relatively scarce. Solidary incentives may also become less attractive as traditional communities disintegrate and other leisure-time activities multiply. Hence parties have encountered new problems in recruiting activists and officers, and membership numbers in many parties have gone down.

Large-scale changes in voters' resources have been accompanied by new political attitudes and behaviors. With urbanization, affluence, secularization, and the expanded role of women in public life, the traditional issue agenda of party politics has been decisively altered. Traditional bread and butter issues have been supplanted by concerns with lifestyles, community, equality, and freedom. In a number of cases, such issues have provided the basis for the mobilization of new interest groups.

Traditional party politics has been challenged by new social values and preferences concerning political action. Well-established parties, as, for example, the social democrats of northern Europe, often have severe problems adjusting to new issues that cut across their traditional constituencies. At the same time, their organizations are undermined by the increased popularity of modes of political action that lie beyond the repertoire of conventional party politics.

Many individuals in the postwar generations hold values that are very distant from the formative concerns of established party systems. Many younger and more affluent citizens engage in, or at least tolerate, forms of political behavior that violate the traditional rules of parliamentary politics. Political parties have difficulty in relating to, or incorporating, such modes of political expression as direct action, boycotts, and even violence. New generations come into politics whose formative political experiences have been unorthodox. Often, party politics has played a very limited role in these early experiences. Changes in values, like changes in resources, have lowered citizens' interest in many of the benefits parties have traditionally offered their followers.

One of the most significant changes parties must confront is the change in the nature of the political community itself. Not since the advent of universal adult suffrage have Western democracies witnessed such upheavals in the composition of their citizenries. Minority groups have gained recognition and representation; immigrants stream into more prosperous nations. Increased international integration (for example, the evolution of the European Union) and migration may foster cross-national party systems, as migrants bring with them partisan attachments from abroad. In fact, immigrants may not identify with the party systems of their new homelands. On the other hand, the growing importance of international representative bodies such as the European Parliament may encourage the formation of embryonic cross-national party families.

Increasingly, since the 1960s political parties have had to compete not only with one another but also with fundamentally different movements that nevertheless make claims on the same issue agenda. Many of these new movements have much narrower concerns than traditional parties have. Some focus on a single issue, such as separatism, abortion, or environmental concerns. Many also have less defined organizational structures and rely on such methods as direct mail solicitation to reach their audiences.

These alternative groups and organizations challenge the issue agenda traditionally defined by political parties and compete for the attention and contributions of their constituencies. Occasionally, such movements even choose to challenge the established parties directly by entering the electoral arena, as the Greens have in Germany and elsewhere or the anticorruption parties have in Italy and Japan. Within parties, rising levels of mass education and aspirations render party members and activists less deferential to their leaders than they were in the past and less willing to delegate critical party decisions to them.

While citizens are exploring unconventional vehicles of collective action, organizational change has taken place within the existing parties. Political campaigns have become more expensive and professionalized, legislative work is ever more specialized, and surveillance by the media is more immediate and intrusive.

Three technological changes are especially important for electoral politics: the advent of electronic mass media such as television, the increasing ease of travel, and the revolution in information technologies. These technological advances have greatly reduced the symbolic, informational, and temporal distance between political leaders and the rank and file, undermined traditional functions of mass parties, and in turn caused organizational change.

No longer can midlevel party activists and officers effectively serve as transmitters of information and demands. Ordinary citizens have much greater independent access to political leaders and information. Politics has become more candidate-centered and less organization-centered. At the same time, party leaders may have less

use for mass membership organizations. In the age of electronic mass media, labor-intensive electoral campaigns may even have become obsolete. Moreover, professional polling and solicitation techniques make the mass membership organization superfluous for many of its traditional purposes.

See also *Ballots; Candidate selection and recruitment; Dominant party democracies in Asia; Election campaigns; Electoral systems; Participation, Political; Parties, Transnational; Party systems; Polling, Public opinion; Proportional representation.*

Kaare Strøm

BIBLIOGRAPHY

Bartolini, Stefano, and Peter Mair. *Identity, Competition, and Electoral Availability: The Stabilization of European Electorates, 1885–1985.* Cambridge: Cambridge University Press, 1990.

Budge, Ian, David Robertson, and Derek Hearl, eds. *Ideology, Strategy, and Party Change.* Cambridge: Cambridge University Press, 1987.

Castles, Francis G., and Rudolf Wildenman, eds. *Visions and Realities of Party Government.* Berlin: Walter de Gruyter, 1986.

Dalton, Russell J., Scott C. Flanagan, and Paul Allen Beck. *Electoral Change in Advanced Industrial Democracies: Realignment or Dealignment?* Princeton: Princeton University Press, 1984.

Duverger, Maurice. *Political Parties: Their Organization and Activity in the Modern State.* London: Methuen; New York: Wiley, 1954.

Epstein, Leon D. *Political Parties in Western Democracies.* New Brunswick, N.J.: Transaction, 1982.

Laver, Michael J., and W. Ben Hunt. *Policy and Party Competition.* London: Routledge, 1992.

Lipset, Seymour Martin, and Stein Rokkan, eds. *Party Systems and Voter Alignments.* New York: Free Press, 1967.

Sartori, Giovanni. *Parties and Party Systems: A Framework for Analysis.* New York and Cambridge: Cambridge University Press, 1976.

Parties, Transnational

Transnational parties are organizations whose basic membership consists of actively collaborating national parties and affiliated groups, affiliated youth and other fraternal organizations, and compatible observer groups. The organizational structure of transnational parties resembles that of other parties: they are formally organized, elect officers, maintain headquarters, adopt rules of operation, have a regular membership, and promulgate programs of public policy. Member parties pay dues and coordinate program, campaign, and other political activities.

For most of the 400 years of their existence as institutions, political parties have been national, subnational, and local organizations. Although international parties began to gain prominence after World War II, transnational parties are not yet components of an organized world party system. Still, they show many of the attributes of an emergent party system, resembling the loosely organized Federalists and Antifederalists of the early American system. In the past, transnational parties were more commonly referred to as "internationals."

Major transnational parties of the twentieth century have included the Communist International (now defunct), the Socialist International (International Socialist Conference), the Christian Democratic International (Christian Democratic World Union), the Liberal International (World Liberal Union), and the Conservative International (International Democrat Union). Other transnational parties have been smaller and less well organized than these, and in some cases their existence has been brief. Examples include the fascists of Italy, Germany, and their allies in the 1930s and 1940s; the Baʾath socialist parties of the Middle East in the early 1990s; and the European greens.

Political parties usually have as their principal objective the placement of their avowed representatives in governmental offices. In the absence of world government or other supranational governments, transnational parties cannot serve this function, and they do not formally nominate candidates for offices in such bodies as the European Parliament or the United Nations. They do, however, openly and actively support the candidates nominated by their national colleagues.

Evolution

As formal organizations, the transnational parties have emerged at different points in time over the past century and a half. Among the most prominent are the Marxist internationals, the Christian democrats, and the Liberals.

Communist International. The best known of the transnational parties were the Marxist internationals, which for more than a century advocated the overthrow of bourgeois governments and capitalist economic systems. The communists saw their movement as a world party movement and precursor of a world political system in the Marxist-Leninist mold.

The Bolshevik Revolution of 1917 created the first communist-controlled government. Russian leader V. I. Lenin founded the Third International, called the Communist International, or Comintern. It was dissolved in 1943 as a conciliatory gesture to the Allies fighting the common battle against the Axis powers of Germany, Italy, and Japan. In the decades after World War II the transnational communist movement was maintained principally by the Soviet Union. The transnational character of the movement was weakened by hostility between the Soviet and Chinese parties and, in the 1970s, by increasing distance between the Soviet Union and European communists in Italy and France. As a result of democratization in Eastern Europe in 1989, ruling communist parties lost members and elections, disbanded, renamed themselves, or were outlawed. Some former communist parties managed to survive and regain influence by adopting strong nationalist postures. Given their history, ideology, and continuing organization in at least sixty countries, these parties may eventually re-create a modified version of the Comintern.

Socialist International. The Socialist International regards itself as the direct successor of the Second International (1889–1919). Following its demise as a transnational organization between the two world wars, an entirely new Socialist International was founded in 1951. Historically, socialists advocated nonviolent change within the context of democratic parliamentary institutions. Occasionally, however, some socialists have advocated "united fronts" with communists.

In 1994 the Socialist International reported a membership of sixty-six national parties; twenty-four consultative parties; and three fraternal organizations, including the International Union of Socialist Youth. There were regional associations of socialist parties in Europe, Asia, and Africa.

Christian Democratic International. Christian democracy emerged in the nineteenth century as an antagonist of liberalism and socialism. After World War II Christian democrats set aside their Roman Catholic theological origin and emphases and began to win elections to national offices throughout Europe. They gained influence especially in the Catholic countries of Latin America.

Efforts at international cooperation among Christian democrats were initiated as early as 1919 by Luigi Sturzo, a Sicilian priest and founder of the Italian Popular Party. The first international meeting of Christian democrats was held in 1925. In 1947 the International Union of Christian Democrats was established. This became the Christian Democratic World Union in 1961 and was restructured as the Christian Democratic International in 1982.

In the early 1990s the Christian democrats had three regional organizations (in Western Europe, Central Europe, and the Americas), sixty-four member parties, twenty-two associated parties, and seventeen observer groups. Approximately twenty member parties belonged to the Christian Democratic Organization of America, founded in 1949. Some conservative Christian democratic parties associated themselves with the International Democrat Union (Conservative International).

Liberal International. Liberals were the major ideological force in Europe during the nineteenth century, chiefly representing commercial and industrial interests. They did not take steps toward formal transnational organization until 1947, when representatives of nineteen liberal parties and groups, mainly European, signed a Liberal Manifesto in Oxford, England. This became the basic document of the World Liberal Union.

Until the early 1970s the Liberal International was principally European in membership and policy concerns. When the Canadian Liberal Party joined, the leadership began to adopt a global perspective and to reach out to organized liberals on other continents. By the early 1990s the Liberal International reported a membership of thirty-four national parties and twenty-two observer groups. In 1986 the National Democratic Institute for International Affairs, an affiliate of the U.S. Democratic Party, joined as an observer member.

International Democrat Union. The youngest transnational party is the International Democrat Union, also called the Conservative International. Its parent organization was the European Democrat Union, which was established in Salzburg, Austria, in 1978. Members of the European Democrat Union included Europe's conservative parties, certain Christian democratic parties, and center-right parties.

In 1982 George Bush, then U.S. vice president, attended the European Democrat Union annual congress in Munich. Later that year he brought Japanese, Australian, Canadian, and U.S. conservatives together to establish the Pacific Democrat Union. In 1983 delegates from these two groups met in London to found the International Democrat Union. Bush then arranged to host its first annual congress at the 1984 Republican national convention. The International Republican Institute, affiliated with the U.S. Republican Party, became actively involved in International Democrat Union efforts.

A Caribbean Democrat Union was formed in Kingston, Jamaica, in 1986, consisting mainly of parties in the English-speaking countries of the region. By 1994 the International Democrat Union had a membership of fifty-seven national parties, mainly from Europe and the Pacific, and claimed to represent more than 170 million voters.

Activities

The four major operative transnational parties engage in activities typical of parties in democracies. Their officers, representatives, and nominees seek to gain office in world, regional, and national bodies. For example, in the direct elections of national representatives to the European Parliament and the selection of officers within this body in 1979, 1984, and 1989, the transnational parties became increasingly involved in the transnational campaign effort and in the caucus activity of the Parliament. Coordination of policies and programs within transnational parties has been evident in the manifestos produced by their respective international congresses and parliamentary declarations.

Transnational parties also assist party colleagues seeking national office in many countries. Examples include the efforts made by the Socialist International on behalf of socialists in Portugal and Spain in the mid-1970s, the assistance given by the Christian Democratic International to colleagues in El Salvador and Guatemala in the mid-1980s, and the support shown by the Liberal International to associates in Nicaragua and Haiti on the eve of the 1990s.

The transnational parties have been active in developing national, regional, and global party organizations. The late Communist International was perhaps the most systematic, energetic, and experienced in providing training and other resources to party cadres in countries throughout the world. Next were the socialists, somewhat constrained by their tactics of peaceful change and respect for democratic institutions and national self-determination. The Christian democrats devoted more attention to transnational organizing after the 1970s, scoring significant successes in Europe and Latin America.

Transnational parties have been visible and influential at various supranational and international agencies. They have played an active role in the formally organized party groups in the European Parliament. They have also participated in informal collegial consultations at sessions of the United Nations, the Organization of American States, and the Organization of African Unity.

In support of global democratic development, the leaders of transnational parties occasionally issue timely joint statements. For example, in 1984 the presidents of three transnationals—representing Christian democrats, liberals, and social democrats—together applauded democratic developments then occurring in Latin America. They expressed their endorsement of the initiatives of the Contadora group in Central America and lent support to the Democratic Alliance in Chile. In 1993, joined by the newly formed International Democrat Union (Conservative International), the leaders of the transnational parties declared their common concern for the problems being created by unbridled population growth in many parts of the world.

The transnational parties are an increasingly valuable resource for national political leaders seeking to establish or rebuild democratic party systems. In this pursuit, the transnational parties are often aided materially by the democratization programs of the U.S. parties, the German political foundations, and similar organizations in other countries. The National Democratic Institute and the International Republican Institute in the United States have cooperated with their respective transnational party associates as well as with each other in conducting workshops on techniques of party organization, campaign and election laws and practices, and related subjects. Through supportive programs the transnational parties arrange international or regional conferences and other opportunities for consultation, lend national leaders the prestige of affiliation with an international body, provide counsel to national leaders, and channel financial, technical, and intelligence assistance, whenever this is legal and feasible.

The history of party systems indicates that partisan movements have almost always appeared before the founding of democratic constitutional governments. Similarly, transnational parties may be a determining factor in transforming regional and world political institutions into democratic supranational governmental systems.

See also *Christian democracy; Conservatism; Fascism; International organizations; Liberalism; Marxism; Parties, Political; Party systems; Socialism.*

Ralph M. Goldman

BIBLIOGRAPHY

Brown, Bernard. *Eurocommunism and Eurosocialism.* New York: Cyrco Press, 1979.
Fitzmaurice, John. *The Party Groups in the European Parliament.* Lexington, Mass.: Lexington Books; Aldershot: Gower, 1975.
Goldman, Ralph M. *From Warfare to Party Politics: The Critical Transition to Civilian Control.* Syracuse, N.Y.: Syracuse University Press, 1990.
———, ed. *Transnational Parties: Organizing the World's Precincts.* Lanham, Md.: University Press of America, 1983.
Irving, R. E. M. *The Christian Democratic Parties of Western Europe.* Winchester, Mass., and London: Allen and Unwin, 1979.
Pridham, Geoffrey, and Pippa Pridham. *Transnational Party Cooperation and European Integration.* Winchester, Mass.: Allen and Unwin, 1981.
Scott, John H. MacCallum. *Experiment in Internationalism.* London: Allen and Unwin, 1967.
Sworakowski, W. S., ed. *World Communism: A Handbook, 1918–1965.* Stanford, Calif.: Hoover Institution Press, 1973.

Party systems

One or more political parties within a state that interact in contesting elections, organizing legislatures, and controlling the executive branch of the government. Party systems are manifestations of popular organizations that seek to press their demands on those who govern representative democracies. Party systems also reflect the properties of the institutions within which such demands can be made.

Political parties exist in the vast majority of the world's independent states, and the number of nonparty states has shrunk significantly in the 1980s and 1990s. Only military dictatorships (currently most common in Africa), some personal dictatorships (such as Libya), and a few traditional monarchies (such as Saudi Arabia) still do not feature modern political parties. Furthermore, many countries, inside and outside the former Communist bloc, have moved away from one-party dominance toward the kind of party systems most commonly found in established democracies. In such postcommunist countries as Poland and Hungary, communist domination has been replaced by a bewildering array of competing parties. Thus political parties arguably are the most important contemporary political organizations, and competitive party systems have increasingly become the norm worldwide.

Several characteristics of party systems are of particular interest. Among these are the number of political parties in a country, the size of the various parties as they are distributed among the voters and in political assemblies such as legislatures, the number of issue or policy dimensions along which parties compete, the social and political divisions or cleavages expressed in the party system, and the stability of voting patterns. Other matters of interest are the levels of conflict and cooperation among political parties, government formation and public policy, and the consequences for stability and democracy.

The Number of Parties

The simplest classifications of party systems are based on the number of successful parties. Such classifications are also highly influential in the study of party systems, in large part because of the plausible links between the number of parties and many other characteristics of party systems. The simplest classification distinguishes among one-party, two-party, and multiparty systems.

One-party systems are the most clearly distinct. According to many specialists, it is unreasonable to compare such systems with systems that have two or more parties, since the institutions under which they operate may be radically different. Many one-party systems exist precisely because other organizations are constitutionally or effectively prohibited from entering the electoral contest.

We can distinguish between different subtypes of one-party systems according to the security of one-party control. In the extreme case, only one party is legally allowed to operate, and aspiring competitors are more or less vigorously prosecuted. Such conditions are most common in totalitarian or near totalitarian political systems, such as many communist societies or Nazi Germany. The Soviet constitution, for example, outlawed any opposition party until Mikhail Gorbachev's reluctant repeal of this provision in 1990. In other one-party states, although opposition parties may not be legally suppressed, they nonetheless suffer from discriminatory legislation or informal harassment. Mexico under the dominant Institutional Revolutionary Party was at least until the mid-1990s a good example of one-party dominance through discrimination, harassment, and intimidation.

It is customary to distinguish either of these forms of one-party systems from systems in which one party in practice dominates, despite relatively unfettered opportunities for competing parties to enter the fray. One such case is Japan from 1955 to 1993, when the country was continuously governed by the Liberal Democratic Party. A party like the Liberal Democratic Party, which is capable of repeatedly winning relatively open elections, is often referred to as predominant. Similarly, the Social Democratic

Labor Party, with only a four-week interruption, governed Sweden from 1932 to 1976, a forty-four-year stretch, although occasionally it governed in coalitions with other parties.

Among more competitive party systems, a fundamental distinction is conventionally drawn between two-party and multiparty systems. Some critics of the conventional wisdom, like Giovanni Sartori, point out the need to make finer distinctions among multiparty systems. Sartori distinguishes between moderate pluralism, where the number of "relevant" parties typically ranges from three to five, and extreme pluralism, where there are more than five relevant parties. Party systems of moderate pluralism feature relatively modest ideological distances among the relevant parties, party convergence toward middle-of-the-road voters, and two-bloc competition. The fact that parties in moderate pluralism tend to coalesce into two competing blocs means that they still have to cater to centrist voters. Moderate pluralism differs from two-party systems in that governments tend to be coalitions of two or more parties. Also, although some systems of moderate pluralism (for example, Germany) do not frequently experience minority governments, most do. Moderate pluralism is found mainly in the smaller European democracies, including both societies that are relatively homogeneous (the Scandinavian countries) and societies that are more heterogeneous (Belgium and Switzerland).

But whereas moderate pluralism has many of the characteristics of two-party systems, extreme pluralism exhibits antisystem parties, great ideological distance between the relevant parties, semiresponsible governments and irresponsible oppositions, inflated electoral promises ("overbidding"), lack of turnover in government, and ultimately a threat of democratic breakdown. In making distinctions among multiparty systems, Sartori primarily stresses the number of parties but maintains that ideological distance ("polarization") may independently affect the interaction between parties. Where there are many parties with a great ideological distance between them, we find polarized pluralism, which is particularly destabilizing. Stable systems of polarized pluralism are relatively rare, but Italy and Finland (at least in the 1970s) approximated this type.

The Distribution of Parties

All typologies of party systems that emphasize numbers run into the problem of how parties should be counted. Do all parties count equally, or should they be counted differently according to their electoral support, legislative representation, participation in coalition bargaining, or stability over time? Analysts of party systems generally agree that it is unfruitful to give equal weight to all parties that contest general elections. They disagree, however, about how to make the necessary distinctions. There are essentially two schools of thought. Either we must distinguish relevant parties, which deserve to be counted, from irrelevant ones, or we must develop a scheme to count all parties and explicitly weight them by their size or some similar characteristic.

Early studies of party systems often chose a more or less arbitrary numerical threshold of relevance—for example, 5 or 10 percent electoral support. Small but decidedly important parties such as the German Free Democrats cause obvious difficulties. One solution is to count such cases as half-parties. Sartori criticized such ad hoc counting rules and instead proposed the criterion of relevance: relevant parties had to have either coalition or blackmail potential (or both).

In parliamentary democracies parties have coalition potential if they at least occasionally take part in bargaining over government formation (even if they are rarely lucky enough to join the winning coalition). Parties may have such coalition potential because they are large, because they have a favorable policy position, or both. In any case, coalition potential means that they matter for the purpose of forming governments.

Parties have blackmail potential if they influence the bargaining or the campaign strategies of other relevant parties, even if they never get to participate in coalition bargaining. Blackmail potential allowed Sartori to count as relevant large and influential "permanent opposition" parties such as the former Italian Communists. Although Sartori has given the notion of relevance an interesting meaning, its practical use is still problematic. How can independent observers agree on whether a given party has coalition potential? The fact that a party has not participated in actual coalition bargaining does not prove that it has no coalition potential. It may be even more difficult, in the absence of extremely good data on the deliberations of party leaders, to determine whether a party has blackmail potential. How do we know whether other parties try to anticipate its behavior? Such operational problems limit the utility of the relevance criterion.

It is therefore attractive to find a way to characterize party systems without subjective judgments. This alternative route has generated various numerical indicators of party system fractionalization (or fragmentation). The classical and best known such index is Rae's index of fractionalization, or simply Rae's F. This is the probability that two randomly selected members of a population (for example, a population of voters or the members of a legislature) belong to the same party. Like all probability measures, Rae's F ranges from 0 (where each member of the population represents his or her own party) to 1 (where everyone belongs to the same party). The Laakso-Taagepera index simply transforms Rae's F into a more intuitively interpretable "effective number of parties."

These fractionalization measures can be applied to whatever aspect of the party system is of interest. If the population is the electorate, these fractionalization measures will pertain to the party system among the voters (party in the electorate). If, on the other hand, the population is the members of the legislature, we obtain a measure of the fragmentation of the legislative party system (party in government).

Determinants of Party Numbers

The most important determinants of the number of parties are the political cleavages among the citizens and the political institutions, such as the electoral system. The more political divisions there are among the voters, and the more these cross-cut one another, the greater the number of political parties will tend to be. Belgium is a good example of a country where cross-cutting linguistic, religious, and class divisions have generated a highly fractionalized party system.

The second critical factor is the electoral system, or the laws and regulations that determine how candidates for office get access to the ballot and how the voice of the voters is translated into legislative or other representation. The most decisive feature of electoral systems is district magnitude—the number of candidates elected per district. Under single-member district elections, such as the elections to the House of Commons in Great Britain or the U.S. Congress, two parties tend to dominate, and it is very difficult for smaller parties to gain representation or even to survive. Single-member district systems greatly reduce the effective number of parties in the legislature, compared with the number of parties among the voters, through underrepresentation of smaller parties, such as the British Liberal Democrats.

At the other extreme, where the entire country is one district of more than 100 representatives, as in Israel and the Netherlands, even very small parties can secure stable representation, and party systems are likely to be much more fragmented. Most electoral systems with multimember districts use proportional representation methods for allocating the seats in each district among the parties, and most such systems have district magnitudes in the intermediate range (that is, five to twenty seats). Typically, the country may be divided into several dozen electoral districts, often along existing regional boundaries. Some allocation methods, such as the Sainte-Laguë highest average formula, are more generous toward small parties than others, such as the d'Hondt method. Consequently, the former method is also associated with more fragmented party systems.

Other features of electoral systems that tend to foster party system fragmentation are pools of supplementary seats for higher tier seat allocation (at the national level), as in Germany; generous public subsidies of political parties; and regulations that make it easy and inexpensive to register a party and run candidates. On the other hand, electoral thresholds, which deny representation to parties gaining less than a predetermined share of the national vote (for example, 5 percent in Germany and 4 percent in Sweden), have the opposite effect.

Issue Dimensions and Cleavages

Party systems differ according to the number of issue dimensions on which parties compete, as well as with respect to the number of salient political cleavages among the voters. Although these aspects of party systems typically are closely related, they are analytically distinct. The number of issue dimensions is a function of the positions taken by political parties in their election programs and other public statements, whereas the number of political cleavages reflects the socioeconomic characteristics of the parties' supporters. Issue dimensions are best analyzed through scrutiny of official party policy statements, such as election platforms or programs (manifestos in British parlance); cleavages are identified through surveys of the demographic characteristics and partisan preferences of voters.

Cross-national research on the contents of party election programs shows that in many countries, the parties' most authoritative policy statements focus on a conventional set of issues, such as economic ownership, regulation, and taxation. In northern European countries especially, the contents of party programs tend to correspond closely to traditional definitions of the left-right spec-

trum. Particularly in countries with a strong Roman Catholic tradition, however, there are other important issue dimensions. In recent decades, new issue dimensions have emerged that cross-cut the conventional left-right axis. Such dimensions include stronger concerns for group representation (especially of women and minorities), environmental concerns, foreign policy orientations, and civil liberties.

The political cleavages underlying partisan preferences in advanced democracies are still linked to ascriptive (that is, acquired passively and early in life) social distinctions such as ethnicity, religious denomination, and language, as well as with quasi-ascriptive traits such as class and region. In an influential study of mass partisan alignments in Western European states, Seymour Martin Lipset and Stein Rokkan sought their roots in the historical resolution of two major social and economic revolutions: the national revolution, associated with the Reformation and the emergence of modern nation-states, and the Industrial Revolution, associated with industrialization, urbanization, and the growth of socialist working-class political movements.

The national revolution generated conflicts between the centers of the emerging nation-states and the outlying areas they conquered. It also led to a confrontation between the church and anticlerical forces, particularly in Catholic societies. The Industrial Revolution divided the new cities from the countryside and workers from managers, as manifested in the class conflict. These various cleavages remained important through the centuries. In the party politics of the twentieth century they have found expression in such issues as language rights and decentralization (center-periphery); secular versus religious education (church-state); tariffs and agricultural subsidies (urban-rural); and nationalization, redistribution, and welfare state policies (class). Different party systems feature different interactions among these cleavages, but the class cleavage is the most uniform in the advanced industrial democracies.

Mass suffrage and institutional reforms such as proportional representation and parliamentary government had reached most industrial democracies by the 1920s. By that time Western, and specifically Western European, parties had developed into remarkably stable cartels, in which each organization had its own well-defined and loyal constituency. The party systems and the underlying social cleavages of Western Europe appeared to be largely frozen from the 1920s to the 1960s. Few new parties arrived on the scene, and voters' attachments seemed to be remarkably stable.

The party systems of the 1960s still largely reflected the cleavage structures of the 1920s. This stability reflected a high degree of loyalty and commitment to political parties among a citizenry prepared to come to the polls in impressive numbers and vote in predictable ways. Since the late 1960s, however, the party systems of many democracies have changed substantially, and cleavage structures no longer appear frozen. New parties have appeared, and many established parties—among them traditional communists, social democrats, and Christian democrats—have suffered substantial losses.

We can assess the relative strength of different political cleavages by such means as the Alford index and the related measure of party-group linkage. The Alford index of class voting subtracts the percentage of left-party supporters in non–working-class households from the percentage of left-party supporters in working-class households (defined as those in which the head of household is a manual worker). Robert Alford's original study of four English-speaking democracies in the 1950s and 1960s thus found the class cleavage to be stronger in Britain and Australia than in North America. Similar indices can be developed for other background characteristics that bisect the population (for example, sex and in some cases religion). Cross-national research shows that class is the most consistently significant political cleavage in Western democracies, but identities such as race, language, or religion are often more powerful predictors of voting where they divide the population.

Party System Change

Students of electoral politics disagree about whether recent changes in voting behavior reflect realignments or dealignments. In a realignment, new social cleavages would replace traditional conflicts based on class, religion, and the other divisions of the national and industrial revolutions.

Generational differences may be a new division. Many new parties, including the German Greens and the Italian Radicals, appeal overwhelmingly to younger voters, whereas many established parties, such as the Scandinavian Social Democrats and the Italian Christian Democrats, receive most of their support from older groups. One possible explanation lies in the radically different so-

cial conditions under which different generations have grown up. Arguably, those who came of age in the affluence of the decades following World War II often have different political concerns from those of earlier generations, who were influenced by their experience of the Great Depression and World War II.

The political mobilization of women and their demands for equal or preferential treatment have generated new differences between the sexes in voting behavior. Such differences are most notable among the youngest generations, among which women are disproportionately drawn to parties of the left and men to those of the right.

Another increasingly important division runs between groups inside and outside the labor force, with the former supporting parties favoring market principles and more limited governments and the latter favoring enhanced welfare state services. Finally, within the labor force, conflicts between those who are employed in the largely protected public sector and those who work in the private sector—who are more exposed to market competition and are therefore less secure in their employment—have become increasingly evident. All these conflicts have become more prominent in shaping voter behavior than they were in the past.

In the case of dealignment, the various social divisions would lose their effect on voting behavior altogether. Election surveys show that more and more voters in modern democracies identify themselves as independents, and that far fewer of today's voters express a strong identification with any political party. Electoral volatility rates have increased sharply in recent elections, as more and more voters change their party preference from one election to the next. The parties have lost most of their ability to shape public opinion, and electoral results fluctuate more than before, subject to such short-term factors as the personalities of candidates, the management of campaigns, and economic circumstances.

Party System Dynamics

Democratic party systems function as channels of representation and accountability. Different types of party systems give priority to different processes of representation. First, party systems differ with respect to how clear a policy choice they offer the electorate. Second, party systems differ with respect to whether one party regularly wins a legislative majority. Even multiparty systems can routinely give one party a legislative majority, as in Japan for most of the period since the mid-1950s. In contrast to systems of more than two parties, however, two-party systems feature a purely competitive situation, in which single-party majority governments can be expected. When the choice is clear and one party obtains a majority, electoral accountability is high. These conditions do not necessarily apply when more than two parties effectively contest elections. The more complex bargaining situations, lessened accountability, and frequent coalitions of multiparty systems have conventionally been considered liabilities.

Four alleged virtues of two-party systems figure prominently in the existing literature: policy moderation, government stability, clarity of choice, and political accountability. Two-party systems promote policy moderation because both parties must try to appeal to centrist voters (technically, the median voter) to win elections. Because in pure two-party parliamentary systems one party always controls a legislative majority, single-party majority governments are the norm. Such governments tend to be more stable than interparty coalitions or minority governments. The voters have a simple choice between two distinct options and can never rationally regret voting for the party they most prefer. Finally, policy responsibility is lodged cleanly with one party, and the voters know whom subsequently to hold accountable.

Since the 1960s such concepts have increasingly come under challenge. Arend Lijphart has shown that two-party systems are neither necessary nor sufficient for these virtues. Many of them can be attained even in multiparty systems, although they may be less likely there. A number of smaller European states with multiparty systems (including the Netherlands and Switzerland) have attained an enviable record of government stability and policy moderation. Besides, policy moderation and clarity of choice are contradictory values, and two-party systems can at most satisfy one of these conditions. If both parties converge toward the policies preferred by the median voter, they effectively offer the voters no choice.

Yet there are clearly cases in which multiparty politics has caused severe problems of political stability. Such problems are most obvious in cases of polarized pluralism. According to Sartori, the clearest cases of such party systems are the German Weimar Republic (1919–1933), Italy, France's Fourth Republic (1946–1958), Chile (1932–1973) in the years before Augusto Pinochet, and Finland. Even a cursory glance at these cases warns us that systems of polarized pluralism seem particularly susceptible to democratic breakdown. Yet the reasonable stability of Italy and, particularly, Finland in recent years shows that such dire consequences are not inevitable. More systematic quantitative studies confirm that strong extremist parties, a critical feature of polarized pluralism, are associated with unstable governments and high levels of political violence. The number of parties in itself, however, does not lead to such undesirable outcomes.

See also *Coalition building; Cube law; Dominant party democracies in Asia; Duverger, Maurice; Election campaigns; Electoral systems; Government formation; Hermens, Ferdinand A.; Parties, Political; Proportional representation; Voting behavior.*

Kaare Strøm

BIBLIOGRAPHY

Duverger, Maurice. *Political Parties: Their Organization and Activity in the Modern State.* London: Methuen; New York: Wiley, 1954.

Epstein, Leon D. *Political Parties in Western Democracies.* New Brunswick, N.J.: Transaction, 1982.

Lijphart, Arend. *Democracies.* New Haven and London: Yale University Press, 1984.

Lipset, Seymour Martin, and Stein Rokkan, eds. *Party Systems and Voter Alignments.* New York: Free Press, 1967.

Powell, G. Bingham, Jr. *Contemporary Democracies.* Cambridge, Mass., and London: Harvard University Press, 1982.

Sartori, Giovanni. *Parties and Party Systems: A Framework for Analysis.* New York and Cambridge: Cambridge University Press, 1976.

Patronage

A system of power relationships between individuals or groups in unequal positions. The word *patronage* derives from the Latin *patronus,* which in ancient Rome meant an individual with a higher status who protected his lower-status *clientes,* or clients, before the law and helped them economically. In this sense, patronage is a synonym for clientelism, since both words define a relationship between two individuals with different status, power, and resources. In another sense, however, patronage is a legitimate and formal procedure related to the acknowledged right of political power holders to appoint their followers to positions of public responsibility.

Patron-client relationships have several distinct characteristics. First, they are social interactions based on a personal exchange of favors. As such, they differ from social interactions based on primary solidarities (ethnic, linguistic, religious, family) and from those based on class or sectoral solidarity. Second, patronage relationships are reciprocal: the patron uses personal influence to protect the client, who reciprocates with different kinds of services. Both enter the relationship voluntarily, and the exchange of material benefits is direct but diffuse—that is, it can involve both the simultaneous use of different resources and the accumulation of future obligations. The restitution is not imposed by a contractual obligation but by a personal sense of gratitude and loyalty.

In analyzing patronage, political scientists have focused on the use of public resources by political leaders for their private aims, especially involving an exchange of favors for votes. Gradually the scope of the concept was enlarged to include complex relationships between multiple actors, not only between persons but also between groups. The increasing scope of the concept gave rise to typologies and classifications to take into account various aspects of the patron-client relationship. For example, the resources involved in the exchange may be direct resources (resources that the patron controls directly, such as land, work, skills, or personal prestige) or indirect resources (resources controlled through strategic contacts with those who control them directly).

The characteristics of patronage also vary according to (1) the type of services (economic, military, political, or electoral) that the client renders in return for the favors obtained from the patron; (2) the degree of personal versus formal obligations that link the two actors; and (3) the basis of the relationship—whether it is purely voluntary or has compulsory or ascriptive aspects. Moreover, patron-client relationships can differ in duration, strength, and extent of the reciprocal pact, which sometimes is sanctioned by various types of rituals. In some cases, patronage can assume the characteristics of nepotism, the distribution of public jobs or contracts on the basis of kinship ties.

Types of Patronage

There are two major types of patronage: the traditional patronage of local notables—such as landowners, doctors, lawyers, and other professionals—and the modern forms of party patronage. Traditional patron-client relationships involve two people, one of higher and one of lower status, who interact face to face. In modern society, especially in developed countries, such relationships involve several ac-

tors of equal status, some of whom may be organizations rather than individuals. For example, parties may assume the role of patrons, while interest groups may be the clients, or vice versa.

The two types of patronage are indeed linked to each other, since party patronage has usually followed the historical patronage established by notables. In traditional societies, the notables use their money and prestige to build networks of protégés. Thanks to their social position, they control the peasants in all their capacities, as producers, soldiers, and voters. When the state structure at the center expands, the notables function as mediators between the center and the periphery, bridging communication gaps.

Traditional societies therefore are incorporated into the developing state through the co-optation of the local notables. The central state provides the notables with public resources, which they can then distribute, thereby increasing their power. In exchange, the notables "transfer" their loyalties from persons to the political institutions. As modernization and democratization take place, however, the notables are likely to lose their power, since the distribution of public resources and spoils is organized increasingly by mass parties. Party patronage replaces the patronage of the notables, and consensus is built around professional politicians, who use public resources as their personal belongings.

Environmental Preconditions

Patronage is one way of organizing relationships between the center and periphery of a state, but it is not the only way. For patron-client relationships to develop, some preconditions have to be present. First, patron-client relationships spread in societies where the patrons have a lot to offer and the clients have a strong need for asking (and accepting) favors. In other words, such relationships flourish in societies that have sharp social inequality and a thorough lack of confidence in equal treatment by the state. In some developing countries, extreme class stratification and the absence of a generalized loyalty to the state contribute to the development of various forms of patronage. From an economic point of view, clientelistic relationships tend to develop in extensive and extractive economies, such as those based on agriculture, that have little internal specialization and little propensity for technological innovation.

Societies in which patronage flourishes tend to develop certain cultural characteristics as well. The development of patron-client relationships is accompanied by cultural codes emphasizing honor, reciprocity, mediation, fatalism, and the role of kinship ties. In fact, in environments strongly affected by traditional norms, patrons develop an instrumental "generosity": through their distribution of favors, they bind the clients to reciprocate with their vote and their loyalty.

In particular, patron-client relationships are influenced by the structure of trust in a society. They are more likely to spread when there are low levels of trust within the major social groups and a fragile extension of trust beyond the basic units to broader institutional complexes. In these situations, there is a combination of contractual and precontractual elements, and a confusion between the public and the private spheres, combined with internal conflict. When universal criteria for resource allocation are weak or nonexistent, members of different classes are forced to make alliances across social boundaries.

These conditions are likely to develop in phases of transition, when the capitalist mode of production and a large public bureaucracy have not yet penetrated the whole society, but urbanization and immigration already jeopardize traditional assets. The political institutions are not strong enough to mediate, especially at the local level, between the citizens and the state, and traditional loyalties survive, though weakened. Although the primary groups are no longer able to offer protection, horizontal (class or sectoral) relationships have not yet emerged.

Patronage does not disappear with the development of modern democracies. In the 1960s and 1970s a new wave of sociological studies indicated that in industrial societies the increasing power of the state is accompanied by increasingly aggressive attempts to gain access to public resources through privileged links with power holders. Moreover, political parties try to acquire blocs of votes by granting particular favors to certain groups of electors.

What determines the strategy of a political party choosing between the distribution of collective benefits and the distribution of divisible benefits through patronage? The most important factors in the party's choice are the orientation and preferences of voters, the type and amount of resources available to the party, and the interests and preferences of party activists and allies. In their role as voters, immigrants, displaced peasants, and in some cases the middle class are supposed to be more sensitive to parties that offer divisible benefits, while the industrial working class seems to respond more favorably to parties that offer collective or programmatic benefits. Par-

ty preferences seem to be quite resilient, since the conditions under which a political party arose—and in particular its access to patronage when it began to mobilize a popular base—define its propensity to use divisible or collective goods later in its evolution.

Consequences

If patronage is, as it seems to be, a permanent feature of society, it is important to reflect on its probable consequences. Several studies of the so-called political machines in the largest U.S. cities singled out some positive functions of patron-client relationships. They allow for vertical social integration; offer an alternative to violence in managing social conflicts; foster collaboration between classes; and develop the exchanges between different subsystems, especially between the periphery and the center. The machine's "bosses" thus contribute to the survival of the political system by distributing welfare, integrating new ethnic groups, helping citizens to cope with bureaucracies, and developing interpersonal ties, which they can then transfer to institutions.

Notwithstanding its usefulness in some phases, the development of patronage relationships carries several types of risk for democracy. First, the distribution of individual benefits is a very expensive way of raising consensus and is also intrinsically inflationary, since the number of people who push to be included in the network of privileged exchanges tends to increase continually. Patronage thus requires growing resources, and at the same time it reduces the capacity to plan public expenditures with a view toward general interests. Second, with its paternal, personalistic, and discriminatory use of public resources, patronage deviates from the main principles of modern bureaucracy: universalism, the separation between the private and public spheres, and the distinction of roles and persons. It also undermines political parties, which should function according to some concept of the public good and which become instead the instrument of personal interests. Patronage is a strategy to raise immediate support for particular politicians, but in the long run it delegitimizes democratic institutions in general.

See also *Politics, Machine; Spoils system.*

Donatella della Porta

BIBLIOGRAPHY

Eisenstadt, Samuel N., and Luis Ronigen. *Patrons, Clients, and Friends: Interpersonal Relationships and the Structure of Trust in Society.* Cambridge: Cambridge University Press, 1984.

Merton, Robert K. *Social Theory and Social Structure.* New York: Free Press, 1957.

Scott, James C. "Patron-Client Politics and Political Change in Southeast Asia." *American Political Science Review* 66 (March 1972): 91–113.

Shefter, Martin. "Party and Patronage: Germany, England and Italy." *Policy and Society* 7 (winter 1977): 403–451.

Weingrod, Alex. "Patron, Patronage, and Political Parties." *Comparative Studies in Society and History* 10 (July 1968): 377–400.

Personality, Democratic

Democratic personality describes the type of personality of individuals who actively participate in democratic politics, workplaces, and voluntary associations—and possibly in democratic families. The concept is not a common one, although it appears occasionally in the research literature.

There are various ways in which the term *democratic personality* can be used: one relates to personality dynamics; another to personality traits. The latter approach generally is the one taken here. Personality traits are enduring dispositions (over many years) and appear in many different situations; they structure individual human behavior on a broad scale. They are broader than attitudes, which may be limited to a few situations. (Consider, for example, attitudes toward voting.)

The democratic personality can be seen as a personality syndrome, that is, personality traits that sometimes occur together. By definition here, the democratic personality refers to the type of personality or personality syndrome that leads a person to seek to participate in or create a democratic political structure and democratic processes in politics, the workplace, associations, or the family. The democratic personality also refers to the type of personality that tends to form or develop through participation in such democratic structures and processes. The democratic personality thus occurs both by selection and by socialization.

Although the concept is usually limited to politics and government, the democratic personality in fact appears in all the major sectors of society: in politics and government (for example, participants in local politics); occasionally in business (participants in workplace democracy); in nonprofit organizations (participants in voluntary associations); and in households and families (members of democratic households).

Politics and Government

Harold D. Lasswell, in the early 1950s, was probably the first scholar to discuss the democratic personality at length, although he was interested in what he called the *democratic character,* a part of the larger personality. The democratic character, for Lasswell, specifically referred to four things: identifications with others that make the individual open and sociable; preferences for values and wants shared with others (meaning that the individual is not power centered or focused on any single value); strong confidence in humankind's potential goodness (that is, low apathy and high self-confidence); and support from the unconscious for the foregoing. The democratic character fits with the democratic community or society—growing out of it and operating within it. The democratic character fails to develop when deficient interpersonal relations produce low self-esteem in an individual.

Other versions of the democratic personality or character have been offered over the years. Michael Binford, for instance, argued in the early 1980s for three subtypes of the democratic political personality: cognitive, socially adaptive, and character rooted. But more important are the data on the types of personality traits that characterize those who participate actively in politics. In the 1960s Lester Milbrath reviewed the literature on determinants of political participation, including personality traits, and his findings still seem generally valid.

Milbrath found that individuals who demonstrated certain traits had higher levels of political participation than did other individuals. High levels of participation were found in those who were high in sociability, extroversion, and friendliness; low in anomie, alienation, or cynicism; high in ego strength, self-confidence, and self-esteem; relatively high in sense of competence or efficacy; and relatively low in power motivation or need for dominance (which are better expressed in business and the military).

Other Sectors

Business firms generally are not run democratically. In recent decades, however, some firms have been purchased, often in bankruptcy, by their employees and have been turned into democratic workplaces. Such workplace democratization has a characteristic pattern. Generally, workers participate in decision making, share in profits, elect the board of directors, and have veto power over major board decisions. They also have or develop a particular set of attitudes and values—a type of consciousness, or personality.

This personality could be said to constitute the economic form of the democratic personality. Paul Bernstein, in a literature review in the mid-1970s, found three key traits in the worker's democratic personality: high self-esteem (self-confidence), high self-reliance (which may be seen as efficacy or competence), and high flexibility (low rigidity). People who are attracted to firms run as workplace democracies are likely to be unusual, and such settings are likely to mold "normal" workers into workers who take on the economic democratic personality in a kind of adult socialization.

The nonprofit or voluntary sector has only recently received scholarly attention. Some idea of the breadth of this sector, which ranges from Brownie troops and Lions Clubs to the Smithsonian Institution and the Ford Foundation, can be gained from Michael O'Neill's *Third America* (1989). There are two major types of organizations: volunteer nonprofit organizations, in which most of the work is done by volunteers (as in the Brownies and Lions Clubs), and paid-staff nonprofit organizations, in which most of the work is done by paid workers (as in the Smithsonian Institution and Ford Foundation).

Paid-staff nonprofit organizations depend on people whose attitudes about work are somewhat different from those of the average worker in society. Nonprofit staff members often have a special pride in their organization, a willingness to take a lower salary than they could earn elsewhere because of the value of their organization in society, and a preference for less formality than is typical in government or business.

More research has been done on the personality of the volunteers for paid-staff nonprofit organizations and on members of volunteer nonprofit organizations than on the staff in paid-staff nonprofit organizations. Volunteer participation is higher among individuals with more competence (efficacy), self-confidence (ego strength), sociability, empathy, morality, emotional stability, assertiveness, persistence, and warmth. Since voluntary associations tend to operate democratically, this list of traits can be said to define, for the present, the associational democratic personality.

Some scholars include associational activity in their overall measures of political participation. For the most part, however, except for political parties, committees, and clubs, volunteer nonprofit organizations are separate from the government sector. Yet in certain circumstances any kind of voluntary association can take political stands locally or at higher levels.

A less well recognized sector is the household and family sector, which consists of all the households and families in the nation. Households can be run democratically or in an authoritarian manner. Both spouses in democratic families are likely to have jobs, to share household and child care tasks relatively equally, to make joint decisions on financial and other matters, to discuss decisions in general, and to show respect for each other. Children in democratic families, as they grow, are gradually given more and more responsibility for their own lives. Obedience is a less important goal than responsible behavior, and children participate increasingly in family decision making as they grow older—as responsible "citizens" of the family.

In a very different kind of household, communes or utopian communities, great emphasis is often placed on decision making by democratic consensus. Authoritarian communes, particularly cult communes, do not display democratic traits. Both traditional democratic families and democratic communes tend to be formed by and to produce people with greater self-confidence, efficacy, sociability, flexibility, and morality, and with less cynicism, than other people.

The democratic personality overall is like the active-effective character delineated by David Horton Smith in *Participation in Social and Political Activities* (1980). A person who displays the traits of a democratic personality and who has more "dominant statuses" (higher education, higher income, and so forth) is encouraged by parents, teachers, and peers to participate in all socioculturally approved activities and structures in a democracy. Individuals with democratic personalities are thus the most active in all kinds of valued social and political groups and activities in a democratic society.

Authoritarian Personality

One concept long opposed to the democratic personality is the concept of authoritarian personality, a concept that refers to a complex of traits, including submission to authority, domination of subordinates, and extreme conventionality. According to the classic research by Theodor

Adorno (in *The Authoritarian Personality,* 1950) and his colleagues introducing this idea, authoritarians are more likely to be prejudiced, ethnocentric, and generally rigid than are other people. Authoritarians are basically weak and dependent people who seek a personal sense of security by seeing the world as an orderly place. Authoritarianism can be measured by the F (or fascism) scale, one of the best-known measuring instruments in social psychology. Researchers have paid more attention to right-wing authoritarianism (fascism) than to left-wing authoritarianism (traditional communism).

Milbrath offered some evidence for less political participation among those who score high on the F scale than among those who score low. He conjectured that the lack of structure in democratic politics may not appeal to authoritarians, who prefer a clear hierarchical structure. For the same reason, authoritarians will tend not to like democratic workplaces, associations, or households. Seymour Martin Lipset, in the early 1980s, suggested that authoritarianism sometimes promotes political extremism and sometimes promotes withdrawal from the usual forms of political participation. In the family, authoritarianism is likely to result from a family atmosphere that emphasizes control and strict discipline, while playing down acceptance of and responsiveness to the child as a person. The authoritarian child develops a dependence on parents for things rather than a dependence for love. Authoritarian parents find it hard to give unrestricted love, rather than approval for correct behavior. The resulting authoritarian adult displays, in a number of ways, the antithesis of the democratic personality.

See also *Associations; Authoritarianism; Lasswell, Harold D.; Participation, Political; Psychoanalysis.*

David Horton Smith

BIBLIOGRAPHY

Bernstein, Paul. *Workplace Democratization.* Kent, Ohio: Kent State University Press, 1976.
Conway, M. Margaret. *Political Participation in the United States.* 2d ed. Washington, D.C.: CQ Press, 1991.
Kirscht, John P., and Ronald C. Dillehay. *Dimensions of Authoritarianism: A Review of Research and Theory.* Lexington: University of Kentucky Press, 1967.
Lasswell, Harold D. *The Political Writings of Harold D. Lasswell.* Glencoe, Ill.: Free Press, 1951.
Lipset, Seymour Martin. *Political Man: The Social Bases of Politics.* Expanded and updated ed. Baltimore: Johns Hopkins University Press, 1981; Aldershot: Gower, 1983.
Milbrath, Lester. *Political Participation.* Chicago: Rand McNally, 1965.
Smith, David Horton. "Determinants of Voluntary Association Participation and Volunteering: A Literature Review." *Nonprofit and Voluntary Sector Quarterly* 23 (1994): 243–264.
Stone, William F., Gerda Lederer, and Richard Christie, eds. *Strength and Weakness: The Authoritarian Personality Today.* New York and Godalming, Surrey: Springer-Verlag, 1993.

Peru

See *Andean countries*

Philippines

A nation of Southeast Asia spread over an archipelago of some 7,000 islands, which gained independence from the United States in 1946. Although large numbers of Muslims live on the southern Philippine island of Mindanao, about 90 percent of Filipinos are Catholic Christians. The Spanish brought Catholicism to the Philippines during their centuries of colonialization. After the United States colonized the Philippines, English became the language of the educated. Eventually it became the main language in the school system and in official Philippine government documents. English is the language Filipinos use when they meet other Filipinos who speak a different dialect of the national language, Pilipino.

After independence, the Philippines became known as Southeast Asia's "showcase of democracy." In terms of the formal institutions of government, that description is accurate. In the postindependence period, up to the time of martial law, which began in 1972 under Ferdinand Marcos's administration, and since the administration of Corazon Aquino, who was elected president in 1986, the Philippine government carried out its functions on the basis of constitutional guidelines, the separation of powers, and adherence to a bill of rights.

Colonialism and Dynastic Politics

The reality is different from the formal structure. The Spanish colonized the Philippines almost five hundred years ago, and ever after the nation was ruled by a few family dynasties that controlled both the economic and the political sphere. The Philippines is the only country in Southeast Asia that was colonized before indigenous institutions had been established. From the great haciendas of the Spaniards to the patronage politics during the American period, through the period of independence and continuing in the early 1990s, these dynasties ruled in a baronial, feudal manner, each controlling a particular area of the archipelago.

Even after the People's Power revolt of 1986, which ousted the authoritarian government of Ferdinand Marcos and installed the democratic Corazon Aquino as president, a group of provincial barons commanded the rural areas. In Cebu Province, for example, the governor, the mayor of Cebu City, and the national member of Congress were all named Osmena. All were members of a politically powerful clan once led by a former president. That system remained essentially the same throughout Filipino history.

The nature of the country—spread over thousands of islands, many of them quite small—was partly responsible for its decentralized, dynastic system. In addition, pervasive poverty taught the poor to rely on their wealthy patrons. Dynastic families sponsored the weddings of their laborers and tenants, paid for children's education, and cared for the sick. This kind of aid formed a relationship of dependence that kept the poor deferential and loyal. In the absence of strong government institutions, patron-client relations developed to meet the needs of the poor people who made up the majority of the population.

Culture also helped shape the dynastic character of Philippine politics. A Filipino's loyalty is directed first to family, then to close friends, then to the local community, then to personally known political leaders, and finally to distant, impersonal governmental agencies. All these concentric circles of allegiance place emphasis on the personal nature of loyalty. Still, an individual's family and "patron family" demand the deepest loyalties.

As a result of colonialism, Filipinos often tend to feel that everything Filipino is second-rate, while everything Western is first-rate. Thus many Filipinos have a feeling of national inferiority, so their support for the nation's governmental system is weak compared with support for family and patrons. Filipino elites are often alienated from their roots and from the masses of the people, most of whom they scorn. The first priority of the elites is self-interest, not the public good. Such values are not conducive to democratic rule, a form of government that requires mutual trust and respect for different points of view.

Party Politics from Marcos to Aquino

For democratization to take root in the Philippines, the formal institutions of government will have to become more than façades for oligarchical rule. From independence to Marcos's declaration of martial law in 1972, the Philippines had a two-party system. The Liberal and Nacionalista parties held power in alternation, with neither party able to reelect its presidential nominee. The ideological differences between the two parties were negligible, and neither party appeared to represent the interests of the vast majority of Filipinos. For the most part, the two parties served to get out the vote for specific candidates.

Under Marcos, one party dominated the political scene. Marcos's New Society Movement was a noncompetitive, authoritarian party devoted to keeping Marcos in power. In the post–martial-law era after 1981, the New Society Movement continued to dominate politics. Opposition parties began to emerge, however, the most important of which was the United Nationalist Democratic Organization (Unido), an alliance of establishment politicians. Unido eventually supported Aquino when she became a candidate for president in 1986. Parties played little role in the 1992 election, when seven candidates vied for the presidency.

The remarkable grassroots movement called the People's Power revolt included Filipinos from every socioeconomic class. In February 1986 they succeeded in ousting Marcos and installing Aquino. Nonetheless the election of Aquino was more a restoration of certain families (and the demise of a few who had aligned with Marcos) than a revolution. The overwhelming majority of newly elected senators and representatives in 1986 were members of families that had dominated Filipino politics for centuries. Although the persons in charge of the government changed, the people's power movement marked no fundamental change in the character of the Philippine political system.

The inability of Aquino to restructure the feudal socioeconomic system in the Philippines detracted somewhat from her success in reviving constitutional rule, free elections, freedom of the press, and autonomous institutions accountable to the public. Although personalism remained an integral part of Filipino politics under Aquino, corruption and cronyism declined, compared with the era of Marcos.

Past and Present Problems

Aquino inherited a profoundly difficult and complex situation, one that could not easily be resolved even by the outstanding economists she brought to her administration. The problems that beset the Philippines under Aquino were the same as those of the past: economic inequality, land disputes, monopolistic industries, corrupt leadership, and an elite class concerned more with self-interest than with the public good. Such problems could be resolved only by fundamental changes in all areas of Filipino life, including the social, economic, cultural, and political realms. For most Filipinos, the standard of living remained the lowest in the Association of Southeast Asian Nations. This was a galling fact for a people who live in a country with rich natural resources, who are highly literate and well educated, and who have more experience with democratic rule than other nations in Southeast Asia.

Aquino's rise to power was the quintessential example of democratization in 1986 and may have indirectly encouraged the people of Burma (Myanmar) to stage their own version of "people's power." The triumphs and travails of the Aquino regime, however, were a product of indigenous culture and behavior. The demise of communist states and the new international era played little role in Philippine domestic politics. Only in the realm of foreign relations, particularly with regard to military bases, did the end of the cold war influence Philippine policy making.

The overriding unmet challenge in the Philippines is to fashion a stable political structure that is predictable enough for the development of external economic ties and domestic entrepreneurship. In the past the Philippines has been a model for how not to develop economically. The growth of the gross domestic product (GDP) in the Philippines has been negligible for almost two decades. In 1992 the GDP grew 1 percent in the Philippines, compared with 8 percent in the other countries in the Association of Southeast Asian Nations. The nation's high population growth (2.6 percent per year) also limited real economic growth.

The country's economic difficulties resulted in part from the Marcos years, when the economy was characterized by crony capitalism. Coveted contracts were frequently given to incompetent presidential clients rather than to effective contractors. Marcos gave his best friends monopoly control over the sugar and coconut industries, thus allowing them to amass fabulous riches that ended

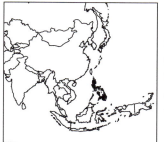

up in Swiss and U.S. bank accounts. The flight of capital subverted the national economy and brought it to the brink of disaster.

In Thailand, Malaysia, Singapore, and Indonesia, capital from Japan, Taiwan, South Korea, and the United States stimulated and sustained economic growth. Such foreign investment, however, never took off in the Philippines. Seven military coup attempts against President Aquino, from 1986 to 1992, frightened away trade, aid, and investment. Thus, even after the fall of President Marcos, the democratic Aquino administration was not able to solve the nation's problems. President Aquino was not a strong enough leader to transform the democratic façade of Philippine government into democratic practice. That goal could be attained only through fundamental changes made by political leaders willing to undercut their own privileged positions.

In the 1980s and early 1990s natural calamities, including floods, hurricanes, and volcanic eruptions, devastated the islands and hampered efforts to build needed infrastructure. Such disasters added to the economic and political morass. The government's inefficient response to the crises also undermined citizen support for the system.

The Philippines is an example of a state that intervened in the economic system with ruinous results. The Philippine government critically hurt the economy through its corrupt intervention and its subservience to the traditional economic dynasties. For their part, the dynasties, with their power bases in the provinces, were often at odds with state authorities.

Domestic insurgency is another of the many problems that subverted political stability in the Philippines in the postindependence period. Although there was evidence of a decline in the number of New People's Army insurgents after President Aquino's election victory, the dire economic conditions suggested that the decline might be temporary. The armed forces managed to capture or co-opt leaders of the New People's Army, and as a result the military became more professional in such counterinsurgency activities. The decision by the Philippine Senate in 1992 to remove U.S. troops from Subic and Clark military bases deprived the insurgents of a principal point of their propaganda: the claim that the Philippine government was a lackey of "imperialist America." Nonetheless insurgency could rise again in the face of economic decline and administrative incompetence.

Still another cause of domestic instability in the Philippines was the excessive administrative centralization of government, which crushed entrepreneurial and creative efforts by the citizenry. The oversized bureaucracy strangled every area it controlled, including such basic services as electricity, water, garbage collection, telecommunications, police protection, and education.

The Ramos Presidency

Fidel Ramos was elected president in May 1992. Like Aquino, he faced the ubiquitous corruption that undercut the legitimacy of every postindependence government. Waiting for the propitious moment to intervene was the army, whose commitment to professionalism and civilian rule was nominal.

In his campaign against six other major candidates for president, Ramos won only 24 percent of the vote. Many of the supporters of losing candidates believed that Ramos was elected through fraud. Six weeks elapsed before a final vote tabulation was announced; the interval provided numerous opportunities for cheating. Moreover, because Ramos's party supporters in the Senate and House constituted a small minority, there was little chance that a coherent program could be enacted. The new president lacked charisma that would help lift the spirit of Filipinos and mobilize them to enact fundamental changes. Furthermore, Ramos did not have the loyal backing of the factionalized armed forces.

Thus after the 1992 elections the chances for needed reform were not good. To pull the Philippines out of its predicament, Ramos needed to reform the economy. Reforms would mean opening the country to foreign investment, ending cronyism by basing economic decisions on merit, eliminating corruption, and creating a workable tax system. The nation's infrastructure, especially the production of power, needed to be overhauled to end the constant electrical brownouts that sapped industrial output. State-owned enterprises needed to be privatized.

Politically, the new president had to modernize the bureaucracy, decentralize decision making, and find ways to make the dynastic families contribute to the nation's best interests. He also needed to reinvigorate ties with the United States, which had deteriorated following rejection of the Military Base Agreement by the Philippine Senate. U.S. aid programs were greatly reduced, and only a diplomat of middle rank (the director of the Peace Corps) was sent to attend Ramos's inauguration. Without support from abroad, the massive problems of the Philippines could not be solved.

See also *Asia, Southeast; Magsaysay, Ramón.*

Clark D. Neher

BIBLIOGRAPHY

Bonner, Raymond. *Waltzing with a Dictator.* New York: Times Books, 1987.

De Guzman, Raul P., and Mila A. Reforma, eds. *Government and Politics of the Philippines.* Singapore: Oxford University Press, 1988.

Greene, Fred, ed. *The Philippine Bases: Negotiating for the Future.* New York: Council on Foreign Relations, 1988.

Hawes, Gary. *The Philippine State and the Marcos Regime: The Politics of Export.* Ithaca, N.Y.: Cornell University Press, 1987.

Johnson, Bryan. *The Four Days of Courage.* New York: Free Press, 1987.

Kerkvliet, Benedict. *Everyday Politics in the Philippines.* Berkeley: University of California Press, 1990.

Kessler, Richard J. *Rebellion and Repression in the Philippines.* New Haven and London: Yale University Press, 1989.

Lande, Carl H. *Rebuilding a Nation: Philippine Challenges and American Policy.* Washington, D.C.: Washington Institute, 1987.

Steinberg, David Joel. *The Philippines: A Singular and Plural Place.* 2d ed. Boulder, Colo.: Westview Press, 1990.

Wurfel, David. *Filipino Politics: Development and Decay.* Ithaca, N.Y.: Cornell University Press, 1988.

Plato

Greek philosopher whose thirty-five dialogues provide the foundation for much of Western philosophy. Born into the Athenian aristocracy, Plato (427–347 B.C.) was expected to pursue a political career. Instead, he withdrew from politics to write his dialogues and founded, about 385 B.C., the Academy, a center for education for young men from all over Greece.

Plato's dialogues often demonstrate a hostility to the Athenian democracy that executed his teacher, Socrates, in 399 B.C. Plato portrays democracy as dependent on the changeable opinions of the many, rather than on the certain knowledge of the philosopher who through the study of dialectic has seen what Plato calls the "forms," the true and unchanging nature of things. In a famous parable from the *Republic,* Plato has Socrates compare the city to a ship whose owner, a large but slightly deaf man, is controlled by those who know nothing about piloting the ship. The "true pilot" who understands the seasons and knows the stars is called a stargazer and is considered useless. Also in the *Republic* Socrates describes how democracy corrupts the young, who see and are influenced by the echoing praise and blame conferred by the assemblies of the many.

In the categories of regimes developed in the *Republic,* Socrates places democracy as the second worst regime, right before tyranny. He caricatures democracy, portraying it as a regime of license and equality where all can do as they wish and no distinctions are made between slaves and freemen, between men and women. It is, however, the only regime in which it would be possible to find a philosopher like Socrates.

In the *Statesman,* Plato presents democracy as the best of the lawless regimes. Because democracy is able to do nothing great, whether good or bad, it causes the least harm if it is without restraint; if orderly, it is the worst, while monarchy is the best when "yoked" by good rules. In Plato's final work, the *Laws,* an Athenian stranger in conversation with a Spartan and Cretan offers a constitution for what he calls a "second best" regime. Its laws incorporate elements of Athenian democracy but always with an emphasis on moderation and limitations.

See also *Classical Greece and Rome; Theory, Ancient.*

Arlene W. Saxonhouse

Pluralism

See *Multiethnic democracy*

Poland

A country with a population of 38 million located in East Central Europe. Poland's twentieth-century history is

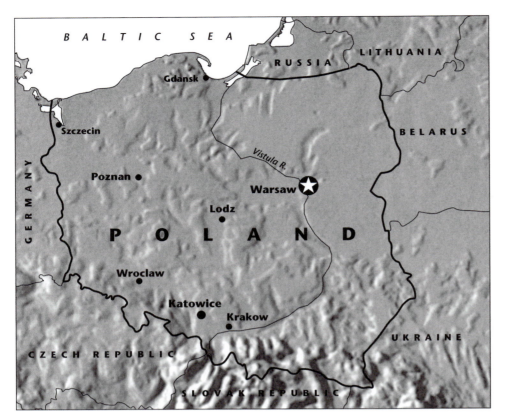

a fascinating case for students of democratization and regime change.

The experiences of the Second Republic (1918–1939) provide a crucial reference point for understanding the country's subsequent development. Poland had been an independent nation-state prior to 1795, when it was divided by the Russian, Prussian, and Austrian empires. After World War I, it was reborn on November 11, 1918, as an independent country with national boundaries contested by its neighbors. At this time, Poland had no state administration or civil service, no parliament, and no constitution or legal system. It was a country without an army, police, national currency, or economic and financial institutions. Its territory comprised three sharply disparate regions inherited from the partitioning powers. The new state faced the enormous task of integrating its peoples as well as its political and economic institutions under the adverse conditions of war and economic disruption.

By 1921, after a series of military confrontations, including a war with the Soviet Union, Poland's borders were established. The country emerged with a Polish ma-jority accounting for roughly 70 percent of the population and sizable Ukrainian, Jewish, Belorussian, and German minorities. Its predominantly agricultural economy was plagued by a multitude of problems common to economically underdeveloped countries: rural poverty, overpopulation, industrial underdevelopment, undercapitalization, and low productivity.

Poland Between the World Wars

The new state was founded as a parliamentary republic; its political elites strongly supported constitutional democracy and broad political participation. The first elections were held in 1919, and a party system comprising a large number of parties from the extreme left to the extreme right developed, reflecting the fragmentation of Polish society. (By 1926 there were twenty-six Polish and thirty-three ethnic-minority parties.) In March 1921 Poland adopted a genuinely democratic constitution that envisioned universal suffrage and a parliamentary system based on the French model.

The country, however, experienced persistent political

instability. The electoral system, which was based on proportional representation, produced political fragmentation and a rapid succession of weak coalition governments. The parliamentary regime lasted until May 1926, when a military coup led by Marshal Józef Piłsudski shifted the locus of power away from representative institutions. The parliament continued to function, elections continued to be held, and opposition to the regime continued to be expressed openly by political parties, trade unions, and the press. Nonetheless, Poland became an increasingly authoritarian state dominated by the bureaucratic political class and the military. The state's powers were expanded in the new constitution adopted in 1935. The Polish regime, however, was not a formal dictatorship, nor was it fascist in its leanings.

The failure to consolidate democracy in the interwar period can be attributed in part to a hostile international environment. Lack of support from Western democracies, claims to Polish territory from Nazi Germany and Soviet Russia, as well as the deteriorating economic situation caused by the Great Depression, all took their toll. Within Poland escalating ethnic conflicts, failed land reform and social distress in the countryside, unemployment in the cities, and political divisions within the elites affected the political situation profoundly.

Despite these inimical conditions and obvious political, economic, and social failures, the achievements of the Second Republic were impressive. Poland was transformed into a unified, modern nation-state with an efficient civil service, a stable legal system, a well-trained army, functioning representative institutions, a free press, and nationwide political parties. During this period an integrated national economy was created. Successful fiscal reforms were instituted, and the state's industrial policies were effective in developing and modernizing many branches of industry in the 1930s. Moreover, a new system of education from elementary schools to universities reduced illiteracy drastically, produced highly educated professional elites, and stimulated a remarkable explosion of cultural and academic creativity.

World War II and the Communist Takeover

The Second Republic was destroyed by Nazi Germany and Soviet Russia in September 1939. The Polish state and its social structure were completely obliterated: the country's political and educational institutions were destroyed, its political parties and civil organizations banned, its in-

tellectual elites scattered and annihilated, and its economy ruined. Poland remained under direct foreign military occupation until 1945, and major military campaigns took place on its territory. During six years of occupation, Poland did not collaborate with Nazi Germany; it had a well-organized resistance movement directed by a government in exile in London, and Polish military units fought against the Germans on most Allied fronts.

During the war, 6 million Polish citizens (of a prewar population of 35.1 million) died or were exterminated, including 3 million Jews who perished as a result of Hitler's "final solution." The wartime German and Soviet deportation programs affected some 3 million people, and the postwar transfer of population—brought about as a result of shifting national borders—affected still more Poles. The devastation of war created favorable preconditions for the coming communist takeover.

Poland's postwar fate was decided by victorious powers at three wartime conferences, held at Tehran, Yalta, and Potsdam. At the end of the war, Poland was liberated and occupied by the Soviet army. Despite Allied promises, a democratic system was not restored. Free political competition was never permitted. Control passed from the German to the Soviet army and then on July 22, 1944, to the Soviet-imposed provisional government (the Polish Committee for National Liberation). The committee ceded the country's eastern provinces to the Soviet Union in exchange for the former German territories east from the Oder-Neisse line. Following the wartime extermination of the Jews, the deportation of Germans, and loss of territories inhabited by Ukrainians and Belorussians, the population of Poland became ethnically homogeneous and overwhelmingly Roman Catholic for the first time.

The committee swiftly set up a civil administration, enacted land reform, and initiated the nationalization of industries. Under the umbrella of the Soviet army, the Polish Communist Party, which in July 1944 had 20,000 members, gained control of key levers of power and unleashed political repression that soon destroyed all resistance. Such actions presented Western powers with a fait accompli and pushed Poland irrevocably into the Soviet sphere of influence. By mid-1946 Communists were firmly in control of the country and held a national referendum to legitimize their policies of nationalization and land reform. The referendum was followed by parliamentary elections in 1947. As a result of intimidation, fraud, and the disenfranchisement of 2 million voters, the communist-led Democratic Bloc won 417 seats while the only surviving opposition, the Polish Peasants' Party, received 27 seats.

Within a few months of the elections, the opposition leader, Stanislaw Mikolajczyk, fled the country, legal political opposition ceased to exist, and all independent organizations were eliminated. By 1948 the consolidation of the communist regime was complete. The Communist Party became a mass organization with an exclusive monopoly of power, the security police established an overwhelming presence, the economy was nationalized, a central planning mechanism was introduced, and forced industrialization policies were implemented. Trade unions became a means of labor control, the independent press was banned, and social life was guided and controlled by mass organizations. Relations with the West were severely restricted. The new institutional status quo was codified in the 1952 constitution, and Poland became a closed society ruled by a Soviet-dependent regime.

Communist Rule

Yet communist rule in Poland had its distinctive features as well. Even when Joseph Stalin's power was at its height, communist practices were less brutal in Poland than elsewhere in Eastern Europe. The Catholic Church was treated more tolerantly, agriculture was not collectivized, and condemned communist officials were not executed. The Stalinist period in Poland ended in 1956, following a bloodily suppressed workers' revolt in Poznan and a dramatic change in the party leadership in October of the same year. Wladyslaw Gomulka, who had been prosecuted during the Stalinist period for alleged nationalist inclinations, became the party's first secretary.

The controlled de-Stalinization reconstituted Poland's political elite, ended discriminatory trade relations with the Soviet Union, and resulted in institutional adjustments and concessions to the Catholic Church, the peasantry and artisans, the youth, and the country's intellectual and academic elites. The effort to collectivize Polish agriculture practically ended, and Poland became the only Soviet-bloc country where most of the arable land (83.7 percent in 1970 and 75.8 percent in 1979) remained in private hands. Furthermore, the private sector's share of retail trade and services remained sizable. The private sector generated a notable portion of national income (5.5 percent in 1970 and 6.0 percent in 1980) and employed nearly 1 million people by 1980. The Polish Catholic Church se-

cured its institutional independence and became a powerful and influential organization. Its place and role in Poland's social and political life was unparalleled in other state-socialist regimes.

Although these concessions and freedoms were significantly curtailed during the 1960s, the Polish government's policies never came close to the rigid ideological policies found in other state-socialist regimes. While the country's political institutions and bureaucratic command economy remained almost completely unaltered, the Gomulka regime's policies became more pragmatic.

The institutional, political, and cultural legacies of the 1956 transition made Poland the most unstable country in Eastern Europe. Political and economic failures led not only to a weakening of the party-state's political position but also to militancy among the industrial working class and lingering dissent among Polish intellectuals. Poland's workers, unlike those anywhere else in the Soviet bloc, were able to defend their standard of living through strikes and demonstrations. Students and intellectuals were also ready to voice their opposition to the party-state's policies. In March 1968 they challenged the cultural policies of Gomulka's regime and its efforts to curtail concessions made in 1956. Street demonstrations by students were followed by political repression in which liberal and revisionist groups within the party and at universities were virtually eliminated.

In December 1970 workers of the Baltic coast launched fierce protests against the state's attempt to raise the prices of consumer goods. The bloody suppression of this protest, in which 45 workers were killed and 1,200 wounded, led to the fall of the Gomulka regime. The new party leadership, headed by Edward Gierek, promised economic reforms and adopted more inclusive policies to improve relations between the party-state and society. Gierek attempted to create a socialist consumer society by importing consumer goods from the West using Western trade credits, but the policy's failure plunged the country into economic crisis.

The growing crisis provoked another workers' rebellion against price increases in 1976 and led to intense defiance on the part of intellectuals and students, anarchy in party-state institutions, the collapse of Marxist-Leninist political discourse, and the moral bankruptcy of the ruling elite. These conditions made the political structure vulnerable to an organized challenge from below. Following the 1976 workers' rebellion, open political opposition emerged centered on the Committee of Workers' Defense. Oppositional activities spread across the country and were protected by institutional resources and moral authority of the Catholic Church. The communist regime's legitimacy eroded beyond repair when Polish-born Karol Cardinal Wojtyla became Pope John Paul II in 1978. His triumphant visit to Poland in 1979 elicited mass manifestations of antiregime feelings.

In July 1980 the Polish regime attempted again to increase food prices. In response, a wave of workers' strikes spread rapidly across the country. The strikes gradually acquired a determined and organized character, and the strikers began to voice political demands. This time, the striking workers had organizational, intellectual, and material resources they had lacked in the past. Opposition groups had independent communication networks linking all segments of the population. They produced grassroots leaders and developed new political and social agendas. The church provided a powerful and independent center of authority.

The Rise of Solidarity

The triple alliance of the church, the workers, and the intelligentsia laid a firm foundation for a successful revolt against the party-state apparatus. For the first time in the postwar history of Eastern Europe, a communist party was forced to negotiate with independent organizations and to surrender control over vast areas of social and political life. As a result of agreements signed with striking workers, the independent trade union Solidarity emerged. It soon had almost 10 million members and represented a majority of Poland's work force.

Solidarity's legal existence brought fundamental changes in Poland's social and political life. The civic fervor sparked by Solidarity spread to all social groups, cities and villages, organizations, and state institutions. A new civil society emerged demanding freedom and political participation. The besieged Polish regime headed by Gen. Wojciech Jaruzelski, under pressure from the Soviet Union and other communist countries, declared martial law in December 1981 and crushed Solidarity. Polish troops entered the cities, Solidarity activists were arrested, all independent organizations were banned, and the country's borders were sealed.

In the long term, martial law did not succeed in pacifying Polish society and reimposing a Soviet-type regime. Jaruzelski's government faced international condemna-

tion and economic sanctions, which further diminished its capacity to deal with Poland's economic crisis. It was not able to destroy or co-opt political opposition and regain the modicum of legitimacy necessary to carry out effective reforms. Compromise with the opposition and limited power sharing were the only viable options for the Jaruzelski regime. In April 1989 the government and Solidarity leaders signed the historic Roundtable Agreements providing for the relegalization of Solidarity and for semifree parliamentary elections, which were scheduled for June 1989. Thus, after a turbulent decade that witnessed the rise of the mass opposition movement, its suppression, and several years of martial law, Poland became the first country in the Soviet bloc to complete a peaceful, negotiated transition of political power.

The Postcommunist Regime

In the June 1989 elections, the Solidarity movement, organized in a network of citizens committees, captured all but one of the 100 seats in the Senate (the new upper chamber of the parliament) and all 161 freely contested seats in the *Sejm* (the lower house). Solidarity-backed Tadeusz Mazowiecki was elected premier. Solidarity's victory, fundamental changes in Soviet policy toward Eastern Europe, and the subsequent collapse of other communist regimes in Eastern Europe made the pathbreaking Roundtable Agreements increasingly obsolete. In the fall of 1989 the new political elites that emerged from the Solidarity movement propelled Poland along the road to liberal democracy and a market economy by introducing a comprehensive package of political and economic reforms.

When Mazowiecki and his ministers took power, the country was near economic collapse and hyperinflation. Their reforms were designed to stabilize the economy and facilitate its transition to a market system. They freed prices, reduced subsidies to enterprises and consumers, put a ceiling on wage increases, reduced social spending and imposed budget discipline, liberalized exports and imports, made the Polish currency partially convertible, and moved rapidly to privatize state enterprises. These policies, however, unfolded in the context of a deepening economic crisis, political chaos, and disintegrating regional economic institutions. In addition, this shock therapy approach produced severe dislocations that directly affected the standard of living and employment security of the majority of the population. Industrial output fell by 24 percent in 1990, unemployment rose from zero to 15.3 percent by 1993, new social inequalities emerged, and a less comprehensive system of welfare provisions was instituted.

The population had embraced economic reform at the beginning of 1990, but as pain followed gain, public support eroded, leading once more to strikes and protests. Popular discontent also produced conflicts among the new political elites, followed by a breakdown of the political consensus that had emerged in the wake of the collapse of the communist regime. Poland's newly established democratic system faced growing popular pressure, political instability, and a significant problem of consolidation. The economic reforms, however, were quite successful. Poland was the first postcommunist country to recover from the severe economic recession that followed the crisis of 1989. After declining 11.6 percent in 1990 and 7.2 percent in 1991, Poland's gross domestic product began to increase steadily, while unemployment stabilized and real income began to rise.

Poland's Political Evolution

Following the Roundtable Agreements, Poland experienced a turbulent political evolution. It had three parliamentary elections, nine prime ministers, and seven governments between 1989 and 1995. After its political triumph, the Solidarity movement disintegrated, and former communists were returned to power in the 1993 elections. Institutionalization of the political system faced significant difficulties. Poland has failed to enact a new constitution, thus leaving many fundamental constitutional issues unresolved. Moreover, the legal situation is chaotic: many laws and regulations inherited from the communist regime are still in force, and many new laws have been introduced ad hoc in response to emerging needs and pressures.

The Polish state has retained its dominant position in the country's politics and has changed very little in its institutional dimension, although reforms introduced in 1990 led to the administrative decentralization and partial autonomy of local politics. The state's capacity to act, however, has declined; it frequently is unable to perform its functions and fulfill people's expectations. Thus, since the initial surge of public trust following the 1989 elections, the polls have registered a gradual and serious decline in the public's confidence in most state institutions, with the exception of the military and the police.

The postcommunist state is facing a serious crisis of legitimacy.

Polish electoral politics reflects the weaknesses of the emerging party system. First, the political spectrum is remarkably fragmented, with more than 200 registered political parties; the larger parties are plagued by internal conflicts, divisions, and frequent splits. This fragmentation is reinforced by an electoral system based on proportional representation. Moreover, the majority of parties, including those influential in shaping the country's politics, have a surprisingly low membership. As a result, party activities have been monopolized by a narrow political class and have concentrated heavily on national-level politics.

Second, clear and stable political cleavages have not emerged. The important cleavage between former Solidarity and former communist forces cuts across other divisions engendered by various visions of the pace and content of economic and social reforms, the relationship between the state and the church, and the definition of national interests. These cleavages blur other, typical political divisions based on ideology (right-left), region (center-periphery), and social class. From 1989 to 1995 blurred cleavages were further complicated by frequent changes in the positions and programs presented by specific parties. The low electoral participation of the people (62.7 percent in 1989, 43 percent in 1991, and 52.1 percent in 1993) may be attributed to political fragmentation and the vague positions articulated by the major parties.

Given the weaknesses of the state and party systems, civil society is becoming strong. Thousands of new organizations and movements have been formed locally and nationally. In 1993 Poland had 1,500 trade unions, of which 200 were nationwide organizations. It is not unusual for the employees of one factory or firm to be represented by more than 10 different union organizations. There are 58 churches and religious denominations with hundreds of affiliated organizations and charities. By the end of 1992 more than 2,000 nationwide voluntary associations were registered in the Warsaw District Court. This number does not include regional and local associations, which are registered by provincial courts. Moreover, there are hundreds of youth organizations, social and cultural movements, business associations, ethnic-minority organizations, and self-help societies. The number of registered foundations increased from 200 in 1989 to more than 3,500 in 1993. These numbers illustrate that civil society has recovered from four decades of communist rule with astonishing speed, strength, and intensity. Its organizations and actors play an increasingly visible and vocal role in the country's politics, often confronting both the parliament and the government.

Polish political turbulence springs from several sources. First, the Solidarity movement, which was the biggest asset of the Polish opposition, was at the same time a serious obstacle to the formation of the party system. By the spring of 1990 the Solidarity coalition had begun to unravel. Political conflicts within the coalition escalated during the summer of 1990, when Lech Walesa (president of Solidarity) challenged the Mazowiecki government for its alleged lack of determination in reforming political and economic institutions. Walesa's challenge led to an open split in the Solidarity camp. The bitter presidential election in November 1990, pitting Walesa against Mazowiecki, not only led to the irreversible collapse of the nationwide movement but also, in the view of many observers, destroyed the consensus regarding the extent, speed, and direction of political and economic transformation.

Second, changing electoral institutions and the lack of clear constitutional rules added uncertainty to the political process. The 1991 elections were held according to a strictly proportional electoral law, and a fragmented parliament was elected with twenty-nine parties holding seats. The electoral reforms instituted before the 1993 elections reduced the number of parties entering the electoral process and forced many to join in electoral coalitions. Only seven parties and coalitions won seats in the lower chamber of the parliament, leaving some important political forces unrepresented.

Third, because Poland was the pioneer in departing from communism, it faced a unique set of problems. The negotiated transition, which led to the "contractual parliament," prevented a clear break with the communist past, delaying and complicating the process. Spontaneous privatization allowed many communist officials to convert their political capital into economic wealth. Moreover, Poland's economic transformation program had no precedent. Finally, Polish society, with its legacies of collective protest and struggle, has been prone to defy the new government through such disruptive means as strikes, occupations, and demonstrations.

Poland still struggles to consolidate its democratic order. Although the return to power of former communists may raise questions about Poland's commitment to democracy, its political achievements should not be judged too harshly. Poland is a true parliamentary democracy: free and fair elections are regularly scheduled; winning parties form governments, and losing parties accept the fact of electoral defeat; and the parliament passes laws. The military is safely confined to its barracks, local governments are empowered, and the new state has granted its citizens full protection of human rights and political freedoms. The country has been free of political violence and does not have antidemocratic political forces; the commitment of all political actors to democracy is genuine.

Continued economic transformations and their cost are powerful sources of conflicts and divisions that may decisively modify the capacity of political actors and affect the consolidation of democracy. The existence of conflicts, however, does not mean that the future of democracy in Poland is in peril. The process of deconstruction of the communist regime began in 1980, or perhaps even in 1956. It is to be expected that the construction of a stable liberal democracy will also be a prolonged and often difficult process.

See also *Europe, East Central; Solidarity; Veto, Liberum; Walesa, Lech.*

Grzegorz Ekiert

BIBLIOGRAPHY

Brumberg, Abraham, ed. *Poland: Genesis of a Revolution.* New York: Random House, 1983.

Davies, Norman. *God's Playground: A History of Poland.* 2 vols. New York: Columbia University Press, 1982.

———. *Heart of Europe: A Short History of Poland.* Oxford: Oxford University Press, 1984.

Kaminski, Bartlomiej. *The Collapse of State Socialism: The Case of Poland.* Princeton: Princeton University Press, 1991.

Kersten, Krystyna. *The Establishment of Communist Rule in Poland, 1943–1948.* Berkeley: University of California Press, 1991.

Kolankiewicz, George, and Paul G. Lewis. *Poland: Politics, Economics and Society.* London: Pinter, 1988.

Kubik, Jan. *The Power of Symbols against the Symbols of Power: The Rise of Solidarity and the Fall of State Socialism in Poland.* University Park: Pennsylvania State University Press, 1994.

Leslie, R. F., ed. *The History of Poland since 1863.* Cambridge: Cambridge University Press, 1980.

Lipski, Jan Jozef. *KOR: A History of the Workers' Defense Committee in Poland, 1976–1981.* Berkeley: University of California Press, 1985.

Sachs, Jeffrey. *Poland's Jump to the Market Economy.* Cambridge, Mass., and London: MIT Press, 1993.

Police power

The power wielded by all states to enforce formal rules of conduct through legally applied coercion, or the threat of coercion. The legal codes of democracies contain limitations on police intended to ensure that police power is applied fairly and in a restrained fashion appropriate to the situation.

The meaning of the term *police* has changed over the past five centuries. The word comes from *polity,* meaning the form of government of a political body. In fifteenth-century Europe *policing* referred broadly to government's interest in matters involving life, health, and property. Order was maintained intermittently by the military, and society was largely unpoliced. In the early eighteenth century, as large modern states with clear national borders began to coalesce, policing became concerned with internal security and the prevention of public dangers. The reach of the law increased during the next several centuries, and police power came to be applied to the prevention and redress of breaches of law. At the same time, the police came to be more closely controlled by the law. In the original British model, policing was to be done by consent, and the police were to be unarmed. Citizens would accept and respect police authority; intimidation would not be necessary.

Although no simple or widely accepted definition of a democratic police exists (indeed, it is easier to define a nondemocratic police force than its opposite), all democratic police systems share the ideal that police powers are to be used according to the rule of law and not according to the whims of the ruler or the police agent. The state's power must be used in a restrained fashion and in proportion to the problem. Some means—torture and summary execution, kidnapping, and harm to a suspect's family—are prohibited in any circumstances. Other means—the use of force, the denial of liberty, and interrogation—must be applied with due process of law. In most countries, actions such as wiretapping or holding a suspect for more than a short period of time must be sanctioned by independent judicial or executive authority. Where required, force must be applied only to the degree necessary for self-defense or to ensure arrest. Punishment is delivered only after a judicial process.

Police Power in Democratic Societies

Social order has multiple sources. These include socialization of citizens to norms, a desire to have others think well of us, reciprocity, self-defense, and the design of the physical environment. Yet the importance of police power in the maintenance of social order increases with the heterogeneity and size of a society.

All industrial societies use a public police force to control crime and to maintain order (for example, by arresting offenders, mediating and arbitrating disputes, regulating traffic, and helping people in emergencies). But the conditions in which police operate, the means they use, and the ends they seek vary greatly between democratic and nondemocratic societies.

In a democratic society the police are subject to the rule of law, rather than to the wishes of a powerful leader or party; they are empowered to intervene in the lives of citizens only in limited and carefully controlled circumstances; and they are publicly accountable. Although the idea of a democratic police includes content as well as procedure, it is easier to specify democratic procedures than democratic content. But at the most general level, content involves respect for the dignity of the person and the ideas associated with universal citizenship, limits on the power of the state to intrude into private lives, and public accountability.

Because the power of the police to use force and to deprive citizens of their liberty offers great temptations for abuse, law enforcement requires a delicate balancing act. The conflicts between liberty and order receive their purest expression in considerations of democratic policing.

It is ironic that police are both a major support and a major threat to a democratic society. When police operate under the rule of law, they may protect democracy by their example of respect for the law and by suppressing crime. But if divorced from the rule of law and public accountability, the police power to use force, engage in summary punishment, use covert surveillance, and stop, search, and arrest citizens can be used to support dictatorial regimes and practices. The toppling of such regimes is invariably accompanied by calls for the elimination of the secret police. The term *police state,* as represented by Germany under National Socialism and the Soviet Union under communism, suggests the opposite of a democratic state. In such regimes the police were subservient to a single party, not a legislature or judiciary. The policing of crime and politics merged, and political nonconformity and dissent became crimes.

In a democratic society, police must not be a law unto themselves. In spite of strong pressures and temptations to the contrary, they must not act in an explicitly political fashion, nor serve the partisan interests of the party in power or the party they would like to see in power. Their purpose must not be to enforce political conformity. Holding unpopular beliefs or behaving in unconventional, yet legal, ways is not adequate cause for interfering with a citizen's liberty. When opponents of democracy operate within the law, police have an obligation to protect their rights as well as the rights of others.

In an important sense a democratic police is a neutral police. For example, police are not to take sides in a racial or labor disturbance, nor should they spy on or disrupt the legal actions of an opposition political party.

Democratic societies strive for equality in law enforcement. Police should be trained to treat citizens equally. Their personal attitudes must not affect their behavior. Police show neutrality if they simply enforce the rules regardless of the characteristics of the persons or group involved (for example, their race, social class, or sex).

But apart from this ideal, there is a sense in which police should not be neutral. They are agents of a particular state and should enforce the laws of that state. To those who disagree with those laws, police actions will not appear neutral because they are applied on behalf of the regime in power. This is one reason why even in a democratic society police are likely to be much more controversial than other agencies of government.

Varieties of and Supports for a Democratic Police

The question of what practices are most conducive to a democratic police (for example, the degree of centralization of the force, the extent of specialization, whether oversight is internal or external, the degree of closeness to the citizenry, and the extent of discretion) has long been the subject of heated debate among democratic theorists. But it is clear that a democratic police can take many forms.

The ideal of a democratic police is supported by a variety of organizational means. These include (1) division of labor among those who investigate, arrest, try, and punish; (2) a military-like bureaucratic structure that limits discretion and promotes accountability; (3) the separation of police from the military and the creation of competing

police agencies; (4) independent agencies (and compartmentalized parts of the organization) that monitor police behavior and that must give permission for certain highly intrusive actions; (5) identification of police (for example, through the use of uniforms with names or identification numbers and clearly marked cars, or, in the case of undercover police whose identity is hidden, a courtroom trial in which police deception is publicly revealed and judged); and (6) rotation of assignments. Such measures reflect the belief that liberty is more likely to be protected if power is diffused, if competing agencies watch each other, and if police actions are visible.

Given the potential for abuse of police power, police forces in democratic societies face numerous external and internal controls. In the United States police are in principle bound by federal and state constitutions, statutes, and common law. Courts attempt to control police behavior by excluding illegally gathered evidence. Underlying this practice is a belief that it is less evil for some criminals to escape than for the government to resort to dubious or illegal practices. Courts may also issue injunctions against particular police actions and may offer citizens compensation for violations. Prosecutors may play a role in police supervision, a practice that is more widespread in Europe. Prosecutors may refuse to accept cases that the police present and may prosecute police for criminal violations. Legislative bodies—through the passage of laws, control over appropriations, the ratification of appointments, and oversight hearings—may also exercise control. Executive branch authorities, such as governors, mayors and city managers, agency heads, police commissions, citizen review boards, and auditors and "ombudsmen" perform similar oversight functions. Police forces seek to exercise self-control through selection, training, procedures, guidelines, and supervision.

In characterizing a given system, we must look beyond formal documents and expressed ideals to actual behavior. For example, in the Soviet Union citizens enjoyed, in principle, many of the same political rights as in the United States. In practice, those rights were routinely denied by the secret police, the KGB, particularly in matters of political conformity.

On the other hand, undemocratic police behavior will occur even in democratic systems. Police organizations in the United States and Western Europe are not without occasional lapses. Unlawful searches and seizures, unrestrained political surveillance, inappropriate use of force, abuse of power for personal gain, and discrimination in law enforcement occur but are concealed because they are contrary to official policy.

Community Policing

The idea of community policing, which gained prominence in the United States after 1980, represents a break with the universalistic, professional-bureaucratic, and technical policing model that sought to separate police from the community in the interest of neutrality and efficiency. This model focused on making arrests after a crime occurred. In contrast, community policing seeks to immerse police into a locality (for example, by having officers walk beats in specific neighborhoods rather than patrol larger areas in cars). Police are encouraged to view themselves as community advocates and to be problem-solving partners with local citizens. They attempt to anticipate community needs and problems and intervene to solve them (for example, by helping potential criminals find jobs or lobbying for lights in a city park). According to the community policing model, police should be generalists rather than specialists, and their organization should be decentralized.

Community policing is an explicit effort to create a more democratic police force. It is based on the assumption that policing will be more effective if it has the support of, and input from, the community and if it recognizes the social-service and order-maintenance aspects of the police role. Of course, this effort can involve sticky issues such as what constitutes a community and how tensions between professional expertise and citizen participation can be resolved—not to mention the danger of police being captured by a segment of the community.

A related development is the spread of private police. In the United States private police outnumber public police, and the gap is widening. This increase raises important questions for democracy. On the one hand, private police can serve as a check on public police. They may also contribute to a more orderly society. Yet they may also undermine democracy. When a basic need such as security is treated as a commodity, the poor are clearly at a disadvantage. Permitting only agents of the state operating under law to use coercion can increase societal equity. The first goal of private police is to serve their employer rather than justice or the public at large. Much of the activity of private police involves informal action and is not subject to judicial review. Private forces are generally subject to far less stringent controls than are public police. They may also enter into questionable alliances, carrying out illegal or unethical actions for public police.

New Threats to a Democratic Police

To do their job effectively, many police believe that they cannot know too much about the community, and they dare not know too little. With their special powers, police (along with the military) represent a much greater potential threat to democratic regimes and practices than do other government agencies such as those concerned with education or welfare. The potential for abuse is ever present. Democratic policing should be viewed as a process, not simply as an outcome.

Guarding against the misuse of physical coercion by the police is an important task of a democratic society. Another task is preventing the "softer" forms of unwarranted surveillance and manipulative control made possible by new technologies. Because these forms are often subtle, indirect, and invisible, preventing them has become an especially difficult task.

To assess the security of democratic freedoms in light of yesterday's technical standards can result in narrow vision and unwarranted optimism. Powerful new technologies that can silently and invisibly pierce boundaries of distance, darkness, time, and economic and physical barriers may encourage police to become less democratic in their behavior. New technologies for the extraction of information make possible significant intrusions on liberty, privacy, and autonomy, even in an ostensibly noncoercive environment with democratic procedures and institutions firmly entrenched.

Video surveillance, computer dossiers, and various forms of biological and electronic monitoring may make police more efficient. Powerful computer data bases that analyze crime patterns may help solve crimes and locate perpetrators. New forms of identification involving DNA or computerized fingerprinting may help convict the guilty and protect the innocent. These technologies may also help to control police. For example, police accountability might be enhanced if all police encounters with citizens were videotaped. Videotapes could serve as a deterrent to misbehavior and offer a new form of evidence in disputed accounts (although it might also mean a more passive police hesitant to innovate or take risks). However, there is no guarantee that the enhancements of police power offered by new technologies will be used to protect rather than to undermine democracy, particularly when they are so subtle.

A democratic society must ask itself, "How efficient do we want police to be?" Democratic societies, which traditionally have been willing to sacrifice a degree of order in the interest of maintaining or increasing liberty, nevertheless experience a constant tension between the desire for order and the desire for liberty. Both are essential, for it is not possible to have a free society without a minimum of order. Democratic policing seeks to avoid the extremes of anarchy and repression.

In an open, democratic society that respects the dignity of the individual and values voluntarism and the nonviolent resolution of conflicts, police, even when they are operating normally, are an anomaly. They are charged with using undemocratic means to obtain democratic ends. Police offer an ethical and moral paradox that will forever make democratic citizens uncomfortable.

Restrictions on police are not a sufficient guarantee of freedom. Taken to the extreme, they may even guarantee its opposite, if private interests reign unchecked or citizens take the law into their own hands. Yet a police whose power is excessive is also a danger. Abraham Lincoln believed that a government must not be too strong for the liberties of its people or too weak to maintain its own existence. There is a paradox in the fact that a democratic society needs protection both by police and from police. On a broader scale, this is one of the major challenges of democratic government.

See also *Accountability of public officials; Human rights; Judicial systems; Justice, Theories of.*

Gary T. Marx

BIBLIOGRAPHY

Bayley, David H. *Patterns of Policing: A Comparative International Analysis.* New Brunswick, N.J.: Rutgers University Press, 1985.

Berkeley, George. *The Democratic Policeman.* Boston: Beacon Press, 1969.

Bittner, Egan. *The Functions of Police in Modern Society.* Cambridge, Mass.: Oelgeschlager, Gunn and Hain, 1980.

Chapman, Brian. *Police State.* New York: Macmillan, 1970.

Donner, Frank J. *The Age of Surveillance.* New York: Knopf, 1980.

Marx, Gary T. *Undercover: Police Surveillance in America.* Berkeley: University of California Press, 1988.

Muir, William Ker. *Police: Streetcorner Politicians.* Chicago: University of Chicago Press, 1977.

Shelley, Louise. *Policing Soviet Society: The Evolution of State Control.* New York: Routledge, 1994.

Silver, A. "The Demand for Order in Civil Society: A Review of Some Themes in the History of Urban Crime, Police, and Riots." In *The Police,* edited by David J. Bordua. New York: Wiley, 1969.

Skolnik, Jerome H., and James J. Fyfe. *Above the Law: Police and the Excessive Use of Force.* New York: Free Press, 1993.

Policy, Implementation of

Implementation of policy is the translation of the laws, money, and other resources of government into actual programs of service. The term *implementation* came into common usage in the field of political science during the 1970s. Although the term is a new one, the fundamental idea underlying implementation is not novel at all. At its simplest, implementation is the practical expression of the intended goals of legislation. Many times these goals are not achieved, which raises the question of why government programs do not work as they were meant to. What would make it possible for governments to reach their goals more often, and more easily? Implementation is essential to a functioning democracy. If the laws passed through a democratic process do not go into action, the democracy may be meaningless.

Generally, the achievement of these goals is considered a problem of public administration, and the principal reason for the failure of programs is thought to be the common pathological behaviors of bureaucratic organizations. Interpreting the intentions of the framers of legislation and dealing with the multiple goals often sought through a single piece of legislation, however, can pose many problems for the administrative organizations charged with implementation. Such organizations are placed in the position of having to define the operational goals of a program and then having to evaluate the achievement of these goals rather than of the goals that the legislature may have been thinking about when it formulated the program. Implementation places the organizations of the public bureaucracy in a central place in democracy. Rather than being simply administrative, they are the link between politics and the public.

The problem of implementation is more than a simple matter of public management; it is also a central question for democratic governance. If governments cannot produce effective action when they hold office, the public is likely to become dissatisfied with those governments and look for alternatives. Even if governments are able to reach their goals, doing so in an excessively expensive, oppressive, or intrusive manner is also unlikely to be popular with their citizens. Thus, in democracies, it is of concern not only whether the goals of the legislation are reached but also how they are reached. Governments and administrative bodies must be aware of the political, administrative, and ethical implications of the choices they make in their implementation of programs.

Not all policy failures are necessarily a function of implementation failures, however. Many programs are designed so poorly by the legislators that they cannot possibly reach their goals, or their goals are so contradictory and ambiguous that inevitably the program can be only partially successful. Also, the success of one program may depend on the existence and success of other programs, especially in complex policy areas like social policy. Therefore, the basic design of programs, and of families of programs, is as central to the effectiveness of the programs as is the manner of implementation.

There are a variety of ways to think about implementation. Three important ways are identification of the barriers to implementation, consideration of implementation from the top down, and consideration of it from the bottom up.

Identification of the Barriers

The oldest and most common way to think about the problem of implementation amounts to enumerating and categorizing all the things that can go wrong in the implementation of a program. Any number of political, managerial, and technical reasons can be brought forth as to why governments do not always function as expected. Identification of these barriers can help implementers avoid potential pitfalls. It can also serve as the essential basis for making decisions about the way to implement a program.

One of the most important barriers to implementation, as well as a potential source of assistance, is the multiorganizational networks that surround any policy area. Some of the members of these networks are interest groups, and some are other government organizations. An organization has a better chance of implementing a policy effectively if it can gain the cooperation of the other actors who have some interest in the policy area. For example, a health program can be better implemented if the medical care providers, social service agencies, and nutrition agencies cooperate.

The Top-Down Perspective

The basic premise of the top-down perspective is that implementation involves the translation of law into the action that was intended by the legislators who framed that law. The success or failure of implementation must therefore be judged from the top down: if actions do not conform to the intentions of the framers, the process has been a failure. In 1973, two scholars, Jeffrey Pressman and Aaron Wildavsky, pointed to the existence of "clearance points" between the writing of the law and the desired action. In the case of the specific program being studied, they found some seventy separate and distinct clearance points at which a decision had to be made that would determine whether action would be taken in an appropriate manner or not.

Even if there were a high probability of success at each clearance point, the need to gain agreement at each point would mean that the overall probability of programmatic success would be quite low. Subsequently, it was pointed out that this analysis assumed that each of the clearance points was independent, whereas a committed politician or administrator could improve the chance of success by packing decisions together or generating a bandwagon effect. Even then, however, the complex networks through which programs must be implemented mean that there are a large number of points at which programs can fail.

In the top-down perspective, any deviation from the intentions of the legislators—whether by inaction or by actions other than those intended—represents a failure of the implementation process. This perspective establishes high standards for the proper conduct of policy implementation, but these may be the only meaningful standards, given that the more evolutionary concepts contained in the bottom-up perspective offer no means of judging whether the process has been a success or not.

The Bottom-Up Perspective

The multiorganizational character of implementation is even more important from the bottom-up perspective. This perspective is composed of two distinct, but complementary, views of policy-making processes. Both reject the legalistic basis of the top-down perspective in favor of a more behavioral view of how the process actually functions. Both have important implications for the understanding of democracy.

One of the bottom-up views of implementation is based on the discretionary power of the lowest echelons of public organizations. Laws are not self-executing; rather, the civil servants in direct contact with the public make countless decisions about such matters as who should be arrested, who should receive benefits, and who should be fined for violating environmental or safety regulations. Thus to understand implementation is to understand the basis on which these government employees make their decisions.

The multiorganizational networks that are responsible for putting laws into effect form the second component of the bottom-up perspective. Although the law may assign the responsibility for implementing programs to a single organization, the success of any one program involves effective coordination with other programs and organizations with similar purposes and target populations.

In this view, to understand implementation requires a comprehension of the interconnections within these emergent structures of programs, sometimes called *implementation structures*. Further, the interconnections that matter are at the lowest levels of the organizations. The interactions of those who actually provide services to clients are perceived to be crucial to the success of any program.

The two parts of the bottom-up perspective began as descriptive interpretations of the implementation process, but the descriptions can turn into prescriptions. If implementation outcomes are so determined by what occurs at the lowest levels of organizations, and by their interconnections with other organizations, it would make sense to design implementation around that level of organization. This orientation has been labeled *backward mapping*. According to this view, if a program is to be effective it is best structured by understanding the values and routines of the lower echelons of the organization(s) and then working backward to determine what the program should look like. This approach appears logical, but it could lead to governments becoming locked into a conservative pattern of doing what is easiest rather than attempting to do what is really needed by the population. Also, contrary to democratic values, the individuals who implement the laws, rather than the elected representatives of the public who debate and vote on them, would become the principal policymakers.

The Implementers

It would be easy to assume that implementation is entirely a function of public organizations, and more particularly that it is the responsibility of public organizations of the government that enacted the legislation being implemented. This simple linear notion is often true in practice, but, increasingly, implementation is conducted through nongovernmental or quasi-governmental organizations. The widespread use of nongovernmental actors increases the importance of multiorganizational aspects of implementation, since it necessitates interaction between the public and private sectors—and often among multiple organizations in both sectors.

Even within the public sector, implementation is often performed through a lower echelon of government than that which adopted the legislation. For example, in Germany the federal government implements very few of its own laws, depending on the state governments for implementation. Likewise, the European Union relies on the member countries to implement almost all of its laws.

The increasing reliance on organizations that have little or no role in the formulation of legislation, and that may have motives (profit, for example) that are quite different from those of the original framers, presents real difficulties for the people in government who want to see laws implemented as they were planned. The use of organizations outside government, especially private and for-profit organizations, for implementation grew rapidly during the 1980s. This growth was due in part to the denigration of the public sector and especially the public bureaucracy common at that time. It was believed that nongovernmental organizations could implement programs better and more cheaply than could the public bureaucracy.

Private organizations often have been as effective as, and less expensive than, public organizations in providing some simple mechanical functions of government—for example, custodial services in public buildings—but they have proved substantially less useful in the discretionary activities of government. Private organizations appear to be good at writing and distributing benefit checks but not very good in deciding eligibility for those checks. Indeed, many recent scandals concerning program implementation have arisen from the behavior of private contractors rather than from the behavior of public officials. The problems encountered with third-party implementation usually do not include blatant corruption, however. More often they concern the differences in goals among organizations and the general lack of a public purpose in nongovernmental organizations.

However, the direct employment of a government organization is far from a guarantee of successful implementation. The common practice of using subnational governments to implement central government programs tends to exacerbate the implementation problems inherent in any policy area. Not only may the policy goals and priorities of the subnational agencies differ from those of the central government organizations that initiated the programs, but their partisan composition may also differ. Such differences may be especially important in countries like Germany or Australia, which have parliamentary governments at both the federal and state levels. With that form of government there is a need to enforce relatively tight political accountability for programs so that subnational governments do not impose their own values on policies. Conflicts also occur within the United States, where, for example, during the administrations of Presidents Ronald Reagan and George Bush in the 1980s and early 1990s state and city governments were fighting with Washington over the interpretation of programs, especially social programs. Of course, variations in policy implementation are generally considered less significant in a federal system than they would be in a unitary regime such as France.

Even within a unitary government, organizational structure may exacerbate some problems of implementation. For example, in Sweden and increasingly in the United Kingdom and the Netherlands, programs are implemented through agencies that are relatively autonomous from the ministries that decide on policy. This organizational autonomy raises the possibility of differing interpretations of legislation and, as a result, outcomes that differ markedly from those intended by the framers of the legislation. Agencies within the cabinet departments of the federal government in the United States also have substantial autonomy in implementing policy, so substantial variations in policy may emerge even within the same department.

Implementation and Democracy

Although democracy is often thought of primarily in terms of the input side of government—including voting and elections and interest group contacts with government—the outputs of government are also crucial for defining the meaning of democracy. If the popular voice as expressed through elections and the legislature is consistently thwarted once the program begins to be implemented, voting may become rather meaningless. Some slippage between legislative intent and administrative action is almost inevitable, and allowing some latitude for administrators may actually improve implementation. The question becomes, then, to what extent is that latitude thought of as a necessary evil—a means to the end of gaining compliance—and to what extent is it seen as a desirable means to redefine the original meaning of the legislation?

The bottom-up perspective on implementation raises some of the classic questions about democracy. In particular, the question of how administrators can be held accountable for their actions to the legislature and ultimately to the voters becomes central. Increasing concern with what may be called discursive democracy and with other means of mass participation in public decisions provides a more direct interpretation of the meaning of democracy than do traditional models of parliamentary accountability. If, however, it is assumed that policy can, and should, be made at the lowest echelons of the public bureaucracy, the question of accountability becomes moot. The only mode of accountability that makes sense in that context is the personal moral accountability of the individuals making decisions at the bottom of the organizations.

See also *Accountability of public officials; Bureaucracy.*

B. Guy Peters

BIBLIOGRAPHY

Bardach, Eugene, and Robert A. Kagan. *Going by the Book: The Problem of Regulatory Unreasonableness.* Philadelphia: Temple University Press, 1982.

Bowen, E. "The Pressman-Wildavsky Paradox." *Journal of Public Policy* 2 (February 1982): 1–22.

Elmore, R. F. "Backward Mapping: Implementation Research and Policy Decision." In *Studying Implementation,* edited by Walter Williams. Chatham, N.J.: Chatham House, 1982.

Hjern, B., and D. O. Porter. "Implementation Structures: A New Unit of Administrative Analysis." *Organization Studies* 2 (1981): 211–224.

Hogwood, Brian W., and B. Guy Peters. *The Pathology of Public Policy.* Oxford and New York: Oxford University Press, 1981.

Hood, Christopher, and G. F. Schuppert, eds. *Delivering Public Services in Western Europe.* London: Sage Publications, 1988.

Kettl, Donald F. *Government by Proxy: (Mis?)Managing Federal Programs.* Washington, D.C.: CQ Press, 1988.

Milward, H. B., and G. L. Walmsley. "Policy Subsystems, Networks, and the Tools of Public Management." In *Policy Implementation in Federal and Unitary Systems,* edited by K. Hanf and T. A. J. Toonen. Dordrecht: M. Nijhoff, 1985.

O'Toole, L. "Policy Recommendations for Multi-Actor Implementation: An Assessment of the Field." *Journal of Public Policy* 6 (May 1986): 181–210.

Pressman, Jeffrey L., and Aaron Wildavsky. *Implementation.* Berkeley: University of California Press, 1973.

Political alienation

A feeling of separation from or nonconnectedness with a political system, or active hostility toward it. The concept of alienation has a long intellectual history, entering social science through Karl Marx's early writings. Marx (1818–1883) believed that industrial workers were oppressed by the mode of production, "alienated" from the work process and the products of their own labor. Consequently, workers became estranged both from themselves and from other human beings.

Beginning in the mid-1960s, as political protest became an increasingly important means of political expression and participation, and many people complained of an inability to affect government policies, some social scientists began to view ideas about the alienation of industrial workers as analogous to the way in which disaffected citizens perceived their relationship to government. Terms such as *powerlessness* and *normlessness* were used to describe political attitudes—powerlessness as the inability to influence government and normlessness as a feeling that political norms had broken down or that leaders did not observe them.

In the United States the civil rights protests that began in the early 1960s were soon followed by protests against the Vietnam War. A major increase in political distrust accompanied the Watergate scandal, which began with a break-in at Democratic Party headquarters during Republican president Richard Nixon's 1972 reelection campaign.

The student protests of these years, primarily from the left, were widespread not only in the United States but also in many countries of Asia, Europe, and Latin America. University students demonstrated against student powerlessness in the face of university rigidity, but they also demonstrated about broader political issues and ideologies. The fall of several governments in different parts of the world was attributed to student activism. In May 1968 widespread protests in France, which began with student uprisings against dormitory living conditions and other university policies, ultimately led to a general strike. The effects of the strike were sufficiently powerful to threaten the government of President Charles de Gaulle.

Research on Political Alienation and Support

As academic research on political alienation increased within political science, it began to merge with two other streams of work. One grew out of "systems theory" and described the political system as an interrelated set of political actors, behaviors, and processes. In one of the most influential of these theories, David Easton argued (in 1965) that the mass public had two major roles: it made demands on political decision makers for policies and programs, and it lent support, which legitimated the policies and programs that decision makers enacted and enabled them to be implemented. Easton argued that a political system could not survive over long periods of time without such support from its citizens, for the implementation of policies would otherwise depend on coercion or on the provision of inducements in the form of policy benefits. As the costs of these escalated, ultimately a system might not have sufficient resources to carry out its policies. For example, military policy could be hindered if there were few volunteers and widespread draft evasion, and implementation of all policies would be made more difficult if there were widespread tax evasion. Easton's ideas influenced political scientists who viewed the protests of the 1960s as an important indicator of an actual or potential loss of support of U.S. government.

A second major influence on the study of political alienation arose from within public opinion research, from studies of "political trust" and "political efficacy." Political efficacy was very clearly the opposite of powerlessness, and political trust seemed more or less an antonym of normlessness. The concepts and measurement of political alienation and political support soon became merged with discussions in public opinion research of political trust, efficacy, inefficacy, futility, cynicism, and other such related terms.

From the late 1960s through the 1970s scholarly debate about the conceptualization, types, and subtypes of political alienation and support, and the ways these ideas should be measured in public opinion surveys, continued, as did research focused on the causes of these attitudes and, to a lesser extent, their consequences and implications. While researchers still continue work on the development of other measures, questions concerning political trust and political efficacy became dominant measuring instruments not only for scholarly research but also in many commercial media polls.

Political Alienation and Support in the United States

Public opinion polls in the United States show that political trust has declined markedly since the 1960s. In 1964, for example, 77 percent of white Americans and 74 percent of African Americans said that the government does what is right "just about always" or "most of the time," and 63 percent of whites and 69 percent of African Americans thought that the government was run for the benefit of all. By 1992, however, only 29 percent of whites and 26 percent of blacks thought the government did what was right that often, and only 21 percent of whites and 20 percent of blacks thought the government was run for the benefit of all. Although it is difficult to obtain reliable national estimates of political trust among other ethnic minorities because their numbers in national samples are relatively small, indications are that trust levels among Hispanic Americans, Native Americans, and particularly Asian Americans are all somewhat higher than those of African Americans and whites. In recent years the percentages of people in these groups reporting that they trust the government in Washington, D.C., have been in the high thirties to mid-forties. Generally speaking, women are slightly more likely than men to think the government can be trusted to do the right thing, but the views held by men and women on who benefits from government activities are the same.

In the United States citizens' feelings of political efficacy, like political trust, have declined during the years from the mid-1960s to the mid-1990s, although not as much. For example, in 1964, 74 percent of whites and 62 percent of African Americans disagreed with the statement that public officials don't care what people think. In 1992 only 39 percent of whites and 35 percent of blacks disagreed. In general, other minorities tend to be closer to African Americans in their sense of their own political efficacy, although Asian Americans score higher in this area than other minority ethnic groups, possibly because of their higher educational levels.

Another popular measure of political support, used primarily in commercial polls but occasionally in academic research, is a question on confidence in institutions. For example, the Gallup Poll asks: "Now I am going to read you a list of institutions in American society. Please tell me how much confidence you, yourself, have in each one—a great deal, quite a lot, some, or very little." In recent polls Americans have generally ranked political institutions lowest and the military, churches, and police highest. But the long-term trend is clear: Americans' confidence in almost all social and political institutions has declined. In 1993 only 18 percent of the public had confidence in the U.S. Congress, down from 37 percent in 1975. At the other extreme, 68 percent had confidence in the military, up from 58 percent in 1975. In 1993 the Gallup Poll added the criminal justice system to its list of institutions. In the 1993 opinion poll this was the only institution that was rated lower than the U.S. Congress. Only 17 percent of the U.S. public expressed confidence in the justice system, a strong indication of frustration over the high crime rate and the nation's inability to deal with it effectively.

As far as what these high levels of political alienation and low levels of political support imply regarding the U.S. public's attachment to the nation as a whole, some insight is provided by David Easton's proposition that there are three basic "objects," or levels, of a political system. The first is the "political authorities," the incumbents of political offices, such as members of legislative bodies or the chief executive of a nation. The second is the "political regime," a system's basic norms and values (such as beliefs in equality, freedom, individualism, achievement, or the work ethic), the "rules of the game" for making political decisions (including the basic documents of a nation, such as the U.S. Constitution), and a system's institutions, such as its parliamentary system or the U.S. Congress and the presidency (not the incumbents of these offices but the institutions themselves). Finally, Easton distinguished the "political community," the people who make up the political system and consider themselves subject to the same political decisions.

Thinking of the political system in this way, it is clearly important to understand which of these three levels people are thinking about when they respond to questions designed to measure their political trust or confidence. After all, it is relatively easy to change the political authorities, as compared with changing the political regime or community. Some scholars believe that when Americans answer in the negative ways, common since the early 1970s, they are thinking of the particular people running the government at the time. According to those who hold this view, these low levels of trust do not mean that Americans have lost faith in the broader aspects of the U.S. political system. Other scholars believe that the low levels of trust that polls have found imply at least some loss of faith in political institutions.

In a remarkable indication of loss of faith in the U.S. government, surveys by the Roper Organization found that agreement that the U.S. Congress "is about as good a representative body as is possible for a large nation to have" dropped from 44 percent of the American public in 1937 to 17 percent in 1990. Agreement that "congressmen spend more time thinking of their own political futures than they do in passing wise legislation" rose from 16 percent to 41 percent over the same time period. And, in 1993, 69 percent of Americans agreed that "the federal government creates more problems than it solves."

Some analysts argue that the U.S. Congress is a handy target of blame for a variety of social and political problems and that most Americans recognize at a deeper level that the Congress does a reasonable job in trying to resolve most problems. This interpretation is consistent with the fact that incumbent members of the U.S. Congress who stand for reelection are usually returned to office. It seems that people tend to trust their own member of Congress even though they give low marks to the body as a whole (and, implicitly, to members from other districts). Despite their apparent attachment to incumbents, however, in recent years citizens in almost half the states passed laws and amendments to state constitutions that would limit the number of terms legislators may serve. These were clearly serious attempts to change the rules of the political game. However, in May 1995 the U.S. Supreme Court held that states could not change the qualifications for members of Congress and that these state laws were therefore unconstitutional.

Despite these indications that low political trust is impinging on the regime level of the U.S. political system, questions addressing the political community level have revealed far stronger public attachment. During the early 1990s, for example, more than 90 percent of Americans declared themselves proud to be an American, considered themselves patriotic, and said they would rather live in the United States than anywhere else. Furthermore, 89 percent said that their love for their country was strong, and 79 percent said that seeing the American flag flying made them feel good. These results suggest that patriotism, loyalty, and attachment to the United States at the level of the political community remain quite high among the American public.

Political Alienation and Support in Other Countries

Levels of political trust and confidence in many other nations are similar to those in the United States or even lower. In surveys during 1993, 63 percent of Britons said their country was not going forward along the right lines, 76 percent of Italians thought that the state was functioning worse than it had five to ten years before, 70 percent of Canadians were dissatisfied with the direction of their country, 61 percent of the French public thought that things in France had a tendency to get worse, and 44 percent of the Japanese public said their country was headed in the wrong direction. In December 1992 only 15 percent of Japan's citizens thought the government could be trusted to do what is right most of the time, and 75 percent said that corruption in government was how things worked in Japan.

Nevertheless, majorities in almost all countries say they are quite proud of their nationality. In a 1981 cross-national study, 91 percent of Ireland's citizens said they were proud to be Irish nationals. Of eight other countries in this study, the Dutch had the lowest level of pride, at 60 percent, and 62 percent of Japan's public said they were proud of their nationality. In a 1985 cross-national study, 97 percent of Americans, 88 percent of Britons, 62 percent of West Germans, and 81 percent of the French reported having pride in their respective countries. Thus, while majorities in each nation express pride in their country, the extent of emotional attachment varies somewhat. That attachment is more likely to be expressed (if not necessarily to be felt) by Americans than by many other national groups among the Western democracies.

The Consequences

Why does low trust matter? In the 1960s, when political protest was rising, research showed that protesters frequently had lower trust but higher feelings of their political and personal efficacy than did nonprotesters. Now that protesters are not studied so much, it is harder to find major consequences of low trust in mass populations.

It is known, however, that people with feelings of low political efficacy are less likely to vote, which is important because a democratic nation's political system is legitimated by popular participation. In the United States the two-party system is often credited as a stabilizing political force. Although people with low trust are no less likely to vote than those with high trust, they are more likely to support third-party or minor candidates for president, such as George Wallace in 1968, John Anderson in 1980, or Ross Perot in 1992, and to vote against incumbents, particularly if the challengers present themselves as opponents of the political establishment, as Barry Goldwater did in 1964 and George McGovern did in 1972. If political trust is focused on the current political authorities, it makes sense that people with low trust are more inclined to "throw the rascals out." Low trust can therefore lead to more frequent changes in government and some tendency to weaken the established parties, possibly increasing political instability. Moreover, to the extent that campaigns revolve around issues of trust and corruption and debate is focused on which candidate is more trustworthy, citizens may become distracted from other important political issues and programs. This distraction may result in the weakening of an important function of election campaigns: to chart a policy direction for political leaders.

People with low trust are also somewhat less likely to obey government mandates, such as voluntarily paying their full measure of taxes, driving at the speed limit, complying with energy-saving measures, or taking flu vaccines or AIDS tests during national campaigns. As Easton hypothesized, low public trust can make it harder for democratic governments to carry out their policies and programs, thus making them less effective.

Demands for constitutional change to achieve policy goals may also be sought by citizens who do not trust their political leaders to implement their policy demands. Distrusting groups who feel the rules are stacked against them and who fail to achieve policy goals may turn not to compromise and continued use of normal political processes to achieve their goals but to attempts to change the "rules of the game" (regime-level changes). Demands to amend the U.S. Constitution to mandate balanced national budgets, permit prayer in schools, limit congressional terms of office, and prohibit abortion are among these sorts of proposals that were on the U.S. political agenda in the mid-1990s. This result is problematic because demands to amend basic documents such as the Constitution to include specific policy goals probably increase political divisiveness: people who oppose the policies in question are likely to feel considerably more threatened by constitutional change than by legislative action, if only because legislative action is much more easily reversed. Thus, when political distrust leads people to try to change the political regime, the consequences can be far-reaching, even leading to weakening the ties that bind together the members of the political community.

Regardless of any potential consequences of such regime changes, however, they can hardly be compared to armed or other violent actions against large populations, the quintessential behavioral expression of political alienation. In extreme cases, as political trust, efficacy, and confidence in institutions hit bottom and political alienation grows, the ultimate end can be the disintegration of the political community itself, either through civil war, widespread emigration, or generalized collapse of the political system. The collapse of the Weimar Republic and the rise of the Nazi regime in Germany in the 1930s have been interpreted in these terms, and lack of faith and trust in the political regimes of the Soviet Union, and the bloc of nations associated with it in Eastern and Central Europe, contributed at least partly to the breakdown of these political systems.

Because political alienation ultimately can have these kinds of dire consequences, the stability of every nation, democratic or not, depends in important ways on the level of trust and support among its citizens. In individual cases, political alienation can motivate horrific actions, such as the release of sarin nerve gas in the Tokyo subway and the bombing of the federal building in Oklahoma City, Oklahoma, in the spring of 1995.

Yet it is no easy matter to determine how low trust is or how high alienation is. Many personal, cultural, political, and methodological factors affect how people respond to public opinion polls. Even when similar wording is used, the interpretations given to questions by people in different countries may differ. Moreover, although public opinion affects the stability of political systems, it is not the only factor to be considered. Economic, political, social, and technological factors; political culture; world events; and the complex currents of international affairs preclude attempts to draw a simple, one-to-one relationship between political alienation and support, on the one hand, and political stability, on the other. For all of these reasons, caution must be used in interpreting the results of any public opinion polls and speculating about their implications, particularly when comparing results from different countries where social, economic, and political conditions and institutions; forms of expression; cultural understandings; and meanings of questions may be quite dissimilar.

A national public opinion poll in the Soviet Union in

November–December 1989 found that 31 percent of Soviet citizens thought the Supreme Soviet always made decisions in the interests of the people, and 34 percent thought that the Congress of People's Deputies always acted in this way. (The choices were "always," "sometimes," or "never.") A September 1989 Gallup Poll revealed that 32 percent of Americans had confidence in the U.S. Congress. Two years later, at the end of 1991, Americans' confidence in the U.S. Congress had declined to 18 percent—yet the country was about to embark on a campaign to elect its forty-second president, whereas the Soviet Union lay in ruins without ever having elected one national leader. Political alienation and political trust certainly do matter; however, the extent of democracy or the strength of a political system cannot be judged by public opinion questions alone. Nor should comparisons of public opinion in very different nations, in isolation from other fundamental considerations, be considered a meaningful basis for predicting the future of nations.

See also *Immigration; Political culture; War and civil conflict.*

Ada W. Finifter

BIBLIOGRAPHY

Bottomore, T. B. *Karl Marx: Early Writings.* New York: McGraw Hill, 1964.
Craig, Stephen C. *The Malevolent Leaders: Popular Discontent in America.* Boulder, Colo.: Westview Press, 1993.
Easton, David. *A Systems Analysis of Political Life.* New York: Wiley, 1965.
Finifter, Ada W. "Dimensions of Political Alienation." *American Political Science Review* 64 (June 1970): 389–410.
———, ed. *Alienation and the Social System.* New York: Wiley, 1972.
Finifter, Ada W., and Paul R. Abramson. "City Size and Feelings of Political Competence." *Public Opinion Quarterly* 39 (summer 1975): 189–198.
Finifter, Ada W., and Bernard M. Finifter. "Pledging Allegiance to a New Flag: Citizenship Change and Its Psychological Aftermath among American Migrants in Australia." *Canadian Review of Studies in Nationalism* 22 (1995).
Lipset, Seymour Martin, ed. *Student Politics.* New York: Basic Books, 1967.
Lipset, Seymour Martin, and William Schneider. *The Confidence Gap: Business, Labor, and Government in the Public Mind.* Rev. ed. Baltimore: Johns Hopkins University Press, 1987.
Sniderman, Paul M. *A Question of Loyalty.* Berkeley: University of California Press, 1981.

Political culture

The sum of the fundamental values, sentiments, and knowledge that give form and structure to political processes. The intellectual history of political culture is closely related to that of democratic theory. The classic study of political culture, a work that established the concept in political science, is Gabriel A. Almond and Sidney Verba's *Civic Culture* (1963). This book identifies the essential cultural and attitudinal bases for a stable democracy.

In most theories about democratic development a critical variable is the basic orientation of the culture: whether it is consistent with democratic practices or opposed to them. Moreover, theories that relate democracy to social and economic development presuppose that certain social and economic conditions will produce the psychocultural attitudes and values essential for stable democracy. Thus to understand democratic development requires some appreciation of political culture.

Political culture is distinct from the more general culture of a society in that it is more narrowly focused on the people's understanding of how power and authority operate, in principle and in actuality. Indeed, political culture sets the ground rules for the play of politics, and it establishes the shared assumptions and beliefs that are the foundations of a country's political life. In most societies there is a dual pattern of political culture: an elite culture is made up of the leadership and the active participants, and a mass culture consists of the rest of the people. A key issue in democratic development is the relationship between the elite and the mass cultures. The elite culture may be the more sophisticated, but it must still resonate to the mass culture.

Intellectual Roots

Long before the term *political culture* was coined, political theorists were exploring the political mores and norms of societies, seeking to determine especially which attitudes are essential preconditions for a stable democracy. Aristotle, for example, in the fourth century B.C. associated democracy with the values and outlook of a middle class. Montesquieu in the eighteenth century identified integrity and trustworthiness as the critical values for a democracy.

Alexis de Tocqueville, in *Democracy in America* (1835–1840), probably went furthest of the classical social theorists in spelling out the essentials of a democratic political culture. He noted that one precondition for democracy was the ability of free citizens to form associations, working together to advance their own interests while respecting the larger needs of the political system as a whole. Tocqueville furthermore recognized the danger that egalitarianism might conflict with the standards of good government, but he insisted that good government was not the same thing as popular government.

The coming together of psychology and anthropology in the development of the theory of political culture was a central feature of the scholarship of the 1940s and 1950s. World War II heightened American interest in other societies. The need to train people in a hurry to operate overseas led the military to turn to anthropology and area studies. At about the same time, anthropologists were strengthening their concepts of culture by incorporating the insights of Freudian depth psychology to explain the socialization processes by which individuals are taught how to be effective members of their culture. Personality and culture came to be seen as opposite sides of the same coin.

In the immediate postwar environment there was also great interest in national character studies. Ruth Benedict's *Chrysanthemum and the Sword* (1946) was a remarkably insightful and solid analysis of Japanese character. It was soon followed by studies of German and Russian national character. Some of these works were highly speculative; for example, Geoffrey Gorer and John Richman suggested in 1945 that primary features of Russian behavior could be traced to the practice of swaddling babies. In 1954 work on national character was thrown into question by Alex Inkeles and Daniel Levinson, who in their article "National Character" called for extremely—indeed, prohibitively—high scientific standards in the field.

Studying Political Culture

The introduction of the concept of political culture opened the way for renewed research into the psychological and cultural basis of political behavior. Instead of making the extreme jump from childhood socialization practices to elite political behavior, as those who wrote national character studies had done, those who studied political culture employed a theory of political socialization and recruitment that incorporated more mature political learning experiences and that recognized the role of the political communication process in shaping opinion. Whereas national character studies were often imaginative

in treating all aspects of popular behavior as relevant for explaining political life, the concept of political culture was focused on the specific practices of political life. The more speculative traditions of national character study evolved into a school of psychohistory in which general cultural trends were examined to explain historical developments.

Almond and Verba's comparative study of five nations (the United States, Britain, Mexico, Germany, and Italy) delineated the cultural basis of stable democracies by identifying the essential components of what they called the civic culture. They tested that concept through sample surveys in the five countries and thereby advanced a solid empirical theory about the political culture of democracy. The work was a landmark study not only because it was an early application of the sample survey method of comparative analysis but also because it identified the theoretical components of a democratic political culture.

In their theory of civic culture, Almond and Verba identified a pattern of citizens' orientations toward government and politics that included a high level of political awareness, a strong sense of competence, and considerable skill in civic cooperation, combined with rational participation in civic and political life. Almond and Verba demonstrated that a relationship existed between their concept of a civic culture and democratic stability. Their analysis of the five-nation surveys showed that Britain and the United States ranked high on the civic culture scale, while the other countries were characterized by more alienation and passivity. Some criticized the study, arguing that the civic culture concept was so closely tied to Anglo-American traditions that it was not appropriate for understanding other, equally legitimate, forms of democracy. Over time, however, experiences throughout the world have shown that almost without exception advances toward more stable democracy have in fact involved the strengthening of what Almond and Verba called a civic culture.

Studies of political culture took on added vitality in the 1960s, as they focused on the less industrialized nations and the problem of political development. The approach offered a solid basis for analyzing the prospects for nation building among the emerging states of the former colonial world. These countries were forced to combine their traditional cultural arrangements with influences from the West. Modernization challenged such countries to create transitional political cultures.

In the late 1960s and early 1970s the study of political

culture lost favor among political scientists. In part, this shift was a reaction to the Vietnam War and the popularization of radical views in some of the social sciences. Political culture was characterized as a conservative, if not a reactionary, concept by those who believed that revolutionary leaders, such as Mao Zedong in China and Fidel Castro in Cuba, were successfully transforming their societies virtually overnight. Any suggestion about the enduring power of culture was therefore seen as hostile propaganda by opponents of revolutionary change.

Political Culture and Democracy

It became obvious by the late 1970s, especially with the opening of China in the post-Mao era, that much of Chinese culture had survived the Maoist attacks on it. During the 1980s the abandonment of communism in many countries (which was to culminate in the collapse of the Soviet Union) reignited interest in questions about the relationship of political culture to democracy.

Samuel P. Huntington was a leader in the revived interest in political culture. In the 1980s and 1990s he produced important works focusing on American politics and on democratization in the world, notably *American Politics* (1981) and *The Third Wave* (1991). This revival of political culture studies briefly conflicted with the new interest in rational choice theory, a field in which the methods of economics were applied to the study of politics. Aaron Wildavsky demonstrated that the two approaches are in important respects compatible because culture determines the political preferences of individuals. Therefore rational choice theorists must look to culture to understand the goals of rational choice.

Ronald Inglehart, in *The Silent Revolution* (1975) and *Cultural Shift in Advanced Industrial Society* (1990), advanced the revival of political culture theory by demonstrating that with the rise in affluence in the Western democracies, cultural matters—such as abortion, ethnic identity, the environment, and women's rights—have come to command greater political attention, while the salience of economic class and more materialistic issues has receded. Therefore politics in postindustrial societies will increasingly revolve around cultural issues and values, not just economic interests.

Probably the most rigorous study of the connection of political culture to democracy that has yet appeared is Robert Putnam's analysis of civic traditions in Italy, *Making Democracy Work* (1993). By carefully evaluating the democratic performance of the twenty regional governments established throughout Italy in 1970, and then testing for statistical relationships involving such factors as levels of income, industrialization, urbanization, available resources, and the like, Putnam and his associates discovered that the most critical variable for explaining democratic successes was the level of development of what he called a civic community. In short, the key to making democracy work was the political culture, and more particularly the existence of attitudes not too different from those Almond and Verba included in their civic culture. Incredibly, this essential civic tradition had been part of the culture in Italy as early as the fourteenth century.

Yet countries need not have a centuries-old civic culture in place in order to democratize. Democracy comes in many forms, and the political cultures of countries that come late to democracy will produce forms of democracy that are somewhat different from those that developed in the West. For example, in East Asia, from Japan to Singapore, there has been greater emphasis upon communitarian values and less on individualism. That is to say, recent history shows that considerable national differences in political cultures can still be consistent with stable democracy. The basic values of democracy—such as belief in popular sovereignty, commitment to the equality of citizens, and respect for minority rights even as decisions go to the majority—can all be found in countries with somewhat different cultural attitudes about community and authority.

There are several other ways to classify differences among democratic political cultures. Some cultures, for example, stress hierarchy and others equality. Both the Japanese and the British political cultures tend to legitimize hierarchy, while the American political culture is more egalitarian. Attitudes toward the role of the state vary among cultures: some, like Sweden, expect extensive state intervention in citizens' affairs, including the providing of extensive public welfare; others, like the United States, idealize a minimal role for the state.

Whatever variables democratic theorists use to classify cultures, two cultural values emerge as critical for stable democracy. The first is tolerance, particularly a willingness to accept the articulation of opposing views. Tolerance must include a readiness to participate in adversarial relationships without allowing feelings of aggression to take over. People must learn to disagree without becoming disagreeable.

The second fundamental value is trust. The ability to trust others is crucial not only as a foundation for building civic associations but also for reinforcing a people's sense of political efficacy. If the people do not have a sense of efficacy—the belief that their participation is worthwhile—democracy cannot be stable. Skepticism about the integrity of leaders is acceptable as long as it does not reach the level of alienation and the end of participation. Alienation is a threat to democratic stability because it signals the end of efficacy. The danger signal for democracy—alienation—is so widely appreciated that a common tactic of dissatisfied elements is to profess alienation. That is, by threatening to break with the spirit of democracy, the dissidents hope to gain leverage.

Political Culture and Political Science

Beyond questions about the role of political culture in the establishment of stable democracies lie questions about the more general importance of the subject itself. First, does the study of political culture meet the scientific standards of political science? For that matter, how scientific is political science? Some critics charge that any talk of political cultures is simply an expression of stereotypes or prejudices about national differences. A slightly less harsh criticism is that political culture is a residual concept that is brought into play when all the "more scientific" explanations have been exhausted. Yet the model of physics, which is often upheld as the ideal of the scientific pursuit, is a rather limited version of science, and attempts to apply that approach to the social sciences often result only in proving the obvious. In fact, advances in physics generally have been characterized by imaginative speculation and hypothesizing about matters that could not yet be tested.

Applying scientific principles to the study of political culture or to other human pursuits is complicated by the uncertainties of human behavior. Paradoxically, human beings can be very predictable, in large part because of the role of purpose and intention, which have no counterpart in the physical sciences. For example, if we know the commitments and obligations of a person, we can at times make very precise predictions. If we have access to a person's daily schedule, we can predict that person's whereabouts with some accuracy. Yet knowing so much may tempt us to believe we know more—for example, about the person's goals and motivations. To an extraordinary degree both scholars and journalists write as if they knew the real purposes of political leaders. Yet the game of politicians is to mask their motives. The problem of motive or purpose exists for all political scientists, including

rational choice theorists who assume that they know the preferences and interests of those they seek to analyze.

Another challenge to the study of political culture comes from those who insist that structures, as formal or informal institutions, should have primacy in political analysis. Structure and culture are, of course, both important, and their relationship is something of a chicken-and-egg problem. Culture influences structures, and structures help shape cultures. Structures are in essence highly institutionalized behavior patterns, and behavior patterns are the products of cultural learning.

The theory of political culture is sometimes attacked because its implicit comparative focus is said to mask prejudicial criticism. The critics claim that the identification of differences is really a way of suggesting peculiarities and inferiority. Yet the political culture approach recognizes the universal qualities of humanity, even as it takes into account the rich variety of cultures and societies. Recognizing the differences between cultures is not an insult to others but an acknowledgment of their distinctiveness. Indeed, it could be argued that to declare that all peoples are exactly alike is the real insult, for it is a way of taking away their unique sense of national identity.

Along this line of argument, it should be pointed out that political culture is not a racist concept. In fact, the anthropologists who developed the powerful concept of primary socialization as the basis of culture were reacting against the racist theories of the Nazis. Basic to the whole approach of culture was an absolute denial of any role for genetic factors, including race. Instead, all cultural differences had to be explained by nurturance. The concept of culture basic to the study of political culture insists that the socialization process passes a culture from generation to generation and that there is no role for biology in that process.

Political Culture and Change

The power of culture and the continuity inherent in the socialization process raise the question of how to explain political change. Critics often say that political culture theory implies the existence of a static polity in which actions are frozen into the mold of an unchanging culture. This view puts the emphasis in the wrong place. Some cultures are static, while others are dynamic. Indeed, in some societies there is a constant imperative for change that is driven by cultural predispositions. Thus political culture can help to explain both continuity and change. Change, as it comes about, takes place in the context of the political culture. The features of the particular culture determine which changes are the most likely and which are the least likely.

There are considerable variations in analyses of political cultural. The use of sample surveys to study mass cultures, as practiced by Almond and Verba in their path-breaking study, has been continued by Inglehart and others. The survey approach is especially useful for comparative studies. Unfortunately, the cost of cross-national studies is high, especially if care is taken to ensure that a questionnaire measures the same things in different places. Therefore the number of cross-national studies has been limited.

Interpretive analysis by specialists who are knowledgeable about particular countries has become more common. In such studies the skills of the individual analyst are critical to the quality of the work. Such an approach rarely produces solid comparative work because few scholars are knowledgeable enough about several countries.

Political culture theory has become a recognized discipline, and the field has the potential to contribute to the advancement of political science. In the pursuit of viable hypotheses, scholars need to keep before them several considerations. First, hypotheses must meet the test of utility in explaining significant developments in a particular political system. Second, hypotheses should build on general theories of culture and personality as well as on comparative findings. Third, research on political culture should be sensitive to what is known about all the related aspects of culture and society in the country being studied. Although the academic world is divided into disciplines, political life in societies is never entirely separated from other aspects of social and economic life.

The perspective of culture is both broad enough to embrace the whole of society and focused enough to penetrate the subtleties of politics. Thus political culture studies can summarize the outstanding features of a political system. They can also highlight the nuances of leadership style and the distinctive subtleties of national political communications.

See also *Elites, Political; Political alienation; Psychoanalysis; Rational choice theory.*

Lucian W. Pye

BIBLIOGRAPHY

Almond, Gabriel A., and Sidney Verba. *The Civic Culture: Political Attitudes and Democracy in Five Nations.* Princeton: Princeton University Press, 1963.

Eckstein, Harry. *Regarding Politics: Essays on Political Theory, Stability, and Change.* Berkeley: University of California Press, 1992.

Huntington, Samuel P. *The Third Wave: Democratization in the Late Twentieth Century.* Norman: University of Oklahoma Press, 1991.

Inglehart, Ronald. *Cultural Shift in Advanced Industrial Society.* Princeton: Princeton University Press, 1990.

Inkeles, Alex, and Levinson, D. J. "National Character." In *Handbook of Social Psychology,* edited by Gardner Lindzey. Cambridge: Addison-Wesley, 1954.

Lipset, Seymour Martin. *Political Man: The Social Bases of Politics.* Expanded and updated ed. Baltimore: Johns Hopkins University Press, 1981; Aldershot: Gower, 1983.

Putnam, Robert. *Making Democracy Work.* Princeton: Princeton University Press, 1993.

Pye, Lucian W. *The Mandarin and the Cadre: China's Political Culture.* Ann Arbor: Center for Chinese Studies of the University of Michigan, 1988.

Thompson, Michael, Richard Ellis, and Aaron Wildavsky. *Culture Theory.* San Francisco: Westview Press, 1990.

Wildavsky, Aaron. "Choosing Preferences in Constructing Institutions: A Cultural Theory of Preferences Formation." *American Political Science Review* 81 (1987): 3–21.

Politics, Machine

Machine politics is organized, orderly activity designed to control public offices and their benefits. The word *machine* was first applied in the latter part of the nineteenth century to political organizations that emerged in the United States. Although attributes ascribed to the political machine could be ascribed to parties elsewhere, the composite came to be seen as peculiarly American.

The metaphor of the political party as a machine implied efficiency, coordination, regularity, and replaceable parts—as well as difficulty for those who did not perform according to its rules. It also implied a preoccupation with the mechanics of holding office rather than with policy. The metaphor of the party as a machine and its leader as a "boss" suited a country that stood at the forefront of the Industrial Revolution, where enterprising capitalists were taking over production by establishing machine-run factories.

Characteristics of Machine Politics

Political observers see the heyday of the "model" political machine as the period from the post–Civil War years through the 1930s. During these years throughout the country there emerged political organizations that controlled all the public offices of a particular political jurisdiction. The establishment of such an organization was often credited to an individual who might or might not hold public office. Observers associated machines mostly with local government, although some were associated with states. The list of political bosses who ran machines included William L. Tweed of Tammany Hall in New York City and Thomas C. Platt of the state of New York, Boies Penrose of Pennsylvania, Tom Pendergast of St. Louis, Frank Hague of Jersey City, and, most recently, Richard Daley of Chicago.

The machines these men operated divided the political labor among individuals, who were assigned discrete tasks in small political units or precincts that constituted the larger governmental unit. Their principal task was to ensure that within their precincts voters supported the machine's candidates for elective office. The strength of the machine rested on its ability to reward its workers with public jobs. Workers might even be expected to return a portion of their salaries to the machine. The machine's strength rested also on its ability to supply its workers with the resources to attract voters, including wide-ranging benefits from welfare to legal aid. With its control of governmental decisions on such matters as public works, zoning, and licensing, the machine could, in addition, attract financial support from business.

The two most important factors facilitating the emergence of the machine were universal male suffrage and the large number of elective public offices. The extension of the right to vote beyond an elite meant that public office seekers had to devise ways to reach out to a mass electorate. Every state and many local governments had bicameral legislatures. The independent election of state and some local executives and the indirect election of the national executive by state presidential electors increased the number of names on the ballot. Moreover, throughout the nineteenth century, in response to the democratic impulse, state and local administrators and judicial officers were added to the ballot. Thus a multitude of office seekers needed ways to reach out to a mass electorate that in turn needed help with a bewildering array of choices.

The solution for office seekers was the creation of political parties, whose activities, as a result of the federal character of the electoral system, were concentrated in the states and local communities. Electoral procedures—decisions about who could vote and the format of the ballot and determinations of where people would vote and how the ballots would be counted—were entirely state and local matters. Moreover, national legislative office was closely linked to local and state jurisdictions. For senators, the link was compelling, since they were chosen by state legislatures until 1913, when the Seventeenth Amendment, providing for the direct election of senators, was adopted. But the House of Representatives was also under strong local surveillance, and most representatives returned home after one or two terms. Even the national executive was linked to the states by the electoral college, which provided for the choice of the president by state electors. The result was decentralized party organization readily susceptible to the domination by a machine.

Party Conditions

Once party organization surfaced, the development of political machines was encouraged by the parties' control of access to the ballot in states and localities. Until the end of the nineteenth century, parties prepared and presented voters with the ballot. Preparing the ballot made it easy for the party to encourage straight party-line voting for the dozens of offices on the ballot. Even after most states took over the printing of ballots, the ballot format still allowed for straight party voting, thus favoring unified party behavior.

Another factor favoring unified party behavior was the number of public jobs and public works controlled by the local and state officials elected on partisan ballots. The disposal of public jobs made it possible to attract loyal party workers who could be expected to continue to work for party officials while on the public payroll. The power to fund public projects ranging from roads and bridges to schools and firehouses made it possible for the party machine to attract financial resources from business. Indeed, the complexity of local political jurisdictions—which included counties, cities, and townships as well as special districts for schools, water, and parks—made it useful for businesses to deal with an organization whose control might well span several jurisdictions.

Finally, the concentration of an expanding electorate in urban centers strengthened the partisan machine. During the nineteenth and early twentieth centuries waves of European immigrants filled U.S. cities along with migrants from the farms. Living in close proximity, often sharing a strong sense of group identity, these new urban dwellers could be mobilized with relative ease. They provided the votes essential to the political machine in exchange for assistance, from welfare to jobs, which they needed to adjust to their new life.

The fuel on which the political machine ran, then, was not national public policy. As long as control of national offices depended on procedures in the control of the states and localities, there was no incentive for the emergence of a national machine. The local focus of the machine was reinforced because few patronage jobs were available to national officials, including the president. Most government jobs were in state and local government. Even federal appointments became hostage to senatorial courtesy, the practice that gave senators of the president's party control over appointments in their own state.

The American two-party system that developed after the Civil War also encouraged the creation of machines at the local level, as each party demonstrated the capacity to stake out areas for its own. Once states and localities demonstrated their willingness to elect continuously only Republican or only Democratic candidates, the machine flourished. In a noncompetitive environment, where their nominees were assured of election, Republican machines prospered in Pennsylvania and Illinois, while Democratic machines did well in New York and Missouri. In the wake of the partisan realignment brought about by the New Deal after 1932, machines in such former Republican strongholds as Philadelphia and Pittsburgh followed the electorate and became Democratic, sometimes using the same personnel.

In effect, the American federal system was nurturing federal parties whose units specialized. The presidency encouraged the semblance of a national organization capable of addressing major national issues and defining national policy. On the other hand, the decentralization of most offices and their electoral procedures left the "stuff" of politics, the bread-and-butter matter of winning elections, to state and local organizations. Free of debilitating internal quarrels, endowed with the capacity to attract compliant workers and financial support as well as votes, the machine had little difficulty in conducting its activities in an orderly, businesslike manner. Not surprisingly the machine became identified with party organization in the United States.

Abuses and Criticisms

During the late nineteenth century the concept of the machine grew in importance because it offered an explanation for the poorly understood phenomenon of the political party spawned by democracy. The party was difficult to understand because it encompassed two seemingly conflicting goals. Popular elections required that candidates and the organizations that sponsored them appear interested only in the electorate's general good. At the same time, the organized effort needed to win office required that the party also serve the private ambitions of those expending the effort. From the outset of the republic the failure to grasp this inherent conflict provoked severe criticism of the notion of party. Even the Founders of American parties, Alexander Hamilton, Thomas Jefferson, and James Madison, expressed their contempt for parties, which they equated with selfish factions, while building their own machinery. Because the Founders had never observed organized efforts continuously competing for the votes of a mass electorate, their failure to appreciate the new phenomenon was understandable.

The division of labor between the national and local party that progressed after the Civil War caused observers to focus on the most tangible evidence of organized political activity. Two foreign students of American politics, James Bryce and Moisei Ostrogorski, concentrating on local organization, described the machinelike traits of the American political party. This description did nothing to improve the party's image. Their charge that the political machine was built on and maintained through the unvarnished appeal to self-interest offended those who felt that selfless concern for the public good was the only proper motive for seekers of public office. In contrast, many Americans were willing to consider self-interest the proper motive for economic pursuits.

The identification of the political machine with unvarnished self-interest was often carried a step further to the identification of the machine with corruption and fraud. Involved as machines were with the use of public jobs, contracts, and benefits to accrue votes and financial support, it was easy to make the connection. Machines often committed such corrupt acts as selling public contracts, miscounting votes, and misusing public funds for private purposes. But it should be added that officials who were not associated with machines also committed such acts. And not all machines necessarily engaged in corruption. Although the Kelly-Nash machine of Chicago in the 1930s and 1940s was reputedly corrupt, its successor, Richard Daley's machine, was not. Then, too, honest politicians could be the products of reputedly corrupt machines. Harry S. Truman, a man who came to establish a legendary reputation for public honesty, was associated with

Tom Pendergast's machine during the time it was under federal indictment for corruption.

Reforms and Decline

Although we should distinguish machine politics from outright corruption and fraud, the equation did lead to a variety of political reforms that ultimately weakened the machine. The elimination of a patronage base began with the Pendleton Act of 1883, which established a merit system for federal employees. The merit system spread slowly to state and local governments during the twentieth century. The registration of voters and the Australian or state-printed ballot, both nearly universal in the United States by 1900, were aimed at reducing voting fraud and thereby the power of the machine. So too were primary elections. Primary elections to select candidates for state offices were made mandatory in Wisconsin in 1903 and spread rapidly through most of the states for most offices. By the middle of the twentieth century they were almost universal. Primary elections took the vital decision about who would be the party's candidate for office away from the machine's easily controlled caucus or convention and gave it to the voters. Further reforms aimed at reducing the power of the machine were nonpartisan elections for local government and judicial positions and the introduction of the city manager to depoliticize local government.

For the first half of the century the machine had little difficulty in adapting to electoral reforms. Voter registration actually solved many of the problems of bookkeeping for the machine and facilitated keeping tabs on the electorate. The state-printed ballot, with its official designation of the party label, assured the regular party organization of the protection of the state, thereby weakening dissident factions. Primary elections were easy to control, given the low turnout of voters. Furthermore, primaries reinforced the areas of one-party dominance in which the machine thrived. They allowed competition to take place within parties rather than between parties during the general election. Elimination of the party label through nonpartisan elections did not reduce the ability of entrenched local organizations to control these elections.

More damaging to the machine was the expansion of the civil service. Because party leaders were less able to reward precinct workers with public jobs, the machine lost essential personnel. Although local political organizations were able to find other ways of attracting and holding workers—using union members, hiring people with funds collected by political action committees—none were as efficient as the machine's use of public employees. Court cases during the 1970s and 1980s further weakened the power of officials to discharge employees for failing to live up to political obligations.

Other changes in the political climate contributed to the decline of the machine. Of considerable importance was the alteration in competitive conditions for elective office that undermined the machine's security. From the 1950s on, one-party dominance declined, and neither party could be sure that all the offices of a particular state would remain securely in its grasp for long periods of time. The uncertainty introduced by increased competition was particularly damaging to an organization whose control depended on the ability to ensure electoral outcomes. Uncertainty intensified in the 1960s, with the one-person, one-vote decisions that provided for the regular reshaping of electoral districts.

Uncertainty went along with changes in rules that placed a more glaring spotlight on elective officeholders, making an association with the machine more a liability than an asset. These changes involved longer tenure for elective state executives and longer sessions (with higher pay) for state legislators. Such changes also affected local and county governments. In turn, the professionalization of legislative bodies meant that services that had been provided by the machines would be obtained in other ways. State legislators, as well as members of Congress, could increasingly count on paid staffs to monitor their constituencies for electoral trouble spots and to deal with constituents' problems. These staffs were supplemented by the growing number of organized interest groups willing to provide specific candidates with services formerly supplied by the machine—unions, particularly those representing public employees, and various business groups, for example. The political role of these organizations was strengthened by the attention directed at campaign financing in the 1970s. The creation of political action committees (PACs) allowed interest groups to funnel financial contributions directly to candidates.

Candidates, as well as organized interest groups, benefited from the technological revolution. Television, the computer, and the fax machine made it easy to design organizations that met the candidate's specific needs. For along with these devices emerged the specialist who could manipulate the technology to provide candidates with a continuous view of the attitudes of their own electorates and advice about which campaign techniques might win them over. In many ways the tailor-made organization was more efficient and more useful than the machine, without the machine's political liabilities.

The machine's success and its decline were therefore attributable largely to the changing ways of winning and holding on to elective offices, and to the changing needs of the machine's principal beneficiaries, elective office seekers. These beneficiaries proved able to win election and re-election with or without the machine. While the machine was prominent, observers attributed its success to the presence of an urban population, largely but not entirely composed of recent immigrants, that was dependent on the benefits supplied by the machine. Indeed, the decline of the machine paralleled the slowdown in European immigration and the emergence of New Deal welfare programs. Yet, as urban social problems reemerged after the 1960s with new waves of migration, while governmental welfare programs slowed due to budgetary constraints, the need appeared as great as ever for some organization to play the machine's reputed social role. The failure of the machine to reemerge, therefore, is better explained by changes in the needs of elective office seekers.

The strength of the machine in American politics has, in any event, always been difficult to assess because both its opponents and its supporters sought to exaggerate its strength. Reformist critics such as the muckraking journalist Lincoln Steffens claimed they could find a machine in every city. Political bosses and officeholders in turn found it useful to further the view of their own invincibility, if only to ward off competitors. Moreover, scholars have had difficulty in distinguishing machines from the orderly, disciplined political organizations that exist in some form wherever offices are to be filled. Such organizations abound, for example, in legislatures. Yet most observers agree that in the United States of the late twentieth century the model political machine, capable of controlling the range of elective offices in a city or state, is probably extinct. In his survey of party organizations in the United States conducted in 1986, David R. Mayhew concluded that "traditional" political organizations were important in eight northeastern states, along with Illinois and Indiana. Although these organizations might display some of the traits of the machine—having party workers on the public payroll, for example—few organizations, if any, were in complete control of governmental units.

If, for all intents and purposes, the machine no longer

exists, it is because the political party in a democracy will always reflect the most effective means of winning election at a particular time. The machine that flourished in American politics for nearly a century was a creature of a certain mix of institutional and electoral rules. Certainly some of the machine's traits are characteristic of all political parties in democracies—coordinated behavior to achieve public office and the use of the benefits of public office to attract loyal supporters. The distinctive characteristic of the American machine was the extent to which such traits became dominant and localized. Once the political atmosphere in the United States changed, so did the form of political organization.

See also *Ballots; Bryce, James; Civil service; Corruption; Election campaigns; Elections, Monitoring; Federalism; Government, Levels of; Ostrogorski, Moisei Yakovlevich; Parties, Political; Patronage; Spoils system.*

Joseph A. Schlesinger

BIBLIOGRAPHY

Banfield, Edward C., and James Q. Wilson. *City Politics.* Cambridge, Mass., and London: Harvard University Press, 1963.
Bryce, James. *The American Commonwealth.* New York: Macmillan, 1915.
Epstein, Leon. *Political Parties in the American Mold.* Madison: University of Wisconsin Press, 1986.
Gosnell, Harold F. *Machine Politics: Chicago Model.* 2d ed. Chicago: University of Chicago Press, 1968.
Mayhew, David R. *Placing Parties in American Politics.* Princeton: Princeton University Press, 1986.
Ostrogorski, Moisei. *Democracy and the Organization of Political Parties.* Vol. 2. Edited and abridged with an introduction by S. M. Lipset. Garden City, N.Y.: Anchor Books, 1964.
Schlesinger, Joseph A. *Political Parties and the Winning of Office.* Ann Arbor: University of Michigan Press, 1991.

Polling, Public opinion

Public opinion polling is a research method designed to understand opinions of large publics by collecting information from representative samples (also called public opinion surveys). Polling is useful for political leaders, whether democratically elected or not, to help them in understanding the opinions of those they govern. Therefore public opinion polling is increasingly popular, not only in democracies but in many other nations as well.

In democracies, public opinion polls have become a staple of mass media reporting, and public opinion about major issues often guides public policy formation. Where leaders are popularly elected, public opinion may constrain what they do. Few elected leaders want to sponsor or be associated with policies that attract very little public support or widespread opposition; they are more likely to back policies with high public approval. Polls provide the information such leaders need. Dependence on polling has become so widespread that candidates occasionally make a point of not using them; they may label their opponents mere followers of the latest poll and themselves as true leaders because they do not "follow the polls." Much more often, however, especially in the United States, candidates at all levels rely on polls to help them understand what their electorates are concerned about.

On the other hand, some argue that public opinion may be manipulated by the mass media and by political, economic, religious, and other elites to achieve their own ends. The issues emphasized in the media, and the slants taken, may influence which issues the public cares about and how the public evaluates those issues. If (or when) this occurs, public opinion may reflect, rather than determine, elite actions. Others point out that in a poll the public can respond only to issues as formulated by the poll takers and that voting, protests, and activities of public interest groups may be more valid indicators than polls of public opinion—especially the opinions of that part of the public that cares enough to participate in some way.

In most democracies, polling reaches a peak during election campaigns. In the United States, for example, just before a presidential election, polls sponsored by the mass media are reported daily. Polls announcing "winner" and "loser" are reported immediately after each presidential debate. Such "instant" polls have been facilitated by the advent of computer-assisted telephone interviewing, in which telephone interviews are conducted from a central location. Interviewers enter responses directly into networked computers, thus permitting the immediate and constant updating of results. Nevertheless, instant or overnight polls may be misleading: it is difficult to get a representative sample when there is no time for repeated calls to people whose telephone numbers fall into the sample but who do not answer at the time of the first call.

Concern that elections will be influenced by poll outcomes has led some nations to take preventive steps, ranging from forbidding the publication of polls during the week before an election (France) to voluntary news blackouts of polls conducted on election day until all voting places are closed (the United States).

Methods

In addition to rigorous sampling methods designed to increase the probability that the sample selected is representative of the population of interest (after all, it is the population in which we are interested, not the sample), there are many other methodological requirements for a good poll. Methodology includes the construction of the sample, determination of how respondents are contacted (by telephone or in person), wording of the questions, placement of the questions within the interview, determination of the refusal rate, and so on. Every aspect of the methodology can affect the findings.

Polling reports are frequently accompanied by a measure of sampling error—an estimate of the difference between the "true" value in the population and the value in the sample. For example, if 54 percent of a national sample of 2,500 cases approves of the job the president is doing, and the sampling error is plus or minus ($\pm$) 3 percent at the 95 percent level of confidence, there is only a 5 percent chance that the population percentage is smaller than 51 percent or larger than 57 percent. This figure depends on the sampling having been done correctly and refers only to probable error due to sampling. Errors introduced by other methodological problems are not included in sampling error. Although there are few practical ways to estimate the error caused by these other factors, reputable researchers are well aware of the problems and take steps to minimize them or adjust their results for them.

Many newspapers and television stations persist in using the term *poll* or *survey* for a simple call-in tally. Because anyone who wants to call in can do so (that is, the sample is self-selected), one cannot know how representative such a "sample" is. Any results obtained through this technique are worthless as an indication of general public opinion.

Development and Implications

Many pioneers of public opinion polling—Louis Harris, Burns Roper, Hadley Cantril—made significant contributions to the field, but none is so identified with the development of political polling as George H. Gallup. Gallup's first public opinion poll during a national election took place in the United States in 1936. By publishing his public opinion analyses in syndicated newspaper columns, Gallup played a major role in popularizing the public opinion poll. The company he founded remains the world's preeminent commercial polling organization, with branches in many countries. (Indeed, as newer, indigenous polling organizations form around the world, their founders are frequently called the Gallups of their nations.)

Polling is now conducted in every developed nation of the world and in most developing nations. Even in China there are social and political polls, although they do not receive much media publicity; most polls in China are conducted for marketing purposes. In the nations of the former Soviet Union, polling has increased dramatically, and polls are reported frequently in the press and on television. Interestingly, in both China and Russia, refusal rates are reported to be much lower than in the United States—probably because polling is more of a novelty and people have relatively fewer ways to express their opinions. In countries without well-developed forums for public input, polls can provide a valuable informal means of expression.

In democracies, polls can provide elected officials with feedback from the public between elections. Even if political elites do affect public opinion, as long as there are competing elites—one of the criteria of democracy—polls are an important and valid way for public opinion to be expressed.

See also *Accountability of public officials; Media, Mass; Political alienation; Public opinion.*

Ada W. Finifter

BIBLIOGRAPHY

Asher, Herbert. *Polling and the Public: What Every Citizen Should Know.* 3d ed. Washington, D.C.: CQ Press, 1995.

Brehm, John. *The Phantom Respondents: Opinion Surveys and Political Representation.* Ann Arbor: University of Michigan Press, 1993.

Cantril, Albert H. *The Opinion Connection: Polling, Politics, and the Press.* Washington, D.C.: CQ Press, 1991.

Lavrakas, Paul J., and Jack K. Holley, eds. *Polling and Presidential Election Coverage.* Newbury Park, Calif.: Sage Publications, 1991.

Mann, Thomas E., and Gary R. Often, eds. *Media Polls in American Politics.* Washington, D.C.: Brookings Institution, 1992.

Margolis, Michael, and Gary A. Mauser, eds. *Manipulating Public Opinion: Essays on Public Opinion as a Dependent Variable.* Pacific Grove, Calif.: Brooks/Cole, 1989.

Martin, L. John, ed. "Polling and the Democratic Consensus." Special issue. *Annals of the American Academy of Political and Social Science* 472 (March 1984).

Polyarchy

A form of government in which there is broad political participation, the right of political opposition, free elections, and control of public policy by elected officials. The word *polyarchy* (literally, "rule by many") has existed in English since at least 1609 but was seldom used before World War II. The term came into more general usage among political scientists and sociologists after the 1953 publication of Robert Dahl and Charles Lindblom's *Politics, Economics, and Welfare,* which used *polyarchy* rather than *democracy* so that it would be possible to analyze and compare real-world "democracies" without implying that such countries fulfilled all the numerous and inconsistent ideals associated with democracy. Although *polyarchy* has not replaced *democracy* even among scholars, it remains the most rigorously defined and analyzed alternative concept and is frequently used by those who wish to clarify that they are speaking of political democracy as it is practiced by actual states rather than democracy as an ideal.

Dahl and Lindblom first described polyarchy as a process through which nonleaders exercised control over leaders. Dahl continued to refine the concept in his work over the next forty years, culminating in *Democracy and Its Critics* (1989), which offered an exhaustive justification of the democratic process and of polyarchy as the best feasible approximation of it in large communities. The essential definition of polyarchy, however, changed little after the publication of Dahl's *Polyarchy* (1971), which examined the historical, social, economic, and cultural conditions for stable polyarchy.

Polyarchy exists when the following conditions are met: (1) only elected officials have the constitutional authority to control public policy; (2) free, fair, and frequent elections are the exclusive means for selecting these officials; (3) the suffrage is extended to practically all adults; (4) practically all voters are eligible to run for public office; (5) the right of citizens to express their political opinions on even the most fundamental issues is protected; (6) citizens are guaranteed access to sources of information that do not reflect official biases; and (7) citizens have the right to form political parties, interest groups, and other relatively independent associations.

Countries that satisfy these requirements well are polyarchies, but countries can also be said to be more or less polyarchic, or even hardly polyarchic at all. Degrees of polyarchy vary along two dimensions. One is what Dahl called public contestation, or the degree to which elections, freedom of association and expression, and access to alternative sources of information combine to guarantee the right to oppose the government effectively. These practices form a single dimension because they tend to vary together: the greater the freedom of expression, the greater the freedom of association, the diversity of the media, and the fairness of elections. The second dimension of polyarchy is breadth of participation, which varies independently of public contestation. For example, countries that hold fair elections do not necessarily allow everyone to vote in them, as was the case in South Africa before 1994. As suffrage restrictions have become increasingly rare in elections, contestation has become the more relevant dimension for comparisons.

Contrast with Democracy

Polyarchy is a narrower concept than democracy, and necessarily so, for the ideals of democracy originated in a broad variety of historical periods and cultures. Some of the ideals are legacies of ancient Athens and other small city-states, which have all but disappeared. Some are derived from republican Rome and its laws. Others build on experience with parliaments and other institutions with roots in a predemocratic era. Still others are purely theoretical ideas about political equality. No synthesis could possibly iron out all the inconsistencies inherited from these diverse traditions. Rather than attempt such a comprehensive synthesis, Dahl proposed his own selective synthesis of the characteristics of a fully democratic process. In his view, a democratic process would provide for voting equality, effective participation, an enlightened understanding of the issues, control of the agenda by the voters, and inclusion of all adults who are compelled to obey the law. Certain ideals associated with the broader democratic tradition are not therefore included in the idea of democracy that polyarchy is said to approximate, much less in polyarchy itself.

For example, polyarchy does not share the Athenian belief in a natural social harmony that would allow the democratic process to attain "the common good." This belief has proved to be unrealistic in larger and more diverse communities. Polyarchy makes a virtue of this inevitable diversity: groups that were once despised as factions are now valued as the components of competitive party systems and pluralism.

Pluralism (the existence of many relatively autonomous associations), however, creates a dilemma in a polyarchy. On the one hand, pluralism is an inevitable and desirable consequence of freedom of association and is therefore an indispensable feature of polyarchy. On the other hand, if these associations gain too much autonomy from government control, they may reinforce social inequalities, undermine identification with the larger community, manipulate the public agenda for their own benefit, or usurp the government's authority to make policy on certain issues.

In addition, unlike some concepts of democracy, polyarchy derives its moral justification from its institutions and procedures rather than from any particular substantive outcome, whether it is justice, efficiency, growth, or socioeconomic equality. Dahl reasoned that because there has never been a consensus about which goal should be made a higher priority than democracy, any decision to establish such a priority would have to be made in a political process, and the legitimacy of that decision then would depend on the nature of the process through which the decision was to be made. When moving from abstract ideals to practical realities, all questions of substance ultimately involve questions of procedure. For this reason, polyarchy is considered a type of procedural democracy.

Polyarchy does not, however, prescribe any specific political institutions, procedures, or rules beyond the seven listed earlier. Polyarchies may be presidential or parliamentary, unitary or federal. They may allow judicial review or prohibit it; hold referendums or not; and elect representatives by majority, plurality, or proportional rules. In fact, Dahl concluded that not even majority rule was required for polyarchy to exist. Specific institutions can affect how polyarchic a country is, but it is not possible to state which of these institutions are best for a given country without knowing its history and other characteristics. Nor does polyarchy provide any guidance on where to draw the borders of the country or whom to include in it: the parameters of the country must be established according to some criterion other than polyarchy.

Standards of Democracy

The narrow criteria for the fully democratic process proposed by Dahl could be perfectly realized only in a rather small community in which all members participated directly in decision making and in which wealth, information, education, and other political resources were distributed equally. No polyarchy has ever lived up to these strict standards. Neither did ancient Athens, where most of the adult population (women, slaves, and resident foreigners) were denied citizenship and attendance at meetings was far from perfect. Contemporary "democracies" are merely polyarchies, which approximate the ideals of democracy in certain respects.

For example, the ancient Greeks, as well as the eighteenth-century French philosopher Jean-Jacques Rousseau, believed that the direct participation of the members of the community in decision making and even administration was essential to democracy. The logistics of participation therefore limited the size of the community to no more than a few thousand members. This ideal had to be abandoned when communities grew to include large territories and millions of citizens. It was no longer feasible to assemble all citizens in one place and permit everyone to take part in a debate, so most citizens had to be content to elect representatives who would debate and make policy for them. Polyarchy can be understood as the result of attempts to adapt the institutions of the large modern state to the ideals of democracy by instituting representation, broadening the suffrage, making elections fair, holding executives and legislators accountable to voters, and guaranteeing rights to free expression and association.

Dahl argued that increasing support for the notion of universal rights partially compensated for the loss of many opportunities for direct participation. Nevertheless, the drastic compromises that were made in order to accommodate the shift in scale should not be minimized. Dahl lamented the inadequacy of polyarchy as a substitute for direct, small-scale democracy.

Justifications and Conditions

Although polyarchy is a rather low standard for democracy compared with the ideal, polyarchies do provide some minimal civil liberties and make it difficult for a government to carry out extremely unpopular policies over a long period of time. While far from perfect, polyarchies are the closest approximations of democracy in the modern world. Moreover, it is possible that some polyarchies will eventually become better approximations of democracy. Dahl speculated that further democratization could occur if governing units became smaller, political resources (wealth, education, access to information) were distributed more equally, or nondemocratic institutions, such as the workplace, were run more democratically.

Dahl also argued that polyarchy was superior to the two major alternatives, anarchy and guardianship. Anarchy is appealing because it promises complete respect for each individual's autonomy, but Dahl considered the condition a practical impossibility, on the grounds that sooner or later some groups would impose statelike control over everyone else. If states are inevitable, he reasoned, they should be the best states possible. "Guardians" from Plato in ancient Athens to Mao Zedong in twentieth-century China, who have claimed superior competence in the art of governing, have offered seductive alternatives to the imperfect polyarchies of the world, but Dahl argued that actual regimes should not be compared with imaginary ones. In a fair comparison, ideal democracy is superior to ideal guardianship, and polyarchy is superior to actual nondemocratic forms of rule, which can be brutal.

With all its flaws, polyarchy is still a difficult standard to attain. There were 67 polyarchies or near polyarchies among the world's 186 countries as of 1993, according to the rating criteria developed by Michael Coppedge and Wolfgang Reinicke (in "Measuring Polyarchy," 1990). These included the countries of Western Europe, the United States, Canada, Australia, New Zealand, Cyprus, India, Israel, and Japan; the Baltic states, Slovenia, and the Czech Republic; most of the Caribbean and Latin America; six Pacific microstates; and Benin, Botswana, Cape Verde, Gambia, Madagascar, Malawi, Mauritius, Namibia, Papua New Guinea, the Philippines, São Tomé and Principe, and the Solomon Islands. Most measures of democracy produce similar lists.

Polyarchy is not necessarily limited to countries. In principle, organizations ranging from neighborhood associations to a world government could be considered polyarchies if they satisfy all seven criteria. In practice, however, the term is almost always applied to government at the national level.

There is no single set of conditions that has been proved invariably to lead to polyarchy. Certain conditions, however, are believed to make stable polyarchy more likely in the long run. Among these are the gradual expansion of participation in a competitive oligarchy, a high level of economic development, a pluralistic social order, and an elite subculture in which there is an atmosphere of trust and cooperation and strong support for political democracy.

In developing countries, culture was often greatly influenced by a former colonial power. Countries that experience revolutions or win independence in a violent war are less likely to possess these favorable conditions. Gross social and economic inequalities, concentrations of wealth or military force, and deep and mutually reinforcing religious and ethnic cleavages are also thought to make polyarchy less likely, although deep social cleavages have sometimes been bridged by elites committed to power sharing and consultation. Intervention by foreign powers has furthered polyarchy in some cases and destroyed it in others. Some countries have become polyarchies for short periods of time without having many of these conditions in their favor.

See also *Classical Greece and Rome; Critiques of democracy; Dahl, Robert A.; Elite theory; Justifications for democracy; Theory, Postwar Anglo-American; Theory, Twentieth-century European; Types of democracy.*

Michael J. Coppedge

BIBLIOGRAPHY

Coppedge, Michael, and Wolfgang Reinicke. "Measuring Polyarchy." *Studies in Comparative International Development* 25 (spring 1990): 51–72.

Dahl, Robert A. *Democracy and Its Critics.* New Haven and London: Yale University Press, 1989.

———. *Dilemmas of Pluralist Democracy: Autonomy vs. Control.* New Haven and London: Yale University Press, 1982.

———. *Polyarchy: Participation and Opposition.* New Haven and London: Yale University Press, 1971.

———. "Polyarchy, Pluralism, and Scale." *Scandinavian Political Studies* 7 (December 1984): 225–241.

———. *A Preface to Democratic Theory.* Chicago: University of Chicago Press, 1956.

Dahl, Robert A., and Charles E. Lindblom. *Politics, Economics, and Welfare.* New York: Harper and Row, 1953.

Popper, Karl

British philosopher of science. Sir Karl Popper (1902–1994) made influential contributions to the theory of democracy. All of his work is informed by the belief that truth and freedom are concomitant and must be protected from the perils of tyranny.

Born in Vienna, Austria, Popper fortuitously took up an appointment as lecturer at Canterbury College, New Zealand, in time to escape the overrunning of his native land by the Nazis. On hearing of Hitler's invasion of Austria he resolved to write *The Open Society and Its Enemies* (1945), which set forth his analysis of, and opposition to,

Karl Popper

political tyranny. This two-volume scholarly critique of the enemies of democratic freedom drew on Popper's preceding work in the philosophy of science. At the end of World War II, Popper moved to England, where he taught at the London School of Economics until his retirement in 1969. He was knighted in 1965. Diverging from the two prevailing intellectual trends, logical positivism and language philosophy, Popper sought to demarcate science from pseudosciences by advocating a "critical-rationalist" methodology.

The linchpin of Popper's methodology is his famous rebuttal of inductivism using the principle of "falsification." First highlighted by eighteenth-century philosopher David Hume, the problem of induction undermines the claim that science stands on a secure empirical footing. The problem is easily understood: no matter how many times we have witnessed an event or occurrence in the past, we cannot conclude that in the future it must occur in the same way. To use Popper's own example, no matter how many white swans we have observed, we cannot, on the basis of this experience, claim that all swans are white. Popper's dismissal of this fundamental problem is brilliant and beguiling in its simplicity. Although no quantity of evidence can ever conclusively verify a claim, argued

Popper, just one contradictory piece of evidence can prove it false. (One observation of a black swan proves beyond doubt that not all swans are white.) Falsification, rather than verification, provides science with a secure footing.

Popper saw science as a series of conjectures open to future refutation. Progress is achieved by discovering, for certain, what is untrue. Science is demarcated from disciplines having scientific pretensions by the phrasing of conjectures that are open to refutation.

Much Marxist political theory—although, in Popper's view, not necessarily Marx's own work—cannot be considered a true science because it cannot be falsified by empirical evidence. Popper's seminal critique of Marxism, clearly informed by his own disillusionment with the prewar Austrian left, contains two more significant arguments. These are, first, that because we cannot predict what our future scientific knowledge will be (if we could, we would already know it), we cannot predict the future course of history; and, second, that history unfolds as a unique series of events, so there are no true laws of sociohistorical evolution. Any political theory based on laws of historical change must therefore be erroneous.

Popper's opposition to the notion of inevitable laws of history—a school of thinking he termed "historicism"—was buttressed by his views on the nature of human beings. He viewed humans as problem solvers and saw social evolution as fueled by this human propensity. The continual attempts to resolve problems give rise, however, to unforeseen and unintended consequences, which present us with new opportunities and new, unanticipated problems.

The "open society" is Popper's conception of how society should be organized so as to protect the freedom of the individual. Such a society must be a pluralistic democracy in which criticism can be voiced freely with the expectation that it will be given due weight. Politicians must be alert to the unintended consequences of their policies and programs and should be prepared to modify or abandon a course of political action if events falsify their expectations. Policy should be directed not toward maximizing happiness, a notoriously difficult objective, but toward minimizing avoidable suffering. Policy should be formed and pursued in small, clearly stated stages so that the "falsifiable" premises of policy can be tested.

The converse, the "closed society," is best exemplified by the Stalinist state, wherein state officials, secure in the knowledge that their political position was fundamentally correct and confident that they could discern the laws of social evolution, brooked no criticism of their policies.

Because the state could never be proved wrong, those voicing criticism could be regarded as in some way at fault and in need of "reeducation" or punishment.

In Popper's eyes, democracy is preferable not because the majority is entitled to rule but because, in a democracy, it is possible to dismiss bad or incompetent rulers. Democracy is simply a label given to the arrangement of social institutions that allows for the dismissal of bad rulers without bloodshed and without threat to the persistence of those institutions. This justification helped Popper overcome the "paradox of sovereignty" posed by a democratic society in which the majority chooses to be ruled by a dictator. For Popper, if the sovereignty of freedom is threatened from any quarter, the citizen has the right and duty to resist and to protect those democratic institutions, which stand as a bulwark against tyranny. Furthermore, the state must intervene if the freedom of individuals is threatened by the economic system.

Popper emphasized the need to protect the freedom of the individual and the individual's capacity to voice effective criticism. The strength of his contributions to democratic theory derives from their unique philosophical underpinning and from the clarity, coherence, and elegance of his ideas.

John Mattausch

BIBLIOGRAPHY

Popper, Karl. *Conjectures and Refutations: Growth of Scientific Knowledge.* London: Routledge, 1972.
———. *The Open Society and Its Enemies.* 5th ed. 2 vols. London: Routledge, 1966.
———. *The Poverty of Historicism.* London: Routledge, 1972.
———. *Unended Quest: An Intellectual Autobiography.* Glasgow: Fontana, 1981; London: Routledge, 1992.
———. *A World of Propensities.* Bristol: Thoemmes Press, 1990.

Popular sovereignty

The principle that government must be authorized by the people. The concept of popular sovereignty is fundamental to any conception of democratic government and to the history of American democracy in particular. The formula of the American Declaration of Independence (1776)—that governments derive power from the consent of the governed and that the people can alter or abolish their government for cause—heralded the coming of democracy in the American colonies and eventually throughout the contemporary world. For example, in the 1850s popular sovereignty was the central issue in the debates between Stephen A. Douglas and Abraham Lincoln over the extension of slavery to new states of the union. More recently appeals to popular sovereignty played a major role in populist movements in the German Democratic Republic in 1989, when demonstrators—chanting "we are the people"—challenged their communist government.

Although popular sovereignty clearly assigns the ultimate authority to the people, the concept is inconclusive as to exactly how this government by the people is to be realized. Douglas argued, for example, that it should be left to the people of a territory on the verge of statehood to decide whether they wanted their state to be slaveholding or free. Lincoln, however, declared that spreading slavery to new territories was a matter of concern to the whole nation. Aside from their obvious differences on the moral issues of introducing slavery to Nebraska, Douglas wanted to leave the decision to the consent of Nebraska voters, while Lincoln preferred that the issue be decided by the consent of all Americans of the Union, presumably through their representatives in the Congress.

Questions Raised by Popular Sovereignty

Just as popular sovereignty does not specify whether to seek the consent of local or regional people, or of the nation, or even of the whole world, it is vague or silent on all the other instrumentalities of modern popular government. It does not even answer the question clearly whether the people should determine only the basic form and mission of government—for example by ratifying a written constitution—or whether their consent is also required for the government's policies or the appointments of its leaders. Some early advocates of popular sovereignty, for example, the twelfth-century English cleric and scholar John of Salisbury, believed that the power of a medieval monarch was conferred fundamentally by the people and that kings were somehow kept in line by the people and the clergy. But these advocates shied away from granting the people the right to rebel against a tyrannical king or queen, to dismiss high government officials, or to change the old monarchic order itself.

The principle of popular sovereignty also leaves open to conflicting interpretations the question of whether an elected president or a British-style parliamentary government is more likely to ensure government by consent. The American-style system separates the powers between an elected president and an elected congress. Many knowledgeable observers view these competing popular mandates as an invitation to irresponsibility or gridlock. Parliamentary government, on the other hand, clearly removes the selection of executive officers and governmental policies a notable degree from the direct influence of the people and leaves it to the elected legislators. The choice between the two also raises questions about the usefulness to popular government of strong parties and a bipolar party system (preferable to a multiparty system) that may empower the voters by presenting distinctive alternatives in leaders and policies rather than the almost indistinguishable choices of the U.S. party system.

Popular control in the era of complex modern industrial societies obviously requires heavy reliance on intermediary organizations such as political parties, interest groups, and the media. However, none of these have yet been subdued reliably, if at all, to serving the popular will and not just their own purposes. Although there is almost universal agreement that the popular will must be delegated to representatives rather than exercised directly, the principle of popular sovereignty is mute as to exactly how these representatives are to be chosen, by what type of electoral law, for what offices, and for how long. Most significantly, the popular principle by itself does not resolve the question of how far even popularly legitimated rule should be permitted to intervene into the rights and interests of individuals.

Evolution of Popular Government

The idea of popular government has evolved through a long historical process of secularization and differentiation. For the peoples of European antiquity and even the Middle Ages, functions of politics and government were rarely as clearly discernible and separate from social and spiritual life as they have become in the past two centuries. Consequently, even though one can find many quotations of thinkers and writers relating to the people as an important source of legitimate authority, these statements were either largely descriptive of a rather undifferentiated and unreflected social reality enshrouded in tradition and religious beliefs, or they were detached from any practical consideration of how one might enable the people to rule.

Greek historians and medieval writers often described

settings of apparent power sharing in which hereditary elites, and sometimes religious establishments, habitually deferred to the popular sentiments without giving the people any formal leverage, except perhaps in major crises or breakdowns of authority. In the sixth through fourth centuries B.C., Greek city-state democracy—such as it was, with its small scale and the presence of large slave and foreign resident populations—had notions of popular sovereignty, even though the Greek concept of citizenship was vague and undeveloped. Aristotle's *Politics*, for example, defines democratic freedom only as the right to rule and be ruled in turn. Aristotle did not advocate democracy, though he distinguished it from other kinds of regimes, such as monarchy and oligarchy (rule by the few). A rapidly changing setting of economic transformation and political crisis in his day marked Greek democracy as the least stable form of government unless it was "mixed" with strong elements of oligarchic or monarchic rule. In the midst of what Plato described as the tensions between the poor and the rich, popular government was bound to be associated with unruly and anarchic mob rule rather than with an institutionalized process of constitutional democracy.

Roman civilization in the republican era, which lasted from about 500 B.C. until 44 B.C., was much closer to the institutional and legal formulas that might give practical significance to notions of popular sovereignty, but there seemed to be little interest in popular rule. Instead, a strong tradition of law and shared governance between the aristocratic Senate and the popular tribunes evolved. With the arrival of imperial absolutism, under Julius Caesar and his successors, popularly legitimated law became an empty shell, its authority usurped by senatorial and imperial decrees without popular sanction. The rise of the absolute authority of emperors and of the rapidly expanding empire swallowed up the republican concern, for example, of the Roman orator Cicero (106–43 B.C.) with creating a well-ordered republic and with its common virtues. Cicero's references to popular sovereignty, like the Athenian leader Pericles' praise of democracy in his funeral oration (431 B.C.) on the first soldiers killed in the Peloponnesian War (reported by Thucydides), were expressions of nostalgia rather than prescriptions for practical political action.

The revival and reinterpretation of important Roman legal concepts in the Middle Ages, nevertheless, helped the idea of popular sovereignty to an unexpected renaissance amid the restraints of religious faith, customary law, and feudalism. The Roman Catholic Church, with its great councils that represented the priesthood, contributed by its example the most distinctive instrument of the secular popular governments of the future—namely, representative government and clear notions of who was being represented and against whom. Feudalism and custom further sharpened ideas of rights and privileges, at first only of lords and corporate bodies, but this precedent provided a basis for future development of all individual rights. Some city republics of the Italian Renaissance experimented with forms of government that would give the ultimate power of lawmaking to "weightier" members of the citizenry of the town. Marsilius of Padua, in his *Defender of Peace* (1324), supplied the theory behind this principle. Thus many of the conceptual prerequisites for the practical realization of popular sovereignty were beginning to emerge from the Middle Ages and the Renaissance, even though their practice was limited to feudal parliaments, courts, and occasional French or Italian examples of municipal self-government or the ancient town meetings of some Swiss cantons.

The Victory of the British Parliament

What was still missing for popular government to come into its own was a widespread sense of the emancipation of the individual from the fetters of religion and traditional social bonds. Massive social and political upheavals in the sixteenth, seventeenth, and eighteenth centuries accomplished this liberation. Thus self-governing individuals, now many in number, granted popular consent to a government that itself had become a secular state, differentiated from religious authority and social control and increasingly abstract in its own authority. One of the harbingers of this great change was the emergence of a democratic political theory espoused by agrarian defenders of the English village commons against the wave of enclosures of common land in the seventeenth century. The Diggers and Levellers not only argued for the birthright of the lower classes against greedy landowners but they struggled for a kind of constitutional convention and solemn enactment that would keep kings and parliaments from taking away the rights of the people. Their protests were to little avail in the midst of the civil wars between king and Parliament but, along with the other political theories generated by that turbulent century, they set the stage for the American and French Revolutions of the eighteenth century.

The great struggle between the kings of England

(James I and Charles I) and Parliament was fought in the battlefields and resulted in the establishment of a kingless commonwealth under a supreme, elected Parliament. The latter, consisting of nobles and the merchant classes, was not elected by all the people. Nevertheless it clearly derived its authority from this fact of "popular election," and a number of the most distinguished political philosophers of that age drew their conclusions from the signal defeat of the divine-rights claims of the king.

Among these was John Locke who, in his *First Treatise of Government* (1689), attacked arguments by Thomas Hobbes and Robert Filmer in the defense of the absolute, divine right of kings, the very opposite of popular sovereignty. As Hobbes had done with a very different outcome, Locke in his two treatises resorted to the fiction of individuals "in a state of nature." He used this device to state both their "natural" rights and their deliberate consent to a social contract that brought them together in a society and under the political obligations of an organized state. To Locke and the English Whigs (the party of the nobility who wanted to limit the power of the Crown), the social contract enabled them to spell out the civil liberties and property rights they wished to protect—not only from a monarch but even from the people whose ultimate, residual authority they readily acknowledged. Monarchy in England eventually made a comeback in spite of republican arguments, such as those of James Harrington and John Milton, who believed in popular sovereignty. But it did so only at the pleasure of Parliament, which derived its authority from popular election—from "the consent of the majority," according to Locke.

The Revolutionary Spirit

On the European continent the new individualistic thinking had flourished in the Low Countries. Benedict de Spinoza, in his *Theologico-Political Treatise* (1670), argued that only democracy gives individuals some say in their own government. But most of Europe was still under strong absolutist governments. In France the political side of the Enlightenment came to the fore only with the advancing eighteenth century—and nowhere as radically as in the writings of Jean-Jacques Rousseau in his *Social Contract* (1762).

Rousseau believed that popular sovereignty was inalienably vested in the people, and, unlike the English Whigs, he believed it could not be delegated to a legislature because the legislature likely would act only in its own interest or in the interests of a select group. No true law can be made without the consent of the people. Rousseau described the process by which a community makes law as the emergence of the general will, which is intrinsically moral and suffers no dissenting minorities. A mystifying mélange of determined dedication to the public interest and of the civic virtue of republicans (from Rome to the soon-to-be-born American Republic), this doctrine of the general will has been called totalitarian by some and blamed for the fanaticism of the French Revolution by others. Some of the Jacobins, the most radical wing of the French revolutionaries, who were responsible for the Reign of Terror, such as Maximilien Robespierre, were disciples of Rousseau.

In the meantime, however, the American Revolution and Constitution had developed along a rather different path. The successful War of Independence and establishment of popular sovereignty, it seems, led the Framers of the Philadelphia convention to follow the counsel of Locke and of the French political philosopher Montesquieu rather than that of Rousseau. Their celebrated Constitution, which fell far short of establishing democratic government, went to great lengths to curb the power of the elected people's representatives in the House of Representatives. The Constitution established checks and balances by the other bodies, which were not directly elected: senators, the president (elected by the electoral college), and the federal judiciary. A prime example of an attempt at mixed government along lines suggested by Aristotle and Montesquieu, the U.S. Constitution heralded a new trend of moderate liberal thought and constitutional government. After centuries in which the practice of popular government had lagged far behind its theories, theories were devised to rein in its practice.

The French Revolution and its Terror drew many critics who, like Edmund Burke and David Hume, challenged the philosophical foundations of individualism and popular rebellion on which they were founded. The most important of the postrevolutionary political thinkers were moderate liberals, such as Benjamin Constant de Rebecque and Alexis de Tocqueville. They defended popular sovereignty but preferred to hem in its exercise. Like many nineteenth-century writers, Constant preferred a constitutional monarchy on the British model, but he favored one that protected civil liberties against arbitrary government action. Tocqueville's astute observations about American mass democracy in the days of Andrew Jackson revealed his fear of a tyranny of the majority despite his support for the coming of democracy. John Stuart Mill perhaps expressed the moderate liberal perspective best when he warned in *On Liberty* (1859) that the true tyrant is the collective mass of individuals composing society itself.

Each of these nineteenth-century thinkers wanted institutional safeguards for individuals and minorities against an oppressive majority of the sovereign people. Tocqueville also praised the power of voluntary associations to protect the rights of minorities and nonconforming individuals. Unlimited popular sovereignty, along the lines of Rousseau and the French Revolution, according to Lord Acton, one of Tocqueville's best-known disciples, was to be avoided at all costs.

Twentieth-Century Questions

At the end of the twentieth century a return to seeking the ultimate political authority in tradition or religion seems remote. Nevertheless religious fundamentalists of many stripes are pursuing a revival of theocracy, subordinating their political system to their God and religious revelations. Moreover, vast popular mobilizations behind ideologies such as communism, fascism, and revolutionary nationalism have invoked the authority of "the people," if in dubious ways and without any legal or constitutional safeguards. On the other hand, the concept of popular sovereignty continues to play a major role in the making of modern constitutions, whether they are radically democratic or hedged with checks upon the exercise of popular authority.

Religious fundamentalists differ from each other not only in their respective religions but also in the extent of their otherworldliness, which leads most of their sects to abstain or withdraw from politics. In some cases, however, the intent was indeed to create a theocracy. For example, Allah and Islamic law were to be the ultimate source of all authority in the Shiʿite Muslim revivalist movement of the Ayatollah Ruhollah Khomeini that began in Iran in 1979. Khomeini's Iran was to be a "theodemocracy" of "limited popular sovereignty under a paramount God," who remained the true sovereign. The ideal Islamic community was conceived as a community of believers in the Word, as interpreted by *imams,* or spiritual leaders, such as Khomeini.

Although shared beliefs and community values created a strong bond between the rulers and their subjects, dis-

sension among rival Muslim interpretations and groups inevitably drew the transmission of theocratic authority into question. Who would decide which *imam* was the right one and whether the community consensus was true or false if such questions could not be resolved by a majority vote of the people? Other politically interested, religious fundamentalists, including some in the United States, have faced similar problems: How shall we know the true messenger of God and his message in case of a challenge? It would be blasphemous to subject the truth of religion to a majority vote of the people. Theocracy and democracy do not mix.

The vast mobilizations of communism and interwar fascism brought countless revolutions and immensely destructive wars on the twentieth century, much of it in the name of the people or, by implication, of popular sovereignty. Communist parties everywhere fought and ruled by the authority of the historical advance and eventual triumph of the downtrodden, international industrial proletariat, or so they said. Once established in power, the parties proceeded to manufacture majority consent by a mixture of ceaseless agitation and propaganda, with iron-fisted repression against those who challenged or resisted them. European fascist and revolutionary nationalist movements after World War I similarly claimed to represent the defeated peoples against their victors, or the allegedly downtrodden ethnic communities against other ethnics who presumably rose to power over them in Eastern Europe. They also learned the techniques of mass mobilization and the manufacture of consent, not to mention of massive repression, from the communists and from each other.

After World War II revolutionary nationalist movements worldwide made similar appeals to the popular sovereignty of their colonial or otherwise oppressed peoples against the domination of colonial empires or of ethnic majorities in their countries. In all these cases, the invoking of popular sovereignty was linked to a community of shared values—proletarian, ethnic, or racialist—and always promoted with massive propaganda. In nearly all these cases, this process of legitimation fell short of any real democratic affirmation and of constitutional protections for minorities and individuals. Even the communists who shared some of the legacy of Rousseau and of the French Revolution, and of populism in various settings, would not hear of submitting to genuine procedures of popular consent or to the constitutional controls on arbitrary governmental power that have long been the hallmark of the contemporary practice of popular sovereignty.

Aside from these dubious alternative applications, then, is the concept of popular sovereignty still relevant to the political life of today's constitutional democracies? The answer undoubtedly is "yes," even though the great battles over the theory and practice of popular government have long been won and popular sovereignty, in one form or another, reigns supreme almost everywhere. The concept is so fundamental to today's democratic practice that we can hardly expect it to be an issue of ordinary electoral campaigns or of parliamentary debates anymore. Even when populist appeals of various sorts tax political elites for ignoring the interests of the people, those elites are unlikely to challenge the ultimate authority of the people to give themselves a particular political order in harmony with their beliefs and values and to intervene when their "general will" is thwarted.

In the sixteenth century, when the Protestant French Huguenots had to defend themselves against an oppressive Catholic king, they presented their argument of a "right of revolution" as the last resort of a community of believers against religious and political repression. As with the Calvinists of Scotland, their right of revolution inevitably became the fundamental right of a God-fearing people to resist and rebel against their tyrannical government, an assertion of popular sovereignty with religious justification. It did not take long, given the rise of differentiated modern state organization with rational administrative and legal structures, for this claim to become secularized. The upheavals of the seventeenth and eighteenth centuries, and the political theories reviewed earlier, revived and refined older traditions of thinking in terms of a rational constitutional order in which the place of popular sovereignty was spelled out. The rise of constitutional enactments couched the concept, in legal language, as the constituent power, the fundamental right of the people to sanction their basic political order with their consent.

In terms of constitutional law, this right meant and still signifies three things. First, the people have the right to make or influence the making of a new constitution. To be sure, some constitutional systems, for example, Great Britain, still operate without a written constitution, and in other countries constitutional drafts are often worked out by a committee of constitutional experts rather than by a popularly elected constitutional assembly.

Second, the sovereign people have the right to ratify their constitution, after extensive public debate and possibly some modification of the original draft. Again, there are exceptions, such as the Federal Republic of Germany's Basic Law of 1949 (and now the Constitution of unified Germany), which was not sanctioned by popular ratification in 1949. It was not ratified because the Federal Republic was still occupied by the three Western powers, and the German leaders wanted to emphasize the provisional character of their Western rump state until reunification. When unification occurred in 1990, the leaders once more avoided popular sanction for reasons of expediency.

Third, the people have the right to be consulted about constitutional changes and amendments. The people's constituent power is usually enshrined in the carefully prescribed process by which constitutional amendments have to be solemnly ratified. Again there are exceptions and various methods of amendment, such as by two-thirds majorities of parliament or, in federal systems, with the states (provinces, cantons) having a constituent power of their own—derived from each state's people—with regard to the federal constitution. The biggest exception, perhaps, is found in major constitutional changes that occur over long periods of time and without a particular act of popular consent. An example is the dominance of the twentieth-century American presidency over Congress and the rise of federal preeminence over the states. Before 1900 Congress was more important than the president, and the states mattered more than the federal government. These changes were not decreed by constitutional amendments but came about through long-range social and economic changes.

Gross abuses of this constituent power have also occurred in the form of system-changing plebiscites (direct votes of the people). For example, plebiscites were used to legitimate the dictatorial powers of Napoleon Bonaparte and Napoleon III and later of Adolf Hitler, who clearly intended to destroy the constitutional order. Such plebiscitary democracy does not fairly represent popular sovereignty because its effect usually depends on the personal popularity of a man on horseback—and often on fraud and coercion as well. Ordinary initiatives and referendums may also trivialize the constituent power of the sovereign people where these devices are used with excessive frequency to add minor technical or policy prescriptions to a constitution (as in California and other western states in the United States).

The final major aspect of popular sovereignty today lies in the use of popular elections to determine the government's officers, party strengths in legislatures, and major policy programs. Although elections do not involve the constituent power in the same sense, they are capable of changing existing regimes in fundamental ways, not only by "throwing the rascals out" but also by instituting major reforms and major new policies, at least for the duration of the legislators' terms of office. For the day-to-day assertion of the popular will short of constitutional change today, elections provide the powerful control leverage so that "the government of the people," to quote Abraham Lincoln, "shall not perish from the earth."

See also *Consent; Fundamentalism; Legitimacy; Levellers; Locke, John; Montesquieu; Populism; Revolution, American; Revolution, French; Separation of powers; Virtue, Civic.* In Documents section, see *Pericles' Funeral Oration (431 B.C.); American Declaration of Independence (1776); Constitution of the United States (1787).*

Peter H. Merkl

BIBLIOGRAPHY

Barker, Ernest. *Principles of Social and Political Theory.* London: Oxford University Press, 1965.

———. *Social Contract: Essays by Locke, Hume, and Rousseau.* With an introduction by Sir Ernest Barker. New York and London: Oxford University Press, 1960.

Friedrich, Carl J. *Constitutional Government and Democracy.* 4th ed. Waltham, Mass.: Blaisdell, 1968.

Hansen, Mogens Herman. *The Athenian Democracy in the Age of Demosthenes.* Oxford: Blackwell, 1991.

McIlwain, Charles H. *Constitutionalism, Ancient and Modern.* Rev. ed. Ithaca, N.Y.: Great Seal Books, 1958.

Sabine, George H. *A History of Political Theory.* 3d ed. New York: Holt, Rinehart and Winston, 1961.

Populism

A political movement that emphasizes the interests, cultural traits, and spontaneous feelings of the common people, as opposed to those of a privileged elite. For legitimation, populist movements often appeal to the majority will directly—through mass gatherings, referendums, or other forms of popular democracy—without much concern for checks and balances or the rights of minorities.

The Nineteenth-Century Origins

The term *populism* was first used in Russia in the 1870s to refer to the beliefs of a heterogeneous group of thinkers and political activists, called *narodniki,* who rejected the use of foreign ideologies in the struggle for democracy or socialism. Most of them believed that capitalism was not necessarily a progressive stage of development and that a better social system could be built on the basis of national popular traditions and institutions, such as the village landowning community.

Aleksandr Herzen (1812–1870) pioneered most of these ideas, which clashed with the Marxist tenet that a revolution in a backward country had to be capitalist because no historical stages of development could be skipped. A later generation incorporated elements of anarchism as interpreted by Mikhail Bakunin (1814–1876). Bakunin valued the spontaneity of the masses, including the large socially uprooted population in Russia, over the meticulous and deadening organizational skills of the Germanic social democrats.

In a completely different context, the term *populism* was also applied to a political movement that thrived in the United States at the end of the nineteenth century. American populism had many anticapitalist components, though its doctrines did not converge with those of socialism. Its leaders espoused traditional values, and many held authoritarian views, including elements of anti-Semitism and white supremacy.

The U.S. populist movement had no single, towering national leader; rather, it relied on local organizers, many of whom had little formal education, to undertake necessary tasks and provide its intellectual orientation through an independent press. The movement was based on the support of farmers and small-town businesspeople. It flourished at a time when the growth of capitalism was hurting producers who could not compete with modern industry.

Farmers in particular resented their indebtedness to merchants and bankers. They also disliked the high cost of rail transport, which they blamed on monopoly operation. To act on their views, the farmers organized a widespread movement. They formed cooperatives, engaged in intensive educational efforts, and developed a partisan press.

In 1892 a People's Party was formed, supporting looser money and credit policies. It also proposed state or municipal ownership of major transport, communications, and other utilities. In 1896, after much internal debate, the party supported William Jennings Bryan for president. Bryan was a Democrat who had renovated his party by breaking with the more conservative orientation of President Grover Cleveland. Bryan accepted part of the Populists' program, especially in matters relating to free silver coinage, but he did not go along with the more radical points of the new party's platform.

Activists resisted the decision to become involved in traditional politics. Electoral defeat followed, and the Populist movement began to deteriorate, becoming internally divided. By the end of the nineteenth century both the movement's political program and the farmer cooperative organization that had backed it were moribund. In several states, Populist traits persisted for decades after the movement's demise, most notably in Louisiana under Huey Long's authoritarian reign as governor in the late 1920s and early 1930s.

One possible development of the basic populist mentality was the adoption of socialist values. This is what happened in Canada in the second quarter of the twentieth century, with the growth of the Cooperative Commonwealth Federation. Similar populist inspiration can be traced in the more conservative Social Credit Party, a strong element in the Canadian province of Alberta, and in other political groups formed in Quebec.

Populism in Developing Nations

Today, the term *populism* generally refers to a third kind of political phenomenon, common in Latin America and, in a different form, in Asia and Africa. In this sense it refers to political parties that are not socialist but are based on the support of the common people and are hostile to the dominant classes. On closer inspection, these parties are seen to be based on a constituency that has little experience of associating for civic purposes—in sharp contrast to the basis of American populism.

Because populist movements in developing countries are not based on autonomous self-organization, they need some other way of holding supporters together. That social cement is the presence of an undisputed leader, who establishes a charismatic relationship with followers. Such movements have two additional requirements. First, the mass of common people must be socially mobilized, that is, cut off from traditional loyalties and prepared to accept new types of leadership. Second, the leaders must emerge from the upper or middle layers of society, but they must be at odds with the majority of their own class of origin.

Situations that may produce this effect are a traditional aristocracy menaced by upstart moneyed sectors, a clergy swept aside by modernization processes, industrialists in dire need of protection against foreign competition, military personnel whose economic position does not equal their potential power, high school or college graduates with few job opportunities, or ethnic elites deprived of recognition by a racist ruling class.

Depending on how the first and second requirements are combined, four different kinds of populist parties may emerge: multiclass integrative parties, middle-class populist parties, working-class populist parties, or social revolutionary parties.

Multiclass integrative parties. Multiclass integrative parties include a large portion of the bourgeoisie and the middle class. They are likely to emerge when there has been a nationwide confrontation against a closed oligarchical regime, as in Mexico, or against foreign domination, as in India. The corresponding parties, the Mexican Institutional Revolutionary Party and the Indian Congress Party, have been capable of mustering widespread popular support, though controlling their followers through state-dominated mass organizations. Typically, small parties at the right and left complete the political system, without much capacity to compete for power. In the long run, as economic development takes place and new entrepreneurial and bureaucratic groups are consolidated, the multiclass integrative party tends to grow more conservative and eventually to become divided.

A variation of this kind of movement is a military national popular regime, which occurred in Egypt under Gamal Abdel Nasser, who came to power in the 1950s. This situation is typical of developing Asian and African countries, where the military replaces the nonexistent bourgeoisie. The military creates a bureaucracy, which often branches off into private enterprise. In Asia and Africa both religion and ethnicity separate the local upper classes from the foreign dominant powers, helping to recruit leaders into this type of anti–status quo political movement. But long exercise of power may blunt the movement's cutting edge and create the conditions for the emergence of an alternative form of military regime or a fundamentalist theocracy. Such conditions gave rise to the Iranian revolution, which in 1979 established Shi'ite Islam as the official state religion.

Middle-class populist parties. In countries torn by internal class divisions, if a multiclass integrative party has not taken hold, a populist movement must be based on the experience of the middle class. Most likely, it will recruit support from among the less well-off provincial members of that class, as well as unemployed or underemployed intellectuals and college graduates. This is the case of Peru's Aprista Party, which combined a tightly organized middle-class component and a popular component united to its leader, Víctor Raúl Haya de la Torre (1895–1980), by a strong political religion. Venezuela's Democratic Action, Costa Rica's National Liberation Party, and Bolivia's Nationalist Revolutionary Movement are other cases of parties formed according to this pattern.

Generally, these parties receive little support from the bourgeoisie and from the better-off members of the middle class. As a result, there is ample room for a more conservative party, or parties, capable of winning elections. The conditions for a democratic alternation in power are thus more likely to develop in this situation than when a multiclass integrative party rules the scene. As the party system settles down within a democratic format, and economic growth and modernization continue, the populist character of these parties tends to diminish, particularly after the death of their founder. Their organization becomes stronger, new leaders emerge in a more routine fashion, and they may move toward another form of party.

Working-class populist parties. The best example of a working-class populist party is Argentina's Peronist movement. Argentina has a relatively high level of urban and educational development and a strong working class that easily becomes a significant actor in politics. In such a milieu a populist movement cannot hope to include both the majority of the working class and large numbers of the middle or upper classes. Strategic minorities of the middle and upper classes, and of the military, however, can be an integral part of this kind of party. After the death of its leader, Juan Domingo Perón (1895–1974), Peronism became, like the Aprista Party in Peru, a more moderate movement than it had been originally. It lacks strong support among the upper and middle classes, leaving an opening for a centrist or conservative party. A conservative party, however, has not yet proved its ability to win a sizable vote in Argentina.

Brazilian Varguism is often considered a populist movement, comparable to Peronism. In fact, the two are quite different. Brazil has a much lower level of urban and educational development than does Argentina. Its populist movement was an alliance of two parties, the Social Democrático and the Trabalhista Brasileiro (Brazilian Labor Party), set up in 1945 by Getúlio Vargas (1883–1954). The alliance resembled a multiclass integrative coalition, along the lines of the Mexican Institutional Revolutionary Party. The Trabalhista Brasileiro branch of Varguism evolved toward a working-class populist party, especially under João Goulart's presidency (1961–1964), but it has not been able to gain more than a small slice of the electorate. It has lost most of its union support to a leftist party, the Partido dos Trabalhadores (Workers' Party).

Social revolutionary parties. Social revolutionary parties are found in developing countries, such as Cuba, Central American countries, Caribbean nations, and some parts of South America. Their strategic component is a determined elite, recruited from parts of the middle class experiencing severe occupational tensions. Under a highly repressive regime, an explosion is likely to occur, if and when the dictatorship faces a crisis. These parties usually have a Marxist-Leninist ideology, so it might seem wrong to classify them as populist. But the charismatic relationship between these parties' leaders and the mass of followers is typical of populist movements. The organizational structure of social revolutionary parties is generally solid, with strong control from the top. After decades of exercise of power they tend to become multiclass integrative parties, including postrevolutionary classes.

Historical and Comparative Evidence

Since the early nineteenth century, forms of populism have often appeared in Latin America. Many have been conservative movements, notably the regime led by Juan Manuel de Rosas (1793–1877) in Argentina or the more radical but short-lived one initiated by José Gervasio Artigas (1764–1850) in Uruguay.

Another well-studied forerunner of populism is the political movement built by Louis Napoleon (1808–1873), who staged a coup in France in 1851 and was confirmed by a massive vote. His case is often seen as an early example of plebiscitary democracy, making a direct appeal to voter support without regard for due legal process and checks and balances. His regime, however, is better seen as a combination of authoritarianism and mass consensus, that is, popular Caesarism. He built his following in opposition to the traditional conservatives and liberals as well as the socialist left. To describe the process by which Louis Napoleon obtained such overwhelming support, Karl

Marx coined the term *Bonapartism*. Marx argued that Bonapartism could develop when there was a peculiar equilibrium between classes, thus allowing an apparently non–class-determined political leader to appear as an arbiter of conflicting interests. Marx saw Bonapartism as a temporary phenomenon, coinciding with the final crisis of capitalism, when classical conservative or liberal-conservative parties could no longer obtain the support of a large part of the electorate.

A later generation of Marxist scholars, especially the Austro-Marxists of the period between World Wars I and II, such as Otto Bauer (1881–1938) and Karl Renner (1870–1950), explored the issue of national self-determination. They were concerned about the lack of internationalist revolutionary spirit among the working class. They saw that with increasing democratization, nationalism, which had been restricted to bourgeois parties, would also take hold of popular parties. As democratization grew, the mass of the population would be freer to assert themselves. Until that time internationalism had been a trait of working-class parties because such parties represented only a minority of their class and deferred to the intelligentsia. Nationalism might occur under the banner of social democracy, but it could also express itself in populist, or "national popular," movements.

Fascism and Nazism have sometimes been seen as having a populist component. Nazism can be described as an extremist movement of the center, with enemies on both sides. Its main foe, however, has been the trade union–organized left. The term *populism* as used today refers to political movements born of confrontation with conservative elements, even though the populist groups may eventually come to terms with their opponents or even form alliances with them.

The spread of populism in developing countries is sometimes attributed to their lack of civic traditions and to cultural traits that emphasize individual leaders. It has also been seen as the result of military dominance, because in many cases the leader of a populist party comes from the armed forces.

Without denying these facts, a sociological analysis of the underlying causes of populism must consider other aspects of the social structure. It should also explain the absence of populism in some developing countries. According to Gino Germani, a founder of this type of study in Latin America, populism results mainly from social mobilization. Social mobilization is a process by which large masses of the population, affected by internal migra-

tion or improved mass communication, break with their traditional loyalties and become available for new involvements. Since they have had little experience with voluntary associations, they are likely to follow some highly visible national leader, preferably one who wears the trappings of the dominant classes but sets himself against the elite. The leader emerges as the result of social tensions, which set some members of the upper classes against the majority conservative opinion of their peers.

Populism must not be confused with other types of popular parties, which rely largely on autonomous organization by workers and intellectuals. Examples of such parties are the social democrats and reborn communists of the developed world. In Latin America, Chile's socialists and communists approach this pattern, and so do the Uruguayan Broad Front and the Brazilian Workers' Party.

The Democratic Party in the United States provides a model of a popular party that is neither populist nor social democratic, has strong trade union support, and holds wide appeal across classes. In Latin America some populist movements are evolving in that direction after the death of their leaders; they are dropping their mobilizational and charismatic features. Examples of such movements are Venezuela's Democratic Action and Argentina's Peronism.

Populism has a paradoxical aspect. It is usually authoritarian and antimodern, thus representing a threat to democracy. Yet it often provides the working class or the peasantry with their only available political channel. In such cases it becomes a necessary element in building a democratic polity.

See also *Anarchism; Andean countries; Argentina; Authoritarianism; Brazil; Caribbean, Spanish; Central America; Costa Rica; Egypt; Ghana; Iran; Iraq; Leadership; Majority rule, minority rights; Marx, Karl; Mexico; Party systems; Separation of powers; Social democracy; Venezuela.*

Torcuato S. Di Tella

BIBLIOGRAPHY

Bottomore, Tom, and Patrick Goode, eds. *Austro-Marxism.* Oxford: Clarendon Press, 1978.
Collier, Ruth Berins, and David Collier. *Shaping the Political Arena: Critical Junctures, the Labor Movement, and Regime Dynamics in Latin America.* Princeton: Princeton University Press, 1991.
Di Tella, Torcuato S. *Latin American Politics: A Theoretical Framework.* Austin: University of Texas Press, 1990.
Germani, Gino. *Authoritarianism, Fascism, and National Populism.* New Brunswick, N.J.: Transaction, 1978.
Goodwyn, Lawrence. *Democratic Promise: The Populist Moment in America.* New York: Oxford University Press, 1976.

Ionescu, Ghita, and Ernest Gellner, eds. *Populism: Its Meanings and National Characteristics.* London: Weidenfeld and Nicolson, 1969.

Venturi, Franco. *Roots of Revolution: A History of the Populist and Socialist Movements in Nineteenth-Century Russia.* London: Weidenfeld and Nicolson, 1960.

Zeldin, Theodor. *The Political System of Napoleon III.* London: St. Martin's, 1958.

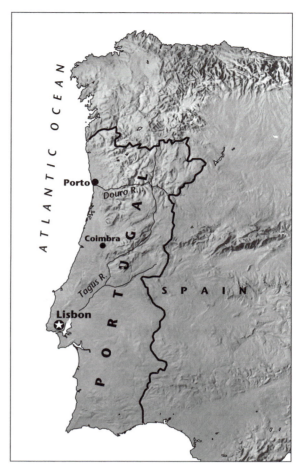

Portugal

An independent republic located on the Iberian peninsula, the westernmost country of continental Europe, which has a short history of democracy. Portugal came to democracy through a military coup in 1974, which led to a revolution that changed the old society and government and subsequently allowed for the formation of a pluralist democracy. The democratic system was consolidated in the decade after the revolution. Portugal became part of the European Community (now the European Union) in 1986 and thereafter began to modernize rapidly.

Bounded by Spain on the east and north and the Atlantic Ocean on the west and south, Portugal has a population of more than 10 million. Most of the population is Roman Catholic; Portuguese is the official language.

Historical Background

Despite Portugal's impressive colonial expansion in the fourteenth and fifteenth centuries, by the twentieth century the country was no longer an international leader and was characterized by both underdevelopment and dictatorship. Although it maintained colonies in Africa and Asia right up to 1974, Portugal was the poorest country in Western Europe with the lowest income per capita.

Liberal political ideas were implemented in Portugal beginning with the Constitution of 1822, which established a hereditary monarchy with a government responsible to the parliament. A consensus on a liberal form of government was not broadly established until the middle of the nineteenth century, however, after which a system known as *rotativismo* was instituted, whereby loose coalitions of notables exchanged, or rotated, offices. This process allowed for governmental stability and was generally influenced by liberal orientations.

The system collapsed in 1890 after a confrontation with Portugal's oldest ally, Great Britain. At issue was the publication by Portugal of a map on which Portugal's territorial claims in Africa were shown to extend across southern Africa from Mozambique to Angola. From the 1870s Portuguese expeditions had explored those areas, and the coloration of the map indicated that they belonged to Portugal. These claims contradicted Cecil Rhodes's plans. Rhodes, a British entrepreneur in Africa, had designs on the region. The Portuguese government acquiesced in a British ultimatum of 1890 and withdrew many of the claims made on the map. The loss of credibility of the government in this episode was an important factor in the collapse of the constitutional monarchy in 1910.

The republic that followed the violent overthrow of the monarchy was the most unstable in Europe at that time. It was finally overthrown in 1926 by a military coup that received popular support. Unable to deal with the economy, the military handed over power in 1928 to an austere economist from the University of Coimbra, António de Oliveira Salazar. By 1930 Salazar had established the foundations of a conservative authoritarian regime, in which he governed as prime minister for almost four decades. He concentrated power in the executive. The parliament and a corporative chamber, with representatives from various corporations, workers groups, and other interests, were virtual rubber stamps for his policy. Parliamentary elections were held periodically, but there were no parties, and only one official movement existed, the National Union. The Salazar regime was conservative in all respects, including its lack of interest in promoting modernization and its emphasis on maintaining the traditional and rural society. The regime was also committed to retaining the colonies, even when much larger and more powerful countries were granting independence to their colonies.

In 1968 Salazar was incapacitated after a stroke. He was succeeded by a law professor, Marcello Caetano. Caetano at first attempted to liberalize the regime and modernize the economy. His administration deemphasized the colonies and began to turn toward the European economies. By 1973, however, these efforts were being frustrated by hard-line opposition from within. As a result, the regime became increasingly repressive. Portugal refused to negotiate colonial independence despite having to fight wars in the three African colonies for more than a decade. On April 25, 1974, approximately 200 junior officers led a virtually bloodless coup that overthrew the old regime within twenty-four hours. The primary goal of these officers, who called themselves the Armed Forces Movement, was to stop the wars in Africa and enter into negotiation with the guerrillas. To stop the wars they first had to overthrow the intransigent regime in Lisbon.

The Coup and the Revolution

Within a year of the coup, Portugal was undergoing a revolution. When the old regime collapsed, the structures of power disintegrated, the repressive apparatus was abolished, and the armed forces were politicized and split into diverse groups. The colonies became independent, and—with civil wars raging in Angola and Mozambique—Portugal received at least 500,000 "returnees" who became an additional burden on its weak economy. The banks and insurance companies were nationalized, along with the more modern sectors of the economy. Lands in southern Portugal were occupied by peasants. Political parties and movements, unions of peasants and urban workers, and a variety of other groups emerged rapidly. Indeed, the same factors that caused the coup to evolve into a revolution—destruction of the old regime and proliferation of a wide variety of actors seeking power—also served to propel the revolutionary process.

Between the fall of 1975 and the summer of 1976 this maelstrom of new and disjointed processes and competing actors began to coalesce into a democratic regime. This positive evolution required the commitment of political actors, both within Portugal and abroad. The interaction was complex, and no single factor caused the configuration that resulted in democracy. Several significant factors were involved.

First, the original program of the Armed Forces Movement stipulated the goal of establishing democracy. Although the Armed Forces Movement later split, and some sectors sought to implement a military-directed regime, politicians could refer to the original program and pressure the officers to seek democracy.

A second factor was the emergence of political parties. The program did not envision the creation of political parties, but they emerged in any case. Some, such as the Portuguese Communist Party, came out from a clandestine existence. Others were formed from earlier groups or movements; these included the Portuguese Socialist Party, Social Democratic Party, and Social Democratic Center Party. Still others were newly created. By 1976 there were twelve functioning parties. Except for the Portuguese Communist Party, all of these required a democracy in order to be viable political actors, and they worked to achieve this outcome.

Third, the parties sought the support of moderate elements in the Armed Forces Movement, which had been superseded by radical factions during the revolutionary fervor of the spring of 1975. Partly as a result of the interaction with civilian politicians, and partly because of the dynamics within the armed forces as they recognized the risks of civil war, these moderate elements became predominant by late 1975. By early 1976 the armed forces were seeking their own depoliticization and the inauguration of a democratic system.

A fourth factor was action by a wide spectrum of international actors. This was a key confining element, which established the parameters of political action and supported the politicians of the democratic parties and the moderates in the armed forces. The actors involved included several governments, with the United States and Germany in the lead; international institutions, such as the North Atlantic Treaty Organization (NATO) and the European Community; and other organizations, such as German political parties.

By the summer of 1976 democracy had been initiated in Portugal. The constitution was promulgated in April, and parliamentary elections were held that same month. Elections for the presidency were held in June. The first constitutional government took office in July: a minority government of the Socialist Party.

Dynamics of Portuguese Democracy

Portuguese democracy soon proved to be unstable, with relatively short-term governments. Between mid-1976 and 1987 there were ten governments and five parliamentary elections. No government completed its term of office, and all possible coalitions were attempted except for one including the Portuguese Communist Party. The instability did not jeopardize the development of democracy, but it did impede the formulation and implementation of policy to modernize the country.

The causes for the instability were varied. One factor was that no political party received a majority of the seats in the parliament. Thus government had to be minority, a coalition, or one imposed by the president. More broadly, democracy was new in Portugal and required time to establish the patterns of elite interaction and popular support common to more mature democracies. Furthermore, Portugal was buffeted with serious demands that would be difficult for any democracy to meet. These included the negative economic, social, and even psychological impact of rapid and haphazard decolonization after 500 years as a colonial power. The revolution, with its nationalization and politicization, left a legacy of disjointed economic structures and processes. Many concerns from the revolution were written into the very long and programmatic constitution, and the document itself became a political issue that further encouraged governmental instability.

Gradually, with many tensions and difficulties, the regime began to be sorted out. International actors provided economic support, and some allies helped professionalize the armed forces. A coalition was patched together in 1982 that allowed the constitution to be revised. This revision resulted in a better arrangement between the presidency and the government, and the armed forces were gradually removed from political power.

Only in 1987, however, with the achievement of a majority government by the Social Democratic Party, were major changes implemented in the dynamics of party interactions. These resulted in governmental stability. The Social Democratic government served its full four-year term and was returned with a majority in 1991. The party benefited in 1987 from the resolution of its internal leadership issues and also from the frustration of the population with governmental instability. Its reelection in 1991 was a recognition of four years of competent governing and an acknowledgment of the dramatic improvements in living standards and modernization brought by Portugal's membership in the European Community.

Today Portugal is a full-fledged democracy with all the characteristics of more established democracies. The constitution is generally adhered to, groups and associations are free to form, and freedom of the press exists. There are several political parties, and elections for all decision-making bodies are held at regular intervals. Neither the military nor any other nonelected organization wields undue influence over the political process. With political stability and the benefits of membership in the European Union, the country is modernizing quickly. The Portuguese people understand the meaning of the elements constituting democracy, and they participate in elections. Overall, and particularly in light of the absence of a democratic tradition, Portugal is a success story of democratic consolidation and socioeconomic modernization in the latter part of the twentieth century.

See also *Democratization, Waves of; Europe, Western; European Union; Military rule and transition to democracy.*

Thomas C. Bruneau

BIBLIOGRAPHY

Bruneau, Thomas C., and Alex Macleod. *Politics in Contemporary Portugal: Parties and the Consolidation of Democracy.* Boulder, Colo.: Lynne Rienner, 1986.

Higley, John, and Richard Gunther, eds. *Elites and Democratic Consolidation in Latin America and Southern Europe.* Cambridge and New York: Cambridge University Press, 1992.

Lijphart, Arend, Thomas Bruneau, P. Nikiforos Diamandouros, and Richard Gunther. "A Mediterranean Model of Democracy?" *West European Politics* 11 (January 1988): 7–25.

Maxwell, Kenneth, ed. *Portugal in the 1980s: Dilemmas of Democratic Consolidation.* New York and London: Greenwood, 1986.

———, and Michael H. Haltzel, eds. *Portugal: Ancient Country, Young Democracy.* Washington, D.C.: Woodrow Wilson Center Press, 1990.

Portuguese Africa

See *Africa, Lusophone*

Postmodernism

A philosophical, cultural, and political movement marked by aversion to absolute truths, fixed meanings, and the authority of Western reason. The term *postmodernism* is a general label applied to a broad range of ideas encompassing academia, politics, and the arts that developed in reaction to modernism. Postmodernism's skepticism in regard to absolute truth has made it a natural ally of democratic thinking.

Modernism itself was a broad-based movement in which linguistic philosophers, anthropologists, architects, and composers sought to define meaning and truth by means of fixed rules of interpretation. The term *postmodernism* achieved widespread recognition as a movement only in the 1980s, when it began to be used by those thinkers who questioned the very possibility of finding such rules or lawlike scientific principles. Postmodern philosophers, literary critics, anthropologists, and psychologists, often under the name "deconstructionists," have followed the French philosopher and literary critic Jacques Derrida in teasing out linguistic tensions that simultaneously make possible and undermine fixed meanings.

Derrida's best-known example traces Western philosophy's preference for speech over writing (because writers are not there to explain their words). Since Plato, philosophers have viewed speech as a transparent conveyor of meaning and thus a necessary component of rationality. But, according to Derrida, the concept of transparency (or the immediate ability to understand) can convey its "meaning" only if the listener already understands the degree to which transparency is not opacity. In other words, the meaning of "transparency" must always already have within it its difference from the word "opacity." But, if so, then "transparency" cannot simply be transparent. In order for speech to be transparent, it must (and yet cannot) harbor "opacity," or writing. All language,

Derrida argues, is constituted by this essential instability: presence could not be presence without already subsuming the concept of absence, soul could not be soul without body, enlightenment without madness, democratic freedom without pathological repressiveness. Western thought has celebrated the first term in each of these pairs, without realizing that each term must depend impossibly on the second.

Academics on both sides of the Atlantic have further developed Derrida's ideas. Jean-François Lyotard, the French philosopher and social theorist, noted that postmodernists treat with skepticism all grand theories that claim to have discovered Truth or the nature of Reason or the Good. In particular, Lyotard denied that there is a unique solution to the problem of political justice. In his view, even democratic efforts to forge consensus through free discussion illegitimately constrict other language games that might not aim at consensus at all. In the United States, Richard Rorty has echoed Lyotard's views but with a somewhat liberal political twist. Because no one view on politics, religion, or aesthetics holds the Truth, the only remaining policy is to keep public conversation going without excluding anyone from speaking.

Linking postmodernism to open conversation appeals to many educators and has particular appeal to some feminists. In the United States, and to a lesser degree in Western Europe, postmodernists have questioned the traditional list of great books, which in their view sustains a particular concept of Western reason. Their efforts have contributed to the controversial movement for "political correctness"—an effort to ensure that minorities are treated with respect by those with power. Feminists contend that politics, even so-called democratic politics, tends to represent a conversation of white males with one another, excluding what Carol Gilligan, an American scholar of education and psychology, has termed the "female voice." More radical postmodern feminists have tried to undermine the very notion of an essential male or female voice. Following Jacques Lacan (1901–1981), the French psychoanalyst, they stress the dynamic quality of all identities. They look to a politics beyond the division of women and men, as Derrida looks for the play of meaning beyond the traditional binary pairs of subject and object or truth and falsity.

The influence of postmodernism has spread beyond universities and politics. In art and music and especially in architecture, it refers to a genre in which a deliberate effort is made to disrupt the conventional, to break up any uniformities, to celebrate the dynamic and even the chaotic over the systematic or the ordered. In the work of artists such as Robert Rauschenberg, musicians such as John Cage, and architects such as Philip Johnson, one finds multiple themes superimposed upon one another, absence (or silence) juxtaposed with presence, and an ironic, almost playful, mixing of styles and periods.

The postmodern rejection of traditional truths in philosophy, literature, politics, and ethics has stimulated a strong counterreaction from people convinced that postmodernism promotes indiscriminate relativism. In the view of these critics, democracy's vitality depends on certain habits of discipline and responsibility that postmodern views threaten to undermine. These critics are unlikely to be moved by a thinker such as the Italian philosopher Gianni Vatimo, who seeks "an accomplished nihilism" as the source of new values. Instead, critics point out that postmodernism offers no coherent set of political ideas, limited by its suspicion of fixed programs.

Finally, detractors can point out that, at least in its philosophical forms, postmodernism begins with Martin Heidegger (1889–1976). Heidegger tried to undo the entire tradition of Western philosophy, suggesting that we need to rethink the nature of existence itself. He made a crucial distinction between Being and beings—the things that actually appear in our world. Heidegger argued that the occurrence of any being (humans included) owes an absolute debt to that which is absent, that which opens the possibility for those beings to exist, namely Being itself. Supporters find in Heidegger a thinking as profound as that of Plato. But critics note that Heidegger's questioning of traditional metaphysics failed to prevent his membership in and sometime support for the Nazi Party of Germany in the 1930s.

See also *Critical theory; Existentialism; Feminism; Historicism; Relativism; Technology.*

David M. Steiner

BIBLIOGRAPHY

Benhabib, Seyla, and Drucilla Cornell, eds. *Feminism as Critique.* Minneapolis: University of Minnesota Press, 1991.
Derrida, Jacques. *Dissemination.* Translated by Barbara Johnson. Chicago: University of Chicago Press; London: Athlone, 1981.
Harvey, David. *The Condition of Postmodernity.* Oxford and Cambridge, Mass.: Blackwell, 1989.
Heidegger, Martin. *Being and Time.* Translated by John Macquarrie and Edward Robinson. New York: Harper and Row, 1962.
Lyotard, Jean-François. *The Postmodern Condition: A Report on Knowledge.* Translated by Geoff Bennington and Brian Massumi. Manchester: Manchester University Press, 1992.
Rorty, Richard. *Philosophy and the Mirror of Nature.* Princeton: Princeton University Press, 1979; Oxford: Blackwell, 1981.

Pragmatism

An American philosophy or philosophical method that claims that the meaning of ideas is found in their consequences. Unlike other philosophical methods, pragmatism avoids the search for the ultimate or highest reality, for eternal truth, and for the all-comprehensive system of knowledge. Instead, it tests the truth of concepts and theories by examining their consequences.

The term *pragmatism* also is used to denote a style of action that gets results by adapting to circumstances or by doing whatever it takes without too much concern about fixed rules or principles. The most famous exponents of pragmatism as a philosophy were Charles S. Peirce (1839–1914), William James (1842–1910), and John Dewey (1859–1952).

Because it developed and evolved over time, pragmatism is difficult to define. For example, Peirce chose at a certain point in the evolution of pragmatism to indicate his disagreement with James's position by renaming himself a pragmaticist instead of a pragmatist. The most widely influential, brief descriptions of pragmatism come from James's essay *Pragmatism: A New Name for Some Old Ways of Thinking.* The pragmatic method, according to James, tries "to interpret each notion by tracing its respective practical consequences. What difference would it practically make to anyone if this notion rather than that notion were true?" From a pragmatic perspective, then, ideas are true if they work—that is, if the ideas join various parts of people's experience together in a way that satisfies them. Thus an idea's truth is not a timeless attribute but something that happens to an idea. The idea becomes true when it proves itself—when results and events show it to be helpful, useful, or satisfying in giving people guidance or orientation in their experience.

In the first chapter of the second volume of *Democracy in America* (published in 1835–1840), French political observer Alexis de Tocqueville gives his now-famous characterization of Americans' philosophical method. This method, according to his analysis, grows out of the basic equality of Americans' social condition and the consequent tendency for each to rely on his or her individual intellectual efforts rather than to accept the direction of supposedly higher intellectual, moral, or political authorities. Americans, he wrote, tend to free themselves from intellectual systems, from habits, from class opinion, and even, to some extent, from national prejudices. They do not simply let tradition guide them but take it as one among many pieces of information and eagerly seek improvements over traditional ways. They try to achieve results without being overly concerned about the means employed, and they downplay the importance of forms or formalities in favor of the substance of things or the bottom line. In this way Tocqueville sketched, half a century before it emerged, the striking features of pragmatism, the first distinctively American philosophy. Pragmatism was often described in the first half of the twentieth century as *the* American way of thinking.

John Dewey

Any examination of the implications of pragmatism for democracy is probably best centered on the thought of philosopher and educator John Dewey, who developed a pragmatic political teaching. His political thought came most clearly to light when he engaged politically the thought of the American Founders and contemporary practices in American democracy.

Dewey, on the one hand, endorsed and admired several important traits of the American Founders. They were progressive, democratic, and liberal. They aimed at increasing the opportunities for the American people to develop their capacities freely. And they were innovators and experimenters, eager to develop a new science of politics that would expand liberty and increase human well-being in the emerging circumstances of their times.

On the other hand, Dewey rejected fundamental principles as enunciated and elaborated by the Founders. Their concept of the human individual as naturally endowed with certain unalienable rights, their thinking on natural rights and natural law, their crucial teachings that legitimate government must be instituted by a compact or social contract and that the primary purpose of government is to secure individuals' rights—all these basic convictions were described by Dewey as useful and progressive at the time they were prescribed but not later. The deepest difference between the Founders and Dewey, then, was that the Founders believed they had uncovered certain decisive truths about human nature and had derived from them some important true consequences for the foundations of a good society. Dewey, by contrast, denied that any such permanently true insights into human nature, the human individual, and the foundation of legitimate government were available to them (or to people today).

Dewey's position stemmed from his acceptance and application of Darwinian evolutionary science, which questions whether there is any definite human nature that one can know, and Hegelian historical philosophy, which teaches that the human world and all its ideas, institutions, and practices change fundamentally in the course of history. Accordingly, what is good or true politically, even on the level of the most fundamental principle, is different in different historical epochs. German philosopher G. W. F. Hegel believed that he had understood history through grasping its movement toward a final synthesis. Dewey rejected any such conception of a final outcome. He kept a notion of progress—but an open-ended one. Accordingly, Dewey could praise the ideas of, say, Founder Thomas Jefferson as good and progressive in 1776, while holding that these same ideas in the twentieth century obstructed further progress or even served as reactionary slogans.

The crucial area of economics or political economy, which often drew Dewey's attention, illustrates his pragmatist approach to democratic politics in contrast to the Founders' constitutionalism. According to Dewey, the eighteenth-century ideas of individual personal and property rights and the insistence on securing these rights against encroachment by political power were good for the time and circumstances of America's first decades. But later, given the rise of large industrial corporations, for example, the defense of individual liberties and property rights against abuses of political power no longer addressed the people's real needs. Individuals were no longer the decisive economic actors; they were weak and ineffective in the face of these massive new concentrations of economic power. Thus just as the abuse of political power may have been the crucial danger requiring vigilance in the 1780s, in the twentieth century the dangers of unchecked private economic power likewise required sustained attention.

Pragmatism in the Twenty-first Century

What, then, might pragmatism prescribe for the political economy of democracy in the twentieth-first century? There is no simple answer because pragmatism seems to call for a series of experiments that test the various ways of handling problems (and seizing opportunities) as they arise in conjunction with new developments in production, ownership, organization, and the like. Dewey believed that greater social control of economic forces was needed in order to bring about a more equitable distribution of the goods that society produced, counteract the imbalance of power between weak individuals and strong corporations, and remedy such ills as inhumane working conditions.

Greater social control of the economy, however, should not be limited to goals that are ordinarily thought of as merely economic. For example, Dewey hoped that pragmatic approaches to society's problems could improve everyone's participation in the expanding possibilities of culture. The pragmatic endeavor to improve the education of all in a democratic society, in fact, was the unifying theme in Dewey's philosophy of democracy. Indeed, democracy's highest purpose is to provide the best possible education for its citizens. Correlatively, genuine democracy, as distinguished from a mass society variously manipulated by propagandists and exploiters in positions of political and economic leadership, depends on the education of citizens. Today, education is even more important than at the time of America's founding because the social and economic lives of Americans have become more complex and more difficult to understand on the basis of ordinary life experience than in the past.

With its claim that the nature of man or the limits of human potentiality cannot be determined, pragmatism cannot understand education in its traditional sense as that which guides its students toward attaining the perfection of human nature. How then does pragmatism understand the goal of education? Dewey suggested that education does not aim at an end but is itself the end. Good education is that which makes further education possible; growth is for the sake of further growth. Indeed, the best education is a life-long process. The appeal of this position lies in its depiction of human well-being as consisting of activities that develop a person, sustained throughout a whole life. But the problem with this position is that it may not leave one equipped with any clear way of distinguishing healthy growth from malignancies or other changes for the worse.

According to Dewey, a democratic education should model itself on experimental natural science. Democracy needs the pragmatic methods of science if it is to deal successfully with its problems and to meet new challenges. The practical efficacy of science, engineering, and technology is reflected in their demonstrated power. That power, however, can be used for bad ends, such as domination, as well as for good ones, such as the improvement of democratic society. Accordingly, science needs to be guided by democratic moral values. And, in fact, scientific researchers and politicians who have a genuinely democratic character show certain moral traits: honesty, fairmindedness, open communication, willingness to innovate and experiment, and devotion to progress.

Pragmatism insists—almost on principle—that people remain open to revisions of and challenges to their fundamental economic, political, and moral concepts. For democracy, the strengths of pragmatism lie in its promotion of innovation and adaptability and its opposition to thoughtless rigidity and easygoing complacency. But costs tend to accompany these benefits. The pragmatic spirit makes it difficult to enjoy the benefits of venerable tradition and assured stability. James Madison, himself a great constitutional innovator, nonetheless recognized that even the wisest and freest governments might not possess enough stability without the veneration that only the passage of time can bestow (*Federalist* No. 49). Pragmatism leaves everything up for grabs and displays an eagerness to experiment with social engineering untrammeled by limits that were accepted in the past. If, as the French philosopher Montesquieu wrote, the political liberty of a citizen is the tranquillity of mind that arises from each person's opinion of his security, one must wonder whether pragmatism does not conflict to some extent with the notion of political liberty.

The ambiguous significance of pragmatism for political life is revealed in the ways pragmatism is both praised and blamed. When a politician or diplomat is praised for being pragmatic, he or she is compared favorably to people who are absolutist, rigidly doctrinaire, ideological, or "true believers." Someone pragmatic can adapt flexibly to changing circumstances. But political discourse also suggests that pragmatic adaptability can be carried too far—as when a politician is accused of "unprincipled pragmatism." When he was charged with being unprincipled, U.S.

senator Everett Dirksen retorted that he was a man of principle and that one of his main principles was his flexibility. In the same way, French president Charles de Gaulle was often attacked and often defended for his pragmatism. These complexities of political judgment on pragmatic flexibility testify to the fact that the political action most admired requires both principle and prudence.

After World War II pragmatism as a philosophy lost prominence and vitality in American intellectual life. Within the academic discipline of philosophy, linguistic analysis moved to the forefront and pragmatism declined. More recently, however, pragmatism has regained philosophical respectability in the wake of postmodernist arguments that most earlier philosophy was caught up in an allegedly impossible search for the ultimate eternal reality or for permanent foundational principles. The writings of Richard Rorty are noteworthy for seeking to restore Dewey's philosophy to its former importance. Rorty shares Dewey's democratic commitments, but in line with the postmodernist view he discards Dewey's faith in science and scientific method. Thus pruned of its connection with science, pragmatism might still aid democracy by criticizing the claims of antidemocratic movements. But such a weakened pragmatism seems unlikely to offer much positive guidance for democratic institutions and policies.

See also *Dewey, John; James, William; Postmodernism; Tocqueville, Alexis de.*

James H. Nichols, Jr.

BIBLIOGRAPHY

Dewey, John. *Democracy and Education.* New York: Macmillan, 1916.

————. *Freedom and Culture.* New York: Putnam's, 1979.

————. *Individualism Old and New.* New York: Minton, Balch, 1930.

————. *Liberalism and Social Action.* New York: Putnam's, 1935.

James, William. *Pragmatism and Other Essays.* New York: Washington Square Press, 1963.

————. *The Varieties of Religious Experience.* New York: Modern Library, 1936.

Nichols, James H., Jr. "Pragmatism and the U.S. Constitution." In *Confronting the Constitution: The Challenge to Locke, Montesquieu, Jefferson, and the Federalists from Utilitarianism, Historicism, Marxism, Freudianism, Pragmatism, Existentialism,* edited by Allan Bloom. Washington, D.C.: American Enterprise Institute Press, 1990.

Rorty, Richard. *Consequences of Pragmatism: Essays, 1972–80.* Minneapolis: University of Minnesota Press, 1982.

Presidential government

A democratic system in which the position and powers of both chief of state and head of government are vested in a president whose election, duties, and powers are constitutionally independent of the legislature. The oldest instance of presidential government is the United States of America, but other prominent examples include Finland, France under the Fifth Republic, and such Latin American democracies as Argentina, Brazil, Chile, Costa Rica, Mexico, Uruguay, and Venezuela. (Switzerland has a hybrid of presidential and parliamentary government that most scholars classify as closer to a presidential system.)

Selection and Tenure of Presidents

The presidents of most presidential democracies are directly elected by the voters. France and Finland, for example, hold two-ballot elections. Any number of candidates contend on the first ballot, and if one receives a majority of the votes cast he or she is elected president. If no candidate receives a majority, a second ballot is held later between the two candidates with the most votes on the first ballot. Similar systems are used in most of the other presidential democracies.

The president of the United States is elected indirectly through an electoral college. Each state is assigned a number of votes in the electoral college equal to the total of its senators and representatives in Congress. (Since 1961 three electoral votes have also been assigned to the District of Columbia, which has no voting members of Congress.) Since the 1790s the major parties have selected national candidates for president and vice president, and the parties' organizations in each state have nominated slates of candidates for presidential electors pledged to vote for their national tickets. In November the voters nominally vote directly for the candidate of their choice but legally for the slates of electors pledged to that candidate. With minor exceptions, in each state the slate that wins the most popular votes is elected; in December the electors in each state cast their ballots, which are then sent to Washington to be counted by the House of Representatives (for president) and the Senate (for vice president). Whichever candidate receives a majority of the electoral votes (270 out of 538) is elected. If no candidate for president receives a majority, the House of Representatives, with each state delegation regardless of size casting one vote, ballots among the three top candidates until one receives a majority.

The U.S. president is elected for a four-year term. Before 1951 there was no formal limit on the number of terms a president could serve, though only one served more than two terms. (Franklin D. Roosevelt was elected to a third term in 1940 and a fourth term in 1944.) The Twenty-second Amendment, ratified in 1951, limits the president to two elected terms. France and many of the Latin American presidential governments do not limit the number of terms the president may serve.

The American system of indirect election was originally designed to elevate presidential selections above partisan squabbling and produce a president to whom all the people would be loyal, like the subjects of a constitutional monarch. For many years Finland used a variation of the American system in the hope that it would produce that kind of president. In 1993 Finland abandoned its American-style system of indirect presidential election and replaced it with a direct vote, two-tiered election modeled on the French system. Despite the differences in their formal selection processes, however, the presidents of Finland, France, and the United States all have considerable political power, and in all three nations the presidents are partisan and controversial.

Presidents as Chiefs of State

With the exception of Switzerland, all democracies, presidential and parliamentary, have a single chief of state, a person who performs the symbolic function of personifying and speaking for the entire polity rather than for any particular party, interest, or other segment. The chief of state also performs many ceremonial functions, such as representing the nation at the highest level in its dealings with other nations and awarding military medals, titles, and other honors to people chosen for special recognition. Most chiefs of state also "reign": when one set of political officials must be replaced by another, the chief of state formally designates which officials are to leave and which are to take office.

In some parliamentary democracies, such as Belgium, Denmark, Japan, the Netherlands, Norway, Sweden, and the United Kingdom, the chief of state is a hereditary monarch. In other parliamentary democracies, such as Austria, Germany, India, Ireland, Israel, and Italy, the chief of state is what might be called an "elected monarch"—an official, usually called the president, who is elected by the parliament for a limited term to perform the same symbolic, ceremonial, and reigning functions as a hereditary monarch.

In addition to the chief of state, each of the parliamentary democracies also has a different person as head of government, its highest political official. Usually called prime minister but in some instances chancellor (Germany) or premier (Italy), the head of government leads and supervises the officers and agencies that initiate and enforce the government's policies.

In the parliamentary democracies, the positions of chief of state and head of government are always separate and distinct. In the presidential democracies, however, they are combined in the single person of the president. This combination of positions and roles makes presidents quite different from the monarchs and prime ministers of the parliamentary democracies. When acting as chief of state, for example, the president of the United States is, like hereditary and elected monarchs, entitled to the honor and respect that all the nation's parties and citizens pay to their country; but, like a monarch, the president must speak for the whole country, not for any part of it, and should be above political controversy. On the other hand, when acting as head of government, presidents, like prime ministers, are required to act as partisan leaders, pressing their party's policies over the objections of competing parties and policies. Thus the president is inevitably the chief warrior in the nation's political combat. The mingling of the two roles makes presidents in the presidential governments more venerated than prime ministers and more powerful but less venerated than monarchs.

The U.S. President as Head of Government

The government of the United States is the oldest and most studied of modern presidential governments. Many commentators have described the U.S. president's main roles and powers as chief executive, chief legislator, commander in chief, and chief diplomat.

Article II of the U.S. Constitution states that the president has executive power. As chief executive, the president appoints the heads of the major executive and administrative departments (the counterparts of ministries in the parliamentary democracies), and they are collectively known as the president's cabinet. That cabinet is quite different from the cabinets in parliamentary democracies, however. Parliamentary prime ministers choose other leaders of their parties (or, in the case of coalition governments, leaders from all the parties forming the coalition). Although they are appointed by prime ministers, cabinet members retain a considerable independent political following and influence; decisions are usually made collectively by cabinets and sometimes override the prime minister's desires. The resignation of one or more prominent cabinet members can wound the prime minister politically or can even cause his or her government to collapse. Department heads in the U.S. cabinet have no such power. They are designated by the president; the president can remove any or all of them at any time without jeopardizing his tenure in any way. If the policy preferences of some or all of them differ from the president's, only the president's count.

U.S. presidents can make a good deal of law on their own authority: they can issue proclamations, directives, and regulations, all of which are as legally binding as any congressional enactment on the people and organizations to whom they apply. More important, the president exerts considerable influence over the actions of Congress and is often called chief legislator. While no president gets all that he wants from Congress, most of the major public bills considered there are conceived and drafted by the president's advisers and guided through the chambers by the president's legislative party colleagues.

Moreover, the president has the veto power. The U.S. Constitution stipulates that the president can disapprove any proposed law passed by Congress. If he does so, Congress can reenact the law only by mustering two-thirds majorities to override in both chambers. The veto is a highly effective weapon: fewer than 10 percent of all presidential vetoes have been overridden. It is, however, a blunt instrument: the president can veto only entire bills. Unlike the governors of many American states, the president does not enjoy the "item veto"—the power to veto only the objectionable parts of bills while approving the rest. This weakness has opened the door for Congress's counterweapon of "riders": when majorities in Congress want to save legislative proposals they believe the president will veto, they attach them as amendments to bills— notably appropriations bills—they know the president is not likely to veto. Most presidents have urged Congress to grant them the item veto, but no Congress has yet been willing to give up such a powerful check on the president's formidable policy-making power.

The U.S. Constitution makes the president commander in chief of the nation's armed forces. The Framers intend-ed thereby mainly to establish the principle, essential to democratic government, of civilian control of the military. In times of war some presidents (for example, Abraham Lincoln and Franklin D. Roosevelt) have played active roles in formulating military strategy and even ordering troop movements, while others (for example, Woodrow Wilson and George Bush) have left such matters entirely to the generals and admirals.

The Constitution gives Congress the power to declare war. Even so, many presidents have on occasion ordered American forces to engage in combat operations on foreign soil without any prior congressional declaration of war (including Harry S. Truman in Korea in 1950, and John F. Kennedy and Lyndon B. Johnson in Vietnam in the 1960s), and the U.S. Supreme Court has consistently held that such actions are within the president's powers as commander in chief. As a result, most analysts agree that the power to commit the nation to a foreign war has effectively been moved from Congress to the president. To be sure, the War Powers Resolution of 1973 requires that the president notify Congress of any commitment of troops and gives Congress the power to refuse support, but Congress has not yet used its refusal power and seems unlikely to do so in the future.

The U.S. president dominates the nation's relations with other nations. As chief of state, the president represents the country in dealing with other chiefs of state and, as head of government, he is the main negotiator with the heads of other governments. The president appoints all ambassadors and other official representatives abroad. All ambassadors of foreign nations present their credentials to him, and, by deciding which of them he will receive, he determines which foreign regimes the United States recognizes as legitimate. The president's power over foreign policy is thus very strong, but it is not unlimited. Presidential nominees for secretary of state and for ambassadors must be approved by the Senate. Any treaties negotiated by the president must be ratified by the Senate before they become effective. Whatever commitments the president makes for economic and military aid to other nations become effective only when both houses of Congress appropriate the necessary funds. Even if the president has no monopoly, however, his dominance over the foreign policy of the world's only remaining superpower strongly supports the assertion that the president is the most powerful democratically elected official in the world.

Other Presidencies

Generally speaking, the presidential governments in various Latin American democracies were modeled on and remain similar to the U.S. system, though in some respects their presidents are even more powerful. They have all the U.S. president's formal powers as chief of state, chief executive, commander in chief, and director of foreign relations. They also have legislative veto powers, some have the item veto, and some are authorized to introduce bills directly in the legislature. Some can make all or most executive appointments without approval by the legislature. The legislatures tend to enact laws in much broader and more permissive language than the U.S. Congress uses. As a result, the Latin American presidents generally have powers greater than those of the U.S. president to issue decrees and administrative regulations without legislative participation or approval.

One significant formal limitation on most of these presidents is the cap on presidential tenure. A common rule is that presidents cannot be reelected until a specified time after they leave office, ranging from four years in Colombia to forever in Mexico. Their power is limited in other ways as well. Like the U.S. president, they must persuade legislatures to support many of the major parts of their programs. Their tenure in office is limited, and they have little or no say in the choice of their successors. In short, the Latin American presidents are powerful heads of government, but they are not dictators.

France (since 1958) and Finland have mixtures of presidential and parliamentary institutions. The presidents of both are directly elected by the voters independently of the legislature and serve fixed terms. Both are heads of state and also independently exercise a number of significant executive and legislative powers, including the power to dissolve the legislature and hold new elections. As chiefs of state, both presidents are not only the symbolic and ceremonial heads of their nations but are also the principal makers and conductors of foreign policy. In addition, the French president can submit constitutional amendments for popular referendums without the consent of the cabinet and the parliament. In an emergency he can suspend regular government procedures and take whatever measures he thinks fit.

The presidents of Finland and France have complicated relationships with their legislatures. Each appoints the premier, who presides over the coalition of parties constituting a legislative majority. The Finnish (but not the French) president appoints the members of the cabinet and can remove them from office at any time.

The real test of whether the French and Finnish systems are fundamentally presidential or parliamentary would come if the premier and a majority of the legislature were unalterably committed to a policy that was totally unacceptable to the president. In such a situation, the president of Finland has the power to dismiss the entire cabinet, but only once has a president dismissed a cabinet that clearly enjoyed the confidence of the parliament. Presidents of France have so far been careful to avoid any such political powder keg. On two occasions (1986–1988 and beginning in 1993) the National Assembly has been controlled by a coalition of parties opposed to the president, and on both occasions President François Mitterrand appointed a premier from an opposition party rather than from his own.

Most analysts have concluded that the Finnish and French systems are best regarded as mixtures of presidential and parliamentary government, with the presidential ingredient somewhat greater in Finland than in France. In any case, parliamentary, not presidential, governments predominate among the democracies: at present about 110 nations have democratic systems, and of those only about 15 have presidential governments. A majority of the nations emerging from the breakup of the former Soviet Union are now trying to build new democratic systems, and most of them appear to favor presidential governments. Even if they continue and succeed, however, parliamentary government will remain the system used by most modern democracies.

See also *Election, Indirect; Electoral college; France; Parliamentarism and presidentialism; Switzerland; United States Constitution; United States of America.* In Documents section, see *Constitution of the United States (1787).*

Austin Ranney

BIBLIOGRAPHY

Andrews, William G. *Presidential Government in Gaullist France.* Albany: State University of New York Press, 1982.

Arter, David. *Politics and Policy Making in Finland.* New York: St. Martin's, 1987.

Duverger, Maurice. "A New Political System Model: Semi-Presidential Government." *European Journal of Political Research* 8 (Summer 1980): 165–187.

Kellerman, Barbara. *The Political Presidency.* New York: Oxford University Press, 1986.

King, Anthony, ed. *Both Ends of the Avenue.* Washington, D.C.: American Enterprise Institute, 1984.

Lijphart, Arend. *Democracies.* New Haven and London: Yale University Press, 1984.

Neustadt, Richard E. *Presidential Power and Modern Presidents.* New York: Free Press, 1990.

Polsby, Nelson W. *Congress and the Presidency.* 4th ed. Englewood Cliffs, N.J.: Prentice Hall, 1986.

Private governance of associations

The exercise of authority over the members of a private organization is distinguished from the governance of public or state organizations by the fact that membership in, and withdrawal from, private associations is usually voluntary. Although all organizations possess some degree of authority over their members, there is a profoundly important difference between public or state organizations and private associations in the relationship between those who wield authority and those over whom it is exercised. Membership in private associations is freely chosen by each individual, at least in principle, and, again in principle, each member may withdraw more or less at will. In the case of the state, by contrast, entry and exit are far more tightly constrained.

Because no one is forced to join most private associations and members can exit when they please, it is sometimes necessary to design governing arrangements that attract and retain individuals if the organization is to survive. Membership in private associations is not always completely voluntary. Lawyers in some states of the United States, for example, must join the bar association in order to practice. And under union-shop contracts, workers must join the union in order to retain their jobs.

The Problems of Voluntary Organizations

Two kinds of difficulty confront those who would build a voluntary association. One, identified by Mancur Olson (in *The Logic of Collective Action,* 1965), is the problem of the "free rider." Except in relatively small groups, or when the costs are trivial, or when the members are philanthropic (or misled), rational individuals will have little reason to join a group to support lobbying or other collective efforts, the fruits of which can be enjoyed whether or not one contributes to the effort.

A second problem is raised by the prospect of "unraveling." In any group of individuals with a given distribution of preferences regarding an acceptable dues structure or policy stand, the leadership may promulgate a position at, say, the midpoint of those preferences. To do so, however, assures that nearly half the members will find the dues too high or the policy too radical and threaten to quit or never to join in the first place. Taxation and other policy decisions of the state, on the other hand, are not so easy for individuals to evade; one must move offshore, or perhaps emigrate permanently. Association dues can be avoided simply by exiting the voluntary organization.

Three distinct solutions to the problems of the free rider and of unraveling may be noted. Members may be attracted and retained by means of selective benefits available only to those who belong to the organization. These benefits may include material goods, sociability, and the value of giving support to a candidate or policy of one's choice. Second, voluntary associations are often formed for the purpose of accomplishing some particular task, discrete or ongoing, and for that accomplishment some people may be fully prepared to subordinate their narrow self-interest to the collective purpose.

A third way of resolving the difficulties confronting the development and maintenance of voluntary associations is by the use of mechanisms of democratic control. Members may join an organization because they believe they will have a say in its decisions. Having thereby accorded its policies legitimacy, they will be willing to remain within its ranks. Moreover, an organization perceived to be democratic in its internal procedures may be more likely to be accepted by others as legitimately representative of its members. Accordingly, its policy statements might have greater impact in the larger polity.

Legal Constraints and Democratic Control

Many nongovernmental organizations, though private and voluntary, are constrained by law. Business firms are incorporated under the terms of state laws which specify, among other things, how boards of directors shall be chosen and what their duties are toward employees and stock holders. Labor unions are regulated in considerable detail regarding their governance; in the United States the elections of their officers and the rights of members against the leadership are sometimes directly supervised by federal officials. Even religious organizations may find that when denominational factions clash over control of church property, the conflict must be settled in court, that is, by public authority.

The aggregate impact of these factors has been to impose on voluntary associations an impressive body of democratic institutional arrangements and procedures that allow for substantial membership control over association leaders. Formal democratic procedures do not guarantee democratic practice, of course, and the realities of association practice must be assessed along with the forms.

The most common mode of democratic control of organizational authority is through election of leaders by members. In the United States the vast majority of voluntary groups hold regular elections to fill leadership positions, and nearly half report holding contested elections at least part of the time. In many organizations, official slates of candidates are presented—a practice that may effectively preempt would-be competitors—but a few, such as Common Cause, have tried to enhance electoral competition by nominating more than the number to be elected and leaving it to the members to decide which nominees will serve.

Elections are especially effective ways for members to exercise control over leaders when competition for office is sustained over a period of time. In their 1956 study of the International Typographical Union, Seymour Martin Lipset, Martin Trow, and James Coleman found a two-party system in operation that produced alternation in office and genuine membership influence over decisions. In some other labor unions, insurgents have occasionally won election contests, but sustained competition has been rare. Some academic professional associations have developed de facto two-party systems, based partly on differences of age and professional prospects and partly on ideological grounds. The result has been to broaden participation in the decision-making processes of the organizations but also, ironically, to shift and in some cases to distort group goals by "politicizing" the associations and rendering them more responsive to activist pressure. In general, it must be said that elections are only occasionally meaningful methods by which association members constrain leadership action.

Membership impact on association decisions can be enhanced in other ways, however. For example, David Knoke (in *Organizing for Collective Action,* 1990) reports that just over half the national associations in his survey of more than 400 American voluntary groups held general membership meetings annually at which policy decisions were made. Others, too large to get everyone into the hall at once, employed some method of choosing delegates to represent the members in convention decisions. Knoke found, in addition, that 37 percent of the organizations he surveyed had held a referendum election during the past three years. Thus substantial opportunity to participate existed. Nevertheless, there seems little basis for rejecting the essential argument advanced by Robert Michels (in *Political Parties,* 1915) that only a distinct minority takes an active part in shaping the policies of most voluntary groups.

Levels of Participation, Decentralization, and Efficiency

Several factors may be adduced to explain the degree to which associations in both fact and form try to bring their members into significant participatory roles. First, to what extent is the organization dependent on its members for financial or other means of support to survive? Jack L. Walker in 1991 found that member dues accounted for only half the income of the more than 800 groups he surveyed. Least dues-dependent were the citizens groups, a finding that accords well with Jeffrey M. Berry's 1977 report that 30 percent of the citizens groups he studied had no members at all, only financial contributors. Further, by providing services of value or simply by taking policy positions that some find appealing, leaders may satisfy members and be able to escape the constraints of member insistence on participation.

A second variable affecting membership involvement in private association governance is the degree of centralization in decision making. Knoke finds that large organizations with multiple goals and complex environments are more likely to develop democratic processes of governance. It may be, of course, that associations with democratic procedures are more successful in attracting members and thus become large, but in any case, size and complexity are closely connected not only to democracy but to decentralization. The devices employed to achieve decentralization are numerous. Federalism is one such device, whereby authority is divided between the central body and geographically defined subunits. In the United States a federal structure for private groups fits well with the federal political system. Many voluntary associations that call themselves federal, however, are actually confederal, with the central body possessing only that authority delegated to it by the constituent units. The AFL-CIO is an example. In many other associations the national body may have little real power over state or local units.

When the organization is centralized but is threatened

by divisive tendencies among the membership, a common practice is to create special-interest groups to allow a degree of functional or substantive autonomy for the more insistent subsets. Professional associations in law, medicine, and assorted academic disciplines, faced by the demands of specialists, have often adopted this institutional form. Business firms and other complex organizations often decentralize operations also, not because of the need to democratize but in order to accommodate interests and objectives within the corporate boundaries that cannot be pursued as efficiently through centralized machinery.

Democratic participation and control may come at the expense of efficiency. Group leaders often feel that member demands for participation are a nuisance, and perhaps ill-informed or strategically unsound. Organizations that find themselves in intensely competitive or conflictual situations may be less likely to adopt democratic practices than those less embattled. Thus labor unions have often felt it necessary to sacrifice some degree of member participation—by holding conventions only every third year, for example—in order to present a disciplined, united face to corporate management.

Surely the most effective constraint on the exercise of authority in voluntary associations is the fear that if members become frustrated by their inability to control the group's direction, they will publicly challenge the representational claims of the leadership or drop out altogether. Potential oligarchs, whether elected by an apparently passive membership or appointed to staff positions by an otherwise preoccupied board of directors, must ever be cognizant that keeping the organization in good health and its members happy is necessary to everything else the group's leaders might attempt to do. Moreover, if the society in which the association operates values democratic norms highly, voluntary associations are likely to reflect those norms in their governing practices.

See also *Associations; Civil society; Communitarianism; Corporatism; Interest groups; Michels, Robert; Rational choice theory.*

Robert H. Salisbury

BIBLIOGRAPHY

Berry, Jeffrey M. *Lobbying for the People.* Princeton: Princeton University Press, 1977.
Knoke, David. *Organizing for Collective Action.* New York: Aldine de Gruyter, 1990.
Lipset, Seymour Martin, Martin Trow, and James Coleman. *Union Democracy: The Internal Politics of the International Typographical Union.* New York: Free Press, 1956.
Olson, Mancur. *The Logic of Collective Action.* Cambridge, Mass., and London: Harvard University Press, 1965.
Schlozman, Kay L., and John Tierney. *Organized Interests and American Democracy.* New York: Harper and Row, 1985.
Truman, David B. *The Governmental Process: Political Interests and Public Opinion.* New York: Knopf, 1951.
Walker, Jack L. *Mobilizing Interest Groups in America.* Ann Arbor: University of Michigan Press, 1991.
Wilson, James Q. *Political Organizations.* New York: Basic Books, 1973.

Privatization

See *Regulation*

Progressivism

A wide-ranging series of efforts to make democratic political systems the basis for a more just, efficient, and cohesive socioeconomic order. The Progressive movement, which dominated U.S. politics between 1900 and 1920, was one manifestation of progressivism. The causes and concerns that fostered the Progressive movement remain a potent source of reform impulses at the end of the twentieth century.

Progressivism is a distinctive reform spirit expressed in activism at all levels of government in the United States and throughout much of American society and culture. Amidst intense political, social, and intellectual ferment, early-twentieth-century progressivism helped lay the foundations for the modern American regulatory and social welfare state and is generally considered the precursor of contemporary American liberalism.

Progressive Politics

Progressivism grew out of the political crisis that intensified during the 1890s as U.S. political institutions struggled to adjust to the closing of the western frontier, the rise of large-scale industry, the growth of cities, massive new waves of immigration, and rapid technological change. It assumed its most characteristic forms about the turn of the century as growing discontent with the effects of these developments—discontent first dramatized by the agrarian Populist movement of the 1880s and early 1890s—galvanized middle- and upper-class activists who were confronting more specifically urban and industrial problems. Over the next twenty years indignation at commercial abuses, symbolized by business monopolies, and at government corruption, epitomized by boss-led political machines, generated an array of reforms that have been closely identified with progressivism ever since.

Progressivism's origins lay in the cities, where activists and reform-oriented mayors sought honest and efficient administration of urban affairs and campaigned for improved streets, lighting, water, and parks; firmer regulation of gas, electric, and public transit services and rates; and stricter housing, sanitation, and workplace standards. Many localities instituted nonpartisan city-manager governments as means to these ends; a few pressed for direct public ownership of selected utilities and for comprehensive programs of urban beautification and planning.

Meanwhile Progressives in numerous statehouses promoted electoral reforms, such as the Australian, or secret, ballot and curbs on campaign-related corruption. They worked to expand state regulatory powers through new public utility, railroad, and corporation commissions; labor laws to benefit women and children; and new provisions for employers' liability and workers' compensation for industrial accidents. But state-level Progressives were best known as champions of such innovations as the primary election, initiative, referendum, and recall—mechanisms that allowed citizens to nominate candidates directly, put policy questions to a general vote, pass judgment on legislative proposals, and call special elections to vote politicians out of office.

The presidency of Theodore Roosevelt (1901–1909) brought progressivism to national government. A growing contingent of Progressives in Congress helped pass laws to expand the federal regulation of interstate commerce and monopolistic business practices. Roosevelt's 1912 independent Progressive Party campaign for a third presidential term pressed his "new nationalist" argument that strong government regulation could harness the industrial efficiency of the trusts in the national interest. Roosevelt lost to Woodrow Wilson, whose own version of progressivism called for a "new freedom" through more limited government intervention to oppose the formation of commercial trusts. Yet, during his first term (1913–1917), Wilson pursued a reform agenda comparable to Roosevelt's, extending federal commerce regulation through the Federal Trade Commission, creating the Federal Reserve system of national banking regulation, and levying the first peacetime federal income tax.

Efforts to make public authority both more accountable and stronger also involved new techniques for its acquisition and exercise. Progressives at all levels relied on executive leadership as a way around obstructionist courts and inefficient and corrupt legislatures. Roosevelt and Wilson redefined the role of the presidency and greatly increased its powers through their initiatives, administrative innovations, and personal styles. Reformers also strove to place larger areas of government activity in the hands of independent commissions staffed by, or heavily reliant upon, nonpartisan experts in specific policy fields. Along with the rest of the expanding public sphere, these new commissions felt the influence of increasingly powerful private interest organizations. The rapid proliferation of business and professional groups, of single-issue citizens' campaigns, and of federations of interest groups was a central feature of the Progressive Era. Roosevelt's attempt to unite Progressives under a single party banner proved short-lived, and although Wilson's presidency saw the Democratic Party replace the Republicans as the party of reform, interest group politics was beginning to eclipse party politics.

The Progressive Ethos

Pervading all this diverse reform activity was a distinctive spirit or ethos which John Whiteclay Chambers has aptly described as a blend of Protestant evangelical fervor, a faith in scientific inquiry, and a belief in the power of organization. Nothing captured this spirit better than the urban settlement-house movement, which became one of the earliest vehicles for Progressive causes. The same groups that worked to provide some of the nation's worst slums with civic amenities, educational opportunities, and a sense of community also surveyed urban social conditions and investigated the causes and effects of poverty. In the process, they created institutional outlets for growing numbers of men and women willing to make the spiritual and material salvation of the masses a full-time occupation.

Over time, analogous energies drove large-scale, official attempts to regulate social and economic life and found expression in distinctive ways of talking about socioeconomic problems and their solutions. In his seminal essay, "In Search of Progressivism," Daniel Rodgers argues that three themes linked otherwise disparate participants in Progressive reform. These were hostility toward monopolies and special privilege, belief in social cohesion and individual interdependence, and faith in social efficiency and engineering. It was through these themes that Progressives defined and conveyed their varied discontents, aspirations, and activist enthusiasms.

At the peak of the Progressive Era, between 1905 and 1915, elements of this ethos infiltrated virtually all walks of American life. Progressive jurisprudence called for the interpretation and enforcement of law to reflect concrete social realities and democratic consensus rather than abstract logic or reasoning from precedent. Preachers of a new "social gospel" awakened organized religion to the needs of the working and poorer classes and to the crusade for a more ethical industrial order. Progressive educators sought to make schooling compulsory, comprehensive, and better organized as well as to transform learning from rote absorption to creative preparation for practical life and democratic citizenship. A new journalism pursued "muckraking" investigations into political corruption, business abuses, and social vices in the name of informing the citizenry and invigorating public debate. Art and literature strove for greater realism and naturalism in attacking old taboos and depicting new conditions. Business sought both higher profits and better labor relations through "scientific management" aimed at efficiency in production. Organized labor built on its increasingly secure legal position by seeking reform through political activity. Finally, professional academic disciplines spawned new fields of specialization in sociology, economics, political science, and history, many of which were geared to reform advocacy and public service.

Indeed, nowhere was the ferment more intense than in the realm of ideas. Progressivism made important innovations in political, economic, and social thought. New theories elaborated on the central Progressive conviction that human conduct and development were determined by the surrounding environment rather than by innate character. At the same time, reformers pressed the equally vital Progressive claim that human beings could alter their environment through conscious collective effort. An important corollary of both beliefs was the historicist argument

that the principles and practices adhered to by one generation could prove wholly inappropriate for another living in changed conditions. A further corollary was that society could progress only by abandoning fixed axioms and learning from experience and experiment.

All these themes converged in the philosophy of pragmatism as articulated by John Dewey, a leading Progressive who insisted that both society and individuals advanced best through the collective participation of all in the continuing experiment of democratic governance. Similar themes ran through what many consider the most important presentation of Progressive political theory, Herbert Croly's *The Promise of American Life* (1909), which argued that the active use of national power for domestic reform did not subvert American democratic traditions but represented their highest fulfillment. All this reasoning challenged deeply rooted American antipathies toward active government and countered the individualistic, anti-interventionist ideologies that dominated the nineteenth century. But it by no means produced agreement on any single doctrine or program of social reform.

Competing Interpretations, Continuing Dilemmas

Many of the conceptual innovations central to Progressive thought borrowed heavily from European intellectual trends. Many Progressives drew on European social science and European social policies in setting an American agenda for reform. This borrowing, along with the emergence in turn-of-the-century Great Britain of a self-styled Progressive alliance of labor, nonsocialist liberals, and revisionist socialists has led some to identify American progressivism with a broader transatlantic effort to reconcile capitalism and socialism. But American Progressives drew at least as deeply on American liberal, republican, popular-democratic, and religious traditions in addressing uniquely American problems of political development. And, despite their occasional collectivistic and antibusiness rhetoric, American Progressives rarely questioned the basic structure of capitalism as vigorously as did their European counterparts. On the contrary, the point at which expansion of the public sphere implied extending democracy to social and economic as well as political life marked the site of American progressivism's deepest ambivalence.

Indeed, many American Progressives consciously tried to avoid any hint of socialism through timely reform and occasional repression. They were, if not hostile to organized labor, "neutral" toward labor and management at a time when management was clearly in command. As many commentators have noted, major elements of the business community not only benefited from efforts to regulate competition and set commercial standards but actually championed the reform agenda and turned it to their advantage. The most strenuous "corporate liberalism" interpretations depict progressivism as a movement to reconstruct American society in the name of corporate interests, according to corporate capitalist values, and around the business corporation as model for virtually all social and political institutions. Although it is misleading to overlook the hostility many Progressives felt toward the influence of business or to attribute reform solely to business interests, progressivism clearly helped legitimize a corporate presence in the American polity that continues to vex American democrats.

Perhaps the most compelling interpretations of progressivism focus on its general organizational imperative and the contradictions that resulted from the almost religious fervor of many Progressives. Progressives believed both that a democratic society could consciously control its destiny and that honest and competent exercise of that control would elicit the support of an enlightened democracy. But when such support proved equivocal and democratic processes seemed to hinder rather than advance the rule of reason, a strong current of elitism surfaced to contradict Progressives' democratic rhetoric. Moreover, the evolution of Progressive reform revealed differences among Progressive elites themselves over the purposes of collective action. Several commentators have emphasized the tension between progressivism's pursuit of social justice and its yearning for social control, and they have noted the often deeply complicated relationship Progressives saw between the two goals. Others have pointed to conflicts within the Progressive outlook between a desire to restore and preserve traditional values and a determination to embrace and master modernity and change.

Traces of the tensions between social justice and social control are visible in many Progressives' ambivalence toward the increasing pluralism of American society and their hesitancy to take up the claims of disenfranchised and minority groups. Many women were prominent reformers, and feminist crusades for women's suffrage and other rights became central to the Progressive agenda. Progressive women, however, divided over whether reform should aim mainly at social and economic equality between the sexes or at extending women's distinctive nurturing and protective roles to new areas of social life. Male, or female, Progressives rarely challenged prevalent racial stereotypes and sometimes embellished them with new theories of race discrimination. Southern Progressives improved opportunities for white citizens while aggressively and systematically disenfranchising and segregating African Americans.

Throughout the country, meanwhile, new waves of immigrants represented, with African Americans, "problems" to be addressed. It was sometimes difficult to separate honest assaults on urban machine "corruption" from nativist attacks on the new ethnic arrivals whom those machines often served or to differentiate the humane aspects of the push to "Americanize" immigrants through education from the less noble instincts behind immigration quotas and policies of exclusion.

Progressivism's recognition that true democracy might require an expanded public sphere occasionally pointed in the direction of a paternalistic state. The conflicting impulses behind progressivism are evident in the constitutional changes the Progressives helped bring about: amendments that gave women the vote, that provided for direct election of U.S. senators, that facilitated new social policies by permitting a federal income tax, and that strictly prohibited the sale or consumption of alcoholic drink.

The terms on which President Wilson led the United States into World War I in 1917 were likewise emblematic of such conflicting impulses. Wilson and other Progressives who loathed militarism nevertheless celebrated conscious, organized intervention to "make the world safe for democracy." World War I and the surge of nationalism and reaction it ushered in also put an end, for the moment, to sustained reflection on the tensions at the core of Progressive thought. When some elements of the earlier progressivism reemerged during the 1930s in President Franklin D. Roosevelt's New Deal, they brought with them the unresolved dilemmas that are a major part of the Progressive legacy.

Progressivism Today

The tensions between expertise, social justice, and democratic control remain within progressivism today, but they have taken new forms since the end of World War II. Progressivism developed before the invention of modern welfare economics and the creation of policy analysis. Yet its ideas are reflected in present-day justifications for activist government derived from economics.

In addition to the inefficiencies of monopoly, modern progressives point to the presence of spillover effects, such as air and water pollution, and to the public's limited access to information about risks and product characteristics. They are also concerned with disparities in the distribution of income and wealth and with inequities in the way such basic goods as education are provided. These failures of the market justify government action to improve the efficiency and fairness of society.

Many modern scholars and political commentators cast a critical eye on some of the policy initiatives of the Progressive Era and the New Deal. They argue that regulation is unnecessary for such potentially competitive industries as airlines and trucking. While the deregulatory mantle is sometimes appropriated by the libertarian right, responsible arguments for deregulation are as much in the progressive tradition as the social regulation of the 1970s expanding the federal role in controlling environmental pollution and protecting the health and safety of workers and consumers. In both cases, the aim is to ground government intervention in sound economic principles. Along these lines, many progressives join with libertarians in supporting free trade and arguing against market restrictions that lack an efficiency rationale.

Progressivism accepts as given an economic system based on private property and capitalist production. It does not, however, make a fetish of either institution. Thus private property rights can be rearranged to improve the fairness or efficiency of the system, and private capitalist firms can be required to pay the costs of the damage they impose on society. The existing distribution of entitlements has no special legitimacy in progressive thought.

But if the government does intervene, it should do so in a cost-effective way. Thus one aspect of modern progressive thought is the design of efficient public programs—a process that requires both expert knowledge and regulatory techniques that minimize the amount of expertise needed. Programs should be designed to economize on information as well as to allocate resources efficiently. For example, economists recommend the use of pricing systems to regulate environmental harms and to allocate scarce government resources, such as rights to use the airwaves or to graze cattle on public land. For redistributive programs, they favor monetary subsidies rather than in-kind benefits. Such programs limit the information needed concerning regulated firms, ranchers, and the poor. Nonetheless, expertise can never be entirely avoid-

ed. The state must fix the price or determine the quantity. It must set eligibility standards for subsidies and monitor compliance. Marketlike strategies cannot entirely overcome the market failure that justified the public program in the first place. Progressives recognize the value of marketlike incentives without assuming that they will eliminate the need for bureaucratic expertise and judgment.

A final strand in postwar progressive thought concerns the political system itself. The public choice movement in the social sciences, as expressed in the work of James M. Buchanan, Gordon Tullock, and others, has posed a challenge. By pointing out that politicians, bureaucrats, and experts may have interests opposed to those of citizens, these mostly conservative scholars argue that government will not invariably further the public interest. To them, the best solution is limited government.

Progressives are too sensitive to the failures of private organizations and the market to accept this conclusion. Yet they have had to respond to this negative view of government. One response has been a revived interest in ideology and professionalism as checks on raw self-interest. The second response is a heightened concern for procedures. If even experts can be self-interested, one cannot rely on unconstrained delegation to resolve the technical problems of a regulatory law. Bureaucratic procedures must be accountable to the public. If we cannot assume the good will of political and bureaucratic actors, we can, at least, seek procedures that minimize the conflict between self-interest and public values even when the market cannot function.

Although economics has set the stage for modern progressivism, it is insufficient to resolve the political dilemmas facing the modern regulatory welfare state. Progressivism in the late twentieth century needs the insights of political science and philosophy as well as economics. It is still engaged in the search for a balance between competence and democratic legitimacy.

See also *Ballots; Dewey, John; Politics, Machine; Roosevelt, Theodore; Welfare, Promotion of; Wilson, Woodrow.*

Frederick Bartol and Susan Rose-Ackerman

BIBLIOGRAPHY

Buenker, John D., and Edward R. Kantowicz, eds. *Historical Dictionary of the Progressive Era, 1890–1920.* Westport, Conn., and London: Greenwood, 1988.

Chambers, John Whiteclay, II. *The Tyranny of Change: America in the Progressive Era, 1900–1917*. New York: St. Martin's, 1980.

Crunden, Robert. *Ministers of Reform: The Progressives' Achievement in American Civilization, 1889–1920*. Urbana: University of Illinois Press, 1984.

Gould, Lewis L., ed. *The Progressive Era*. Syracuse, N.Y.: Syracuse University Press, 1974.

Kloppenberg, James. *Uncertain Victory: Social Democracy and Progressivism in European and American Thought, 1870–1920*. New York: Oxford University Press, 1986.

Link, Arthur S., and Richard L. McCormick. *Progressivism*. Arlington Heights, Ill.: Harlan Davidson, 1983.

Rodgers, Daniel. "In Search of Progressivism." *American History* 10 (December 1982): 113–131.

Rose-Ackerman, Susan. *Rethinking the Progressive Agenda: The Reform of the American Regulatory State*. New York: Free Press, 1992.

Sklar, Martin. *The Corporate Reconstruction of American Capitalism, 1890–1916*. Cambridge: Cambridge University Press, 1988.

Wiebe, Robert H. *The Search for Order, 1870–1920*. New York: Hill and Wang, 1967.

Property rights, Protection of

Protection of property rights is a concept that is concerned with the legal relationship between individuals or collectives and material resources. Property rights define the interest an individual or group has in a material good with respect to the rest of the world. To say that someone owns a particular piece of private property is to imply that the person has a greater interest in that object than anyone else. The nature, justification, and implications of this interest are complex. The organizing principle of a system of private property is that each object belongs to one person. Yet the system also provides for numerous forms of joint ownership. Some concepts of property rights do not even provide for individual ownership. Instead they assign ownership either to a collective, based on some common interest, or to society at large, based upon some interest in the object that all people share equally.

Property is often owned jointly by a collection of individuals, such as business partners, or a husband and wife. A property owner need not even be a human being: Much property is owned by collective entities created by the state, such as privately or publicly held corporations, joint stock companies, cooperatives, or trusts. Even in countries committed to private ownership of property, the state itself is a property owner.

Methods of Allocation

Why is it desirable or necessary to give one person or group a greater interest in an object than anyone else? Most of the philosophers who have thought that the protection of private or collective property rights is necessary and desirable—with the exception perhaps of Karl Marx—have traced this system of organizing rules to the phenomenon of scarcity. Because human demands are greater than the supply of material resources, there must be some method to determine how these goods are allocated among competing claimants. Given that people's prosperity, and even their survival, can be at stake, profound disagreements can arise over the use of scarce resources. Property rights are the method a society uses to decide, in a fair and predictable manner, who is to have access to what resource. This method of allocation varies across societies, depending upon the principles of distributive justice to which a society subscribes. These principles describe each individual's rights and duties in a society's institutions and determine the appropriate distribution of the benefits and burdens that accompany membership in the community.

A society's provision for any right to property, private or otherwise, to resolve this allocation dilemma indicates a commitment to the individual that sets it apart from societies based on other theories of justice. A society in which resources were distributed according to need or merit would produce another allocation of goods and would not necessarily justify private ownership. To understand the significance of the right to property, it is important to understand what it means to have a right at all.

States must justify allocating scarce resources to one person or group over others. The justification usually rests on one of three types of political theory: goals based, duty based, and rights based. Under goals-based political theories, actions that advance a society's goals, such as economic efficiency, are encouraged, while actions that undermine the goals are prohibited. Under a duty-based political theory, acts that fulfill a set of duties individuals may have, such as following the biblical Ten Commandments, are encouraged even at the expense of goals such as economic efficiency. Under a rights-based political theory, the aims of the state are based on individual claims to a certain way of life, regardless of the effect on other goals or the diminution of the general welfare. Rights-based political theories focus on individual autonomy rather than on conformity with some moral code (as in duty-based theories) or on the advancement of general welfare (as in goals-based theories).

To guarantee a right to property is to give an individual claim to a material resource regardless of the effects on other goals of society. This very strong claim is probably what the eighteenth-century English jurist Sir William Blackstone had in mind when he described private property as "that sole and despotic dominion which one man claims and exercises over the external things of the world, in total exclusion of the right of any other individual in the Universe."

Yet few states, if any, conceive of property rights so broadly or protect them so strongly at the expense of other moral duties or social goals. The fact that the state will enforce someone's property right in a baseball bat does not permit that person to whack anyone over the head with it. Both the goal of public safety and the moral duty not to harm others override a property owner's "sole and despotic dominion" over an object with respect to the rest of the world.

The state thus can restrict the use of property rights without weakening the concept of ownership of an object. This suggests that the nature of this right is more complex than complete control over a material good. Indeed, property rights can better be viewed as a bundle of different rights, which—depending upon the political and economic aims of a particular society—can be enjoyed in greater or lesser measure without undermining the overall conception or protection of private property.

Even though the right to property rarely means despotic control over a good, the total bundle of rights that makes up property ownership does entail various forms of dominion. The components of the bundle may vary. The standard elements of the liberal concept of ownership, as set forth by the contemporary English legal philosopher Anthony Honoré, would include possession, use, management, income, capital, security, transmissibility, absence of term, prohibition against harmful use, liability to execution, and residuary rights. These terms are defined as follows.

Possession is the exclusive physical control of an object. *Use* means the enjoyment and benefit of the object owned. *Management* is the right to decide how and by whom the thing owned shall be used. *Income* means the right to benefits derived from sacrificing personal use and

enjoyment of an object and allowing others to use and enjoy it. *Capital* is the power to alienate the object and the liberty to consume, waste, or destroy all or part of it. *Security* means immunity from expropriation so that the owner can look forward indefinitely to retaining ownership. *Transmissibility* is the owner's right to devise, bequeath, or alienate the interest in an object to other people at will. *Absence of term* means that the owner's rights are not limited to a certain term. *Prohibition against harmful use* means that the owner has a duty not to use property in a manner harmful to others. *Liability to execution* means that the owner's interest in an object is subject to confiscation for payment of a debt. And *residuary rights* means that when lesser interests in an object that have been transferred to others lapse, they revert to the owner with the greatest interest.

Justifications

Although no society guarantees the entire bundle of rights, historical and anthropological data suggest that some elements of property rights are protected nearly everywhere. The degree to which any of these are protected—or even whether schemes of collective or communal ownership are favored—depends upon the larger concept of justice that property rights are designed to serve.

Attempts to justify property rights are as old as political theory itself. Aristotle in the fourth century B.C. provided an early utilitarian defense of private property rights against communal ownership. Utilitarianism aspires to maximize the total or average happiness of society by preferring any political aim that improves the general welfare. Aristotle based his rejection of communal ownership on the grounds that the net total productivity of land would be higher and the level of social conflict lower if each person owned his or her own plot of land. He thought it was natural that people would work hardest at what was theirs. Nevertheless, some people would always work harder than others, and they would resent the freeloaders. Aristotle advocated private property rights in order to achieve the social goods of peace and productivity, not to protect some crucial aspect of individuality. Indeed, Aristotle was willing to divide the bundle of property rights and distribute the use of resources communally in order to preserve social cohesion.

Another famous defense of property runs contrary to Aristotle. One of the most distinctive aspects of this argument, developed by the seventeenth-century English philosopher John Locke, is the justification of private ownership in terms of the individual rather than the general welfare. Locke set out to show how individuals can come to have property rights in what God has given to everyone in common.

Rejecting the notion that all property, including people, belonged in the first instance to the king, Locke argued that all people belonged to themselves and had a right to own material resources even before the rise of civil society—that is, in the state of nature. This natural right comes from the need to use these material resources to survive. Locke claimed that when a person took objects from their natural state and mixed his or her labor with them, part of what that person owned became mixed together with the object in such a way as to exclude the common right of other people to own it and to make that object his or her property. So, for example, if a pioneer cleared some land of trees and rocks, he or she would own the land. Similarly, if that pioneer became a farmer and labored in the field to plant a crop, he or she would own the harvest. In Locke's view, property rights are so important that no one would consent to any government that failed to protect those rights, and any government that did fail to do so would legitimately be the object of rebellion.

Although Locke justified property rights based on the individual, he did not base his justification on what all individuals have in common. Rather, he based his argument on what some individuals might happen to do. If no one mixed his or her labor with an object or acquired an object legitimately from someone who did do so, then no property rights would exist.

A modern variation proposed by the American philosopher Robert Nozick justifies property ownership based on historical entitlement. Asking whether a particular distribution of property is just means asking how people acquired it. If each individual got it fairly, through some just principle of acquisition or through transfer from someone else who had justly acquired the property, then no one's freedom has been violated, and there is no cause for complaint. If the pedigree of a piece of property is tainted, it undermines the property right of the owner.

Because of the immensely long span of time that separates today's societies from the prehistoric "state of nature," it is impossible to know the lineage of most property. Hence, the justice of the distribution must be taken on faith—something that those excluded from ownership are unlikely to accept. Moreover, like all special rights, historical entitlement does not justify property based on some universal human trait. Rather the right is justified by a special or contingent set of circumstances, such as mixing one's labor with the property or purchasing it from someone who has already done so. Some people may or may not find themselves in a position to satisfy these conditions for reasons beyond their control. For example, there may be no unclaimed land left or no willing sellers.

Under these theories, large portions of the population who do not satisfy the specific conditions will not enjoy the right to property. This is inconsistent with the notion of fundamental rights that protect some aspect of human nature everyone possesses. Rights to speech and privacy, for example, are not normally conditioned upon actions beyond a person's control. Property could also be seen as a crucial component of some other right that is considered fundamental, such as freedom or democracy. If so, societies would have to balance their commitment to property rights against these other goals.

According to the early nineteenth-century German philosopher G. W. F. Hegel, justice requires more than a system of property rights protecting individual entitlement. Ownership of property is seen as necessary for everyone. For Hegel, property was a basic aspect of ethical development that enabled people to act freely in the world. This view of property led him to oppose poverty in part because lack of property undermined individual freedom, to which everyone was entitled.

Property and Justice

If the right to private property is justified because it supports a more general right, such as freedom or democratic participation, then societies that maintain inequalities of property ownership may be in danger of undermining these universal values. Many philosophers before and since Hegel have connected property rights with personal freedom in some manner. These include many of the Framers of the U.S. Constitution and modern political theorists from Milton Friedman to John Rawls.

To see how property was designed to protect individual freedom, it is important to recall that in the ancient world and in the Middle Ages, citizenship did not afford equal status to all members of society. Citizens in ancient Rome and Greece had independent power based primarily on property ownership. Feudalism imposed a complex legal relationship between lord and serf, which essentially made the serf the property of the lord. The general right to property advocated by Locke and his successors gave people ownership over themselves first of all and then the right to own objects—thus freeing them from dependence upon the state. This independence is seen as a precondition of democratic participation, whereby each person is able to participate in the political process as an equal. *Equal* in this sense does not mean that each person has exactly the same material means. Rather, each person has access to property, and this access provides the foundation for freedoms of speech, assembly, and so forth, which are the groundwork of democratic government.

There is, however, a paradox in the relationship between property rights and freedom that has been observed by both libertarians and socialists. If people are to have the freedom to possess and transfer as a key aspect of owning property, some people will work harder than others or use their talents to make better use of their property. In short, the freedom of action that private ownership entails necessarily leads to inequality of property ownership.

Theorists from Aristotle through Seymour Martin Lipset, the contemporary American political sociologist, have doubted whether stable government can survive alongside profound material inequality. There is also some doubt about whether democratic political rights and individual freedoms can survive if these inequalities become extreme. If property rights provide the basis for independent political participation, this foundation will be removed under situations of extreme inequality. Independence will evolve into dependence by the poor upon those who control great wealth. This dependence is troubling if it is the natural result of people freely exercising their property rights.

The U.S. Supreme Court addressed this issue in *Marsh v. Alabama* (1946). The case involved a large corporation that owned a company town for its workers. The company excluded from its property people who were trying to exercise their First Amendment rights to freedom of speech, assembly, and religion. The right to exclusive possession is one of the basic elements of ownership. Yet in this and later instances the Court took note of the clash between rights to speech and private property. The Court determined that when private property owners assumed the functional powers of the state, they lost some of their control over their property in deference to the constitutional freedoms of others.

Clearly, inequality of economic power among individuals can undermine the basis of freedom and democratic participation that property rights were originally designed to secure. Still, the concept of property is sufficiently complex and versatile to endure and to fulfill its various roles.

Owners who must yield part of their right to exclude can still enjoy the use, income, and transmissibility of their property in their bundle of property rights. A state that supports property rights for the role they play in protecting individual freedom and political participation may decide to protect an extensive bundle of property rights that achieve this goal.

See also *Aristotle; Hegel, G. W. F.; Locke, John.*

David Fagelson

BIBLIOGRAPHY

Ackerman, Bruce A., ed. *Private Property and the Constitution.* New Haven: Yale University Press, 1977.

Demsetz, Harold. "Toward a Theory of Property Rights." *American Economic Review: Proceedings and Papers* 57 (1957): 347–359.

Dworkin, Ronald. *Taking Rights Seriously.* Cambridge, Mass.: Harvard University Press; London: Duckworth, 1978.

Honoré, Anthony M. "Ownership." In *Oxford Essays in Jurisprudence,* edited by A. G. Guest. Oxford: Oxford University Press, 1961.

Locke, John. *Two Treatises of Government.* Edited by Peter Laslett. Cambridge and New York: Cambridge University Press, 1960.

Nozick, Robert. *Anarchy, State, and Utopia.* Cambridge: Harvard University Press, 1974.

Rawls, John. *A Theory of Justice.* Cambridge: Harvard University Press, Belknap Press, 1971; Oxford: Oxford University Press, 1973.

Ryan, Alan J. *Property and Political Theory.* Oxford and New York: Blackwell, 1984.

Waldron, Jeremy. *The Right to Private Property.* Oxford and New York: Oxford University Press, 1988.

Proportional representation

A category of electoral systems designed to translate voters' preferences proportionally into representatives' seats in multimember representative bodies. The most common forms of proportional representation (PR) use list PR formulas, according to which political parties are awarded seats proportionate to the numbers of votes cast for the different party lists. The less common alternative is the single transferable vote (STV) formula, in which voters cast votes for individual candidates instead of party lists. In STV arrangements, as in list PR, the aim is to achieve a proportional correspondence between votes and seats.

List PR formulas can be classified into systems based on highest averages (or divisor) and largest remainders (or quota), and subclassified according to their particular divisor or quota. As far as their effects are concerned, the main difference is the degree of proportionality. It is important to remember that the degree of proportionality in PR systems is affected not just by the particular PR formula but also, and more strongly, by the district magnitude (the number of representatives elected in a district) and electoral thresholds (commonly defined as a minimum percentage of the vote a party needs in order to receive any seats). Proportionality increases as district magnitude increases and the electoral threshold, if any, decreases.

The various forms of list PR as well as STV can be explained best by means of the five simple illustrations in Tables 1, 2, and 3. These five examples represent the vast majority of the PR systems that have actually been in use. For simplicity, the examples use the hypothetical case of a six-member district for list PR and a three-member district for STV. These are at the extreme ends of the normal range of average magnitudes: most list PR systems have magnitudes that are much higher than six, and most STV systems have average magnitudes of about four or five.

List PR Formulas

The two main highest-average formulas are d'Hondt and modified Sainte-Laguë. The rules of both specify that seats are awarded one at a time to the party that has the highest "average" numbers of votes per seat; each time a party is given a seat, its average goes down. This procedure continues until all seats are allocated. These averages are not normal averages (means) but are defined in terms of a particular set of divisors prescribed by the methods.

The d'Hondt divisors are the integers 1, 2, 3, 4, and so on. The first "average" of each party is its vote total divided by 1, that is, its original vote total. In Table 1 the first seat (indicated by the number in parentheses) is awarded to party A, the largest party. Party A's votes are then divided by 2, the next divisor. The second seat goes to party B, because its average (which equals its original vote total) is higher than A's new average and also higher than C's and D's averages. The third seat goes to party A because its vote divided by 2 is now higher than B's new average and also higher than C's and D's averages (which are still their original vote totals). The procedure—using each new divisor in turn as needed—is repeated until all six seats are allocated. The final seat distribution is 3, 2, 1, and 0 seats for the four parties, respectively.

TABLE 1.   Seat Allocation by Two Highest-Average Formulas in a Six-Member District with Four Parties

Party	Votes (v)	D'Hondt allocation			Total seats
		v/1	v/2	v/3	
A	42,000	42,000 (1)	21,000 (3)	14,000 (6)	3
B	31,000	31,000 (2)	15,500 (5)	10,333	2
C	15,000	15,000 (4)	7,500		1
D	12,000	12,000			0
TOTAL	100,000				

Party	Votes (v)	Modified Sainte-Laguë allocation			Total seats
		v/1.4	v/3	v/5	
A	42,000	30,000 (1)	14,000 (3)	8,400	2
B	31,000	22,143 (2)	10,333 (5)	6,200	2
C	15,000	10,714 (4)	5,000		1
D	12,000	8,571 (6)			1
TOTAL	100,000				

TABLE 2.   Seat Allocation by Two Largest-Remainder Formulas in a Six-Member District with Four Parties

Party	Votes	Hare quotas[a]	Full quota seats	Remaining seats	Total seats
A	42,000	2.52	2	0	2
B	31,000	1.86	1	1	2
C	15,000	0.90	0	1	1
D	12,000	0.72	0	1	1
TOTAL	100,000	6.00	3	3	6

Party	Votes	Droop quotas[b]	Full quota seats	Remaining seats	Total seats
A	42,000	2.94	2	1	3
B	31,000	2.17	2	0	2
C	15,000	1.05	1	0	1
D	12,000	0.84	0	0	0
TOTAL	100,000	7.00	5	1	6

a. Hare quota = 100,000 (votes) / 6 (seats) = 16,667
b. Droop quota = 100,000 / (6 + 1) = 14,286

A useful shortcut, especially when many more than six seats are to be allocated, is the Hagenbach-Bischoff method: first give all parties the numbers of seats that equal their Droop quotas (to be explained) and then continue by using the number of seats already won plus 1 as the next divisor. Although the Hagenbach-Bischoff procedure differs from the d'Hondt method, the results of the two are always identical.

The modified Sainte-Laguë divisors are 1.4, 3, 5, 7, and successive odd integers. (The pure Sainte-Laguë formula, which is rarely used in practice, has 1 rather than 1.4 as the first divisor.) The sequential procedure for awarding seats to parties is the same as in the d'Hondt method. In the example of Table 1, the first five seats are allocated in the same order, but the sixth seat is won by party D instead of party A. Hence the final seat allocation is 2, 2, 1, 1.

The two most common largest-remainder formulas, using the Hare and Droop quotas, are illustrated in Table 2. The first step in quota systems is to determine the quota of votes that entitles parties to receive a seat. Parties are given as many seats as they have quotas of votes, and any unallocated seats are given to those parties that have the largest numbers of unused votes (remainders). The Hare quota is the total number of valid votes divided by the number of seats; the slightly lower Droop quota divides the total number of votes by the number of seats plus 1.

The easiest method for calculating the results is to divide each party's votes by the quota (the results are shown in the third column of Table 2). Parties receive one seat for each full quota, and any unallocated seats go to the parties with the largest fractions of a quota. In the first part of Table 2, using the Hare quota, three seats are awarded initially on the basis of full quotas, and the remaining seats are allocated on the basis of largest remainders. In the table's second example, using the Droop formula, five seats are awarded on the basis of full quotas and one seat on the basis of largest remainders. An even lower quota has been used in Italy, the Imperiali quota, which is the total number of votes divided by the number of seats plus 2. The Imperiali formula, if it were applied to the example of Table 2 (it is not shown in the table), would allocate all seats on the basis of full quotas, but the final allocation of seats would be identical to that obtained with the Droop formula.

The examples of Tables 1 and 2 show that the choice of

PR formula can affect the allocation of seats. Such differences do not always occur. For instance, in a slightly larger district that elects seven representatives, all four formulas yield exactly the same result, namely, 3, 2, 1, and 1 seats for the four parties. When differences do appear, they occur within the two groups of divisor and quota formulas rather than between them, and they systematically affect the degree of proportionality of the election outcome.

Among the highest-average formulas, d'Hondt is the least proportional and gives the greatest advantages to larger parties. It contrasts with the pure Sainte-Laguë formula, which is highly proportional and treats large and small parties evenhandedly. Modified Sainte-Laguë makes it harder for small parties to gain their first seats by raising the first divisor from 1 to 1.4 and thus reduces proportionality to some extent.

Among the largest-remainder formulas, Hare is highly proportional and impartial between small and large parties. Proportionality decreases as the quota decreases. Lower quotas mean that there will be fewer remaining seats, and hence also more wastage of remaining votes—which is especially harmful to small parties because the remaining votes are a relatively large portion of the small parties' votes. The Imperiali quota is so low that often there will not be any remaining seats. When the quota is lowered to such an extent that all seats are full quota seats and all remaining votes are disregarded, the outcome becomes exactly the same as that of the d'Hondt formula. To sum up, d'Hondt and Imperiali are the least proportional, and pure Sainte-Laguë and Hare the most proportional, of the list PR formulas; modified Sainte-Laguë and Droop are in an intermediate position.

Single Transferable Vote

The proportionality of STV is more difficult to compare with that of the other PR formulas because voters cast preferential votes for individual candidates instead of party list votes. Table 3 contains a simple illustration of STV's rules: a three-member district, 100 voters, and five candidates. The voters' preferences appear at the top of the table. There are 23 ballots with candidate P as the first preference, Q as the second preference, and T in third place, with no further preferences indicated. Some other ballots also contain three preferences, but the rest contain only one or two preferences.

Like largest-remainder formulas, STV requires the choice of a quota, which is almost always the Droop quota. The STV Droop quota, however, differs slightly from

TABLE 3. Seat Allocation by Single Transferable Vote in a Three-Member District with Five Candidates

Droop quota = $[100 / (3 + 1)] + 1 = 26$

Preferences

23 ballots P, Q, T
23 ballots P, R, S
16 ballots Q, R
5 ballots R, S
20 ballots S, T
8 ballots T, Q, R
5 ballots T

Candidate	First count	Second count	Third count
P	46	− 20 = 26	26
Q	16	+ 10 = 26	26
R	5	+ 10 = 15	+ 8 = 23
S	20	20	20
T	13	13	− 13 = 0
Nontransferable	—	0	+ 5 = 5

Candidates elected: P, Q, and R.

the largest-remainder Droop quota: the quotient arrived at by dividing the total vote by the number of seats plus 1 is rounded up; if the quotient is an integer, 1 is added. In the example of Table 3, the largest-remainder Droop quota would be 25, but the STV Droop quota is 26. (In mass elections with thousands of votes, the difference between two Droop quotas is so tiny that it can be ignored.)

In the first count the ballots are arranged according to first preferences. Candidates who have a Droop quota or more of these first preferences are elected: this applies to candidate P with 46 votes. In the second count, P's 20 surplus votes are transferred to the next preferences, half to Q and half to R, because the original 46 ballots with P as first preference were also split equally between Q and R as second preferences. With the help of the transferred votes, Q is also elected in the second count with exactly 26 votes (and hence no surplus votes). Because, in the third count, there are no surplus votes to be distributed, the weakest candidate (T) is eliminated and T's 13 votes are available for transfer; 8 of these ballots show Q as second preference, but because Q is already elected, they are credited to the third preference, R; since the other 5 ballots contain no second preference, these votes become nontransferable. Now only four candidates are left, and S is next in line for elimination; this means that no further calculations are necessary and that R is the third candidate to be elected.

Because STV voters vote for individual candidates, they can vote for candidates of different parties. However, STV can be compared with the other PR formulas on the basis of the simplifying assumption that party votes lost by transfers to candidates of other parties are gained back by transfers from other parties. That is, assume that voters cast their votes entirely within party lines. The results then become very similar to those of the Droop largest-remainder formula. STV therefore can be placed in the same intermediate category of proportionality as Droop and modified Sainte-Laguë. However, since STV requires the rank ordering of candidates, having a very large number of candidates would make the voters' task extremely difficult. Hence STV tends to be applied in low-magnitude districts—which results in a considerable reduction in its proportionality.

The Popularity of D'Hondt

The PR formulas are not used with equal frequency. By far the most popular formula for national legislative elections is d'Hondt: it is used in Belgium, Finland, Iceland, Israel, Luxembourg, the Netherlands, Portugal, Spain, and Switzerland, and it was used in Germany until 1987. Modified Sainte-Laguë has been used mainly in Norway and Sweden. Of the largest-remainder formulas, the main examples of Hare quotas are Costa Rica, Denmark, and, since 1987, Germany. Droop was used in Austria until 1971 and in the 1989 and 1990 elections in Greece; Imperiali has been used only in Italy.

Some of these systems use two levels of districts—relatively small lower-tier districts and large, often national, upper-tier districts—to ensure a high degree of nationwide proportionality; they may use different formulas at the two levels. It is also worth noting that several PR systems, such as the Finnish, Spanish, and Swiss, have one or a few single-member districts in which, by definition, PR cannot be used. The exceptions are so minor that these systems can still be called PR systems.

One reason d'Hondt is the most popular PR formula is

that it favors the larger parties to a greater extent than the other formulas—and large parties have more influence on electoral laws than do small parties. The importance of partisan self-interest should not be exaggerated, however. If the largest parties in PR systems really wished to maximize their gains, they would abolish PR altogether. Although d'Hondt is relatively advantageous for large parties, it is still fundamentally a proportional method.

D'Hondt has two additional properties that have contributed to its popularity. One is that it discourages parties from splitting or presenting more than one list per party as a tactical ploy. For instance, under the Hare formula, as in Table 2, with a five-member district, party B can double its seats from 1 to 2 by presenting two separate lists, each receiving half of the votes of B's supporters. Under d'Hondt a party can never benefit from splitting into separate lists.

D'Hondt is also free from the so-called Alabama paradox. This paradox is the possibility, which occurs fairly often, that when the total number of seats in a district is increased by one, one of the parties may actually lose a seat. All quota formulas suffer from this paradox. But divisor formulas award seats sequentially; hence, when a seat is added to a district, the allocation of the other seats cannot change. The Alabama paradox has received the greatest attention in the context of assigning legislative seats to election districts rather than allocating district seats to parties, but the two processes are conceptually identical.

A distinction that cuts across all list PR systems is the degree of voters' influence on the selection of candidates within lists. In closed-list PR, as in Germany and Israel, voters cannot change the order of the candidates' names on the lists. In partly open list PR, voters can express a preference for one or more individual candidates, but these candidates have to obtain a large number of votes in order to be chosen ahead of candidates who have a higher position on the list, as in Belgium and the Netherlands. In completely open list PR, of which Finland is the best example, the election of candidates from a list depends entirely on the voters' preferences. In this respect, open-list PR is similar to STV, another system in which it is entirely up to the voters to decide which candidates of a particular party will be elected.

Semiproportional Formulas

In the debate about the merits of electoral systems, the main split divides PR advocates and supporters of the plurality single-member district system (in which the candidate with the most votes wins regardless of whether he or she has received an absolute majority). The former emphasize the advantages of proportionality and minority representation, whereas the latter praise the pressures toward two-party systems and the close voter-representative contact of their favorite system.

Semiproportional systems can be seen as intermediate systems that try to combine some of the advantages of both PR and plurality; they can therefore also be labeled semiplurality systems. These systems provide for minority representation without formal PR by adjusting the rules of plurality. The principal semiproportional methods are the cumulative vote, limited vote, and single nontransferable vote.

The cumulative vote resembles plurality in multimember districts (in which each voter has as many votes as there are seats to be filled), except that voters are allowed to cumulate their votes. The classic example is the method by which the lower house of the Illinois state legislature was elected from 1870 to 1980. Three-member districts were used, in which each voter could cast his or her three votes for one candidate (receiving three votes), for two candidates (receiving one and one-half votes each), or for three candidates (receiving one vote each). The main reason for instituting the cumulative vote system was to give Democrats in heavily Republican areas and Republicans in heavily Democratic areas an opportunity to elect representatives: the party could nominate one candidate per district and ask its supporters to cast all their votes for that candidate.

The limited vote is also similar to multimember plurality except for one important feature: the voters are given fewer votes than the number of seats at stake in the district. The best-known examples are a few districts in British parliamentary elections in the late nineteenth century (mainly three-member districts in which each voter had two votes) and the Spanish Senate (most of the members of which are elected in four-member districts with three votes per voter).

The single nontransferable vote (SNTV), used for the election of the Japanese House of Representatives from 1947 to 1993, is a special form of the limited vote in which each voter has one vote in districts that generally have three to five members. SNTV makes it relatively easy for small parties to be elected. For instance, in a four-member SNTV district, a candidate has to poll only slightly more than 20 percent of the vote to be guaranteed to win. This is the same as the Droop quota in STV, which is also suffi-

cient for election. Moreover, SNTV entails two special problems for large parties that small parties do not face: they have to decide how many candidates they can safely nominate and then instruct their supporters to divide their votes equally among these candidates. Overnomination, undernomination, and unequal vote distribution can all be costly to large parties. In practice, Japanese SNTV and Irish STV, which have used districts of similar magnitude, have been about equally proportional.

On the other hand, the minority representation made possible by the cumulative vote and the limited vote applies mainly to the second largest party. In the typical Illinois three-member district, the first party would get two seats and the second party would get one; in the typical Spanish senatorial district, the first party wins three seats and the second party wins one. Neither formula does much for third, fourth, and smaller parties.

To summarize, SNTV is similar in its main effects to STV and hence much closer to PR than to plurality. The cumulative and limited votes disproportionately favor the large parties—much like plurality. These formulas are therefore not truly intermediate systems in the sense of being roughly in the middle of the wide gap between PR on the one hand and single-member district plurality on the other.

See also *Districting; Duverger, Maurice; Electoral systems; Hermens, Ferdinand A.*

Arend Lijphart

BIBLIOGRAPHY

Amy, Douglas J. *Real Choices/New Voices: The Case for Proportional Representation in the United States.* New York: Columbia University Press, 1993.

Balinski, Michel L., and H. Peyton Young. *Fair Representation: Meeting the Ideal of One Man, One Vote.* New Haven: Yale University Press, 1982.

Bogdanor, Vernon. *What Is Proportional Representation? A Guide to the Issues.* Oxford: Martin Robertson, 1984.

Finer, S. E., ed. *Adversary Politics and Electoral Reform.* London: Anthony Wigram, 1975.

Hallett, George H., Jr. *Proportional Representation: The Key to Democracy.* Washington, D.C.: National Home Library Foundation, 1937.

Katz, Richard S. *A Theory of Parties and Electoral Systems.* Baltimore: Johns Hopkins University Press, 1980.

Lakeman, Enid. *How Democracies Vote: A Study of Electoral Systems.* 4th ed. London: Faber and Faber, 1974.

O'Leary, Cornelius. *Irish Elections 1918–77: Parties, Voters, and Proportional Representation.* New York: St. Martin's, 1979.

Reed, Steven R. "Structure and Behaviour: Extending Duverger's Law to the Japanese Case." *British Journal of Political Science* 20 (July 1990): 335–356.

Rose, Richard. *What Are the Economic Consequences of PR?* London: Electoral Reform Society, 1992.

Protest movements

A form of activity organized to influence politics outside conventional political institutions such as elections, parties, lobbying, and patronage. The protest movements that concern us here are those directed at wielders of power in democracies. Increases in education, improved communications, and changing values have encouraged a participatory revolution among citizens. Many are not content to limit their political involvement to voting and other activities carried out principally within political parties. They seek to influence political decision making directly by engaging in what is variously referred to as political protest, direct action, aggressive political participation, or grassroots or elite-challenging activities.

Modern democratic societies contain public organizations—governmental or state—as well as other politically relevant institutions, such as parties, interest groups, and various types of associations, that are not a part of the formal machinery of government. These institutions of political and civil society play a major role in the political process by providing channels of communication between individual citizens and holders of elected, appointed, and bureaucratic positions. Protest movements often bypass these channels, though they may seek to work through them as well.

What Protest Movements Do

People have always protested against unpopular authorities, laws, and regulations. History is full of slave revolts, peasant uprisings, urban riots, tax revolts, and the like. Likewise, history is full of repression of these manifestations of popular opinion: engaging in such activities is dangerous under nondemocratic regimes. Democracies provide popular control over authorities and regular channels of communication between the public and those who wield power. Elections, parties, personal contacts, and interest group politics would seem to make protest activities unnecessary.

The availability of these multiple paths of access to power holders has not prevented the development of more aggressive forms of direct action by protest movements. These include shutting down offices, plants, factories, and schools by occupying buildings; preventing the movement of trains, buses, and planes by lying down on the roads and runways; boycotting and picketing shops and products of firms that engage in activities opposed by the movement; trying to shut down abortion clinics; disrupting meetings; marching in demonstrations; and many other acts.

Much protest activity is directed at public authorities, but private individuals, corporations, and associations may also feel the ire of demonstrators. Although many of the policy goals of movements are general and national or even international, action can take place at any level. The following discussion concentrates on attitudes and behaviors that have been researched extensively and about which considerable empirical information is available.

So-called conventional participation includes such acts as voting, discussing politics with friends, attending rallies, following politics in the press and on television, working for a party or candidate, and contacting political figures. The "unconventional," or protest, forms of participation can be divided into two categories—legal and illegal. Legal forms include gathering and signing petitions (hardly unusual in some countries but rare in others), engaging in lawful demonstrations, picketing or boycotting stores or companies or products, and engaging in rent strikes. Illegal forms include violence against persons and property damage. These categories are not always distinct: what is legal in one country may be prohibited in another, though patterns are similar in the long-established democracies. Some actions, such as occupying buildings and blocking traffic, may vary in legality from one country to another.

There is very little support in present democracies for illegal forms of protest that involve violence against people or property; fewer than 2 percent of the citizens of contemporary democracies approve of these actions or claim to engage in them. Riots may be associated with protest movements, but they are seldom planned events. Rather, they are usually triggered by passions and frustrations stemming from confrontations between the public and authorities, and sometimes they are fueled by desire for the material rewards of looting. Terrorism, which is politically motivated violence by individuals or groups against symbolic or substantive targets, is supported only by a small portion of the general population, though it may be approved of widely within particular subgroups. A major goal of protest movements is to gain support from the undecided or indifferent, so protest groups seldom encourage extreme forms of action. Most citizens of democratic countries have come to accept legal forms of protest as legitimate and useful.

Although protest is often viewed as elite-challenging, or "bottom up," political action, protest activities require leadership, organization, skills, and other resources. Protest movements are usually led by political entrepreneurs for whom activism is a career. Others who participate hold political attitudes and policy preferences that are consistent with the goals and activities of the protest movement. But individuals and groups must still be mobilized; they must be brought into the movement, made to feel enthusiasm for its goals, and encouraged to take part in its activities.

Publicity is the fuel of successful protest. Given a grievance that would be widely shared by substantial groups in society, the problem remains of converting potential protest into real action. Coverage in the media, especially television coverage, assumes immense importance for the success of a protest movement. Thus much of the activity of protest movements is undertaken to gain publicity. Often the more outrageous a protest group's activity, the better.

One reason protest movements attract participants is that individuals are often frustrated in trying to affect government decision making. Local direct action against a known opponent often brings satisfactions not easily available on a larger stage. Many issues, such as war and peace or large economic problems, may seem so distant from the world of the average citizen as to be beyond influence. More local issues—an environmental hazard or a discriminatory practice or the construction of a jail in the neighborhood—may seem both more pressing and more amenable to direct action. Hence much protest activity is local, organized for a limited purpose, devoid of ties with larger concerns, and often short lived.

However, protest activities may possess a larger national or international dimension. The civil rights movement in the United States, the worldwide environmental movement, the struggle for rights for gays and lesbians, and the feminist movement all exhibit some of the characteristics of protest movements. Large social movements like these may include many different types of organizations and behaviors. They often incorporate interest organizations, associations, and even political parties.

The ecology, or green, parties of several countries, for example, use their party and sometimes parliamentary status as much to publicize movement goals as to advance themselves electorally. Other parties and associations may appear to be different things at different times. The line between parties and protest movements is seldom clearcut, since the latter specialize in fluid and often changing patterns of relationships with other participants in the political sphere. Parties seek to place candidates in office. Protest movements seek to achieve diverse goals, of which placing people in office may be one. Parties often seek to co-opt popular protest movements. Indeed, one measure of success for a movement is to have its goals adopted by major political forces.

Explanations of Protest Movements

There are as many explanations for protest movements as there are grievances in the world. However, ascribing the protest merely to the grievance is as simplistic as ascribing revolt to tyranny. Grievances and tyranny have long been with us; the protest movements we are discussing are a product of the age of mass politics, the short period in human history in which the preferences and behaviors of ordinary citizens have influenced political outcomes.

Although protest has been widespread in history, the age of mass politics has barely exceeded two centuries. Mass politics is associated with the destruction of the feudal order, the establishment of constitutional systems with limited suffrage, and the later democratization of these systems through the development of mass parties to mobilize the newly enfranchised. That is, mass politics coincides with the growth both of competitive politics and of inclusive politics.

The New Politics as Explanation

Voters in the age of mass politics needed well-organized parties that could compensate for the individual's poorly developed personal skills and resources. In Europe, these parties were largely socialist, communist, and Christian democratic; in the United States, city machines and personal followings achieved the same results. When many people could not read—and, of course, before radio and television came along—people communicated face to face. Most people interacted mainly with others who shared a number of personal characteristics, such as belonging to the working class or being of the same religious or linguistic or ethnic group, or identifying with a particular part of the country.

With democratization, the mass of people shifted from being objects of politics to being subjects with legal rights on their way to becoming citizens. In addition to rights, people had ways to participate fully in the political decisions that affected them. People's involvement in politics was based largely on their social group characteristics, a condition referred to as *social mobilization.* As parties developed ties with their supporters, patterns of mobilization became increasingly political—that is, based on direct ties between the individual and party with less intervention of the social groups. Changes in the personal characteristics of citizens led to what has been called *cognitive mobilization* based on the individual's personal understanding of his or her interests and preferences, without a party as intermediary.

The present period is the era of the "new politics," a time not only of cognitive mobilization but also of rising expectations concerning participation on the part of a well-educated and "postmaterialist" citizenry. As elaborated by political scientist Ronald Inglehart (in *The Silent Revolution* and other works), postmaterialism is prominent among younger citizens who were reared under conditions of physical and economic security and who are well educated. Postmaterialists are not opposed to material well-being but take it for granted; they value more highly other things such as self-realization, participation in decisions that affect them, interesting jobs, and personal freedom.

Postmaterialists are present in the electorate in large numbers. Their numbers increase with time because of generational replacement. (Those who die off are more materialist, while the young are postmaterialist.) They also possess the skills and resources to further their values in the political process. Proponents of the new politics explanation argue that postmaterialists are largely responsible for the waves of protest that have swept the United States and Europe since the 1960s and that democracies are faced with continued growth in the potential for protest as postmaterialist cohorts age. Of course, there are limits to the growth in the number of postmaterialists: economic downturns can delay and perhaps reverse that number.

A consequence of these changes is a shift in the social basis of protest. The working class has long been engaged in protest politics, not only against employers but also against political authorities because of the large role of the modern state in economic life. Today in many countries the working class represents the relatively materialist portion of the population. Working-class people fear that job losses may result from environmental, trade, and other policy shifts—changes that postmaterialists are likely to favor strongly.

Thus the force of the motive for change shifts from a conservative and fearful working class to a segment of the middle class with postmaterialist values and a concern for self-realization, a commitment to environmentalism, participatory democracy, and freedom in matters of sexual orientation. Because many of their positions on the issues are opposed by the traditional parties and politics, postmaterialists are likely to pursue their political goals outside as well as inside conventional channels.

Relative Deprivation as Explanation

Another view of the origins of protest movements focuses on the injustices, inequalities, and grievances in society that affect some groups far more than others and thus give rise to feelings of relative deprivation. There are many versions of this concept. A person who is not personally deprived may identify with a group that is, as a whole, deprived; therefore, we can speak of *fraternal deprivation.* And in discussions of deprivation, we must specify our frame of reference. Do we compare our achievements with those of others who are similar on some objective measure—same job but different income, for example—or do we focus on what we would like to have? Do we compare our situation with the best possible condition we can imagine? Notions of fairness can be very complex to sort out.

Reality is less important than perceptions and expectations in influencing behavior. Whether one feels deprived is affected by many factors, including socialization and culture. Perceptions are filtered through expectations, and these in turn are established by a complex process of individual and group interactions and assumptions.

Protesters usually have some resources that can be mobilized to make some level of success more probable. The extremely deprived are often too preoccupied with survival to become involved in protest movements. Some writers argue that acts of protest are a product of improving conditions; these acts relate especially to disappointments that emerge when a period of rising expectations is hit with sudden downturns. It is the discrepancy between aspirations and achievements that propels protest. Where aspirations are low, there is little protest.

The Rational Actor as Explanation

The rational actor approach has exercised great influence on thinking about protest in recent years. According to this approach, individuals often seek to satisfy their needs and preferences through collective action. It is the utility to the individual that accounts for involvement: the citizen receives personal rewards from the protest activity. These rewards may be material, in that the success of the activity would result in material benefits for the citizen. The citizen's involvement must also be important to the success of the movement: rational actors do not waste their time and other resources pursuing goals that either are impossible to achieve or will be achieved whether the citizen is personally involved or not.

The rational actor will be a "free rider" when possible—that is, he or she will leave collective action to others because one person will not be the determining factor in success and because if the collective action is successful he or she will benefit from it anyway. Scholars following the rational choice approach deal with this problem in part by emphasizing the noncollective, personal benefits the actor receives from participating. Aside from the material benefits mentioned above, these may include the simple satisfaction of being involved in a worthwhile cause and other subjective benefits.

By bringing in the subjective feelings of individuals as well as the material rewards of protest activities, the rational actor explanation begins to merge with the psychological and cultural explanations associated with the new politics and relative deprivation explanations. The different explanations point to the mixed motivations of protest activity. For many, protest is certainly largely instrumental—that is, it is a means to an end. For others, however, the movement, like all social activity, has important emotional elements that make activity valuable for its own sake. Indeed, it is likely that for many citizens political activity, including protest activity, is intimately tied up with personal identity and self-realization.

None of the three explanations adequately explains the process of mobilization. Individuals must be recruited into a movement; they must be socialized to its goals; their expectations must be raised. Although any particular segment of the population may have the potential for joining a protest movement, nothing will happen unless opportunity arises. Participation in protest movements is heavily dependent on context. City versus country, university community versus factory town, social science faculty versus engineering school—all these make a difference in how likely people are to realize their protest potential.

Who Protests?

The principle of democratic pluralism assumes that democratic politics opens the political system to the influence of individuals and groups with interests that demand representation. Many scholars and activists have criticized this view, pointing out that even in pluralist democracies there are many factors that favor the wealthy, well placed, and resourceful. Some democracies have other patterns of interest representation. Corporatist systems, for example, grant a preferred status to particular trade unions, employers' associations, and other groups in return for agreement to certain constraints on their behavior. Clientelist systems give privileged access to those with the right personal or party connections to those in power. In short, all systems, even the most democratic, offer uneven access to decision makers.

A long tradition of research on involvement in politics, including voting and other aspects of conventional participation, has demonstrated the dominance in political action, with only a few exceptions, of those with resources. This socioeconomic model predicts—correctly—that those with greater wealth, higher education, centrality of position, and higher status are more likely to participate in politics than those without these characteristics.

Historically, involvement in protest movements seems to have been concentrated in groups that rank low in socioeconomic status, and for whom presumably the conventional channels were closed. These have included industrial workers; ethnic, religious, and linguistic minorities; people on the geographical or cultural periphery; and beleaguered peasants and farmers. However, the societal evolution associated with the new politics seems to be changing the social origins of protesters. Studies since the 1960s indicate that the socioeconomic model explains involvement in protest movements as well as in conventional politics. Protest in democracies is now dominated by well-educated citizens of middle-class backgrounds. They possess the resources of skills, money, time, and general knowledge, as well as, perhaps, a clearer understanding of their interests than other citizens.

This change in the social basis of protest involvement may be a product of the particular historic period that began in the 1960s. It witnessed widespread student revolt, exacerbated by the large size of the baby boom cohort, combined with anti–Vietnam War, disarmament, antinuclear, environmental, sexual liberation, and, in the United States, civil rights movements. These affected people of all ages, but most of these movements had a special appeal to the young. The great material prosperity of the period encouraged postmaterialism and discouraged labor unrest.

An era of shrinking material possibilities may alter the demographic profile of protesters, with a rise in labor protest a likely consequence of the economic restructuring accompanying the internationalization of economies. The massive migrations now under way in Europe and America could also trigger mobilization along these lines. For the past generation, protest has been dominated by the educated young, but more recently antiabortionists and the Christian right, who recruit from all age groups, have become active.

The percentages of national populations that approve of protest and that are willing to engage in protest are far higher than the percentages that actually take part in protest actions. The demographic profiles of the two groups, however, are roughly similar. Both are dominated by educated young males. Men participate more in both conventional and protest politics than women, though the massive changes in the educational levels of women, their participation in the work force, and the impact of feminism should reduce these gender differences rapidly. Surprisingly, the gender gap is narrower with regard to protest than with regard to conventional political participation.

Students have the skills and other resources, including free time, to be active in politics. Young people, especially students, are relatively easy to mobilize. At least during the past generation, the student environment has been quite supportive of protest behavior. Becoming involved has not been demanding. Some generations of students, however, have been very conservative or even apathetic. The young in general, however, are low on conventional participation, including voting. It is only in the domain of protest that they dominate.

Many people engage in both protest activities and conventional forms of participation such as electoral politics. Far from being an alternative form of political action, engaged in largely by people shut out of conventional forms of political involvement, protest activities are for many only one part of their political involvement. Moreover, citizens who engage in both protest and conventional forms of participation are of higher socioeconomic status than those who engage only in protest behaviors.

The Consequences of Protest Movements

Protest movements place on the political agenda issues that the electoral and party processes seek to brush aside. Whether this is a good thing or a bad thing depends on one's point of view. The conventional political process functions in such as way as to aggregate demands and also to filter them, to soften some and reject others, and often to keep off the agenda issues for which no good solution seems forthcoming. For citizens with strong feelings about these issues, such outcomes are unacceptable. Movements that are successful in mobilizing large numbers of people cannot be ignored. Thus protest movements provide an antidote for the inadequacies of representative democracy or even of majority rule. Intense minorities matter in politics. To succeed, they must pay close attention to public opinion, to the impact that their actions are having on those not firmly for or against their goals. Given the widespread public opposition to violence, protest movements tend to remain moderate in their actions.

It is hard to conclude that political systems are seriously threatened by protest movements that operate within the rules of the game as they have emerged since the 1960s. Yet there can be no guarantee that ways of protesting will not change in less benign directions in the future.

In light of the ease with which a cause can gain visibility with the general public, and considering the benefits of material and emotional satisfaction for participants, political entrepreneurs are likely to continue to find it advantageous to exploit the potential of protest movements. The combination of educated and resourceful citizens who crave influence over matters that affect them and a complex governing structure that is heavily bureaucratized, often unresponsive, and, perhaps of necessity, remote is certain to encourage the search for alternative methods of influencing political outcomes. Nonviolent protest has widespread legitimacy among the public. Protest movements are too good an invention for serious political activists to ignore. They are part of the repertory of today's citizens.

See also *Civil society; Dissidents; Interest groups; Participation, Political; Rational choice theory; Revolutions; Social movements; Women's suffrage in the United States.*

Samuel H. Barnes

BIBLIOGRAPHY

Barnes, Samuel H., Max Kaase, et al. *Political Action.* Beverly Hills, Calif.: Sage Publications, 1979.

Gurr, Ted Robert. *Why Men Rebel.* Princeton: Princeton University Press, 1970.

Inglehart, Ronald. *Culture Shift.* Princeton: Princeton University Press, 1990.

———. *The Silent Revolution.* Princeton: Princeton University Press, 1977.

Kaase, Max. "Mass Participation." In *Continuities in Political Action,* edited by M. Kent Jennings et al. Berlin: Walter de Gruyter, 1990.

Muller, Edward N., and Karl-Dieter Opp. "Rational Choice and Rebellious Collective Action." *American Political Science Review* 80 (June 1986): 471–487.

Opp, Karl-Dieter. *The Rationality of Political Protest.* Boulder, Colo.: Westview Press, 1989.

Verba, Sidney, Norman H. Nie, and Jae-on Kim. *Participation and Political Equality.* Cambridge: Cambridge University Press, 1978.

Zimmermann, Ekkart. *Political Violence, Crises, and Revolutions.* Cambridge: Schenkman, 1983.

Protestantism

The beliefs and practices of most non-Catholic Western Christian churches. Protestantism, which is usually associated with devotion to the Bible as the source and norm of teaching, began as a reform movement within Western Christianity early in the sixteenth century. It has been a major contributor to the rise of modern democracy.

The political allegiances of Protestantism have been diverse, however. Some elements of original Protestantism supported monarchy and other old orders of polity, while some sided with advocates of democratic freedom and republican polities. The political allegiances have remained diverse. Some Protestants draw on their sources and texts to argue for authoritarian regimes and to support law and order, while, across the battle lines, other Protestants quote scriptures about liberty to justify their leanings toward revolution and their hope of establishing democracies.

Original Protestantism and Democracy

Protestantism is the name usually applied to the impulse and eventually the set of churches that resulted from efforts to reshape Catholic Christianity in northwest Europe and the British Isles beginning early in the sixteenth century. Various pre-Reformation movements, such as those begun in the fourteenth century by Jan Hus (1372?–1415) in Bohemia and John Wycliffe (1330–1384) in England, supported the authority of lay persons and thus were seen by the church and the emperor or king as subversively democratic. But the larger and permanent outbreak of Protestantism—named after a document of protest at the Diet of Speyer in Germany in 1529—vastly extended the voice and power of the laity against the power-holding clergy and thus contributed to the development of democratic thinking.

Martin Luther (1488–1546) of Saxony has attained an almost mythical reputation as a (or the) pioneer, although historians are cautious about favoring one part of Protestantism or one hero (or villain, to the Catholics of his day) over another. By challenging the papacy, which he argued was corrupt in its teaching and practice, and the emperor, at the Diet of Worms in 1521, Luther began to unsettle assumptions about the control of human destiny. For centuries, emperor and pope, king and bishop, magistrate and priest, had had official and often cooperative (but also frequently competitive) relationships with one another. Although lay nobles sometimes acquired power that made them almost independent of such a relationship, ordinary people had little control over their own political destinies. But when the relationship itself was challenged, more of them began to find ways to assert individual liberties.

Individual liberties, which were asserted first and chiefly with respect to human beings' dealings with God, soon were regarded as important in human beings' dealings with each other. (In a sense Protestantism set out to eliminate the middleman by attacking the priesthood as the sole link between human fate and divine judgment or grace.) It was a heady experience for lay people to be urged to read the Bible, which contained many texts that spoke of individual responsibility and personal freedom. But if one looked only at the German Reformation of Luther's time, little actual realization of democracy would be found.

The Protestant impulse developed coincidentally and semi-independently in many areas in the sixteenth century: in Switzerland under the French reformer John Calvin (1509–1564); in Scotland urged on by John Knox (1513–1572); in Britain under many theological influences after the separation of Henry VIII from Roman authority (1534); and in the Netherlands and Scandinavia. In almost every case, issues of political freedom accompanied the central impetus toward finding and declaring new relationships between believers and their God.

Most notable among these advocates of reform was

John Calvin, who carried on the bulk of his work in Geneva. From some viewpoints, Calvin was anything but an enhancer of democracy. In Geneva he and his colleagues, together with civic leaders, disempowered Catholic rule and rulers. But in their place the Calvinists set up a kind of theocracy, in which only the saints—Reformed Protestants—were to rule. The civic authorities, working alongside and under the theological cover of systematic Calvinism, tried to enact and enforce laws that explicitly bound people to one version of faith, now the Reformed one. That policy by itself would mark original Calvinism as antidemocratic. Dissenters—agents of religious liberty and anticipators of political democracy—were unwelcome. One of them, Michael Servetus (1511–1553), was burned as a heretic with as much punitive zest as had been displayed by the Catholic inquisitors who had hounded him earlier. Where there was no room for dissent, there was no room for democracy.

The Second Phase: Protestant Dissent

Calvinism included other impulses, however, and some of these came to light and fulfillment when a special branch of Calvinist Reformed theology informed an English movement called Puritanism. As early as the 1570s some Puritans were effectively protesting the Elizabethan Settlement, named after Elizabeth I, who had established the Anglican Church. To Puritans, the Anglican bishops and policies seemed as repressive as pre-Reformation Catholicism had been. Soon, after they attacked episcopacy and much of the ritual of the church as half-reformed, Puritans became the new victims of repression. Some of them migrated to the Netherlands and others to the Atlantic shores of North America. They went for freedom—their own freedom. But, far from being democrats, they set up in ideal circumstances, such as those provided by the Massachusetts Bay, theocracies as efficient and complex—and perhaps as punitive—as the one in Geneva.

Puritanism, however, carried within it the seeds of new democratic plantings, which its more established leaders themselves tried to stunt or uproot. At the heart of this version of Protestantism was the concept of a covenant, in which the God witnessed to in Christian faith reached down and made an agreement with the people in the body politic. The people also made a covenant with each other, as in the celebrated Mayflower Compact agreed upon by the first and more radical "Pilgrim" Puritans in Plymouth Colony in 1620. This covenant, while it bound God to demonstrations of care for the people, also bound the people to be responsible in their lay vocations and their civil life. But if they were to be responsible, they must be free.

The advocacy of freedom, based on such concepts as the priesthood of all believers (in part an import from the Lutherans), the freedom of the laity to read and interpret scriptures, and the insistence that local congregations and their leaders were the final authorities in church life, over which no pope or bishops could rule, all combined to cultivate democratic impulses. While all this was occurring, from the time of Luther and Calvin to the time of Massachusetts Bay governor John Winthrop (1588–1649), the more radical Reformed and Puritan types carried the incipient democratic logic of Protestantism further—and certainly further than old-line established Protestant authorities wanted it to go.

On the Continent most of these groups were called Anabaptists because they rebaptized adults who had been baptized as infants. Anabaptism also was a half-unveiled move toward democracy; it was assumed that even in matters of the soul, individuals must make rational decisions and act independently of actions taken on their behalf as infants by their parents and a parental kind of church. In England and New England and wherever else Puritan forces spread, the more radical groups were called Baptists or Congregationalists. The congregational concept was important in the spread of democracy because it again empowered individuals on the local scene, independent of and often against the central authority of church and state. Among the best known of these more radical sorts was Roger Williams (1603–1683), who, after founding Providence in 1636 with a few faithful sympathizers, ended up as a "seeker" without clear churchly ties in Rhode Island. His anti-establishment colony countered the originally more authoritarian Massachusetts Bay, New Haven, and Connecticut colonies.

The most decisive step in the realization of Protestant impulses to democracy occurred in the British colonies that became the United States of America with the signing of the Declaration of Independence in 1776 and the war and Constitutional Convention that followed. The establishment Calvinists of New England and their dissenting compatriots; the Presbyterians and other Protestants in New York, Pennsylvania, and other middle colonies; the Anglicans or Episcopalians in the southern colonies—except for some clergy who, having taken an oath to the Crown, fled to Canada or elsewhere or were silent or silenced—united to oppose king and monarchy. With that opposition came declarations not only of independence from Britain but also of support for equality and rights, bedrock assertions of the developing democracy.

The Enlightenment

The vast majority of the free population of the thirteen American colonies was Protestant. (Catholics numbered perhaps 30,000 in a population of more than 4 million.) It was natural, then, that Protestants should claim a patent on the ensuing democratic polity and practice. They did so with some warrant since they argued their case for political independence, liberty, and responsibility both in church and theology, and in daily life and politics, on the basis of biblical texts. These texts described a God of judgment and mercy who by covenant worked through human agents. But such agents needed liberties in order to be obedient and creative.

Because the same biblical texts were on the scene in 1517 when Luther began the work from which so many date Protestantism, there are good reasons to ask why they were not acted on and their democratic thrusts not realized until about 1787, well over two and a half centuries later. That kind of embarrassing question implies its own answer: Protestantism by itself did not "pull off" democracy, even though most branches of Protestantism cooperated in its development, profited from it, argued the case for it, and contributed to its realization and extension.

By most accounts, the main contemporary or corollary element in the rise of modern democracy was a movement that was in part complementary to and often quite competitive with the churches: the Enlightenment. In northwestern Europe outside France the Enlightenment was often of a Protestant or post-Protestant sort: friendly to the man Jesus, welcoming of the support of dissenting Protestant church people, and frequently successful even within the establishment. But instead of accenting the Bible as the source of divine and human truth alike, it looked at the figurative book of Nature and established freedoms on the basis of reason, or, as in the Declaration of Independence, on the basis of self-evident truths. The more radical thinkers simply opposed the church, but some linked up with Protestant dissenters in criticizing religious establishments. Thus, as was the case in the Virginia colony, they worked together to separate church and state.

Beginning in the late eighteenth century, Protestantism broke its northwestern European and Anglo-American bounds. Thanks to missionary and colonizing activities, it spread to many shores on most continents during the nineteenth century. Wherever its beachheads developed into full-blown churches, Protestantism brought with it— at least as ideals if not always in practice—an accent on the laity, the freedom to read the sacred texts, the validity of earthly vocations (as opposed to merely the quest for heaven), the strength of the local congregation as a kind of town meeting, the empowerment of citizens, the separation of church and state, freedom of speech, and rejection of religious authoritarianism.

The Mixed Record of Later Protestantism

In practice, as noted, various strains of Protestantism have not always been fully the friends of democracy. Thus in late twentieth-century Guatemala, historically a Catholic country, evangelical Protestants, growing in numbers and influence, at least twice elected one of their own to high public office. Working with the army to suppress liberties, they remained members in good standing of their Protestant organizations and for a time were seen as heroic defenders of law and order by many fellow believers. Yet they were repressive and permitted anything but biblical and Protestant advocacies of democratic freedom to be voiced.

The divisions within Protestantism make it very difficult to describe one systematic approach to democracy. Legally established Protestant churches, when they fought to hold on to privilege, feared anarchy and did what they could to put down dissent that might lead to democracy. Luther set a precedent for this repression when he opposed the mass of people in the peasants' uprising in Germany in 1525; Calvin did the same when he concurred with the execution of Servetus. So did New England Puritan Congregationalists in their exiling of Roger Williams, dissenter Anne Hutchinson, and any other upstart voices for freedom—even as they advocated a kind of democracy in town and church meeting. Yet the peasants, Servetus, Williams, Hutchinson, and the persecuted Quakers had equal claims on the name and traditions of Protestantism.

Variations based not on situation but on the theology itself existed as well. Luther, who could never say enough about the freedom of the believer in matters of faith, feared anarchy more than he feared authoritarianism, and Lutherans—with notable exceptions—often went along with and sometimes spoke up for authoritarian and even totalitarian regimes. Indeed, many Lutheran "German Christians" supported the führer principle in the days of Hitler—and nothing could have been more undemocratic. The Lutherans believed that they could not progressively bring in the Kingdom of God or utopia and often were resigned to living passively in an evil world. Thus it was possible for a Lutheran political ethic to be lived out without much protest against authority.

The Calvinist and Baptist forms of Protestantism, in contrast, are readier to see themselves as agents of world transformation. They generate social gospels and social Christianity, and they speak of bringing in the Kingdom of God, or of Christ transforming culture. When they connect notions of Kingdom and Christ-and-culture with human responsibility and freedom, they almost have to speak up for some kind of democracy. How can people who are captive of pope and emperor, regime and established church, be responsible for their actions if all their actions could be commanded and regulated?

This being said, the two poles described here may be a bit too neatly defined; real life is lived in the messiness of circumstance, complexity, and compromise. Some Protestants may speak a good line for democracy, but when they reach power, acting on the basis of the Original Sin that they have inherited—a widespread Protestant notion—they often forget that line. In such circumstances, however, some still give lip service to and often practice what theologian Paul Tillich called the Protestant principle of prophetic protest. In other words, they use the critical word of God to call to judgment all elements of power, including their own nations and churches. Against that standard all governments and religious institutions are seen as finite, limited, errant, and in need of perpetual reform even as they command some measure of loyalty. (Tillich did not believe that only and all Protestant churches upheld this principle. He named it as much after ancient prophesy as after Protestantism.)

Protestantism and Democracy

Protestant theology tends to include some common features. Basic is this: God is God and humans are not. Protestantism is theocentric in design, not human-centered. God judges kings and popes and autocrats and does not let them have complete control. Next, humans, while sinful, have potential both as the redeemed and, even in the natural order, as servants of God acting responsibly through proper dealings in the human sphere. This belief means, for most humans, establishing governments that ensure a place for freedom and creativity.

Beyond these tenets, Protestantism sets out to serve democracy as a political form by putting limits on it. As one book title put it, "Everything is political but politics isn't everything." Protestants may put great energy into democratic government, but because their souls are not saved by it and because they see themselves as an enemy of idolatry, they protest against governments or polities—including those set up and advocated by largely Protestant populations—when they appear to attract too much energy and devotion. Protestants reason that citizens who are freed of the notion that they are gods or godlike and that their governments and nations deserve unqualified support are more likely to encourage democracy than are those for whom democratic government is the be-all and end-all of life.

In any systematic look at Protestantism and its role in democracy, therefore, certain themes stand out. Protestants are meant to be independent, guided by their reading of scripture: the laity are to have a major voice, with few limits on their democratic expression in church—a kind of parallel theater to the political arena. The characteristic Protestant accent on the local as well as on the separation of church and state, or on drawing a line of distinction between religion and the civil authority, has been and remains a strong contribution to democracy.

Through the four and a half centuries of Protestant growth before the Declaration on Religious Freedom issued by Catholics at the Second Vatican Council in 1965, Protestants consistently—and, it might be said, easily—dismissed Catholic claims on democracy and saw Catholicism as always and everywhere their enemy. Yet through much of the twentieth century, in occasional if persistent opposition to fascist, Nazi, communist, and other kinds of totalitarianism, Protestants often joined with Catholics in defending democratic futures. Although the two Christian communions may make their case on somewhat different grounds, in most nations they see themselves on the same side in the defense of democracy. The historically honest among them simply do not make monopolistic claims. For that, they could thank the rationalists of the Enlightenment and the circumstances of modern pluralism, which militate against churchly monopolies and the authoritarian expression that characteristically goes with them. Protestantism, in truth, wants to be seen as pro-democratic. In practice, it has been pro-democratic more often than not and remains so.

See also *Catholicism, Roman; Federalism.* In Documents section, see *American Declaration of Indepedence (1776).*

Martin E. Marty

BIBLIOGRAPHY

Brown, Robert McAfee. *The Spirit of Protestantism.* New York: Oxford University Press, 1961.

Forell, George. *The Protestant Faith.* Englewood Cliffs, N.J.: Prentice Hall, 1960.

Marty, Martin E. *Protestantism.* New York: Holt, Rinehart and Winston, 1972.

Tillich, Paul. *The Protestant Era.* Chicago: University of Chicago Press, 1957.

Tocqueville, Alexis de. *Democracy in America.* New York: Vintage Books, 1945.

Yoder, John Howard. *The Politics of Jesus.* Grand Rapids, Mich.: Eerdmans, 1972.

Psychoanalysis

The system of psychological theory developed by Sigmund Freud (1856–1939). Psychoanalysis has profoundly influenced many aspects of twentieth-century ideas and challenged the concepts of rationality underlying the premises of democracy. Freud, through clinical observation, formulated theories that transformed the contemporary image of human beings.

The Freudian Method

Freud studied in Paris with the neurologist Jean-Martin Charcot and later in Vienna with Josef Breuer. Building on Charcot's and Breuer's work, he proposed that patients become ill when they are unable to accept certain aspects of their past. He hypothesized that the root of neuroses is unexpressed strangulated affect caused by unconscious emotions. By examining the history of a patient's symptoms, Freud aimed to awaken memories and thus root out what was troubling the patient. At first he thought hypnosis was the best technique for approaching neuroses. Gradually, however, he left it to the patient to choose the subject of each session's work. Patients were supposed to "free associate" about any ideas that came into their heads. Freud appealed to the rational strengths of his patients, an effort, through understanding the past, to free their energies for the future.

One of Freud's greatest mistakes was temporarily to think that the source of his patients' troubles was a childhood sexual trauma. He soon came to believe that such seduction tales were fantasies, products of infantile desires

The Austrian psychiatrist Sigmund Freud founded the psychoanalytic method, which has greatly influenced twentieth-century cultural thought. Freud's views of the unconscious and rationality have implications for traditional views of democracy.

rather than actual events. By 1897, when Freud treated sexuality as part of the inner world of his patients, the ideas that we have come to know as the foundation of psychoanalysis were formulated. The therapy was designed to uncover childish fantasies beneath neurotic façades. Freud proposed that the internal world of patients, rather than external events, was the chief source of neurotic difficulties. Sexual longings became mobilized in the therapeutic relationship because the patient transferred to the therapist, as the surrogate for parental figures, all those infantile fantasies that have come to be known as the Oedipus complex.

Freud believed that dreams, like symptoms, are a compromise attempt at wish fulfillment. Each dream contains hidden meanings that are disguised because of the patient's internal conflicts. To understand a dream requires the conquest of a resistance to self-knowledge. The wishes giving rise to dreams, as well as neuroses, are the manifestations of an unbridled egoism. In Freud's view, self-centeredness is an inevitable part of the structure of personality.

Psychoanalysis involved the exploration of hidden self-deceptions. Freud held that the lengthy phase of human dependency and immaturity has lasting effects and that all humans retain the child within themselves. Freud's description of the egoism of the unconscious fits his concern with the persistence in adulthood of childish modes of reaction. He believed that people were unnecessarily hobbled by neurotic illness and prevented from the full flowering of their mental powers. He simultaneously called attention to the strength of the childhood past and held out the ideal of individual self-realization.

Freud said that psychoanalysis elicits the worst in everyone. He believed that, however reasonable someone might appear, the analytic situation he invented would reveal the presence of infantile modes of feeling. His preferred method was first to arouse transferences and then to dissolve them through the power of the analyst's interpretations. He thought people could benefit from the rational insights that analysis made possible.

Implications for Democracy

After Freud contracted cancer of the jaw in 1923, his work shifted toward speculative rather than clinical concerns. He liked to think he had created a science that was independent of philosophic presuppositions, but he also had ambitions to transform how people think politically and socially. In terms of his own habits and commitments, he was a classical liberal. (As a young man, he had translated one of John Stuart Mill's volumes into German.)

The implications of psychoanalysis, however, were to challenge traditional democratic thought. Freud believed, for example, that the ties that bind people together are not the products of rational consent but rather are the result of unconscious identifications. He also thought that shared values and beliefs, and a collective absorption of heroic models from the past, account for the powerful forces that underlie democratic communities. Instead of believing that the ways in which people behave and think are products of rational choice, Freud pointed out the extent to which options are determined by forces about which people have little awareness.

Freud's work bears considerably on the traditional defense of democratic principles: if we are shaped by unconscious desires, those who govern and those who vote are similarly influenced by nonrational factors. If Freud is correct and our motivations arise largely from our instinctual depths, can we count on either those who rule or those who ostensibly choose them to operate on rationally explicable principles?

Democratic theory rests on the premise that leaders follow their self-interest and that to get reelected they will pay attention to the public's mood. The theory behind elections rests on rational conduct on the part of those who rule. Democratic thought also implies that people choose their governments rationally, mindful of their own best advantage. The more people cannot be counted upon to act in behalf of their own welfare, the greater the plausibility of philosophies that are unfriendly to democracy.

Undoubtedly Freud's theories have conservative implications. He believed, for instance, that conscience is the result of an individual's internalization of aggression: the more upright we are, the more repressed we must be; thus anxiety and suffering are essential components of being civilized and decent. At the same time, however, Freud posed radical theories, which Marxist critical theorists such as Herbert Marcuse built on. Freud believed that religion was an unnecessary neurotic crutch that human beings could do without. Attacking religion as a neurosis, Freud expressed utopian hopes for the future. He aimed to protect individual autonomy from unconscious threats.

Liberal theorists such as Harold Lasswell hoped to find in psychoanalysis a technique that would eliminate neurotic suffering and also provide experts with the knowledge to shape society in a way that would minimize the obstacles to promoting human dignity. The rise of Adolf Hitler prompted other thinkers to use Freud's theory to delineate the nature of authoritarianism and explain how people can fear freedom. An explicit aim was to use psychoanalysis to express the possibilities for assisting the development of the democratic personality in the sense of making people more genuinely the masters of their fate.

Although Freud's work points in many ideological directions, psychoanalysis has to challenge the complacencies of traditional democratic thought. To the extent that we are creatures of our unconscious, and that unknown mental regions are defined by our childhood past, we will always be in the grip of powerful irrational forces. Freud held out the hope of gaining a measure of control through the insights that come from psychoanalytic enlightenment, but it would be a distortion to think that his work can easily comfort democratic beliefs.

According to Freud, human rationality is weak. Neither leaders nor the people can be expected to behave in the idealistic fashion that classic democratic thought anticipated. Since Freud's death, revisionist analysts, tracing their intellectual lineage back to those like Carl Jung and Alfred Adler who broke with Freud before World War I, have taken a different view of the unconscious than did Freud. If one sees in the unconscious not just self-deception but also possibilities of self-healing, psychoanalysis is less threatening to presuppositions about the possibilities of rational human conduct.

See also *Authoritarianism; Critical theory; Lasswell, Harold D.; Personality, Democratic; Postmodernism; Rational Choice Theory.*

Paul Roazen

BIBLIOGRAPHY

Ellenberger, Henri. *The Discovery of the Unconscious.* New York: Basic Books, 1970.
Freud, Sigmund. *The Standard Edition of the Complete Psychological Works of Sigmund Freud.* Edited by James Strachey. 24 vols. London: Hogarth Press, 1953–1974.
Fromm, Erich. *Sigmund Freud's Mission.* New York: Harper, 1959.
Jones, Ernest. *The Life and Work of Sigmund Freud.* Vols. 1–3. New York: Basic Books, 1953–1957.
Minutes of the Vienna Psychoanalytic Society. Edited by Herman Nunberg and Ernst Federn. 4 vols. New York: International Universities Press, 1962–1967.

Public opinion

The political values, attitudes, or opinions of the general public of a country or other political unit, usually understood to include voting patterns and other political behavior. In light of the central importance of "the people" in democracy, the role of public opinion and its influence on political decisions must be considered in evaluating the extent of democracy in any political system.

Direct Democracy and Its Drawbacks

In the contemporary world there are few, if any, significant political units in which the people rule directly on a regular basis. However, public opinion does have a direct influence from time to time when important issues are decided by ballot referendums. In the United States there are no national referendums, but most of the states use them. Using the initiative, citizens can petition to place issues on the ballot. California is known for the large number of propositions placed on the ballot for public decision, and state policy has been strongly affected by some of them. Perhaps the most famous is Proposition 13, which arose as part of a public tax revolt in 1978. By limiting property taxes, Proposition 13 has had important effects on the state's ability to fund a variety of public programs. Following Californians' precedent, voters in several other states passed similar propositions.

Another important popular movement is the effort to limit the number of terms elected officials may serve in a particular public office. By the mid-1990s term limits proposals had passed in twenty-three states in the United States, most limiting elected officials to about twelve years in office. Despite the widespread public support for term limits, however, in May 1995 the U.S. Supreme Court held by a narrow majority (5–4) that states could not add to the qualifications specified in the U.S. Constitution for members of Congress. Therefore, state laws or amendments to state constitutions setting limits on the number of terms federal elected officials can serve were declared unconstitutional. Ironically, even while striking down these popular laws, the majority on the Court reasoned that the states may not interfere with the right of the people to choose their representatives. According to this ruling, changes in the qualifications for members of Congress may be made only by amendment to the U.S. Constitution. Public pressure may ultimately force such an amendment to be passed in Congress, but to take effect it would also have to be ratified by three-quarters of the state legislatures.

In various countries, referendums have been held on a range of issues, from whether to adopt daylight savings time to moral issues such as abortion laws and prohibition of liquor. Switzerland considers itself a direct democracy (as opposed to a representative democracy), and has relatively frequent referendums, as does Italy.

In some cases, national referendums have decided issues of major national and international significance. In various European countries the public voted on membership in the European Community (now the European Union), and its political viability hung in the balance on close votes in Denmark and France. In Canada there have been referendums on the status of Quebec. A referendum in South Africa was part of the ongoing transformation of that nation from apartheid to racial equality and democracy. In these cases, public opinion as expressed in referendums has decided one of the most important political questions of all—how a political system should be defined and whom it should include.

Nonetheless, popular participation in political decisions does not ensure that democratic ideals of fairness will be preserved. Where large numbers of people are intolerant of others, popular votes can limit the rights of unpopular minorities. For example, in 1992 Colorado voters passed an amendment to their state constitution that barred local governments from prohibiting employment or housing discrimination against gay men and lesbians. But in the United States one role of the courts is to check the majority when others' rights are at stake. A court injunction prevented the measure from taking effect, and two years later the Colorado Supreme Court ruled it unconstitutional.

Cases such as this highlight the importance of political tolerance in a democracy. Public opinion research shows that most people support democratic ideals, including tolerance of various types of minority groups, when asked about them in the abstract. However, when groups that people dislike, or perceive as threatening, are involved, tolerance declines. In many democratic nations, including the United States and most countries in Europe, there is significant intolerance of disliked groups. Some of these groups, such as Nazis, have committed horrific crimes or caused other substantial misery in the past, and it is understandable that many people would dislike them. Nevertheless, democratic theorists point out that it is precisely because some groups are disliked that tolerance is an important quality in democratic societies. Moreover, in many cases, intolerance exists even when a disliked group does not pose a real threat to others. Recent examples of the results of intolerance of disliked groups can be seen in the violence among various ethnic groups in the former Yugoslavia and Soviet Union after the ruling apparatus in those countries broke down. Intolerance even among relatively small groups can significantly detract from democratic ideals, as in "skinhead" violence against immigrants in Germany and other countries.

Fortunately for democracy, political leaders are generally more tolerant than members of the mass public, perhaps because they have higher levels of education, they have experience with diverse people and ideas, they are self-selected from among those who are less dogmatic, and they are socialized into a microculture (the legislature or other political environment) where civility and democratic norms are generally prized. Some researchers also note, however, that democratic political leaders are more aware of the "acceptable" or "politically correct" answer to survey questions about tolerance, and part of their apparently greater tolerance may stem from an unwillingness to appear intolerant when asked such questions by interviewers. Nevertheless, being unwilling or ashamed to express intolerance is at least a step toward increased tolerance.

Channels for Expressing Public Opinion

The use of referendums is increasing, but considering the vast number of decisions made by contemporary governments, only a few significant questions can be decided through referendums. If the people rule, it is generally through elected officials in a system of representation. Representative systems are faced with one of the core challenges of democracy: to ensure that there are enough effective channels, both formal and informal, for public opinion to be expressed to elected leaders, that the behavior of these leaders can be monitored, and that there are regular opportunities for the people to change leaders if they are not satisfied with their responsiveness to popular opinion (or for any other reason). The success with which a political system meets this challenge is a measure of the extent to which it is a democracy.

Some channels for the expression of public opinion are not governmental. For example, political opinions can be aired in letters to newspapers and magazines. One of the difficulties with this type of forum is that letter writers are not a representative sample of the population: very few people are inclined to take the time to write letters or have their opinions aired in the public media. By selection of the letters to print, editors may further narrow the viewpoints expressed. An estimation of "public opinion" based on letters printed in newspapers would be distorted. Even if different times and issues stimulated different people to write, it is doubtful that this source could ever supply an accurate picture of the opinions of the public as a whole.

Many people belong to organizations that take public positions on issues or lobby government officials in an attempt to influence policy decisions and implementation. Alexis de Tocqueville, the nineteenth-century French political theorist, described Americans as a nation of joiners; in fact, people in many other countries are as likely as Americans to belong to political groups.

In the United States groups compete for public support and to spur or discourage particular governmental actions on important political issues, such as health care, abortion, crime and poverty, prayer and other expressions of religion in public schools, taxation and budget policies, and protection of the environment versus business and property interests. Some groups advocate policies that will benefit specific groups, such as religious, racial, and ethnic groups; members of labor unions; or occupational groups, such as doctors, lawyers, or teachers. Advocates of full civil rights for women and members of racial or ethnic minorities played an important role in the development of American civil rights law. Even people with particular health problems, such as AIDS and breast cancer, have mobilized to influence health policy and increase the amount of public money devoted to research on these diseases. In many countries, industry trade groups are among the most powerful lobbies. Sometimes a prominent goal of industry groups is to decrease government involvement in a particular industry or policy area.

Groups that advocate particular political positions are frequently referred to as *special interests*. Even though each may be only a small part of overall public opinion, many groups represent important constituencies, bringing the point of view of their segment of the public to the attention of officials who make policy choices. The power of these groups, however, is frequently disproportionate to their size in the population, and the sum total of their activities does not provide effective representation of public opinion as a whole.

The interests of large numbers of people are not well represented in organized groups. Typically, diffuse and heterogeneous sectors of the population such as consumers, students, medical patients, and poor people are not well organized even though they have many common

interests in public policy. Moreover, the large sums of money that many powerful interest groups give to finance the election campaigns of public officials raise substantial concern that they are "buying" access and thereby undermining popular democracy. Because democratic systems must permit people to lobby their government, in addition to curbing inordinately large financial contributions from powerful organized interests, more group organization rather than less is the likely cure for inequities in influence. In the United States older people, welfare recipients, students, and even crime victims now have important advocacy groups that bring the interests and opinions of their members to public attention.

Consensus and Discord

That there are strong policy disagreements among active political groups does not mean that there are no areas of consensus in public opinion. On basic values such as national identification and loyalty, there is broad agreement. Such attitudes are very important in keeping the citizens of a nation together in a political unit. Large majorities of the public in almost all modern democracies feel patriotic and express love for their countries. Although members of various racial and ethnic groups may differ on policy issues, and citizens' opinions may differ by class, age, or other social and political characteristics, the differences among groups in most democratic societies are overshadowed by support for their nation.

One frequent manifestation of national loyalty is the "rally round the flag" phenomenon. During international crises, approval ratings of political leaders rise, particularly when they are seen to be taking action to resolve the crisis. For example, in the United States both President George Bush, during the Persian Gulf war, and President Jimmy Carter, when American hostages were taken in Iran, enjoyed extremely large increases in their approval ratings. Bush's rose to an extraordinary 89 percent at the end of the war. However, this effect can be quite temporary, and may be more an expression of support for the nation itself than for the leader: neither Carter nor Bush was reelected.

A widely shared sense of nationhood keeps people together even when they disagree strongly on specific issues. When many people feel that they really do not "belong" to a nation, that they are inadequately represented in the government, or that the government is illegitimate, political systems can disintegrate through civil war or mass emigration. The American Civil War resulted in part from Southerners' feeling that political differences with the North were so great that they could no longer share one political system. The long and violent dispute in Northern Ireland over union with Britain is another example of the difficulty of keeping people in a political system to which they do not wish to belong.

Mass emigration to West Berlin was such a problem for communist East Germany after World War II that the regime finally, in 1961, built a wall between East and West Berlin. This concrete and barbed wire structure was guarded day and night by armed military patrols. The Berlin Wall lasted almost thirty years, a monument to a political system that could not command the loyalty of a sufficient number of its citizens. It was both a symbolic and a literal reminder of the importance of public support for the viability of political systems. Thus many theorists argue that feelings of national identification and loyalty are of more fundamental importance than agreement or disagreement on policy issues. For such reasons, political alienation and political support are important areas of public opinion research.

Political Ideology and Sophistication

Although the political process can be seen in part as an effort to reconcile group differences about political issues, not all members of the mass public hold strong views on issues. In democratic systems, however, those who hold strong views must have the opportunity to express and advocate them. An important debate in public opinion research concerns how knowledgeable ordinary citizens are about political issues. This research investigates whether political attitudes in the mass public are structured enough to be described as belief systems or political ideologies. In general, the research seeks to determine the public's level of political sophistication.

Public opinion researchers disagree about sophistication and ideology among the public. In an early study, Philip Converse concluded on the basis of data from public opinion surveys in the United States in the 1950s that the mass public was relatively unsophisticated in its political views. Three decades of follow-up research were stimulated by his work. Some political scientists who used data collected in the 1960s argued that the American public had become much more politically aware and sophisticated. They pointed to changes in political campaigns as the reason: more ideological campaigns provided a sort of po-

litical education for many people. For a while, this "revisionist" position was widely accepted. When subsequent researchers evaluated the methods used in the different studies, however, they noted that the studies had not been comparable. In some cases the survey questions used in the later studies were clearly better, but because they were not comparable to the original ones, it became difficult to assess the degree to which political sophistication had really changed. Some scholars in the field today believe that the original position is more accurate, while others point to the weaknesses of the early methods and argue that the lack of sophistication of the mass public was overstated.

Disagreement about the validity of the methods used to measure political ideology and attitudinal structure has led some researchers to attempt to assess how much people know about important political issues or institutions and then to infer their sophistication from the extent of their knowledge. Unfortunately, most information tests show that many people do not know much about political issues. Although increased education since World War II has led to some overall increase in political knowledge, Michael Delli Carpini and Scott Keeter have shown that people at each educational level today are no more knowledgeable than people with the same amount of education were in the 1940s and 1950s, despite the much larger amount of political information available today. In general the average person's knowledge of politics is not impressive. Most of this research has occurred in the United States, but where comparable data are available, they do not suggest that publics in other democracies are very different.

Whether or not they fit information and opinions about political issues into an overall ideology or belief system, however, most people manage to make sense of the issues that matter to them. Many people evaluate issues according to how they affect the groups with which they identify—for example, "average people," "the middle class," "working people," or labor union members; ethnic, racial, or religious minorities; or small business owners. Others are primarily concerned about one dominant issue or a cluster of related issues, such as "reproductive rights" or "family values."

Benjamin Page and Robert Shapiro have argued that even if most individuals in a mass public are not particularly well informed, have conflicting positions on different issues, and do not necessarily integrate their political ideas into an overall ideology, the public in the aggregate nevertheless makes reasoned judgments about most important political issues. These political scientists reason that people whose evaluations of political issues are inconsistent or random tend to cancel each other out. Therefore, as more information becomes available, the public as a whole, as represented by overall distributions of opinion in public opinion polls, is sufficiently well informed and rational in its attitudes on political issues.

Voting Behavior

Voting behavior is perhaps the most important indication of public opinion and participation in a democracy. Many political scientists have focused on this aspect of the public's relationship with government. One of the enduring questions is, Why do people vote the way they do? Which is most important—issues, candidates, or parties? Early researchers in this field concluded that most voters were not issue oriented because they were often unaware of candidates' positions on the issues. More recently, researchers have argued that the public responds to the information presented in a political campaign. If candidates do not make their positions clear and articulate their differences, the public is not given enough information to vote on the basis of issues.

Research by Paul Abramson, John Aldrich, and David Rohde shows that there are substantial differences from election to election in the United States in the number of people who have enough information to cast an issue-based vote. They attribute the differences to the varying amount and quality of information provided by candidates and parties in different election campaigns. At most, 50 to 60 percent of the public have positions on important issues and understand correctly where the candidates stand relative to each other on these issues. Many of these people may be called *issue voters,* since they are very likely to select the candidate who is closest to their own position on issues. There can be no issue voting among people who do not have positions of their own or who do not correctly assess where the candidates stand. Sometimes voters do not care or do not pay enough attention to get information about candidates, and sometimes candidates do not make their positions clear.

Other influences on voting behavior include how well a candidate or a candidate's party has done in the past, the state of the economy, and whether the country is at peace or war. When the country is perceived to be in bad times, the electoral fortunes of candidates of the party in power will suffer. Evaluations of the personal qualities of the candidates and feelings about the parties are also important.

For many people the main connection to the world of politics is through their party identification, a sense of attachment or belonging to a particular party. An individual's family may have a history of voting for a party. Or party identification can be based on how well the country has done when that party has been in power, how people feel about a party's positions over time, or how people think the parties will deal with issues of particular importance to them. Party identification tends to mobilize people to vote because it gives them a stake in the outcome. Public opinion research shows that people who identify with, or at least lean toward, a political party are more likely than people who consider themselves true independents to be informed, to vote, and to participate in political life in other ways.

Most American voters consider themselves Republicans or Democrats or lean toward one party or another; only about 12 percent consider themselves complete independents. The party label can provide a shortcut to evaluate candidates, events, and issues in the political arena and is closely related to how people vote. Identification with an established party makes people more resistant to the appeals of minor party or "independent" candidates and thus tends to make a political system less susceptible to change. For example, very few strong party identifiers voted for Ross Perot in the 1992 presidential election in the United States. Perot did get almost 20 percent of the total vote, and among independents who had no leaning toward either major party, more people voted for Perot than for either Bill Clinton, the Democratic candidate, or George Bush, the Republican candidate. Perot might even have won had there been a larger number of Americans who considered themselves true independents. Nevertheless, there are signs that the pull of party is declining somewhat in the United States and in some other countries as elections have become more candidate oriented, as structural and social changes have weakened party organizations, and as people have become less confident of the parties' abilities to solve social and economic problems.

It is somewhat paradoxical that democratic systems provide for public input—indeed voting is compulsory in some countries (including Australia, Belgium, and Italy)—yet politics and political issues are peripheral to the concerns of many citizens. Many people do not exercise their right to vote. Among the Western democracies, Switzerland and the United States have the lowest rates of voting. In recent U.S. presidential elections, only slightly more than half the eligible electorate has turned out to vote, and turnout in Switzerland is frequently even lower. In many other industrialized democracies, turnout is far higher.

Whether low participation and lack of public interest are threats to democracy is a topic of disagreement among scholars. Some students of democracy interpret low participation and the lack of political interest to mean that people are generally satisfied with political outcomes. Others argue that many people feel that it is useless to try to figure out political issues, form opinions on them, and vote. Some people who do not participate feel that the system is rigged against them; that it is controlled by powerful groups, large financial donors, and others with private interests; and that the average citizen has very little political influence.

The idea that low political interest among the citizenry is not a serious concern for democratic political systems would be more persuasive if participation rates, political interest, and other indicators of political sophistication were evenly distributed in the population, but they are not. People with higher incomes and education generally take more of an interest in politics, are better informed, and participate more. For these reasons, their views are made known more effectively to political leaders and therefore have a greater chance of influencing policy outcomes.

Voting is an important way to increase the chances that one's political views will be registered. A key motivation of elected officials is to stay in office. Therefore, officials must be attentive to the views of those who vote. Research by Kim Quaile Hill and Jan Leighley has shown, for example, that welfare policies are more generous to the poor in U.S. states where the poor and the wealthy do not have very different rates of voting. State by state, as the gap in participation between income groups grows, welfare policies are less likely to be generous. The results suggest that where the poor vote at lower rates their interests have less influence on state welfare policy. This is an example of the general proposition that elected officials are more likely to work for policies particular groups favor when those groups demonstrate, by voting, that they can affect the political careers of the elected officials.

Public Opinion Polls

In recent years a nongovernmental channel of expression for public opinion, the public opinion poll, has become increasingly important. Since their beginnings in the 1930s, particularly with the pioneer work of George Gallup, polls have become ubiquitous in contemporary democracies. In the United States, where they are used most widely, no significant political event occurs without numerous polls of public opinion about it. In many emerging democracies that do not yet have mature representative institutions, such as the countries that became independent as part of the collapse of the Soviet Union in 1991, polls have been one of the only ways in which public opinion as a whole could be expressed.

In general, democratically elected political leaders have a vested interest in paying attention to public opinion polls, since their reelections can be jeopardized if their votes or other actions diverge too greatly from what is acceptable to their constituencies. But legislators and other officials pay differing amounts of attention to the polls (or so they say).

Some legislators admit to paying close attention to polls, arguing, for example, that, because they are "representatives," they should represent their constituents by most often voting as a majority of their constituents would want them to. This model of representative behavior is sometimes referred to as the *instructed delegate model*. Other lawmakers argue that they were elected to apply their judgment and intelligence to decision making, acting for the "public interest" or the constituency interest as they understand it. This model is sometimes referred to as the *trustee* or *Burkean model* (after the eighteenth-century British political philosopher Edmund Burke, who advocated this role for members of Parliament).

Members may also disagree about whether they should represent the public interest of the nation as a whole or the narrower interests of the people in their districts. Presidents and other chief executives also follow polls closely, both to assess support for their policies or legislative programs and to gauge voters' likelihood of supporting them if they run for reelection.

Philosophies aside, it is the rare elected official who does not feel more comfortable when his or her views are consistent with the majority's than when they are opposed. Nevertheless, research in both France and the United States has demonstrated that although legislators and constituents generally agree about the role of government in society, the correlations between overall opinion on specific issues in the constituencies and the votes of legislators from those constituencies are generally not very high. When many constituents feel strongly about an issue, legislators are likely to take constituency opinion into account before casting votes on bills. Some research has also found that legislators pay special attention to their own supporters and to the opinions of state party officials.

When political leaders have the support of the public for what they are doing or would prefer to do, they frequently attempt to endow their policies with a certain amount of moral legitimation by pointing out the public support. They may cite poll figures as justification for not undertaking a contrary course (which they may not wish to pursue in any case). Conversely, poll data from a representative's district may be so one-sidedly opposed to the representative's party's position, and the next election feared to be so close, that party leaders may excuse a representative from voting with the party on an important and close issue, in deference to their mutual interest in the representative's reelection.

Public opinion polls are particularly important during election campaigns. Candidates may not shape all their policy stances according to what is popular at any given moment, but at the least, they emphasize issues on which there is agreement between their views and those of the public, and they play down issues on which there is significant disagreement. For this reason, candidates in a race for the same office sometimes appear to be speaking past each other, one candidate emphasizing one issue and the other candidate another issue. Each is trying to appeal to that part of the public that agrees with him or her. For example, if one party has been in power during an unpopular military undertaking or war, a candidate of that party will generally emphasize some other issue on which the record will be received more sympathetically by potential voters. The candidate of the opposition party in the same election may very well decide to focus on the opposition's stance on the war issue, on which the incumbent party is vulnerable, or on his or her party's own record on foreign policy. Thus public opinion influences the candidates' choice of issues to emphasize. Because of this tendency, media and polling organizations that do public opinion polls also play a role in shaping the political agenda by their decisions about which issues to ask about and what questions to ask.

Polls are also used during election campaigns to encourage financial donations. Most people and groups prefer to donate money to a candidate who is likely to be elected. Therefore, potential donors may be shown that one candidate is better known than the opposition, is ahead in "trial heats," or is favored on the issues. Many candidates commission private polls because they must begin collecting money for election campaigns far in advance of the time the mass media begin testing public opinion about particular contests. Furthermore, if the candidate is seeking a minor office, the usual campaign polls may not even cover the race.

Role and Effects of Public Opinion

Most people are occupied in their daily lives with jobs, family, health, and other day-to-day concerns. Unless a crisis develops, political issues may remain peripheral to their concerns. Public opinion, therefore, is often said to be permissive. That is, political officials can pursue policy making without having to be concerned that large numbers of constituents are evaluating their every action or vote.

But from time to time, issues arise that motivate large numbers of people to political activity. In the United States the matter of abortion rights, pitting those supporting "the right to choose" against those favoring "the right to life," has perhaps been the most prominent in recent years. Another important issue has been health care, especially for elderly people. At one point during the Bush administration (1989–1993), Congress passed, and the president signed into law, a bill that would have increased Medicare costs for elderly people. Immediately following this law's passage, the elderly community was mobilized in protest. The outcry was so great that the law was quickly repealed.

A similar incident occurred in Britain in 1989–1990. Prime Minister Margaret Thatcher's government passed a community charge, a tax on every person of voting age in all households, with some exceptions for hardship. This extraordinarily unpopular measure, quickly dubbed a poll tax by its opponents, led to demonstrations throughout the country and riots in London. The public uproar contributed to Thatcher's subsequent loss of the Conservative Party leadership. Two years later John Major's government abolished the community charge and adopted a council tax, basically a return to the prior system of taxation based on property.

Issues of critical importance to particular groups can become "voting issues." These are issues on which some members of the public will base their vote regardless of their ideas about any other issues and regardless of their other attitudes about particular candidates or parties. When people feel so strongly, group and individual advocacy, letters to newspapers, contacts with representatives, and public demonstrations are most likely.

The newest outlet for the expression of political views in the United States is "talk radio," which so far has been dominated by conservative groups. Like those who write letters to newspapers, vocal political groups who use public media like radio to express their views can appear to be much larger than they really are, judging by the number of people who agree with their point of view in a representative public opinion poll.

Small groups who are very vocal about their political beliefs are called *intense minorities,* and they can have influence out of proportion to their numbers if they are willing to make their issue the primary or only factor in their voting decisions. If members of an intense minority vote for or against a particular candidate, basing their votes on the candidate's position on one issue, and if the rest of the public is indifferent, supports the opposing point of view only mildly, or is not concerned enough about the issue to base their votes on it, the intense minority can have a disproportionately large influence on the election. On the electoral level, such strongly held feelings are perhaps the functional equivalent of the large amounts of money donated to candidates by specific interest groups with large stakes in current legislation.

In many cases, public opinion is permissive only until something happens to which people strongly object, and then a major role for public opinion develops after the fact. Public disapproval or policy failure may result in the electorate's "voting the rascals out" at the next election. The election is thus the ultimate weapon or bottom line of public opinion. In other cases, public opinion is mobilized much earlier in the policy formation process. For example, in the United States public opposition to the size of the government's role in President Clinton's original health care plan was at least partly responsible for the proposal's failure.

In combination with the vote, the effects of public opinion ripple through the entire political system. For example, research in the United States suggests that the level of approval or disapproval of a president's job performance, as measured by the Gallup Poll or other public opinion polls, has an important effect on the president's political power. When the president's approval ratings are high, members of Congress are more likely to support the presidential legislative program, because legislators fear retribution from their constituents if they do not support a popular president. Conversely, when presidential approval declines, legislators are more likely to feel free to oppose the president.

Not only does low public support make it more difficult for the president to get a legislative program passed, but Congress is also more likely to pass legislation that the president opposes, the president is therefore more likely to veto legislation, and Congress is more likely to override the president's veto. If Congress does not pass the legislative initiatives of a popular president, the president can appeal to the people, as Ronald Reagan did, to contact their representatives and urge support of his program. If enough people do this, members of Congress learn that their own political futures may depend on their support for the president's program. Mobilization of public opinion is a club the president cannot wield when approval ratings are low. Thus, even as simple an indicator of public opinion as the level of approval for the president affects the president's power, the types of legislation Congress passes, and the dynamics of presidential-congressional relations.

In parliamentary systems, parties are stronger than in presidential systems and have a larger role, and the fortunes of members of parliament of the prime minister's party are closely tied to the prime minister's success. Thus it is easier to impose party discipline on the members in parliamentary systems. Nevertheless, public opinion still plays a role in determining the amount of support the prime minister gets. For example, if public opinion disapproves of the job the prime minister is doing, opposition members may be more likely than otherwise to vote against the prime minister's program because they are less fearful of losing their seats if an election is called.

Public Opinion and Government Policy

For most people in most democratic political systems, voting is the primary way in which they express their political views. But in a true democracy many other avenues are available for the effective expression of public opinion. These include voting in referendums, contacting public officials, working in political campaigns and with organizations interested in public policy issues, supporting political parties, and joining vocal political demonstrations and protests. Public opinion polls also bring the attitudes of the public at large and of particular groups to the attention of political leaders. However, any given method may not affect the public policy debate at a particular time, and some individuals or groups may feel that their views are not taken into account, perhaps even over long periods of time. Indeed, where the public is socially and politically heterogeneous, and where there are sharp differences of opinion, there will always be groups who are not satisfied with the outcomes of particular political decisions.

Although public opinion and public policy are generally congruent in a democracy, it is not easy to establish that public opinion is the driving force in policy formation. Nonetheless, of all systems of government, democracies provide the most effective means for the expression of public opinion and the best chance that the policies and programs of government will be consistent with the aspirations and goals of a large part of the population.

See also *Accountability of public officials; Interest groups; Polling, Public opinion; Referendum and initiative; Types of democracy; Voting behavior.*

Ada W. Finifter

BIBLIOGRAPHY

Abramson, Paul R., John H. Aldrich, and David W. Rohde. *Change and Continuity in the 1992 Elections.* Washington, D.C.: CQ Press, 1994.

Campbell, Angus, Philip E. Converse, Warren E. Miller, and Donald E. Stokes. *The American Voter.* New York: Wiley, 1960.

Converse, Philip E. "The Nature of Belief Systems in Mass Publics." In *Ideology and Discontent,* edited by D. E. Apter. New York: Free Press, 1964.

Converse, Philip E., and Roy Pierce. *Political Representation in France.* Cambridge, Mass., and London: Harvard University Press, 1986.

Delli Carpini, Michael X., and Scott Keeter. "Stability and Change in the U.S. Public's Knowledge of Politics." *Public Opinion Quarterly* 55 (1991): 583–612.

Erikson, Robert S., Norman R. Luttbeg, and Kent L. Tedin. *American Public Opinion.* 4th ed. New York: Macmillan, 1991.

Finifter, Ada W., and Ellen Mickiewicz. "Redefining the Political System of the USSR: Mass Support for Political Change." *American Political Science Review* 86 (1992): 857–874.

Hill, Kim Quaile, and Jan E. Leighley. "The Policy Consequences of Class Bias in State Electorates." *American Journal of Political Science* 36 (1992): 351–365.

Kinder, Donald R. "Diversity and Complexity in American Public Opinion." In *Political Science: The State of the Discipline,* edited by Ada W. Finifter. Washington, D.C.: American Political Science Association, 1983.

Miller, Warren E., and Donald E. Stokes. "Constituency Influence in Congress." *American Political Science Review* 57 (1963): 45–56.

Mueller, John. *Policy and Opinion in the Gulf War.* Chicago: University of Chicago Press, 1994.

Page, Benjamin I., and Robert Y. Shapiro. *The Rational Public: Fifty Years of Trends in Americans' Policy Preferences.* Chicago: University of Chicago Press, 1992.

Ranney, Austin, and David Butler, eds. *Referendums around the World: The Growing Use of Direct Democracy.* Washington, D.C.: American Enterprise Institute, 1994.

Smith, Eric R. A. N. *The Unchanging American Voter.* Berkeley: University of California Press, 1989.

Sniderman, Paul M. "The New Look in Public Opinion Research." In *Political Science: The State of the Discipline II,* edited by Ada W. Finifter. Washington, D.C.: American Political Science Association, 1993.

R

Racism

A pattern of beliefs, behaviors, and institutional practices in which one group of people denigrates and subordinates another solely on the basis of physical differences with which they are born. Racism and the struggle against it have plagued and helped to shape societies since people of apparently different races first came into contact with one another. Throughout recorded history lighter skinned people have sought to subordinate darker skinned people, culturally as well as politically. That tendency is deeply troubling for all societies, but it is especially problematic for modern democracies, which are predicated on the assumption of the political equality of all citizens.

A society that fosters or tolerates racism among its members cannot be considered democratic (even given democracy within the dominant group). But efforts to root out racism and its consequences have proved so difficult as to destabilize would-be democratic societies.

Controversies over Racism in Democracies

The pernicious effects of racism on democracy are most apparent in systems that sanctioned racially based slavery or programs of extermination. The Western Hemisphere's institutionalization of slavery and the Nazis' "final solution" for Jews in Europe are obvious examples. Beyond this general assertion, however, controversies abound.

One dispute addresses the relationship between racism and class domination. Some analysts argue that slavery was essentially an economic relationship, reinforced and stabilized by racial denigration and hostility. At least two variants of this claim have been advanced: owners and capitalists used slavery to exploit not only slaves but all workers, or free workers used slavery to enhance their position at the expense of other (enslaved) workers. Others argue that slavery or racial subordination derives primarily from psychological or political motives and that racism persists even when it is not economically profitable to the dominant race.

A second controversy addresses the relationship between racism and democracy. To most democrats, racism and democratic values are direct opposites in moral terms and are likely to destroy each other in daily practice. In this view, governmentally sanctioned racism (which occurred in the Jim Crow era in the United States and under apartheid in South Africa) is an anomaly to be eliminated from a fundamentally sound democratic system. A polity that purports to be democratic is strengthened when it repudiates racism because it thereby permits the political equality of all citizens.

Some argue that, to the contrary, racism is essential to the successful functioning of at least some purportedly democratic polities or even that democratic values are deeply rooted in racist presumptions. On the former point, for example, the fledgling United States might not have survived without the economic resources and political strength of the slave-holding South. Regarding the latter point, some claim that the idea of individual freedom followed directly from the experience of slavery or that the values of republicanism and democracy would have failed in the American colonies had not the wealthiest and most powerful members of society found a way, through racially based slavery, to ensure that the poorest and least powerful members of society could not displace them. If such arguments are correct, the question remains whether democracies can abjure racism and still remain robust.

A third controversy, growing out of that question, revolves around the necessary and acceptable measures for uprooting racism from democratic societies. Abraham Lincoln abhorred slavery, but he believed that the U.S. Constitution required the federal government to keep out of the internal affairs of southern states. More recently some Americans have argued that strong forms of affirmative action in employment, or mandatory reassignment of children to public schools to promote racial balance, interfere so severely with other democratic values that such measures should not be used even to eliminate racism.

It is clear that as South Africa eliminates racially based apartheid, it must abandon its traditional governmental practices and create new ones. In the eyes of some white South Africans, that move will destroy a functioning democracy in favor of an uncertain future that may or may not be more broadly democratic. In all these cases, people who see themselves as sincere democrats disagree over how far their society can go to eliminate racism without harming other cherished values.

Manifestations and Possible Solutions

Until the 1960s most white Americans conceived of racism in individual terms. Racism was seen as a problem of prejudice in beliefs and discrimination in actions. Scholars sought to understand the origins of prejudice in psychological traits such as authoritarianism, in economic interests, or in social phenomena such as educational levels. Proposed solutions to prejudice and discrimination combined individual and governmental actions. Individuals should be taught tolerance through moral exhortation and increased familiarity with members of other races. Governments should prohibit public officials and perhaps private actors from taking discriminatory actions against identifiable people.

By the 1970s some African Americans and their allies argued that individual prejudice and discrimination were only part of racism. They developed the concept of institutional racism, which implies that societal practices and rules promote and maintain racial disparities even when individual actors are not prejudiced or do not discriminate. Instances of institutional racism included basing public school attendance zones on neighborhoods rather than on ensuring that all schools in a community were racially integrated and using citywide elections rather than district elections for municipal government. In these and other cases, apparently neutral rules worked systematically and predictably to the disadvantage of blacks and the advantage of whites.

Since the 1970s definitions of racism have grown still broader than these. Some see any racially disparate effect of a rule or practice as racism, even if those who promulgated the rule did so for reasons having nothing to do

with race. For example, rules that members of a police force must be of a certain height make it harder for Latinos to become police than for Anglos; home mortgage deductions from federal income taxes disproportionately benefit whites, who are more likely than blacks with the same level of income to own homes. Others see cultural racism in the fact that European forms of art, such as symphonies and ballets, have higher status and receive greater public subsidies than do African or Native American forms of art. Some perceive insidious racism in the daily practices of coworkers. Not being invited to a meeting, not receiving eye contact during a conversation, not receiving a positive evaluation or a challenging assignment all can be taken as evidence of racism that persists long after Jim Crow laws or apartheid has disappeared.

Proposals for eliminating these subtle forms of racism are highly disputed. Suggestions range from changing the scoring procedures on employment tests to ensure that as many blacks as whites "pass" the tests to teaching black students that Africans contributed more to classical civilization than did the ancient Greeks. At the extreme, this view of pervasive racism implicates all democratic institutions and all citizens either as perpetrators (witting or not) of racial subordination or as fighters against it. Most controversially, those who define racism very broadly define the appropriate response as heightened color consciousness combined with compensatory action rather than as color blindness combined with strict equality of treatment.

Consequences

Even if one retreats from very broad definitions of racism, it is easy to see its consequences in the daily lives of members of both subordinated and dominant races. In the United States, despite several decades of legal equality and the growth of a substantial middle class, African Americans hold only one-fourth as much wealth per capita as do white Americans, and that fraction has barely changed since the 1960s. German law makes it extremely difficult for even German-born descendants of Turkish "guest workers" to become German citizens, whereas people of German ancestry who have resided outside the country for decades may readily return to German citizenship. White South Africans have enjoyed a huge array of privileges and an exaggerated perception of their own worth, as a consequence of the minuscule wages and lack of power of their African servants and employees. The Romany people of eastern Europe have been forcibly deprived of their land, traditional trades, language, and culture by governments that tolerate them, if at all, only if they blend into the native populations as much as possible. The Harijans (formerly "untouchables") of India still suffer indignities and poverty despite decades of strict affirmative action mandates from the Indian government. The Burakumin of Japan were formerly known as Eta, meaning "full of filth," and were treated accordingly. As these examples suggest, racism is not sharply separate from ethnic hostility since despised ethnic groups are often seen as racially distinct.

Examples could proliferate. But the main point is that racism creates or reinforces deep social, cultural, political, and economic inequalities that democratic governments find difficult to eradicate for at least two reasons. First, those who gain from these inequalities have a hard time recognizing the illegitimacy of their position even as they denounce the sentiments and practices associated with racism. In such cases, legislatures and chief executives, who are basically responsive to the will of the majority of citizens, can do little to offset the effects of racism even when they want to. Their responses to this dilemma range from turning the problem over to branches of government that are less directly democratic (for example, the courts in the United States) to secession or even to civil war.

Second, the ill effects of racism may take on a life of their own, as the urban underclass in the United States or the social problems associated with the Romany population in eastern Europe illustrate. If a racially oppressed group is kept poor, powerless, and socially stigmatized long enough, it may develop a culture of poverty or an oppositional culture. In that case, its members reject the possibility of joining the mainstream society even when racial oppression is lifted. Even if they do not reject the rest of society, members of an underclass may lack the skills, discipline, and cultural capital needed to hold a job in the dominant economy—thus reinforcing the links between racial and class subordination. In the worst case, racism so perverts the racially oppressed that they reject both conventional morality and any alternative or revolutionary morality. They choose instead violent nihilism, with terrible consequences for all.

Current Questions

Questions about the meaning and practice of racism remain. Analysts dispute whether members of racially oppressed groups can be racist. If racism is a system of hierarchical structures designed to subordinate some racial groups to others, the subordinated cannot, by definition, be racist even if they hate the dominant racial group. If, however, racism is defined as prejudice and discrimination, the subordinated can be as racist as the dominators.

A second question focuses on the meaning of race and its implications for the practice of racism. Races may be socially constructed categories rather than sharply etched biological entities. After all, Americans in the nineteenth century perceived Irish immigrants to be a different race from themselves, and German Nazis defined Aryans as the master race, distinct from Jews and eastern Europeans alike. The definition of who is black has changed over time in the United States and in South Africa. If race is a collective convention, what counts as racism is even less clear than if racial differences are empirically determinable. For example, Brazilians of all colors and heritages deny that racism pervades Brazilian society. Yet darker Brazilians, compared with lighter Brazilians, are disproportionately poor, powerless, and socially stigmatized. In this case, racism is manifested by the absence of consciousness of either racial differences or racial discrimination.

Other questions address practice rather than concepts. Can members of previously subordinated races learn to live with their "double consciousness" in a way that neither tears them apart nor forces them to deny either their distinctiveness or their shared citizenship? Can members of previously dominant races learn to accommodate previously despised groups on their own terms and to accept the idea of sometimes losing status or position to a member of the darker race? Should the policies of a democratic polity aim toward color blindness or toward egalitarian color consciousness?

Most important of all, can democracies correct their own historical flaws through democratic means? To answer in the affirmative requires a society to jump at least four hurdles. Those who have benefited from racism by virtue of their race, even if not through their own choice, must accept the measures needed to compensate the victims of racism. The victims must accept compensation and renounce their own desire for moral or institutional superiority. Elected leaders must have the wisdom and determination to implement the policies needed to achieve the first two conditions. And, finally, these goals must be achieved without unduly sacrificing other equally cherished goals.

These are the challenges facing democracies in the next century. Some nations have made progress against racism since the slavery of past centuries and the extermination policies of this century. Others are embarking on wars of "ethnic cleansing." Racism is commonly, but not universally, abhorred. Martin Luther King, Jr., of the United States and Nelson Mandela of South Africa have shown the way for others to rise above racially inspired hatred. But others, such as the late Meir Kahane of Israel and Slobodan Milošević of Serbia, remind us that racism as individual prejudice and public policy is not dead.

Cultural forms ranging from fundamentalist Protestantism to jazz music demonstrate that people of different races can mingle to the benefit of all, but institutional barriers from housing segregation to the erection of new national boundaries demonstrate that they do not very often so mingle. Whether the effects of racism can be ameliorated (if not eradicated) and democracy correspondingly enhanced remains to be seen.

See also *Affirmative action; Civil rights; Furnivall, John Sydenham; King, Martin Luther, Jr.; Mandela, Nelson; Nationalism; Slavery; Theory, African American.*

Jennifer L. Hochschild

BIBLIOGRAPHY

Adorno, Theodore, Else Frenkel-Brunswick, Daniel Levinson, and R. Nevitt Sanford. *The Authoritarian Personality.* New York: Harper and Row, 1950.

Du Bois, William E. B. *Writings.* Edited by Nathan Huggins. New York: Library of America, 1986.

Fredrickson, George. *White Supremacy: A Comparative Study in American and South African History.* Oxford and New York: Oxford University Press, 1981.

Horowitz, Donald. *Ethnic Groups in Conflict.* Berkeley: University of California Press, 1985.

Jordon, Winthrop. *White over Black: American Attitudes toward the Negro, 1550–1812.* New York: Norton, 1968.

King, Martin Luther, Jr. *A Testament of Hope: The Essential Writings and Speeches of Martin Luther King, Jr.* Edited by James M. Washington. New York: HarperCollins, 1986.

Morgan, Edmund. *American Slavery, American Freedom.* New York: Norton, 1975.

Patterson, Orlando. *Freedom in the Making of Western Culture.* New York: Basic Books, 1991.

Rational choice theory

A theoretical system that assumes that political actors (individuals, states, groups, and so forth) have goals and that they will adopt effective and efficient means for achieving these goals. Rational choice theory is deductive: from basic premises about purposive goal-oriented behavior we can deduce explanations for political events, such as the functioning of democracy.

Game theory, often employed by rational choice theorists, models the behavior of political actors engaged in cooperative or conflictive interactions. In game theories, political actors are assumed to be aware that their fates are affected by what other actors do, they adjust their behavior to take this interdependence into consideration, and they recognize that other political actors are also sensitive to this interdependence. An example is a game of chicken. You understand that if you opt to continue on a head-on course, your rewards are very much determined by what your opponent decides to do. Of course, your opponent is engaged in exactly the same kind of reasoning.

Rational choice theory has contributed to our understanding of democracy by addressing three questions: Why do governments exist? Why do societies adopt democratic institutions? And what political outcomes occur in democratic settings?

Rationality and Government

Rational choice theory characterizes government as a solution to the problem of collective action within a society. The general problem of collective action is that individuals have every incentive not to cooperate in the provision of collective goods but rather, in the term used by Mancur Olson, to "free ride." If other citizens contribute to the provision of a collective good (for example, by paying a "tax"), an individual might be tempted to cheat on the assumption that her noncompliance would have a negligible effect on the provision of the collective good.

The flaw in this analysis, of course, is that all rational citizens will engage in a similar reasoning. Hence no individual citizen will be willing to contribute to the provision of the collective good if he expects others to free ride. If you expect others to cheat, your best strategy is to cheat as well, even if society as a whole would be better off if everyone cooperated by paying the tax. Thus, without some external enforcement of cooperation, individuals will not cooperate and pay the tax. Government, then, is an external solution to the problem of collective action. A monarchical or totalitarian government, for example, can enforce cooperation by imposing severe costs for free riding. Alternatively, societies can adopt democratic solutions to the problem of collective action.

The Choice of Democracy

Why do some societies develop democratic institutions to enforce cooperative behavior in place of monarchies or authoritarian structures? According to Olson, democracy emerges in those unique historical circumstances when two conditions are met: when a dictator is overthrown, and the conspirators are a heterogeneous group with no single leader or dominating party. If no one faction can suppress the others or segregate itself into a separate country, the choice for all the factions is either to engage in pointless conflict or to agree on a way of coexisting.

Hence the development of representative institutions is predicted in those circumstances where small groups of actors (for example, the nobility of seventeenth-century England) with relatively equal resources (for example, land) expect to interact with each other well into the future. This expectation makes these political actors more inclined to agree to representative institutions in which they can resolve conflicts over issues of collective concern (such as defense or protection of private property). This rather unique set of circumstances, which characterized England after the Glorious Revolution of 1689, when James II was overthrown and William and Mary were invited to assume the throne, provides an explanation for the country's early development of democratic institutions.

Rational choice models also attempt to explain why democratization fails. One school of inquiry employs rational choice models to explain the successful (or unsuccessful) transition from authoritarianism to democracy. The focus of this inquiry is on the major groups and parties involved in negotiating the transition. For example, using game theory one can treat the major factions negotiating the transition as actors in a two-person game. The cooperative agreements possible in the transition depend upon the coalitions into which the various factions are inclined to enter. Adam Przeworski points out that the struggle for democracy involves conflict both between the authoritarian regime and its opponents and among the allies who are vying for a favorable position once democracy has been established. He divides the opponents of authoritarianism into moderate and radical factions. The supporters of authoritarianism are divided into reformers and hard-liners. Depending upon how these factions coalesce, the transition to democracy will be successful, troubled, or a failure. For example, if moderates within the opposition bloc and reformers within the authoritarian bloc are too suspicious of each other to cooperate, the transition to democracy will likely fail.

At issue here are the types of political structures and procedures that these factions agree upon. The initial rules of the political game that are agreed upon in these new democracies will not be neutral with respect to election outcomes and legislative policy decisions. For example, certain electoral laws can favor one faction over another. In Spain's transition to democracy in the 1970s after Francisco Franco relinquished power, conservative-rural parties were initially favored by electoral laws that set a minimum number of representatives that could be elected from the country's multimember constituencies. Hardliners had more of an influence on initial legislation than they would have had if there had been strict proportionality between constituency size and number of representatives elected to the national parliament.

Although new democratic institutions are not neutral, they must be designed so that, at a minimum, they make all major political factions comfortable with the prospect of losing power. Democracies fail when certain important political factions fear that if they lose the contest for political power they will have little chance to regain power in subsequent elections. For these factions the benefits of revising the rules of the political game are relatively high.

Collective Decisions Under Democratic Rules

Rational choice theory suggests that although individuals are able to rank their preferred outcomes from most favored to least favored, society is unable to deal with these individual rankings in any coherent fashion. When citizens' preferences are translated into collective decisions under democratic rules, the outcomes are not stable or coherent.

Lack of stability, or coherence, in voting is often illustrated by the voters' paradox. As an example, take the 1994 U.S. presidential election. Assume there are three voters. Voter 1 prefers George Bush to Ross Perot and ranks Bill Clinton last. Voter 2 ranks Clinton over Bush and Bush over Perot. Finally, voter 3 prefers Perot to Clinton and Clinton to Bush. When Bush is pitted against Perot, the coalition of voters 1 and 2 results in a victory for Bush. A contest between Perot and Clinton results in a Perot victory. If majority rule generated coherent outcomes, we would expect Bush to beat Clinton in a two-person contest. Paradoxically, Bush defeats Perot, Perot defeats Clinton, and Clinton defeats Bush. Although individuals are able to rank their preferences from best to worse, groups are unable to do so.

In certain circumstances, voting outcomes are coherent. The median voter theorem predicts that candidates in a majority rule contest will adopt policy positions closest to the position of the median voter. (The median voter is the voter who falls right in the middle of all voters aligned on a single policy continuum.) This theorem supports the notion that the ideal point of the median voter represents the equilibrium outcome under majority rule.

Consider the ideal points of the same three voters arrayed on a single dimension, with voter 1 on the left, voter 2 in the middle, and voter 3 on the right. In a two-candidate election between Bush and Clinton, both candidates would adopt issue positions that converge to the ideal point of the median voter 2 because that voter can form a coalition with voter 1 to defeat alternatives to the right or with voter 3 to defeat alternatives to the left. Hence the ideal point of voter 2 is the equilibrium outcome; it cannot be defeated.

But we can only be sure that majority rule generates coherent outcomes when there is only one issue dimension. When there is more than one dimension, an individual who is the median voter on one dimension is not necessarily the median voter on the other dimension(s). Thus, with majority rule, in a multidimensional issue space a coalition can win on one issue and be outvoted on another. There is, as was the case with the voters' paradox, no stable outcome; we cannot predict which coalition of voters will form and whether it will last for any length of time.

These insights into democratic voting mechanisms suggest that voting results become "incoherent" when more than two candidates are running or when more than one issue dimension is being considered. Believing that democratic outcomes are not as chaotic as these findings might suggest, rational choice theorists have refined these early models. In particular, they argue that the institutional setting in which voting takes place can reduce instability, or the degree to which outcomes can cycle.

For example, formal and informal procedures in a legislature can promote more coherent outcomes by reducing the number of choices voted upon or by reducing the issue dimensions. The use of specialized legislative committees makes outcomes more stable because votes on one issue dimension are separated from those on other dimensions. An agriculture committee, for example, will consider legislation that typically can be evaluated in terms of one single issue dimension (such as relative support or opposition to agriculture subsidies).

Rational choice theory has made two major contributions to our understanding of democracy. First, democracy is essentially a set of institutions designed to allow citizens to make choices. Rational choice theory has generated elegant and powerful explanations, many of them surprising, for the outcomes we can expect from these democratic procedures. Second, the emergence of democracy is the result of bargains struck among various political actors. Once again rational choice theory, particularly game theory, offers nonobvious, if not counterintuitive, explanations for why these actors choose democratic forms of government and for why these democratic institutions either succeed or fail.

See also *Utilitarianism*.

Raymond M. Duch

BIBLIOGRAPHY

Black, Duncan. *The Theory of Committees and Elections*. Cambridge: Cambridge University Press, 1958.

Downs, Anthony. *An Economic Theory of Democracy*. New York: Harper and Row, 1957.

North, Douglass C. *Institutions, Institutional Change, and Economic Performance*. Cambridge and New York: Cambridge University Press, 1990.

Olson, Mancur. "Dictatorship, Democracy, and Development." *American Political Science Review* 87 (September 1993): 567–576.

———. *Logic of Collective Action*. Cambridge, Mass., and London: Harvard University Press, 1965.

Przeworski, Adam. *Democracy and the Market: Political and Economic Reforms in Eastern Europe and Latin America*. Cambridge and New York: Cambridge University Press, 1991.

Riker, William. *Liberalism against Populism*. San Francisco: W. H. Freeman, 1982.

Shepsle, Kenneth A., and Barry Weingast. "Structure Induced Equilibrium and Legislative Choice." *Public Choice* 37 (1981): 503–520.

Referendum and initiative

Instruments through which citizens may be consulted on matters of public interest. A referendum denotes a question put to a popular vote. An initiative is a referendum launched by the action of citizens, usually by signing a petition. Many national and state constitutions provide for the holding of referendums. A few provide for initiatives. There are many ways in which such popular consultations, which have existed since ancient Athens, are conducted.

Democracy, the ideal of universal self-government involving every citizen, has always been faced with the obstacles of numbers and time. Sites do not exist for the assemblage of the whole population of any political unit except for small cities and towns, and people are reluctant to devote long hours to public meetings. Every democracy has therefore turned most of the business of government over to elected representatives. Yet it often seems desirable for the actions of a community to be founded on some fuller demonstration of popular consent.

In the United States in the 1890s the Progressives' cries against corrupt politicians prompted many states to make constitutional provision for referendum, initiative, and recall. President Woodrow Wilson's principle of self-determination fostered the spread of the referendum idea in Europe after World War I. At some time or other in the past hundred years almost every nation has turned to the specific and comprehensive test of public opinion that a referendum provides.

Incidence and Success

In the history of the civilized world there have been almost 1,000 referendums at the national level. Half of these have been in one country, Switzerland. Although the United States is one of the few major democracies never to have held a national referendum (the others are Japan, India, Israel, and the Netherlands), many American states have used the referendum.

Referendums usually come about when the government or the legislature decides that a particular issue should be put to a popular vote. Some countries have a binding requirement that constitutional amendments (and sometimes other matters) must be endorsed by referendum; that is why Australia, with forty-four referendums, comes next after Switzerland. Some constitutions make provision for a popular initiative: a given number of signatures can be enough to force a newly passed law to a popular vote. In a few cases there is provision for a measure actually to be proposed by ordinary citizens. Italy has turned increasingly to such measures since 1970. And initiatives in California have attracted much attention—notably Proposition 13 in 1978, which set limits to property taxes.

Referendums may be advisory or mandatory. In other words, they may merely be a very comprehensive opinion poll on a public issue, or their verdict may have the full force of law. In the latter case, the outcome may depend on a simple majority among those voting, or on achieving a two-thirds or three-quarters majority of those voting, or on a majority of the total electorate (so that abstention is equivalent to a negative vote). In federal states, such as Australia and Switzerland, the support of a majority of states or cantons as well as of voters is required for the electorate's approval of a measure to be valid.

Most referendums have produced a heavy "yes" vote. Surprisingly few fall into the middle range of 45 to 55 percent support. The places where the most referendums have failed to secure approval have been Australia and Switzerland, the countries that have made the greatest use of the device.

Legislatures and governments usually pass matters on to the people only when they are confident of the answer. But occasionally a referendum has provided a convenient way to pass on the responsibility when those in power are divided over a moral or practical issue. Letting the people decide offers a neat way of avoiding a party split. In 1975 Britain's Labour government solved its problems over membership in the European Community (now the European Union) by holding the country's first (and so far only) nationwide referendum. In the 1920s several Scandinavian nations and Canadian provinces dealt with the thorny problem of prohibiting alcoholic beverages by holding direct popular votes, which at first tended to say "yes" and later to say "no."

American states vary widely in their use of referendums and initiatives. A majority allow for them in their constitutions but only a few, mainly in the West, make regular use of them. More and more have been occurring, however. In the first enthusiasm of the 1910–1919 decade there were 269 state referendums, but the number fell to a mere 85 in the 1960s. The number jumped to 193 in the 1980s, and the trend appears to be holding. Historically, about 60 percent of American state referendums have won a "yes," but in the 1990s the approval rate has declined to less than half.

Types of Referendums

The subject matter of national referendums tends to fall into four categories: constitutional reform, territorial change, moral issues, and other policy issues.

Constitutional reform is the most important field for referendums. After a national upheaval, a country may seek legitimation for the new regime and the rules under which it is to run (as occurred in France in 1945–1946 after World War II and in Spain in 1977 in the transition after

Gen. Francisco Franco's regime). It may also refer other major constitutional matters to the people: for example, the form of the electoral system (New Zealand in 1992 and 1993; Italy, 1993); the power of the Senate (France, 1959); the status of the monarchy (Belgium, 1950; Greece, 1974); or voting age (Denmark, 1978).

Territorial change has been a key area. Some European nations and ethnic groups were consulted on post-1918 frontier settlements, or more recently on membership in the European Union. Moral issues—such as prohibition (Sweden, 1922; Finland, 1931); divorce (Italy, 1974); and abortion (Ireland, 1992)—have also been conveniently moved from legislative to popular decision.

Other policy issues have been settled by referendum from time to time. Rule of the road, to determine which side of the road cars were driven on, was voted on in Sweden in 1955; nuclear power was an issue in Austria in 1978; and membership in the North Atlantic Treaty Organization (NATO) was put to the vote in Spain in 1986. Most of the questions for referendums in American states fall into this heterogeneous category.

Implications

Contrary to popular belief, referendums are usually not habit forming. Most countries have held one or a few referendums to solve particular problems. These usually have clear-cut, indeed overwhelming, results. They are not radical instruments; the establishment view usually prevails. Money does not, by itself, prevail; the less well financed side often wins.

Referendums have been abused. Dictatorial regimes have often held them to demonstrate their legitimacy and, lacking the safeguards of secrecy or honest counting, have secured 99 percent endorsement. But in Switzerland and some American states they have become a way of life, accepted as an essential part of the democratic process. The price of holding nationwide referendums three or four times a year has been a decline in participation; the Swiss turnout has often been under 40 percent.

Referendums are not a panacea. But they are a useful device that has been used worldwide to defuse tensions and to give legitimacy to constitutional, territorial, or political settlements. They have been abused by tyrants and demagogues and exploited by some disingenuous democratic politicians. But they have often solved problems in the only way that could guarantee popular acceptance.

See also *Participation, Political.*

David E. Butler

BIBLIOGRAPHY

Butler, David, and Austin Ranney, eds. *Referendums: A Comparative Study of Practice and Theory.* Washington, D.C.: American Enterprise Institute, 1978.
———. *Referendums around the World.* Washington, D.C.: American Enterprise Institute, 1994.
Lijphart, Arend. *Democracies: Patterns of Majoritarian and Consensus Government in Twenty-one Countries.* New Haven and London: Yale University Press, 1984.
Magleby, David B. *Direct Legislation: Voting on Ballot Propositions in the United States.* Baltimore: Johns Hopkins University Press, 1984.
Ranney, Austin, ed. *The Referendum Device.* Washington, D.C.: American Enterprise Institute, 1981.

Reformation

The religious revolt, inaugurated by the German theologian Martin Luther in 1517, that permanently divided Western Christendom between Roman Catholicism and various branches of Protestantism. The Reformation was, at its core, a fight for freedom—freedom of the individual believer from Catholic canon law and clerical control, freedom of the political official from ecclesiastical power and privilege, and freedom of the local clergy from central papal rule. Although this Protestant fight for freedom drew only marginally on democratic ideas or institutions, the theological teachings that inspired it were filled with democratic implications.

The leading reformers of the early sixteenth century—Luther, Philipp Melanchthon, Huldrych Zwingli, John Calvin, Martin Bucer, and others—taught that a person is at once saint and sinner. On the one hand, each person is created in the image of God and has equal access to God. Each person is called by God to a distinct vocation, which stands equal in sanctity and dignity to all others. Each person is a prophet, priest, and king and responsible to exhort, minister, and rule in the community. Each person therefore is vested with a natural liberty to live, to believe, to serve God and neighbor. All people are entitled to the Scripture in their own language, to education, to work in a vocation. On the other hand, all persons are inherently sinful and prone to evil and egoism. They need the restraint of the moral and civil law to deter them from vice and drive them to virtue. They need the association of others to exhort, minister, and rule them with law and

Martin Luther, German leader of the Protestant Reformation, questioned the authority of the pope.

with love. Humans are thus by nature communal creatures and belong to families, churches, schools, and other associations. Such associations, which are ordained by God and instituted by human covenants, are essential for the individual to flourish and for the state to function.

In the early 1560s French Huguenots, Dutch pietists, Scottish Presbyterians, and other Protestant groups began to derive democratic theory from this Reformation theology. The early Reformation theology of the person was cast into democratic social theory. Because all persons stand equal before God, they must stand equal before God's political agents in the state. Because God has vested all persons with natural liberties of life and belief, the state must assure them of similar civil liberties. Because God has called all persons to be prophets, priests, and kings, the state must protect their freedoms to speak, to worship, and to rule in the community. Because God has created people as social creatures, the state must promote and protect a plurality of social institutions, particularly the church, the school, and the family.

The early Reformation theology of the covenant was cast into democratic constitutional theory. Societies and states must be created by voluntary written contracts or constitutions, to which parties swear their allegiance before God and each other. Such constitutions must describe the community's ideals and values, delineate the citizen's rights and responsibilities, define the officials' powers and prerogatives.

The early Reformation theology of sin was cast into democratic political theory. The political office must be protected against the inherent sinfulness of the political official. Power must be distributed among self-checking executive, legislative, and judicial branches. Officials must be elected to limited terms of office. Laws must be clearly codified, and discretion and equity closely guarded. If officials abuse their office, they must be disobeyed; if they persist in their abuse, they must be removed, even if by force of arms.

These ideas of the early Reformation helped to inspire the creation of several democratic church polities in the later sixteenth and seventeenth centuries. Anabaptist churches, notably the Amish and Mennonites, separated themselves from secular society into small democratic communities, which featured popular election of church officers, public participation in ecclesiastical governance, and intensely egalitarian organizations and activities. Calvinist churches, particularly those of English and American Puritan stock, were often created as democratic polities. Church congregations were formed by ecclesiastical constitutions. Church power was separated among pastors, elders, and deacons, each of whom was elected to a limited term of office and held a measure of authority over the others. Church law was codified and administered through a variety of public or representative bodies. Church members convened periodic popular meetings to assess the performance of church officers and to deliberate changes in doctrine, liturgy, or government. Several Puritan writers in colonial New England, from Thomas Hooker to John Wise, drew ready political lessons from this democratic understanding of the church.

These ideas of the Reformation also helped to inspire a number of democratic political reforms in early modern times. Lutheran beliefs and believers encouraged several Scandinavian and German cities to pass new laws that broke centuries-old feudal and ecclesiastical controls over local politics and properties, revamped criminal and civil procedural protections, introduced a modicum of religious toleration, and expanded public schools and civic social welfare programs. Calvinist preachers and politicians led the seven northern provinces of the Netherlands into revolt against the Spanish king in 1567. They also helped to create, through the 1579 Union of Utrecht and the 1581 declaration of independence, a confederate structure of government for the Dutch republic and the framework for new political and civil rights for its citizens.

Puritan Calvinists, particularly the radical Levellers, were among the leaders of the English Civil War in the 1640s that truncated royal prerogatives, augmented parliamentary power and representation, and yielded the famous 1689 Bill of Rights and Toleration Act. Baptists, Quakers, and other Protestant groups introduced religious toleration to colonial America and were instrumental in securing the guarantees of freedom of religion, speech, assembly, and press in several American state constitutions and in inspiring the First Amendment to the U.S. Constitution. Protestant beliefs and believers, from many denominations, were at the heart of both the American Revolution and the great democratic constructions of the early American republic.

The Reformation was certainly not the sole source of democracy in the early modern Western world. Yet it was a fertile seedbed from which grew an impressive array of familiar democratic ideas and institutions.

See also *Catholicism, Roman; Christian democracy; Levellers; Protestantism; Religion, Civil; Revolution, American.*

John Witte, Jr.

BIBLIOGRAPHY

Franklin, Julian H., ed. *Constitutionalism and Resistance in the Sixteenth Century.* New York: Pegasus, 1969.

Kingdon, Robert M., and Robert D. Linder, eds. *Calvin and Calvinism: Sources of Democracy?* Lexington, Mass.: D. C. Heath, 1970.

Klaasen, Walter. *Anabaptism in Outline: Selected Primary Sources.* Scottdale, Penn.: Herald Press, 1981.

Sanders, Thomas G. *Protestant Concepts of Church and State: Historical Backgrounds and Approaches for the Future.* New York: Holt, Rinehart and Winston, 1964.

Skinner, Quentin. *The Foundations of Modern Political Thought.* Vol. 2 of *The Age of Reformation.* Cambridge: Cambridge University Press, 1978.

Tonkin, John. *The Church and the Secular Order in Reformation Thought.* New York and London: Columbia University Press, 1971.

Walzer, Michael. *The Revolution of the Saints: A Study in the Origins of Radical Politics.* Cambridge: Harvard University Press, 1965.

Witte, John F., Jr., ed. *Christianity and Democracy in Global Context.* Boulder, Colo.: Westview Press, 1993.

Regulation

Regulation and issues involving deregulation and privatization are fundamental concepts underlying the core questions about the power to make economic decisions. What should be the role of the state in societal decision making? Who shall decide how a society's resources will be used? Who shall decide which products and services are to be produced, in what quantities, and with what qualities? Who shall produce them, using which methods of production? Who shall decide the prices of these goods and services? What are to be the safeguards to prevent the abuse of economic power, and what is to be the mechanism of accountability to ensure that private decisions are in the public interest?

In the kind of private enterprise economy envisioned in Adam Smith's *Wealth of Nations* (1776), self-interest and individual freedom are seen as the central motive force of economic growth and development, and market competition is seen as the principal regulator of economic activity. Not the state but the free play of market forces should determine the kinds and quantities of goods to be produced, the means of production to be employed, and the distribution of income. Individual economic activity is to be coordinated through a market mechanism that is external to human control, manipulation, or perversion. The individual appetite for private gain is to be harnessed for social ends by an "invisible hand"—the incentives and compulsions of a competitive market. As the economic analogue of constitutional checks and balances, the competitive market regime pits producers against each other in serving consumer wants and the public good.

The market, however, is not a natural, spontaneous, or self-generating mechanism. If it is to perform its regulatory function, the invisible hand must be supplemented by government, acting as a rule maker and umpire, creating a framework in which individual freedom is not used to destroy the freedom of others or to subvert the entire system of freedom. Without rules to protect competition from conspiracies, cartels, and monopolies, the market cannot discharge its regulatory functions.

Beyond that, as Smith recognized, government must shoulder certain critical responsibilities that cannot be relegated to the market. Government has duties to protect the citizens from violence and invasion by outsiders; to protect each member of the society from injustice and oppression at the hands of other members; and to undertake certain works which, although critically important, would not be in the economic interest of private individuals to undertake on their own. Even Adam Smith, the patron saint of private enterprise, recognized that, in some instances, the play of self-interest and market competition does not produce socially beneficial results and may require direct government intervention to protect the public.

The Need for Regulation

In a perfectly functioning free enterprise system, a minimalist role for government may be sound public policy. But in an imperfect world some regulation is necessary. For example, market preference—consumers casting dollar votes to determine what goods are produced in what quantity—may be a reliable means for deciding whether resources shall be used to make baseball bats or snowmobiles, but it is hardly a workable guide for stocking the nation's defense arsenal. Only government can make efficient decisions with respect to such collective goods as battleships, missiles, and bombers. In addition, at least three major market imperfections, or market failures, may have to be corrected by direct regulatory intervention by government. These are natural monopolies, imperfect information, and externalities.

So-called natural monopolies are situations in which enforced competition would entail wasteful inefficiencies and would impose intolerable costs of duplication. A single electric company, for example, can deliver electricity to a community far less expensively than could multiple competing providers, each with a separate system of lines, poles, and generators. Similarly, one large pipeline can transport petroleum between given points at a fraction of the cost that would have to be incurred by a myriad of small, competing parallel lines. In such situations, technological constraints militate against competition, and public policy must choose an alternative economic governance system. It may permit private ownership alone, trusting to the monopolist's sense of social responsibility not to exploit the public. It may subject private ownership to public regulation. Or it may put both ownership and operation of the natural monopoly in the hands of government authority.

Where information is imperfect, government has to exercise its traditional police powers to protect the health and safety of the citizenry. For example, information on product safety and dangers may not be available. Certainly those with best access to product safety information—the producers—have little incentive to publicize such information, or even to collect it in the first place, because it obviously would do little to enhance their sales. Even if full product safety information were available, consumers might still lack the technical sophistication needed to assess its significance. In that event, buyers' choices would not be rational, nor would the mix of goods produced be socially optimal. In matters such as clean air, pure water, airline and automotive safety, and licensing of physicians and surgeons, government has a legitimate role to play in protecting consumer health, safety, and welfare.

Externalities are costs imposed or benefits bestowed on third parties by the economic activities of an individual or group. If negative externalities and costs are involved, there is no assurance that decentralized competitive market decision making will produce socially optimal results. Those competing in the market have every incentive to keep costs low and maximize profits. This may mean, for instance, using production processes that generate toxic waste and dumping that waste in the adjacent community. Environmental pollution is a classic example of the problems posed by negative externalities and by the severing of the link between private advantage and public welfare.

Efforts by government to correct these market imperfections are rarely called into question except by ideological extremists. In these instances, as Adam Smith put it, government regulations that curb individual liberty may be justified in the interest of promoting the welfare of the society generally.

Deregulation

The practical problem arises when private interests lobby government to go beyond its necessary and economically proper functions. In a utopian world, government's economic role would be determined strictly in accordance with scientific economic principles. In the hurly-burly real world of democratic lobbying and pressure politics, however, the coercive power of the state is an attractive prize for private interests bent on fashioning public policy so as to subvert the competitive market and escape its discipline. The problem then is where to draw the line between economically legitimate government intervention and antisocial special-interest protectionism. In some circumstances, the dictum that "the government that governs least governs best" may be the essence of wisdom.

The government, for example, may subject inherently competitive industries such as trucking and airlines to public utility regulation, not to protect the public from victimization by a natural monopoly but to shield existing firms from competition. As a result, prices are higher, quality is lower, technological innovation is reduced, and the public is worse off. Conversely, government may continue to regulate an industry at that industry's behest, even though far-reaching innovation has destroyed the older technology that initially gave rise to natural monopoly conditions and the need for regulation by the state. In addition, government may be lobbied by private economic interests for state subsidies or by collapsing corporate giants for bailouts (for example, Penn Central, Lockheed, and Chrysler in the United States in the 1970s). This situation promotes the reverse of economic Darwinism—survival of the fattest, not the fittest—because the firms involved are considered too important to be allowed to fail.

These are the central issues in the debate over regulation versus deregulation, an activist versus a minimalist state, government intervention versus laissez-faire. They confront a democratic society with a perennially vexing dilemma in economic policy making: How can government be held accountable and responsive to the citizenry yet, at the same time, be rendered resistant to encroachment on its sovereign power by special-interest factions demanding private economic advantages? And how can government be insulated from the plundering of powerful private interests, without at the same time being rendered less representative and more despotic? Obviously, these are questions that cannot be resolved by simplistic slogans.

Privatization

Similar issues bedevil the question of who shall perform certain key functions and who shall own a nation's production facilities. In a private enterprise economy, government's direct economic role is generally held to a minimum—on the assumption that private entrepreneurs have the necessary incentives to use their resources efficiently and to make the investments necessary to ensure economic growth. Harnessed by competition, private profits (and losses) serve as the invisible hand to discipline individuals and to compel them to employ their property and energies in ways that promote both their own interest and that of the public.

At times, however, governments may decide either to build production facilities at the outset or to take over and nationalize already existing private production facilities. There are a variety of reasons for these decisions: lack of sufficiently developed private infrastructure to build

them, an aggressive modernization and industrialization effort, or national prestige.

National policy may change, and governments may embark on privatization programs to transfer these state-owned facilities to private parties. Great Britain under Margaret Thatcher's government privatized approximately a dozen large state enterprises during the 1980s, including British Aerospace, British Airways, British Gas, British Petroleum, British Telecom, and Jaguar. In Latin America some 800 state-owned enterprises were privatized during the 1980s, in actions that included the sale or liquidation of more than 400 of Mexico's 1,155 public enterprises; the privatization of some 500 state-owned enterprises in Chile; and the privatization of telecommunication, airline, and public utility operations in Venezuela and Argentina.

The central economic question is whether society can, and should, rely on the private sector rather than government to perform certain functions. In some instances (for example, trash collection), the analysis may be a relatively straightforward comparison of costs and efficiency between public and private providers of the services involved. In other cases, such as prisons and schools, however, the problem is more complex, and the answer may hinge as much on overarching questions of state sovereignty, morality, and social legitimacy as it does on financial and economic analysis.

The challenge of privatization is most dramatically highlighted in Eastern Europe and the former Soviet Union, where formerly communist nations are struggling to transform entire command-and-control economies into Western-style market societies. The dilemmas are vexing. For example, the cash-strapped state may be tempted to maximize the revenues it receives from the sale of giant monopoly enterprises. But if it does, it will be led to sell these monopolies intact, even though their market power, now in private hands, will expose the public to economic exploitation. If the state attempts to reorganize these monopoly enterprises into competitively structured industries before privatizing them, however, it will reduce their attractiveness to private bidders along with the price that can be obtained from their sale.

Ownership of state enterprises may be transferred to their workers in order to create incentives for them to be efficient and productive. But what happens to workers employed in hopelessly antiquated and inefficient state enterprises? Alternatively, if ownership is transferred to all citizens equally, there is the problem of how a far-flung network of millions of individual owners can effectively monitor the firm's management and its use—or misuse—of their assets.

State properties can be sold to the highest bidder, on the grounds that those who are best suited for managing the enterprise will pay the highest price. But this policy entails the political risk of concentrating wealth and power in the hands of a privileged few. Or it may subject citizens to domination by foreign interests that can outbid potential domestic owners. In addition, massive privatization will destroy the extensive but unprofitable social safety net formerly provided by state enterprises in the form of schools, stores, and medical care. Ironically, in this respect, the move to a market system may require a more expansive government role in providing desperately needed services. In addition, the enormous shock and suffering that large-scale privatization will inflict on the populace may require that political liberalization be delayed in order to prevent social protest from undermining the economic transformation process.

Economic Policy and Democracy

In a democratic society the issues of individual versus state, freedom versus restraint, and private interest versus public good will not be resolved on narrow economic grounds alone. Their reconciliation cannot be found in some handbook of economic solutions, nor can it be deduced from abstruse model building or complicated mathematical equations. The process of resolution will be raucous, comprising conflict and compromise, and will follow a tortuous path—a path on which rigid ideology is an obstacle, not an aid. The acceptable resolution will vary with time, place, institutional circumstance, and cultural tradition.

All national economic policies ultimately boil down to two fundamental challenges: to produce wealth and to distribute it. The core problem, of course, is how to attain these twin objectives. If history is any guide, it is apparent that, over the years, whether liberals or conservatives were in power, the United States and other capitalist nations have had more activist governments than laissez-faire purists would prescribe. At the same time, they have, and in the foreseeable future are likely to have, a predominantly free economy: government assumes responsibility for moderating unemployment and inflation, for providing defense and other public goods, for marginally redistributing income and providing some minimal assistance for the poor, and for regulating where there are major, clear cases of failure by free markets to yield socially beneficial results.

How best to do these things, and how far to go with them, are proper questions for discussion. But within the range of options likely to be considered, none of the choices will add up to radical departures from this moderate approach. With pragmatic realism, the search will continue to be guided by the limits of what government can do as well as by what government must do.

See also *Laissez-faire economic theory.*

Walter Adams and James W. Brock

BIBLIOGRAPHY

Adams, Walter, and James W. Brock. *Adam Smith Goes to Moscow: A Dialogue on Radical Reform.* Princeton: Princeton University Press, 1993.
———. *The Bigness Complex: Industry, Labor, and Government in the American Economy.* New York: Pantheon Books, 1986.
Adams, William J., and Christian Stoffaës, eds. *French Industrial Policy.* Washington, D.C.: Brookings Institution, 1986.
Greer, Douglas F. *Business, Government, and Society.* 3d ed. New York: Macmillan, 1993.
Litan, Robert E., and William D. Nordhaus. *Reforming Federal Regulation.* New Haven: Yale University Press, 1983.
Shepherd, William G. *Public Policies toward Business.* 7th ed. Homewood, Ill.: Irwin, 1985.
Smith, Adam. *An Inquiry into the Nature and Causes of the Wealth of Nations.* 2 vols. Oxford: Oxford University Press, 1979.
Vickers, John, and George Yarrow. *Privatization: An Economic Analysis.* Cambridge: MIT Press, 1988; Chicester: Wiley, 1988.

Relativism

The view that value is subjective and that no way exists to establish the objective worth of human goals by reason or science. Relativism thus denies that one can prove democracy to be superior to other forms of government. The modern doctrine, though distinct, has antecedents almost as old as human thought. For example, the Sophists of ancient Greece, criticized by Plato and Aristotle in the fourth century B.C., held that traditional morality was merely a matter of conventions. Yet many thinkers believed that nature was knowable and that certain human strivings were objectively good because they were natural.

Much later, Niccolò Machiavelli (1469–1527), the Florentine originator of modern political philosophy, proposed to speak of human beings as they really acted rather than as they should act. Although he celebrated realism, he entertained few doubts about the knowability of what human beings should do, and his work abounds with moral evaluations he thought of as objective.

We come closer to modern relativism in the thought of the Scottish philosopher David Hume (1711–1776), who in his *Treatise of Human Nature* (1739–1740) objected to a practice he found common in deductive reasoning on human morality: a movement from considerations of what exists to conclusions as to what should exist. Hume thus described a gulf between "is" and "ought," but his own moral reasoning was not relativistic, for he wrote that laws of nature and principles of justice exist objectively.

The Social Science Approach

In the late nineteenth century relativism came of age, as the doctrine of the unbridgeable gulf between "is" and "ought" became part of the project to make the study of human beings as rigorous as the study of the natural sciences. Under the influence of positivism, a doctrine asserting that all reliable knowledge must be based on sense perception, a new social science arose. The most prominent methodologist of this new discipline was the German sociologist Max Weber (1864–1920), who articulated the distinction between fact and value.

In principle, a fact can be measured and can otherwise be objectively observed and described as well as communicated between subjects. Values, on the other hand, are subjective and are not amenable to either rational or scientific verification or disproof. To say that X is six feet tall is to state a fact, but to state that X is good is to express a value judgment; those who make it mean no more than—though also no less than—that they like X. Science therefore must confine itself to dealing with means because it is impotent when it comes to establishing the true worth of human ends.

According to Weber and other social scientists, this conviction does not by any means imply that science has nothing to say about human ends. Scientific analysis can, first of all, enumerate human ends and describe them in ever more exacting detail. Second, it can elaborate the potential or actual conflicts among the various human values; for example, it can dissect the tensions between liberty and equality. Third, it can point to the consequences of acting on certain values; so one can objectively state that when one rules by the principles (values) of tyranny one perpetrates fear among one's subjects. Finally, scientific analysis may be able to demonstrate that certain ends cannot be attained by certain means; for example, it may be impossible to bring about an atmosphere of love by the

generation of fear. Nevertheless, there is no rational-scientific basis for preferring one ideal or way of life over another. Justice may be preferable to injustice, but there is no objective or absolute answer to the classical question, Why should one be just?

Relativism and Democratic Values

Relativism gained prominence in Germany rather than in the United States, where the translations of much of Weber's work did not appear until after the end of World War II. In Germany the doctrine was used as a weapon against influential extremism in the universities; its proponents pointed to the fact that the autocratic rhetoric of radical professors, especially those on the political right, was not an authentic part of the sciences they professed. In the United States, by contrast, a great consensus reigned about democratic values; moral and social science thus could develop without extensive debate on fundamentals. The fiercest probing into the goals espoused by American democracy seems to have come in the years after World War II, following the great victory of that democracy over fascist powers.

Relativists do not, of course, understand themselves as enemies of democracy. They are much more likely to stress their neutrality—at least as scientists—to competing values and to emphasize the benign uses and consequences of the doctrine they espouse. The first of these is the growth of solid knowledge about human beings—knowledge that is no longer clouded over by ideological blinders, political passions, or excessive predispositions. Relativists maintain that techniques such as interviews, opinion sampling, and voting studies become more sophisticated and reliable as one abandons the bootless attempts to distinguish between virtuous and vicious respondents, wise and foolish citizens.

Relativists can and do go further by pointing to a kind of kinship between their credo and the fundamental democratic value of equality. Because no significant superiority in anything but brute strength can be established objectively, a presumption arises that all hierarchies are conventional rather than natural, that another human being's inequality is always, as it were, in the eye of the beholder. Indeed, an intimacy seems to exist between egalitarianism and relativism. Egalitarians find solace in relativism's rejection of the very idea of anyone's innate superiority over anyone else, and relativists view favorably egalitarianism's rejection of the orders in rank that they dismiss as arbitrary and unwarranted.

What is more, both relativism and democracy are linked to the idea of progress. Relativism understands itself as an advance over previous human thought, which in spite of all its variety had in common a false idea that reason can decipher objective human goods. Relativism views itself as the provider of objective truth about the lack of objectivity in previous thinking about values and hence as the agent of liberation from the dogmatism of the past.

Finally, relativism views itself as beneficial to democracy in that it counsels toleration for the diverse ways of humanity. Democracy, after all, entails not only majority rule but also minority rights. Relativism teaches that before the bar of reason all ways of life are equal in being rationally baseless. Hence relativists are likely to think that any one way of life, being as good (or bad) as any other, is entitled to as much respect as any other. Relativism is innately favorable to the slogan "live and let live."

The Dilemma of Relativism

A series of problems arise, however, that expose what even some relativists call the seamy side of relativism. For example, relativism favors toleration, but it confesses to be at a loss to demonstrate why tolerance ought to be preferred to intolerance. Moreover, it is not at all clear whether one ought to extend the protection of tolerance to those who oppose toleration in either theory or in practice. If one tolerates the intolerant, one may act against the very principles that one supports, and if one refuses to protect those who do not believe in toleration, one becomes intolerant oneself, even of most of the great political philosophers of the Western tradition. Relativism does not excel in resolving this dilemma.

The so-called seamy side of relativism comes to light especially when the very foundations of a political regime or of a way of life are challenged. At such times the questioning goes deeper than the worth of a particular value, such as progress, and engulfs all values. Thus, when in the twentieth century liberal democracy was exposed to threats from both the right and the left, relativism was at a loss to show why human beings should refuse to accept either fascism or communism. Its own premises forced it to state that a choice of extremism was as defensible as a preference for moderation.

Unable to say decisively what is good about democracy, or bad about its foes, relativism has been accused of providing only cold comfort for the political decencies. Traditionally, democrats have believed that a vigorous democracy entails a belief in the kinds of principles enshrined in the American Declaration of Independence of 1776. Relativism finds itself unable to endorse these principles because they are not objective truths; it is incompatible with beliefs that natural or divine rights exist.

Moreover, relativism has been accused of playing into the drawbacks of democracy catalogued by Alexis de Tocqueville's *Democracy in America* (1835–1840). Tocqueville deplored the leveling effects he associated with the rule of the many. Relativism can be said to contribute to this leveling by withholding support from any notion of human greatness. It may also contribute to the growth of conformity by denying that good reasons for certain choices exist beyond the craving for approval by other human beings.

Increasing awareness of the seamy side of relativism has led to vigorous attempts to overcome it. Weber acknowledged his debt to Friedrich Nietzsche (1844–1900), and the latter's critique of rationality, but strangely enough he did not react to Nietzsche's implicit criticism of the distinction between facts and values. The traditional criticism of the fact-value distinction had been that objective knowledge of values is available to human beings, though it may have to be attained by methods different from those used by the natural sciences. The distinction between facts and values therefore is spurious because there can be moral facts.

Nietzsche's approach is radically different. Instead of denying that there are values, he played with the idea of denying that there are facts. What we call facts, according to Nietzsche, are merely fictions on which we agree. Science is unable to overcome the basic human situation in which all knowledge depends on one's perspective. We think what we must think because of the historical situation in which we find ourselves. The certainties that the so-called hard sciences propound are illusory because they are not indisputable. Different historical dispensations, for example, lead to different kinds of physics, and they certainly produce different moral evaluations. What Weber calls facts are merely uncontroversial values that generate little debate because nobody cares enough about them to contest them seriously.

When relativism loses its bedrock foundation in the sciences, it gradually changes into historicism, the doctrine that all thought is historically determined or at least conditioned. Historicism can avoid relativism only by supposing an absolute moment in history when the final truth becomes available. That thought was explored most profoundly by G. W. F. Hegel (1770–1831), but the ongoing process of history prevented it from being accepted. Without an absolute moment, historicism is simply the most radical form assumed by relativism. In a sense it can be said to restore the dignity of values because they turn out to be more profound than the shallow conventional agreements of what are called facts. But when relativism sheds, or is deprived of, the last vestiges of objectivity, it turns into nihilism. Nihilism asserts that human beings cannot justify what they do or will and that ultimately nothing matters. In that case, democracy is as meaningless as any other human contrivance.

Thus relativism's convergence with historicism fails to resolve the crisis that attends the awareness of its seamy side. The search for a solution shows no signs of terminating. The yearning for previous certainties solves nothing, because the naïveté that is lost is impossible to recover. Some, however, continue to find their ultimate meaning in religion and attempt to refute Nietzsche's assertion that God is dead. Others cling to the hope that philosophy is progressive and that future thinkers will discover an objective grounding for value. Still others cultivate a stance of irony, clinging to the common decencies of life, while conceding or even asserting the absurdity of valuing these without any objective basis.

See also *Egalitarianism; Hegel, Georg Wilhelm Friedrich; Historicism; Machiavelli, Niccolò; Nietzsche, Friedrich; Tocqueville, Alexis de; Weber, Max.*

Werner J. Dannhauser

BIBLIOGRAPHY

Ayer, A. J., ed. *Logical Positivism.* Glencoe, Ill.: Free Press, 1959; London: Greenwood, 1978.
Brecht, Arnold. *Political Theory: The Foundations of Twentieth-Century Political Thought.* Princeton: Princeton University Press, 1959.
Cohen, Morris, and Ernest Nagel. *An Introduction to Logic and Scientific Method.* New York: Harcourt, Brace, 1934.
Rorty, Richard M. *Contingency, Irony, and Solidarity.* Cambridge and New York: Cambridge University Press, 1989.
Strauss, Leo. *Natural Right and History.* Chicago: University of Chicago Press, 1953.
Weber, Max. *From Max Weber: Essays in Sociology.* Translated and edited by Hans H. Gerth and C. Wright Mills. New York: Oxford University Press, 1946; London: Routledge, 1991.

Religion, Civil

Civil religion is a theme in the history of political thought that concerns the political utility of religion. Religion, from this view, is seen as supplying an essential basis for civic ties and obligations.

Going back to Plato's *Laws* in the fourth century B.C., political philosophers have been concerned with the function served by religion in helping to secure political order. In the sixteenth century, Niccolò Machiavelli, in important respects the founder of modern political philosophy, acknowledged the problem of the political function of religion in his *Discourses on Livy*, in which he discusses the political advantages of Roman paganism relative to Christianity. Notwithstanding the process of secularization that has been characteristic of modernity and the secularism of modern thought, this issue has been an important one in modern democratic theory as well, notably in the writings of Jean-Jacques Rousseau and Alexis de Tocqueville.

Rousseau

Contemporary liberal democracies generally are committed, either in practice or by constitutional doctrine, to a separation of church and state. Rousseau, one of the first great theorists of democracy, concluded his political masterpiece, the *Social Contract* (1762), with an argument to the effect that republican politics must strive to unify temporal and religious authority. It may help to shed light on the relationship between religion and democracy to review Rousseau's analysis of the problem of a civil religion.

Rousseau concludes the *Social Contract* with a stunning notion: no state has ever been constituted without religion serving as its base. This statement occurs in the context of a penetrating analysis that lays out an exhaustive survey of religious-political possibilities. Rousseau sets forth two main alternatives: the first, which he calls *natural divine right,* is strictly otherworldly in its focus and finds its purest embodiment in the Christianity of the Gospels. The second, which Rousseau refers to as *civil,* or *positive, divine right,* embraces a variety of more worldly theocratic regimes. These divide basically into two types: local pagan religions like that of ancient Rome and more universalistic, and therefore potentially imperialistic, theocracies such as Islam and Judaism. All national religions will appear parochial relative to the universalism of Christianity, but as the contrast of Judaism and Islam with paganism shows, this parochialism can have either a (relatively) tolerant or an aggressive cast.

Rousseau also presents a third possibility, *mixed right,* which divides authority between church and state. In practice, this hybrid type of religion means that the priests are tempted to usurp temporal authority for themselves and to this extent undercut the established authority of the state. Rousseau calls it the religion of the priest, and like Thomas Hobbes denies to this worldly-otherworldly religion any moral claim whatsoever on the ground that sovereignty as such cannot be divided. The most blatant target of this polemic is Catholicism, but Rousseau concedes that the dividing of sovereignties is latent in Christianity in general.

Rousseau's statement that no state has ever been founded that is not based on religion rules out the possibility of a sound politics in the absence of a civil religion. A religion that is neither strictly worldly nor strictly otherworldly (namely Catholicism) is vehemently rejected. A religion that is strictly otherworldly (non-Catholic versions of the Christianity of the Gospels) is religiously true but, at best, is politically useless. It fails to make available the civil religion that Rousseau insists is politically indispensable. Rousseau goes to great lengths to show that attempts to reconcile Christianity with the requirements of politics are hopeless. It makes no sense to speak of a Christian republic: the two words are mutually exclusive. This belief might suggest that Rousseau, as a partisan of republican politics, would be forced to embrace some species of theocracy, either of the pluralistic, pagan variety or of the imperialistic, monotheistic variety.

Although Rousseau voices sympathy for Roman religious practices, and declares that the views of Muhammad, the founder of Islam, were sound, he ultimately repudiates theocracy as an option. Theocracies breed intolerance, and intolerance is morally unacceptable. In this respect, Christian universalism embodies a moral truth that must be retained. All good politics is parochial, and a religion that encourages this parochialism, rather than helping us to transcend it (as true Christianity does), would diminish our humanity. So, although Rousseau accepts and restates the analysis of the antipolitical character of Christianity presented in Machiavelli's *Discourses on Livy,* he is too sensitive to the perils of neopagan politics to be able to follow Machiavelli in the latter's unqualified desire for a return to some kind of paganism (or some other radical alternative to Christianity). As Rousseau points out, the Crusades show what results when Christianity is turned in a pagan direction, and the Crusades were an abomination.

But even if we could conceive of a civil religion that was not subject to this criticism—that is, some kind of morally and politically attractive theocracy—Rousseau says that we would be seeking a possibility that is no longer attainable. Christianity has definitively superseded all other religions. So we are left with the two unhappy alternatives of a morally true religion that is in its essence subversive of politics and a sound civil religion that is morally unattractive and historically an anachronism.

The standard reading of the *Social Contract* is that Rousseau does offer a civil religion. This comes in the closing paragraphs of the penultimate chapter of the book, in which Rousseau seems to try to combine the idea of a civic cult, in at least a minimalist version, with a strong emphasis on the ideal of tolerance found in John Locke. But it remains puzzling how any civil religion, if it is to be robust enough to satisfy Rousseau's political requirements, can be rendered compatible with the moral imperative of tolerance. Moreover, it is hard to see how such a civil religion can succeed in eluding the powerful Rousseauian arguments reviewed above. It would have to be at the same time as particularistic as Machiavelli's political vision and as tolerant as Locke's, a feat that seems to be squaring the circle.

One presumes that in urging the adoption of a civil religion Rousseau had in mind a "real" religion, one that could shape the motivations of citizens, thus fostering good citizenship and helping to consolidate the foundations of the state. But what he offers is a diluted, "phantom" religion, an Enlightenment-style religion of tolerance, one might say, in which liberal or negative tenets prevail over those that might positively build republican citizenship. In Rousseau's embracing of this thin quasi religion, it is as if he has bid farewell to his republican ideal, with the hearty parochialism and potential illiberalism that it implies. He fails to explain how the liberalized and anemic religion that he conjures up can possibly satisfy the need for a robust political religion hailed through most of his argument. Thus, in typical fashion, Rousseauian politics ends with a paradox rather than a proposal.

We can summarize Rousseau's analysis of religious possibilities in the *Social Contract* as follows: Rousseau rejects politics without a civil religion. He accepts "pure" Christianity morally but rejects it politically. He forcefully rejects corrupted Christianity, which contests the sovereign's claim to undivided political authority. (The chief example is Catholicism, but Rousseau refers also to Shinto and Tibetan Buddhism.) He rejects monotheistic theocracy, which is either conquering and proselytizing (the warrior religion of the Quran) or simply conquering or genocidal (the warrior religion of the Old Testament). And he rejects as historically anachronistic a benign theocracy such as Roman paganism, despite his evident sympathy for this kind of national religion.

One is left somewhat baffled as to the basis upon which Rousseau thinks any politically useful religion can be sustained. He has rejected vigorously any possible compatibility between Christianity and sound republican politics while dismissing all the obvious alternatives to Christianity.

Tocqueville and a Modern Civil Religion

To locate a workable civil religion for modern democratic societies, we might turn to Tocqueville, a thinker deeply immersed in Rousseauian thought. Like Rousseau, Tocqueville highlights the function of religion in fostering attachment to the laws and institutions of the political community and in providing a pillar of decent republicanism. Indeed, various contemporary theorists (Robert Bellah, William Galston, Wilson Carey McWilliams, and Thomas Pangle, to name a few) have been inspired by Tocqueville to see the attractions of an American civil religion of just this kind.

Tocqueville tries to show, in the face of Rousseau's challenge, that Christianity, and even Catholicism, can meet the test of political utility applied to religion at the end of the *Social Contract.* Yet only in a very qualified sense does Tocqueville share in the enterprise of civil religion as Rousseau defines it. For Tocqueville places religion firmly within the sphere of what liberals tend to call *civil society,* as opposed to the realm of the state. And, like Locke, he strongly supports the strict separation of church and state, a principle that Hobbes and Rousseau severely criticized. Tocqueville tries to show, in response to Rousseau, that one can have a political religion that is both Christian and moderately this worldly, both tolerant in spirit and politically useful in securing the required ethos of a democratic state. To this modest Tocquevillean vision of a civil religion, Rousseau no doubt would reply that it offers a much watered down version of Christianity in the service of a much watered down version of republicanism.

It is perhaps easy to assume that we live in a radically secularized age in which religion and politics inhabit mutually exclusive spheres of life. Indeed, the very question of the relationship between religion and politics seems anachronistic in a world in which religion has been thoroughly privatized by Protestant Christianity in alliance with political liberalism. Yet perhaps the question has been brought to life with the contemporary vitality of political Islam asserting, once again, the possibility of a theocratic regime. If liberal democracies with their secularized politics are to address the claims of this renewed theocratic politics, they may have to avail themselves of that whole dimension of theorizing made available in Rousseau's acute analysis of the various civil religions, with their advantageous and destructive contributions to political life.

See also *Communitarianism; Hobbes, Thomas; Locke, John; Machiavelli, Niccolò; Republicanism; Rousseau, Jean-Jacques; Tocqueville, Alexis de; Virtue, Civic.*

Ronald Beiner

BIBLIOGRAPHY

Bellah, Robert N. "Civil Religion in America." *Daedalus* 96 (winter 1967): 1–21.

Hobbes, Thomas. *Philosophical Rudiments concerning Government and Society.* In *Man and Citizen,* edited by Bernard Gert. Garden City, N.Y.: Anchor Books, 1972, chaps. 15–18.

Kolakowski, Leszek. "Politics and the Devil." In *Modernity on Endless Trial,* edited by Leszek Kolakowski. Chicago: University of Chicago Press, 1990, chap. 15.

Locke, John. *A Letter concerning Toleration.* Edited by James H. Tully. Indianapolis: Hackett, 1983.

Löwith, Karl. *Meaning in History.* Chicago: University of Chicago Press, 1949.

Machiavelli, Niccolò. *The Discourses.* Edited with an introduction by Bernard Crick; translated by Leslie J. Walker. Harmondsworth: Penguin Books, 1970; New York: Modern Library, 1950. Book 1, chaps. 11–15.

Rousseau, Jean-Jacques. *On the Social Contract.* Edited by Roger D. Masters; translated by Judith R. Masters. New York: St. Martin's, 1978. Book 2, chap. 7; Book 4, chap. 8.

Tocqueville, Alexis de. *Democracy in America.* Edited by J. P. Mayer; translated by George Lawrence. Garden City, N.Y.: Anchor, 1969.

Representation

The mechanism by which the people participate indirectly in government through representatives. Modern democracies, or republics as they also are called, are based on elective representation. Not all public officers are elected by the people in such governments, but those who are not elected must be chosen by those who are so elected.

In the United States, for example, the people elect members of the House of Representatives and the Senate—the two branches of the federal legislature—and the electors who choose the president. In effect, the people may be said to elect the president, inasmuch as presidential electors almost always act as rubber stamps for the preferences of those who elected them. All other officers in the federal government are chosen by elected officials, the most important of them by the president with the Senate's consent. In modern representative government, all officers must be responsible to the people. In the United States and most other democracies, all elective and some appointed officers serve for limited terms or at the pleasure of those who appointed them or, in the case of judges, as long as they demonstrate good behavior. Put another way, democratic or republican government, as it is commonly understood today, excludes hereditary offices and offices held for life.

It is possible to combine hereditary and life offices with elective ones, but such a government would not be wholly republican. The British government, for example, includes an elective House of Commons, a cabinet drawn mainly from the Commons, a hereditary monarchy, and a House of Lords based in part on heredity and in part on life appointments. Strictly speaking, the British have a mixed form of government, though in view of the predominance of its elective elements, it is commonly described as democratic. The French philosopher Montesquieu, writing in the mid-eighteenth century, was so impressed with the importance of the House of Commons that he called Great Britain a republic under the cover of a monarchy. We may say the same of countries like Denmark and the Netherlands whose public business is conducted almost entirely by elective legislatures and cabinets drawn from one or both legislative chambers, and whose monarchs play mainly ceremonial parts.

It is also possible for an elective or representative government to serve as a cover for one that is independent of the people. Such a government ruled the former Soviet Union and the "people's democracies" of Eastern Europe. They are still found in some countries today, not limited to those of a communist cast. For example, in Indonesia the same person, backed by the power of the military, has been easily reelected at five-year intervals since he and the army seized power in 1965; and this military government dominates legislative proceedings.

Origins of the Popular Assembly

The citizens of the ancient republics of Greece and Rome governed themselves directly, in the assembly. Direct representation limited the size of the city-state, or *polis,* as it was called in Greece, to the distance that citizens could travel to meet together. In the assembly they made laws; decided questions of war and peace; chose ambassadors, generals, and magistrates; and reviewed these officials' performance of duties. Some offices in the city-state were filled by lot on a rotating basis. This method of rotating offices was especially prevalent in the democratic city-states, which believed that every citizen should have an equal chance to hold office.

Modern governments' experience with "direct democracy" is pretty much limited to the use of juries drawn more or less randomly from the population, but only the British government and those influenced by British legal practice go this far. Most nations (for example, Italy and France) do not go this far and rely solely on the decisions of judges, sometimes acting in conjunction with "lay judges," as in Sweden. Modern juries, moreover, are small in number and are under the direction of government attorneys (in places where grand juries are used) or judges (in the case of trial juries). By contrast, ancient juries were large in number, and their members acted in effect as judges as well as jurors. The Athenian jury that convicted Socrates of impiety and corrupting the youth in 399 B.C. numbered more than a thousand.

Some writers have said that the existence of elections and selection by lot in the ancient city-states is evidence that the ancients understood the concept of representation. Why, then, it has been asked, did the Greeks not use representation to expand their states beyond the narrow compass imposed by the need to assemble all the citizens for the conduct of government? Had they formed a single national government, it has been said, they would have been more secure against powerful monarchies such as Persia. Instead, they had to rely on leagues and loose confederations, which were liable to disunity among their members. Furthermore, it has been suggested, an extensive republic would have made citizens more secure against domestic factions and the danger of anarchy or tyranny posed by such factions. In short, why did the ancient Greeks not do what Americans did in 1787? The newly independent American states formed a large republic, rather than continuing under the Articles of Confederation, forming several smaller confederations, or allowing the thirteen existing states to go their separate ways.

It is not at all clear that the Greeks understood elections, whether conducted by citizens or by lot, as a means for representing the people in government. They seem to have employed these devices for participatory, not representative, purposes, to ensure that all or almost all citizens would have a chance to rule as well as to be ruled. Moreover, they considered the city-state to constitute a natural society. Citizens knew each other directly or through immediate acquaintances and therefore were connected by trust.

The modern counterpart of the ancient assembly is the lower house of the legislature. It is everywhere elected by the people, whereas the upper chamber is often chosen by local governing bodies. It is primarily this lower house that represents the people in government. Thus the American Founders sometimes referred to the House of Representatives as "an assembly" or "a popular assembly," and the French and Pakistanis have formally designated their lower house as the National Assembly. Lower chambers usually are entrusted with preponderant legislative power. The British House of Lords, for example, may delay legislation enacted by the House of Commons for only a year (thirty days in the case of financial bills); the Japanese House of Representatives may overcome the opposition of the upper House of Councillors by repassing legislation by a two-thirds majority (or by its original simple majority for financial legislation). The American Senate is rather exceptional in this respect: its powers are roughly coequal to those of the House of Representatives.

Early Americans generally considered the institutions of government to be more or less representative as they measured up to the assemblies of the ancient republics. The Senate was a representative body, in the eyes of early Americans, but less so than the House of Representatives, for it represented the states directly and the people indirectly. Furthermore, the Senate's small size (two members from each state) and long term of office (six years) distanced it from the people. In the early years of the American Republic the president was not often viewed as a popular representative. Never, apparently, was the term *representative* applied to judges. Judges operated in that part of the government most removed from the people, and (unlike the president, who had the veto) they were given no share in the legislative power.

Hobbes and Representation

The doctrine of representation was the invention of the English philosopher Thomas Hobbes, who used the term in his *Leviathan* (1651). For Hobbes, representative government was a government authorized by the people. It could be hereditary as well as popular, entrusted to one person or to an assembly, so long as power was not shared. Hobbes preferred a sovereign individual to a sovereign assembly because he believed that a monarch would be better able to achieve the purpose of government, to protect the people from threats to each other and from foreign nations. Thus Hobbes has been associated with the defense of absolute monarchy. What made government representative for Hobbes was that the people had empowered it to act in their behalf.

Hobbes's doctrine of representation was developed further by John Locke, later in the seventeenth century. Locke agreed that a people could place the supreme power of society, which he identified as the legislative power, in whatever hands they wished, but he indicated that it was best entrusted to an elective body. Representative government for Locke was also directed toward security, but Locke emphasized the security of individual rights. The American Declaration of Independence (1776) incorporates Locke's improvement upon Hobbes. It proclaims the right of a people to base the foundations of government on such principles and to organize governmental powers in such a form as they think will provide for their safety and happiness.

Thomas Jefferson, the Declaration's author, later said that he would not question a people's choice even when it was reposed in a Napoleon Bonaparte or an Alexander the Great. The Declaration, however, does unobtrusively provide guidance. How many kinds of government, after all, profess a belief in the equality of birth and inalienable rights to life, liberty, and the pursuit of happiness? And if legitimate government must derive its powers from popular consent in the first place, would it not likely occur to a people to insist on a government that required their consent on a continuing basis? In any event, toward the end of his life Jefferson stated that the issue had been settled, for modern experience had demonstrated that only government chosen by the people could secure equal rights.

And yet Hobbes's notion of the representative ruler, as contrasted with the representative assembly, has had its influence. Locke stated in his *Second Treatise of Government* (1689) that when the executive consists of a single person possessed with the power of veto, it is as if the executive reflected the polity as a whole. If this executive is made elective and accountable to the people, we have a sketch of the American presidency. Indeed, instilled with "energy," the president was intended by the Framers to fulfill Hobbesian and Lockean ends; he was to be essential not only in executing the laws but in providing security against external and internal dangers.

Andrew Jackson, U.S. president from 1829 to 1837, held the view that, as president, he was as much the representative of the people as was Congress. Jackson was the first president openly to press his positions on the legislative body and to carry his quarrels with it to the people. Today it is widely accepted that the president represents the national interests of the people, while Congress represents their local and particular interests.

So, too, the executives of other modern democracies who are elected directly by the people are generally regarded as representatives of their nations. Elected presidents have achieved such ascendancy in relation to the legislature in governments that contain this office that these governments frequently are called "presidential" governments, to distinguish them from the parliamentary kind, with their plural executives responsible to the lower house of parliament.

Such are the governments of nations influenced by the American political example. Most of these are in Latin America, but they also include, since World War II, the governments of the Philippines, the Republic of Korea, and Nigeria. Most nations copied the British model or (in the case of European countries) had it implanted on their soil. A few governments (for example, France and Russia) combine a popularly elected executive with an executive chosen by parliament. Purely parliamentary governments themselves have felt the impulse toward a strong popular executive: they are sometimes referred to as "cabinet" or even "prime ministerial" governments.

Most democracies other than the United States have displayed more confidence in their lower legislative chambers. As we have noted, they have entrusted them with greater power than they have their second chambers, which typically are less directly under popular control. Also, most of these democracies have been unwilling to give their judges the power to strike down legislative enactments, and the small number that do hedge the exercise of that power much more than is done in the United States.

It might be said that representative government today features the interplay of two models: Hobbes's single ruler and the ancient assembly, both made accountable to the people through elections, can be seen in modern representative governments.

Trends

Representative government, then, replaces the people with persons who act for them. Some early Americans explained representation as a necessity, required by the size of the nation. And yet nearly all Americans at the founding regarded representation as an improvement upon direct rule by the people. They would have preferred a representative republic even if America had been the size of the Athenian city-state. *The Federalist,* a series of essays written to support the ratification of the Constitution in 1787 and 1788, maintains that representation improves the public debate by causing ideas to be refined through a select body of citizens (*Federalist* No. 10). The people are competent to choose their governors and to judge how well they have been served by them, but not to govern themselves.

Representation by itself, however, was not sufficient to produce good government, for what it produced was the House of Representatives, a large and changeable body that in the view of the Framers contained many of the defects of the ancient popular assembly. To make their government more stable, the Founders made the Senate, executive, and judiciary somewhat more distant from the people, and they added energy to stability by placing the executive power in the hands of a single person. The Senate, president, and judiciary were given the task of restraining the people when they needed moderation by restraining the House of Representatives.

All representative government places some distance between the people and their representatives. This distance seems inevitable, however short the terms of office and however few the checks on legislative bodies. The heart of the matter perhaps lies in representation itself. We need no philosopher to tell us that our representatives are not ourselves, as the eighteenth-century French philosopher Jean-Jacques Rousseau, a critic of representative government, pointed out. Their opinions, ambitions, and interests cannot be identical to those of the electorate, no matter how they are chosen. And, as we have noted, the American Founders thought that representative popular government conducted by popularly elected representatives was superior to government directly by the people.

Attempts are being made today to allow the people to act in place of their elected representatives or, at least, to become active participants in making government policy. Nowhere has this effort been carried further than in the United States. Some American reformers have suggested having members of Congress chosen by lot or allowing citizens to vote on legislative issues electronically after watching them debated on television. More moderate changes, actually in operation, allow citizens to communicate their views to government on a continuing basis, not just at times of election, through public opinion surveys, radio and television talk shows, informal telephone voting on issues presented on television, and demonstrations covered by the media. Government officials use these sources of information in framing their policies and conduct their own televised "meetings" with the people. A striking trend in American politics is the extent to which government officials, including some members of the Supreme Court, "go public," that is, seek popular support for themselves and their views. And self-appointed representatives of the people mediate between the people and government, explaining government to the people and instructing government as to what the people want. Members of the media play a crucial role in this activity, mediating among the contending parties and making their own contributions.

To state the current situation in a somewhat exaggerated way, America has become a new Athens. Its citizens are informed about each other by the media and carry on public deliberations in a vast assembly whose proceedings have been made possible by television. Interested parties vie for attention in this assembly, government officials along with private citizens, and they stage "media events" to attract attention. Officials, including members of Congress, thus are not representatives of the people, chosen to deliberate in their stead, but magistrates, chosen, like those in the ancient city-states, to carry out the popular will.

See also *Classical Greece and Rome; Hobbes, Thomas; Locke, John; Mill, John Stuart; Montesquieu; Participatory democracy; Proportional representation; Separation of powers; United States Constitution.* In Documents section, see *American Declaration of Independence (1776); Constitution of the United States (1787).*

Robert Scigliano

BIBLIOGRAPHY

Barber, Benjamin R. *Strong Democracy: Participatory Politics for a New Age.* Berkeley: University of California Press, 1984.
Fustel de Coulanges, Numa D. *The Ancient City: A Classic Study of the Religious and Civil Laws of Ancient Greece and Rome.* Baltimore: Johns Hopkins University Press, 1980.
Hamilton, Alexander, James Madison, and John Jay. *The Federalist.* New York: Modern Library, 1937.
Mansfield, Harvey C., Jr. *The Spirit of Liberalism.* Cambridge: Harvard University Press, 1978.
Mill, John Stuart. *Considerations on Representative Government.* London: Longmans, Green, 1873.
Pitkin, Hanna F. *Representation.* New York: Atherton Press, 1969.

Representative democracy

See *Types of democracy*

Republicanism

A tradition of thought concerned with the celebration and preservation of free states that originated in ancient Greece and Rome. Republicanism was revived in the city-states of medieval Italy and influenced the founding of modern republics in America and Europe. Although overshadowed by the rise of liberalism as the dominant Western ideology, it has recently been revived as part of a critique of modern democratic politics that attacks liberal individualism and appeals to older notions of citizenship.

Classical Republican Theory

The original meaning of republicanism depended upon a contrast with monarchy. Republics were free states in the sense that they were run by citizens who were not subject to arbitrary power. Instead of being a king's personal possession, government was in principle the common business *(res publica)* of the citizens. Although the word *republic* is Roman in origin, the principle was established earlier in the Greek city-state, or *polis*, where a variety of elaborate institutions diffused power so that, as Aristotle observed, citizens could rule and be ruled in turn. If such a state was to remain free in a world of despots and tyrants, its citizens had to be prepared to defend it and to participate in its government.

Classical republican theory, drawing upon the experience first of the small city-states of Greece and then of the expansionist Roman Republic, had two connected aspects: first, the celebration of free states and, second, discussion of how they could best be preserved in a world where they were always exceptions and always threatened with tyranny as a result of internal divisions or external conquest. In the fourth century B.C., Aristotle maintained in his *Politics* that life in a *polis* is a necessary condition of human fulfillment. On the whole, however, the achievements celebrated in republican literature were military glory and heroism, reflecting the fact that ancient republics were above all warrior bands whose freedom from conquest and tyranny depended upon their military prowess.

In such circumstances it was out of the question that citizenship, which entailed military and governmental responsibilities, could be extended to the entire population. Even where (as in Athens) the state was considered to be democratic, the *demos,* or people, did not include women, slaves, or resident aliens. Democracy in the sense of inclusiveness was a lower priority within republican thought than the qualities that enabled free states to flourish and persist. Liberty was inseparable from courage, patriotism, and public spirit, and republican heroes were praised for their willingness to sacrifice their private interests for the common good.

Republican thinkers were preoccupied with the question of how freedom could be preserved. Alongside emphasis on the virtue of the citizens went interest in the social and institutional structure of successful republics. Aristotle, surveying the experience of 158 examples of the Greek *polis,* identified the division of wealth among citizens as an important source of strife, with cities liable to predatory rule either by oppressive oligarchs or by confiscating democrats. Lasting harmony seemed to him most likely where a large middle class of independent landowners flourished and where the extremes of oligarchy and democracy were avoided. Speculations about the virtues of constitutional mixed regimes were popularized by the Greek writer Polybius, reflecting in the second century B.C. upon the success of the Roman Republic. Instability, according to Polybius, was the natural condition of city-states, with forms of government changing into one another in an endless cycle. Rome had been able to break out of this cycle because its constitution contained monarchical, aristocratic, and democratic elements. In this view, Rome owed its greatness to the complexity of its political system as well as to the virtue of its citizen-soldiers.

The Middle Ages and Renaissance

In the twelfth century A.D., after a thousand years dominated by the presence or memory of the Roman Empire (during which time the dominant political ideal had come to be Christian monarchy), republicanism came to life again in the city-states of northern Italy. Like the ancient cities, they diffused power among their citizens, developing elaborate institutional devices such as multiple councils and executive officers elected for short terms. Again like the ancient cities, they were democratic in the sense that a large proportion of citizens at some time or other held public responsibility, but they were undemocratic in that citizenship was never extended even to the whole adult male population. Drawing on Roman writers such as Sallust and Cicero, their spokesmen celebrated the greatness of free states, stressing the need for concord among the citizens, fostered by impartial justice.

By the late Middle Ages, however, the Italian city-republics were increasingly under threat from tyrants at home and powerful new monarchies abroad. The Florentine humanists, who drew heavily on classical learning, found themselves in a situation similar to that of many ancient republican thinkers, trying to explain the eclipse of republican freedom and to provide prescriptions for preserving free states. Like their predecessors, they stressed both the moral qualities of citizens and the ingenuity of constitutions. One notably long-lived and stable republic was Venice, whose success many republicans attributed to her institutional balance: the three-part system of a leader *(doge),* Senate, and Council was interpreted as a classic mixture of monarchical, aristocratic, and democratic elements.

Although Renaissance republicanism was in many ways a revival of classical themes, a note of novelty was injected in the early sixteenth century by Niccolò Machiavelli, whose *Discourses on Livy* became an influential source of republican ideas for the next two centuries. Concentrating on the Roman example of military glory achieved by a free state, Machiavelli asserted the need for public-spirited citizens to be prepared to fight in defense of their city. He also advanced more controversial ideas: that the struggles between Rome's patricians and plebeians had contributed to the city's greatness, that republican citizens needed a civic religion considerably fiercer and more secular than Christianity to motivate them, and that republics (and especially the leaders who founded or revived republics) must be prepared to suspend justice and morality when politically necessary.

Beginnings of Modern Republican Thought

After the end of the Florentine republic in 1520, the republican ideal of a free state of patriotic citizen-warriors lived on as an alternative tradition of political thinking alongside mainstream monarchism. One of Machiavelli's most influential followers was James Harrington, whose republican utopia *The Commonwealth of Oceana,* published in 1656 after the English Civil War, adapted classical principles to contemporary English conditions. Armed freeholders, in possession of enough land to secure their independence, were cast as the citizen-warriors of classical tradition, and Harrington devised elaborate institutions to secure the diffusion and rotation of power among them. Although *Oceana* was intended as the blueprint for a new republic to replace the much-disputed unwritten English constitution, it had become by the early eighteenth century the source of a convenient vocabulary in terms of which that constitution could be defended against developments that were seen as a threat to freedom.

In the eyes of publicists who claimed to represent the "country" against the corrupting influence of the king's court, England was itself a kind of republic, its parliamentary monarchy standing for the traditional mixed constitution, and the freeholding electors of the shires for classical citizens. From this point of view, freedom was increasingly under threat from the monarchy, which had established a standing army instead of relying for defense upon a citizen militia. These critics, seeing in financial speculations and venal politicians the luxury and corruption that proverbially destroyed republics, looked to the virtuous freeholders to safeguard freedom by regaining control of Parliament.

One of the major issues of eighteenth-century political thinking was the extent to which this antique vocabulary of classical republicanism could still be applied in what was seen by some as an age of progress and improvement. Montesquieu's *Spirit of the Laws* (1748), which describes virtuous republics in traditional terms, nevertheless locates political liberty elsewhere, in the mixed constitution of the English parliamentary monarchy, presiding over a nonvirtuous commercial society. In his *Social Contract* (1762), Jean-Jacques Rousseau revived the classical ideal, complete with mythical lawgiver, direct participation in government, civil religion, and heroically patriotic Spartan citizens, but he made clear that this ideal was unattainable in decadent modern times. His followers among the French revolutionaries tried nevertheless to revive the militaristic heroes of ancient republicanism, but elsewhere a new kind of liberal republicanism was emerging, one much less heroic and more businesslike in tone. At the opposite extreme from Rousseau, Jeremy Bentham and his followers understood a republic simply as the most efficient solution to the problem of government. Taking for granted that both rulers and subjects will be selfish, they placed no reliance on public spirit, concentrating instead on devising means whereby power holders could be made responsible to those whose interests they represented.

The American Experience and the New Republicanism

The Founders of the United States occupied a space somewhere between Rousseau's classical idealism and Bentham's cynical modernism. Although both the authors and the opponents of the U.S. Constitution were aware of the classical emphasis on a united body of citizens leading independent and frugal lives, and feared the possible corrupting effects of size and riches, James Madison argued in *Federalist* No. 10 (1787–1788) that a large, federal, representative republic was an improvement on the small, intensely communal states favored by classical nostalgia because it would allow self-interested factions to cancel one another out. Similarly, the elaborate checks and balances built into the system could turn self-interest to the common good rather than relying on an improbable degree of public spirit. At the time, the Constitution was subjected to a great deal of criticism based on republican traditions. To critics accustomed to a suspicion of executive power that traditionally had expressed itself in duplication of authority or in rapid rotation in office, the position of the president seemed little short of monarchy.

Although republicanism remained throughout the nineteenth century a cause to be fought for against monarchical government, it showed less and less of its classical ancestry. The difference between classical republicanism and modern liberal republicanism was spelled out in 1819 by the French political thinker Benjamin Constant de Rebecque. In his time, Constant observed, liberty was an individual matter, enjoyed in private and in peace, whereas in the ancient republics liberty meant collective public activity, largely concerned with war. Constant saw clear evidence of progress in the difference between the two.

This new republicanism became increasingly associated with democracy in the sense that the rights of citizenship were claimed for wider and wider sections of the population. Classical republicanism had always been democratic in the sense that power was in the hands of citizens rather than in those of a monarch. Citizenship, however, normally had meant membership in one of several different orders with different rights and had always been a privilege carrying with it specific duties. As this condition ceased to be the case, political thinkers, led by Alexis de Tocqueville, began to worry whether public spirit (even of the minimal kind required to maintain freedom in a modern republic) was compatible with the historic trend toward democracy in the sense of a society without hereditary ranks. Tocqueville feared that in a democratic society individuals would tend to become isolated, impotent, and indifferent to public affairs, thus allowing tyrants to establish themselves. In America in the 1830s, however, although worried by signs of a "tyranny of the majority," Tocqueville observed a level of participation in political parties and voluntary organizations of all kinds that bore witness to the active citizenship needed to sustain a free state.

Tocqueville's concerns have been revived in recent decades by political thinkers (from Hannah Arendt to contemporary communitarians) who have once again adapted the themes of classical republicanism to new circumstances. Faced with societies in which politics can be portrayed as a matter of bidding for the votes of indifferent and atomized masses, critics of modernity have reasserted an ideal of active citizenship and public spirit. As a revival of classical republicanism, this reappearance is highly selective: contemporary republicans do not seek to resurrect the Spartan warrior, to reinstate slavery, or to deprive women of citizenship, and their stress usually is on the satisfaction to be got from participating in public affairs—an Aristotelian theme, but one that can be given a modern, individualistic slant. Meanwhile, as faith in inevitable progress toward freedom for all humanity falters, another aspect of classical republicanism is beginning to look topical: inquiry into the conditions in which political liberty can be instituted and preserved.

See also *Antifederalists; Aristotle; City-states, communes, and republics; Classical Greece and Rome; Federalists; Machiavelli, Niccolò; Montesquieu; Property rights, Protection of; Republics, Commercial; Revolution, American; Revolution, French; Rousseau, Jean-Jacques; Theory, Ancient; Tocqueville, Alexis de; Virtue, Civic.*

Margaret Canovan

BIBLIOGRAPHY

Aristotle. *The Politics.* Edited by Stephen Everson. Cambridge and New York: Cambridge University Press, 1988.

Hamilton, Alexander, James Madison, and John Jay. *The Federalist.* Edited by M. Beloff. Oxford and New York: Blackwell, 1987.

Harrington, James. *The Commonwealth of Oceana, and A System of Politics.* Edited by J. G. A. Pocock. Cambridge: Cambridge University Press, 1992.

Machiavelli, Niccolò. *The Discourses.* Edited by Bernard Crick; translated by Leslie J. Walker. Harmondsworth: Penguin Books, 1970.

Montesquieu, Charles-Louis de Secondat, Baron de. *The Spirit of the Laws.* Translated and edited by A. M. Cohler, B. C. Miller, and H. S. Stone. Cambridge and New York: Cambridge University Press, 1989.

Pocock, J. G. A. *The Machiavellian Moment: Florentine Political Thought and the Atlantic Republican Tradition.* Princeton: Princeton University Press, 1975.

Rahe, Paul A. *Republics Ancient and Modern: Classical Republicanism and the American Revolution.* Chapel Hill: University of North Carolina Press, 1992.

Rousseau, Jean-Jacques. *The Social Contract, with Geneva Manuscript and Political Economy.* Edited by R. D. Masters. New York: St. Martin's, 1978.

Republics, Commercial

Commercial republics are political orders in which there is private ownership of property, relatively free transfer of ownership, and a legal system to enforce contracts; in which business and commerce are not dishonored; and in which more than one social order or rank is involved in public decisions. Commercial republics typically involve some type of representative government. What we today call liberal democracies are more properly commercial republics.

The first genuine commercial republics were the Dutch republic in the seventeenth century and Great Britain somewhat later. The Dutch republic established a pattern that often has been followed: it had few natural resources; its people were a heterogeneous group of immigrants drawn by its religious tolerance, and its wealth came almost entirely from trade. Britain's story is somewhat different. Despite its aristocratic history, neither monarch nor lords held absolute power, and English common law protected property rights effectively. The British political system, although a monarchy in name, was actually a hybrid with many republican elements. Its "ordered liberty" was admired by the first great theorist of modern commercial republics, Montesquieu (1689–1755). Along with Montesquieu, the thinkers of the Scottish Enlightenment reflected most profoundly on the place of commerce in a political order. Any account of the idea of a commercial republic must rely principally on their writings.

The phrase *commercial republic* was, before the eighteenth century, a contradiction in terms. The word *republic* is derived from the Latin *res publica* (the common business). The classical view contrasted the public or political with the private, the realm of economics. The word *economics* derives from the Greek word for household, *oikos*, where life's necessities are taken care of. A commercial republic allows the pursuit of security and well-being by free individuals. Such a political order seems to emerge everywhere when a political regime does not regard (or ceases to regard) religious or moral instruction as one of its primary tasks.

The relation between democracy and commercial republics is paradoxical. In the strictest sense of democracy, there is no connection; indeed, the two are antithetical. In a looser sense, however, liberalization of traditions and the spread of democratic institutions generally have accompanied the economic progress, urbanization, and mobility brought about by the commercial republican way of life.

Commerce and Enlightenment

Some scholars assert that commercial republics can be found in antiquity. Carthage and Tyre are sometimes so described, but there are grounds for doubt. All political communities require some commerce to satisfy their material requirements, but until the modern period (beginning about A.D. 1600), at least in the West, commerce and trade were understood to be the low but necessary foundation for the more truly human activity of politics. Aristotle in the fourth century B.C. declared in his *Politics* that human beings are by nature political animals and that political activity is what distinguishes humankind from other animals. Politics thus for many centuries (in the Christian as well as the classical tradition) was associated with the freedom and dignity of human beings, while economics was seen as something to be disdained by a well-born citizen. Even in Athens, a relatively free, open, and democratic ancient city, trade and commerce were carried on by resident aliens who had none of the privileges of citizens. Political life was concerned with loftier matters: war and peace, moral education, the arts and religion.

In the sixteenth and seventeenth centuries the ancient and medieval republics began to be regarded in a different light: they presented a scene of endless strife and bloodshed, conquest and slavery. The turbulence within and among ancient republics, the expansion and contraction of empires such as the Roman, were fueled by the striving for political dominion, honor, and glory. The devastating religious wars of the early modern period began to raise questions about the beneficial effects of the connection of politics with virtue or human excellence.

The early modern thinkers of what came to be called the Enlightenment presented a new view: politics should be regarded not as the chief concern of a noble life but as a means to the fulfillment of more important, because more fundamental, human requirements, namely, security and prosperity. All individuals have a natural right to preserve themselves as best they can. They organize themselves into political communities merely as a way to secure their lives, liberty, and property. Politics is to be understood as an instrument to supply the conditions for security and prosperity—formerly private matters. This conception of politics was a direct assault on the classical conception, which had long held sway, and it was part of the great theoretical revolution of modernity, which culminated in the Enlightenment.

The new understanding of politics meant the elevation of commerce and trade, which would now be of central importance in the political realm and a concern of statesmen and sovereigns. Not surprisingly, many objected to this development. Commerce produces wealth, which seemed inseparable from luxury; luxury appeared to many almost the same as self-indulgence. It was widely believed that ancient Rome's decline from greatness began when Roman conquests brought luxury into the heart of the empire: the eventual result was that the public spirit was sapped, and the people were no longer willing to sacrifice for the public good.

Opponents of the new understanding decried what they saw as the eclipse of virtue by commerce and trade. The French philosopher Jean-Jacques Rousseau (1712–1778) captured the spirit of this reaction in his *Discourse on the Sciences and Arts* (1750). Rousseau claimed to be a defender of virtue, by which he meant an individual's autonomy or authenticity. Truly virtuous individuals, according to Rousseau, are not found in an enlightened commercial society because the complex economy of such a society undermines individual autonomy by rendering each individual dependent on others. Only in a simple society, where needs are few and no one is dependent on anyone else, can individuals be free and virtuous. According to Rousseau, autonomy means self-government; a genuine democracy can exist only when individuals are equal to one another. The inequalities accompanying commerce and wealth make true participatory democracy impossible.

Rousseau asserted that communities as well as individuals cannot remain free if they welcome commerce, science, and the arts. These elements soften citizens, undermine religion and patriotism, and make a community easy to conquer. Although Rousseau's conception of virtue is nothing like that of the ancients, his condemnation of commerce (as well as of the sciences and the arts) is reminiscent of the classical belief in the inappropriateness of trade or commerce as concerns in the noble life of politics. Rousseau's advocacy of a democracy consisting of free and equal citizens, combined with his passionate condemnation of business and wealth, highlights the tension between commerce and democracy in the strictest sense of the word.

Political Economy

By the middle of the eighteenth century liberal ideas had made some headway, and the Industrial Revolution was under way. In monarchies such as France commerce could not flourish because it was held to be less honorable than birth, title, or place. A trader who made his fortune typically might try to buy a title or office and ignore his commercial past. The aristocratic view was still powerful in England too. The landed gentry, reluctant to relinquish political power, saw themselves as defenders of the civic virtue against the inroads of the commercial classes.

A number of deeply held beliefs stood in the way of wholehearted acceptance of the new principles of liberal or commercial society. Many believed that wealth and luxury could not extend far through the ranks of society without weakening the civic order. There was widespread admiration for the ancient republics, especially Sparta and Rome, with their emphasis on patriotic virtue and self-sacrifice. Trade seemed a dangerous thing: gold, the wealth of the kingdom, might flow overseas to pay for the very luxuries that enervate the citizens. Trade and commerce would disrupt stable and familiar arrangements. In a free commercial market who would see that just prices are charged for commodities? Many must have felt the wise course was to avoid the turmoil of a commercial society.

Such fears and concerns provoked an impressive response. In the middle decades of the eighteenth century statesmen, scholars, and pamphleteers wrote a large number of tracts and books with titles like "A Vindication of

Commerce." The greatest of these writings were contributed by thinkers of the Scottish Enlightenment, in particular David Hume (1711–1776) and Adam Smith (1723–1790), who were among the founders of the science of political economy. The term itself suggests the combination of two things long seen as antithetical. In 1752 Hume published a collection of essays that included "Of Commerce," "Of Luxury," "Of Money," "Of Interest," and "Of the Balance of Trade," to dissolve the fears and misconceptions blocking acceptance of commercial societies. Smith's celebrated *Wealth of Nations* (1776) attempted systematically to establish the foundations of the new science.

The political economists used the history of human progress to explain the superiority of commercial society. Smith's "four-stage theory" is perhaps the clearest formulation (the four stages are hunting, shepherding, agricultural, and commercial). Adam Ferguson (1723–1816), in his *Essay on the History of Civil Society* (1767), also presents a progressive account beginning with "rude nations" (before property was established) and ending with "polished" (commercial) nations. In his *History of England* (1754–1762), Hume depicts the era when England was in the grip of the feudal order as rude and barbarous. He traces the evolution of the rule of law, property rights, and an independent judiciary, as the nation progressed to what he considers a more humane commercial order.

A second contribution of the Scottish philosophers was a critical account of the ancient republics, intended to counter the arguments of those who praised small, participatory republics. Hume suggested that the ancient republics were less attractive than their admirers admitted. They depended on slavery, and they maintained armies of citizen soldiers only at great cost in individual liberty and personal happiness. The petty republics of antiquity were torn by factional conflict and subject to constant threats from other republics, requiring considerable sacrifice to remain on a wartime footing. They purchased the freedom of their cities by giving up individual freedom. More of individual freedom is found in the civilized modern commercial republics, the Scottish philosophers maintained, than in the ancient republics.

The Scots argued that luxury or refinement is not a threat to the political order because commerce, which promotes refinement, encourages frugality and the love of gain rather than dissipation and corruption. Sumptuary laws to curtail luxury (or wealth and inequality) merely discourage the energetic attempt by individuals to improve their circumstances. These laws generally do not produce virtue but succeed only in replacing one set of vices with another: sloth and indolence supplant greed and vanity. The vain display of riches is more likely when wealth is fixed in the estates of a permanent nobility than in a commercial order, where property owners direct their attention to productive investments. Human relationships are more civil when personal dependency (of the serf on the lord) is replaced by hired service, since paid workers can find other buyers for their services if they are not treated well.

As for the dangers trade poses to the strength of a commonwealth, the Scots advanced powerful arguments undermining mercantilism—the view that a nation's wealth consists in gold and that the government has an interest in suppressing trade, which would cause gold to be traded for other goods. Genuine wealth consists in productive capacity, the Scots argued, and productivity is enhanced by trade. The annual fund of labor in any society is the wealth of a nation. Wealth depends on the skill, dexterity, and judgment with which labor is applied. These capabilities in turn depend on the division of labor.

Smith and others used the example of pin manufacturing. Even within so small an enterprise, specialization multiplies the productivity of individuals by a factor of thousands. In a commercial society a surprising degree of cooperation among hundreds of individuals goes into the production of even so simple an object as a woolen coat. But the division of labor is limited by the size of the market in which goods can be circulated: no village could support a pin factory except in a market large enough to consume all the pins produced by half a dozen skilled pin makers. Thus trade—even or especially foreign trade, which vastly enlarges the market—contributes to the productivity of a commercial economy and enhances the prosperity of all who participate in it. A wise sovereign will not in normal circumstances be concerned with flows of gold, since real wealth consists in productive capacity.

The scale of cooperation in a commercial or market economy calls attention to something directly relevant to democracy. The ancient republics took moral education very seriously, because the bond uniting citizens depended upon their sharing a commitment to civic virtue or excellence, sanctioned by the gods. The suppression of private interests in favor of the public good was regarded as a necessary condition of civic virtue because private interest leads to faction and discord. The Scots suggested, and both Dutch and British practice confirmed, that the cooperation necessary in a commercial society does not require the suppression of private interests. A market economy requires only that individuals pursue their private interests within the bounds of the law. Individuals seeking to improve their own circumstances do so by catering to the needs and desires of others. Thus they will be led as if by an invisible hand to promote the good of society.

The increase in the wealth of a nation depends on maximizing the productive use of scarce resources, including human labor or energy. This optimization takes place most efficiently when each individual strives to satisfy the needs of others as indicated by freely fluctuating prices. When prices are regulated, for example, by magistrates adhering to a doctrine of "just price," there is no mechanism to signal more pressing needs or desires. But when the high price for some product or service indicates it is in demand, individuals are drawn to supply it. The benefit that ensues is the result of human action, indeed, but not of human design, to paraphrase Ferguson.

The Scots observed a similar phenomenon in other human institutions, such as law and language, where "spontaneous order" arises as an unintended consequence of human activity, without any supervising intelligence. This idea lies behind Smith's view that in a commercial society organized according to the system of natural liberty individuals can be left alone to pursue their lives as they wish, as long as the society is secured against foreign invasion and a legal system is in place to protect against fraud and oppression. This doctrine is sometimes known as *laissez-faire*. Although the government should be responsible for providing certain public works (which it will be in no individual's interest to supply even though such works are of benefit to a mercantile society), the importance of government is diminished in proportion as the role of politics is diminished in the lives of average men and women.

Doubts and Drawbacks

The great advantage of a commercial republic, as Montesquieu and the Scots saw it, is the naturalness of such an order. It conforms to the most universal human passions and sentiments. Self-interest is more common than benevolence, to say nothing of self-sacrifice. The commercial republic thus is the regime that most accords with human nature. But even the most optimistic theorists expressed some doubts. Rousseau's objections to a commercial republic have already been mentioned: commerce and wealth corrupt by rendering individuals dependent on one another and thus making politeness and civility indispensable; bourgeois society fosters dishonesty and slavishness.

Smith and Ferguson voiced a more specific version of this fear, centered on the extensive division of labor found in polished commercial nations. As workers become ever more specialized, the narrowness of some occupations might become so stultifying as to reduce workers to the level of animals. The individual virtues of courage and prudence would find no room to develop, and workers would be incapacitated for lives of human dignity, much less for citizenship. To remove such a danger, Smith proposed that the sovereign in a commercial order should provide for education for all members of the society.

A more subtle problem was spelled out by Alexis de Tocqueville (1805–1859) in *Democracy in America* (1835–1840). Tocqueville observed that in a commercial republic with no aristocracy (where landed wealth is not protected by inheritance laws), wealth changes hands rapidly. All men and women, whether rich or poor, are induced to think about wealth more than ever before. Wealthy individuals must take pains to keep their wealth; those without will think about nothing else. Tocqueville feared the materialism that would result. He associated materialism with a restlessness, even rootlessness, that could have dangerous political consequences. Ferguson had written earlier about the danger of the relaxation of national spirit in a commercial nation. Both foresaw the possibility of a paternalistic despotism, one that timid and selfish individuals might even welcome to spare them the trouble of the exertion required for freedom.

Commercial republics, or liberal democracies, have also been accused of posing a danger to the human spirit. The focus on security and bodily goods, which played so large a part in the original justification for this type of political order, has, according to some critics, degraded human beings to the level of animals. The contemporary Russian writer Aleksandr I. Solzhenitsyn has attacked Western societies for their materialism and their forgetting of God. The great French novelist Gustave Flaubert bitterly attacked enlightened commercial societies in *Madame Bovary* (1856). He portrayed society as having made a mockery of everything grand and beautiful so that the deepest longings of the soul find no outlet.

Tocqueville observed that the most dangerous tendencies of commercial society, such as materialism and political apathy, were effectively countered in America in the 1830s by religion and by the American instinct for political association. But the erosion in the twentieth century of the conditions that Tocqueville considered indispensable to democracy—religion and political decentralization—raises questions about the future of such political orders. Proponents of liberal democracy often see it as the only legitimate political order, and their claim is buttressed today by the collapse of communism, the chief alternative of the past century. The twenty-first century may settle the question whether commerce is compatible with a healthy political order, or whether it leads to soulless materialism and, as Tocqueville feared, a new kind of paternalistic despotism.

See also *City-states, communes, and republics; Enlightenment, Scottish; Laissez-faire economic theory; Locke, John; Montesquieu; Rousseau, Jean-Jacques; Spinoza, Benedict de; Tocqueville, Alexis de.*

John W. Danford

BIBLIOGRAPHY

Caton, Hiram. *The Politics of Progress: The Origins and Development of the Commercial Republic, 1600–1835.* Gainesville: University of Florida Press, 1988.

Hamowy, Ronald. "Progress and Commerce in Anglo-American Thought: The Social Philosophy of Adam Ferguson." *Interpretation* 14 (January 1986): 61–87.

Hont, Istvan, and Michael Ignatieff, eds. *Wealth and Virtue.* Cambridge: Cambridge University Press, 1983.

Hume, David. *Essays: Moral, Political and Literary.* Edited by Eugene Miller. Indianapolis: Liberty Classics, 1985.

Lerner, Ralph. "Commerce and Character: The Anglo-American as New-Model Man." *William and Mary Quarterly* 3d ser., 36 (1979): 3–26.

Montesquieu, Charles Secondat, Baron de. *The Spirit of the Laws.* Translated by Thomas Nugent. New York: Hafner Press, 1949.

Pangle, Thomas L. *The Spirit of Modern Republicanism.* Chicago: University of Chicago Press, 1988.

Rahe, Paul A. *Republics Ancient and Modern.* Chapel Hill: University of North Carolina Press, 1992.

Smith, Adam. *An Inquiry into the Nature and Causes of the Wealth of Nations.* 2 vols. Oxford: Clarendon Press, 1979.

Revolution, American

The American Revolution is the political movement and war (1775–1783) that resulted in the independence of the thirteen original United States from British colonial rule. Although not fought in the name of democracy, the American Revolution ushered in the founding of the preeminent democratic republic of the modern world.

Constitutional Dispute

The Revolution originated in a constitutional dispute between Great Britain and the American colonies concerning the rights of the colonists and the reach of Parliament's authority, especially the authority to tax. Faced with enormous debt from the Seven Years' War with France, and expecting the colonies to pay for protecting their western frontier, the British in 1764 set a high duty on molasses and in 1765 taxed legal documents and publications under the Stamp Act. These measures met stiff resistance from the colonists, who insisted that their rights as Englishmen included a privilege against taxation without representation. After vehement colonial protests, Parliament repealed the Stamp Act in 1766 but reasserted its claim to authority.

The colonists' theory of the imperial constitution allowed Parliament the power to regulate and thus tax trade, but it reserved for the colonial legislatures the power to lay internal taxes for the purpose of raising revenue. Their political link to Great Britain was held to be established through the king, who appointed a royal governor and other officials for most of the colonies.

Yet these officials too earned the colonists' ire, both for their attempts to enforce the despised duties and for other actions held to impinge upon the colonists' liberties as Englishmen. The landing of British troops in Boston in 1768 was seen to violate the constitutional prohibition against standing armies in time of peace without legislative consent. Recourse to the Admiralty courts against smugglers was held to violate the common law right to trial by jury. Dismissal of colonial assemblies abridged the people's right to secure their liberties and properties by law. Parliament's grant of a monopoly on the American tea trade to the East India Company in 1773 was challenged not only for the tax involved but also as a violation of the right to trade freely. The attempt to land tea in Boston provoked direct action: the dumping of the tea, by a disguised band, into the harbor.

Parliament responded sharply. It closed the port of Boston, reorganized the government of Massachusetts, and protected royal officials from local courts. The colonies' delegates, meeting in Philadelphia in 1774 as a Continental Congress, declared these acts as violative of their rights under the laws of nature, the English constitution, and the colonial charters. Congress pledged to avoid or suppress all commerce with England until the acts were repealed.

Fighting broke out in Massachusetts the following April, when patriot militia at Lexington and Concord repelled an attempt by British troops to seize their military stores. In August the king proclaimed the colonies to be in open rebellion.

Revolutionary War

Several military victories by the colonists, the evacuation of British troops from Boston, rejection by the Crown of colonial attempts at reconciliation, and the widespread popularity of Tom Paine's pamphlet *Common Sense* led the reassembled, Second Continental Congress to take the steps that would establish American independence. In June 1776 the Congress issued a call to the colonies to write constitutions for themselves as states. On July 4 it adopted the Declaration of Independence.

Drafted by Thomas Jefferson, this brilliant document reiterated the constitutional case against the British, but, as befit the moment of severing political ties, it rested that case on universal principles (in its terms, "self-evident truths" anchored in "the Laws of Nature and of Nature's God"): "that all men are created equal, that they are endowed by their Creator with certain unalienable Rights, that among these are Life, Liberty, and the pursuit of Happiness." Since governments derive their powers from the consent of the governed, the people may withdraw consent when government becomes destructive of its ends and may establish new forms. The Declaration did not repudiate the British constitution, as the Americans had understood it, nor renounce their claim to the common law rights of Englishmen, but it reformulated the basis of their rights from immemorial custom to the natural law of human equality and the political choices that register popular consent.

Clarity of principle did not ensure success in practice. New York City fell to the British in the autumn of 1776 and remained occupied for the duration of the war. George Washington, commander in chief of the Continental army, surprised the British and their German mercenaries at Trenton, New Jersey, on Christmas night in a daring attack that revived patriot spirits. Americans stopped a British invasion from Canada the next summer and foiled the imperial strategy of driving a wedge down the Hudson River between the states.

Still, the end of 1777 found the British in temporary control of Philadelphia and the remains of the Continental Army encamped in poverty at Valley Forge west of the city. Training of the regulars there by the Prussian baron von Steuben and the entry of the French into the war, secured by Congress's envoy in Paris, Benjamin Franklin, fortified the American cause in 1778. The British, having largely withdrawn from New England and facing stalemate in the middle states, turned to the South as their theater of operation. They captured Savannah, Georgia, and Charleston, South Carolina, and won occasional battles inland.

When, in 1781, General Cornwallis finally made his move into Virginia, he was met by armies under Washington and the French commanders the Comte de Rochambeau and the Marquis de Lafayette, who, supported by French naval victories offshore, forced the British to surrender. The Battle of Yorktown effectively ended the land war. In the Treaty of Paris of 1783, Great Britain recognized American independence and agreed to withdraw its troops from the occupied cities and from the western garrisons. Britain was able to secure an American pledge of repayment of debts owed British merchants.

Americans fought the Revolution under the general direction of Congress, an unchartered body of state delegates that lacked authority to tax and thus relied on contributions of men and money from the states. (Supplies and loans also came from European allies—France, the Netherlands, and Spain.) State militia did much of the fighting, but Washington's success in persuading Congress to support an army gave the war the continental focus necessary for victory. Scholars estimate that between one-fifth and one-third of the free population remained loyal to Great Britain. These loyalists met with different fates, some going into exile, others suffering confiscation of their goods and expulsion, many eventually reconciling themselves with the patriots and becoming citizens. Leadership of the Revolution was largely in the hands of prominent citizens, acting through the state assemblies; even the "mobs" were known to include merchants in disguise. The franchise was broad in most states, but not universal. Except for some Anglicans, Methodists, and members of the pacifist sects, the clergy were largely supportive of independence, often giving it the authority of a divinely ordained cause in their sermons.

Founding Democratic Republics

The governments of the new states showed variety: Pennsylvania's was the most democratic, with a unicameral legislature and an executive committee. Most of the others established an upper legislative house, in which property owners had special weight, and a governor, usually elected by the legislature.

In 1781 the Articles of Confederation, drafted four years earlier, were finally ratified by all the states, giving Congress written authority in law. As the decade proceeded, the loose confederation proved inadequate. Its inability to tax and to enforce its law by judicial process left Congress at the pleasure of the state legislatures. Its lack of authority to regulate commerce among the states contributed to economic disarray, as did issues of paper money in the states and other legislative measures for debt relief.

An armed rebellion of western Massachusetts farmers who were unable to pay their debts because of economic recession lent an atmosphere of crisis to the meeting of the Federal Convention in Philadelphia in 1787. Called to propose amendments to the Articles, the Constitutional Convention quickly settled on a plan to reconstitute the federal government. Presided over by Washington and led in its work by James Madison, it drafted a new Constitution that would strengthen federal power as it transformed a league of states meeting in Congress to a full republican government with a bicameral legislature, a single executive, and a system of independent courts. Honoring a pledge made by Federalists (those who supported the new Constitution) to Antifederalists (those who opposed it) during the course of the debate over ratification, the new Congress in 1789 proposed, and the states soon ratified, a series of amendments known as the Bill of Rights.

An ongoing subject of debate is whether the Constitution fulfills or betrays the democratic promise of the Declaration of Independence and the Revolution. From the outset it was seen that the Constitution's compromise on slavery—giving the institution legal protection but never calling it by name—went against the Declaration's principle of equality. But Congress after all had removed from Jefferson's draft of the Declaration a condemnation of the slave trade.

Those who see reaction in the Constitution's protection of property rights overlook the fact that, to the founding generation, security of property was held to be not only the end of government but also the precondition of political freedom. Besides, as the nineteenth-century political observer Alexis de Tocqueville remarked, a rough equality of conditions characterized America from colonial times, and the universal dedication of its people to commercial pursuits was widely noted by the Founders.

Although it is true that the term *democracy*—which the Founders seem to have defined as majority rule without regard for individual rights—often met with scorn in their writings, and although they showed the sophistication of the Enlightenment in their sober understanding of the power of self-interest, it might also be said that the Founders aimed to summon virtue from the people through republican forms of government. What is undeniable is that in every subsequent democratizing movement in American history, from Jeffersonian republicanism to Jacksonian democracy, from abolitionism to demands for equal rights for women and African Americans, appeal has been made to the Declaration of Independence and often to the American Revolution itself.

See also *Antifederalists; Burke, Edmund; Colonialism; Declaration of Independence; Federalists; Jefferson, Thomas; Madison, James; Paine, Thomas; Revolution, French; Tocqueville, Alexis de; United States Constitution; United States of America; Washington, George.* In Documents section, see *American Declaration of Independence (1776); Constitution of the United States (1787).*

James R. Stoner, Jr.

BIBLIOGRAPHY

Bailyn, Bernard. *Ideological Origins of the American Revolution.* Cambridge and London: Harvard University Press, 1967.

Greene, Jack P., ed. *The American Revolution: Its Character and Limits.* New York: New York University Press, 1987.

———. *Colonies to Nation, 1763–1789: A Documentary History of the American Revolution.* New York: Norton, 1975.

Jaffa, Harry V. *How to Think about the American Revolution: A Bicentennial Cerebration.* Durham, N.C.: Carolina Academic Press, 1978.

Lerner, Ralph. *The Thinking Revolutionary: Principle and Practice in the New Republic.* Ithaca, N.Y.: Cornell University Press, 1987.

Sandoz, Ellis. *A Government of Laws: Political Theory, Religion, and the American Founding.* Baton Rouge: Louisiana State University Press, 1990.

Wood, Gordon. *The Creation of the American Republic, 1776–1787.* Chapel Hill: University of North Carolina Press, 1969.

———. *The Radicalism of the American Revolution.* New York: Knopf, 1992.

Revolution, French

The French Revolution is the period of upheaval between 1787 and 1799 that overturned the old order of the nobility and the church in France on behalf of "the people" and "the nation." The revolutionary movement, based on liberal, democratic principles, established a constitution in 1791 and proclaimed the Declaration of the Rights of Man and of the Citizen. After a phase of reform, it entered a period known as the Reign of Terror. The revolution ended in 1799 with the overthrow of the First Republic by Napoleon Bonaparte.

The Beginnings

The French Revolution began modestly. In February 1787 the controller general of finances called an emergency assembly of people of rank to avert a financial crisis. The assembly rejected reforms imposing higher taxes on the privileged classes and demanded a call of the Estates General, an advisory assembly of deputies from the three estates (the clergy, the nobility, and the common people); it had last met in 1614. Despite ministerial efforts to enforce the reforms, and a reduction of the power of the resisting aristocrats, Louis XVI agreed to a meeting of the Estates General. He also permitted the publication of pamphlets on proposals to reconstruct society. The Abbé Emmanuel-Joseph Sieyès's *What Is the Third Estate?* (1789) became a rallying point for the new French nation.

The notices of election to the Estates General brought a further initiative. Each parish in France drew up a list of grievances. Among the chief frustrations were ministerial despotism, the influence of the clergy, hereditary offices, the concept of the divine right of kings, and the burdens carried by the peasantry. These grievances were prepared energetically and with high expectations of reform. This step marked the beginning of the revolutionary democratic movement on behalf of "the nation" in France. It would soon revolutionize all of Europe.

The Estates General opened May 5, 1789, with 600 elected deputies for the third estate and 300 each for the nobility and the clergy. On June 17 the third estate declared itself the National Assembly, the acknowledged representative of the French nation, and asserted its sovereign power to determine which taxes were legitimate. Although Louis XVI dispersed the third estate, it reassembled and resisted further orders to disband. Liberal members of the nobility and the clergy joined the ranks of the Assembly. The king surrounded Paris with foreign soldiers, but on June 27 he sanctioned the meeting.

Other circumstances contributed to an air of discontent and expectation. Poor harvests in 1787 and 1788, rising prices for inedible bread, the near-bankruptcy of the monarchy, and rumors of a conspiracy of the aristocracy to overthrow the third estate fueled popular irritation. The suffering caused by unrelenting hunger as well as tales of looting brigands produced widespread anxiety. When

German troops attempted to enforce order in the Tuileries, popular revolt ensued.

Revolt and Reform

The Bastille was the symbol of autocratic rule. In it and other prisons throughout France people could be imprisoned without due process. On July 14, 1789, the Bastille was stormed. Its governor was executed and a small number of inmates were released. The army did little to oppose the insurrection. Seizure of artillery from the Hôtel-de-Ville by the "French nation" met with a similar disinclination to fire on the people. Louis XVI entered the Assembly and declared that he entrusted himself to them.

Resistance against the nobility spread and was defended by intellectuals. The Comte de Mirabeau invoked Jean-Jacques Rousseau's principle that the people's "collective will" is right and reason itself. So empowered, the National Constituent Assembly undertook to abolish feudal privileges, special tax exemptions, and annual taxes paid to the church. When it met with opposition from the king and his supporters, the revolutionaries marched to the palace at Versailles and, under the command of the Marquis de Lafayette, forced the royal family to return to Paris to hear of the misery of the people.

The Assembly began the wholesale reconstruction of France. It abolished the feudal orders of chivalry, craft guilds, and inherited offices. Historical regions were renamed. Associations of citizens and towns formed federations. Under a plan produced by Abbé Sieyès, France was divided into departments administered by elected assemblies. The French Guard was replaced by a National Guard in which the nobility were denied membership. Civil marriage was introduced. In an effort to control the church, the Assembly reduced the number of dioceses and parishes, redistributed stipends from wealthy to rural parishes, opened church offices to popular election, and denied it standing as an order. Charles-Maurice de Talleyrand and Mirabeau led the initiative to expropriate church lands (that is, to declare that they belonged to the nation). A system set up to distribute mortgages on church property in exchange for new notes printed by the Assembly gave the people an incentive to remain committed to the revolution.

Debate and Dissension

The Assembly was not unanimous in the measures it was undertaking on behalf of the revolution. When, for electoral purposes, it distinguished between active citizens (those satisfying certain property qualifications) and passive citizens, Maximilien Robespierre and Jean-Paul Marat resisted. Others questioned restrictions placed on opposition newspapers, religious houses, and trade unions. The clergy who opposed the civil constitution were ordered to swear loyalty to it or resign. Deputies could not agree whether the king should have a legislative veto. Moderates sat at the right of the president's chair, while the "advanced" sat on the left. Later, dispute between the left and the right would erupt more violently.

Political clubs, notably the Jacobins, the Feuillants, and the Cordeliers, formed to reflect the range of opinion. Through their large network of provincial affiliations, the clubs served as means of public surveillance and agitation. Much of the debate among the clubs revolved around whether the king should be dethroned, an issue fanned by the king's aborted escape from Paris in June 1791 and his brother's successful flight out of France. The people's agitation increased when copies of the king's record book were made public. Illegal payments to émigrés, aristocrats who had fled the country, seemed to confirm the rumor that the royal family was conspiring with foreign states against the French people.

After demonstrations, petitions, and bloodshed, the king accepted the constitution in September 1791. Under the constitution, the king relinquished power. As executive, he retained a limited veto, but the executive was effectively subordinate to the legislature. The flagship of the constitution was the Declaration of the Rights of Man and of the Citizen. It set forth all the characteristically modern democratic principles: all are born with equal rights; public office is accessible to all; freedom of thought, speech, and the press and of work and ownership are inalienable rights; sovereign power resides in the nation; law is the expression of the general will; the citizens or their representatives determine taxation; the executive, legislative, and judicial powers are separate.

The revolutionaries did not intend to confine their actions to defining and implementing the political rights of the French nation alone. In 1790 the National Constituent Assembly declared that it denounced any undertaking of war that had as its objective conquest or diminishing the liberty of any people. In addition, the Assembly made French nationality available to all those wishing to be free.

French opponents of the radical cause attempted to mobilize the European powers to resist the spread of the revolution. Many of the revolution's supporters in these countries were identified as Jacobins, the most radical of the French political clubs, and were persecuted. At first, the European monarchs responded weakly to the threat posed by the revolution. But in 1792, when France announced its opposition to the remaining monarchical dynasties of Europe, coalitions were formed to resist the new republic.

The Terror

The mixed success of the international confrontations produced stresses on the domestic front. The revolutionaries, believing that the king and the aristocracy were colluding with the foreigners, imprisoned the royalty. A split arose between the Girondins, who favored a bourgeois republic in France as the model of a new Europe, and the Montagnards, who, led by Robespierre, responded more favorably to the demands and political aspirations of the lower classes but wanted to confine the revolution to France. A set of unanticipated vetoes by the king, and an increase in support for the royal family from *émigrés,* led Georges-Jacques Danton to push for the overthrow of the monarchy.

In August the Paris Commune was established. Its purpose was to suspend the power of the king, call a national convention, and revise the constitution. Believing that the commune's effectiveness depended on the suppression of sympathy for the king, Danton and Mirabeau organized the First Terror. They aimed to stamp out the remaining Royalists by organizing a wide net of arrests, seizures, and executions. As a result, the European monarchs cut diplomatic ties with France. The revolutionaries sought approval elsewhere, by awarding honorary citizenship to those intellectuals favorable to the French cause.

The National Convention met September 20, 1792. In the following days, with Danton, Robespierre, Marat, and Louis-Antoine-Léon Saint-Just at the helm, it abolished the monarchy. In its new calendar, 1792 was recognized as the first year of the new republic. Under pressure from the Montagnards and the commune, Louis XVI was tried for treason. Robespierre addressed the Assembly as it heard evidence against the king. He argued that its duty was not to pronounce for or against a man, but to enact a measure of public safety and to protect the nation itself. Despite resistance by the Girondins, the king was executed for treason on January 21, 1793.

In the same year France annexed or occupied Belgium, the Rhineland, and Savoy. Acting on its Edict of Fraternity, which guaranteed assistance to all those desiring liberty, and on its policy of extending the republic to its "natu-

The guillotine, a device for beheading a person, became the symbol of the Reign of Terror during the French Revolution.

ral" frontiers, France declared war on Britain, Holland, and Spain. The French met defeat, however, and suffered further hardship as a result of a crippling trade blockade imposed by the British.

Mounting international pressures produced a new round of internal strife. The extremist position in France became stronger, and the Girondins were expelled from the National Convention. The Montagnards, led by Danton, Robespierre, and Marat, allied themselves with the working class and assumed power. Under their direction the convention introduced radical economic and social reform: state limits on prices, national assistance for the poor, heavy taxes on the rich, confiscation of the property of *émigrés,* and universal, compulsory education. The convention drafted a new constitution, ratified by national plebiscite, announcing universal suffrage, a single assembly chamber, and the rights of the nation. Funded through the national purse, 22,000 revolutionary committees ensured the enforcement of the social reforms.

In response to organized regional resistance, the National Convention issued a proclamation in October 1793 legitimating any means it deemed fit to continue the revolution. Power was centralized in the Committee of Public Safety, which worked with the Committee of General Security and the Revolutionary Tribunal to subdue or execute enemies of the people. The revolutionaries' fear of conspiracy gave rise to a new political practice, the public exhibition of professed sincerity. Treason trials proliferated. Even appeal to the good of "the nation," once so powerful a way to garner the people's support, could not stem the refusal to pay dues and rents. Violent opposition spread—from insurrection in the Vendée in western France to uprisings in Normandy, Provence, Lyon, Bordeaux, and Brittany. Much of the opposition was supported by the Catholic clergy, who seized the opportunity to persecute Protestants. Thousands died at the guillotine, and the country was plunged into civil war.

Counterrevolution

Robespierre, the "Incorruptible," was overthrown and executed on July 27, 1794. Power shifted to the moderates, who expelled the directors of the Terror, rescinded the limit on prices, and allowed the enforcement of many of the committees' laws to lapse. The National Convention undertook to create a new constitution. Interpreting the climate as favorable, the Royalists attempted to restore their power, instituting their own form of agitation, the White Terror. Despite the turmoil, the convention in these last months accomplished much: it established an elementary and secondary school system, professional academies and training schools, various cultural institutions, and the National Institute of Science and Arts. In August 1795 the National Convention, now wary of the abuses of one-chamber assemblies, approved a new constitution that placed executive power in a five-member Directory and legislative power in a Council of Ancients and a Council of Five Hundred. It added a statement of duties to the declaration of rights in the constitution of 1791.

But the Directory faced crippling problems: the burdens of the European wars, a debt crisis unalleviated by loans forced from the remaining property holders, Jacobin and Royalist counterrevolutionary unrest, and its own growing reputation of decadence and corruption. An insurrection by Royalists and reactionaries was quelled by Napoleon Bonaparte in October 1795. Among those outraged by the extravagance of the Directory were followers of the communist François-Nöel Babeuf, who unsuccessfully plotted the overthrow of the government in May 1796. The Directory was strained by revolving alignments of pro-Royalist and pro-Jacobin forces.

In the meantime, conflict between revolutionaries and counterrevolutionaries escalated throughout Europe, further exacerbating the domestic conflict between the Directory and the legislative councils. Directors pursued the Girondin policy of spreading revolution over Europe, and in 1797 French troops conquered large parts of Austria, Switzerland, and the Papal States, establishing these states as republics.

A campaign conceived with a view to conquering the Ottoman Empire was aborted with Britain's resistance, specifically by Horatio Nelson's triumph in 1798 over one of Bonaparte's convoys in the Battle of the Nile. That same year also brought French military defeats at the hands of Austria, Russia, and Turkey. Bonaparte returned to France and in November 1799 executed a coup d'état, expelling the Royalists from the Directory and councils. The Directory was abolished, and Bonaparte declared that the revolution was at an end. His own empire, however, would convey its most important principles throughout Europe.

Consequences

The Revolution signaled a turning point in modernity. Observers were awed by a power that could sweep away and install a new order, fulfilling the expectation of modern political philosophers that, in René Descartes's words, it was possible to tear down the edifices of the ancients and begin anew. Indeed, this was every bit a philosopher's revolution, and with it came a new political breed: intellectuals who mediated philosophy and power through ideology. Mirabeau and Sieyès saw themselves as completing the philosophic work of Voltaire and Rousseau. The French Revolution became the model for all future revolutions. It was the first revolution built on the principle of total reconstruction, not only overhauling political and legal institutions but overseeing the smallest details of social and personal life. And it was the first revolution that recorded the valiant action of the women involved.

Its achievement was the democratic principle that the constitution is the will of the people and that, as Thomas Paine said, any government violating the constitution exercises "power without right" and thus is a despotism. Central to the declaration of right was the recognition that humans have the prerogative to institute such right. The French revolutionaries' vision of democracy was new. It was based not on the English model of the separation and balance of powers, nor on representative government, but on the general will. From this revolutionary theory, and the experience of diverse peoples in the European wars, emerged the consciousness of nationalism—the recognition of the nation as sovereign over the law. The success of the French Revolution announced the incompatability of hereditary right and privilege with citizenship. After the revolution true democracy could mean nothing less than the equal admission of all members in a state to full political participation.

The French Revolution demonstrated the strategic effectiveness of organizing a crowd. It was, arguably, the first revolution to use systematic terror to purge every vestige of an existing regime. Its success came from the potent but volatile emotions it tapped—pity, enthusiasm, resentment, and panic—and the virtues it exploited—sincerity, natural goodness, and compassion. The revolutionaries—self-styled Roman founders—understood the ardor produced by professions of "virtue," but they also knew how to harness that ardor to murderous ends. What made the republic so sinister was the ease with which the idea of "the people and the nation" could be evoked to agitate and mobilize the crowd, while brutally extinguishing the lives of human beings.

The French revolutionaries believed they had undertaken a revolution of reason against Christianity, though they erected their own Temple of Eternity and instituted their own cults of reverence. Succeeding generations of political thinkers and actors would inherit this substitution of ideology for religion. For some, this shift would raise the question whether ideology can truly satisfy the deepest human longings, while for others it marked the permanent overthrow of despotism and superstition.

See also *Burke, Edmund; Egalitarianism; Nationalism; Paine, Thomas; Popular sovereignty; Rousseau, Jean-Jacques; Sieyès, Emmanuel-Joseph; Tocqueville, Alexis de.* In Documents section, see *Declaration of the Rights of Man and of the Citizen (1789).*

Peter C. Emberley

BIBLIOGRAPHY

Acton, Lord John Emerich. *Lectures on the French Revolution.* London: Macmillan, 1910; New York: Gordon Press, 1972.

Arendt, Hannah. *On Revolution.* Harmondsworth: Penguin Books, 1963.

Burke, Edmund. *Reflections on the Revolution in France.* Indianapolis: Hackett, 1987.

Goodwin, Albert. *The French Revolution.* London: Hutchinson, 1966.

Hampson, Norman. *A Social History of the French Revolution.* Toronto: University of Toronto Press, 1963; London: Routledge, 1966.

Lefebvre, Georges. *The French Revolution.* 2 vols. Translated by John Hall Stewart and James Friguglietti. New York: Columbia University Press, 1962–1964; London: Routledge and Kegan Paul, 1967.

Michelet, Jules. *History of the French Revolution.* Translated by Charles Cocks. Chicago: University of Chicago Press, 1967.

Sydenham, M. J. *The French Revolution.* London: Batsford, 1965.

Taine, Hippolyte Adolphe. *The French Revolution.* 3 vols. Translated by John Durand. Gloucester, Mass.: Peter Smith, 1962.

Williams, Gwyn A. *Artisans and Sans-Culottes: Popular Movements in France and Britain during the French Revolution.* New York: Norton, 1969; London: Libris, 1989.

Revolutions

Rapid, basic transformations of a nation's governmental institutions and ideals—and perhaps its social structures as well. *Political revolutions* suddenly change governmental arrangements. *Social revolutions* transform both political and class structures, and they are accompanied and in part carried through by popular revolts from below.

Have revolutions during modern times contributed to the democratization of social and political life? Or have they, instead, reinforced or created tyranny, betraying the libertarian and egalitarian hopes of many of their supporters? These questions are a perennial subject of passionate debate among modern social theorists and politically engaged people. The classical Marxist vision on these matters was optimistic. "Bourgeois revolutions" were thought to lay the basis for historically progressive but socially limited forms of liberal democracy, while subsequent "proletarian revolutions" would create conditions for universal political and social democracy. Proletarian revolutions, Marxists believed, would be accompanied by a "withering away of the state" as an organ of coercive domination of the many by the few.

After World War II, Western social scientists used theories of modernization to develop a very different vision of the relationship between revolutions and democracy. They were reacting to the obvious facts of history that contradicted Marxist expectations. S. N. Eisenstadt, for one, argued that democracy had been furthered only by moderately disruptive revolutions in Western European countries that were undergoing smooth economic modernization. Such early modern revolutions as the Dutch (1555–1585), English (1640–1689), American (1775–1789), and French (1787–early 1800s) were often cited as examples of democratizing revolutions in this sense. By contrast, modernization theorists argued that more thoroughgoing and violent revolutions in later modernizing nations, such as Russia and China, had given rise to tyrannical dictatorships, defeating possibilities for democratization.

Since the 1970s much comparative historical scholarship has been devoted to understanding the causes and outcomes of political and social revolutions in modern times. The results offer a more nuanced view of the complex interrelationships of political authoritarianism, democracy, and revolutionary change than was provided by either classical Marxists or modernization theorists. Early modern political revolutions in the Netherlands, England, and America appear to have furthered liberal governmental institutions for the upper classes, but they did not directly institutionalize democratic political participation. Social revolutions—from the French Revolution through the Russian and Chinese revolutions of the early twentieth century to the Vietnamese, Nicaraguan, and Iranian revolutions of the latter half of the century—have led to greater degrees of popular political participation. Yet they have almost always culminated in more centralized, bureaucratic, and authoritarian national states than the old regimes they displaced.

Social revolutions have invariably broken out in countries where most people were previously excluded from rights to political participation (though they certainly have not occurred in all such countries). But liberal forms of democracy—involving freedom of speech, freedom of association, and competitive elections—have not usually been immediately furthered by social revolutions. After brief interludes of political freedom, the political and class struggles of these social revolutions have led to the installation of authoritarian regimes. Examples include the military dictatorship of Napoleon Bonaparte that followed the French Revolution, the dictatorships of communist parties that followed the Russian, Chinese, and Vietnamese revolutions, and the theocratic dictatorship of Islamic clerics that followed the Iranian revolution.

Some events of the late twentieth century may be exceptions to the generalization that social revolutions always culminate in authoritarian regimes. Before considering these cases, however, let us examine the relationships among political authoritarianism, revolution, and democracy during the past several hundred years.

Early Modern Political Revolutions

The English revolution of the seventeenth century is often cited as a prime example of a moderately disruptive revolution that furthered the cause of democracy. Broadly viewed, the conflicts and settlement of this revolution stretched from the calling of the Long Parliament in 1640 to the removal of James II in the "Glorious Revolution" of 1688–1689. Yet the English revolution can be considered to have had a democratic outcome only if it is stretched into the nineteenth century to include much later developments. For example, Eisenstadt included the following among the "outcomes" of the English revolution: the rise of the middle classes (a gradual development of the seventeenth through the nineteenth centuries), the creation of an urban proletariat (late eighteenth and nineteenth centuries), and the broadening of political access and civil rights for both of these nontraditional classes (which came about almost entirely through parliamentary reforms during the nineteenth and twentieth centuries).

Actually, the seventeenth-century English revolution was a political revolution against absolute monarchy. Its strengthening of parliamentary sovereignty furthered the social and political dominance of property holders, landlords, and merchants. Because principles of parliamentary decision making triumphed over the arbitrary rights of kings, this revolution's political outcome can certainly be called liberal. But it was liberal rule by and for an upper-class oligarchy. During the revolution, there was a challenge from the Leveller movement, which aimed to extend political participation to all property-holding men, whether small or large property holders. But this was decisively defeated, as were other, more radical movements claiming rights for all nondominant groups, including the propertyless. Thus the result of the English revolution was not democracy, although the revolution did further the important principle that subjects have rights to dissent and to participate in governance.

The victory of oligarchic parliamentary liberalism weakened authoritarianism and set precedents for further political democratization much later in British history. But that came only after England's pioneering capitalist industrialization, which was accompanied by major social dislocations for rural and urban lower classes. If these groups had gained democratic political rights during the English revolution, they might well have resisted—or slowed down—the capitalist industrialization of England. Democratic rights were extended to the lower classes only after capitalist England had gained primacy in the world capitalist system and after the formation of an economically disciplined and politically organized industrial proletariat. Major social movements demanding democratization, as well as World War I, were catalysts for full political democratization in Britain, which occurred in steps taken by Parliament between the 1830s and the 1920s. Thus to suggest that democratization was a direct outcome of the much earlier English revolution is to understand history in a deterministic fashion—claiming that all later "progress" somehow flows automatically from one arbitrarily designated previous event.

Comparable difficulties accompany any attempt to attribute democratic outcomes to the early modern Dutch and American revolutions. Both of these political revolutions liberated "new nations" from imperial powers (Spain in the case of Holland, Britain in the case of the United States). Both also established upper class–dominated representative political systems. Democratization in the Netherlands, as in England, came much later. In the United States universal suffrage for white males did emerge between the 1820s and 1840s, a few decades after the revolution. The spread of manhood suffrage, however, was not a direct result of the revolution. Rather, it resulted from the distinctive political legacies of British colonial rule and the preponderance of small property holders (mostly farmers) in most U.S. states. Moreover, the constitutional settlement in 1789 of the American Revolution included the institutionalization of black slavery in the South, entrenching a set of antidemocratic structures that were not fully overcome for 170 years. The elimination of slavery and its legal aftereffects in the United States required the cumulative effects of the Civil War, two world wars, the New Deal of the 1930s, and the civil rights struggles of the 1960s.

One can plausibly argue that early modern political revolutions, such as the Dutch, American, and English revolutions, removed the obstacles to democratization that were inherent in rule by absolute monarchs or foreign imperial powers. These political revolutions created liberal governmental arrangements that left open the possibility of later shifts toward liberal democracy. But democratic social and political movements were defeated as part of the victories of upper-class liberals in these revolutions. And as the U.S. case vividly shows, part of the price of institutionalizing a liberal political outcome could be the firm denial of even the potential for equal rights to a large part of the population. Landlords in the American South would never have accepted the U.S. Constitution in 1789 if the document had not included provisions for their ownership of slaves and the exclusion of blacks from social and political rights.

Social Revolutions in France, Russia, and China

The word *revolution* today is generally understood to mean a fundamental sociopolitical change accompanied by violent upheavals from below. Yet it did not take on this connotation until the French Revolution of the late eighteenth century. Unlike its English, Dutch, and American counterparts, the French Revolution was a social revolution in which class-based upheavals from below, especially those of peasants against landlords, propelled sudden transformations in the class structure and resulted in the centralization of state power. In this respect the French Revolution can be grouped with revolutions in Russia (1917–1930s) and China (1911–1960s). From this point of view the French Revolution was not primarily "bourgeois" or "liberal." Nor was the Russian Revolution "proletarian" in the Marxist sense of furthering working class–based democratic socialism. Rather, the French, Russian, and Chinese revolutions, despite important variations, displayed striking similarities of context, cause, process, and outcomes.

All three of these classic social revolutions occurred in large independent monarchies with predominantly agrarian economies and societies. The monarchical states were partially bureaucratic, and they were authoritarian because their subjects, except for a few of the most privileged, were excluded from political participation and decision making. In the decades before their revolutionary outbreaks, moreover, the old regimes of Bourbon France, Romanov Russia, and Qing China found themselves pressured militarily by countries with more highly developed economies: France by England, Russia by Germany, and China by Japan and various Western powers.

The social revolutions in these three agrarian bureaucratic monarchies had similar characteristics. First, the centralized, semibureaucratic administrative and military organizations of the old regimes disintegrated because of international pressures and disputes between monarchs and landed-commercial upper classes. Second, widespread popular revolts occurred, including peasant revolts against landlords. After lengthy struggles by political forces trying to consolidate new state organizations, all three revolutions resulted in more centralized and mass-mobilizing national states, more powerful than prerevolutionary regimes in relation to all domestic social groups and to foreign competitors. None of these revolutions had a liberal-democratic outcome, and none resulted in a socialist democracy.

The political phases of the French Revolution from 1789 through 1800 certainly included attempts to institutionalize civil liberties and electoral democracy, as well as the legalization of private property rights for peasants and the bourgeoisie alike. Because the French Revolution furthered a private-propertied society—rather than a party-state that owned and managed the national economy—it allowed for the eventual emergence of liberal-democratic political arrangements in France. But the immediate result of the revolution was Napoleon's nationalist dictatorship, which left the enduring legacy of a highly centralized and bureaucratic French state with a recurrent tendency to seek national glory through military exploits.

During the French Revolution, democratization—in the sense of social equality and participation in national politics—was perhaps most dramatically furthered through "careers open to talent" in the military officer corps, the institution of mass military conscription, and the greater efficiency of the state in collecting taxes from all citizens. From a European continental perspective, the most important accomplishment of the French Revolution was the capability to launch highly mobile armies of citizen-soldiers, coordinated with the deployment of artillery forces.

These social and military changes were launched between 1792 and 1794 by the revolutionary party called the Jacobins. Even though they did not stabilize their "Republic of Virtue," the Montagnard faction of the Jacobins fended off the most pressing domestic and international counterrevolutionary threats. Their fall from power in 1794 was not the end of military mass mobilization in France. Before long, Napoleon consolidated a conservative bureaucratic regime and came to terms with private property holders and the Roman Catholic Church. Then he expanded military mobilization, deploying citizen armies of an unprecedented size and capacity for rapid maneuvering. The increased popular participation and the sense of French nationalism and democratic mission unleashed by the revolution were thus directed outward, toward overthrowing monarchs and aristocracies in other countries. Before their eventual defeat in Russia, French citizen armies redrew the political map of modern Europe and inspired the emergence of other European nationalisms in response.

Russia and China both experienced social revolutionary transformations that resulted in the rule of communist-directed party-states. Both the resulting regimes were authoritarian and aimed to mobilize mass energies for national economic development and military participation. Nevertheless, from the point of view of peasants—who were the vast majority of people in both countries—there were differences between the Russian and Chinese communist regimes.

Because the Russian Bolsheviks came to power in the cities, they lacked political ties to the peasantry. They regarded peasants as "backward" and as an obstacle to national development. During the late 1920s and early 1930s Russian peasants were coerced into joining collective farms, at the same time as an autocratic dictatorship was installed under the leadership of Joseph Stalin. Thereafter, Russian workers and peasants alike were subjected to terror and bureaucratic oppression to promote the rapid heavy industrialization of the Soviet Union.

In China the Communist Party developed a partnership with the peasantry before it came to power in 1949. It pursued agricultural collectivization with less terror and coercion than was used in the Soviet Union. Chinese communist development strategies after the 1950s placed more emphasis on agriculture and small industries, allowing some economic benefits to, and local participation by, peasants and rural leaders. Eventually, the Chinese communists gave up on collective agriculture, allowing the return to private farms and market processes in the national economy. The Chinese communists, however, have not allowed their governmental system to become democratic. And during the Cultural Revolution of the 1960s, Mao Zedong's faction of Chinese communists waged a campaign of terror and violence, especially against intellectuals and urban middle-class Chinese.

Social Revolutions in Developing Nations

During the twentieth century, social revolutions occurred from time to time in small countries located in relatively peripheral economic and geopolitical positions within the international system. Some occurred in nations emerging from colonial domination; examples include Algeria during the process of separation from French rule during the 1950s and early 1960s, Mozambique and Angola during struggles against Portuguese rule in the 1970s, and Vietnam during struggles against French and Japanese rule in the 1940s and 1950s. Other social revolutions occurred in nominally independent, dictatorial regimes with close ties to international patrons. Examples of this type include the Mexican revolution against the rule of Porfirio Díaz, starting in 1910–1911; the Cuban revolution of the late 1950s against the rule of Fulgencio Batista; the Nicaraguan revolution of 1979 against the rule of Anastasio Somoza; and the Iranian revolution of 1979 against the rule of the second Pahlavi shah.

All the twentieth-century social revolutions in developing nations overthrew authoritarian regimes that excluded most people from political participation. Still, many countries in Asia, Africa, Latin America, and the Middle East had (and have) such authoritarian, nondemocratic governments. Only a few of them have been challenged by strong revolutionary movements or popular revolts. Fewer still have experienced actual transfers of state power from old regimes to new ones run by revolutionaries. Fortunately, comparative studies by scholars such as Jeff Goodwin, Timothy Wickham-Crowley, and Jack Goldstone help determine which kinds of authoritarian, developing states have been most likely to experience social revolutions.

Among countries formerly subjected to colonial rule by Western European nations or by Japan, there were crucial variations. Some colonies—especially those of Britain—were ruled indirectly, as partnerships between the colonial authorities and domestic upper-class groups. Other colonies—especially those of France, Portugal, and Japan—were ruled much more directly by the colonizers. In these colonies, even the domestic propertied and educated elites were excluded from political and governmental participation.

It appears that social revolutions were more likely to occur during the decolonization of directly ruled colonies. In such colonies, guerrilla movements led by nationalistic communists were often able to mobilize widespread rural and urban support, including some elite support. When World War II (or international developments afterward) weakened directly ruled colonial governments, vacuums of power emerged that gave an opening to the nationalist revolutionaries.

By contrast, indirectly ruled colonies often experienced less violent transfers of power to nationally independent regimes run by domestic elites that already had had some influence in the earlier colonial systems. In some of these cases democratic political systems were instituted as well. The best example is India, a former British colony that became the world's most populous democracy.

Among nominally independent developing nations, a certain type of authoritarian regime has proved especially susceptible to revolutionary overthrow: the personalistic dictatorship. According to Goodwin, all regimes in developing nations are vulnerable to challenge from revolutionary movements if they exclude most of their citizens from routine political participation and if they repress reformist groups, such as trade unionists, opposition political parties, or church-based groups. Thus would-be revolutionary movements exist in many developing countries.

Some authoritarian regimes have such great military strength and such secure international borders that they can get away with political repression for a long time. Some military dictatorships in developing nations spread influence fairly broadly across military officer corps and allied groups of landlords and capitalist property holders. But other dictatorships in developing nations have been very narrowly based—especially personalistic, or patrimonial, regimes.

In a personalistic dictatorship a single ruler holds sway, supported by a special, nonprofessional armed force. Such patrimonial rulers often coerce and exclude even upper-class people in their societies. They use divide-and-rule tactics to manipulate military officers and to try to prevent coups d'état. They provide economic favors only to family members and friends, often treating other upper-class families very badly. So exclusive and manipulative are these patrimonial dictatorships that they are likely to generate strong revolutionary movements that include upper- and middle-class supporters, along with workers and peasants.

Compared with collective military dictatorships, personalistic regimes are much more likely actually to be overthrown by revolutionary challengers. This can happen, for example, if the ruler dies, or if foreign allies of the ruler suddenly withdraw their support. Thus, for example, patrimonial dictatorships such as those of Díaz in Mexico, of Batista in Cuba, of Somoza in Nicaragua, and of Mohammad Reza Pahlavi in Iran all fell from power. In each case, once the ruler was gone, the old military and administrative institutions suddenly fell apart and the revolutionary movement could move in and take power.

What happened after direct colonial regimes or personalistic dictatorships were overthrown? The course of events resembled that of the social-revolutionary displacements of agrarian-bureaucratic monarchies in France, Russia, and China. Violent political and military struggles accompanied, and often followed, the birth of revolutionary regimes in developing countries. "Democratization" of a sort accompanied such struggles, as masses of ordinary people previously excluded from politics were drawn in. Guerrilla revolutionary movements tapped the support of peasants, students, and often urban dwellers in such places as Algeria, Cuba, Mexico, Vietnam, Portuguese Africa, and Nicaragua. Peasant villages were the sites of autonomous popular revolts during revolutions in Mexico, Ethiopia, and Bolivia. Worker's unions played a key role in Bolivia, while the Iranian revolution was carried through by Islamic clerics and a broad alliance of urban social groups.

Whatever the varieties of groups and alliances that participated in overthrowing the old regimes, social revolutions in developing nations tended to result in authoritarian dictatorships by revolutionary leaders. These leaders typically forced into exile or killed off their competitors, even former allies against the old regime. Communist parties established dictatorships following revolutions in Cuba, Angola, Mozambique, and Vietnam. A single nationalist and populist party came virtually to monopolize national political power in Mexico after its revolution. Military rulers eventually took over in Bolivia. In Iran a dictatorship of militant Islamic clerics took power and shaped the rules of the new regime.

All these postrevolutionary regimes continued to mobilize popular groups into domestic political struggles and often into wars with foreign powers. Communist Vietnam channeled popular energies into lengthy military struggles against noncommunist South Vietnam, which was backed by the United States. Islamic Iran threw millions of its people into a costly war with neighboring Iraq. All revolutionary regimes in developing countries tried to assert national independence against great powers on the world stage. Their supporters would argue that such national assertion by formerly colonized or dominated peoples is a component of "democratization." Nevertheless, most social revolutions in developing nations did not culminate in liberal democracies, with constitutional procedures, civil rights, and free elections—any more than the French, Russian, or Chinese revolutions did.

Are Some Social Revolutions Leaning Toward Democracy?

The relationship of revolution and democratization may have begun to change in the late twentieth century. The Nicaraguan revolution that overthrew the Somoza dictatorship had first brought to power a guerrilla movement led by the Sandinistas, a loosely communist group of intellectuals and politicians. During the 1980s the Sandinistas entered into international agreements to allow elections. When their party lost an election in 1990 to a non-Sandinista coalition led by Violeta Chamorro, the Sandinistas—an armed revolutionary movement—agreed to step down from presidential office. As a result of this remarkable decision, a kind of electoral democracy took root in Nicaragua—thus, perhaps, belying the generalization that social revolutions always lead to authoritarian rule.

Of course, the circumstances in Nicaragua were special. The original revolution against Somoza had been made by a broad alliance, including upper- and middle-class reformers as well as guerrilla and urban movements led by Sandinistas. The Sandinistas themselves included a variety of political tendencies. What is more, the agreement to hold elections was more or less forced on the Sandinistas because the United States sponsored a counterrevolutionary military force, the contras. The Sandinistas agreed to hold elections in return for U.S. agreement to stop sponsoring the contras. More typically, foreign pressures after a social revolution lead not to compromise but to greater militancy and authoritarian rule by revolutionaries. Threatened revolutionaries typically mobilize mass support for military struggles against foreign powers. This is what happened in both Vietnam and Iran.

The other place in the contemporary world where revolutions may be promoting liberal democracy is Eastern Europe. For several reasons, analysts do not agree on whether the overthrows of Eastern European communist regimes that occurred in 1989 were really social revolutions. First, these overthrows became possible only when an imperial-colonial power, the Soviet Union, withdrew its military protection for the communist dictatorships of Eastern Europe. Second, except for the revolution against a personalistic communist dictator in Romania, most of the Eastern European revolutions of 1989 occurred suddenly, without violence from below. Third, the former communist elites were not always fully displaced. Nonetheless, fundamental changes in government and social structure did coincide in Eastern Europe. The political authorities that emerged after 1989—as well as most of the social movements and new political parties—espoused the values of market capitalism and Western-style constitutional democracy.

That revolutions against communist dictatorships finally occurred may mean that democratization will be furthered (rather than frustrated) by such transformations. In the mid-1990s it was still too early to tell whether civil rights, competitive elections, and truly constitutional government would prove stable in revolutionized polities of Eastern Europe. And it was certainly too soon to tell whether their national-economic and property arrangements would make a full transition from state ownership to smoothly functioning capitalism.

Nevertheless, the overthrow of communist dictatorships in the name of national, economic, and political freedom inaugurated a "new day" in the annals of revolution in modern history. At last, perhaps—and in a thoroughly ironic way—Karl Marx's dream of revolution leading to democracy may be realized.

See also *China; Mexico; Revolution, American; Revolution, French; Russia, Pre-Soviet; United Kingdom.*

Theda Skocpol

BIBLIOGRAPHY

Adelman, Jonathan R. *Revolution, Armies, and War: A Political History.* Boulder, Colo.: Lynne Rienner, 1985.

Eisenstadt, S. N. *Revolution and the Transformation of Societies: A Comparative Study of Civilizations.* New York: Free Press, 1978.

Goldstone, Jack A., ed. *Revolutions: Theoretical, Comparative, and Historical Studies.* New York: Harcourt Brace Jovanovich, 1986.

Goldstone, Jack A., Ted Robert Gurr, and Farrokh Moshiri, eds. *Revolutions of the Late Twentieth Century.* Boulder, Colo.: Westview Press, 1991.

Goodwin, Jeff. *States and Revolution in the Third World: A Comparative Analysis.* Berkeley and Los Angeles: University of California Press, forthcoming.

———, and Theda Skocpol. "Explaining Revolutions in the Contemporary Third World." *Politics and Society* 17 (December 1989): 489–509.

Huntington, Samuel P. *Political Order in Changing Societies.* New Haven and London: Yale University Press, 1968.

McDaniel, Tim. *Autocracy, Modernization, and Revolution in Russia and Iran.* Princeton: Princeton University Press, 1991.

Marx, Karl, and Friedrich Engels. "Manifesto of the Communist Party." In *The Marx-Engels Reader.* 2d ed. Edited by Robert C. Tucker. New York: Norton, 1978.

Moore, Barrington, Jr. *Social Origins of Dictatorship and Democracy: Lord and Peasant in the Making of the Modern World.* Boston: Beacon Press, 1967; London: Penguin Books, 1991.

Skocpol, Theda. *Revolutions in the Modern World.* Cambridge and New York: Cambridge University Press, 1994.

———. *States and Social Revolutions: A Comparative Analysis of France, Russia, and China.* Cambridge and New York: Cambridge University Press, 1979.

Snyder, Richard. "Explaining Transitions from Neopatrimonial Dictatorships." *Comparative Politics* 24 (July 1992): 379–399.

Wickham-Crowley, Timothy P. *Guerrillas and Revolution in Latin America: A Comparative Study of Insurgents and Regimes since 1956.* Princeton: Princeton University Press, 1992.

Wolf, Eric R. *Peasant Wars of the Twentieth Century.* New York: Harper and Row, 1969.

Rhetoric

Rhetoric is the art of speaking well or of speaking persuasively. But since the difficulty of the case to be made might cause even the best possible speech to fall short of successfully persuading its audience, a more precise definition of *rhetoric* is the capacity to see and to use in each case all the available means of persuasion.

Clearly, though, some people speak better than others, whether by natural gift, experience, or some other cause. While any effort or ability to speak well could be considered rhetoric, the term is best applied to an art, skill, or science that has consciously and explicitly reflected on what is required to speak persuasively. Rhetoric as such an art emerged within the Western tradition among the Greek Sophists of the fifth century B.C., most notably Protagoras and Gorgias.

Although rhetoric can, in a sense, play a role in any and all persuasion, it has from the beginning attracted the most attention and seemed of greatest importance in its public and political dimensions: forensic or judicial rhetoric in courtrooms; deliberative or political rhetoric in legislatures and assemblies; and ceremonial rhetoric in funeral orations, Independence Day speeches, and the like. Rhetoric has flourished most vigorously in republics, as it did above all in the democracy of ancient Athens. Democratic political life provided many opportunities for the exercise of rhetoric, from the full assembly of the people to the councils and courts, and well-developed rhetorical skills often paved the road to positions of political leadership. Although political rhetoric may contribute in valuable ways to democratic deliberation, democracy nonetheless harbors a certain suspicion of rhetoric. If, as democrats tend to believe in one way or another, all people are equal in their basic political rights and capacities, why should an *art* of rhetoric be needed? It is not the kind

Lenin proclaims Soviet rule at the second all-Russian Congress of Soviets in Petrograd following the 1917 overthrow of the Provisional Government.

of specialty, such as medicine or military engineering, to which nonexperts must defer. Indeed, if rhetoric works, does it not disrupt democratic equality by benefiting the privileged few who have the wealth and leisure to study it?

Plato criticized Sophistic rhetoric in two well-known dialogues in which Socrates, his teacher, plays a leading role. In *Gorgias,* Socrates attacks rhetoric for not being a genuine art or knowledge. Separated from genuine political science, whose goal is the search for justice, rhetoric simply flatters the people. Demagogues use it irresponsibly to provide pleasure without real benefit or regard for the common good. In *Phaedrus,* Socrates criticizes rhetoric for its fragmentary and unsystematic character. It lacks, for example, an adequate account of all the various types of human character and an orderly inventory of the means of persuading each type. These two critiques considered together point toward the need for an ordered, philosophically grounded art of rhetoric, informed and guided by a political philosophy that aims at justice and the common good. Aristotle sought to meet that need in his own *Rhetoric,* the first comprehensive treatment of the

subject and by far the most influential. It focuses on the arguments and examples used to persuade, but it also discusses how the speaker should present his or her own character and appeal to the audience's passions.

Rhetoric is thus conceived as the key means by which knowledge and intelligence might influence the course of practical life, the bridge linking philosophy and science to the political community. At the same time, this classic conception of rhetoric subordinates the art of persuasion to philosophy or to knowledge about ethics and politics. Education in rhetoric so conceived cannot provide a sure guarantee against rhetoric's misuse, but it seeks to elevate and inform rhetorical practices. This rhetorical tradition was taken up later by the Romans, most illustriously by the great writer, orator, and statesman Cicero.

In the universities of medieval Europe rhetoric held a secure place, but it played a lesser public role under monarchies than in ancient republics. The revival of classical letters and learning by Renaissance humanists of the fifteenth and sixteenth centuries renewed reflection on the possible civic function of rhetoric.

In more modern times rhetoric suffered a certain eclipse and loss of status. The Enlightenment thinkers of the seventeenth and eighteenth centuries, with their hopes for the advancement of science in harmony with political and social progress, considered rhetoric useful at first, but less so later as the light of science spread. From the standpoint of nineteenth-century romanticism, which valued the creative individual's unique vision, rhetoric appeared a lowly device indeed.

As the discipline and status of rhetoric declined, political scientists nonetheless had to examine the political phenomena once addressed by rhetoric: political communication and propaganda. *Political communication,* a broad and neutral term, obscures the special importance of persuasion in politics. *Political propaganda* suggests the calculating manipulation of passive human material, in contrast with classical rhetoric's focus on persuading people assumed to be free to make deliberate judgments.

Under the influence of postmodernism in the last quarter of the twentieth century, rhetoric has become a hot academic topic. Postmodernist discussions typically define rhetoric in very broad terms: it is the study and practice of discourse in any area whatsoever, articulating the prevailing rules of discourse and accounting for how they came into being and continue to change. For those filled with Enlightenment hopes that science and philosophy could do everything, rhetoric was nothing; for postmodernists who deny to science and philosophy any sound foundations or permanent truths, rhetoric is everything—or, rather, everything is rhetoric.

In the beginning, rhetoric applied to public speaking, but authors from Plato on have applied it to written discourse as well. Changes in the media of communication affect the circumstances or the character of rhetoric. With the rise of periodical publications, for example, journalists began to engage in political rhetoric that was no less important than that practiced by politicians. A new medium often fosters the emergence of a new rhetorical style: radio broadcasts made possible President Franklin D. Roosevelt's fireside chats, and the peculiar features of television were put to effective use by Ronald Reagan (the Great Communicator). Many observers fear that the characteristics of television as a communication medium encourage brief snippets (sound bites) and visual effects at the expense of substantive speech, turn news into entertainment, and perhaps diminish people's capacity to follow extensive arguments.

Rhetoric is as controversial today as in Plato's time, and it remains forever exposed to the charge of deception. It is therefore easy to feel impatient with any claims advanced on its behalf. But if human beings must coordinate their activities with each other, and if the two basic means of doing so are persuasion and force, surely a strong case can be made for the value of rhetoric, especially in the processes of democratic self-governance.

See also *Postmodernism.*

James H. Nichols, Jr.

BIBLIOGRAPHY

Aristotle. *On Rhetoric: A Theory of Civic Discourse.* Translated by George A. Kennedy. New York: Oxford University Press, 1991.

Ceaser, James W., et al. "The Rise of the Rhetorical Presidency." In *Rethinking the Presidency,* edited by Thomas Cronin. Boston: Little, Brown, 1982.

Cicero, Marcus Tullius. *De Oratore (On the Orator).* Translated by E. W. Sutton and H. Rackham. Cambridge and London: Harvard University Press, 1979.

Cole, Thomas. *The Origins of Rhetoric in Ancient Greece.* Baltimore and Northampton: Johns Hopkins University Press, 1991.

Plato. "Gorgias." In *Lysis, Symposium, Gorgias.* Translated by W. R. M. Lamb. Cambridge: Harvard University Press, 1961.

———. "Phaedrus." In *Euthyphro, Apology, Crito, Phaedo, Phaedrus.* Translated by H. N. Fowler. Cambridge, Mass., and London: Harvard University Press, 1982.

Roh Tae Woo

The leader who ended South Korea's military dictatorship and introduced the country to democracy. Roh (1932–   ) was born into a peasant family in Taegu. As a student at the Korean Military Academy, he became friendly with Chun Doo Hwan. Years later, as an army officer, Roh helped Chun become president of South Korea in a coup d'état that took place in 1980. Chun's regime turned out to be the most repressive in the history of Korean political development.

After his retirement from the army in 1981, Roh was appointed minister of state for national security and foreign affairs. He also held numerous other positions in the Chun government and later became chair of the ruling Democratic Justice Party, which ensured his selection as the party's presidential candidate in 1987.

Antigovernment demonstrations were frequent at that

In the presidential election of December 1992, Kim Young Sam of the Democratic Liberal Party won a three-way race, becoming the first civilian president of the Republic of Korea in thirty-one years. His legacy from Roh included a lagging economy, increased crime and social disorder, and spiraling inflation, but he also inherited a firm foundation for completing South Korea's transition to democracy.

Ilpyong J. Kim

BIBLIOGRAPHY

Kim, Ilpyong J., and Eun Sung Chung. "Establishing Democratic Rule in South Korea." In *Establishing Democratic Rule: The Emergence of Local Governments in Post-Authoritarian Systems,* edited by Ilpyong J. Kim and Jane Shapiro Zacek. Washington, D.C: Washington Institute Press, 1993.

Kim, Ilpyong J., and Young Whan Kihl, eds. *Political Change in South Korea.* New York: Paragon House, 1988.

Roh Tae Woo

time, with members of the middle class joining students to demand an end to the military regime and establishment of a democratic government. Under Roh's leadership the Democratic Justice Party joined with other political parties to write a constitution incorporating such reforms as direct presidential elections and the decentralization of power. The first presidential election in sixteen years was held on December 17, 1987. Roh won, with 36.6 percent of the popular vote.

During his five years in office (1988–1993), Roh hosted the summer Olympic games in Seoul in 1988; established diplomatic relations with the Soviet Union, Eastern European nations, and China; and opened negotiations with North Korea. These negotiations resulted in a nonaggression pact signed on December 13, 1992. In addition to his achievements in foreign relations, Roh presided over a successful realignment of South Korea's political parties in 1990, when the Democratic Justice Party merged with two opposition parties to create the ruling Democratic Liberal Party.

Rokkan, Stein

Norwegian political scientist and sociologist, known for his work on state formation, nation building, and the genesis of democracy in Europe. Rokkan (1921–1979) is remembered for his efforts to facilitate international cooperation in the social sciences. He served as vice president of the International Sociological Association (1966–1970), president of the International Political Science Association (1970–1973), and president of the International Social Science Council (1973–1977). He founded the European Consortium for Political Research and was its chairman from 1970 to 1976.

Rokkan was born in the Lofoten Islands, in northern Norway. Throughout his life, he was preoccupied with the relationship between social divisions, interests, and conflicts (cleavage structures), on the one hand, and the pattern of alliances and oppositions (party systems and voter alignments), on the other. The rich variety of historical trajectories and political forms in Europe triggered his lifelong pursuit of devising parsimonious models to explain the differences in the style and structure of mass involvement in European politics.

Rokkan examined the growth and structuring of mass politics in Western Europe in two steps. First, he mapped the sequence of steps in the institutionalization of formal mass democracy in Europe: the establishment of safeguards to allow organized competition, the broadening of the franchise, the standardization of the secret ballot, the lowering of thresholds of representation, and the introduction of various measures of parliamentary control over the national executive. Second, he documented the timing of the growth and the stabilization of organizations that were instrumental in mobilizing mass support through these new channels, and he mapped the formation and "freezing" of organized party alternatives within each national political system.

Rokkan and Seymour Martin Lipset's "freezing" thesis was that the party systems of the 1960s reflected (with few but significant exceptions) the cleavage systems of the 1920s, despite massive changes in the social structure since the establishment of the party organizations. Rokkan argued that those parties that were able to establish mass organizations and entrench themselves in local government before the final drive toward electoral mobilization proved the most viable. In a sense the political system was deprived of "political space" after the final thrust toward full-suffrage democracy. Hence, when the Fascist and National Socialist Parties entered the scene in the 1920s and 1930s, they were left with little choice but to try to create a new niche for themselves by borrowing ideological elements from the existing parties and becoming the first "catchall" parties in Europe.

Rokkan went back in history to unravel the preconditions for the development of stable representative political institutions. He believed that the chances for democracy were critically affected by differences in the initial conditions of state building, the early processes of territorial consolidation, and later alliances among crucial sociopolitical groups. Equally important were the timing of the inevitable crises of development and each nation's success in dealing with them.

Democracy, in Rokkan's view, can be studied as the work of a loose combination of competing elites, operating through political parties with different social, cultural, and territorial bases. Democratic stability is explained first and foremost by the strategies of elites rather than by individual political preferences. Although Rokkan brought Marxism into the analysis, he did not find Marxism interesting in itself.

Toward the end of his life, Rokkan tried to explain violent breakdowns in the transition to democracy and to specify preconditions for viable democracy. He attempted to locate—and then to classify—European nation-states along two axes of time and space: the South-North axis and the East-West axis.

The South-North axis located territories on the basis of distance from the influence of Rome and measured conditions necessary for rapid cultural integration. Rokkan interpreted the Reformation as the first major step toward the definition of territorial nations because Lutherans and Calvinists broke with the Roman Catholic Church and merged ecclesiastical bureaucracies with secular territorial establishments. This action closed the "exit options" on the cultural front and accentuated the cultural significance of the borders between nations; hence it was of critical importance for the nation-building process. The East-West axis differentiated the economic resource bases of state building. The West extracted resources from long-distance trade, while the East, because of the weakness of its cities, based its state-forming efforts on landowners and the resources they could offer—food and a labor force.

In Rokkan's view, this contrast in the resource bases went a long way toward explaining the difference between the Western and Eastern systems, both in their internal structures and in their later transitions to mass politics. Western Europe developed a number of strong centers of territorial control at the edges of an old empire, the Roman Empire, and the decisive steps toward state formation and nation building took place on the peripheries of the territories. What proved critical for the later development of Western European political systems was the low level of overall mobilization at the time of state building. The consolidation of the machineries for territorial control took place before the economy was fully monetized, before mass literacy was realized, and before the lower social strata could articulate any claims for participation.

The timing and sequence of developmental crises were of vital importance. The national elites had time to build up organizations before the next challenges came to the fore: the strengthening of national identity at the mass level, the opening of channels for mass participation, the development of a sense of national economic solidarity, and the establishment of a workable consensus on the need for a distribution of resources and benefits. In other words, the Western nations had a chance to solve some of the most difficult problems of state building before they faced the ordeal of mass politics.

In the countries that were late in unifying, however, these conditions did not exist. Austria, Germany, Italy, and

Spain had weak centers. This condition set the stage for Fascism and National Socialism—a politics of imperial restoration through military-industrial alliances and authoritarian, mass mobilizing party fronts.

See also *Lipset, Seymour Martin; Theory, Twentieth-century European.*

Bernt Hagtvet

BIBLIOGRAPHY

Eisenstadt, S. N., and Stein Rokkan, eds. *Building States and Nations.* 2 vols. Beverly Hills, Calif., and London: Sage Publications, 1973.

Hagtvet, Bernt, ed. *Politikk mellom økonomi og kultur: Stein Rokkan som politisk sosiolog og forskningsinspirator.* Oslo: Ad Notam, 1992.

Rokkan, Stein. *Citizens, Elections, Parties.* Oslo: Universitetsforlaget, 1970.

———. "Dimensions of State Formation and Nation-Building: Possible Paradigm for Research on Variations within Europe." In *The Formation of National States in Western Europe*, edited by Charles Tilly. Princeton: Princeton University Press, 1975.

———, and Bernt Hagtvet. "The Conditions of Fascist Victory: Towards a Geo-Economic, Geo-Political Model for the Explanation of Violent Breakdowns of Competitive Mass Politics." In *Who Were the Fascists? Social Roots of European Fascism,* edited by Stein Ugelvik Larsen, Bernt Hagtvet, and Jan Petter Myklebust. Bergen: Universitetsforlaget, 1980.

———, and Seymour Martin Lipset, eds. *Party Systems and Voter Alignments.* New York: Free Press, 1967.

———, and Derek W. Urwin. *Economy, Territory, Identity: The Politics of West European Peripheries.* Beverly Hills, Calif., and London: Sage Publications, 1983.

———. *The Politics of Regional Identity.* Beverly Hills, Calif., and London: Sage Publications, 1981.

Romania

See *Europe, East Central*

Rome, Classical

See *Classical Greece and Rome*

Roosevelt, Franklin D.

President of the United States from 1933 to 1945, during the Great Depression of the 1930s and World War II. The contributions made by Roosevelt (1882–1945) to modern democracy include his energetic collaboration with the international coalition that defeated Germany and Japan in 1945. He also decisively influenced the redirection of American liberal democracy toward the welfare state.

A member of the "progressive," reform-oriented wing of the Democratic Party, Roosevelt was also generally on good terms with the machine politicians and was therefore well positioned to make a bid for the Democratic Party's presidential nomination in 1932. He used his terms as president to lead the creation of a new Democratic Party coalition. This coalition—known as the New Deal coalition—was the basis of the Democratic Party's majority status in American politics into the 1990s. Roosevelt's New Deal program, in response to the economic depression, promised to make the federal government more responsible for managing the economy, for regulating financial institutions, and for relieving the distress of victims of economic misfortune.

In effect, Roosevelt's political leadership and policies

formed the basis of the "safety net" of the welfare state in the United States. His actions provided the material for some of the most important controversies in American politics in the remainder of the twentieth century—controversies about the proper role of liberal democratic government in general and in particular about the role of the U.S. federal government in economic management and the provision of welfare. Roosevelt voiced the pragmatic and progressive argument that historical changes in the industrialized world, especially the inevitable growth of large private business corporations, meant that responsibility for both economic prosperity and economic fairness had to be given to public agencies of the federal government. Otherwise, he argued, the right of every citizen to make a comfortable living would be neither sufficiently recognized nor reliably secured by large and uncaring private economic enterprises.

Roosevelt's New Deal institutionalized progressive intellectuals' skepticism about America's business-oriented culture and tried to elevate enlightened public administrators over the captains of industry as the true heroes of the postindustrial state. The New Deal succeeded in redefining American liberalism as the progressive belief that government should intervene actively in the workings of the economy and that justice demanded aiming at equitable results as well as equitable procedures.

Roosevelt's politics had an important effect not only on substantive policy controversies but also on the institutions of American democracy. In the pursuit of his policies, he greatly enhanced the American political system's reliance on the modern presidency as the initiator of policy and the enunciator of moral visions to shape public opinion. He thus perfected the progressive approach to executive power that Woodrow Wilson had first elaborated.

See also *Politics, Machine; Pragmatism; Presidential government; Progressivism; Welfare, Promotion of; Wilson, Woodrow; World War II.*

John Zvesper

BIBLIOGRAPHY

Frisch, Morton J. "Franklin Delano Roosevelt." In *American Political Thought: The Philosophic Dimension of American Statesmanship,* edited by Morton J. Frisch and Richard G. Stevens. Dubuque, Iowa: Kendall/Hart, 1976.

Greer, Thomas H. *What Roosevelt Thought.* East Lansing: Michigan State University Press, 1958.

Rosenman, Samuel I., ed. *The Public Papers and Addresses of Franklin D. Roosevelt.* 13 vols. New York: Random House, 1938–1950.

Zvesper, John. "The Liberal Rhetoric of Franklin Roosevelt." In *Rhetoric and American Statesmanship,* edited by Glen Thurow and Jeffrey Wallin. Durham, N.C.: Carolina Academic Press, 1984.

Roosevelt, Theodore

Twenty-sixth president of the United States from 1901 to 1909. Roosevelt (1858–1919) is remembered for his reform efforts, for antitrust legislation, and for winning the Nobel Peace Prize. The son of a wealthy New York investment banker, Roosevelt studied at Harvard University. His interests in politics and history led him to write several books, including *The Naval War of 1812.* When his father died in 1878, he inherited his family's fortune.

Before becoming president, Roosevelt served in various offices. He was elected to the New York Assembly, he was deputy sheriff in the Dakota Territory, and he headed the New York City police commission. Under President William McKinley he served as assistant secretary of the navy. When the United States declared war on Spain in May 1898, Roosevelt became lieutenant colonel of the Rough Rider regiment; he led the charge up San Juan Hill in Cuba.

In 1898 Roosevelt was elected governor of New York, and in 1900—in part because Republican leaders wanted to get him out of the way—he was nominated for vice president of the United States. When President McKinley was assassinated in September 1901, Roosevelt became, at age forty-two, the youngest U.S. president.

In both domestic and foreign policy Roosevelt was more active than most presidents before him. He set aside vast acres of forest reserves, brought antitrust actions against several giant corporations, signed the Pure Food and Drug Act of 1906, and pushed through a ban on railroad rebates. His foreign policy initiatives were far reaching. Roosevelt energetically promoted U.S. interests abroad, where his foreign policy watchword was "speak softly and carry a big stick." In 1903 he engineered the creation of the Republic of Panama, negotiated a treaty authorizing the United States to build the Panama Canal, and began construction. He won reelection easily in 1904. In his second term he negotiated the Treaty of Portsmouth, thereby ending the Russo-Japanese War in 1905. In 1906 he persuaded France and Germany to attend a conference at Algeciras to settle disputes over Morocco. His work earned him the Nobel Peace Prize.

After winning reelection in 1904, Roosevelt had proclaimed that he would not run again. He secured the 1908 Republican nomination for his protégé, William Howard Taft. For the next couple of years Roosevelt toured Africa and Europe. After returning to the United States, he quarreled publicly with President Taft and decided to run for president, in part to unseat the incumbent. Defeated at the Republican convention in June 1912, he ran as a candidate of the new Progressive (or Bull Moose) Party. The Progressives favored women's suffrage and other reform measures. Although Roosevelt ran well ahead of Taft, the split Republican vote enabled Democrat Woodrow Wilson to win the presidential election. In 1916 Roosevelt again ran unsuccessfully for the Republican presidential nomination.

Roosevelt remained politically active throughout his life. He strongly favored U.S. participation in World War I on the side of the Allies. In April 1917 he sought but was denied command of a division in World War I. He died on January 6, 1919.

See also *Progressivism*.

Michael Barone

BIBLIOGRAPHY

Beale, Howard K. *Theodore Roosevelt and the Rise of America to World Power*. Baltimore: Johns Hopkins University Press, 1984.
Blum, John M. *Republican Roosevelt*. 2d ed. Cambridge, Mass., and London: Harvard University Press, 1977.
Chessman, G. Wallace. *Theodore Roosevelt and the Politics of Power*. New York: Harper, 1969.
Gould, Lewis L. *The Presidency of Theodore Roosevelt*. Lawrence: University Press of Kansas, 1991.
Morris, Edmund. *The Rise of Theodore Roosevelt*. New York: Coward, McCann and Geoghegan, 1979.

Rousseau, Jean-Jacques

Geneva-born French philosopher, critic of modern philosophy and politics, and proponent of both extreme individualism and extreme collectivism. Rousseau (1712–1778) ran away from home at age sixteen and spent his youth wandering among various employments and cities of southern Europe before settling in Paris. The publication of his *First Discourse* (1750) made him an overnight sensation; twelve years later the publication of *Emile*, with its attack on revelation, led to his expulsion from France. He spent much of his remaining years fleeing persecution, real and imagined.

The philosophical and political revolution known as the Enlightenment had plenty of enemies, but Rousseau was its first defector. In criticizing it from within, using its own principles against itself, Rousseau inaugurated the "radical tradition" of Western political philosophy. He began the tendency, reproduced in every generation after him, to denounce modern humanity as fundamentally unhealthy, to blame its ills not on human nature or original sin but on the character of modern society, and to seek a solution through a still more radical application of the new ideas and principles that had given rise to that society.

Rousseau was both heir and opponent of the political ideas of Thomas Hobbes and John Locke. He shared their realist and activist orientation toward politics, their empiricist theory of knowledge, their egoist psychology, their rights-based individualism, and their contract theory of the state. But he argued that these principles fostered a society of restless, materialistic individuals who were enslaved to their rulers, in conflict with each other, and divided within their own souls. By interpreting and applying these principles more intransigently, Rousseau turned them squarely against their first authors and derived a radical (and seemingly self-contradictory) set of prescriptions that pointed simultaneously toward a highly collectivized, militantly patriotic, and rigidly democratic republic and toward a hyperindividualistic life of withdrawal from society and communion with nature and one's inner self.

To understand the inner logic of this complex Rousseauian rebellion, we shall begin with the central idea of Rousseau's philosophic system: the natural goodness of man.

The Argument for Natural Goodness

Human beings are wicked and unhappy, Rousseau maintains, but this condition is wholly the work of society. By nature, people are good, both for themselves and for others. They are good for themselves because they are at one with themselves and self-sufficient; they are good for others because they have no natural desire to harm others and lack the artificial passions, needs, and prejudices that now put their interests in conflict with others. Moreover, although altruism and morality are not natural, compassion is, and compassion leads people to avoid inflicting needless harm on others.

Rousseau argues for the doctrine of natural goodness in his *Discourse on the Origins of Inequality* (1755), in which he implicitly attacks the church's doctrine of original sin and explicitly confronts Hobbes's teaching on the state of nature. Hobbes had argued that human beings are selfish, asocial individuals, that their natural condition is a brutal state of war, and that absolute monarchy is the only form of government strong enough to create peace and order. Rousseau responds that precisely on the Hobbesian premise of human asociality, the state of nature and its inhabitant, "natural man," must have been good and not bad. He reasons that if one subtracts from man's present character all that could have been acquired only in society, what remains is a simple, self-sufficient creature, devoid of language, reason, foresight, and vanity, and thus lacking all the passions and social relations that, in Hobbes's account, produce enmity and war.

In support of his doctrine, Rousseau also appealed to the evidence of solitary introspection, which seemed to reveal that humans are fundamentally peaceful and contented creatures who take an elemental joy in the mere sentiment of their existence. What seems to have confirmed Rousseau in his belief in human goodness, however, was his new understanding of the origin of human evil. Only by systematically explaining existent human evil—which Rousseau considered to be great—in terms of the effects of society, could he free nature of all blame.

Rousseau's general argument runs as follows. If we accept the modern premise of human asociality, we must explore more fully than heretofore the possibility that all human evil is simply a derangement caused by the unnatural environment—civil society—into which human beings have evolved. Human asociality means that by nature we do not love or care for others and that we do not need them. We are naturally solitary and self-sufficient: that is why we are good. But society, by bringing us together and stimulating the development of our faculties and artificial desires, makes us need others without making us love them. This social condition of mutual selfish need is the true source of all the evil we do to others and to ourselves.

Society makes us need others by stimulating the development of three characteristics: foresight, which fills us with new cares and worries; imagination, which teaches us new hopes and pleasures; and vanity, which makes us obsessed with our rank and merit in the eyes of others. To provide for these new needs, humans eventually develop a system to divide up various tasks; this division of labor, by making all individuals into "specialists" who live by exchange, deals the final blow to natural self-sufficiency and institutionalizes mutual dependence. All subsequent "progress" of society only further heightens our faculties, our needs, and thus our interdependence.

Mutual dependence might not be a bad thing if human beings were naturally social and so inclined to love and help one another. But Rousseau is exploring the assumption that people are naturally selfish; and society only intensifies this egoism. Consequently, this social condition of mutual dependence, in which self-concerned individuals find themselves other-dependent, is unnatural and self-contradictory. Rousseau believes that in this fundamental "contradiction of the social system" he has discovered the true, social source of human evil, the historical cause that destroyed the natural goodness of human beings, making them exploitative toward others and divided against themselves.

Society makes people exploitative because the needy selfishness it fosters makes them need others more while loving them less. All are driven to use others, knowing that others are likewise driven to use them. In such an environment, people are forced by their self-interest to be enemies. This condition often compels individuals to make mutually beneficial agreements. But it also compels them to wish to avoid delivering on their part of the agreement. It is to this end that the strong devote all their strength and the weak all their ruses. In short, society is a community of secret enemies: it is formed and held together by each individual's need to use the others. It thus systematically forces everyone to be deceitful and exploitative.

At the same time, society makes individuals bad for themselves. Social men are all actors and hypocrites; they are divided against themselves by the contradiction between their intense self-concern and the obsession with others that this very selfishness necessitates. As other-directed egoists, they spend their lives serving and manipulating others precisely because they care only about themselves.

In sum, civil society produces and builds upon mutual selfish dependence and, in so doing, compels people to falsify and divide themselves in a constant effort to ma-nipulate and exploit others. Because this structural contradiction in society explains all the evil we now observe in human beings, it is unnecessary to suppose them evil by nature. Impelled by this evidence and his other inferences, Rousseau concluded that man was naturally good.

Rousseau's Two Solutions

Rousseau's analysis of the problem of human evil has revolutionary implications for its solution. Generally, by arguing that all evil arises from the effects of society, Rousseau transforms the problem into a social or historical issue, whereas before it had seemed a natural or divine one. This change raised radical and potentially totalitarian hopes—albeit less in Rousseau than in thinkers who followed him—that through political action one might transform the human condition itself.

More specifically, by tracing evil to the contradictory social condition of mutual dependence, Rousseau's analysis points rigorously to two diametrically opposite solutions. The contradiction of selfish other-directedness can be resolved either by making individuals wholly self-concerned and self-dependent or wholly other-concerned and other-directed. People must be either totally separated or totally united, but they must never depend upon others while caring only for themselves. Thus Rousseau's search for solutions branches into two opposite ideals: extreme collectivism and extreme individualism.

The Collectivist Solution

The collectivist solution is the subject of Rousseau's political writings, especially the *Social Contract* and the *Discourse on Political Economy*. Its overall strategy is to eliminate the phenomenon of selfish dependence by eliminating human selfishness, at least to the extent possible. To this end, Rousseau makes a variety of proposals designed to rework our malleable human nature, to transform naturally selfish individuals into patriotic citizens who love and live for the community. These proposals include smallness of size of the political unit (akin to the Greek city-state), relative equality and homogeneity of the population, an agrarian economic base, public education that cultivates virtue and patriotism more than talents, strict republican morals, patriotic public festivals, a civil religion, and censorship of the arts and sciences.

These institutions—both in their moralizing intention and in their invasive effect—involve a clear break with the "limited government" of liberal political theory. Indeed, they are consciously modeled on the practice of the ancient republics, especially Sparta and Rome. Yet Rousseau's return to ancient practice, combined as it is with modern theories of the radical asociality and malleability of human nature, constitutes something new and portentous. It is not altogether unfair to say that, in his conception of the state as an instrument for overcoming human nature, Rousseau planted the first seeds of modern totalitarianism.

Still, Rousseau, a fierce opponent of every form of oppression, was fully aware of the dangers posed by a state powerful and meddlesome enough to accomplish the crucial task of transforming men into citizens. To counteract this danger, he proposed to maximize the power of the citizenry over the state by placing the sovereign power in the hands of what he called the "general will." The meaning of this most famous Rousseauian institution is notoriously obscure. It can best be approached by taking up Rousseau's formal doctrine of the state from the beginning.

Because human beings are by nature asocial and arational, the state does not exist by nature and there are no natural titles to rule. For essentially the same reasons, there are no natural rules of justice or natural law. In making the latter claim, Rousseau brings to completion a crucial and fateful tendency of early modern thought: he liberates politics and morality from nature, indeed from all higher or transcendent standards.

Given the absence of natural rule and natural law, and given the state of war that prevails in their absence in the final stage of the state of nature, human beings are compelled to create the state through the conclusion of a social contract. The ruling power thus created must be "sovereign" in the strict sense: it freely creates the rules of morality, without reference to any higher or external standard. It makes things just, by commanding them, or unjust, by forbidding them.

But how can it be safe to create so free and awesome a power, and where should it be lodged? Rousseau argues that, paradoxically, the sovereign freedom of this power is the key to its safety. Liberated from the need to do justice to our natural inequality and individual uniqueness, the social contract is free to impose an artificial equality and conventional equivalence. In so doing, it makes the state a homogeneous unity that can be ruled through general laws, which, coming from all, apply identically to each. These laws are the expression of the general will: the will of the whole community regarding the community as a whole.

Consider, for example, a state of five individuals. If one rules, it is a monarchy; if two, an aristocracy; if three or more, a democracy. Each of these traditional forms of government involves the rule of a part over the whole and thus easily can become tyrannical. But if the five agree to be governed by general rules on which all vote and that apply equally to each, there is no longer the rule of a part—of some over others—but of all over each: the general will. This will, although it may be mistaken regarding what is good, cannot be tyrannical or ill intentioned because no one wishes to harm himself or herself. The general will, then, should be made sovereign.

To this end, Rousseau proposes that the laws be made by an assembly of the people in which all have the right to vote. But he knows that factions in the assembly can easily prevent the general will from being expressed and that supplemental institutions, tailored to local needs and conditions, must be added to ensure the right outcome. These supplemental institutions include the requirement of more than a simple majority for passing laws, the proper management of subpolitical groups (clans, parties, interest groups), the artful apportionment of votes among the different segments of the population, and, above all, the creation of a virtuous, or patriotic, citizenry.

Because extraordinary wisdom would be required to arrange all these elements properly, Rousseau suggests that the main body of the laws must be drafted by a great legislator and then ratified by the people. Furthermore, he argues that the executive power, which enforces the laws made by the sovereign general will, ideally should be placed in the hands of an elective aristocracy. This executive, he implies, should attempt indirectly to lead and improve the people, much as the legislator does at the beginning. In these ways, Rousseau tempers the extreme egalitarianism of his primary principles and, without granting special rights to virtue or wisdom, grants them a special role in the state.

A healthy political order, in Rousseau's view, is extremely rare and difficult, to be found only a few times in ancient history and scarcely at all since. In the modern world, he believed, the predominance of large nation-states, the rise of materialistic individualism, and the combination of atheism and universalistic religion (Christianity) had all but destroyed the possibility of genuine republican morals. Accordingly, Rousseau was a historical pessimist with few hopes for the political improvement of the large monarchies of Europe, notwithstanding the revolutionary role that his writings would play shortly after his death.

Ultimately, his political writings illustrate the tragic tensions and contradictions that beset all political life as such: the conflict between the need for transformative political power and the inevitable abuse of that power, or between the need for freedom and equality and the need for superior wisdom or virtue. These inevitable shortcomings of the collectivist solution encouraged Rousseau to turn to the individualist solution.

The Individualist Solution

If human beings cannot be wholly united, they must be wholly separated, to avoid the corrupting effects of selfish dependence. Obviously, this solution is not practicable for the vast majority but works only for the rare, gifted individual—the solitary philosopher or artist—as exemplified by Rousseau himself. Indeed, this way of life is elaborated primarily in Rousseau's autobiographical writings: the *Confessions; Rousseau, Judge of Jean-Jacques;* and, above all, the *Reveries of a Solitary Walker.* These works describe how Rousseau, by dint of philosophic genius and extraordinary strength of soul, freed himself from the false needs and hopes that arise in society and enslave us to it. He withdrew from society to live in natural freedom, unity, and goodness as did natural man, immersing his soul in the sweet and simple plenitude of the "sentiment of existence." But his faculties, artificially extended in society, also took him beyond natural man. He expanded his existence over the communities of kindred spirits painted for him in reveries by his highly developed artistic imagination, and he contemplated and identified with the spectacle of nature.

In *Emile,* his treatise on education, Rousseau presents a more accessible and egalitarian, if also less perfect, form of the individualistic solution by showing how the ordinary individual, without superior qualities of mind or character, might remain relatively healthy and happy even within society if reared from birth with the proper method. Emile is brought up in total spontaneity and freedom, without ever being submitted to the overt will or command of another human being. Thus his natural independence and self-directedness is preserved. But all along, his tutor, by manipulating the physical environment, supervises and controls Emile's every experience. The tutor uses this power to fabricate for Emile a limited sociality that makes him genuinely care for others, and so refrain from using them, while still leaving him whole within himself. For this purpose, the tutor makes primary use of two natural but highly malleable impulses: compassion and sex.

As Emile matures, the tutor teaches him to read hearts and to see the weakness and suffering that people hide behind their masks of respectability and cheerfulness. So, when the age of vanity, envy, and competition arrives, Emile, seeing and responding to the inner man, will feel only a generous compassion. At the same time, the tutor endeavors to delay, purify, and elevate Emile's sexual desires, sublimating them into love. Emile will become a romantic lover and then a bourgeois family man, possessing a moral idealism composed in equal parts of lofty erotic longings and solid patriarchal interests. This complex idealism will culminate in a love of God. Thus, living with his family in rustic retreat, Emile will be protected by relative isolation, compassion, love, and religion from all tendency to selfish other-dependence, the social source of human evil.

Ultimately, Rousseau's individualist writings, like his political ones, illustrate the intractability of the problem more than they provide a practicable solution. In civilized society the healthy individual, it seems, must either be a philosopher or be raised by one. Still, through this side of his teaching, Rousseau became the ideologist of such institutions of modern individualism as romanticism, bohemian intellectualism, the sentimental and child-centered family, the cult of compassion, and the pursuit of authentic selfhood through introspection and self-disclosure.

See also *Censorship; Communitarianism; Hobbes, Thomas; Montesquieu; Natural law; Religion, Civil; Revolution, French; Spinoza, Benedict de; Tocqueville, Alexis de.*

Arthur M. Melzer

BIBLIOGRAPHY

Gildin, Hilail. *Rousseau's Social Contract: The Design of the Argument.* Chicago: University of Chicago Press, 1983.

Kelley, Christopher. *Rousseau's Exemplary Life: The Confessions as Political Philosophy.* Ithaca, N.Y.: Cornell University Press, 1987.

Masters, Roger D. *The Political Philosophy of Rousseau.* Princeton: Princeton University Press, 1968.

Melzer, Arthur M. *The Natural Goodness of Man: On the System of Rousseau's Thought.* Chicago: University of Chicago Press, 1990.

Shklar, Judith N. *Men and Citizens: A Study of Rousseau's Social Theory.* Cambridge: Cambridge University Press, 1969.

Starobinski, Jean. *Jean-Jacques Rousseau: Transparency and Obstruction.* Translated by Arthur Goldhammer. Chicago: University of Chicago Press, 1988.

Russia, Post-Soviet

Known as the Russian Federation, the largest, richest, and most powerful of the fifteen successor states to the Soviet Union, which broke apart in 1991. The territory of the Russian Federation stretches across eleven time zones, from the Baltic Sea to the Pacific Ocean, and from the Arctic Ocean to the Black Sea. Russia's population of some 150 million consists of a majority of Russians and includes substantial numbers of other ethnic groups, such as Bashkirs, Chechens, Jews, Ossetians, Tatars, Ukrainians, and Yakuts.

Lacking natural frontiers in both Europe and Asia, Russia throughout its history has repeatedly found itself at war with its neighbors. Thus post-Soviet Russia inherited a nostalgia for empire and many undemocratic values, habits, and routines from its czarist and Soviet past. Establishing a robust democratic system therefore was bound to be an uphill struggle.

Democracy in post-Soviet Russia has been unconsolidated at best; at worst, it has been an empty claim. Given the brevity, the fluidity, and the novelty of multiparty democracy there, it is hardly surprising that political life in Russia is marked by contradictory trends and an uncommon measure of uncertainty regarding the prospects for democracy. Although the departure from Soviet norms has been enormous, by many criteria the gap between Russian practice and democratic theory remains vast.

The Rocky Road of Democratization

The process of transforming the political system from the totalitarian model to a more democratic one began in the years of Mikhail Gorbachev's leadership (1985–1991). Accurately described as democratization, that process included such landmarks as the elimination of censorship in the pursuit of glasnost (openness) and the appearance of differing and competing publications; the mushrooming of literally thousands of grassroots organizations, some of which gave rise to social movements and ultimately political parties; and the abolition of Article 6 of the Soviet constitution of 1977, which had affirmed the Communist Party's monopoly of power. In spite of their serious deficiencies, the parliamentary elections of 1989 and 1990, and the Russian presidential election of June 12, 1991 (which brought Boris Yeltsin into office, a year after the Russian Federation had declared its sovereignty within the frag-

menting Soviet Union), were further milestones in this process.

The democratization process was incomplete in that it left essentially unchanged many of the old institutions and attitudes toward decision making, accountability, and representation. Furthermore, it was bounded by the continued commitment of the Gorbachev leadership to the Communist Party and its role in society and, more broadly, to the guidance and control of change from above. In August 1991 a powerful coalition of civilian and military leaders—including the vice president, the head of the secret police, the defense minister, and the minister of the interior—attempted a coup d'état to reverse the reforms and, in particular, to forestall the adoption of a new union treaty that would have given the constituent republics of the Soviet Union considerably greater autonomy.

The defeat of the coup in the name of duly constituted authority signaled, and in turn contributed to, the collapse of the Gorbachev regime, of the Soviet Union itself, and of the Communist Party, with its vast network of incumbents and privileges. In Russia the prompt suspension of the ruling party and the seizure of its records and property by the Yeltsin regime both dramatized and pushed forward the democratization process. The process soon stalled, however. On the one hand, the "democrats" who had come to power had not been prepared to take over and were not sure what to do; on the other, resistance soon developed—in the bureaucracy, in parliament, and elsewhere—to the institutionalization of a new democratic order.

Prior to the coup, "democrats" (and "democracy") had been the label used (by both the democrats and their enemies) to identify the political universe of anticommunists of all stripes. An untidy usage, which lumped together a vast variety of reform communists, dissidents, and authoritarians of the right, it did provide the basis for the broad coalition that, under the name of Democratic Russia, rallied diverse popular elements in 1990–1991 to ensure Yeltsin's June 1991 electoral victory. With the collapse of the communist system in the second half of 1991, the common cause of the democrats—their antiregime orientation—lost its reason for being. What was meant by a democratic orientation thereafter was much harder to tell.

One reason democratic reforms in Russia stalled in 1992–1993 was the virtual deadlock between the executive branch (in this instance, the proponent of further reforms) and the legislatures (both the larger Congress of

Post-Soviet Russia

People's Deputies and the smaller Supreme Soviet of the Russian Federation). Indeed, the parliament—elected before the collapse of the Soviet Union—comprised a substantial cohort of former Communist officials who not only feared losing their positions and privileges if a new constitution was adopted or a new election held but also opposed political and economic reforms.

Given its impatience with the near paralysis of the legislature, the Yeltsin administration was increasingly tempted to act by decree, laying itself open to charges of usurpation of power. Thus the gridlock between the branches of the central government acquired overtones of a constitutional confrontation, in addition to a political-ideological tug-of-war between the dominant groups in the two branches. With political ambitions of his own, the speaker of the parliament, Ruslan Khasbulatov, led an effort to impeach President Yeltsin that came perilously close to succeeding. The newly established Constitutional Court, a welcome innovation, wound up being sadly politicized and drawn into the duel.

Crisis, Elections, and Constitution

The Yeltsin team found encouragement in the results of the national referendum held on April 25, 1993, which in substance gave President Yeltsin a vote of confidence. When a new stalemate developed, Yeltsin on September 21 dissolved the parliament and called for new elections. A substantial fraction of deputies, supported by Vice President Aleksandr Rutskoi, refused to comply and instead called for an armed strike against Moscow television and city government. The entire Russian government found itself in considerable jeopardy and confusion, and only after some hesitation and soul searching did army and secret police contingents on October 3–4, 1993, obey Yeltsin's order to shell and seize the parliament building and place the remaining deputies under arrest.

Although carried out in the name of democratic reforms, the traumatic siege and capture of the parliament

Russian soldiers stand guard in front of the burned-out parliament building in Moscow in October 1993.

building scarcely served to enhance the democratic reputation of the Yeltsin regime. If the ensuing parliamentary elections and the simultaneous plebiscite to approve the new constitution, on December 12, were intended to provide a validation of the October operation, the results were a troubling disappointment to the democrats.

The new constitution of the Russian Federation, hastily rewritten by Yeltsin's staff, provides for a pluralist political system and an elaborate array of civil and human rights, including the right to run for public office, the right of assembly, and the right to own private property. It establishes a popularly elected presidency and a bicameral parliament, with the lower house (the State Duma) elected by universal suffrage—one-half its members by party lists, the other half by single-member districts—and the upper house (the Council of the Federation) composed of two deputies from each of Russia's eighty-eight regions and republics. Party results of December 1993 are listed in Table 1.

The constitution is heavily weighted toward a presidential system, minimizing the role of parliament even in legislative and budgetary matters and greatly complicating the process of amending the constitution. It also omits the Treaty of Federation, which would formalize the relationship between the federal center and the constituent parts. Opinion on the desirability of ratifying the constitution was greatly divided among democrats; its major support came from the pro-Yeltsin Russia's Choice coalition and from Vladimir Zhirinovsky's extremist Liberal Democratic Party. The official count indicated approval of the constitution by some 58 percent of those voting; only some 54 percent of those eligible to vote took part in the plebiscite. In fact, later reports suggested that the figures had been doctored, but the major political groupings were prepared to accept the official results.

The Failure of the Democrats

The major disappointment of the election results, for the democrats, was the poor performance of the reformers and the upsurge of antidemocratic groupings, both on the far left (Communist Party of Russia) and on the far right (above all, Zhirinovsky's group, since some of the other "national-patriotic" groups had been barred because of their antiregime position in the October crisis).

The apparent weakening of the democratic forces between 1991 and 1995 had a variety of causes. For one thing, the layer of democrats who had been in the forefront of politics during and after the coup of August 1991 turned out to be unexpectedly thin. For another, the following three years had given others time to organize, including both the national-patriotic forces of the far right and the resurgent neocommunists and their allies. Often their efforts produced a new antiregime amalgam opposing democracy, economic reform, and the West. Likewise, the years 1992–1993 witnessed an acceleration of forces within the Russian Federation—both regional and ethnic—defying, or more often simply ignoring, the political center. Moreover, the oftentimes arbitrary, boorish, inconsistent, and petty behavior of Yeltsin and some of his close advisers did not help.

The democrats came to be widely identified in the public mind with growing chaos, crime, and ineffectiveness; with a serious decline in living conditions; and with the Western powers, whose help had proved to be disappointing. Western models and values were increasingly perceived as faulty, unsuitable, or at best a mixed bag in bringing to Russia—along with fast food and comput-

TABLE 1. Russian Parliamentary Seat Distribution, in Elections of December 12, 1993 (by party)

Party (Leader)	State Duma[a] (Lower chamber)		Council of the Federation[b] (Upper chamber)
	By party lists	In single-member districts[c]	
DEMOCRATIC PARTIES			
Russia's Choice (Yegor Gaidar)	40	56	40
Yabloko (Grigori Yavlinsky)	20	13	3
Unity and Concord (Sergei Shakhrai)	18	9	4
Movement for Democratic Reform (Anatoli Sobchak)	0	8	1
CENTER / MODERATES			59
Democratic Party (Nikolai Travkin)	14	7	—
Civic Union (Arkadi Volsky)	0	18	—
Women of Russsia (Alevtina Fedulova)	21	4	—
FAR LEFT AND FAR RIGHT			22
Agrarian Party (Ivan Rybkin)	21	26	—
Communist Party (Gennadi Zyuganov)	32	33	—
Liberal Democratic Party (Vladimir Zhirinovsky)	59	11	—
OTHERS, INDEPENDENTS	—	34	47
TOTAL	225	219	176

SOURCES: ITAR/TASS, December 25, 1993; and Radio Free Europe/Radio Liberty, *Research Report* 3 (January 1994).
a. Voters in each of 225 electoral districts elected one representative by name to represent their district in the State Duma. All voters also cast a second vote for a party by name; 225 Duma seats were apportioned to the parties according to the proportion of this vote they received. Six candidates subsequently were disqualified.

b. Voters in each of 88 territorial jurisdictions elected 2 members to the 176-seat Council of the Federation. A majority of council members claimed no specific party affiliation.
c. Includes independents who later adhered to a party group.

ers—pornography, prostitution, and privilege, in a dramatic departure from Soviet ideals of social justice. In the electoral campaign the democrats were aloof, smug, divided, and unable to establish rapport with the rank and file.

Finally, it became clear that, while the old Communist Party of the Soviet Union was officially gone, many of its former officials and adherents had found new and often powerful and comfortable niches in the government or the economy. These people constituted a new underground nomenklatura (the term for the Soviet office-holding elite) that was informally but effectively obstructing the country's transition to a democratic regime.

Nevertheless, Russia had taken tremendous strides. Transitions to democracy are bound to take time: nowhere have institutions been invented, processes agreed on, and behaviors learned overnight. Nor should one minimize the habit-forming impact of a free press, television, and radio and of open policy debates by rival speakers and parties. Although the danger of mass violence remains, especially if economic conditions deteriorate fur-

ther, the transformation of the Soviet system has taken place with a remarkably low level of bloodshed and coercion. Finally, there were—for democrats—encouraging grassroots developments in some municipalities that led to the victory of self-styled democrats in local elections.

Many of these problems were highlighted by the crisis occasioned in December 1994 by the forcible conquest of Chechnya, in the Northern Caucasus, where a separatist movement under Dzhokar Dudaev had defied Moscow's authority. It illustrated the extent of executive dominance, the prevalence of extremist advisers around the president and their erratic miscalculation, the weakness of the democrats, a politicization of the army's command, and—in the aftermath of the bloody fighting and the crisis of confidence in the country's leadership—a lack of attractive alternatives to Yeltsin.

Russia as a Democracy

A stable democracy, it has been suggested, must be institutionalized and elicit the informed cooperation of all involved. In these terms, Russia has not qualified as a stable democracy. Its governmental institutions are a messy mix, some dating back to the old regime, coexisting with new improvisations. There is only partial acceptance of the government's authority. The notion of citizens' rights and obligations has yet to be clearly articulated, let alone accepted by the population.

Intermediary associations—essential to political competition—are emerging but are still at an early stage. In the public mind, political parties remain suspect and unattractive. The multiplicity of political organizations is largely based on ideological postures or personalities, but organizations are beginning to appear based on ethnicity, territorial (regional) interests, and economic interests, such as the new stratum of successful business owners. The mass of workers is still without an institutional voice.

If democracy requires not only majority rule (however circumscribed) but also the protection of minority rights, here again current practice leaves something to be desired. More broadly, there is a lack of protection for individual as well as for group (and especially ethnic) rights, giving rise to widespread confusion regarding the relative priority of entitlements. The problem lies not only in the codification of rights but also in their implementation. In the absence of an independent judiciary and the rule of law, intolerance is bound to be translated into discrimination.

Finally, it is a matter of some debate to what extent civil servants, managers of enterprises, or military and police officers can subvert or sabotage decisions of elected officials and whether they could be counted on to support the legitimate authority in future crises.

Attitudes Toward Democracy

The discovery of popular attitudes toward democracy is subject to the familiar vagaries of survey research and opinion polling, as well as the particular hazards of sampling in as vast and varied—and unfamiliar—an environment as post-Soviet Russia. Moreover, it is virtually impossible to separate democratic values from attitudes toward current policies and particular actors. Still, although the results are contradictory and bitterly debated, certain findings appear to be solidly based.

Although there is a widespread yearning for a strong leader, as part of the broader quest for law and order, both among elites and in the population at large, this desire is not incompatible with a commitment to democracy. No

doubt the notion of democracy for many respondents defies specification; preference for democracy does not reduce intense intolerance of certain ethnic, demographic, or political groups; and the desire for democracy coexists with a lingering antipathy to all political parties (a product of both Soviet experience and post-Soviet pragmatism).

The most sophisticated surveys, as well as exit polls at the time of elections and referendums in the post-Soviet years, show a predominant pro-democracy sentiment, although in the mid-1990s both cynicism and extremism were clearly on the rise. It is interesting that, despite the strong concern about crime and violence, the suspension of civil liberties for the sake of combating organized crime, in June 1994, aroused widespread opposition from both supporters and opponents of the Yeltsin regime. No less important, democratic values correlate significantly with lower age and better education—a plausible finding, given the more extensive Soviet exposure of older age groups, and one that may justifiably be seen as a source of optimism.

The significance of these findings must not be exaggerated. They tell us nothing about the depth of democratic values or about the extent to which people expressed support of democracy because it was fashionable to do so. But they do make an important point in the protracted debate over Russian political culture. Russia has a long past in which parliamentary and other democratic institutions found little place. Yet, on the basis of contemporary survey research, one may at the very least assert that (perhaps because of economic development, educational attainments, or other changes that have intervened in this century) such a legacy need not be an impregnable obstacle to the growth and rooting of democracy in Russia. By the same token, democratic values would not necessarily forestall an authoritarian takeover in the future.

A Balance Sheet

Though halting, incomplete, and inconsistent, Russia's evolution toward democracy has been real. For those who had insisted that Russians were not culturally or historically prepared to understand, assimilate, or practice democracy, the events of recent years have provided sobering correctives. Events have also shown that the transition to democracy is a far more complex and unsteady process than was formerly surmised—especially in as vast a land, as heterogeneous a population, as catastrophic an economy, as isolated a polity, and as authoritarian a tradition as those of post-Soviet Russia. Such a transition is particularly difficult when democracy is identified, in the popular mind, with a number of disappointing experiences. The main obstacles to stable democracy in Russia might be summed up with the following points.

There is a general failure on the part of all branches of the government to educate both the bureaucracy and the population at large about the meaning of democracy, either by example or by instruction. Indeed, there remains a widespread failure to understand what democracy is, let alone to teach it in and out of the schools.

The population lacks the common values, myths, and symbols that would serve to unite people as dedicated members of a new democratic community. Citizens have no experience with democratic procedure, including in particular the priority of process over outcome and tolerance of heterodoxy. Also lacking is a sense of citizenship, with its customary rights and duties.

Many people have become impatient with the new system, partly out of a mistaken assumption that democracy is bound to bring a variety of benefits beyond the dimension of politics (in particular, wealth or at least consumer goods). The "democratic" experience to date is associated, in many minds, with a striking increase in crime, corruption, and anarchy, a staggering decline in per capita gross domestic product, and a dramatic loss in international standing.

The drive of regions, ethnicities, and localities to maximize their autonomy frequently involves an effective refusal to accept the central government's authority in such matters as tax collection and military service. Regions and republics also insist on dealing directly with foreign governments and companies when desired. This is a set of challenges not easily resolved, both because of the problem of states' rights in a federation and because of the tension between rival ethnic and regional pulls.

The structure of the central government is not conducive to real democracy. Both the new constitution and the political reality permit the president and his considerable staff to rule in relatively arbitrary fashion, without effective constraints on executive authority (except for criticism in parliament or the media). Although this presidential authority responds to a widespread yearning for a firm hand and for political stability, it opens the door to unchecked abuse and to the influence of unelected pressure groups—especially economic and military groupings—and of individuals of dubious qualifications. On the other hand, authoritarian tendencies are mitigated by the pervasive ineffectiveness of government.

Finally, the failure to institutionalize a proper separation of powers is particularly blatant in the virtual absence of an independent judiciary as a coequal branch of government. Even within the executive branch the prime minister and the cabinet have become increasingly dependent on the wishes and whims of the president and his staff.

See also *Gorbachev, Mikhail Sergeyevich; Russia, Pre-Soviet; Union of Soviet Socialist Republics; Yeltsin, Boris Nikolayevich.*

Alexander Dallin

BIBLIOGRAPHY

Brudny, Yizhak. "The Dynamics of 'Democratic Russia,' 1990–1993." *Post-Soviet Affairs* 9 (April-June 1993).

Colton, Timothy J., and Robert H. Legvold, eds. *After the Soviet Union.* New York: Norton, 1992; London: Norton, 1993.

Dallin, Alexander, ed. *Political Parties in Russia.* Berkeley: University of California International and Area Studies, 1993.

Dawisha, Karen, and Bruce Parrott. *Russia and the New States of Eurasia.* New York: Cambridge University Press, 1994.

Fish, Steven M. *Democracy from Scratch: Opposition and Regime in the New Russian Revolution.* Princeton: Princeton University Press, 1995.

Gibson, James L., et al. "Emerging Democratic Values in Soviet Political Culture." In *Public Opinion and Regime Change: The New Politics of Post-Soviet Societies,* edited by Arthur H. Miller et al. Boulder, Colo.: Westview Press, 1993.

Lapidus, Gail, ed. *The New Russia.* Boulder, Colo.: Westview Press, 1994.

McFaul, Michael, and Sergei Markov. *The Troubled Birth of Russian Democracy.* Stanford, Calif.: Hoover Institution Press, 1993.

Schmitter, Philippe C., and Terry Karl. "The Conceptual Travels of Transitologists and Consolidologists." *Slavic Review* 53 (spring 1994): 173–185.

Russia, Pre-Soviet

The large region, then state, in eastern Europe and northern Asia (from 882 to 1917), which had a long and difficult experience with democracy, even before the trials of the Soviet period. The first state structure among the East Slavs was created by Viking marauders along the Dnieper River in ninth-century Eurasia. The glorious inheritance of the resulting polity, known as Kiev Rus', has been contested between Russian and, more recently, Ukrainian scholars. Each of the two nationalities claims to be the rightful heir of Kiev Rus'.

Kiev Rus' and Muscovy

Kiev Rus' was a federation of commercial city-states that also controlled substantial territory beyond the river routes of the region. The lifeblood of Kiev Rus' was international commerce. The city-states of the Kievan federation, although dominated by Scandinavian and Slavic elites, had democratic elements in their political structure, most notably the *veche*, an urban popular assembly bearing a certain resemblance to citizens' assemblies in classical Greece and even to the New England town meeting. The *veche* seems to have derived from the earliest period of East Slavic history, but it did not become politically significant in the cities of Kiev Rus' before the eleventh century.

The assembly achieved its greatest importance in Novgorod, a northern commercial city. There the status of the ruling prince, who was always selected from a non-Novgorod family, was virtually reduced to that of mercenary military commander whose role was defined contractually. The neighborhood-based urban assembly, which evolved into a large bicameral body, ran the city government and controlled the surrounding "empire." The surroundings consisted almost entirely of thinly populated lands useful largely for the trapping of fur-bearing animals, an important aspect of Novgorodian commerce. Novgorod eventually became the easternmost depot of the Hanseatic League, a medieval organization of commercial cities (including Bremen, Hamburg, and Lübeck) that stretched from London along the Baltic Sea to Kiev Rus'. Novgorod's government may be compared with that of some other Hanseatic cities or with those of Italian cities of a slightly later period.

Whether Novgorod's system was a true democracy has long been a matter of controversy. In the eighteenth and nineteenth centuries, radical and liberal critics of Russia's autocratic government frequently lamented the subjugation of Novgorod by Moscow, where monocratic government increasingly prevailed, in the fifteenth century. They denounced Czar Ivan III for extinguishing the citadel of indigenous Russian democracy. Soviet historians, by contrast, tended to regard Novgorod as a commercial oligarchy that was not very democratic. They stressed the rise of a kind of upper chamber within the *veche*, known as the Council of Lords, and the virtual monopoly of important city offices by the rich and powerful, in alliance with the influential Novgorodian church. However one estimates the democracy of such systems, the memory of the vital civic and commercial life of Kiev and Novgorod gave rise to traditions different from, and even opposed to, the powerful fact of autocratic Russian development.

Feuds among the rulers of Kiev Rus's principalities and shifting trade patterns weakened the federation, which was ultimately destroyed by the Mongol conquest of 1237–1240 and the subsequent occupation. As the Mongols' grasp of the region gradually slipped between 1390 and 1480, the rulers of the principality of Muscovy gained control of the region.

The Muscovite autocracy, a form of absolutism extreme in its theoretical claims, at least, is usually considered to have been consolidated by the mid-sixteenth century, in the reign of Czar Ivan IV, known as Ivan the Terrible (1533–1584). In Muscovite Russia the sort of representational "estates" organization often found in Western European monarchies, by which the crown negotiated with different groups of its subjects, was extremely weakly developed.

In particular contrast to Great Britain and its Parliament (but even to the French Estates General), the Russian Assembly of the Land (Zemsky sobor) never achieved any real independence in relation to the czar, nor was it ever able to serve as a rallying point for political or social interests other than those of the autocracy. Only a few of its meetings were even preceded by elections. Far more often the czar or his officials simply chose "representatives," who happened to be in Moscow, for information-gathering purposes. The body was never very influential, except during the so-called Time of Troubles (1598–1613), when dynastic struggles combined with invasions by Poland and Sweden threw Russia into chaos.

Among the many features of Russian cultural history, however, has been the episodic Russian effort to reinterpret the state's autocratic development. Slavophile and populist intellectuals in the nineteenth century often argued that early Russia was characterized by a variety of popular and conciliar organizations that brought the views of "the land" or even "the people" to the foot of the czar's throne, the Assembly of the Land being only the best known. But these are really ideological claims, based on very little substance. Some Soviet scholars counted many more meetings of the Assembly of the Land than their Western colleagues and even understood the Russian autocracy as an estate-representative monarchy between 1549 and 1684, but their views are extreme indeed for the modern period. The Assembly of the Land lapsed entirely in the second half of the seventeenth century, as the czars consolidated autocratic power after the Time of Troubles and its aftermath.

The Imperial Period

The "Westernizing" emperor, Peter the Great (1682–1725), may be said to have promoted the growth of liberal and radical points of view intimately (though often ambiguously) connected with democracy. But he did so by promoting a hegemony of European ideas and values in Russia that would bear democratic fruit only over the longer run. His deepest sympathies at the institutional level lay with European absolutism and, in a complicated sense of the term, with militarism. His military exertions and financial needs strengthened the hold of serfdom on Russia, and the country was scarcely more democratic at his death than before his succession.

Despite the well-known flirtation of Catherine the Great (1729–1796) with the French *philosophes* and the diffusion of Enlightenment ideas in court circles of the late eighteenth century, Russia's encounter with democratic ideas began only in her reign and was far from enjoying her approval. Her harsh treatment of Aleksandr Radishchev (1749–1802), author of Russia's first radical classic, *A Journey from St. Petersburg to Moscow* (1790), gave rise to the martyrology that would play a large role in the subsequent development of a Russian revolutionary movement.

Before the emancipation of the Russian serfs in 1861, Enlightenment points of view continued to spread among Russia's elite. They were very evident in the so-called Decembrist revolt of 1825. In that important event a group of aristocratic officers, inspired by a mix of French, English, and American ideas of liberalism, democracy, and constitutionalism, attempted to replace the new emperor, Nicholas I, with his brother Constantine.

In the aftermath of the Decembrists' failure, less activist and more romantic points of view, also Western in derivation, began to compete with the inheritance of the Enlightenment for the hearts and minds of Russia's increasingly Westernized upper class. The process resulted in the emergence of two points of view: those of the Slavophiles and the Westerners, or Westernizers. The Slavophiles created what the sociologically minded historian Andrzej Walicki called a "conservative utopia," based primarily on German romantic writings. They criticized the whole Westernization process, beginning with Peter the Great, and urged Russia to return to its proper historical path: religious and social communalism and patriarchalism. The Westernizers, by contrast, urged Russia to persevere along its path toward full membership in Western civilization. The most important of the Westernizers, furthermore, inspired by G. W. F. Hegel and his more left-wing followers, and eventually by Karl Marx, hoped for a drastically democratized Russia that would be a leader in a future democratic Europe.

In retrospect, both the Slavophile and the Westernizing points of view (which have proved strikingly durable in Russian culture) contained democratic elements but also dangers to democracy. The Slavophiles idealized "the people" and implicitly criticized the dynasty, but they were hostile to capitalism, markets, contractual thinking, and competition. The Westernizers were in theory radical democrats, but their visionary historicism was vulnerable to left-wing elitism and paternalism, visible already in the populist phase of the Russian revolutionary movement and particularly apparent in the rise of Bolshevism, which called for a vanguard of elite revolutionaries to lead the masses.

Meanwhile, the social and industrial structure of Russia began to change significantly after 1861. The emancipation of the serfs made it necessary for the government to undertake a sweeping series of measures known to non-Soviet scholars as the Great Reforms. In the course of a decade or more, the army was significantly democratized, the legal system was overhauled along British and French lines, new structures of urban administration and local government were created, and censorship was somewhat lessened. More or less simultaneously the government attempted to put its fiscal house in order and to create financial institutions that would make industrialization possible. Although the matter has recently been contested, most scholars still find that the industrialization that ensued in Russia was driven by state policy far more than was the case elsewhere in Europe. Late czarist economic policy foreshadowed the extreme centralism of the Soviet economic model and its emulators among the developing economies of the cold war era.

The End of Imperial Russia

Students of nineteenth-century Russia agree that what resulted from the interaction of so much reform activity was the beginning of civil society in Russia. Civil society

Czar Nicholas II and Czarina Alexandra pose with their entourage. Nicholas (reigned 1894–1917) was the last czar to rule Russia. He grudgingly instituted superficial democratic reforms following the Revolution of 1905, but never renounced absolutist principles or relinquished any substantial powers.

was late and slow in developing, no doubt, but it had shown real progress by 1914. The term *civil society* refers to a whole sphere of human activity, between the family and the state, and a set of private activities that are economic, social, and political in nature. Civil society in Russia meant the development of professions (comparable to those in Western Europe), of philanthropic and civic organizations, of private industry and business, and (after the 1905 revolution) of limited political parties and semi-parliamentary government.

To some scholars these developments suggested that after an extremely slow start, Russia was on the road to achieving a Western European type of modernity, in which democracy would play a key role. Only the catastrophe of World War I, they argued, prevented such a development. Others, such as the historian Leopold Haimson, viewed Russia's problems as too deep for such an op-

timistic evolutionary scenario. They argued that fundamental oppositions still existed between elite and nonelite Russia, between rural and urban Russia, between the tiny minority with significant political power and the vast majority with little or none.

Whether Russia's shattering defeat in World War I derailed what might otherwise have turned into a stable Russian democracy, or merely exacerbated virtually unresolvable conflicts, has been much debated and can never be known for certain. What we do know is that, in the chaos of defeat and revolution, the monarchy and the privileged groups that supported it were unable to withstand a militantly leftist and authoritarian challenge. We also know that the new elite that was formed under Vladimir Ilich Lenin and Joseph Stalin was likewise not up to the task of creating either democracy or stability in Russia. The road to what Mikhail Gorbachev poignantly called the "common European home" will be long and winding; the end is not in sight.

See also *Kerensky, Alexander Fedorovich; Russia, Post-Soviet; Union of Soviet Socialist Republics.*

Abbott Gleason

BIBLIOGRAPHY

Clowes, Edith, Samuel Kassow, and James L. West. *Between Tsar and People.* Princeton: Princeton University Press, 1991.

Freeze, Gregory. "The Soslovie (Estate) Paradigm and Russian Social History." *American Historical Review* 91 (1986): 11–36.

Lincoln, W. Bruce. *The Great Reforms.* DeKalb: Northern Illinois University Press, 1990.

Malia, Martin. *Alexander Herzen and the Birth of Russian Socialism, 1812–1855.* Cambridge: Harvard University Press, 1960.

Pipes, Richard. *Russia under the Old Regime.* New York: Scribner's, 1974; Harmondsworth: Penguin Books, 1990.

Rogger, Hans. *Russia in the Age of Modernisation and Revolution, 1881–1917.* London and New York: Longman, 1983.

Rwanda

See *Africa, Subsaharan*

INDEX

INDEX

Denaturalization, 592
Deng Xiaoping, 209, 286–287, 365, 749
Denmark, 452
    candidate selection and recruitment, 164, 165
    censorship, 190, 191
    cultural background, 1103–1104
    democratization, 1104, 1105, 1363
    European Union membership, 455, 462, 476, 1028, 1107
    German relations, 524, 525
    government formation and policy making, 257, 458, 459, 461
    Icelandic politics, 1106–1107
    measures of democracy, 818
    modern democratic practice, 1107–1108
    monarchy, 844, 1055
    Norwegian politics, 843, 1447
    political parties, 457
    political structures and practices, 309, 417, 456, 476, 738, 1055, 1302
    referendum and initiative, 1044
    social welfare effort, 460
    tax revolt, 1108, 1213, 1218
    taxation, 1215, 1216
    voting behavior, 1348, 1351
    voting rights, 1105, 1355, 1356
    women's suffrage and other rights, 1381, 1383, 1384, 1386
    World War II, 1107, 1395
Depression, 1930s, 489, 747
    Argentina, 71
    Bolivia, 65
    Brazil, 135
    China, 206
    Colombia, 260
    economic policies and, 804, 1083
    Germany, 229, 525–526
    Japan, 664
    Latin America, 827
    Poland, 949
    political socialization affected by, 937, 1156
    Puerto Rico, 180
    Scandinavia, 1108
    United States, 1191
Deregulation, 1047–1048
Deroin, Jeanne, 487
Derrida, Jacques, 82, 319, 992
Descartes, René, 434, 567, 1071, 1112
Despotism
    Africa, 36
    Burke views, 147–149
    mass society as, 814, 815
    regime characteristics, 69, 104, 850, 1072
    utilitarianism and, 1335
Dessouki, Ali, 645
De-Stalinization, 329, 950, 1297
Destourien Socialist Party, 1269
Determinism, 727
Deutsche, Karl, 333
Development, economic. See Economic development
Development of the English Constitution (Ostrogorski), 901
Developmental democracy, 784
Developmental state, 246, 803
Devolution, 335
Dewey, John, 206, 356, 390, 571, 816, 924, 993–996, 1004, 1250
Dewey, Thomas E., 405, 871
Dewey Commission of Inquiry, 572
Dhlakama, Afonso, 22

d'Hondt method, 936, 1011–1014
Dia, Mamadou, 1117
Diagne, Blaise, 1117
Diamond, Larry, 49, 353, 388
Díaz, Porfirio, 826, 1076
Dicey, A. V., 139
Dickens, Charles, 403
Dictatorship of the proletariat, 1150, 1152
Dictatorships
    dissident movements, 361–367
    economic development hindered by, 802
    legislatures in, 739
    military rule, and transition to democracy, 836–841
    modern rise of, 722, 765
    regime characteristics, 104, 350, 357–359
    revolutionary overthrow, 1076
    Roman Republic, 254, 727
    socioeconomic development in, 388
Diderot, Denis, 1130
Diefenbaker, John, 161
Dienstbier, Jiří, 330
Diets, 444
Diffusion, 36
Digger movement, 981
Dilthey, Wilhelm, 80, 566
Diodotus, 1243
Diop, Mahjmout, 1118
Diouf, Abdou, 1118–1120
Diplomacy. See Foreign policy
Direct democracy, 814
    anarchism and, 61
    features and mechanism, 278, 1278–1281
    France, 498
    Gandhi preference, 522
    representative democracy compared, 319
    teledemocracy, 278, 824–825, 1281
    See also Participatory democracy
Dirksen, Everett, 996
Disability discrimination, 397
Discourse ethics, 319
Discourse on Political Economy (Rousseau), 1087
Discourse on the Origin of Inequality (Rousseau), 307, 566, 1086, 1255
Discourse on the Sciences and Arts (Rousseau), 1062
Discourses on Davila (Adams), 12
Discourses on Livy (Machiavelli), 218, 251, 321, 783, 1052, 1053, 1059, 1343
Discrimination. See Affirmative action; Racism
Disraeli, Benjamin, 290, 292–293, 359–360, 1364
Dissidents, 184, 1260
    Aung San Suu Kyi, 96–97
    China, 208–210
    country comparisons, 361–367
    Sakharov, 1101–1102
    Soviet Union, 504, 1290, 1297, 1298–1299
Distributive justice, 686–689, 1139–1142
Distributive politics, 742
District of Columbia, 199, 410, 411, 915, 916, 996
Districting
    African American representation, 1239
    Canada, 160
    country comparisons, 367–372, 397, 457
    cube law, 327–328
    Duverger's rule, 380–382
    gerrymandering, 370–371, 412, 418, 421, 791
    Hungary, 579, 580
    majority rule, minority rights, 790–791
    malapportionment, 412, 418
Divided government, 742, 1226

Divine law, 878
Divine right of kings, 182, 445, 446, 503, 691, 773, 774
    Confucian mandate contrasted, 283
    conservatism view, 290
    popular sovereignty versus, 980, 982
Divorce, 184
    Ireland, 637
    Italy, 213, 1044
    women's rights, 489, 490, 1383
Djibouti, 17, 20, 1314, 1384
Djiboutian National Movement for the Installation of Democracy, 20
Djilas, Milovan, 363
Dobb, Maurice, 385, 386
Doe, Samuel, 31
Dollfuss, Engelbert, 103, 104
Domestic policy, 493
Dominant party democracies, 934
    Africa, one-party state democracies, 1236, 1237, 1284
    Asia, 372–376, 1124–1126
    authoritarianism and, 105–106
    communist countries, 1283–1284
    Israel, 648–649, 668
    Italy, 668
    Japan, 665–670
    Malaysia, 794–795
    in multiethnic societies, 862
    Sweden, 668
    Tunisia, 1269–1270
Dominica, 171, 476, 1135
Dominican Liberation Party, 377, 378
Dominican Republic, 104, 176–178, 180, 263, 376–378, 476, 625, 1226
Dominican Revolutionary Party, 178, 377, 378
Dominion, 268, 270
Doriot, Jacques, 472
Dorr, Thomas, 1324
Dorr's Rebellion, 1324
Dorso, Guido, 324
dos Santos, José Eduardo, 22
Dossou, Robert, 366
Dostoyevsky, Fyodor Mikhailovich, 470
Double jeopardy, 595
Douglas, Roger, 102
Douglas, Stephen A., 727, 762, 980
Douglas, William, 595
Douglass, Frederick, 729, 1238, 1387
Doukhabors, 160
Downs, Anthony, 378–380, 1256
Drahomanov, Mykhaylo, 1289
Dred Scott v. Sandford (1857), 231, 1190, 1325, 1389
Dress codes, 505
Dreyfus, Alfred, 614
Droop quota, 1012–1015
Drug trade, 66, 259, 261, 331, 512
Dual-executive government, 913
Duarte, José Napoleón, 354
Duarte, Juan Pablo, 177
Dubček, Alexander, 329, 363, 1147
Du Bois, W. E. B., 232, 1233–1234, 1239
Dudayev, Dzhokhar, 188
Due process, 595, 756, 757, 807, 1318
    police power, 954–957
Duhamel, Georges, 1124
Duignan, Peter, 264
Dunleavy, Patrick, 336, 1303
Dunlop, John, 611
Dunn, John, 1252

of U.S. involvement in Southeast Asia, 1250
of welfare state, 1212
See also Polling, public opinion
Public Opinion (Lippmann), 764, 765
Public Opinion and American Democracy (Key),
707
Public Philosophy, The (Lippmann), 765
Public sector, 460
Public service, 234–235
See also Bureaucracy; Civil service
Public spirit. *See* Civic virtue
"Publius," 483
Puerto Rico, 176, 177, 179–180, 263, 476, 477
Pulatov, Abdurakhim, 84
Punitive Medicine (Podrabinik), 362
Puritans, 1022, 1045, 1046, 1304, 1320–1321
Putnam, Robert, 967

Q
Qatar, 640, 831, 833
Qoboza, Percy, 366
Qu Yuan, 202
Quadafi, Moammar, 1514
Quadragesimo Anno (Pius XI), 212–213
Quadros, Jânio, 136, 138
Quakers, 1023, 1046
Qube system, 825
Quebec, 157–162, 264, 480, 481, 615, 986, 1028
Quebec Bloc Party, 160
Quesnay, François, 435, 719
Quirino, Elpidio, 787
Quran, 638, 643, 831
Qureshi, Mooen, 907
Qutb, Sayyid, 644–645

R
Rabin, Yitzhak, 649, 1413
Rabuka, Sitiveni, 271
Racism, 1037–1040
fascism and, 473, 474
France, 501, 502
hate speech, 189, 191, 503
liberalism opposed, 757, 758
nationalism and, 876–877
political inequality, 1253, 1278
progressivism and, 1005
racist aspects of democratic theory, 496
South Africa, 129–130, 708, 1162–1164
South West Africa, 867
United States, 708–710, 855, 1238–1240, 1254,
1318, 1377, 1398
Radical Civic Union, 71–74, 839
Radical empiricism, 662
Radical Liberal Party, 1108
Radical majoritarian democratic theory, 91
Radical Party
Chile, 201, 506
Italy, 937
Radicalism, 292, 765, 767, 1369
Radio. *See* Mass media
Radishchev, Aleksandr, 1097
Rae, Douglas W., 416, 419, 420
Rae's F, 935
Raffles, Stamford, 1124
Rahman, Mujibur, 904, 906
Rajk, László, Jr., 582
Rakhmanov, Imamali, 85
Rákosi, Mátyás, 581
Rally for the Republic, 292
Ramalho Eanes, António, 913

Ramaphosa, Cyril, 366
Ramaswami, V., 594
Ramgoolam, Seewoosagur, 39
Ramos, Fidel, 946
Ramphal, Shridath, 270
Ran Wanding, 365
Ranke, Leopold von, 566
Rastokhez Party, 84
Rational actor theory, 1019
Rational choice theory, 1040–1042
voting behavior, 379–380, 1346–1353
Rationalism, 319
abstract, 434
conservatism antipathy to, 289, 291, 293
See also Idealism, German
Rationality, 505
Rauchenbusch, Walter, 1149
Rauschenberg, Robert, 993
Rawlings, Jerry John, 27, 31, 46, 529–531
Rawls, John, 219, 289, 306, 308, 686–689, 1009,
1140, 1335, 1345
Ray, James Earl, 710
Raynal, Guillaume-Thomas François, 1130
Reactionary despotism, 192
Reagan, Ronald, 75, 354, 496, 572, 577, 597, 804,
960, 1034, 1080, 1141, 1374
Real World of Democracy, The (Macpherson), 785
Realist (Progressive) Party, 813
Realists, 323, 324, 1378
Realpolitik (power politics), 1378
Reason, 432, 466, 469
Reasonableness of Christianity, The (Locke), 775
Recall, 319, 336, 811, 916, 922, 1280, 1326
Recollection (Tocqueville), 1265
Red Cross, 134
Reed, John Shelton, 389
Referendum. *See* Initiative and referendum
Reflections on the Revolution in France (Burke),
147, 149, 322
Reflections on the Revolution of Our Time (Laski),
723
Reform Party
Canada, 160
New Zealand, 101
Reformation, 444, 453, 478–479, 523, 568, 936,
1044–1046, 1082, 1370
Regime, 1241–1246, 1257
Regionalization, 335
Regulation, 760, 1046–1049
economic. *See* Markets, regulation of
laissez-faire theory contrasted, 719–721,
802–803
Progressive ethos and politics, 803–804,
1002–1007, 1083–1084, 1377
Regulus, 1342
Rehnquist, William, 233, 596
Reid, Thomas, 432
Reinicke, Wolfgang, 977
Relativism, 396, 565, 698–699, 993, 1049–1052,
1224
Religion
American Revolution and, 1067
American society, Tocqueville analysis, 815,
1267–1268
and civic education, 393–394
civil religion, 1052–1054, 1059, 1065, 1087, 1344
dissident movements and, 366
European cleavages, 453
existentialism and, 466–470
French Revolution and, 1072

institutional role, 850
Rousseau criticism, 1088
Spinoza scientific principles, 1176
See also Separation of church and state;
specific religions
Religious freedom
Catholic Church endorsement, 183
Japan, 665
Jefferson view, 673
Leveller movement, 755–756
liberalism and, 279, 756, 757, 759, 773, 775
as measure of democracy, 303, 688
Ukraine, 1292
United States, 574, 1046, 1318
Religious intolerance, as threat to democracy,
513–514
Renaissance. *See* Middle Ages and Renaissance
Renaissance Movement, 1271
Renaissance Party, 84
Renascent Africa (Azikiwe), 109
Renaut, Alain, 1258–1259
Renner, Karl, 427, 988
Report on Manufactures (Hamilton), 557
Representation, 1278
African Americans, 1239
ancient and medieval republics, 788
Antifederalist view, 69–70
Bagehot analysis, 111–112
Belarus, 124
consent to taxation and, 1211–1212
consocial democracy, 1283
corporatism, 1282–1283
critiques of, 322–324
Dahl theory of random selection, 334
direct or participatory democracy compared,
319, 921
districting, 367–372
doctrinal development, 567, 574, 575, 727,
1054–1058
European Union, 465
federal systems, 481
Federalist view, 483–484
French government distinguished, 1072
functional representation, 1282, 1283
India, 522
legislatures and parliaments, 736–747
mass democracy avoided by, 814
minority interests. *See* Majority rule, minority rights
models of representative behavior, 322, 1032,
1253–1254
participatory democracy and, 1280–1281
proportional formulas, 1010–1016
statistical representation, 1281–1282
supplemental representation, 367
United States, 1316, 1319–1320, 1330
Western Europe, 456–457
"Repressive Tolerance" (Marcuse), 191
Republic (Cicero), 217, 321, 878, 1244
Republic (Plato), 189, 217, 320, 357, 468, 504, 686,
947, 1241, 1242, 1246
Republic of China. *See* Taiwan
Republic of Korea. *See* South Korea
Republican Party
Bolivia, 63
Costa Rica, 313, 314
Germany, 528
Italy, 653, 656
Kazakhstan, 84
Ukraine, 1290